Coping with Chronic Illness

Overcoming Powerlessness

Edition 2

JUDITH FITZGERALD MILLER, Ph.D., R.N.
Associate Professor and Research Scholar
Marquette University College of Nursing
Milwaukee, Wisconsin

F.A. DAVIS COMPANY • **Philadelphia**

F. A. Davis Company
1915 Arch Street
Philadelphia, PA 19103

Printed in the United States of America

Last digit indicates print number: 10 9 8 7 6 5 4

NOTE: As new scientific information becomes available through basic and clinical research, recommended treatments and drug therapies undergo changes. The author and publisher have done everything possible to make this book accurate, up-to-date, and in accord with accepted standards at the time of publication. The author, editors, and publisher are not responsible for errors or omissions or for consequences from application of the book, and make no warranty, expressed or implied, in regard to the contents of the book. Any practice described in this book should be applied by the reader in accordance with professional standards of care used in regard to the unique circumstances that may apply in each situation. The reader is advised always to check product information (package inserts) for changes and new information regarding dose and contraindications before administering any drug. Caution is especially urged when using new or infrequently ordered drugs.

Library of Congress Cataloging-in-Publication Data

Miller, Judith Fitzgerald.
    Coping with chronic illness : overcoming powerlessness / Judith
Fitzgerald Miller.—Ed. 2.
       p.   cm.
    Includes bibliographical references and index.
    ISBN 0-8036-6192-4 (softbound : alk. paper)
    1. Chronic diseases—Nursing. 2. Control (Psychology)—Health
aspects. 3. Chronic diseases—Psychological aspects. I. Title.
    [DNLM: 1. Chronic Disease—nursing. 2. Chronic Disease—
rehabilitation. 3. Models, Psychological. 4. Nurse-Patient
Relations. 5. Sick Role. WY 152 M648c]
RT120.C45M55   1991
610.73′61—dc20
DNLM/DLC
for Library of Congress   91-35317
                                            CIP

TO PATRICK AND OUR CHILDREN,
KIM, ELIZABETH, AND PATRICIA

■ P R E F A C E ■

The purpose of this book is to facilitate understanding of the world of the chronically ill and to develop nursing's repertoire of strategies to care for persons with long-term health problems. The ultimate goal of nursing care is to maintain and enhance client/family quality of life. As for other individuals, quality of life for the chronically ill includes playing roles important to the individual, giving and receiving love, balancing dependence with independence, being satisfied with self, being at peace, having a feeling of self-worth, having energy to enjoy life's special pleasures, coping effectively, and having hope.

Although there are some undeniably negative characteristics associated with chronic illness such as uncertainty, declining physical trajectory, dependence, role transition, and feelings of powerlessness, an expanded perception is needed that takes into account the rich attributes of human life such as the ability to think, create, rationalize, experience joy, learn, and appreciate art and music. Humans have limitless potential for growth, unfolding, and being. During illness a special caring advocate can support adaptation and nurture that unfolding, enabling growth to occur through confronting adversity. Persons who are ill are to be viewed as having multiple resources to enable them to be in control of their lives. Despite a compromised physical integrity, other resources such as social support, psychological stability, knowledge, self-esteem, energy, and hope can be developed and maintained, and certain chapters are devoted to developing client/family power resources.

Client autonomy characterizes the current era of health care: benevolent paternalism from an omnipotent physician, health care team, or health care system determining client/family decisions and directing passive clients/families is no longer the norm. Client/family autonomy is safeguarded by nursing care.

This second edition of *Coping with Chronic Illness: Overcoming Powerlessness,* contains five new chapters on coping with specific chronic health problems and strategies to alleviate powerlessness. Creative strategies are explored in these chapters such as the use of imagery, literature, behavior change, and unique coping modalities. All the other chapters have been expanded with current research reviewed and new models described.

Related theories are explored in this revision including uncertainty (Mishel, 1988); self-regulation (Levanthal & Johnson, 1983), cognitive control (Meichenbaum, 1985); adaptation (LoRocca, Kalb & Kaplan,

1983) and behavior change, to name a few. Endurance factors such as hardiness and salutogenic factors are reviewed.

New models presented in this revision include care of the patient with multiple sclerosis, a model of factors affecting functioning in persons with COPD, healing through bibliotherapy, enhancing self-esteem, and inspiring hope.

In addition to the previously selected prototypical chronic health problems discussed in the first edition, client/family responses to AIDS and cancer are explored in relation to coping and control. In-depth analyses of persons with multiple sclerosis and chronic lung disease including the pathophysiology, factors influencing coping, and adaptation have been added. Nursing assessment, diagnoses, interventions, and related research are the foundations of the subject of this book.

Analyses of client/family exemplars provide "real world" clinical decision-making, application of research findings, and generation of nursing strategies, all geared to promoting holistic caring. The case study method is a useful research approach to document a sequence of events and responses over time to validate indicators of nursing diagnoses and the immediate and long term effects of nursing. Diverse methods of client/family coping are also documented in this book.

More precise and in-depth assessments of clinical phenomena are presented as are reviews of research instruments to measure coping, stressors (of hemodialysis) fatigue, helplessness (of arthritis), quality of life, self-esteem, and hope.

Despite the linking of a diagnostic category such as energy with a specific health problem (arthritis or chronic lung disease), it is hoped that readers study the chapters transferring insights regarding nursing diagnoses and treatments to other clients/families and do not restrict the nursing content to a medical diagnosis.

Part I provides a model of persons comprised of power resources and a foundation for understanding coping and powerlessness. Part II includes developmental vulnerabilities to powerlessness in children with select mobility impairments, middle-aged women, and the elderly. Client/family responses to specific prototypical chronic health problems are reviewed in Part III. Caring strategies are presented in Part IV with an emphasis on maintaining client/family control.

Some sections of this book are entirely new but despite additions and revisions in each chapter, a work of this nature is never complete. Various theories and perspectives need continued exploration, research, and discovery. More ideas for nursing interventions need to be developed. Expanded perceptions of the chronically ill client/family are needed. It is hoped that this work will provide an impetus for continued work and development. Expansion of nursing's healing power is limited only by the bounds of one's creativity.

Judith Fitzgerald Miller

References

Leventhal, H., & Johnson, J. (1983). Laboratory and field experimentation: Development of a theory of self-regulation. In P. Wooldridge, M. Schmitt, J. Skipper, & R. Leonard (Eds.), *Behavioral Science and Nursing Theory* (pp. 189–262), St. Louis: CV Mosby.

LoRocca, N., Kalb, R., & Kaplan, S.R. (1983). Psychological changes. In L.C. Scheinberg (Ed.), *Multiple sclerosis: A guide for patients and their families* (pp. 175–194). New York: Raven Press.

Meichenbaum, D. (1985). *Stress innoculation training.* New York: Pergamon Press.

Mishel, M.H. (1988). Uncertainty in illness. *Image: Journal of nursing scholarship, 20,* 225–232.

■CONTRIBUTORS■

Diann Recker Baumann, M.S.N., R.N.
Maternal Child Clinical Nurse Specialist
OB/GYN, S.C.
Milwaukee, Wisconsin

Debra Hastings, M.S.N., R.N.
Doctoral Student
University of Wisconsin-Milwaukee School of Nursing
Milwaukee, Wisconsin

Ruth Hobus, M.S.N., R.N.
Instructor
South Dakota State University
Brookings, South Dakota

Anne McMahon, M.S.N., R.N.
Clinical Supervisor
Marquette University College of Nursing
Milwaukee, Wisconsin

Judith Fitzgerald Miller, Ph.D., R.N.
Associate Professor and Research Scholar
Marquette University College of Nursing
Milwaukee, Wisconsin

Christine Bohm Oertel, M.S.N., R.N.
Racine, Wisconsin

Polly Ryan, M.S.N., R.N.
Doctoral Candidate
University of Wisconsin-Milwaukee, School of Nursing
Clinical Nurse Researcher
Milwaukee County Medical Complex
Milwaukee, Wisconsin

Patricia S. Schroeder, M.S.N., R.N.
Nursing Quality Consultant
Quality Care Concepts, Inc.
Thiensville, Wisconsin

Susan R. Stapleton, M.S.N., C.N.M., R.N.
Certified Nurse Midwife
Reading Birth and Women's Center
Reading, Pennsylvania

Rebecca Stephens, Ph.D., R.N.
Assistant Professor, Adult Health Nursing
The Florida State University
Tallahassee, Florida

■ C O N T E N T S ■

xiii

■ P A R T ■

I

Current Status

A model for understanding nursing care of the chronically ill patient that promotes patient control through development and support of the individual's power resources is presented in Chapter 1. A common core of patient resources is presented in the power resource model; however, it is not possible to enumerate all the human strengths that are to be supported by nurses. The model provides a frame of reference for the book in that some chapters are devoted to developing select resources.

Coping with perceived powerlessness is a major demand throughout chronic illness. All persons have a capacity for coping. Coping is stimulated in individuals with chronic health problems. Unlike acute crises, during which denial of the impact of the threat is the usual means of coping, chronic illness brings about a confrontation with reality, adaptation, and participation in care. The individual and family must respond to the requirements of the external situation (e.g., adhere to the medication regimen, participate in exercises, maintain a weight-reduction program, or complete treatments such as self-dialysis), as well as respond to one's own feelings about the situation (powerlessness, depression, or low self-esteem). Other specific coping tasks that have been identified in chronically ill patients are discussed in Chapter 2.

The research base and the resulting theoretical propositions and nursing practice speculations are presented in Chapter 3. Although the research base about concepts of powerlessness, locus of control, helplessness, and reactance theory has been derived from behavioral science literature, its relevance to nursing is noted. Development of a nursing diagnostic category on powerlessness appears essential and valid.

■

Patient Power Resources
■ JUDITH FITZGERALD MILLER

There are varied theoretical perspectives on chronic illness that include emphases on patient response processes and integration, patient and family adjustment and adaptation, and anticipation of illness-related demands and crises aversion (Brown, Rawlinson, & Hilles, 1981; Charmaz, 1983; Craig & Edwards, 1983; Lawrence & Lawrence, 1979; Radley & Green, 1987; Strauss et al., 1984). A model of chronic illness that stems from the commonsense viewpoints of the patient and family suffering with the illness has particular relevance to the focus of this book on patient empowerment. Turk and associates (1986) proposed a four-dimensional structure of illness interpretation based upon patient/family perceptions: seriousness, personal responsibility, controllability, and changeability. These dimensions, derived from Leventhal, Meyer, and Nerenz's (1980) commonsense representation of illness, were validated using the Implicit Model of Illness Questionnaire (Turk, Rudy, & Salovey, 1986). *Seriousness* refers to the individual's knowledge about the degree to which the illness is difficult to manage and the amount of intense medical surveillance that is needed. *Personal responsibility* is the degree to which individuals perceive themselves to cause or cure the illness. *Controllability* is the extent the illness is viewed to be controllable by the ill person or other agents. *Changeability* refers to knowledge about the rate and degree to which symptoms vary over time. The expected trajectory of illness events and desired treatment effects may be included in the changeability dimension. The degree of powerlessness perceived by patients is influenced in part by their interpretation of each of these four dimensions.

There is a way for individuals with chronic illness to be and feel in control of what is happening to them; power is a resource for living that is present in all individuals. In the most elemental sense, power is the ability to influence what happens to oneself. May (1972) described five

3

types of power: exploitative, manipulative, competitive, nutrient, and integrative. The type of power that is relevant to this book is nutrient power. May defines nutrient power in terms of providing for, caring for, or having concern for the welfare of others. For our purposes, power will be defined as nurturative, that is, providing for and caring for self, directing others regarding self-care, and being the ultimate decision maker regarding care. With power comes the ability to effect change or prevent it; power and control are used as synonymous terms.

Powerlessness is the perception that one lacks the capacity or authority to act to affect an outcome. The greater the individual's expectation to have control and the greater the importance of the desired outcomes to the individual, the greater the perceived powerlessness experienced when the individual does not, in fact, have control (Wortman & Brehm, 1975). Powerlessness in chronically ill patients occurs for a variety of reasons. The patient may experience uncertain health with remissions and exacerbations or, in some instances, progressive physical deterioration. There are physical and psychologic losses. Overwhelmingly strange, invasive, and threatening experiences may occur as part of ongoing diagnostic and treatment measures. What is routine to the health-care worker may be anything but routine to the patient. The language system of health workers may create the impression that they are sophisticated masters of the situation, while patients feel isolated and unaware of what is happening to them. Some or all of these factors may influence the chronically ill person's perceived lack of control.

Chronic Illness Defined—Select Factors Influencing Responses

Chronic illness refers to an altered health state that will not be cured by a simple surgical procedure or a short course of medical therapy. Although each chronic illness presents unique demands on the patient and family, two generalizations can be made: (1) the person with a chronic illness experiences impaired functioning in more than one— often multiple—body-mind (Turk, Sobel, Follick, & Youkilis, 1980) and spirit systems; and (2) the illness-related demands on the individual are never completely eliminated. Lubkin (1986) critiqued traditional definitions of chronic illness and suggests that chronic illness is "the irreversible presence, accumulation, or latency of disease states or impairments that involve the total human environment for supportive care and self-care, maintenance of function and prevention of further disability" (p. 6).

Many demands are made on the patient and family. The patient must endure close medical scrutiny regarding symptoms, response to therapy, and compliance, and acquire a knowledge of self and therapy so that self-monitoring is possible. The family also needs to develop and refine skills for daily monitoring and management. Finally, all these efforts must be directed toward keeping the problem controlled and in remission while also controlling anxiety over the threat of full-blown incapacitation during exacerbations.

Reif (1975) identifies three general features of chronic illness: (1) the disease symptoms interfere with many normal activities and routines, (2) the medical regimen is limited in its effectiveness, and (3) treatment, although intended to mitigate the symptoms and long-range effects of disease, contributes substantially to the disruption of the usual patterns of living.

Individuals and families have varied responses to the stress of illness; Antonovksy (1980) suggests that this is because of varied resistance resources that are salutary (promote health and prevent illness). The resistance resources include the following variables: physical, biochemical, artifactual-material (money, shelter), cognitive-emotional, valuative-attitudinal, interpersonal-relational, and macrosociocultural (place in the world, familiar rituals). For example, cognitive-emotional characteristics include knowledge and intelligence, ego identity, and a sense of coherence. A sense of coherence is an enduring perception that one's life has worth, meaning, and purpose. A feeling of being in control is part of coherence as is confidence that "things will work out well." In addition to the variables identified by Antonovsky, another personality variable, hardiness, may promote coping and enable patient/family resistance to stress. Kobasa and associates described three components of hardiness: control, commitment, and challenge (Kobasa, 1979a, 1979b, 1982; Kobasa, Maddi Puccetti, & Zola, 1985). Hardy persons tend to believe in their own ability to influence life events rather than being helpless; they are actively involved, not passive or alienated, and they perceive change as an opportunity for growth. Pollock (1986; 1989) extended the construct to include a disposition toward health and resistance of illness. Hardiness in the chronically ill is said to influence the use of social resources for successful coping (Pollock, 1986), psychologic health (Nowack, 1989), and psychologic well-being (Lambert, Lambert, Klipple, & Mewshaw, 1989; Lambert & Lambert, 1987). Hardiness bolsters endurance throughout unpredictable challenges of chronic illness.

Unpredictable dilemmas that characterize chronic illness and promote powerlessness include symptom exacerbation, failure of therapy, physical deterioration despite adherence to the prescribed regimen, the side effects of drugs, iatrogenic alterations, breakdown in the patient's family or significant-other support network, and breakdown in the patient's psychologic stamina.

Mishel's work on uncertainty has particular relevance for understanding the individual's cognitive and coping response to chronic illness (Mishel, 1988; 1983; 1981; Mishel & Braden, 1988; 1987; Mishel, Hostetter, King, & Graham, 1984; Mishel & Murdaugh, 1987). Mishel's middle-range theory views uncertainty as the inability to arrive at meaning in the illness-related events. Sources of uncertainty stem from inconsistency in symptom patterns; inconsistency between expected and experienced illness-related events; and unfamiliarity and complexity of cues and events. Persons with chronic illness experience remissions and exacerbations, disrupting a predictable pattern of their symptoms. Event congruence in the chronically ill may not take place if the patient expects to be healed yet experiences recurrence of the illness, or when treatment does not produce immediate desired results. The treatment setting remains alien as complexity of surveillance of the chronic condition continues over long periods of time. The patient's cognitive capacity is affected by the illness, pain, nutrition, and fear. All these incongruities and decreased cognitive capacity create uncertainty. Select mechanisms referred to as *structure providers* can increase or decrease uncertainty. These include use of education, social support from significant others, and trust in the nurse and health-care providers as "credible authorities." Uncertainty is appraised by patients by use of inference and illusion. Inferences are based upon personality dispositions such as a sense of mastery and general beliefs about oneself and control of the environment. Illusion results in viewing uncertainty as positive. It protects persons when they encounter situations that are difficult to accept such as during the downward trajectory of chronic illness. Coping strategies utilized by patients will be determined in part by whether uncertainty was appraised as a danger or an opportunity. If viewed as a danger, methods to control negative emotions may be used. If viewed as an opportunity, buffering coping strategies including avoidance, selective ignoring, reordering priorities, and neutralizing are used. The desired end result is adaptation (Mishel, 1988).

Psychodynamics of chronically ill patients have not been well described. Strain (1979) identified the following eight categories of psychologic reactions to chronic medical illness:

- Perceived threat to self-esteem and body intactness that challenges individuals' beliefs that they are masters of their own bodies
- Fear of loss of love and approval that evolves from patients' fears that illness and dependence on others will cause significant others to withdraw
- Fear of loss of control of achieved body functions and/or parts with resulting loss of independence
- Anxiety resulting from separation from loved ones and familiar environment that provided support, gratification, and a sense of intactness
- Guilt and fear of retaliation for having incurred the health problem in the first place or for having lost control

- Fear of pain
- Fear of strangers providing intimate care

A prevalent theme throughout all these reactions is a lack of control. The lack of control seems to pervade all aspects of chronic illness—from etiology of the disease itself, to events and experiences within the health-care system while the patient seeks treatment for the disease.

Strain (1979) explains the regressive behavior that occurs in children during stress is likely to occur in chronically ill adults. Lack of involvement in their own care promotes regression in chronically ill patients. The regression to unwarranted dependency and passivity can be prevented through nursing care. Nursing measures to prevent negative dependency are discussed throughout this book, and specific measures to empower the chronically ill person are described in Part IV.

Feldman (1974) uses the term readaptation in referring to rehabilitation of chronically ill patients. He stated that readaptation "is coming to terms existentially with the reality of chronic illness as a state of being, discarding both false hope and destructive hopelessness, restructuring the environment in which one must now function." (287). Readaptation for chronically ill patients requires reorganization and acceptance of self on a level that transcends the illness. This is a sizable challenge, in light of the multiple stresses and unpredictable dilemmas that accompany chronic illnesses.

Factors that are said to influence positive adjustment to chronic illness include knowledge, coping resources, problem-solving attitude, sense of personal mastery, and motivation (Turk, 1979). *Knowledge* of the illness and desired effects of therapy, as well as understanding patient and family roles, facilitates adjustment. Turk (1979) attests that personal meaning is imposed when individuals have the cognitive structure to accurately assign such meaning. *Coping resources* are those which are available to help persons master, tolerate, or reduce a problem or demand. Merely knowing that a coping response is possible helps reduce the threat of a situation. *Problem-solving attitude* is a perspective of active resourcefulness in confronting problems. Persons with this attitude perceive problems accurately, have the ability to pose several alternative responses to problems, and have a history of success in confronting problems. *Personal mastery* means individuals have confidence in their ability and demonstrate a sense of control and self-efficacy to handle situations related to their illness. Although most patients become depressed at times and question the worth of their involvement with illness treatment, these thoughts serve to *motivate* adjusted persons to continue with requisite behaviors compliant with therapy demands, while persons who are poorly adjusted tend to manifest a negative, defeated, demoralized attitude.

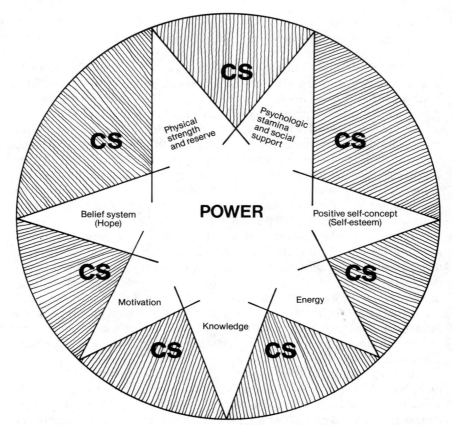

FIGURE I ■ I   Patient power resources. CS refers to the individual's unique coping strategies utilized when resources are compromised.

Perceptions of greater personal control over the care regimen in 92 persons with rheumatoid arthritis were associated with positive mood states and psychosocial adjustment. In contrast, perceptions that health providers had control over patients' daily symptoms were associated with negative mood states in patients (Affleck, Tennen, Pfeiffer, & Fifield, 1987).

Despite the unpredictable dilemmas of living with illness, chronically ill persons have goals similar to those of any well person: to live life fully and to function optimally in all aspects of life, that is, to have quality of life. Quality of life encompasses being able to engage in roles that are important to individuals: perceiving themselves as worthwhile; achieving a sense of independence; feeling satisfaction with self, accomplishments, and relationships; and having a sense of well-being despite the limitations imposed by illness. The central focus of nursing in empowering the chronically ill is to maintain and enhance the quality of life.

Instruments to assess quality of life in various types of chronically ill persons and in the elderly have been developed (Ferrans & Powers, 1985; George & Bearon, 1980; Padilla, Presant, Grant, Metter, Lipsett, & Heide 1983). A perception of lack of control over most aspects of one's life interferes with achieving quality of life.

Maximizing the patient's power resources facilitates the patient's ability to cope with chronic illness. An individual's power resources (Fig. 1-1) include physical strength (physical reserve), psychologic stamina and social support, positive self-concept, energy, knowledge, motivation, and belief system–hope. Individuals with chronic illnesses may have deficits in several power resources, that is, physical strength and energy; therefore, remaining power components may need to be developed to prevent or overcome powerlessness. The patient's unique and varied coping strategies compensate for deficient resources and build up remaining resources such as hope and positive self-concept (specifically self-esteem). Because the power resources are discussed in more detail in later chapters, they will be described only briefly here.

Power Resources

PHYSICAL STRENGTH

Physical strength refers both to the individual's ability for optimal physical functioning and to physical reserve. When any body system is compromised by illness, the individual's power to act is decreased. The present status of an individual's physical strength will influence the patient's power—whether the patient is on a downward course with more physical symptoms arising (a deteriorating health state) or the patient is improving physically. Physical reserve is the ability of the body to maintain physical balance when confronted with threats or extra demands. For example, individuals with acquired immunodeficiency syndrome (AIDS) or those on long-term therapy with immunosuppressive drugs have less reserve in fighting infection than others. Persons with arthritis may have an accompanying muscle atrophy and weakness.

PSYCHOLOGIC STAMINA—SOCIAL SUPPORT

Psychologic stamina refers to a unique resiliency present in humans. Despite the crisis of illness and day-to-day uncertainty, some patients are able to maintain psychologic equilibrium. Somehow, events that could be viewed as threats are interpreted as being meaningful. At the other extreme, chronic illness may cause psychologic imbalance. Depression and anxiety are two prevalent symptoms in chronically ill individuals (Adams & Lindemann, 1974). The patient with a chronic health problem may need help to maintain a positive outlook and to prevent or alleviate paralyzing anxiety, depression, and hopelessness.

Social support refers to relationship qualities of attachment, social integration, opportunity for nurturance, reassurance of worth, sense of reliable alliance, and guidance from a trustworthy, caring person (Weiss, 1974). Additional perspectives describe types of social support to include tangible support (instrumental support such as help with activities of daily living), emotional support, and informational support (Schaefer, Coyne, & Lazarus, 1981). Social support is said to both buffer the stress of illness and enhance health regardless of the level of stress (Cohen & Syme, 1985). Corbin and Strauss (1984; 1988) noted that couples who worked together were able to prevent and resolve problems and were able to manage the chronic illness demands. Social support has been found to be related to coping effectiveness (McNett, 1987), quality of life (Burckhardt, 1985), and adaptation (Bramwell & Whall, 1986; Dimond, 1979; Maybury & Brewin, 1984; Northouse, 1988; Winert, 1983; Zedlow & Pavlou, 1984) in the chronically ill. Pattison (1974) found that the life spans of patients with chronic obstructive lung disease were not predicted by the amount of remaining respiratory function (extent of pathology), but rather depended on their having someone in their social network who cared about them. Maintaining intact social support systems and supporting the family coping with the burden of caring for and worrying about their chronically ill family member is a challenge for nursing.

POSITIVE SELF-CONCEPT

Self-concept is the individual's total thoughts and feelings about self (Rosenberg, 1979). Components of self-concept include physical self (body image), functional self (role performance), personal self (moral self, self-ideal, and self-expectancy) (Driever, 1979), and self-esteem (self-worth). Epstein (1973) states, "There is a basic need for self-esteem which relates to all aspects of the self systems, . . . in comparison to which, almost all other needs are subordinate." (p. 404). Self-esteem is therefore a crucial component of self-concept and a determinant of functioning. Feeling worthwhile is basic to taking action to achieve improved health.

Chronic illness has an impact on self-concept. The illness may promote a feeling of being "permanently different" or of having less worth— as compared with a defective mechanical device. Cooper (1976) refers to the world of chronic illness as the "fourth world." The fourth world is made up of millions of persons alienated from ideal everyday life and denied interactions because of the effects of disease and its treatment.

Self-concept reconstruction is one phase of adjusting to the illness.

The goal in self-concept reconstruction is to integrate an accurate perception of the altered body part into a positive concept of self, while understanding that the ability or potential ability for managing care of the health problem resides within the self. Allowing the illness to be the dominant component in defining self needs to be avoided. Individuals with multiple sclerosis, for example, may need nurses' help to define themselves in terms of continuing roles, strengths, abilities, and goals, rather than simply in terms of the neurologic impairment. Chapter 15 discusses enhancement of self-esteem as a method of alleviating powerlessness.

The nature of an individual's personality influences self-concept. One personality characteristic that is directly related to this subject is locus of control. Unlike powerlessness, which is a situationally determined perception that outcomes are beyond the individual's control, an internal locus of control is a stable tendency to perceive events and outcomes to be within the person's own control regardless of the situation. Persons with internal loci of control tend to perceive positive and negative life events as being a result of their own actions—under personal control (Lefcourt, 1966; Rotter, 1966). Persons with external loci of control tend to perceive life events as being unrelated to their own behavior and instead being contingent on chance, fate, or the powers of others. It is important to determine the individual's usual perceptions of life events and how much or how little control and/or involvement in self-care management the ill individual needs. In caring for chronically ill patients, nurses need to be concerned with whether or not the individual with an internal locus of control experiences more intense feelings of powerlessness when dealing with the illness than does an individual with an external locus of control. Locus of control is discussed in more detail in Chapters 6, 8, and 9.

ENERGY

Energy is the capacity of a system for doing work; energy potential is stored energy. There must be a balance between energy uptake and energy expenditure. Energy sources include nutrients, water, rest, and motivation. Energy is expended to restore or heal physical states, to actively cope with daily living demands, and to cope with unusual stress. Energy is also spent for growth through learning, work, and play (Ryden, 1977). Absence of energy for the most basic levels of energy utilization, referred to as the compensatory level needed for physical balance, contributes to powerlessness of the individual and prevents energy utilization for higher-level expenditure needs, for example, growth and learning. Action is possible if strength and energy are present. Actions of the ill person include measures initiated by the person to protect and/or improve health. Coping with uncertainty of energy availability is discussed in Chapter 11.

KNOWLEDGE AND INSIGHT

Having knowledge and insight about what is happening to them enables patients to feel more in control and helps to alleviate the anxiety of uncertainty. It has been documented many times that patients who were informed and had accurate expectations about an anticipated experience would exhibit less anxiety during the stressful event (Johnson, 1972; 1973; Johnson, Morrissey, & Leventhal, 1973; Johnson & Rice, 1974; Johnson, Kirchhoff, & Endress, 1975).

The care regimens chronically ill persons are required to implement are difficult in that they require learned skills, are time-consuming to execute, usually require changes in habits and routines, and entail physical and psychologic stress (Reif, 1975). The regimen's difficulty is not only due to the individual's having to learn psychomotor skills such as an injection technique or having to learn technical information such as actions of drugs, but is due also to the individual's having to cope with psychologic reactions to the health problem. Engaging in the learned therapy is a constant reminder of being different and of having the chronic illness.

Patient knowledge allows for involvement in decision making and awareness of the alternatives and the anticipated consequences of each alternative course of action. Knowledge is one "structure provider" that decreases uncertainty (Mishel, 1988) and enables development of a cognitive map for ongoing interpretation of events, enabling persons to find meaning in illness-related events (Turk, 1979). Lack of understanding contributes to lassitude and inaction, both of which are characteristic of powerlessness. (See Chaps. 12 and 16.)

Internal awareness (Kinsman, Jones, Matus, & Schum, 1976) is a concept for discussion in relation to the power of knowledge and insight. Internal awareness is the ability to detect and interpret physical and psychologic cues so as to take appropriate action to control symptoms and maintain psychologic balance (Miller, 1982). This refers to developing a sensitivity to one's own body and means having an accurate perception of alterations in health such as changes in fatigue, pain, appetite, skin color, elimination, mood states, tension, anger, depression, guilt, and other physical and psychologic states. For example, a young patient with insulin-dependent diabetes may discover that circumoral numbness is the earliest symptom of impending insulin shock. Taking the appropriate action—ingesting glucose, followed by a protein food, for example—could avoid an emergency-room visit. Internal awareness also means knowing the desired effect of the therapy and self-monitoring in light of this effect. The patient on diuretics with congestive heart failure who noted a daily weight increase of 2 pounds would be aware of the seriousness of this sign and would contact the physician. The patient would not wait a week until the respiratory distress could be severe. Having this sensitivity to one's own signs and symptoms and reactions to therapy empowers the person to take action to control symptoms and avert crises.

MOTIVATION

The theory of motivation based on competence and self-determination was reviewed by Deci (1976). This theory of motivation is congruent with approaches proposed in this book, namely, to develop the patient's sense of control over self and environment. Competence theory refers to the individual's ability to deal effectively with the environment by manipulating the environment not only to meet basic needs (e.g., food and comfort) but also to have a feeling of efficacy (Deci, 1976).

Kagan (1972) describes the human being as having a motive for mastery. He proposed that the origins of mastery were human beings' desires to achieve standards, predict the future, and define themselves. Reduction of uncertainty is a component of Kagan's concept. In the same sense, deCharms (1968) states that individuals strive to be their own causal agents (for producing change in the environment, as well as in self and self-behavior). The desire to control one's destiny influences all other human motives. Deci also describes competence behaviors as being geared to "dissonance" reduction. That is, the individual strives to reduce the amount of incongruity among beliefs, expectations, and actual actions and outcomes of events. Deci (1976) concludes his review of motivational theories by stating that intrinsically motivated behaviors enable persons to feel competent and self-determining. He summarizes intrinsically motivated behaviors as two kinds: (1) those seeking stimulation, and (2) those reducing incongruity (dissonance).

In chronic illness, motivation is important in maximizing potential, promoting social and work roles, and developing self-confidence through risk taking (e.g., being able to risk rejection when applying for a new job despite the chronic illness). Motivation is also needed to learn new skills and engage in therapies. Humanistic means of motivation especially relevant for nurses are discussed in Chapter 16. Motivation is one aspect of enabling behavior, that empowers individuals.

BELIEF SYSTEM

The belief system of the individual encompasses belief in God to provide strength and ability to cope with stress and overcome it; belief in therapeutic regimens, with the accompanying autosuggestion that the therapy will be effective; belief in care givers; and belief in self, that is, confidence in one's own capabilities. Kraines (1943) stated if the patient believes strongly in a care giver, by that very belief the patient obtains moral support and can face problems with a new degree of equanimity.

Frank (1975) describes how patients' expectations for therapy influence outcomes. Patients' self-suggestions about success of therapy may have self-fulfilling prophecy effects. The psychiatric patients' expressed optimism about treatment was a determinant in their symptomatic improvement in a 6-week course of therapy (Uhlenhuth & Duncan, 1968).

Spiritual malaise does not appear to be conducive to healing (Frank, 1975). The chronically ill person needs relief from the isolation of suffering, and having a relationship with God may alleviate this aloneness. Some individuals may find meaning in the misfortune of chronic illness through religion and faith. The knowledge that chronic illness affects mind, body, and spirit systems directs nurses' attention to developing spiritual well-being in their patients. "Spiritual well-being is the affirmation of life in a relationship with God, self, community, and environment that nurtures and celebrates wholeness" (Moberg, 1979, p. 5). A new hope is derived from renewed spiritual well-being. The presence of faith and hope empowers an individual to have a perceived sense of control and may enhance therapeutic results. Inspiring hope is discussed in Chapter 17.

The more power resources that are compromised in an individual, the more nursing strategies will be needed to help the patient overcome a lack of control. These nursing strategies must consider the individual's unique coping style and focus on specific deficient power resources.

Summary

The continuous ups and downs of chronic illness present a threatening sense of uncertainty that may range from an inablity to predict whether one will have enough physical energy for an upcoming event, pain or comfort, nausea resulting from chemotherapy, or the internal motivation needed to follow through with an expectation. Not being able to predict how well symptoms will be controlled often prevents the individual from planning and engaging in social activities. Because social activities play a role in the development of a positive self-concept, these types of interactions are especially important for chronically ill persons. However, the uncertainty that accompanies the illness may cause ill individuals to isolate themselves. Eventually, the cure-oriented medical profession may demonstrate its own discouragement to the patient.

The ultimate uncertainty in the question, "When will this end in death?" is always with the patient. How much more loss the family and patient will suffer before death is an unspoken query seldom voiced. Psychologic stability and social support help patients balance these fears with recognition of abilities and potential in their lives. The three-staged progression of the chronically ill person's relationship with health workers of *naive trust*, to *disenchantment*, and finally *guarded alliance* (Thorne & Robinson, 1989; 1988) is not the type of full partnership, participative relationship envisioned to be created by nurses to empower patients. All care is dependent upon a helping, caring nurse-patient relationship that becomes the vehicle for patient empowerment.

Patients who are chronically ill need to have power to be managers of their own care. They should not forfeit this role to health-care personnel. Nurses can maximize patients' resources for power by developing the strengths that remain as well as by supporting the patients' select coping strategies while recognizing that individual patient and family responses are influenced by salutary resources (Antonovsky, 1980), hardiness, and their developed coping ability.

The power resources model provides the general framework for this book. Chapters are devoted to examining causes, indicators, and measurement of power resource deficits in specific health problems and/or age groups. Strategies to alleviate powerlessness are described for specific chronic health problems. Empowerment strategies specific to components of the power resources model are developed; individual chapters are devoted to enhancing self-esteem, inspiring hope, overcoming energy deficits, and developing enabling strategies (motivation and knowledge), all of which are directed at alleviating powerlessness of chronic illness. The many explicit challenges confronting chronically ill patients are discussed in Chapter 2, in which a presentation of a typology of coping tasks for chronically ill patients is presented.

References

Adams, J., & Lindemann, E. (1974). Coping with long-term disability. In G. Coehlo, D. Hamburg, & J. Adams (Eds.), *Coping and adaptation* (pp. 127–138). New York: Basic Books.

Affleck, G., Tennen, H., Pfeiffer, C., & Fifield, J. (1987). Appraisals of control and predictability in adapting to a chronic disease. *Journal of Personality and Social Psychology, 53,* 273–279.

Antonovsky, A. (1980). *Health, stress and coping.* San Francisco: Jossey-Bass.

Bramwell, L., & Whall, A. N. (1986). Effect of role clarity and empathy on support role performance and anxiety. *Nursing Research, 35,* 282–287.

Brown, J., Rawlinson, M., & Hilles, N. (1981). Life satisfaction and chronic disease. Exploration of a theoretical model. *Medical Care, 19,* 1136–1146.

Burckhardt, C. S. (1985). The impact of arthritis on quality of life. *Nursing Research, 34,* 11–16.

Charmaz, K. (1983). Loss of self: A fundamental form of suffering in the chronically ill. *Sociology of Health and Illness, 5,* 168–195.

Cohen, S., & Syme, S. L. (1985). Issues in the study and application of social support. In S. Cohen & S. L. Syme (Eds.), *Social support and health* (pp. 3–21). Orlando: Academic Press.

Cooper, I. S. (1976). *Living with chronic neurologic disease.* New York: WW Norton.

Corbin, J., & Strauss, A. (1988). *Unending work and care: Managing chronic illness at home.* San Francisco: Jossey-Bass.

Corbin, J., & Strauss, A. (1984). Collaboration: Couples working together to manage chronic illness. *Image: The Journal of Nursing Scholarship, 14,* 109–115.

Craig, H. M., & Edwards, J. E. (1983). Adaptation in chronic illness: An eclectic model for nurses. *Journal of Advanced Nursing, 8,* 397–404.

deCharms, R. (1968). *Personal causation: The internal affective determinants of behavior.* New York: Academic Press.

Deci, E. (1976). *Intrinsic motivation.* New York: Plenum Press.

Dimond, M. (1979). Social support and adaptation to chronic illness. The case of maintenance hemodialysis. *Research in Nursing and Health, 2,* 101–108.

Driever, M. (1976). Theory of self-concept. In C. Roy (Ed.), *Introduction to nursing: An adaptation model* (pp. 169–191). Englewood Cliffs, NJ: Prentice Hall.

Epstein, S. (1973). The self-concept revisited: Or a theory of a theory. *American Psychologist, 28,* 404–416.

Feldman, D. (1974). Chronic disabling illness: A holistic view. *Journal of Chronic Disease, 27,* 287–291.

Ferrans, C., & Powers, M. (1985). Quality of Life Index: Development and psychometric properties. *Advances in Nursing Science, 8,* 15–24.

Frank, J. (1975). *Persuasion and healing.* New York: Schocken Books.

George, L., & Bearon, L. (1980). *Quality of life in older persons.* New York: Human Sciences Press.

Johnson, J. (1973). Effects of accurate expectations about sensation on the sensory and distress components of pain. *Journal of Personality and Social Psychology, 27,* 261–275.

Johnson, J. (1972). The effect of structuring patients' expectation on their reactions to threatening events. *Nursing Research, 21,* 499–504.

Johnson, J., Kirchhoff, K., & Endress, M. (1975). Altering children's distress behavior during orthopedic cast removal. *Nursing Research, 24,* 404–410.

Johnson, J., Morrissey, J., & Leventhal, H. (1973). Psychological preparation for an endoscopic examination. *Gastrointestinal Endoscopy, 19,* 180–182.

Johnson, J., & Rice, V. (1974). Sensory and distress components of pain: Implications for the study of clinical pain. *Nursing Research, 23,* 203–209.

Kagan, J. (1972). Motives and development. *Journal of Personality and Social Psychology, 22,* 51–66.

Kinsman, R., Jones, N., Matus, I., & Schum, R. (1976). Patient variable supporting chronic illness. *The Journal of Nervous and Mental Disease, 163,* 159–165.

Kobasa, S. (1982). Commitment and coping in stress-resistance among lawyers. *Journal of Personality and Social Psychology, 42,* 707–711.

Kobasa, S. (1979a). Personality and resistance to illness. *American Journal of Community Psychology, 7,* 413–423.

Kobasa, S. (1979b). Stressful life events, personality, and health: An inquiry into hardiness. *Journal of Personality and Social Psychology, 37,* 1–11.

Kobasa, S., Maddri, S., Puccetti, M., & Zola, M. (1985). Effectiveness of hardiness, exercise and social support as resources against illness. *Journal of Psychosomatic Research, 29,* 525–533.

Kraines, S. (1943). *The theory of neuroses and psychoses.* Philadelphia: Lea & Febiger.

Lambert, C., & Lambert, V. (1987). Hardiness: Its development and relevance to nursing. *Image: Journal of Nursing Scholarship, 19,* 92–95.

Lambert, V., Lambert, C., Klipple, G., & Mewshaw, E. (1989). Social support, hardiness and psychological well-being in women with arthritis. *Image: Journal of Nursing Scholarship, 21,* 128–131.

Lawrence, S. A., & Lawrence, R. M. (1979). A model of adaptation to the stress of chronic illness. *Nursing Forum, 18,* 33–42.

Lefcourt, H. (1966). Belief in personal control: Research and implications. *Journal of Individual Psychology, 22,* 185–195.

Leventhal, H., Meyer, D., & Nerenz, D. (1980). The commonsense representation of illness danger. In S. Rachman (Ed.), *Contributions to medical psychology* (Vol. 2, pp. 3–26). Oxford: Permagon Press.

Lubkin, I. (1986). *Chronic illness: Impact and interventions.* Boston: Jones and Bartlett Publishers.

May, R. (1972). *Power and innocence.* New York: WW Norton.

Maybury, C. P., & Brewin, C. R. (1984). Social relationships, knowledge and adjustment to multiple sclerosis: An exploratory study. *Social Science and Medicine, 11,* 245–250.

McNett, S. C. (1987). Social support, threat, and coping effectiveness in the functionally disabled. *Nursing Research, 36,* 98–193.

Miller, J. F. (1982). Categories of self-care needs of ambulatory patients with diabetes. *Journal of Advanced Nursing, 7,* 25–31.

Mishel, M. H. (1988). Uncertainty in illness. *Image: Journal of Nursing Scholarship, 20,* 225–232.

Mishel, M. H. (1983). Parents perception of uncertainty concerning their hospitalized child. *Nursing Research, 32,* 324–330.

Mishel, M. H. (1981). The measurement of uncertainty in illness. *Nursing Reseach, 30,* 258–263.

Mishel, M. H., & Braden, C. J. (1988). Finding meaning: Antecedents of uncertainty. *Nursing Research, 37,* 98–103.

Mishel, M. H., & Braden, C. J. (1987). Uncertainty: A mediator between support and adjustment. *Western Journal of Nursing Research, 9,* 43–57.

Mishel, M. H., Hostetter, T., King, B., & Graham, V. (1984). Predictors of psychosocial adjustment in patients newly diagnosed with gynecological cancer. *Cancer Nursing, 7,* 291–299.

Mishel, M. H., & Murdaugh, C. (1987). Family experiences with heart transplantation: Redesigning the dream. *Nursing Research, 36,* 332–338.

Moberg, D. (1979). *Spiritual well-being: Sociological perspectives.* Washington, D.C.: University Press of America.

Northouse, L. L. (1988). Social support in patients' and husbands' adjustment to breast cancer. *Nursing Research, 37,* 91–95.

Nowack, K. (1989). Coping style, cognitive hardiness, and health status. *Journal of Behavioral Medicine, 12,* 145–158.

Padilla, G., Presant, C., Grant, M., Metter, G., Lipsett, J., & Heide, R. (1983). Quality of Life Index for patients with cancer. *Research in Nursing and Health, 6,* 117–126.

Pattison, E. M. (1974). Psychosocial predictors of death prognosis. *Omega, 5,* 145–159.

Pollock, S. E. (1989). The hardiness characteristic: A motivating factor in adaptation. *Advances in Nursing Science, 11,* 53–62.

Pollock, S. E. (1986). Human responses to chronic illness: Physiologic and psychosocial adaptation. *Nursing Research, 35,* 90–95.

Radley, A., & Green, R. (1987). Illness as adjustment: A methodology and conceptual framework. *Sociology of Health and Illness, 9,* 179–207.

Reif, L. (1975). Beyond medical intervention strategies for managing life in face of chronic illness. In M. Davis, M. Kramer, & A. Strauss (Eds.), *Nurses in practice: A perspective on work environments* (pp. 261–273). St. Louis: CV Mosby.

Rosenberg, M. (1979). *Conceiving the self.* New York: Basic Books.

Rotter, J. (1966). Generalized expectancies for internal versus external control of reinforcement. *Psychological Monographs, 80,* 1–28.

Ryden, M. (1977). Energey: A crucial consideration in the nursing process. *Nursing Forum, 16,* 71–82.

Schaefer, C., Coyne, J., & Lazarus, R. (1981). The health-related function of social support. *Journal of Behavioral Medicine, 4,* 381–406.

Strain, J. (1979). Psychological reactions to chronic medical illness. *Psychiatric Quarterly, 51,* 173–183.

Strauss, A., et al. (1984). *Chronic illness and the quality of life.* St. Louis: CV Mosby.

Thorne, S., & Robinson, C. (1989). Guarded alliance: Health care relationships in chronic illness. *Image: Journal of Nursing Scholarship, 21,* 153–157.

Thorne, S., & Robinson, C. (1988). Health care relationships: The chronic illness perspective. *Research in Nursing and Health, 11,* 293–300.

Turk, D. (1979). Factors influencing the adaptive process with chronic illness. In I. Sarason, & C. Spielberger (Eds.), *Stress and anxiety* (Vol. 6, pp. 291–311). New York: John Wiley & Sons.

Turk, D., Sobel, H., Follick, M., & Youkilis, H. (1980). A sequential criterion analysis for assessing coping with chronic illness. *Journal of Human Stress, 6,* 35–40.

Turk, D., Rudy, T., & Salovey, P. (1986). Implicit models of illness. *Journal of Behavioral Medicine, 9,* 453–474.

Uhlenhuth, E. H., & Duncan, D. B. (1968). Subjective change with medical student therapists: Some determinants for change in psychoneurotic outpatients. *Archives of General Psychiatry, 18,* 532–540.

Weiss, R. S. (1974). The provisions of social relationships. In Z. Rubin (Ed.), *Doing unto others* (pp. 17–26). Englewood Cliffs, NJ: Prentice Hall.

Winert, C. (1983). The physiological and psychosocial stress of long term illness and the effects of social support on the "healthy" functioning of the families. *Western Journal of Nursing Research, 5,* 34.

Wortman, C., & Brehm, J. (1975). Responses to uncontrollable outcomes: An integration of reactance theory and learned helplessness. In L. Berkowitz (Ed.), *Advances in experimental social psychology* (Vol. 8, pp. 277–336). New York: Academic Press.

Zedlow, P. W., & Pavlou, M. (1984). Physical disability, life stress, and psychosocial adjustment to multiple sclerosis. *Journal of Nervous and Mental Diseases, 172,* 80–84.

■

Analysis of Coping with Illness

■ **JUDITH FITZGERALD MILLER**

The unique manner in which individuals and families deal with the demands of chronic illness influences the degree and nature of lifelong adjustment and well-being. Patients and families must develop skills not only to manage the physical care demands and life-style modifications accompanying illness but also to cope with a taxonomy of psychosocial tasks accompanying illness. Some stressors of chronic illness are transitory; however, uncertainty is ever-present (Auerbach, 1989). It may not be possible to reverse disability, but knowledge about coping strategies can moderate the psychologic impact of illness (Johnson, Lauver, & Nail, 1989).

Coping Defined

There are varied clinical and research traditions on coping, each having a slightly different emphasis. Psychoanalysts and some psychologists view coping as a stable personality-based emotional and behavioral mode of responding. Some experimental psychologists study coping as learning escape and avoidance of threatening stimuli (Roth & Cohen, 1986). Physiologic perspectives consider coping as cortical and subcortical stimulation by the hypothalamus resulting in activation of the pituitary and adrenocortical system. Others such as Lazarus and Folkman (1984) view coping as context-specific behavioral and emotional processes in which an individual appraises, encounters, and recovers from contact with a stressor, whether a minor daily hassle or a major life change (Peterson, 1989). Mechanic's (1974) social-psychologic view is that coping deals with social environmental demands. From an education perspective, coping is problem solving; confronting the realities of the problem while maintaining integrity of functioning (Bruner, 1966). Coping is the constantly changing cognitive and behavioral efforts used to manage specific external and/or internal demands that are appraised as taxing and that exceed the resources of the person (Lazarus & Folkman, 1984). Coping is what an individual does about a problem to bring about relief, reward, quiescence, and equilibrium (Weisman, 1979). Focusing specifically on illness, Lipowski (1970) defines coping as all cognitive and motor activities a sick person uses to preserve bodily and psychic integrity, to recover reversible impaired function, and to compensate to the limit for any irreversible loss. Although Haan (1977) differentiates defense mechanisms (defending) from coping, in this book defense mechanisms are viewed as a part of the individual's coping repertoire. Haan views defense mechanisms as rigid psychologic mechanisms regardless of the nature of the problem and defines coping as an open dynamic process that permits new information to be used and behavior modified in light of new insights.

Throughout this chapter, coping refers to dealing with situations that present a threat to the individual so as to resolve uncomfortable feelings such as anxiety, fear, grief, and guilt. Problems precipitating these uncomfortable affects may be thought of as coping tasks. Coping tasks are external stimuli such as dealing with pain, threat of surgery, and impending death, as well as internal psychic phenomena such as threatened body image, perceived alterations in role function, and unresolved anger. Coping strategies are the specific techniques a sick person selects to deal with the illness and its consequences. An individual's coping style is one's enduring disposition to deal with challenges and stress by employing a specific group of techniques (Lipowski, 1970). Weisman (1979, p. 27) states, "Coping combines perception, performance, appraisal, correction, followed by further activity and directed motivated behavior." The aim of coping is mastery, control, or resolution (Weisman & Worden, 1976–1977).

COPING PROCESS

The coping process may include a two-staged cognitive process of primary and secondary appraisals (Lazarus & Folkman, 1984). With the primary appraisal, the individual determines whether the conditions or stimuli are a threat ("Am I O.K.?"), and the secondary appraisal includes a review of choices of action if a threat is perceived ("What can I do?"). Responses include behaviors such as emotional, cognitive, and physical activities.

The coping process may have differing results such as mastery, resilience, or crisis (resolved or unresolved) (Garland & Bush, 1982). If the threat is resolved, the coping behavior will be used in similar situations and a sense of *mastery* will be achieved. In some cases, the threat may not be averted, yet the individual gets through the event without lasting psychic trauma and manifests *resilience* (successful coping). If the threatening situation is not handled effectively (ineffective coping), a *crisis* may result, and if unresolved, psychologic and physiologic disequilibrium may occur. The crisis may be resolved with or without professional intervention, and the individual returns to previous or higher levels of functioning.

COPING FUNCTIONS

The function of coping varies with the differing coping theoretical frameworks used (Lazarus & Folkman, 1984) and may include:

- Reduction of tension and maintenance of equilibrium (adaptation)
- Sound decision making
- Maintenance of autonomy and freedom
- Motivation to meet soical environmental demands
- Maintenance of stable social, psychologic, and physical state
- Control of the meaning of potential stressors before they become a threat, and according to Beutel (1985)
- Avoidance of negative self-evaluation

Pearlin and Schooler (1978) describe four types of functions: (1) prevention of stress from events or situations; (2) alteration of the situation or problem; (3) change in the meaning of the situation; and (4) management of the symptoms or reactions to the stress. Lazarus and Folkman (1984) divided coping functions into emotion-focused and problem-focused coping. Emotion-focused coping is said to be prevalent when persons conclude that they cannot control the stressful stimuli; that is, nothing can modify the harmful threatening event. Examples of emotion-focused strategies include avoidance, minimization, distancing, selective attention, mediating, venting feelings, and increasing physical activity as a distractor. Problem-focused coping is the use of a problem-solving process including defining the problem, enumerating alternatives, comparing alternatives in terms of costs and benefits, and finally, selecting an action. Problem-focused strategies are enacted when the threat is appraised as being changeable. Learning new self-care skills to confront the demand is a problem-focused strategy.

Jalowiec (1989) reported three types of coping strategies as a result of confirmatory factor analysis of her Coping Scale based on 1400 respondents. The three factors were confrontive (e.g., discuss problems, seek information, set goals, maintain control), emotive (e.g., worry, expect the worst, blame others), and palliative coping (e.g., sleep, laugh it off, pray, let someone else solve it).

EFFECTIVE COPING

Coping behavior is effective when the behavior utilized resolves the uncomfortable feeling associated with threat and/or loss, preserves the integrity of the individual, and preserves the ability of the individual to function effectively in relationships, life roles, and maintenance of a positive self-concept. Visotsky and coworkers (1961) described coping as being effective when it (1) kept distress within manageable limits, (2) generated encouragement and hope, (3) maintained or restored a sense of personal worth, (4) maintained or restored relationships with significant others, (5) enhanced prospects for physical recovery, and (6) enhanced prospects for favorable situations (interpersonal, social, and economic). Caplan (1963) identified effective coping strategies such as actively exploring reality issues and searching for information; freely expressing both positive and negative feelings, and having tolerance for frustration; actively invoking help from others; breaking problems into manageable bits and working them through one at a time; being aware of fatigue and tendencies toward disorganization, pacing activities, and engaging in problem-solving efforts; mastering feelings when possible and accepting the inevitable when not; trusting in oneself and others, and maintaining optimism about the outcome.

Coping Styles

Coping changes with situational demands. Flexibility is favored over a rigid style. Some consistency in terms of coping style yet variability in use of select strategies depending upon seriousness of the threat has been noted to be effective. The repeated manner in which the chronically ill individual responds to the presenting coping task is the individual's coping style. Coping style can be identified by noting the individual's range of behaviors over time. Coping styles can be divided into three categories: approach, avoidance, and nonspecific defense (Goldstein, Jones, Clemens, Flagg, & Alexander, 1965; Lazarus, 1966; Lipowski, 1969; 1970; Lomont, 1965). The term approach (Lazarus, 1966) is synonymous with the style Goldstein and coworkers (1965) labeled sensitizer and Lipowski (1970) labeled vigilant focuser. The term avoidance is synonymous with minimization (Lipowski, 1970) and repression (Lomont, 1965). Figure 2-1 illustrates the coping continuum.

To be effective, the coping response should match the nature of the

Approach   Nonspecific defenders   Avoidance
(Vigilant focuser)   (Minimizer)
(Sensitizer)   (Repressor)

FIGURE 2 ■ 1   Continuum of coping styles with synonymous terms identified.

demand (Roth & Cohen, 1986). Mullen and Suls (1982) found that avoidance strategies were effective for short-term outcomes, but approach strategies were more effective for long-term outcomes. Denial might be helpful early in the chronic illness, during an acute traumatic event, or when a threatening situation is uncontrollable (Roth & Cohen, 1986). However, if this method of avoidance continues to such extremes that treatment is not sought or abandoned, then the denial is no longer effective.

Roth and Cohen (1986) summarized the benefits and costs for both extremes of coping. The benefits of approach include: action is taken to alleviate the problem; emotions are accurately perceived and ventilated; and effects of the trauma *may* be integrated, preserving a positive self-concept. The cost or risk of approach may be increased distress and excessive anxiety. Benefits of avoidance include obtaining a reprieve from nonproductive worry and having time to find reasons for hope. Eventually these effects of avoidance may lead to approach methods. The cost or risk of avoidance is that appropriate problem-solving and/or treatment may be delayed; true feelings are not perceived and disclosed; accurate information may intrude and heighten anxiety.

Individuals who practice avoidance use repression. denial, projection, and any other strategy that minimizes the threat. Avoidance includes intellectual strategies that diminish the seriousness of the threat for the individual. Selective inattention and ignoring or rationalizing the facts or consequences of the illness are avoidance strategies (Kiely, 1972).

Approach behaviors on the other end of the coping continuum include tackling, vigilant focusing, and sensitizing. Tackling is an energetic fighting of the illness and an active engaging in therapy. Vigilant focusing refers to an obsessional alertness and compulsive attention to details of therapy. Vigilant focusers need detailed explanations of procedures and treatment (Kiely, 1972) and have more evident anxiety than do minimizers. Sensitizers are those who readily acknowledge threatening emotions of hate, fear, disgust, and love (Andrew, 1973). They are on the approach end of the coping continuum because of their direct confrontation with emotional states.

Neutrals, or nonspecific defenders, use combinations of approach and avoidance strategies. On the Mainord Coper-Avoider Sentence Completion Test (an instrument to measure coping), the individuals classified as neutrals score in the middle; they are neither avoiders nor sensitizers (Andrew, 1973).

Impact of Patient's Coping Style on Care

Does being able to recognize an individual's coping mechanisms serve any real therapeutic purpose? Identifying patients' coping styles and specific coping strategies is imperative for a holistic nursing approach. Nurses need to be made acquainted with how the patient is confronting the ups and downs of chronic illness. Nurses may unwittingly stifle helpful patient strategies, making judgments about what they themselves would do in similar circumstances instead of objectively evaluating the patient's selected strategies and supporting those that are effective.

Judgments cannot be made about the value of approach versus avoidance strategies unless criteria for effective coping are used (see Fig. 2-1). Coping is effective if uncomfortable feelings of anxiety, fear, grief, or guilt are contained; hope is generated; self-esteem is enhanced; relationships with others are maintained; and a state of wellness is maintained or improved. Cohen and Lazarus (1973) studied 61 surgical patients to determine the relationship between the mode of coping and recovery from surgery. Patients were classified as using avoidance, vigilance, or both types of behavior according to results of the Andrew version of the Goldstein Coper-Avoider Sentence Completion Test (1967). The variables studied were number of days in the hospital, number of analgesics used, minor medical complications, and negative psychologic reactions. The 10 vigilant patients had slower recoveries that required more days of hospitalization and had more minor complications than did the 14 patients who used avoidance or the 37 patients who manifested both vigilance and avoidance. There were no significant differences in the other variables (Cohen & Lazarus, 1973).

Nurses need to be aware that patients who are vigilant focusers are active seekers of information who master situations in active roles. Persons using this coping style must be kept informed of minute details of care and alternative methods available. The vigilant focuser needs to participate fully in providing care, setting goals, and evaluating progress. Vigilant focusers may test staff by asking several persons the same questions to compare responses and verify information already received. These patients need the same approaches used by nurses for various personal-care activities. Variation in approaches will heighten already-present anxiety. Being forced into powerlessness situations of pain and disability may be more devastating to the vigilant patient than to an avoider.

It is particularly relevant for nurses to note that instruction programs need to be tailored to the individual's coping style. To give an individual who is an avoider the precise details of an anticipated stress may cause more harm than good. On the other hand, the vigilant focuser needs to feel in control, and the sense of control is rooted in knowledge and competent participation in care. To bombard the avoider with information may diminish ability to cope. To avoid the details of what will occur in dealing with a vigilant focuser heightens anxiety and diminishes coping ability.

Shanan and colleagues (1976) studied 59 terminally ill renal failure patients who were on hemodialysis and a matched sample of 59 subjects to determine if prolonged stress reduced active coping and to determine the effect of the patients' backgrounds on coping. The results of the Shanan Sentence Completion Test indicate that patients on dialysis obtained lower coping scores and had passivity, negative self-perception, and a tendency to withdraw by using denial. The only background variables related to illness and coping were the individual's sex and education. Women were more negative than men. Education helped prepare the patient to cope with specific problems.

Miller and Mangan (1983) studied types of surgical preparatory information provided patients with differing coping style preferences. Persons were assigned to one of two conditions: high amount of presurgical information and low amount of information. Persons whose coping style was consistent with the depth of information presented had less distress than those with a discrepancy between style and the intervention. That is, vigilant focusers needed detailed information whereas avoiders benefited from less detail.

COPING DETERMINANTS

The way a person copes with illness is influenced by the nature of the power resources of belief system (faith and hope); family–social support; psychologic well-being; self-esteem; motivation; type and meaning of the illness; number and seriousness of the illness-related demands; stage of illness progression; developmental and family influences; previous success using varied strategies; accurate appraisal of the threat; self-insight; and self-efficacy. Intrapersonal factors affecting coping may include age, personality, culture, specific self-care skills, values, beliefs, emotional state, and cognitive capacity. Environmental factors may include presence of a support system, access to health services, physical resources for living, and financial resources.

In analyzing the stages of progression of an illness, differences in coping energy utilization can be easily understood. Charmaz (1973) presented a three-stage progression of chronic disease. Stage 1 is labeled interrupted time, when daily activities are temporarily adjusted to obtain a diagnosis. Stage 2 is the time intrusion phase, when daily activities need to be adjusted to control the effect of the disease. The illness consumes time and energy. Stage 3 is time encapsulation, during which the individual is consumed by the illness; the individual is engulfed with care management throughout the day.

The meaning of the illness to the individual affects coping behavior. Differences in coping can be expected if one individual perceives the illness to be a threat to sexual role functioning and another views the illness as insignificant. Illness may be viewed as a loss or gain, or of no significance.

Perceiving illness as a loss refers to loss of pleasures, role fulfillment, functional abilities, self-esteem, self-satisfaction, love, recognition, and normalcy. Illness may be viewed as a threat to life. Grief and anxiety accompany the perception of illness as a loss.

Illness may be perceived by some as a gain if it provides relief from the stress of other life roles. The suffering of illness may be viewed as having spiritual value for the individual and as an opportunity to relieve guilt, repent for perceived past offenses, and to accept this plight as a punishment. Illness may provide respite from intrapersonal conflict or an opportunity to withdraw and resolve conflict. It may also afford some individuals the opportunity to receive kindness, attention, and signs of affection they might otherwise not get.

If the individual views the illness as insignificant, little importance is assigned to the symptoms (Lipowski, 1969) or possible consequences of the illness and treatment.

The nurse's understanding of the patient's perception of the illness will enhance the nurse's ability to identify and support the coping strategy the patient selects. Clear differences in coping would exist between individuals perceiving illness as a threat or loss and those perceiving illness as a gain or as insignificant.

Coping Tasks of Chronically Ill Individuals

Coping tasks are those particular challenges that must be faced and overcome so that the individual preserves integrity, restores or maintains a positive concept of self, and functions effectively in relationships and life roles. Individuals with chronic health problems may be challenged to cope with multiple complex tasks.

Kiely (1972) categorized three types of stresses that initiate coping responses: (1) loss or threat of loss of psychic "objects," that is, personal relationships, body functions and image, and social roles; (2) injury or threat of injury to body involving notions of pain or mutilation; and (3) frustration of biologic drive satisfaction—especially nurturant or libidinal drives—as well as frustration over lack of avenues for aggressive discharge.

To identify the coping tasks of chronically ill persons, nursing diagnoses of 118 chronically ill patients were reviewed. These nursing diagnoses were made by 44 graduate nursing students enrolled in a graduate nursing practicum course entitled "Nursing Strategies for Adults: Long-Term Health Problems." Each student studied and cared for a small caseload of patients (no more than three) for the duration of the academic

TABLE 2 ■ I   Typology of Coping Tasks of Chronically Ill Adults*

Broad Task Category	Subconcepts in the Category
1. Maintaining a sense of normalcy.	Hiding, minimizing illness, and/or responding to curious inquiries of others. Living as normally as possible despite daily therapy and obvious symptoms.
2. Modifying daily routine, adjusting life-style.	Including therapy and symptom control in daily routine. Providing for safety.
3. Obtaining knowledge and skill for continuing self-care.	Having internal awareness. Monitoring effects of therapy.
4. Maintaining a positive concept of self.	Integrating illness into self-concept. Maintaining or enhancing self-esteem.
5. Adjusting to altered social relationships.	Experiencing loneliness and social isolation. Undergoing patient- or other-initiated disengagement. Preserving relationships with friends and family who satisfy dependency needs. Maintaining family solidarity.
6. Grieving over losses concomitant with chronic illness.	Losing physical abilities, function. Losing status. Losing income and social relationships. Losing roles and dignity. Dealing with financial losses.
7. Dealing with role change.	Losing roles—social, work, family. Gaining roles—dependent help seeker, self-care agent, chronically ill patient.
8. Handling physical discomfort.	Handling illness-induced discomfort. Handling pain caused by therapy.
9. Complying with prescribed regimen.	
10. Confronting the inevitability of one's own death.	
11. Dealing with social stigma of illness or disability.	
12. Maintaining a feeling of being in control.	Exerting cognitive control. Exerting behavioral control. Exerting decisional control.
13. Maintaining hope despite uncertain or downward course of health.	Experiencing effects of hope. Finding meaning in physical changes.

*Supported by HEW Grant No. 1 D23 NU00038-62.

semester. Coping tasks were also identified in literature review and through Stapleton's (1978) and this author's clinical practice. Table 2-1 lists the coping tasks identified; each will be discussed briefly.

STRIVING TO FEEL NORMAL

Maintaining a sense of normalcy includes keeping signs and symptoms of illness under control or out of view of persons surrounding the individual. It includes a mental review of existing abilities and functions. When the chronically ill individual engages in a personal reaffirmation of being as capable as coworkers or the individuals in the person's social network, the ideal of being and feeling normal (having abilities similar to others in the social network) is fostered.

Wiener (1975) described individuals with rheumatoid arthritis using the normalizing strategies of covering up, keeping up, and pacing. Covering up means keeping signs of disability and pain hidden and may include not using an assistive device—cane or other external sign of handicap such as a wheelchair. Controlling evidence of discomfort and fatigue is an imperative behavior for successful covering up. Chronically ill individuals expend much energy covering up, not only to maintain a sense of normalcy, but to avoid curious questioners and to avoid making those around them feel uncomfortable. Persons interacting with the chronically ill individual may feel uncomfortable about not knowing how much assistance with mobility to provide, how to respond to obvious evidence of pain, and how to minimize their own vigor and vitality so as to lessen the discrepancy between themselves and the chronically ill person's impairment. Covering up is not a form of denial; it is a refusal to allow the disability to interfere with social interactions.

Keeping up refers to the ill individual's successful carrying through with a planned event (Wiener, 1975), while covering up, expending increased energy, and causing overwhelming fatigue and perhaps exacerbation of symptoms. Events, such as hosting a family get-together or preparing a holiday meal, call for frantic keep-up activity.

Pacing refers to balancing the activities of covering up and keeping up with the rest needed to avoid unnecessary periods of immobilization in order to restore energy wasted in covering up and keeping up. Pacing results from understanding limitations in abilities and appropriately engaging in activities that satisfy ego needs without causing undue exhaustion.

MODIFYING ROUTINES AND LIFE-STYLES

To control symptoms and live as normally as possible, the individual may need to alter habits and routines. Habits of overeating, lack of exercise, lack of relaxation, or smoking may need to be modified. Daily routines may need to be interrupted to obtain needed therapy for the chronic disease, for example, postural drainage and intermittent positive-pressure breathing for individuals with emphysema. Activities that exacerbate symptoms must be learned and avoided. (The elementary teacher with rheumatoid arthritis may need to avoid playground duty on cool, damp days, for example.)

OBTAINING KNOWLEDGE AND SKILL FOR CONTINUING SELF-CARE

Self-care is a key concept for the chronically ill individual's maintenance of optimal health. Achieving desired outcomes depends on the patient's self-care practices and not on the power of the health-care team. Being competent in ministering to self means acquiring the necessary skills, knowledge, and motivation. It also means having an awareness of body cues, interpreting physical changes accurately, and taking appropriate action either to alter therapy or to seek help from health-care resources to prevent a crisis.

MAINTAINING A POSITIVE CONCEPT OF SELF

When previous abilities are gone, energy and ability to successfully engage in desired activities that satisfy ego needs have disappeared, changes in physical self have occurred, and maintaining a positive concept of self is a major coping task. The individual must avoid allowing the disability or illness to become one's entire identity. Instead, the illness, related changes, and therapies must be integrated into a positive concept of self that helps the individual maintain a sense of competence and normalcy. Activities that enhance self-esteem need to be identified; and the remaining personal strengths need to be emphasized. Helping the patient review accomplishments and remaining intact roles enhances self-esteem. Balancing the self-ideal with the altered body image is necessary to maintain a positive self-concept and self-esteem (see Chap. 16).

ADJUSTING TO ALTERED SOCIAL RELATIONSHIPS

Chronic illness may cause social isolation and loneliness. The sick person may withdraw because of a depleted energy reserve or poor self-concept, feeling unworthy of previous social contacts, or simply being physically unable to participate in former social events. As the illness encapsulates more of the person's time, thought processes may be dominated by the illness, controlling symptoms, and obtaining relief. Only the most loyal friends may persist in being supportive during this repetitive pattern of interaction. In other words, isolation may be initiated by significant others' withdrawal to obtain relief from the difficult scene of physical deterioration. Davis (1975, p. 253) quotes a chronically ill woman as saying, "Anyone who is sick for longer than 6 months won't be remembered except for birthdays and holidays."

The ill individual may need to adjust to having fewer interactions with fewer people and to receiving decreased confirmation of being a capable individual. The ill person must also strive to preserve relationships with those friends and family members who satisfy physical and emotional dependency needs.

GRIEVING OVER THE LOSSES OF CHRONIC ILLNESS

Chronically ill individuals grieve over multiple losses. Loss of physical abilities includes losses of mobility, organ functioning, energy availability, physical stamina, sexual attractiveness, and sexual function. Other losses may include loss of self-esteem, role performance, and social relationships. Grief work takes place to deal with these losses and to preserve a sense of personal integrity and dignity. The cumulative effect of significant losses may create doubts in ill persons' minds about their own ability to maintain quality of life. Reformulating goals and examining aspirations requires coping skills.

DEALING WITH ROLE CHANGE

Role changes of chronically ill persons may be analyzed in terms of loss and gain. The role losses may include loss of social roles (church participant, member of bowling team, officer in a community group) and employment role, and diminishing of the role of family decision maker and disciplinarian. The individual has to take on roles of being chronically ill, dependent help seeker, self-care agent, and client of a complex health-care system.

Role change encompasses giving up roles accompanied by grief work, as well as taking on new roles accompanied by role insufficiency. "Role insufficiency is any difficulty in the cognizance and/or performance of a role or of the sentiments and goals associated with the role behavior as perceived by self or by significant others" (Melies, 1975, p. 264). In adoption of the role of self-care agent, rehearsal of role enactment may be an important prelude to actual role taking. Kassebaum and Baumann (1965) point out that Parsons' sick-role theory (Parsons, 1951) is inadequate for the chronically ill person because of Parsons' emphasis on the temporary surrendering of roles and the person's desire to get well. Kassebaum and Baumann identified four dimensions of the sick role in chronically ill persons. The dimensions include dependence, reciprocity (mutual expectations for exemption from some role obligations), role-performance alteration, and denial of sick role. The incapacity for role performance is not a total, temporary incapacity as described by Parsons, but rather may be a partial permanent alteration in roles and performance of roles (Kassebaum & Baumann, 1965).

Learning the role of dependent help seeker, maintaining a positive dependence, is another component of this coping task. Positive dependency "requires honest acceptance of one's differentness and the special needs and conditions it imposes" (Feldman 1974, p. 290). Seeking help for physical and emotional needs without feeling weak and inadequate is necessary. The patient is challenged to resolve feelings of conflict over wanting to be totally independent yet needing to be dependent at a time in adult life when independence is expected. Manipulating a complex health-care system to have needs met is also a challenge to the individual. Accepting the role of being chronically ill and having a less-than-ideal state of health is included in coping with role changes.

HANDLING PHYSICAL DISCOMFORT

Virtually all chronic illnesses are accompanied by some discomfort, either from the disorder itself (e.g., joint pain of arthritis) or from the prescribed therapy (e.g., insulin injections or hemodialysis treatment). The individual needs to discover personally satisfying and adequate means of dealing with pain. Modalities adjunctive to medications that have been effective include relaxation, autosuggestion, distraction (as with music), and biofeedback.

As pain becomes chronic, the sufferer devotes time and energy describing the discomfort so as to reinforce with others that the pain is legitimate. The pain of a specific chronic illness such as arthritis is not as overt as pain of a fracture or surgical incisions. When the pain experience is prolonged and the chronically ill patient's pain experience is not congruent with health-care workers' perception of the usual course of pain, the patient may need constantly to reaffirm that the pain is real.

COMPLYING WITH THE PRESCRIBED REGIMEN

It is one thing to make temporary adjustments in habits and daily patterns and quite another to alter habits for the rest of a lifetime. Acquiring new behaviors, taking medications, and so forth are less difficult compliance problems than altering personal habits and routine behaviors of smoking, drinking, and eating (Haynes, 1976). Helping sick individuals realize that their actions will result in desired outcomes is a challenge to health professionals, especially when the actions demand discipline and result in uncomfortable side effects.

CONFRONTING THE INEVITABILITY OF ONE'S OWN DEATH

Having a chronic illness causes reflection on life's accomplishments and a direct realization of the temporary nature of earthly existence. There may be thoughts of having "little time left," especially in comparison with the life expectancies of healthy friends. The goal is to confront this task, interpreting it as a challenge to make the most of life instead of giving in to paralyzing depression and anticipating one's own demise.

DEALING WITH SOCIAL STIGMA

How does the chronically ill individual handle the second looks, the stares from children, and the embarrassment of being unable to enter buildings or use toilet facilities unassisted? Wright (1983) describes three types of responses of individuals to stigmatizing behavior: (1) ignore it, bury one's head in the sand; (2) overreact with rage, retaliation, and overt hostility; and (3) use humor, which may cause further self-deprecation.

Nurses can help chronically ill persons develop mature acceptance of self and undaunted self-confidence, despite the disability.

MAINTAINING A FEELING OF BEING IN CONTROL

Chronically ill persons may find it difficult to maintain control because of intrusions into privacy by health-care teams and the sharing of intimate information on medical records for all interested onlookers to review. One patient with brittle diabetes stated, "It's as though you're a butterfly with a pin stuck through you. The MDs come around to view you as a specimen on exhibit." The ability to control environmental intrusion while maintaining a sense of privacy preserves personal dignity.

Controlling a deteriorating physiologic state may not always be possible, even in the best of compliance situations. Enhancing the patient's knowledge of what is happening—physiologic changes and improvements, and effects of therapy—increases a sense of control. Having the patient make decisions about routine timing of therapy and altering habits gives the patient psychologic control. Nurses can plan for increasing patient control according to Averill's (1973) categories: (1) behavior control—the individual's direct action on the environment; (2) cognitive control—the way in which an event is interpreted or appraised by the individual; and (3) decisional control—the opportunity to choose among various courses of action.

MAINTAINING HOPE DESPITE UNCERTAIN OR DOWNWARD COURSE OF ILLNESS

As the chronic health problem progresses, and as physiologic deterioration and loss of function continue, hope is a sustaining force that helps the individual avoid despair and actually "prolongs life against all odds" (Korner, 1970). The course of events is unpredictable in chronic illness, in which remissions and exacerbations occur. There may be uncertainty in day-to-day functioning; for example, patients with rheumatoid arthritis may find planning ahead impossible owing to unexpected pain and stiffness. To augment and confirm an individual's values and purposes in life and to help the individual establish realistic goals are challenges to the nurse and the individual's significant others. Pattison (1974) studied three types of predictors of death prognoses in 12 men with pulmonary emphysema over an 18-month period. He found that neither the physiologic measures (blood gases and pulmonary studies) nor the psychologic measure (Inpatient Multidimensional Psychiatric Scale) was correlated with death or clinical improvement. The only measure that correlated with death was the sociologic tool that determined the nature of family and friend relationships. Clinical improvement correlated with an intact and positive family relationships; death correlated with disruption

and negative family relationships. Hope for life and the will to li\
related to having something and someone to live for (Pattison, 1974).

Coping with Chronic Illness: A Descriptive Study

A study of 56 chronically ill adults was completed to determine the specific coping strategies used to deal with the tasks of being ill. The study sample consisted of the caseloads of 19 graduate students enrolled in a seminar-practicum course entitled "Nursing Strategies for Adults: Long-Term Health Problems" during two academic semesters. The graduate students, with the author's guidance, cared for and studied the patients for 3 months. The students used field notes to record the impact of chronic illness on the patient's life; daily activities of leisure and work, family interaction, role disturbances, self-esteem, patterns of self-care, and grief work. Coping behaviors were documented and summarized from a review of field notes that were recorded throughout the semester. The coping strategies were recorded on a data collection tool "Impact of Chronic Illness." The aim of this tool was to enhance the students' understanding of the world of chronically ill persons as well as to collect data about coping.

Adults with chronic health problems hospitalized during exacerbations in a 700-bed metropolitan hospital were included in the sample. Patients in the sample ranged from ages 20 to 79, with the largest number being in the 40- to 69-year-old age group; 25 subjects were men and 31 were women (Table 2–2).

The medical diagnoses reported in Table 2–3 are the patients' major presenting diagnoses, which caused problems and/or incapacitation at the time of the study. Many patients had multiple diagnoses, for example, patients with coronary artery disease also had underlying diabetes. Only one diagnosis was tabulated for each patient. The most frequent diagnoses were cancer, 12 patients; diabetes, 9 patients; coronary artery disease,

TABLE 2 ■ 2   Sample Age and Sex Characteristics

Age	Number of Men	Number of Women
20–29	2	5
30–39	2	3
40–49	5	7
50–59	7	6
60–69	6	8
70–79	3	2
Total	25	31

TABLE 2 ■ 3   Number of Prevalent
Chronic Diseases

*Chronic Disease**	*Number*
Cancer	12
Coronary artery disease	9
Diabetes	9
Ostomies	5
Congestive heart failure	4
Arthritis	3
Chronic renal failure	3
Multiple sclerosis	3
Amputation	2
Paraplegia	2
Cerebral vascular accident	1
Hypertension	1
Peripheral vascular disease	1
Systemic lupus erythematosus	1
Total	56

*Many patients in the sample had multiple diagnoses. Only the major presenting diagnosis of each patient that is causing problems at this time is listed.

9 patients; and ostomies, 5 patients. (See Table 2–3 for complete tabulation.)

Data on coping from the Impact of Chronic Illness tool were analyzed to determine the various coping strategies 56 patients utilized. The intent was not to categorize the patients as minimizers, focusers, or neutrals, but rather to discover as many effective coping strategies as possible. Coping strategies were considered effective if they met any one of the criteria listed in Figure 2–2 as modified from Visotsky and coworkers (1961).

**Uncomfortable feelings
(anxiety, fear, grief, or guilt) contained**

Hope generated

Self-esteem enhanced

Relationships with others maintained

**State of wellness (self-actualized well-being)
maintained or improved**

FIGURE 2 ■ 2   Criteria for effective coping.

More than one strategy has been identified for each patient. The coping behaviors were categorized as approach or avoidance strategies. Approach strategies are behaviors that indicate a willingness to confront the realities of the threat, an awareness of personal reactions and feelings, and an attempt to deal with these feelings. Avoidance strategies are behaviors that protect the individual from conscious confrontation with the threat. Table 2–4 summarizes the approach and avoidance behaviors.

APPROACH STRATEGIES

The approach strategy most frequently used to deal with the tasks of chronic illness had to do with seeking information. Being attentive to the details of care and symptom control, participating in managing requirements of the illness, and raising questions without hesitation are examples of this approach strategy.

Enhancing one's spiritual life was the second most frequently used approach strategy. Specifically, individuals renewed their faith in God, prayed for strength to endure the threats, and received a sense of peace and hope as a result of "asking God for help." Patients related that they felt God's love and had strong convictions about His goodness to all earthly creatures. They felt God would challenge them with tasks He knew they could handle. When individuals interpreted handling the challenge as an expectation of God, they established a self-expectation to be successful.

Methods of self-distraction—diverting attention from illness to other facets of living—included submerging oneself in work and performing mental exercises such as solving problems and meditating. More passive self-distraction activities were watching television and doing needlework. Self-distraction was classified as an approach strategy when the patient consciously selected these activities as a means of dealing with otherwise continuous thoughts about the illness. Another approach strategy is to be keenly aware of emotions and reactions to personal dilemmas and sharing these feelings with a helper. Some patients coped with stress by using a specific routine of physcial relaxation exercises. Other specific strategies are listed in Table 2–4.

AVOIDANCE STRATEGIES

The mental mechanisms of denial, repression, and suppression are included in the most frequently used avoidance strategies. These influence all the avoidance strategies; that is, if the individual denies the fact that diabetes is serious, participation in treatment may be haphazard, or no help will be sought when assistance is needed. Both of the latter are other avoidance strategies. One patient who was blind because of retinopathy of diabetes believed her eyesight would return. Patients avoid

TABLE 2 ■ 4   Approach and Avoidance Coping Strategies of 56 Chronically Ill Adults

Approach Coping Strategies	Number Using Strategy	Avoidance Coping Strategies	Number Using Strategy
1. Seeks information.	14	1. Uses denial, suppression, repression.	11
—Focuses vigilantly on details of care.		2. Minimizes problems, signs, and symptoms of illness.	9
—Eagerly learns illness-related modifications in habits, diet.		3. Social isolation.	6
—Questions rationale for therapy.		—Disengages from previous activities and social relationships.	
—Compares staff responses to same questions.		—Becomes preoccupied with self.	
2. Gains strength from spirituality.	13	—Withdraws.	
—Prayer.		4. Avoids talking about self, feelings or thinking about health problem.	6
—Faith.		5. Passive acceptance.	5
3. Diverts attention.	10	—Belief in spiritual predestination.	
—Recognizes when becoming anxious; engages in extreme physical exertion or compulsive activity.		—It's God's will; nothing can be done.	
—Meditation.		—Shows little or no emotional concern over existing problems.	
—Pain distraction.		6. Sleeping.	3
—Television.		7. Delays decision making on personal health matters.	2
—Needlework.		8. Considers alternative modes of therapy.	2
4. Expresses feelings and emotions.	8	—Unconventional diets.	
—Cries.		9. Blames others.	2
—Expresses hostility, anger.		—Physician.	
—Describes powerlessness.		10. Refuses to participate in treatment.	1
5. Uses relaxation exercises.	6	11. Excessive dependence on significant other.	1
6. Maintains control.	5	12. Manipulates others.	1
—Of environment.		—Significant other performs care tasks the patient could do.	
—Of daily activity schedules in hospital.		13. Sets unrealistic goals.	1
—Of ostomy care.		14. Unrealistic hope for future.	1
—Of advice-giving to spouse and nurse.		—Functional abilities to return.	
7. Verbalizes concerns.	4	—Remission.	
8. Maintains a positive healthy dependence on others.	4	15. Does not actively seek help.	1
—For physical needs (shopping, housework).		16. Uses cigarettes, drugs, alcohol.	1
—For emotional needs (love, support).			
9. Uses positive thinking techniques	4		
—Tries to see good in every situation.			
—Autosuggestion for pain relief.			

10. Seeks help.	4
—From diabetes nurse-specialist when patient determines it is needed.	
11. Maintains realistic independence.	4
—Completes self-care activities within the limitations of illness.	
—Relates past health experiences to future actions in caring for self (responding to insulin reactions).	
—Manipulates prescribed therapy, tranquilizers.	
—Has realistic expectations for outcome of therapy.	
12. Maintains social activities.	3
—Retirement activities.	
—Church activities.	
13. Sets goals, strives to achieve them.	3
—Attacks problems, "digs in" to get things done.	
14. Reminisces over past accomplishments.	3
—Life review.	
15. Conserves energy.	3
—Analyzes daily activity; saves energy for most desirable activity.	
—Daily rest periods.	
16. Uses humor.	3
17. Intellectualization.	3
—Mental mechanisms used to devise rational, personally meaningful explanations for occurrences (physical deterioration).	
18. Engages in activities covering up disability, discomfort.	2
19. Role rehearsal.	2
—Visualizes what it will be like as illness progresses.	
—Rehearses a variety of personal outcomes as a result of therapy.	
20. Utilizes problem-solving approach.	2
21. Finds comfort in realizing there are other persons who are in the same boat.	1

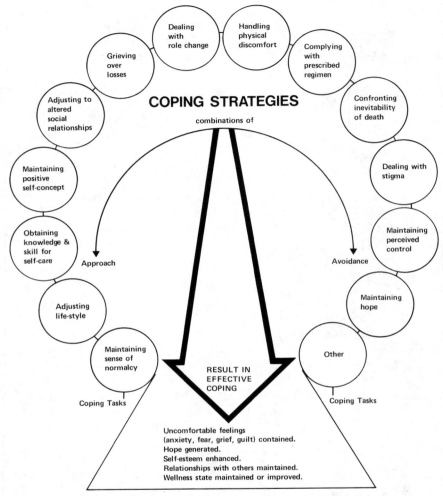

FIGURE 2 ■ 3   A model for coping with chronic illness.

the serious nature of their illness by minimizing symptoms and therapy, playing down consequences of their illness. This is noted in the way the patients describe the illness and refer to their being little affected by it. The third most common avoidance strategy was withdrawing from others, either to avoid disclosure about the impact of the illness or to continue preoccupation with self. In not talking about themselves and their health problems with health-care workers, patients use avoidance; other specific avoidance strategies are listed in Table 2–4.

Although the isolated strategies have been categorized as either approach or avoidance, it should be noted that many patients are in the center of the approach-avoidance continuum, using combinations of approach and avoidance strategies. Figure 2–3 illustrates a model of coping with chronic illness that identifies the tasks and depicts patients' use of coping strategies in which they characterize themselves as approachers, avoiders, or nonspecific defenders (combined approach and avoidance). Criteria for effective coping are included in the model.

Weisman and Worden (1976–1977) studied coping of 120 patients with newly diagnosed cancer. A tool based on the coping scale of Sidle and coworkers (1969) was developed to categorize coping strategies of the patients with cancer. This tool included 15 coping behaviors such as seeking more information (rational inquiry), sharing concerns (mutuality), making light of the situation (affected reversal), doing something else (distraction), taking action regarding the problem (confronting), seeking direction (cooperative compliance), and blaming self (masochism). The coping behaviors used by each patient were compared with their scores on three other indices: (1) the patient's total mood disturbance was measured by the Profile of Mood States; (2) the patient completed a self-rating revealing how adequately the problem was resolved; and (3) the patient's vulnerability index was determined by a psychologic interview. Weisman and Worden concluded that good copers used confrontation, redefinition of the problem (accepting the problem and looking for positive aspects), and compliance with authority. Good copers had high resolution, low vulnerability, and low total mood disturbance. Poor copers used suppression, passivity, submission, and tension-reducing measures (such as drinking and drugs), and had low resolution, high vulnerabiltiy, and high total mood disturbance.

Weisman (1979) described good copers in more detail. Good copers are resourceful and are not rigid; they are characterized by the fact that they avoid denial and take action based on confronting reality, redefine problems into solvable forms—consider alternatives, maintain open communications, seek help and accept support, maintain high morale, and maintain hope.

Assessment and Strategies to Enhance Coping

Nurses are to avoid prescribing a favored coping technique without assessing the patient's perceptions, feelings, suggested ways of dealing with the problem, and usual modes of coping. The nurse needs complete awareness of the nature of the threat. Information about coping can be obtained by select interview questions. Paper-and-pencil coping instruments can be used for a quantitative evaluation.

Examples of coping interview questions to uncover primary and secondary appraisal information may include the following:

- Can you identify what makes you stressful or anxious? If so, what?
- How are you feeling about (mention the specific threat such as impending diagnostic test, treatment protocol, or living with the specific health problem)?
- What helps you deal with these feelings?
- How have you handled these kinds of situations in the past?
- Has this (e.g., arthritis) changed your life? If so, in what way(s)?
- What helps you handle these changes and/or stresses? How do you deal with the ups and downs?
- What has helped you through difficulty in the past? Have you tried these methods now?
- Do you generally like all the detailed information you can get about a difficult event or threatening situation, or do you prefer not facing it head-on?

Specific ideas may be stimulated in the assessment by reviewing a list of strategies and inquiring whether they are meaningful for the patient.

- Is religion and prayer important to you?
- Do you use specific distractions?
- Do you know any relaxation exercises?
- Have you tried mental imagery?
- Do you share your perceptions, reactions, and fears with someone else who is close to you?
- Are you able to find and concentrate on positive aspects of most situations?
- Do you readily seek help from others?
- Do you try to put difficulties out of your mind?
- Do you rely on your problem-solving ability?
- Has daydreaming or fantasizing helped you?

Instruments to evaluate coping to be used in a research context or to validate clinical impressions and nursing diagnoses have been developed. Those most appropriate for nursing include the Jalowiec Coping Scale (Jalowiec, 1989); Coping Strategies Inventory (Quayhagen & Quayhagen, 1982); Ways of Coping Checklist (Lazarus & Folkman, 1984); Coping Responses Scale (Moos, Cronkite, Billings, & Finney, 1984); Coping Strategies Scale (Weisman & Worden, 1976–1977); Coping Scale (Sidle, Adams, & Cady, 1969); Pain Management Strategies (Brown, Nicassio, & Wallston, 1989); Daily Coping Checklist (Stone & Neale, 1984); Chronicity Impact and Coping Instrument, for parents with ill children (Hymovich, 1984); and Family Crisis Oriented Personal Evaluation Scale: F-COPES (McCubbin, Olson, & Larsen, 1987).

EXPANDING COPING REPERTOIRES

Strategies to develop or expand coping repertoires will include use of a self-regulation approach, cognitive control strategies such as stress inoculation, and other miscellaneous approaches.

SELF-REGULATION

Self-regulation theory is based on developing a cognitive scheme (mental map) to guide incoming information, retrieve stored information, focus attention, and guide behavior (Johnson, 1984; Leventhal & Johnson, 1983). Preparatory information and past experience influence the composition of the scheme patients develop regarding impending health-care events, threatening intrusive procedures, or deterioration in health. Patients are helped to focus attention on the objective characteristics of the experience rather than on the subjective emotions provoked and negative evaluative reactions. Information is given in a clear and unambiguous manner, describing as exactly as possible the event to be experienced. Physical sensations to be experienced are reviewed including what will be felt, seen, heard, smelled, and tasted. These physical sensations are those experienced by most persons going through this event. The environment in which the event will take place needs to be described as well as the duration and sequence of happenings during the anxiety provoking event. When possible, self-care activities to promote comfort are also shared (Johnson & Lauver, 1989; Johnson, Lauver, & Nail, 1989). In summary, the self-regulation approach to coping enhancement includes providing concrete objective information about physical sensations to be experienced, environmental features, and temporal characteristics. The goal in implementing this coping strategy is to enhance understanding of the experience, reduce its abstract nature, and increase confidence in dealing with the situation by focusing attention on the objective not on the unpleasant, uncomfortable nature of the experience.

The effects of using self-regulation were evaluated with 84 men having radiation therapy for prostatic cancer who were randomly assigned to an experimental or control group (Johnson, Lauver, & Nail, 1989). The self-regulation procedure used a series of four tape recordings administered: (1) before treatments began, informing patients of the treatment plan; (2) just before the first treatment, describing the size and location of the treatment room, sound of the treatment machine, length of treatment; (3) at the fifth treatment, providing information about the nature, timing, and pattern of side effects of therapy; (4) at the last week of treatment, describing changes in side effects following completion of the therapy. Self-care activities to prevent or minimize side effects were included in the third and fourth tapes. The same researcher spent the same amount of time with men in the control group discussing the patients' well-being and using social conversation. Measurements of function and mood were taken during the first, third, and last week of treatment and at 1 and 3 months posttreatment (Johnson, Lauver, & Nail, 1989). Persons receiving the experimental procedure experienced less disruption in function as measured by the recreation and pastime subscale of the Sickness Impact Profile (Bergner, Bobbitt, Carter, & Gilson, 1981). No differences were found on negative mood scores measured by the Profile of Mood States (McNair, Lorr, & Doppelman, 1971).

The primary purpose of the self-regulation strategies is to create cognitive schemata that enable the person to cope with threatening events. The goal is to decrease any discrepancy between what patients expect and what actually happens to them. Key types of information are (1) physical sensations to be experienced; (2) characteristics of the environment; and (3) temporal information.

COGNITIVE CONTROL STRATEGIES

Stress inoculation training (SIT) is a technique aimed at desensitizing individuals to events they perceive as threatening. It combines teaching, discussion, cognitive restructuring, problem solving, relaxation, behavioral rehearsal, self-monitoring, self-instruction, and self-reinforcement (Meichenbaum, 1985). Persons develop a sense of *learned resourcefulness* and become immune to coping failure when confronting stress. Meichenbaum (1985) highlights the specific purposes of SIT:

- Teach patients that stress and coping are transactional
- Develop patient's skill to monitor maladaptive thoughts and behavior
- Develop patient's problem-solving skills
- Develop emotion regulation and self-control coping skills
- Sensitize patients to recognize and use maladaptive responses as cues to implement substitutive coping behaviors

Overall SIT should help patients become knowledgeable, enabling them to use self-understanding and coping skills to handle the stress of illness. The phases of teaching this coping strategy include conceptualization, skill acquisition and rehearsal, and application and follow-through.

During the conceptualization phase, a helping relationship is established between the patient and nurse. The stress-related problems and

TABLE 2 ■ 5 Examples of Negative and Positive Self-talk

Negative Self-talk	Positive Self-talk
I can't handle this.	I need to take one day at a time.
	I'm doing the best I can.
This is the worst thing that could have happened to me.	I am strong and will not be defeated.
How can this happen to me?	Life on earth means confronting difficulties.
This place is terrible.	I am lucky to be where the latest technology and know-how exist.

the patient's responses and feelings are clarified. Nonthreatening probes may be used by the nurse such as, "Is this what I hear you saying? I get the feeling that repeated doctor visits create anxiety about discovering cancer recurrence; is this the way you see it? Tell me more about that." Patients may be asked to re-create an image of the stress provoking event and share reactions to it. Patients are taught that thoughts and emotions play a role in creating and maintaining a stressful state. After patients are helped to identify their reactions, they are taught to monitor their thoughts, feelings, and behaviors related to stressors of interest.

During the skill acquisition and rehearsal phase, relaxation training, elimination of negative self-talk and substituting positive self-statements (Table 2–5), role playing, and mental rehearsals take place. The newly learned behaviors are then used in stress provoking situations and their effects are evaluated. Modifications of SIT have been effective with cancer patients (Moore & Altmaier, 1981; Weisman & Sobel, 1979) and with patients in rehabilitation (Corburn & Manderino, 1986).

OTHER STRATEGIES

Emotion-focused strategies are those attempts to eliminate or control emotional responses to aversive events by using relaxation, deep breathing, focusing on calmness, practicing calming self-talk ("It will be over soon. I'll be fine. I'm fortunate to be in such good hands."), redirecting attention by using pleasant mental images. *Problem-focused* strategies are those using information providing accurate expectations about sensory and procedural properties of an impending stimulus. Martelli and colleagues (1987) found that combinations of problem-focused and emotion-focused interventions were most helpful in 46 patients' responses to oral surgery. Emotion-focused interventions, when used alone, resulted in the lowest adjustment levels measured by the Krantz Health Opinion Survey Information (Krantz, Baum, & Wideman, 1980). Preoperative anxiety was directly related to postoperative pain and inversely related to postoperative adjustment.

Coping with Specific Health Problems

CANCER

Persons may experience differing stressors (coping tasks) depending on the type of chronic health problem they have. Cancer may provoke emotional distress including depression, anxiety, and anger; physical symptoms; disruption in daily life patterns and relationships including marital and sexual activities; and fears regarding disease progression and death (Meyerowitz, Heinrich, & Schag, 1983). Hinton (1973) identified six major stressors of 100 cancer patients to be pain, disfigurement, concern over the future (dying), loss of work role, dependency, and alienation. Woods and colleagues' (1989) review of living with cancer confirmed sexuality, communication, intimacy, and role changes as family concerns. Living with a chronic illness such as cancer requires behavioral skills such as relaxation, assertiveness, and problem solving (Heinrich & Schag, 1984; Miller & Nygren, 1978). Gotay (1984) discovered that spouses and women with breast cancer used different coping strategies at beginning and advanced stages of the illness. During the early stages, patients sought information, used self-talk, tried to put it out of their minds, found something favorable in their situation, and took firm action. Spouses sought direction, sought information from an authority, took firm action, accepted the inevitable. During the advanced stage, women used self-talk, prayer, had faith and hope, found something favorable about the situation, talked with others. Their mates took firm action, used prayer and self-talk, and shared with others. Taking firm action was prevalent for both spouses in both stages of the illness and refers to taking care of one's business in the early stages, and in the advanced stage involved actions that enabled others to plan for life after death of the patient. Hope was a prevalent coping strategy during the advanced stage for both spouses (Gotay, 1984). Herth (1989) found a significant relationship between hope and successful coping in 120 adults with cancer undergoing chemotherapy.

Forty spouses of men with cancer, identified as having difficulty coping, disclosed in interviews that their major difficulties were emotional, social, family, and financial needs (Kalayjian, 1989). Uncertainty was a problem for 50 percent of the wives. The following nursing behaviors were identified as helpful to their coping: listening, talking, caring, availability, sensitivity, empathy, and honesty. Nursing interventions that family judged helpful to their coping were discovered from 62 family members responding to vignettes of persons with cancer in an initial, adaptational (transitional), and terminal phase of illness (Lewandowski & Jones, 1988). The most helpful interventions during the initial phase were giving a clear explanation of what is being done for the ill member and keeping the ill member comfortable. Being kept informed was the most helpful intervention during the adaptation phase, and providing time alone for the patient and family member was the most important for the terminal phase.

CARDIAC

Perception of adequate social support has been related to effective coping by wives of men with coronary artery disease and myocardial infarctions (MIs) (Riegel, 1989; Riffle, 1988). As a result of studying 40 wives of patients having had an MI, Nyamathi (1987) made the following nursing care recommendations to enhance the spouses' coping:

- Involve the couple in the plan of care particularly planning for postdischarge
- Provide explicit, pertinent information to the couple
- Consistently provide reassurance, concern, and a positive attitude as a communication style
- Prepare for discharge including specifics about diet, exercise, sexual activity, preparation for cardiac emergency, follow-up, and cardiac rehabilitation program as appropriate
- Review existing coping resources such as social support

Of the 60 cardiac surgery patients studied by Anderson (1987), those who were in the experimental groups (receiving preoperative information or the group receiving preoperative information plus coping preparation) had significantly less preoperative anxiety and fear and postoperatively had more positive affect and less incidence of sudden hypertension than the control group.

Preparation of 60 adults for cardiac catheterization using one of five methods was studied to determine the impact of those coping methods on patient anxiety. The experimental group consisted of variations of self-regulation (Johnson & Lauver, 1989) using video tapes presenting (1) sensory procedural information; (2) modeling—a patient describing the experience; (3) cognitive behavioral coping (procedural information plus relaxation, reframing with self-reinforcing statements and distraction); (4) modeling plus coping; (5) attention to placebo group receiving information about the structure and function of the heart. All four of the treatment groups had less anxiety than the placebo group (Anderson & Masur, 1989).

OTHER HEALTH ALTERATIONS

Langer, Janis, and Wolfer (1975) studied the effectiveness of a coping strategy on reducing stress in surgical patients. The coping device was based on use of distraction and perception control. Patients were taught to direct attention toward favorable aspects of the anticipated stressful situation. The patient was made to feel in control by using the strategy of cognitive reappraisal of the anxiety provoking events and calming self-talk. Patients were taught that it is rarely the events themselves that cause stress, but rather the views people take of events and attention given to these views. Patients were taught to rehearse the positive aspects of hospitalization (improving health, receiving care and attention, having a rare opportunity to relax, and enjoying temporary relief from the pressures of the world).

Sixty patients were divided into four groups of preparation. Group 1 received the coping device described. Group 2 received preparatory information only, that is, preoperative skin preparation instructions and information about medications, anesthesia, and how the patient would feel after surgery, with incisional pain, nausea, and constipation described as possible discomforts. Group 3 received a combination of preparation information and the coping device. Group 4 served as a control and received only information about hospital routines. Nurses blindly rated the subjects' anxiety and ability to cope with discomfort before and after the researcher intervention. There was a rapid decrease in anxiety and increase in ability to cope in the group given the coping strategy. Postoperatively, the group given the coping device required fewer pain medications and fewer sedatives than the groups not given the device. There was no significant difference among the groups in the number of days of hospital stay (Langer, Janis, & Wolfer, 1975).

The strategy described by Langer is appropriate for nurses to use to help patients cope not only with stresses that are short term in nature, such as facing surgery, but also with stresses lasting a lifetime, as in the case of chronic disease.

Dimond (1980) studied the effect of two coping strategies used by 36 patients on hemodialysis to adapt to chronic hemodialysis. The two coping strategies were patient-perceived progress in managing dialysis (cognitive control) and patient use of short-term planning (behavioral control). Adaptation was determined by subjects' morale scores (Behavior-Morale Scale), changes in social function (Sickness Impact Profile), number of medical problems, and stability of physical status. Those subjects who used the two coping strategies had significantly higher scores at the 0.05 level on the four measures of adaptation. Dimond emphasized that short-term planning was one way that patients on dialysis could control their daily lives. She suggests that in addition to teaching patients with renal failure about the disease and its treatment, teaching specific skills in short-term planning is important to enhance the patient's perception of personal competence and control.

Does the coping capacity of chronically ill individuals decrease as the illness continues over long periods? Although there is no conclusive answer based on research, it seems logical that nurses should generate specific strategies patients can try out as the illness progresses. Determining the combinations of strategies that are appropriate to the patient's coping style and control orientation is the challenge. Much nursing research on the topic of coping is needed.

Specific tasks confronting chronically ill persons can be labeled coping tasks. Individuals have unique means of responding to the tasks (using coping strategies) in order to master, control, or resolve the tasks. Collectively, the coping tasks of chronic illness precipitate powerlessness. Coping facilitates powerfulness.

References

Anderson, E. (1987). Preoperative preparation for cardiac surgery facilitates recovery, reduces psychological distress and reduces the incidence of acute postoperative hypertension. *Journal of Consulting and Clinical Psychology, 55,* 513–520.

Anderson, K., & Masur, F. (1989). Psychologic preparation for cardiac catheterization. *Heart and Lung, 18,* 154–163.

Andrew, J. (1973). Coping style and declining verbal abilities. *Journal of Gerontology, 28,* 179–183.

Auerbach, S. (1989). Stress management and coping research in the health care setting: An overview and methodological commentary. *Journal of Consulting and Clinical Psychology, 57,* 388–395.

Averill, J. (1973). Personal control over aversion stimuli and its relationship to stress. *Psychological Bulletin, 88,* 286–303.

Bergner, M., Bobbitt, R. A., Carter, W. B., & Gilson, B. S. (1981). The Sickness Impact Profile: Development and final revision of a health status measure. *Medical Care, 19,* 787–805.

Beutel, M. (1985). Approaches to taxonomy and measurement of adaptation in chronic disease. *Psychotherapy and Psychosomatics, 43,* 177–185.

Brown, G., Nicassio, P., & Wallston, K. (1989). Pain coping strategies and depression in rheumatoid arthritis. *Journal of Consulting and Clinical Psychology, 57,* 652–657.

Bruner, J. (1966). *Toward a theory of instruction.* Cambridge, MA: Belknap University Press of Harvard University.

Caplan, G. (1963). Emotional crises. In A. Deutsch (Ed.), *The encyclopedia of mental health* (Vol. 2). New York: Franklin Watts.

Charmaz, K. (1973). *Time and identity: The shaping of selves of the chronically ill.* Unpublished doctoral dissertation. San Francisco: University of California.

Coburn, J., & Manderino, M. (1986). Stress inoculation: An illustration of coping skills training. *Rehabilitation Nursing, 11,* 14–17.

Cohen, F., & Lazarus, R. (1973). Active coping processes, coping dispositions and recovery from surgery. *Psychosomatic Medicine, 35,* 375–389.

Davis, M. (1975). Social isolation as a process in chronic illness. In M. Davis, M. Kramer, & A. Strauss (eds.), *Nurses in practice: A perspective on work environments,* (pp. 253–259). St. Louis: CV Mosby.

Dimond, M. (1980). Patient strategies for managing maintenance hemodialysis. *Western Journal of Nursing Research, 2,* 555–568.

Feldman, D. (1974). Chronic disabling illness: A holistic view. *Journal of Chronic Disease, 27,* 287–291.

Garland, L., & Bush, C. (1982). *Coping behaviors and nursing.* Reston, VA: Reston Publishing.

Goldstein, M. F., Jones, R. B., Clemens, T. L., Flagg, G. W., & Alexander, F. G. (1965). Coping style as a factor in psychophysiological response to tension-arousing film. *Journal of Personality and Social Psychology, 1,* 200–302.

Gotay, C. (1984). The experience of cancer during early and advanced stages: The views of patients and their mates. *Social Science and Medicine, 18,* 605–613.

Haan, N. (1977). *Coping and defending: Processes of self-environment organization.* New York: Academic Press.

Haynes, R. B. (1976). A critical review of the determinants of patient compliance with therapeutic regimens. In D. Sackett & R. B. Haynes (Eds.), *Compliance with therapeutic regimens.* Baltimore: Johns Hopkins University Press.

Heinrich, R., & Schag, C. (1984). A behavioral medicine approach to coping with cancer: A case report. *Cancer Nursing, 7,* 243–247.

Herth, K. (1989). The relationship between level of hope and level of coping responses and other variables in patients with cancer. *Oncology Nursing Forum, 16,* 67–72.

Hinton, J. (1973). Bearing cancer. *British Journal of Medical Psychology, 46,* 105–113.

Hymovich, D. (1984). Development of the Chronicity Impact and Coping Instrument: Parent Questionnaire (CICI:PQ). *Nursing Research, 33,* 218–222.

Jalowiec, A. (1989). Confirmatory factor analysis of the Jalowiec Coping Scale. In C. Waltz & O. Stricland (Eds.), *Measurement of nursing outcomes: Vol. 1. Measuring client outcomes.* (pp. 287–308). New York: Springer.

Johnson, J. (1984). Psychological interventions and coping with surgery. In A. Baum, S. E. Taylor, & J. E. Singer (Eds.), *Handbook of psychology and health: Vol. 4. Social psychological aspects of health* (pp. 167–176). Hillsdale, NJ: L. Erlbaum Associates.

Johnson, J., Lauver, D., & Nail, L. (1989). Process of coping with radiation therapy. *Journal of Consulting and Clinical Psychology, 5,* 358–364.

Johnson, J., & Lauver, D. (1989). Alternative explanations of coping with stressful experiences associated with physical illness. *Advances in Nursing Science, 11,* 39–52.

Kalayjian, A. (1989). Coping with cancer: The spouse's perspective. *Archives of Psychiatric Nursing, 3,* 166–172.

Kassebaum, G., & Bauman, B. (1965). Dimensions of the sick role in chronic illness. *Journal of Health and Human Development, 6,* 16–27.

Kiely, W. F. (1972). Coping with severe illness. *Advanced Psychosomatic Medicine, 8,* 105–118.

Korner, I. (1970). Hope as a method of coping. *Journal of Consulting Psychology, 34,* 134–139.

Krantz, D. S., Baum, A., & Wideman, M. (1980). Assessment of preferences for self-treatment and information in health care. *Journal of Personalality and Social Psychology, 39,* 977–990.

Langer, E., Janis, I., & Wolfer, J. (1975). Reduction of psychological stress in surgical patients. *Journal of Experimental Social Psychology, 11,* 155–165.

Lazarus, R. (1966). *Psychological stress and the coping process.* New York: McGraw-Hill.

Lazarus, R., & Folkman, S. (1984). *Stress, appraisal and coping.* New York: Springer.

Leventhal, H., & Johnson, J. (1983). Laboratory and field experimentation: Development of a theory of self-regulation. In P. Wooldridge, M. Schmitt, J. Skipper, & R. Leonard (Eds.), *Behavioral science and nursing theory* (pp. 189–262). St. Louis: CV Mosby.

Lewandowski, W., & Jones. S. (1988). The family with cancer. *Cancer Nursing, 11,* 313–321.

Lipowski, Z. (1970). Physical illness, the individual and the coping process. *Psychiatry in Medicine, 1,* 91–102.

Lipowski, Z. (1969). Psychosocial aspects of disease. *Annals of Internal Medicine, 71,* 1197–1206.

Lomont, J. (1965). The repression-sensitization dimension in relation to anxiety responses. *Journal of Consulting Psychology, 29,* 84–86.

Martelli, M.F., Auerbach, S.M., Alexander J., & Mercuri, L.G. (1987). Stress management in the health care setting; Matching interventions with patient coping styles. *Journal of Consulting and Clinical Psychology, 55,* 201–207.

McCubbin, H., Olson, D., & Larson, A. (1987). F-COPES: Family Crisis Oriented Personal Evaluation Scales. In H. McCubbin & A. Thompson (Eds.) *Family Assessment Inventories for Research and Practice* (pp. 194–207). Madison: University of Wisconsin Press.

McNair, D. M ., Lorr, M., & Doppelman, L. F. (1971). *Manual for the Profile of Mood States.* San Diego: Educational and Industrial Testing Service.

Mechanic, D. (1974). Social structure and personal adaptation: some neglected dimensions. In G. V. Coelho, D. H. Hamburg, & J. E. Adams (Eds.), *Coping and adaptation.* New York: Basic Books.

Meichenbaum, D. (1985). *Stress inoculation training.* New York: Pergamon Press.

Melies, A. (1975). Role insufficiency and role supplementation: A conceptual framework. *Nursing Research, 24,* 264–271.

Meyerowitz, B., Heinrich, R., Schag, C. (1983). A competency-based approach to coping with cancer. In T. Burish, & L. Bradley (Eds.). *Coping with chronic disease: Research and applications* (pp. 137–158). New York: Academic Press.

Miller, S., & Mangan, C. E. (1983). Interacting effects of information and coping style in adapting to gynecological stress: When should the doctor tell all? *Journal of Personality and Social Psychology, 45,* 223–236.

Miller, M., & Nygren, C. (1978). Living with cancer: Coping behaviors. *Cancer Nursing, 1,* 297–302.

Moore, K., & Altmaier, E. M. (1981). Stress inoculation training with cancer patients. *Cancer Nursing, 4,* 389–393.

Moos, R., Cronkite, R., Billings, A., & Finney, J. (1984). *Health and daily living form manual.* Palo Alto, CA: Social Ecology Laboratory, Department of Psychiatry, Stanford University Veterans Administration Hospital.

Mullen, B., & Suls, J. (1982). The effectiveness of attention and rejection as coping styles. *Journal of Psychosomatic Research, 26,* 43–49.

Nyamathi, A. (1987). The coping responses of female spouses of patients with myocardial infarction. *Heart and Lung, 16,* 86–91.

Parsons, T. (1951). *The social system.* New York: The Free Press.

Pattison, M. (1974). Psychosocial predictors of death prognosis. *Omega, 5,* 145–159.

Peralin, L. I., & Schooler, C. (1978). The structure of coping. *Journal of Health and Social Behavior, 19,* 2–21.

Quayhagen, M., & Quayhagen, M. (1982). Coping with conflict: Measurement of age-related patterns. *Research on Aging, 4,* 364–377.

Riegel, B. (1989). Social support and psychological adjustment to chronic coronary heart disease: Operationalization of Johnson's Behavioral System Model. *Advances in Nursing Science, 11,* 74–84.

Riffle, K. (1988). The relationship between perception of supportive behaviors of others and wives' ability to cope with initial myocardial infarctions in their husbands. *Rehabilitation Nursing, 13,* 310–314.

Roth, S., & Cohen, L. (1986). Approach, avoidance, and coping with stress. *Americal Psychologist, 41,* 813–819.

Seligman, M. (1975). *Helplessness: On depression, development, and death.* San Francisco: W.H. Freeman and Co.

Shanan, J., De Nour, A., Kaplan, A., & Schak, G. (1976). Effects of prolonged stress on coping style in terminal renal failure patients. *Journal of Human Stress, 2,* 19–27.

Sidle, A., Adams, J., & Cady, P. (1969). Development of a coping scale. *Archives of General Psychiatry, 20,* 226–232.

Stapleton, S. (1978). Coping with chronic illness. Unpublished paper. Milwaukee, WI: Marquette University College of Nursing.

Stone, A,. & Neale, J. (1984). New measure of daily coping: Development and preliminary resuts. *Journal of Personality and Social Psychology, 46,* 892–906.

Visotsky, H., Hamurg, D., Goss, M., & Levobits, B. (1961). Coping behavior under extreme stress. *Archives of General Psychiatry, 5,* 27–52.

Weisman, A. (1979). *Coping with cancer.* New York: McGraw-Hill.

Weisman, A., & Sobel, H. (1979). Coping with cancer through self-instruction. A hypothesis. *Journal of Human Stress, 5,* 3–8.

Weisman, A., & Worden, W. (1976–1977). The existential plight in cancer: Significance of the first 100 days. *International Journal of Psychiatry and Medicine, 7,* 1–15.

Wiener, C. (1975). The burden of rheumatoid arthritis: Tolerating uncertainty. *Social Science Medicine, 9,* 97–104.

Woods, N., Lewis, F., & Ellison, E. (1989). Living with cancer: Family experiences. *Cancer Nursing, 12,* 28–33.

Wright, B. (1983). *Physical disability: A psychosocial approach.* New York: Harper & Row.

■

Concept Development of Powerlessness:

A Nursing Diagnosis
■ JUDITH FITZGERALD MILLER

Development of the concept of powerlessness is the focus of this chapter. The process of concept development involves distinct phases such as developing a commitment to study the concept as a result of experienced challenges and/or piqued curiosity, defining the concept in a working-definition format, reviewing the literature to substantiate current concept development, making observations in the field, drawing conclusions from one's own and others' descriptive research, and designing predictive and prescriptive studies. The phases of concept development emphasized in this chapter include reviewing the literature (deriving theoretical propositions and proposing nursing practice speculations), and reporting field observations. Powerlessness manifested in the specific health problems of AIDS and cancer are included as prototypes.

Methods of concept analysis and development have been proposed by Chinn and Jacobs (1987), Norris (1982), Rodgers (1989a, 1989b), and Walker and Avant (1988). Wilson's (1969) technique of concept analysis has influenced nursing's methods in explicating the nature of phenomena of concern for this discipline. See Forsyth's (1980) concept analysis of empathy as an example. This research on concept clarification, analysis, and development has provided for development of nursing's body of knowledge.

Developing and validating new nursing diagnostic categories requires concept analysis and systematic investigation. A descriptive research approach in developing this concept is used throughout this book. Dubin (1969) distinguishes between descriptive and hypothesis-

50

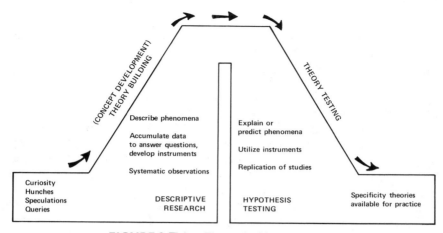

FIGURE 3 ■ I Theory building and testing.

testing research. He states that descriptive research is the questioning, or theory-building, side of research. For purposes of this book, concept development of powerlessness takes place on this side of the model. Hypothesis testing is the answer-seeking, theory-testing side. (Fig. 3–1.)

Before hypotheses can be formulated and tested, systematic observations of phenomena must take place. Observations of patients in states of powerlessness have been made and are reported in this book. Interest and curiosity have been piqued by these observations of individuals whose physical conditions plunged downward despite strict adherence to prescribed regimens.

Nurses are challenged to help patients achieve a sense of control and avoid or alleviate powerlessness. Nurses need to be able to recognize the nursing diagnosis, determine which patients are vulnerable to diagnoses related to powerlessness, design nursing strategies to alleviate the diagnosis, and evaluate outcomes.

Related Theories and Powerlessness Defined

Constructs such as helplessness, learned helplessness, external locus of control, and powerlessness all connote that individuals believe that outcomes of events are not contingent upon their own behaviors. Each construct has some uniqueness and specificity. Learned helplessness and locus of control are presented in the literature as theories.

A person who experiences repeated uncontrollable events may eventually manifest learned helplessness. That is, persons come to expect noncontingency between their actions and the resulting outcome. This expectancy may be transferred to many life experiences. Three deficits result: (1) motivation deficits—hesitancy to take action; (2) cognitive deficits—the inaccurate expectation of uncontrollability is transferred to other life situations; and (3) affect deficits—apathy, withdrawal, depression, and decreased self-esteem (Seligman, 1975). Since persons assigned reasons for their uncontrollability, the concept of attribution was added to the revised theory of helplessness (Abramson, Seligman, & Teasdale, 1978). Persons attribute their helplessness to stable or unstable, global or specific, and personal or external factors. When persons attribute their helplessness to a broad range of situations and helplessness is present in varied situations, the attributions are said to be global and stable. Persons who attribute their lack of control to personal, stable, and global factors will be more vulnerable to depression and have lower self-esteem than persons who attribute powerlessness to universal, unstable, and specific factors (Abramson, Garber, & Seligman, 1980; Maiden, 1987; Murphy, 1982). Cumulative losses, disabilities, and impairments of the elderly and chronically ill renders them vulnerable to perceived helplessness (Slimmer, Lopez, LeSage, & Ellor, 1987).

Locus-of-control theory is founded on social learning theory and posits that potential for a behavior to occur in any situation is a function of the expectancy that the behavior will lead to a valued reinforcement (Rotter, 1975). The generalized expectancy that one's reinforcements are directly the result of one's own behavior is labeled internal locus-of-control orientation. The expectancy that outcomes (reinforcements) are determined by powerful others, fate, luck, or chance is termed an external locus-of-control orientation. Thousands of papers have been published on differences in locus of control, and, generally, people with an internal locus of control (internals) are described as more potent, competent, effective, and able to take action to modify aversive situations (Wallston & Wallston, 1982). Internals seem to be desirable in this age of taking responsibility for one's own health. Wallston and Wallston (1981; 1982) expanded the conceptualization to a multidimensional, health locus-of-control concept by developing the scale to measure Internal Health Locus of Control (IHLC) and two external scales: Powerful Other Health Locus of Control (PHLC) referring to doctors, nurses, family, or friends, and Chance Health Locus of Control (CHLC) measuring health and illness as a matter of fate, luck, or chance. Helplessness and locus of control are based on a reinforcement paradigm, whereas powerlessness is an existential construct (Lewis, 1982). An existential focus refers to the "here and now," the current circumstance or situation rather than to an enduring personality trait such as locus of control.

Powerlessness is the perception that one lacks the capacity or authority to act to affect an outcome of a current situation or immediate happening. When one or more of the power resources of physical strength, psychologic stamina, self-concept, energy, knowledge, motivation, and belief system are compromised, powerlessness is a potential problem.

(See Fig. 1–1.) In contrast to locus of control, powerlessness is situationally determined. Locus of control is directly related to powerlessness and is a rather stable personality trait. Locus of control seems to be a long-term tendency or a stable view of why events take place.

The studies on powerlessness were analyzed in the following categories: powerlessness and learning; individual's beliefs or illusions and control; effects of no control on animals; effects of no control on human's physiologic response and problem solving; control in select health-illness situations; and powerlessness as a precipitant of death.

For each section of literature reviewed, theoretical propositions (Newman, 1979) will be deduced. Theoretical propositions are translations and conclusions drawn from research findings. Some interpretation for nursing practice will be included in each section. These interpretations are labeled practice speculations. They are derived from theoretical propositions, and although they have logical practice relevance, they need to be tested.

Literature Review

POWERLESSNESS AND LEARNING

Seeman (1962) concluded that powerlessness leads to poor learning of control-relevant information. Patients hospitalized with tuberculosis who were high in powerlessness knew fewer facts about the disease and maintaining health than did a matched sample low in powerlessness. The patients low in powerlessness were less satisfied with information given by staff and were rated by the staff as being more knowledgeable about their illness. In Seeman's study of prisoners (1963), there was no difference between high-powerlessness and low-powerlessness prisoners' knowledge of life in the correctional institution; however, prisoners who were low in powerlessness had more knowledge about parole matters, that is, how to get out on parole and conditions while on parole. The premise for Seeman's (1967) studies is that "An individual's generalized expectancy for control of his outcomes governs attention to and acquisition of information available in the environment" (p. 105). Seeman also correlated high powerlessness with low political awareness (1972) and low nuclear survival knowledge (1967).

Phares (1968) studied acquisition and utilization of information in subjects with internal or external locus of control. Both groups were taught information until they had perfect recall. The subjects then had to use the information in a computer simulation task. He found that while the internals and externals did not differ in the acquisition of material, internals provided significantly more reasons for decisions made during the simulation task than did the externals, and differential retention of the

Theoretical Propositions	Practice Speculations
1. Perceived powerlessness leads to poor learning of control relevant information.	Before beginning patient teaching, determine the patient's feelings of powerlessness.
2. Involving learners in decision making regarding content to be learned enhances learning.	Patients with an internal locus of control need emphasis on information that gives them a sense of control.
3. The personality trait locus of control influences ability to utilize control-relevant information.	High-powerless patients may need structured approaches, teaching of self-care in small increments so patients can feel a sense of control without being overwhelmed with care demands.
	Involve patients by having them determine what aspects of care they are ready to learn and when they want to learn them.

FIGURE 3 ■ 2   Powerlessness and learning.

information did not explain the internals' superior utilization of the information.

Nineteen externals and 21 internals were given personality tests and informed of reports containing negative and positive information about their personalities. The externals had greater recall of the negative information given to them about themselves than did internals. The internals were more willing to try remedial behaviors to improve than were the externals (Phares, 1968).

Giving learners a choice, such as determining the series in which to take a test (Stotland & Blumenthal, 1964), resulted in lower anxiety as indicated by palmar sweating than did not giving individuals a choice. Perlmutter and Monty (1973) demonstrated that the group given the choice of lists for word memorization did better than the group given no choice. The theoretical propositions (translation and conclusion statements) and practice speculations are presented in Figure 3–2.

Discussion of Practice Speculations

The phrase "start patient teaching where the patient is" has new meaning when we look beyond motivation, psychologic readiness, and ability to grasp concepts to determine the patient's feelings of powerlessness. Patients with low powerlessness may need multiple avenues of content presentation. They should be encouraged to compare methods of self-care and be given freedom to question and pursue alternate modes of meeting needs for care. Those patients who tend to have an internal locus of control may need added emphasis on information that would give them a sense of control. This may even involve explicit verbalization by the nurse, such as, "Knowing this will give you added ability to be in control of the situation." High-powerless patients, however, may need structured approaches. This could mean teaching self-care in small increments so that patients feel a sense of accomplishment when they are successful with these scaled-down, yet realistic, goals.

A feeling of being controlled by fate, destiny, or others is not conducive to learning new skills such as self-care (Zahn, 1969). Patients with this orientation may believe that learning a self-care skill—such as learning a low-salt and calorie-restricted diet, as well as monitoring the effects of the rest of the antihypertensive regimen—will do no good because what was meant to happen will happen despite patient involvement. Despite their locus-of-control tendency, perhaps all patients must perceive some sense of situation control before they can learn health-control information.

ILLUSIONS OF CONTROL

In situations where personal competence can affect outcomes, individuals tend to perform more actively and competently than in situations that appear beyond their control. What effect does the individual's belief in having control have on arousal, anxiety, and so forth? The reviewed studies on perceived control all report that subjects who believed they had control of an aversive stimulus such as an electric shock or noise manifest less anxiety and tolerate noxious stimuli better than subjects who believed they had no control.

Geer, Davison, and Gatchel (1970) studied autonomic responses of 20 men who perceived they had control over electric shock and 20 men who perceived no control. The subjects in the perceived-control group were led to believe that they could decrease the duration of the shock from 6 to 3 seconds if they pushed a reaction switch with each electric shock. The no-perceived-control group was not given this information. Both groups were told that the researcher was interested in reaction time between receiving the shock and pushing the switch. Even though the perceived-control group did not affect the duration of the shock, their perception of being in control influenced the results. The perceived-control subjects rated the shocks as less painful than did the no-perceived-control subjects; the perceived-control subjects had less galvanic skin response, suggesting they were less aroused by the shocks than were the no-perceived control subjects. This study was replicated by Glass and coworkers (1973) on 48 college students. Subjects in the perceived-control group rated their pain as less and performed better on the Stroop Color Word Test than did those in the no-perceived-control group. Contrary to the findings of Geer, Davison, and Gatchel (1970), there was no significant difference in autonomic response as measured by the galvanic skin response between the two groups.

Glass and Singer (1972) studied the response to belief of control over aversive stimuli. The subjects received 18 electric shocks while trying to solve graphic puzzles. Half of the group was given soluble puzzles, whereas the other half were given unsoluble puzzles. All subjects received the same number of shocks but were told that solving the puzzles would prevent the next scheduled shock. The subjects who perceived control performed better on postshock tasks, making fewer errors on a proofreading test, and having shorter reading times than the subjects who perceived no control.

Procedures that give subjects the choice of avoiding or not avoiding aversive stimuli are equivalent to giving them perceived control over the potential stress of threat (Corah & Boffa, 1970). Forty subjects were divided into two groups: an escape group, which had the choice instructions, and a no-escape group, which had no choice instructions. The escape group was instructed to press a button to escape white noise if the noise became uncomfortable. The choice was up to them. The no-escape subjects were told not to push the button unless the noise "became so uncomfortable you must." The galvanic skin response was used as an indicator of physiologic arousal. The escape group had less arousal than did the no-escape group. The escape group also rated the discomfort as less than did the no-escape group (Corah & Boffa, 1970). A sense of control influences how threats are appraised. This study suggests that choice is a variable that can reduce the aversive quality of the stimulus.

Houston (1972) studied the effects of an illusion of control on anxiety and physiologic arousal as measured by the Zuckerman Affect Adjective Check List and heart rate, respectively. He also used no-control situations to compare the physiologic arousal of individuals with internal locus of control with the arousal in individuals with external locus of control. The 20 subjects in the avoidable-shock group were led to believe that they could avoid an electric shock by not making mistakes on a memory task. The 20 subjects in the unavoidable-shock group were told there was no way to avoid the shock. Despite the fact that both groups received the same number and intensity of shocks, subjects in the latter group reported more anxiety but demonstrated less physiologic arousal. Contrary to Houston's expectations, the group with external locus of control manifested less physiologic arousal than did the group with internal locus of control. This could be attributed to the effects of placing individuals with an internal-locus personality trait in no-control situations. More anxiety, as measured by physiologic arousal, may be caused in subjects with an

Theoretical Propositions	Practice Speculations
1. An illusion of control causes less physiologic arousal during stress events than perceived no control.	Providing patient with alternatives so as to make choices provides an illusion of control.
2. An illusion of control causes threats to be evaluated as less harmful than perception of no control.	Containing anxiety and aversive physiologic arousal is desirable in all phases of health-illness. Helping patients feel a sense of control achieves this end.
3. When individuals are provided with freedom to make choices, an illusion of control is created.	Help the patient feel control over aspects of the immediate environment, personal effects, plants, and so forth.

FIGURE 3 ■ 3   Illusions of control

internal locus of control because they are not resigned to events being contingent on external forces. (See Fig. 3–3.)

DIscussion of Practice Speculation

The illusion of patient control has benefits for patients in terms of creating less anxiety and physiologic arousal and greater ability to learn than does the perception of no control. Helping patients know when specific events will take place provides an illusion of control. The events may be diagnostic tests or treatments such as a dressing change. Patients can achieve some sense of control by knowing about alternatives for self-care and feeling free to make decisions about the alternatives. Nurses need to help patients become aware of alternatives and enable them to make decisions. An example is having the new patient with diabetes realize that a diet restriction of 1200 calories per day involves freedom and variety in meal planning. Good selections will now enhance the patient's nutritional state because food of no nutritional value is not included in the selection of six food-exchange lists.

Helping the patients and families be as informed as health-care personnel about their health states is fundamental. While the perceived absence of control is debilitating, the illusion of control may improve well-being (Langer, 1983).

EFFECTS OF NO CONTROL ON ANIMALS

"The mere knowledge that one can exert control serves to mitigate the debilitating effects of aversive stimuli" (Lefcourt, 1973, p. 419). The reported aversive quality of a stimulus decreases when subjects exercise control over that stimulus.

The original study of control by Mowrer and Viek (1948) demonstrated that rats exhibited less fear of an aversive stimulus (electric shock) if they could exercise control (leap into the air when shocked to terminate the shock). A significant difference in eating inhibition was noted in the group that had no control over the shock. (The animals were presented with food; if they did not eat within 10 seconds, the behaviors were labeled an inhibition.) Mowrer and Viek observed the 20 animals for 15 consecutive days. They described the no-control animals as being helpless, having lost their will, and not actively providing for their self-interest, for example, satisfying hunger.

The effects of subjecting animals to no-control situations have been documented in a series by Seligman, Maier, and Solomon (1969), Overmier and Seligman (1967), Overmier (1968), and Seligman and Maier (1967). In these studies, dogs were restrained in a cloth hammock and given electric shocks by electrodes attached to their feet. The intensity and duration of the shocks varied in the experiments. Another series of shocks was given to the same dogs while they were in an escapable shuttle box. The animals were shocked by a wire grid on the bottom of the box. If the animal crossed the shoulder-high barrier in the center of the box, the shocks would be stopped. Overmier and Seligman (1967) compared responses of dogs that received inescapable shocks and those that received no aversive pretreatment but were placed in the escapable shuttle box. Those animals that had been restrained and shocked when placed in the escape box displayed helpless behavior; at first, they ran around frantically for approximately 30 seconds, and then they lay down and quietly whined. After a few seconds, the dogs seemed to give up and passively accept the shock.

The helplessness induced by the inescapable shock was eliminated if the animal had some experience controlling the shock (Seligman & Maier, 1967; Seligman, Maier, & Geer, 1968). Seligman (1968) tried to overcome the helplessness in dogs previously in no-escape conditions by calling the animal over a lowered barrier in the box to the no-shock side. One in four dogs crossed the barrier. The other three were then leashed and forced to the escape side. The animals were pulled across the barrier 20 times. It then took 20, 35, and 50 trials for the dogs to escape the shock on their own. The animals' behavior was explained as resulting from learned helplessness. Their having learned a lack of control over reinforcement was difficult to reverse.

Not all animal studies reported that the control subjects have the advantage. Brady and coworkers (1958) reported that the four monkeys who pressed levers to escape electric shocks developed ulcers. The paired monkeys who had no control did not develop gastrointestinal lesions. The control monkeys were labeled by Brady and coworkers as

Theoretical Propositions	Practice Speculations
1. Repeated exposure to threat and/or harm induces a state of helplessness in animals.	
2. Reversal of learned helplessness is difficult but can take place with forceful success experiences provided by someone controlling the situation.	
3. Predictability of aversive stimuli decreases the threat of the stimuli.	

FIGURE 3 ■ 4   The effects on animals of helplessness or lack of control.

"executive" monkeys. The findings were refuted by Weiss' study (1971) of 180 rats, in which ulcers were more common and more extensive among the animals with no control.

Seligman and Meyer (1970) studied the effects of unpredictable shock on rats' bar-pressing behavior for food. A variable number of unpredictable shocks were given to 20 rats. Suppression of bar pressing occurred. After being given a fixed number of otherwise unpredictable shocks in each session, rats resumed bar pressing after the last shock, using its occurrence as a safety signal. Bar pressing resumed more quickly in rats that received milder predictable shocks than in rats that received the mild unpredictable shocks. Fear, measured by the suppression of bar pressing, correlated with the amount of gastric ulceration found in the unpredictable-shock animals. (See Fig. 3–4.)

The implications of this research and these propositions will be discussed at the end of the next section.

EFFECTS OF NO CONTROL ON HUMANS

When subjects administered shocks to themselves and selected the level of intensity of shock, they reported less discomfort at higher levels of shock and endured stronger shock intensity than did matched subjects who were administered shocks by the investigator (Staub, Tursky, & Schwartz, 1971). The predictability of self-administered shocks diminished the threat of aversive stimuli (Ball & Vogler, 1971; Pervin, 1963). On a second series of shocks, both control and no-control groups now had shocks administered to them; the groups that previously had control declined in tolerance for shocks and rated shocks as more painful than when they had control. The ability to predict events may reduce the subjective experience of helplessness, even when control is not possible, and may thereby reduce tension or anxiety. When ability to terminate aversive stimuli is lacking, predictability may reduce the impact of the stimuli; and when the abiltiy to predict is lacking, perceived ability to terminate aversive stimuli may have a similar effect (Staub, Tursky, & Schwartz, 1971).

To determine the effect of control over environmental stressors on frustration tolerance and task performance, two groups of subjects were exposed to random noise played on a tape recorder at 110 decibels (Glass, Singer, & Friedman, 1969). One group had control over the noise through use of a button; the other group had no control. The response to the noise stressor was measured by use of the galvanic skin response readings, number of errors made on cognitive tasks, tolerance for frustration by the number of trials made at insoluble puzzles, and a postexperimental questionnaire requesting ratings from the subjects on how distracting, irritating, and unpleasant they felt the noise to be. The group that had control demonstrated much greater tolerance for frustration based on a larger number of trials at solving insoluble puzzles. The percentage of proofreading errors was less for the group with control. The group with control also rated the noise as less aversive than did the group with no control.

Kanfer and Seidner (1973) studied the effectiveness of self-controlling response in 45 women undergraduate students. The subjects were divided into three groups, all of whom had one hand immersed in ice water. Subjects in Group 1 viewed travel slides that they advanced at their own desired rate. Group 2 had the slides advanced by the experimenter. No slides were used for Group 3. Duration of ice-water tolerance was greater for subjects who advanced the slides at their own rate (significant at the 0.01 level). The researchers did not attribute the tolerance for ice water to self-distraction techniques that may have been used by the group controlling the slides. The conclusion was that the self-controlling responses increased tolerance for the aversive stimuli.

Thornton and Jacobs (1971) were able to replicate learned helplessness in humans as had been done in previous animal studies. After pretreatment in which the subjects had no control, humans transferred helplessness to a second task in which they had control, just as the animals had done. Eighty subjects were divided into four groups. One group could avoid the electric shock by pushing a button in a 30-second reaction time; the second and third groups could not avoid the shock. The second group received a fixed shock; the third, a variable shock. The fourth group was given no shock pretreatment. The variable-shock group that had less predictability experienced more stress. Groups 1, 2, and 3 transferred their helplessness to a task in which they had control. In this second phase, pushing a button could eliminate the shock. Fewest attempts to control the shock were made by the variable-shock pretreatment group.

The learned helplessness is due to learning that reinforcement and responding are independent of one another. Miller and Seligman (1973;

1975), in comparing depression and laboratory-induced learned helplessness, determined that learning that reinforcement and responding are independent is central to the symptoms and etiology of both learned helplessness and depression. Seligman (1975, p. 82) draws a parallel between the behaviors of depression and those of learned helplessness, stating that in both there is

1. A lowered initiation of voluntary responses—animals and men who have experienced uncontrollability show reduced initiation of voluntary responses.
2. A negative cognitive set—helpless animals and men have difficulty learning that responses produce outcomes.
3. A time course—helplessness dissipates in time when induced by a single session of uncontrollable shock; after multiple sessions, helplessness persists.
4. Lowered aggression—helpless animals and men initiate fewer aggressive and competitive responses, and their dominance status may diminish.
5. Loss of appetite—helpless animals eat less, lose weight, and are sexually and socially deficient.
6. Physiologic changes—helpless rats show norepinephrine depletion, and helpless cats may be cholinergically overactive.

Hiroto and Seligman (1975) and Gatchel, McKinney, and Koebernick (1977) found that depressed subjects and nondepressed subjects exposed to inescapable noise exhibit similar deficits in attempting to solve anagram puzzles.

Johnson and Kilmann (1975) studied the relationship between locus of control and perceived problem-solving ability in 20 internal men, 20 internal women, 20 external men, and 20 external women. Men who were internal rated themselves as more confident in problem-solving ability than did men who were external. No significant difference was found between internal and external women.

Anderson (1977) studied 90 owner-managers of small businesses that were damaged by a hurricane to determine the relationship among locus of control, perceived stress, coping behaviors, and performance. Externals perceived higher stress than did internals. The externals responded with more defensiveness and less task-oriented coping behavior than did internals. The task-oriented coping behaviors of the internals were more successful in solving the problems created by the stressful event, since the performance of the internals' organizations were better. (Coping was determined by evaluating the economic position of the company. If the company returned to preflood status, coping was considered effective.) Kahn and coworkers' (1964) categorization of coping behaviors was employed to categorize coping. Class I coping responses are

Theoretical Propositions	Practice Speculations
1. Repeated no-control experiences precipitate a state of helplessness.	Be sensitive to how helplessness is induced in patients: strange language system, strange environment, uncertainty of health-illness and treatment situations, unpredictabilty of therapy outcomes.
2. Observed behaviors of helpless animals parallel behaviors of depressed human beings.	Eliminate unpredictability of events by informing patients of scheduled tests and procedures.
3. Coping behaviors may vary depending on the personality trait locus of control.	Helping patients be aware of the sensory events that may accompany a threatening procedure will decrease the perception of threat. Recognize that individuals' coping styles will vary.
4. When aversive stimuli are predictable the stimuli are interpreted by the subject as less threatening than when the stimuli are unpredictable.	Recognize that no control or helplessness in one aspect of the patient's life may be transferred to all aspects, creating generalized helplessness. Help the patient be aware of those aspects that are patient controlled. Prevent generalized helplessness, which is difficult to reverse.

FIGURE 3 ■ 5   The effects on humans of helplessness or lack of control.

aimed at dealing with the objective task situation. In Class I, coping behavior included problem-solving efforts such as obtaining resources to counter the initial loss. Class II coping behaviors deal with emotional or anxiety reactions to the stimulus. Examples include withdrawal, group affiliation, hostility, and aggression. (see Fig. 3–5.)

Discussion of Practice Speculations

Helplessness is a syndrome of behaviors that mimics depression (Seligman, 1975). It is a challenge to the nurse to be aware of how helplessness can be induced in patients in order to take measures to prevent it. This involves the nurse being sensitive to the patient's response to a strange language system, strange environment, uncertainty of health-illness and treatment situations, and unpredictability of therapy outcomes. Planning for patient control by enabling patient decision making and participation is crucial. Determining patients' preferred coping strategies and not suggesting strategies that could be in conflict with their related locus-of-control tendency must also be kept in mind.

Eliminating unpredictabilty of events is possible for most patients. This may involve keeping patients informed of scheduled tests, anticipated sensations during an examination or test, and the expected outcomes. It may involve, for example, helping the patient and family plan for discharge from a health setting to home. The certainty of knowing the date of discharge gives the patient a sense of control. Knowledge about anticipated events allows the patient to direct activities within the family to prepare for the events.

CONTROL IN HEALTH-ILLNESS SITUATIONS

MacDonald and Hall (1971) studied the relationship of locus of control and perception of disability. The Rotter Locus of Control Scale and a Disability Scale were completed by 479 subjects. Externally controlled subjects rated physical disabilities as more debilitating than did the internally controlled subjects. Internals rated emotional disorders as being more debilitating than physical disabilities. The emotional disabilities included having irrational fears, being extremely depressed, and being withdrawn. Physical disabilities included internal disorders such as heart problems and diabetes, sensory disorders such as speech loss and deafness, and cosmetic disorders such as obesity and amputations.

Several studies have been done on the relationship of locus of control to anxiety (Donovan, Smyth, Paige, & O'Leary, 1975; Lowery, Jacobsen, & Keane, 1975; Watson, 1967). Findings of all these studies are the same; that is, external subjects have higher anxiety than internal subjects. In these studies, anxiety was measured by the Taylor Manifest Anxiety Scale and the Zuckerman Affect Adjective Check List. The Lowery, Jacobsen, and Keane study (1975) measured state anxiety in preoperative patients. Both trait and state anxiety are higher in external subjects when self-report is used. Donovan and coworkers (1975) also used an unobtrusive measure of anxiety, the Activity Preference Questionnaire. The results of this anxiety measure revealed no difference in anxiety between internals and externals. These authors raise the issue that the Taylor Manifest Anxiety Scale may measure a dimension of neuroticism and/or negative self-concept rather than anxiety. Yet another consideration is that the subject with internal locus of control may be unwilling to disclose anxiety on tools that overtly measure it.

A scale measuring health locus of control was designed by Wallston and coworkers (1976) and by Wallston, Wallston, and DeVellis (1978). These instruments are area-specific for health and have been used to study health behavior and predict the most helpful approaches for patients desiring weight reduction. Wallston and coworkers (1976) studied 88 subjects and found that internals who valued health sought more information on hypertension as a health risk, by choosing a significantly larger number of pamphlets made available, than did the high- and low-health-value external subjects and the low-health-value internal subjects. The

Theoretical Propositions	Practice Speculations
1. Control is stress reducing.	Ways of ameliorating fear during pain and strategies to enhance control should be used.
2. Individuals with an external locus of control more readily report anxiety than do those with internal locus of control.	Validation of mood states is necessary in that anxiety may not be disclosed by patients with internal locus of control and therefore may not be treated by the nurse.
3. Effectiveness of treatment programs may depend on tailoring the program to an individual's locus-of-control tendency.	Provide support and behavior therapy to patients considering their locus of control. Externals benefit from a group approach, and internals benefit from a one-to-one approach.

FIGURE 3 ■ 6   Control in health-illness situations.

Rokeach (1973) value survey served as a model for developing the health-value scale.

In the study of subjects participating in a weight-reduction program, 34 women completed the Health Locus of Control Scale and were randomly assigned to two different types of weight-reduction treatments. The basic difference in the type of treatment program was that one was self-directed and the other was group-oriented. The 8-week program was completed by 22 women. The externals in the group program lost more weight than did the externals in the self-directed program. The internals in the self-directed program lost more weight than did the internals in the group program (Wallston, Wallston, Kaplan, & Maides, 1976). The results of this study provide some support for the need to tailor diet and behavior modification programs to match the individual's locus-of-control tendency.

In comparing locus of control to pain tolerance, Craig and Best (1977) found that internals had greater pain tolerance to increasing intensities of researcher-administered electric shocks than did the externals. (See Fig. 3–6.)

Discussion of Practice Speculations

Consideration of the unique patient situation and personal meaning of control is necessary for accurate nursing prescriptions. Nurses must recognize that fear of not being in control during painful experiences or of being unable to terminate the pain is a major threat. These fears can be ameliorated somewhat by the nurses sharing information, demonstrating pain-relief strategies, and teaching the patients relaxation, use of autosuggestion, and many self-control techniques.

One of several variables that influence self-disclosure of anxiety is the locus-of-control tendency. Interpretation of mood states must be validated with the patient and not conclusively interpreted and recorded on care plans. Individuals with internal locus of control do not readily self-report anxiety, yet these patients may have more anxiety than patients with external locus of control.

The Health Locus of Control Scale (Wallston, et al., 1976) should be considered for nursing research involving locus-of-control tendencies in patients. This tool is area-specific for health and does not have the global political items that are contained in the Rotter Internal-External Locus of Control Scale (Rotter, 1966). Behavioral indicators of locus of control need to be studied in more detail. An initial study is described in Chapter 8.

As programs on nursing care are prescribed, tailoring the program to patient's control tendency is essential.

Precipitants of Death

Richter (1959) concluded that death in rats resulted from a combination of responses to various stresses occurring in rapid succession, which generates a sense of hopelessness in the animals. In wild (non-laboratory-bred) rats, handling, whisker snipping, and confinement to glass jars to swim without knowing that they would be saved caused the animals to die. The death was not attributed to an adrenal response. When hopelessness was eliminated by removing the rats from the water and then immersing them again, the rats did not die. Removal of the rats caused them to become aggressive in trying to free themselves, showing no signs of giving up. Such rats perceived the situation not to be hopeless and swam for 40 to 60 hours, instead of dying within minutes.

Accounts of deaths in humans due to hopelessness are reported by Seligman (1975), Engel (1968; 1971), Kastenbaum and Kastenbaum (1971), and Lefcourt (1973). A dramatic example of a healthy individual succumbing to hopelessness is reported by Lefcourt (1973):

> A female patient who had remained in a mute state for nearly 10 years was shifted to a different floor of her building along with her floor mates, while her unit was being redecorated. The third floor of this psychiatric unit where the patient in question had been living was known among the patients as the chronic, hopeless floor. In contrast, the first floor was most commonly occupied by patients who held privileges, including the freedom to come and go on the hospital grounds and to the surrounding streets.

In short, the first floor was an exit ward from which patients could anticipate discharge fairly rapidly. All patients who were temporarily moved from the third floor were given medical examinations prior to the move, and the patient in question was judged to be in excellent medical health though still mute and withdrawn. Shortly after moving to the first floor, this chronic psychiatric patient surprised the ward staff by becoming socially responsive such that within a 2-week period she ceased being mute and was actually becoming gregarious. As fate would have it, the redecoration of the third floor unit was soon completed and all previous residents were returned to it. Within a week after she had been returned to the "hopeless" unit, this patient, who like the legendary Snow White had been aroused from a living torpor, collapsed and died. The subsequent autopsy revealed no pathology of note, and it was whimsically suggested at the time that the patient had died of despair.

Ferrari (1962) studied freedom of choice in 75 elderly patients admitted to a nursing home. Of the 17 who said they had no alternative except to move into the nursing home, 8 died after 4 weeks in the home and 16 were dead by the end of 10 weeks. Of the 38 who saw alternatives to being admitted to the nursing home but chose to reside there, only 1 subject died in the 10 weeks. All the deaths were termed unexpected by the nursing home staff. It could be argued that the sicker patients had fewer alternatives and more family pressure to move into a nursing home, yet all the deaths were termed unexpected.

Although skepticism may be expressed by researchers who do not recognize a qualitative approach, it is impossible to validate the happenings with the subjects themselves. To permit these findings to fall on deaf ears would cause needless physiologic deterioration and death in situations in which nurses could intervene by instilling a sense of hope. Is it possible to document the passive surrender of some chronically ill individuals? A case is presented in Chapter 6.

Hopelessness is a feeling of giving up. The individual is filled with despair, a sense of "there is nothing left." A feeling that one is completely responsible for the situation contributes to the feeling that nothing can be done to overcome or change the situation. The individual does not feel worthy of help (Engel, 1962). Hopelessness is loss of autonomy, with a feeling of despair coming from the individual's awareness of an inability to provide gratification to self (Schmale, 1964). If powerlessness is not contained, a cycle of lowered self-esteem and depression occurs, followed by hopelessness. The patient is immobilized in terms of solving problems, setting goals, and taking action. If this state is permitted to continue, isolation, loneliness, and death may ensue.

Engel (1968) has identified five characteristics of a hopelessness complex he labels "giving-in-given-up." This complex includes:
- A feeling of giving up, experienced as helplessness or hopelessness
- A depreciated image of self
- A sense of loss of gratification for relationships or role in life

Theoretical Propositions	Practice Speculations
1. Hopelessness is a temporary failure of mental coping mechanisms.	Helping patients achieve a sense of control, averting a hopeless state, may be vital to their recovery.
2. When helplessness builds over time and results from various situations, a generalized feeling of hopelessness results.	Inspiring hope affects survival.
3. When a cycle of powerlessness, depression, immobility, and hopelessness is not broken, a deteriorated physical health state may result.	Helping patients realize there is someone and/or something to live for prolongs life.

FIGURE 3 ■ 7   Precipitants of death.

- A feeling of disruption of the sense of continuity between past, present, and future
- A reactivation of memories of earlier periods of giving up

Theoretical propositions on powerlessness and death are listed in Figure 3–7.

DISCUSSION OF PRACTICE SPECULATIONS

Having someone or something to live for inspires continued life (Pattison, 1974). Building patient endurance and inspiring survival by instilling hope are familiar to nurses. Strategies for inspiring hope are discussed in Chapter 17.

Averill (1973) specifies three types of control: behavioral, cognitive, and decisional. Behavioral control is the availability of a response that may directly influence or modify the objective characteristics of a threatening event. Providing the patient control over aspects of the environment is an example of behavioral control. Allowing the patient to carry out a procedure such as a colostomy irrigation, in a self-determined, therapeutically effective way, is another example. Cognitive control is the way in which an event is interpreted, evaluated, or used in a cognitive plan. Patients can be helped to interpret events as being controlled by them. Decisional control is the opportunity to choose among various alternatives. Patients need to be aware of alternatives and consequences of alternatives. This categorization of control types may be helpful in guiding nurses to provide for patient control so as to avert hopelessness. Helping patients perceive a sense of control may be vital to their recovery.

The review of literature reveals that powerlessness has devastating effects on the person's physical and emotional states. This is a diagnosis that not only is amenable to nursing but also is unique to nursing—dependent upon nursing as the professional group to take action to alleviate powerlessness. The speculations derived from a research base provide ideas for testing in practice. Whether the interventions proposed alter the powerlessness state needs to be studied.

Field Observations as Another Phase of Concept Development

Making observations in the field verifies or refutes the need for developing the concept of powerlessness. Questions about whether the concept has real-world relevance are answered by initial field observations. These observations were made to identify factors in the health-care environment and actions of health-care providers that could increase or decrease patient control. Averill's (1973) categories defined in this chapter were used to categorize observations of chronically ill patients in one urban hospital. Observations were made 2 to 3 hours a week for a period of 6 weeks. Examples of factors decreasing and increasing control according to Averill's categories are presented in Tables 3–1 and 3–2. These field observations help us conclude that further development and validation of the nursing diagnostic label of powerlessness is warranted.

Indicators of Powerlessness

The indicators or defining characteristics of powerlessness are those signs and symptoms that lead to the conclusion that powerlessness exists. Indicators of the nursing diagnosis of powerlessness were determined by 27 graduate students enrolled in a clinical nursing course on chronic illness. The students had studied powerlessness as part of the course content and made powerlessness diagnoses on 81 chronically ill patients in their caseloads. The graduate students recorded other indicators that led them to believe their chronically ill patients were experiencing powerlessness. Similar specific signs and symptoms were clustered into 17 categories (broad statements or indicators). The indicators were then rated by a panel of 24 experts (graduate nursing faculty and advanced-standing graduate students), to determine which indicators may be characteristic of severe, moderate, low, or no powerlessness. (See Table 3–3.)

The indicators rated as "severe" could be termed "critical indicators" of the nursing diagnosis of powerlessness. That is, when any of these indicators are present, nurses could conclude that the patient has a nursing diagnosis of powerlessness. Although the signs and symptoms categorized as "moderate" and "low" are important cues, they may not lead

TABLE 3 ■ I Factors Decreasing Behavioral, Cognitive, and Decisional Control in Hospitalized Chronically Ill Patients

Behavioral Control	Cognitive Control	Decisional Control
Blind patient was left in a wheelchair in the center of the waiting room and was not told where she was or how long she must wait.	Patient was reprimanded for leaving waiting room to go to restroom after waiting 2 hours. "If you aren't here when we call you, you will miss your turn."	Appointment scheduled in ambulatory care department without asking patient if date and time is convenient.
Patient was left alone in x-ray room on hard table, in cold room, only partially covered.	Patient was not informed of his daily lab values, although he had requested that this be done.	Patient in x-ray department told to "try to hold it" when he asked location of bathroom.
	Health-care personnel more knowledgeable about patient's illness and treatment than he is.	Diagnostic and treatment procedures scheduled without asking patient or explaining why they were being done.
	Health-care personnel walked into patient's room without knocking.	Patient has little or no choice about who will share room.
	Health-care personnel talk "over" patient about their personal activities.	Little choice over scheduling activities—eating, sleeping, bathing, and treatments.
	Health-care personnel are not wearing name tags.	

TABLE 3 ■ 2 Factors Increasing Behavioral, Cognitive, and Decisional Control in Hospitalized Chronically Ill Patients

Behavioral Control	Cognitive Control	Decisional Control
Nursing-care Plan: "Allow patient to sleep until breakfast trays arrive; do not awaken for TPR."	Patient informed of weight, blood pressure, lab values.	Patient given access to refrigerator to get own soft drinks.
Patient moved to another room at her request because of roommate noise.	Patient taught about medications.	Patient given list of all U.S. dialysis centers and given full responsibility for making own vacation arrangements.
Patient in x-ray was told, "We can see you through the window. Hold up your hand if you need something."	Nursing-care Plan: Detailed description of how to do patient's dressing change had been worked out with the patient.	Medications left at bedside for patient to take when ready.
After patients were taught specific procedures, expectation given for them to take full responsibility for catheter care, urine testing, dressing change, shunt care.	Patient given feedback about lab values, taught how to record results on a flow sheet.	

TABLE 3 ■ 3 Defining Characteristics of Powerlessness

Severe	Moderate	Low
Verbal expressions of having no control or influence over situations.	Nonparticipation in care or decision making when opportunities are provided.	Expressions of uncertainty about fluctuating energy levels.
Verbal expressions of having no control or influence over outcomes.	Expressions of dissatisfaction and frustration over inability to perform previous tasks and/or activities.	
Verbal expressions of having no control or influence over self-care.	Expressions of uncertainty about treatment outcomes.	
Depression over physical deterioration that occurs despite patient compliance with regimens.	Dependence on others that may result in irritability, resentment, anger, and guilt.	
Passivity.	Inability to seek information regarding self-care.	
	Inability to monitor progress.	
	Does not defend self-care practices when challenged.	
	Hesitant to plan for future, set goals.	
	Expressions of doubt regarding role performance.	
	Reluctance to express true feelings, fearing alienation of self from care givers.	

the nurse to conclusively make the diagnosis of powerlessness. Validity and reliability of this tool have not been established.

Powerlessness and Specific Health Problems

AIDS

Since AIDS was first diagnosed in the United States in 1981 (Grady, 1988), the illness has been synonymous with uncertainty. The few knowns about this illness to date include methods of transmission, methods of diagnosis, the nature of the debilitating clinical course of the illness resulting in death, effects of specific drugs such as azidothymidine (AZT), and types of opportunistic infections that occur.

Methods of transmission known to date include contact with infected blood or semen. Specifically the human immunodeficiency virus (HIV) is transmitted by sexual contact (vaginal, anal, and oral), blood transfusions, intravenous drug use, and perinatally from infected mother to infant. McMahon (1988) reviewed the literature on body fluids and cells containing HIV and reported it isolated in blood, semen, cervical and vaginal secretions, breast milk, saliva, serum, tears, urine, alveolar fluid, brain tissue, cerebrospinal fluid, and epithelial cells.

It must be noted that data change weekly on AIDS, particularly epidemiologic information on deaths and incidence according to the Center for Disease Control Classification. Groups include acutely infected (Group I), asymptomatic infected (Group II), generalized lymphadenopathy (Group III), HIV with other related diseases such as secondary cancers, infections, neurologic involvement (Group IV). Readers are referred to the Centers of Disease Control AIDS weekly Surveillance Report to obtain the latest statistics (AIDS Program Centers for Disease Control, 1988). Opportunistic infections include *bacterial infections* such as salmonella in the blood, lungs, gastrointestinal (GI) tract, gall bladder; *viral infections* (cytomegalo virus, herpes simplex and zoster) in the skin, mucosa, peripheral nerves, retina, lungs, GI tract, and brain; *protozoal infections* of the brain, lymph nodes, muscle, lungs, and GI tract; *fungal infections* of the brain, lungs, bone marrow, skin, GI tract, mucosa, and reticuloendothelial system (Wolfe, 1989).

The physical and psychosocial complexity of the person with AIDS results in multiple nursing diagnoses and difficult challenges for nurses. It is a multisystem disease having no known cure. Since this health problem has the potential to overload the health-care system as it currently exists and create an economic crisis, AIDS is a concern of all persons. It is a national problem (Lynch, 1989). Three phases of the illness may be considered: (1) diagnosis—HIV antibodies are detected in the blood; (2)

AIDS-Related Complex of symptoms may be experienced such as night sweats, lymph node enlargement; and (3) frank immunologic suppression with rampant opportunistic infections (Lynch, 1989).

Nursing Diagnoses

Nursing diagnoses of persons with AIDS have been described (McLaughlin et al., 1987; Rosenthal & Haneiwich, 1988; Ungvarski, 1989) and include alteration in breathing pattern, alteration in nutrition (less than body requirements), alteration in elimination (diarrhea), impaired skin integrity, alteration in thought processes, alteration in comfort, potential for additional infection, and potential for physical injury. Other nursing diagnoses to consider include activity intolerance and fatigue, ineffective family and individual coping, self-care deficits, spiritual distress, social isolation, sensory deprivation, role deprivation, knowledge deficit, self-esteem disturbance, body image disturbance, hopelessness, depression or suicide ideation, anxiety and uncertainty, anticipatory grieving, bereavement overload, and powerlessness. The body wasting, skin lesions from Kaposi's sarcoma, inability to ambulate without assistive devices, and uncontrolled diarrhea (due to protozoal and other opportunistic infections) may result in body image disturbance. Bereavement overload and powerlessness may be due to the large number of irreversible losses such as loss of body function, social support network, livelihood, role performance, financial security, independence, and anticipation of a future.

Interventions

Consistent symptoms management is central to enabling the person with AIDS to maintain a sense of control (Bennett, 1988). Control begins with prevention of opportunistic infections if possible, being informed of T4 lymphocyte levels. (Normal levels range from 600 to 1200 per millimeter. Persons with AIDS may have a T4 cell range from 0 to 500 per millimeter.) When the T4 cell level drops to around 400 per millimeter, the person is more vulnerable to opportunistic infections such as the prevalent pneumocystis carinii pneumonia (Grady, 1988). Regardless of symptoms and complications, maintaining adequate nutrition is essential for restoring energy reserves and muscle strength. Providing comfort, prevention of falls and injury, anticipating a future, and preserving positive self-worth are categories of nursing interventions. Referrals may be needed to community support agencies specific for AIDS patients and others such as Meals on Wheels, Cancer Care (Bennett, 1988), and Home Hospice Care. Having the person maintain a sense of purpose and meaning in life and feeling in control of the direction of one's own life may be facilitated by reminiscence and goal setting, reflecting on favorable aspects of the past while anticipating a future. Empowerment does not preclude asking for help (Ribble, 1989); patients may need assistance in identifying helpful persons in their social network and soliciting their care.

Information contributes to emotional mastery of uncontrollable events (Furstenberg & Olson, 1984) and is indispensable in enabling coping (Frierson, Lippmann, & Johnson, 1987). Misinformation has contributed to panic, stigmatization, and premature closure of patients' and families' anticipating life's pleasures. Information about the disease transmission and effects, sexual activities that are safe, available community support, treatment choices, compliance with treatments, nutrition, skin care, mouth care, and monitoring for signs of opportunistic infections are examples of information to be provided by the nurse. Providing a climate for ventilation of feelings helps alleviate anger and enables grief work. Grief work also encompasses examining unrealistic guilt, confronting self-protective denial, using peer counseling (Frierson and Lippman, 1987), and avoiding perceptions of illness as punishment. Nurses can help patients plan for a future, helping them realize that AIDS can be a chronic illness and not an immediate death sentence. Listening holistically, providing a caring milieu, and being present nonjudgmentally are meaningful nursing behaviors (Warner-Robbins & Christiana, 1989).

In addition to information, symptom management, stress management, planning for the future, and spirituality can be sources of empowerment. Nurses should establish helping relationships with persons with AIDS and display nonconditional positive regard and respect. Issues sensitive to the patient's well-being can emerge when the qualities of a helping and therapeutic relationship exist. Spirituality may be a sensitive issue yet a valued coping resource. Spirituality is noted to become more valuable to some persons when the diagnosis of AIDS is confirmed (Belcher, Dettmore, & Holzemer, 1989; Warner-Robbins & Christiana, 1989). Some express that "even when no one else can accept me, God will." Spirituality involves a relatedness (connectedness) with something greater than self, a sense of closeness to a higher being and others (Reed, 1986). Reed found that older terminally ill persons had higher well-being than younger persons (1986) and that terminally ill hospitalized adults had a greater spiritual perspective than nonterminally ill hospitalized adults (1987). Similar findings of greater spiritual well-being and higher religious well-being among chronically ill adults compared to healthy adults were noted by Miller (1985). Reed (1986) attributes spirituality to enabling self-transcendence during suffering of a terminal illness. The love and spiritual strength provided by personal religious practices, faith, prayer, and beliefs need to be recognized and encouraged by nurses if this dimension is valued by patients. The spiritual needs of persons with cancer can be applied as well to the person with AIDS. These include having hope, giving and receiving love, and feeling significant to those around them (Epperly, 1983).

Research

Feelings of helplessness or lack of control have been a common research finding in studies on psychologic responses to AIDS (Archer, 1989; Frierson & Lippmann, 1987; Frierson, Lippmann, & Johnson, 1987; Furstenburg & Olson, 1984; Viney, Henry, Walker, & Crooks, 1989). Viney and associates' (1989) review of literature on emotional reactions of persons to physical illness revealed that anxiety, depression, anger, and helplessness are present. Specific psychologic issues of 11 persons with AIDS included social isolation, change in body image, helplessness, sexual concerns, and anger and grief (Frierson & Lippman, 1987). Similar responses were found in 50 family members of AIDS patients. Families manifested psychologic stress related to fear of contagion—anxiety about contracting AIDS; having to reveal private information about self and family to the public; feeling stigmatized; helpless; and filled with grief mixed with anger, guilt, and denial (Frierson, Lippman, & Johnson, 1987). Frierson and associates (1987) describe the response of a wife of 15 years who found out her husband had become bisexually active over the past 5 years and contracted AIDS. "At first I felt like killing him, then I realized he was already dying" (p. 64).

Viney and associates (1989) studied 105 men to compare emotional states of 35 HIV-positive men with 35 chronically ill and 35 healthy adult males. Content analysis scales were developed to analyze transcripts of tape recorded interviews. The two ill groups were more anxious, depressed, and helpless than the well group. The HIV-positive men had more anger yet higher competence than the other patients. Enjoyment was a more prevalent theme (more frequently expressed) in the interviews with the HIV group than the others. Viney and others conclude that expressions of enjoyment should be encouraged by health personnel. Expressions of enjoyment result from effective coping.

A poignant finding of a study of spirituality and well-being of 35 persons with AIDS (Belcher, Dettmore, & Holzemer, 1989) is summarized in a patient's quote, "AIDS is not all that I am" (p. 24). In general, respondents in this study saw the diagnosis as positively enhancing their spirituality not destroying it. Select activities of importance to them were meditation, reading spiritual literature, praying, and visualization.

Empowerment is a process by which persons are supported and valued as they learn about themselves, make decisions, mobilize resources, accept control of themselves, and plan for direction in their lives (Ribble, 1989). Nurses themselves may feel powerless striving to change public policy, counteracting stigmatizing behavior of others, and working on prevention of this public health problem. They witness a difficult illness progression including AIDS dementia and, despite today's technology, know the illness will result in death. These nurses experience repetitive grief (Flaskerud, 1989). Dealing with value discrepancies, fears of contagion, and maintaining confidentialities are all other nurse stresses (Bolle, 1988) that provoke powerlessness in the practitioner. The ANA Guide for Nursing's response to the person with AIDS (Miramontes, Boland, Corless, & McLoughlin, 1988) is a reminder of nursing's history in providing exemplary care to persons suffering from epidemics and difficult conditions from the Crimean to poliomyelitis. AIDS is another opportunity for nursing health-care leadership. Physical and psychologic problems of the patients and families may have a cumulative effect and the affirmation of the goodness of life and continued living may no longer be possible unless skillful nursing intervention takes place.

CANCER

Helplessness in cancer patients may be evident during varied stages of the illness. During the diagnosis phase, patients may experience unfamiliar intrusive procedures. They may feel victimized, having an illness beyond their control. They may view themselves as vulnerable and interpret the diagnosis as synonymous with death. Stoner (1985) provides clinical examples throughout the phases of illness progression. During the diagnostic phase, Stoner described a 65-year-old man who had cared for his wife throughout her long course with cancer, bringing her for chemotherapy three times a week and so forth. Despite all concerted effort, he witnessed her physical decline and death. When he developed lung cancer himself, his initial reaction of helplessness was manifested in his refusal to have treatment and comment "what good will it do anyway, it did nothing for my wife." Perceptions of uncontrollability are extended beyond receiving the diagnosis to experiencing the effects of treatment.

Bombarding patients with chemotherapy, radiation, or bone marrow transplantation, for example, all heighten symptoms and may be a threat to life. Patients and families need to be involved in making informed decisions about treatment choices and know the potential risks involved. If metastasis occurs despite adherence to regimens, feelings of helplessness increase. Cooperating with further treatment may be very difficult for the patient. During the terminal stage, cancer is not controllable (Stoner, 1985). Until a self-actualized acceptance and peace is achieved, powerlessness may reach its peak at this time for patients and families.

Some research on helplessness and control in persons with cancer has been completed. Men with genitourinary cancer who were anxious at the time of periodic cytoscopic follow-up exams also tended to feel *helpless,* hopeless, overwhelmed, and depressed (Scott, Oberst, & Bookbinder, 1984). Lewis (1982) studied 57 persons with late-stage (terminal) cancer and found a positive correlation between experienced personal control and quality of life measured by self-esteem and purpose in life. Similar to Scott and associates' findings, a negative correlation was found between control and anxiety (Lewis, 1982). Lewis concluded that well-being in late-stage cancer patients is not a function of the control they maintain over their health but is a function of a more global sense of control over their lives in general. Relinquishing personal control over health during varied phases of illness may not be negative. Relinquishing control during critical or terminal phases may be a necessary adaptive maneuver. On the other hand, having ability and performing self-care skills is not synonymous with the perception of control (Anderson, 1990). Efficacy training may be used to increase perceptions of control and to reduce anxiety.

Taylor (1983) found that adaptation to chronic illness (cancer) was influenced by cognitive coping processes that enhanced self-esteem and included (1) making social comparisons with less fortunate others; (2) selectively focusing on attributes that make the patient feel advantaged; (3) creating hypothetical worse worlds; (4) construing benefits from the event; (5) manufacturing normative standards of adjustment that make one's own adjustment seem exceptional. Westbrook (1987) found similar coping processes were associated with persons with scleroderma who perceived they had some control over their disease.

OTHERS

The nursing diagnosis of powerlessness is frequently observed in patients with spinal cord injuries (Mahon-Darby, Ketchik-Renshar, Richmond, & Gates, 1988; Richmond & Metcalf, 1986) and other neurological deficits (Boeing & Mongera, 1989; Miller & Hastings, in press).

Summary

This chapter contains initial work on analysis of the concept of powerlessness. Harmful effects of powerlessness were noted in the early literature. That research was comprised largely of studies by psychologists carried out in lab settings. Nurses' clinical observations of factors increasing and decreasing control as well as indicators of powerlessness noted in select chronic health problems such as in persons with AIDS or cancer provide convincing data that nurses can facilitate coping with chronic illness and alleviate powerlessness. These data also challenge continued study of powerlessness as a maladaptive response to chronic illness. Opposing forces, such as self-efficacy as a strategy to combat powerlessness, will be discussed later in this book. The theoretical propositions and practice speculations suggested in this chapter provide direction for nursing. Drawing conclusions that are less speculative but are based on descriptive research is the focus of other chapters as a continued exercise in theory development.

References

Abramson, L. Garber, J., & Seligman, M. (1980). Learned helplessness in humans: An attributional analysis. In J. Garber, & M Seligman (Eds.), *Human helplessness: Theory and applications* (pp. 3–34). New York: Academic Press.

Abramson, L., Seligman, M., & Teasdale, J. (1978). Learned helplessness in humans: Critique and reformulation. *Journal of Abnormal Psychology, 87,* 49–74.

AIDS Program Centers for Disease Control (1988). *AIDS weely surveillance report.* Washington, DC.

Anderson, C. (1977). Locus of control, coping behaviors and performance in a stress setting: A longitudinal study. *Journal of Applied Psychology, 62,* 446–451.

Anderson, J. (1990). Home care management in chronic illness and the self-care movement: An analysis of ideologies and economic processes influencing policy decisions. *Advances in Nursing Science, 12,* 71–83.

Archer, V. (1989). Psychological defenses and control of AIDS. *American Journal of Public Health, 79,* 876–878.

Averill, J. (1973). Personal control over aversive stimuli and its relationships to stress. *Psychological Bulletin, 80,* 286–303.

Ball, T., & Vogler, R. (1971). Uncertain pain and the pain of uncertainty. *Perceptual and Motor Skills, 50,* 1195–1203.

Belcher, A., Dettmore, D., & Holzemer, S. (1989). Spirituality and sense of well-being in persons with AIDS. *Holistic Nursing Practice, 3,* 22–26.

Bennett, J. (1988). Helping people with AIDS live well at home. *Nursing Clinics of North America, 23,* 731–748.

Boeing, M., & Mongera, C. (1989). Powerlessness in critical care patients. *Dimensions of Critical Care Nursing, 8,* 274–279.

Bolle, J. (1988). Supporting the deliverers of care: Strategies to support nurses and prevent burnout. *Nursing Clinics of North America, 23,* 843–850.

Brady, J., Porter, R., Conrad, D., & Mason, J. (1958). Avoidance behavior and the development of gastroduodenal ulcers. *Journals of Experimental Analysis of Behavior, 1,* 69–72.

Chinn, P., & Jacobs, M. (1987). *Theory and nursing: A systematic approach.* St. Louis: CV Mosby.

Corah, N., & Boffa, J. (1970). Perceived control, self observation and response to aversive stimulation. *Journal of Personality and Social Psychology, 16,* 1–4.

Craig, K., & Best, A. (1977). Perceived control over pain: Individual differences and situational determinants. *Pain, 3,* 127–135.

Donovan, D., Smyth, L., Paige, A., & O'Leary, M. (1975). Relationships among locus of control, self-concept and anxiety. *Journal of Clinical Psychology, 31,* 682–684.

Dubin, R. (1969). *Theory building.* New York: Free Press.

Engel, G. (1971). Sudden and rapid death during psychological stress, folklore or folkwisdom? *Annals of Internal Medicine, 74,* 771–782.

Engel, G. (1968). A life setting conducive to illness: The giving up-given up complex. *Annals of Internal Medicine, 69,* 293–300.

Engel, G. (1962). *Psychological development in health and disease.* Philadelphia: WB Saunders.

Epperly, J. (1983). The cell and the celestial: Spiritual needs of cancer patients. *Journal of the Medical Association of Georgia, 72,* 374–376.

Ferrari, N. (1962). *Institutionalization and attitude change in an aged population: A field study on dissidence theory.* Unpublished doctoral dissertation. Cleveland: Case Western Reserve University.

Flaskerud, J. (1989). *AIDS/HIV infections: A reference guide for nursing professionals.* Philadelphia: WB Saunders.

Forsyth, G. (1980). Analysis of the concept of empathy: Illustration of one approach. *Advances in Nursing Science, 2,* 23–42.

Frierson, R., & Lippman, S. (1987). Psychologic implications of AIDS. *American Family Practitioner, 35,* 109–115.

Frierson, R., Lippmann, S., & Johnson, J. (1987). Psychological stresses on the family. *Psychosomatics, 28,* 65–68.

Furstenberg, A., & Olson, M. (1984). Social work and AIDS. *Social Work in Health Care, 9,* 45–62.

Gatchel, R., McKinney, M., & Koebernick, L. (1977). Learned helplessness, depression and psychological responding. *Psychophysiology, 14,* 25–31.

Geer, J., Davison, G., & Gatchel, R. (1970). Reduction of stress in humans through nonveridical perceived control of aversive stimulation. *Journal of Personality and Social Psychology, 16,* 731–738.

Glass, D., & Singer, J. (1972). *Urban stress: Experiments in noise and social stressors.* New York: Academic Press.

Glass, D., Singer, J., & Friedman, L. (1969). Psychic cost of adaptation to environmental stressor. *Journal of Personality and Social Psychology, 12,* 200–210.

Glass, D., Singer, J., Skipton, L., Krantz, D., Cohen, S., & Cummings, H. (1973). Perceived control of aversive stimulation and the reduction of stress responses. *Journal of Personality, 41,* 577–595.

Grady, C. (1988). HIV: Epidemiology, immunopathogenesis, and clinical consequences. *Nursing Clinics of North America, 23,* 683–696.

Hiroto, D., & Seligman, M. (1975). Generality of learned helplessness in man. *Journal of Personality and Social Psychology, 31,* 311–327.

Houston, B. (1972). Control over stress, locus of control and response to stress. *Journal of Personality and Social Psychology, 21,* 249–255.

Johnson, B, & Kilmann, P. (1975). Locus of control and perceived confidence in problemsolving abilities. *Journal of Clinical Psychology, 31,* 54–55.

Kahn, R., Wolfe, D., Quinn, R., Snoek, C., & Rosenthal, R. (1964). *Organizational stress: Studies in role conflict and ambiguity.* New York: John Wiley & Sons.

Kanfer, F., & Seidner, M. (1973). Self-control: Factors enhancing tolerance of noxious stimulation. *Journal of Personality of Social Psychology, 25,* 381–389.

Kastenbaum, R., & Kastenbaum, B. (1971). Hope, survival and the caring environment. In E. Palmor, & F. Jerrers (Eds.), *Prediction of life span* (pp. 249–271). Lexington, MA: Health Lexington Books.

Langer, E. (1983). *The psychology of control.* Beverly Hills: Sage.

Lefcourt, H. (1973). The function of the illusions of control and freedom. *American Psychologist, 28,* 417–425.

Lewis, R. (1982). Experienced personal control and quality of life in late-stage cancer patients. *Nursing Research, 31,* 113–119.

Lowery, B., Jacobsen, B., & Keane, A. (1975). Relationship of locus of control to preoperative anxiety. *Psychological Reports, 37,* 1115–1121.

Lynch, R. (1989). Psychological impact of AIDS on individual, family, community, nation, and world in a historical perspective. *Family and Community Health, 12,* 60–64.

MacDonald, A., & Hall, J. (1971). Internal-external locus of control and perceptions of disability. *Journal of Consulting Clinical Psychology, 36,* 338–343.

Mahon-Darby, J., Ketchik-Renshar, Richmond, R., & Gates, E. (1988). Powerlessness in cervical spinal cord injury patients. *Dimensions of Critical Care Nursing, 7,* 346–355.

Maiden, R. (1987). Learned helplessness and depression: A test of the reformulated model. *Journal of Gerontology, 42,* 60–64.

McLaughlin, F., Grant, A., MacIntyre, R., Miramontes, H., Jorrison, C., & O'Brien, M. (1987). *AIDS resource manual.* San Francisco: California Nurses' Association.

McMahon, K. (1988). The integration of HIV testing and counseling into nursing practice. *Nursing Clinics of North America, 23,* 803–822.

Miller, J. (1985). Assessment of loneliness and spiritual well-being in chronically ill and healthy adults. *Journal of Professional Nursing, 1,* 79–85.

Miller, J., & Hastings, D. (in press). Family and patient response to chronic illness.

Miller, W., & Seligman, M. (1975). Depression and learned helplessness in man. *Journal of Abnormal Psychology, 84,* 228–238.

Miller, W., & Seligman, M. (1973). Depression and the perception of reinforcement. *Journal of Abnormal Psycholgoy, 82,* 62–73.

Miramontes, H., Boland, M., Corless, I., & McLoughlin, S. (1988). *Nursing and the human immunodeficiency virus: A guide for nursing's response to AIDS.* Kansas City, MO: American Nurses' Association.

Mowrer, O., & Viek, P. (1948). An experimental analogue of fear from a sense of helplessness. *Journal of Abnormal and Social Psychology, 43,* 193–200.

Murphy, S. (1982). *Concept clarification in nursing.* Rockville, MD: Aspen.

Newman, M. (1979). *Theory development in nursing.* Philadelphia; FA Davis.

Norris, C. (1982). *Concept clarification in nursing.* Rockville, MD: Aspen.

Overmier, J. (1968). Interference with avoidance behavior: Failure to avoid traumatic shock. *Journal of Experimental Psychology, 78,* 340–343.

Overmier, J., & Seligman, M. (1967). Effects of inescapable shock upon subsequent escape and avoidance responding. *Journal of Comparative and Physiological Psychology, 63,* 23–33.

Pattison, E. (1974). Psychological predictors of death prognosis. *Omega, 5,* 145–160.

Perlmuter, L, & Monty, R. (1973). Effect of choice of stimulus on paired associate learning. *Journal of Experimental Psychology, 99,* 120–123.

Pervin, L. (1963). The need to predict and control under conditions of threat. *Journal of Personality, 31,* 570–587.

Phares, E. J., Ritchie, D. E., & Davis, W. (1968). Internal-external control and reaction to threat. *Journal of Personality and Social Psychology, 165,* 402–405.

Reed, P. (1987). Spirituality and well-being in terminally ill hospitalized adults. *Research in Nursing and Health, 10,* 335–344.

Reed, P. (1986). Religiousness among terminally ill and healthy adults. *Research in Nursing and Health, 9,* 35–41.

Ribble, D. (1989). Psychosocial support groups for people with HIV infection and AIDS. *Holistic Nursing Practice, 3,* 52–62.

Richmond, T., & Metcalf, J. (1986). Psychosocial responses to spinal cord injury. *Journal of Neuroscience Nursing, 18,* 183–187.

Richter, C. (1959). The phenomenon of unexplained sudden death in animals and man. In H. Feifel (Ed.), *The meaning of death.* New York: McGraw-Hill.

Rodgers, B. (1989a). Concepts, analysis and the development of nursing knowledge: The evolutionary cycle. *Journal of Advanced Nursing, 14,* 330–335.

Rodgers, B. (1989b). Exploring health policy as a concept. *Western Journal of Nursing Research, 11,* 694–702.

Rokeach, M. (1973). *The nature of human values.* New York: Free Press.

Rosenthal, Y., & Haneiwich, S. (1988). Nursing management adults in the hospital. *Nursing Clinics of North America, 23,* 707–718.

Rotter, J. (1975). Some problems and misconceptions related to the construct of internal versus external control of reinforcement. *Journal of Consulting and Clinical Psychology, 43,* 56–67.

Rotter, J. (1966). Generalized expectancies for internal versus external control of reinforcement. *Psychological Monographs, 80,* 1–28.

Schmale, A. (1964). A genetic view of affects. *Psychoanalytic Study of the Child, 19,* 287–310.

Scott, D., Oberst, M., & Bookbinder, M. (1984). Stress-coping response to genito-urinary carcinoma. *Nursing Research, 33,* 325–329.

Seeman, M. (1972). Alienation and knowledge-seeking: A note on attitude and action. *Social Problems, 20,* 3–7.

Seeman, M. (1967). Powerlessness and knowledge: A comparative study of alienation and learning. *Sociometry, 30,* 105–109.

Seeman, M. (1963). Alienation and social learning in a reformatory. *American Journal of Sociology, 69,* 270–284.

Seeman, M. (1962). Alienation and learning in a hospital setting. *American Sociological Review, 27,* 772–798.

Seligman, M. (1975). *Helplessness: On depression, development and death.* San Francisco: Freeman.

Seligman, M. (1968). Chronic fear produced by unpredictable shock. *Journal of Comparative and Physiological Psychology, 66,* 402–411.

Seligman, M., & Maier, S. (1967). Failure to escape traumatic shock. *Journal of Experimental Psychology, 74,* 1–9.

Seligman, M., Maier, S., & Geer, J. (1968). The alleviation of learned helplessness in the dog. *Journal of Abnormal and Social Psychology, 73,* 256–262.

Seligman, M., Maier, S., & Solomon, R. (1969). Unpredictable and uncontrollable aversive events. In F. R. Bruch (Ed.), *Aversive conditioning and learning.* New York: Academic Press.

Seligman, M., & Meyer, B. (1970). Chronic fear and ulcers as a function of the unpredictability of safety. *Journal of Comparative and Physiological Psychology, 73,* 202–207.

Slimmer, L, Lopez, M., LeSage, J., & Ellor, J. (1987). Perceptions of learned helplessness. *Journal of Gerontological Nursing, 13,* 33–37.

Staub, E., Tursky, B., & Schwartz, G. (1971). Self-control and predictability: Their effects on reactions to aversive stimulation. *Journal of Personality and Social Psychology, 18,* 157–162.

Stoner, C. (1985). Learned helplessness: Analysis and application. *Oncology Nursing Forum, 12,* 31–35.

Stotland, E., & Blumenthal, A. (1964). The reduction of anxiety as a result of the expectation of making a choice. *Canadian Journal of Psychology, 18,* 139–145.

Taylor, S. (1983). Adjustment to threatening events: A theory of cognitive adaptation. *American Psychologist, 38,* 1161–1173.

Thornton, J., & Jacobs, P. (1971). Learned helplessness in human subjects. *Journal of Experimental Psychology, 87,* 369–371.

Ungvarski, P. (1989). Nursing management of the adult client. In J. Flaskerud (Ed.), *AIDS/HIV infection: A reference guide for nursing professionals* (pp. 74–110). Philadelphia: WB Saunders.

Viney, L., Henry, R., Walker, B., & Crooks, L. (1989). The emotional reactions of HIV antibody positive men. *British Journal of Medical Psychology, 62,* 153–161.

Walker, L., & Avant, K. (1988). *Strategies for theory construction in nursing.* Norwalk, CT: Appleton & Lange.

Wallston, K., & Wallston, B. (1982). Who is responsible for your health? The construct of health locus of control. In G. Sandes, & J. Suls (Eds.), *Social psychology of health and illness* (pp. 65–95). Hillsdale, NJ: L. Erlbaum Associates.

Wallston, K., & Wallston, B. (1981). Health locus of control scales. In H. Lefcourt (Ed.), *Research with locus of control construct.* (Vol. 1). New York: Academic Press.

Wallston, K., Wallston, B., & DeVellis, R. (1978). Development of the Multidimensional Health Locus of Control (MHLC) Scales. *Health Education Monographs, 6,* 161–170.

Wallston, K., Wallston, B., Kaplan, G., & Maides, S. (1976). Development and validation of the Health Locus of Control (HLC) Scale. *Journal of Consulting and Clinical Psychology, 44,* 580–585.

Warner-Robbins, C., & Christiana, N. (1989). The spiritual needs of persons with AIDS. *Family and Community Health, 12,* 43–51.

Watson, C. (1967). Relationship between locus of control, self-concept and anxiety. *Journal of Clinical Psychology, 31,* 682–685.

Weiss, J. (1971). Effects of coping behvaior in different warning signal conditions on stress psychology in rats. *Journal of Comparative Physiologic Psychology, 73,* 202–205.

Westbrook, M. (1987). Belief in ability to control chronic illness: Associated evaluations and medical experiences. *Australian Psychologist, 22,* 203–218.

Wilson, J. (1969). *Thinking with concepts.* London: Cambridge University Press.

Wolfe, P. (1989). Clinical manifestations and treatment. In J. Flaskerud (Ed.), *AIDS/HIV infection: A reference guide for nursing professionals* (pp. 58–73). Philadelphia: WB Saunders.

Zahn, J. (1969). Some adult attitudes affecting learning: Powerlessness, conflicting needs and role transition. *Adult Education Journal, 19,* 91–95.

■ P A R T ■
II

Powerlessness and Developmental Vulnerabilities

Individuals are vulnerable to powerlessness at different times throughout the life cycle. Behavioral manifestations of powerlessness, coping behaviors, and some nursing approaches are discussed in this part for each of three developmental groups: children, middle-aged women, and elderly persons.

A child in whom autonomy has already been well established will have unique reactions to situations where he or she has no control. Nurses must understand these reactions and interpret them for the parents. The child's coping behaviors are also unique to childhood. Coping behaviors of chronically ill adults (Chapter 2) can be contrasted with those of children (Chapter 4).

A prevalent health problem among some middlescent women is obesity. The relationship of obesity to powerlessness is discussed in Chapter 5. Empowerment strategies for women coping with the stressors of middle years who are also struggling with weight control are presented.

The relationship of long-standing, uncontrolled powerlessness and hopelessness is revealed in the detailed case-study analyses of elderly patients (Chapter 6). Nursing care of elderly patients who are experiencing powerlessness is included. The serious consequence of a feeling of futility is that the ill elderly person may actually invite death.

■

Coping Behavior of Children Experiencing Loss of Mobility

■ DIANN RECKER BAUMANN

The physical and psychologic crises of illness in children are compounded when the confronting health problems cause immobility. Children bring their total developmental accomplishments and past experiences to each new situation that affects their ability to cope with new stresses encountered. Expected or normal development is a progression of children's gaining power and control through developmental achievements.

The purpose of this chapter is to identify coping behaviors of children experiencing powerlessness resulting from immobility. Detailed case studies of immobilized children at two different stages in development, toddler and preadolescent, are included, with specific nursing strategies to enhance children's feelings of control.

Coping

Murphy (1962) defines coping strategies as the child's individual patternings and timings of his or her resources for dealing with specific problems, needs, or challenges. This often involves both the methods of dealing with the environment and the devices and mechanisms for dealing with tension aroused by the stimulus. Learning is necessary for children to develop their own coping strategies. Reality testing involves learning and promotes development of coping strategies. It is both a cognitive and

85

a manipulative function and proceeds by creative restructuring in order to test one's potential. Murphy refers to coping as a synthesizing or integrative concept; it deals not only with techniques but with strategy (Murphy, 1962).

Encountering a situation that is new or not yet mastered (an obstacle or conflict) initiates the process of coping, and it may be gratifying, threatening, challenging, or frustrating. Murphy identifies ways in which the child might act when faced with a threatening situation. Various possibilities for action might be reduction of the threat, control of the threat by setting limits, destruction of the threat, or balancing of the threat with security measures.

Once the child learns specific methods of coping successfully, the patterns developed are drawn upon in new situations. The individual child displays variations in coping methods depending on problems encountered (degree of perceived threat), previous experiences, parental involvement, and the child's unique coping abilities.

The Role of Mobility in the Emotional Life of the Child

On the biologic level, Adams and Lindemann (1974) identified movement as the first mechanism necessary for biologic coping: "Virtually all response to environmental challenge involves purposeful movement, either of the total organism or its appropriate parts" (p. 132). Rank's (1949) study of aggression indicates: "The tension and/or anxiety finds its primary expression in motor-expressive discharge" (p. 32). "The blocking of the normal emotional discharge channel of motor activity taxes the adaptive capacities of the child to the utmost" (p. 43). Mobility is thus identified as significant for both biologic and psychologic reasons.

Mobility plays a psychodynamic role in the lives of children and adults. Mittlemann's (1954) study of mobility identifies a "motor urge" present in all age periods. This becomes the dominant urge in the second year of life. The motor urge is seen as one of the most important avenues of exercising such functions as mastery, integration, reality testing, and control of impulses. It is "significantly connected with nearly every other motivational striving, both of physiologic (oral, excretory, genital) and more general emotional nature (love, dependency, etc.) and particularly self preservation" (Mittleman, 1954, p. 142).

Muscular maturation in the second year of life provides the child with the facility for locomotion. It is the period when the sense of autonomy makes significant growth. Mobility for the toddler is important in the development of autonomy, as well as for discharging tension, reality testing, integration, and mastery. The toddler's sense of autonomy is facilitated by the drive and energy to move. Mittlemann (1967) describes the second year of life as including ". . . increase in self-assertion, and independence alternating with continued dependence on the environment, increase in aggression, fear of motor retribution, motor (imitative) identification, the readiness to translate impulses into activity, predominance of motor language in communication with the environment" (p. 284). In a similar fashion, the young adolescent strives to achieve a mature sense of self. Gallatin (1975) states

> The youngster elaborates upon the basic sense of autonomy that emerged during the second crisis of childhood. There is an echo of self-awareness of the adolescent . . . "the toddler's dim recognition that he is an autonomous being" (p. 178).

Mahler (1963) suggests that the child's sense of identity may be traced to the first 2 years of life. She defines this feeling of identity as the cohesive cathexes of our securely individuated and differentiated self-image. In other words, "normal separation-individuation is the first crucial prerequisite for the development and maintenance of the *sense of identity*." In the toddler stage, the child develops the realization of being separate from the object (mother) in the symbiotic union of infancy.

Erikson (1968) defines the stages of child development in terms of an accruing sense of ego strength. He identifies the second stage—the stage of autonomy—as follows:

> A sense of self-control without loss of self-esteem is the ontogenetic source of the sense of free will. From an avoidable sense of loss of self-control and or parental over-control comes a lasting propensity for doubt and shame (pp. 109–110).

Mobility plays a particularly important role in the life of both the toddler and the young adolescent. Motion and activity become significant as outlets and means to work through adolescent energies. The "craving for locomotion" expressed by Erikson (1961) relates to the discontent and searching of youth. Vehicles of motion such as the automobile offer what Erikson calls "passive locomotion with an intoxicating delusion of being intensely active" (p. 11). The nature of young adolescents keeps them seeking adventure and excitement.

Blos (1967) identifies the adolescent's forceful turning to the outside world toward action and bodily motion as a form of resistance against regression. Deutsch (1944) suggests that there is a "thrust of activity" before the sudden increase of passivity that inaugurates the young girl's development into womanhood. "The thrust of activity represents not an increase of aggression but rather an intensive process of adaptation to reality and of mastery of the environment made possible by the development of the ego" (p. 4).

The child's uses of the motor system have a significant relation to perceptions of, and feelings about, self; the intact motor system and the guidance to use it in socially acceptable ways contribute to the development of a healthy self-image and body image (Blake, 1969; Erickson, 1967).

Mobility is shown as an important factor for the child in terms of exploring the environment, gaining a sense of autonomy, and expressing tension and anxiety. The motor urge plays a role in achieving mastery, integration, and reality testing. A healthy self-identity and body image are influenced by the child's mobility—particularly in the toddler and preadolescent stages, when the process of separation and individuation is under way. It is clear, therefore, that the restriction of freedom of mobility can predispose a child to severe anxiety and frustration.

Two children coping with radical threats of powerlessness resulting from immobility are described here. The first discussion focuses on a toddler coping with the powerlessness of traction. The second relates an analytic study of one preadolescent girl's coping behavior during the loss of control from a paralytic illness. The assessments and interventions are presented as they relate to Johnson's model of nursing.

Johnson's Behavioral Systems Model of Nursing

Johnson's behavioral systems model of nursing (Auger, 1976; Fawcett, 1989; Loveland-Cherry & Wilkerson, 1989) identifies the nurse as a person who provides protection, nurturance, and stimulation so that the highest level of behavioral functioning in the child's eight subsystems are provided. These subsystems interact to make the person whole: achievement, affiliation, aggression-protection, dependency, elimination, ingestion, restoration, and sexuality. When the goal of one subsystem is not met, an imbalance in one or more of the other subsystems may occur. This imbalance might consequently manifest itself in maladaptive behavior.

There is a need to regulate and control behavior in children to maintain balance and stability and to achieve the highest behavioral goals appropriate for the child's individual developmental level. A wide variety of variables are taken into account when the nurse assesses the behavior and environment of the child, such as the child's state of biologic (maturation and growth) and psychologic functioning, the nature of the family network, pathology, and culture among other factors.

When the child's needs for functional requirements of protection, nuturance, and stimulation are not met and the child's ability to adapt to stress is weakened by illness, the nurse intervenes to become the external regulator of the child's environment. The overall objective of any nursing intervention is to establish regularities in the patient's behavior so that the goal of each subsystem will be met at the highest possible level.

Clinical Data and Nursing Strategies

CASE STUDY: ONE TODDLER COPING WITH THE RESTRAINT OF TRACTION

Larry is a 3-year-old black boy who sustained a spiral fracture of his left femur as a result of a fall at home while playing wtih his 8-year-old sister. He is the youngest of an intact family of five children. He is described by his mother as a "talkative and outgoing, friendly" child. He has not been noted to have significant shyness with new people. His mother is proud of his ability to sing solos in front of a large group of people in church.

Larry was placed in Russell's leg traction after his admission to a children's hospital. The primary nurse became involved with his care 1 week after admission. The staff nurses reported that his mother visited only "a couple times a week" and that Larry had prolonged (more than a half hour) screaming and crying spells when his mother left. The staff identified Larry as a child who "fussed, screamed, and cried a great deal." One person described him as "spoiled." The staff had difficulty in dealing with Larry's coping behaviors; there was a noted "disturbed staff-family relationship." It was an apparent stress for the parents to cope with the child's hospitalization and injury.

The primary nurse began her care of Larry when he was free of the acute fracture pain. Circulatory and neurologic functions of the left leg were observed and found intact. Skin integrity was maintained in excellent condition. Skeletal alignment was maintained, as verified by follow-up x-ray.

The goal of the nurse-child relationship was to foster the child's highest possible level of behavior. Restricted mobility of traction and separation from his family were the paramount stressors in Larry's altered environment. The nursing process was directed toward assessment of the function of each behavioral subsystem, identification of the primary sources of imbalance, and prescription of the methods of regulation of the external environment. The intervention was directed toward improving the child's ability to cope in general and specifically to cope with immobility.

The assessment was based on the knowledge of biologic and behavioral responses, developmental research, and the interrelationships of the child's behavioral subsystems. Larry had the extraordinarily strong impinging forces of his restricted mobility in traction and the separation from his family. Because of his developmental stage, he was especially vulnerable to these forces. As a result, Larry's behavioral systems were in an imbalance, and his ego integrity was threatened.

A child's efforts to cope with immobility may be successful or unsuccessful. If the child is not successful, there will be further tensions. If the method of coping does not reduce the strain, the external threatening forces and added internal upheavals rapidly become intermingled and reinforce one another. Nursing is to be directed toward assisting the child to cope—to find some tension-releasing activity—in order to stabilize behavioral subsystems and maintain equilibrium.

Maternal separation can result in specific phases of child behavior: protest, despair, and denial. Robertson and Robertson (1971) found that if toddlers were separated from their mothers for 10 to 27 days in an adequate setting with a substitute mother, they did not respond in the protest-and-despair cycle. Another child, who was separated from his mother and subjected to the inadequacies of the residential nursery care, displayed acute distress and despair commonly exhibited by institutionalized children. Larry's screaming and crying episodes were in protest of the separation from his mother. Prolonged separation from the mother can affect the toddler profoundly and can potentially cause physiologic and depressive emotional disturbances.

The major stressors related to Larry's hospitalization were centered on the affiliative, achievement, and aggressive subsystems. The following subsystem assessment illustrates how these imbalances placed stress on the other subsystems. The behaviors noted were observable and, to some degree, functional in Larry's attempt to cope with the pressure of immobilization and separation. Through prescribed nursing intervention, Larry was moving toward improved coping behaviors and was releasing some of his inner tensions while dealing with the feelings of powerlessness.

Achievement Subsystem

Larry's achievement subsystem was interrupted as noted by his regression to lack of bowel and bladder control. The variables in this subsystem related to his developmental stage of autonomy versus shame and doubt. His restricted mobility and autonomy caused frustration. His previous control and powers were lost.

Larry's negativistic expressions, his loud crying and screaming, and his poor eating habits were identified as his striving to gain some control or power. The primary nurse focused on sustaining Larry's available facets of autonomy. Larry was guided to direct his aggressive behavior in compatible ways in an effort to gain some feeling of control and power. Alternative modes of aggressive behavior were supplied through the following nursing directives:

1. Provide choices (for toys and play)

2. Avoid reprimand for his temporary loss of toilet control; do not shame this regressive behavior
3. Accentuate positive reinforcement when he successfully manages bowel and bladder control; assist his ability to do so by offering the bedpan frequently
4. Utilize manipulative play activities with toys and artwork
5. Encourage partial self-care (brushing teeth, bathing, and eating)

The short-term goal was to help Larry use acceptable modes of control and give him a feeling of having some power, some sense of autonomy. The long-term goal was the eventual return of his prehospitalization level of autonomy.

Affiliative Subsystem

The affiliative subsystem was significantly altered as Larry perceived a loss of his primary love object in the separation from his mother. The experience and fear of separation created anxiety. Larry protested by screaming at each separation from his mother. His avoidance of new caretakers was observed in shy, negativistic, turning-away behavior.

An understanding that Larry is highly vulnerable to fear of abandonment is necessary. Cognitively, he has no concept of time, which may have helped him cope with separation. Understanding when he would see his mother again, as well as when he would go home, could have facilitated mastery over his feelings of abandonment. Larry apparently came from an intact family with evidence of good interrelations before the hospitalization. This positive variable was radically interrupted by the hospitalization. Communication was hindered by the family's lack of a telephone and their inability to visit daily.

Nursing focused on maintenance of the mother–child tie and a surrogate relationship to alter the fear of abandonment. The mode was to provide a consistent protective and nurturing relationship with the primary nurse. Directives to maintain mother–child ties include

1. Encourage parents to visit despite the difficulty of leaving
2. Maintain daily visits and interaction with the primary nurse to provide a surrogate relationship
3. Supply items to help the child feel ties with home:
   • Toys from home
   • A family photo album
   • Conversation about the family
   • An article of clothing to signify a plan for leaving the hospital
   • Gifts of artwork from the child's siblings

4. Use the peek-a-boo game cooperatively to assist in working through separataion anxiety
5. Interpret and defend the child's behavior to staff members who appear to misunderstand

The short-term affiliative goal was to maintain the mother–child relationship, and the long-term goal was toward the incorporation of the hospital experience without residual instability.

Aggressive Subsystem

The aggressive subsystem was interrupted by Larry's confinement and immobilization in traction. He was silent and withdrawn at times, exhibiting negativism, while at other times he screamed and threw tantrums. He would often assume an angry facial expression and throw things out of the crib. In Larry's toddler developmental stage, the aggressive system to express frustrations is active. Mobility and expressions in aggressive play would normally provide a toddler with a healthy expression of frustrations.

Nursing care focused on guiding Larry to rechannel aggression in the supportive presence of the caring nurse. Alternative modes of play activity utilized some of the following toys and techniques for expression of aggression.

1. Pounding bench toy
2. Punching bag
3. Pounding on a toy drum
4. Manipulation through drawing and scribbling
5. Motion of playing with cars
6. Manipulation with hanging and pull-push toys
7. Manipulation of wash cloth and water play at bath time
8. Synergistic effect of being in the playroom with others

The short-term goal was to support multiple, acceptable aggressive activities as outlets for his internal frustration. The long-term goal was to have Larry readapt aggressive behavior to a moderate level appropriate for his age and in nondisruptive modes after hospitalization.

At the completion of treatment for the fractured leg, Larry was able to walk happily into his mother's arms, ready to return home. The primary nurse visited Larry's home 1 month later. He apparently was reintegrating well into the home environment, as evidenced by his outgoing and talkative behavior, playfulness, and returned motor ability. His behavioral subsystems balance had returned.

Preadolescence and Coping with Paralysis

Paralysis is identified as a "severe narcissistic wound" (Bernabeu, 1958). The inability to function independently as a result of a sudden onset of flaccid motor paralysis is psychologically traumatizing. This is a crisis that places a significant stress on the individual's adaptive processes.

'   The hospitalized, paralyzed child is faced with normal developmental challenges compounded by both the physical and the psychologic crises of illness. The professional nurse is called upon to assist the child in coping with these stresses. The nursing approach is based on knowledge of preadolescent development and on understanding gained from the scant research on paralysis of children.

YOUNG ADOLESCENT DEVELOPMENT

The "young adolescent" refers to the child between ages 10 and 14. This time span includes variations in sexual development. Individual tempos and styles of maturation are noted in young adolescents. Early adolescence and puberty have been described as a time of heightened conflict between adolescents and parents (Steinberg, 1981; 1987; 1989); yet successful psychosocial maturity is dependent upon a supporting, caring family environment (Greenberger, 1984). Adolescence is a time of conflict, passive aggressiveness, and rebelliousness (Blos, 1979) and is a stage as "change filled" as the stage of infancy (Greenberger, 1984). The so-called turbulence of early adolescence is experienced in varying degrees by different children (Lerner, 1988).

Attainments during the latency period represent the essential precondition for advancement to adolescence. Intellectual development is in transition from the state of concrete operations to one of abstract reasoning through the use of judgment, generalization, and logic. Socially, the child's empathy, understanding, and altruistic feelings have acquired significant stability. The child's physical stature allows for independence and mastery of the environment. Ego functions must have developed an increased resistance to regression and to disintegration under the stresses of the normal, everyday critical situations. Blos (1962) states

. . . the synthesizing capacity of the ego must have become effective and complex; and finally, the ego must be sufficiently able to defend its integrity with progressively less assistance from the outside world. These latency achievements have to yield to the prepubertal increase in drive energy (p. 57).

The prepubertal hormonal alterations elevate the level of drive tension; such intensification becomes apparent both in mental content and in behavior. These matters alert nurses that the initial advances in pread-olescent psychic restructuring are under way. The tentativeness of these processes instills in the preadolescent both the fear of losing familiar ground and the desire to go ahead to the unknown (Blos, 1970).

Blos (1967) describes the psychic development in adolescence as the process of disengagement of libidinal aggressive cathexes from the internalized infantile love and hate objects. This creates ambivalence and emotional lability, which are characteristic of adolescents. Blos states that individuation cannot be accomplished without some regression. This type of regression constitutes an integral part of development at puberty. "The relentless striving toward increased autonomy through regression forces us to view this kind of regression in adolescence as regression in the service of development, rather than service of defense" (p. 173).

Erikson's (1963) epigenetic stages describe young adolescents as having some mastery of basic trust, autonomy, initiative, and industry in their psychosocial development. The young adolescent is at the stage of "identity versus role confusion" in which the question "Who am I?" takes on significant meaning. Rapid body growth and genital maturity present cause for a psychologic revolution. Adolescents' primary concerns then are with both self-concept and with what they appear to be in the eyes of others.

The young adolescent is at a stage of life between a saddening fare-well to childhood and a gradual transition toward as yet unknown adult-hood. A major conflict of this in-between stage of preadolescent devel-opment is in the struggle between the desire to be dependent and the wish to be independent. Preadolescent development displays a strong drive for growth and independence—there is a need to grow up, to achieve on one's own, and to experience and learn from the world. Descriptive of the adolescent attitude and quality are terms such as enthu-siasm, varied interests, a passion for adventure, readiness to be inspired, and eagerness to go all out for a purpose.

The subjective and objective experience of instability in the adoles-cent years is explained by the many internal and bodily changes that occur in puberty. Adolescence is a time of life when the youth has a heightened awareness of what goes on in the body; its rapid changes create stress for adolescents seeking their own identity and control. Adolescents must develop a sense of self-awareness of self-control; they must adapt to phys-ical and psychologic changes.

The preadolescent cognitive developmental stage is an integrated picture constituting a natural culmination of the sensorimotor structures and of the grouping of concrete operations. Young adolescents are build-ing upon and expanding their capabilities. They become capable of rea-soning about propositions they do not yet believe, by means of differen-tiation of form and content. They become capable of drawing the necessary conclusions from concepts that are merely possible. This constitutes the beginning of hypothetic-deductive, or formal, thought. There is an interest in the future, which adds futuristic dimensions to the child's thought process.

The preadolescent is striving to master the situations of life through various coping strategies. This struggle for mastery depends upon available energy and upon expectations and trust in future gratification (Murphy, 1976). This phase is a critical period of both turbulence and potentiality—intrinsically a period of great stress and weakened coping skills. It is also a time of extreme vulnerability.

This is great turmoil and searching in the lives of adolescents as they seek identity, even without the complication of a physical impairment. During preadolescence and adolescence, fluctuations between extreme opposites in feeling are deemed normal.

THE PSYCHOLOGIC THREAT OF PARALYSIS

Langford (1961) studied children's adaptation to illness and hospitalization and identified preadolescent youngsters as tending to express fears of permanent disability. Paralysis, then, might be viewed as an integral deterioration of the body.

Guillain-Barré syndrome is a distinct clinical entity characterized by a subacute development of symmetric paresis or paralysis in subjects of all ages and occurs commonly in young women (Riggs, Gutmann, & Whited, 1989). Guillain-Barré is acute idiopathic polyradiculoneuropathy, manifesting progressive weakness, absence of tendon reflexes, sensory changes and compromised respirations (DeMello, DeFreitas, & Chimelli, 1989). Weakness is identified as the major presenting complaint. The severity of motor weakness covers a wide spectrum from a mild ataxia to a total paralysis of every motor and cranial nerve (Arnason, 1975). The etiology of this disease remains imperfectly defined. Although reversibility is characteristic of this syndrome, respiratory failure without compensation may be a fatal complication. Reversibility of this disease varies for complete recovery ranging from 2 to 18 months. Guillain-Barré syndrome presents a potentially long-term course of rehabilitation for the patient and is potentially fatal. Consequently, the patient is presented with severe threats to self-preservation and psychic equilibrium.

Bernabeu (1958) studied eight paralytic children and identified the "rage" response in reaction to the restraint of paralysis:

The core reactions to the crippling are frustration, anxiety, and rage . . . a major complicating factor in this situation arises from the fact that motor discharge, a major element in a child's normal economy of handling aggression, is either eliminated or seriously curtailed . . . (pp. 176–177).

The crippled motor system, ". . . interfered with in its expressive, performance, and locomotor aspects, fails in its function of serving ego development." The significant function of motility is inhibited by the force of paralysis. Bernabeu (1958) summarized the types of fears identified in the paralyzed children:

> . . . fear of death and suffocation, separation anxiety, fear of fragmentation, the castration anxiety—including the feelings of "difference" and inferiority linked to these. Fear of loss of love is reinforced by fear of physical relapse, since progress always depends on the attention of others. The fear of punishment is related to the fear of their own aggression as well as the onset of the disease (p. 177).

The victim of paralysis experiences a forced dependence on nursing care, which arouses a basic independence-dependence conflict. The child's level of mastery and autonomy is restrained. The paralyzed preadolescent, initiating the developmental task of identity, faces an adaptation crisis.

Coyle and Miller (1966) cautioned nurses caring for patients with Guillain-Barré syndrome to consider the patients' possible disabilities and emotional reactions. Patients may react by becoming apathetic, irritable, and depressed. Their moods frequently range from impatience to overt expressions of hostility and resentment to profound anxiety.

Blake's (1969) empirical study identified immobilization as a crisis. She hypothesized specific tasks related to the immobilization of young persons. The child must learn new ways to cope with frustrations, change in body image, and loss of pleasure from activity. New patterns of interaction are sought to provide control over the child's feelings of helplessness and to promote the restoration of self-esteem and the feelings of self-direction and independence.

Dadich (1972) studied an 11-year-old girl's use of control while immobilized in halo-femoral traction and found that she coped with the anxiety by controlling herself as well as controlling others involved in her care. Mastery of overwhelming feelings was attained only if she had some power to control. Seeley (1973) also found that an 8-year-old immobilized girl used similar coping behaviors. The subject concentrated on the reachievement of motility, control over people, and control over the situation.

Clinical Data and Nursing Strategies

CASE STUDY: LOSS OF CONTROL IN A PREADOLESCENT GIRL

The behavioral responses of an 11-year-old girl coping with loss of control during the reversible paralytic illness of Guillain-Barré syndrome were observed during the intensive-care and recovery phases of a 3-month hospitalization. The primary nurse assumed the role of participant-observer and described the girl's behavioral responses in the form of process recordings.

Joanne is an 11-year-old white girl who is seventh in an intact family of nine children. Joanne's growth and development were reported as normal; she had been healthy during her childhood, was a high scholastic achiever, and led a socially active life before the onset of illness.

Four days before hospitalization, Joanne complained of weakness, vomiting, and feelings of numbness and tingling in her feet and hands. She had difficulty controlling her feet while walking. She experienced progressive weakness and paralysis.

On the day of hospitalization, Joanne experienced dyspnea and was transferred to the intermediate-care unit by ambulance. Four hours later, she was transferred to the intensive-care unit and was totally dependent on a mechanical respirator. A tracheotomy was performed on the fourth day of hospitalization to facilitate ventilation.

Joanne's respiratory-dependent state was just one of her symptoms of paralysis. She was unable to move below her neck, and she had lost both bladder and bowel control. She experienced dysphagia, aphonia, distortion of facial expression, and diplopia. She underwent a multitude of diagnostic and treatment procedures. Joanne was referred to the primary nurse on the fourth day of hospitalization. The referring staff nurse described Joanne as "scared to death."

Data Collection

The primary nurse assumed the role of participant-observer during 32 sessions of recorded observations. These observations were made at varying times of day and evening during 51 days of Joanne's 3-month hospitalization. The length of the observations averaged 1½ hours.

Immediately after the observations, process recordings were written describing both the verbal and nonverbal behaviors of the child. Verbal behaviors of the child included the content and manner in which words and/or sounds were communicated. Nonverbal behaviors included aphonic mouthed words, facial expressions, body movements, and gestures. Verbal and nonverbal behaviors were observed in relation to the events at the time.

Content of the 32 process recordings was analyzed to identify the major coping behaviors manifested by the child. The behaviors were tabulated by frequency of occurrence in relation to the significant events of the illness and its treatment. Behaviors were then analyzed to identify both the modes and the pattern of responses observed over time in relation to the significant events of the illness and of its treatment.

Joanne's methods of coping with the degrees of loss of control and the feelings of powerlessness can be divided into two distinct phases. Phase 1, the acute phase, was the period when she experienced a complete loss of control. The predominant behavioral responses manifested during this phase were to control powerlessness and to focus on activities of daily living. The controlling responses were categorized and will be discussed in the following order of frequency; directive, resistive, and compliant responses.

- Directive responses were those in which the child attempted to direct what was to be done to her, how it was to be done, and by whom.
- Resistive responses were those in which the child opposed care by refusal, postponement, or limitation of action. Grimacing, crying, and clicking of her tongue were classified as resistive. Refusal to participate was considered resistive in an effort to control or in resistive submission when there was no alternative means of control.
- Compliant responses included those indicative of yielding, consenting, or conforming to the caretakers and the caretaking activity.

Three modes of behavior—motion, breathing, and grooming and diversion—were observed in which controlling responses were used. These are specific behaviors within select subsystems of the Johnson framework in that motion is a behavior within the aggressive-protective subsystem, breathing is included in the ingestive subsystem, and grooming and diversion are included within the restorative subsystem. Because only the select components of the subsystem were observed and to enable the reader to more easily follow the data presented, the mode titles of motion, breathing, and grooming and diversion will be utilized instead of the entire Johnson subsystem headings.

Phase 2, the recovery phase, included the period when the child gradually regained control of body functions. The predominant behavioral responses manifested in the recovery phase were to control powerlessness and to focus on activities of daily living. Although the order of frequency of controlling responses is different from the order in the acute phase, the definitions of these categories remain the same in both phases.

Phase I: Acute Phase

The raw data of the acute phase consist of 16 process recordings. This acute phase included the first 25 days of hospitalization. To cope with this paralytic illness and the multiple treatments and caretakers, Joanne attempted to maintain a sense of control. The directive (113), resistive (57), and compliant (34) responses appeared to aid her in maintaining some autonomy.

Directive Responses

The directive responses ranged from 0 to 25 per interaction during the acute phase. Directive responses were related to activities of daily living and occurred in the following order of frequency: motion (59), breathing (37), and grooming and diversional activities (17).

Examples of directive responses related to motion included Joanne's verbal orders regarding range-of-motion exercises, repositioning, and chest clapping, for example, "Turn my neck first," and "Don't clap so hard." Directive responses within the breathing mode while Joanne was respirator-dependent included "Suction my tube," and "Bag me faster, harder."

Grooming was considered an important part of Joanne's care in an effort to maintain her intact body image. Not only was Joanne unable to control body motion, she also experienced significant edema of her hands, feet, and face secondary to adrenocorticotropic hormone (ACTH) therapy. This edema may have presented a threat to Joanne's body image. Diversional activities were methods offered to stimulate her interests in things other than the illness and its treatments. Her directive responses included "Lip gloss my lips" and "Read some more."

Mail from Joanne's peers seemed to give her support. Fewer controlling responses were noted after she received communications from peers.

The most frequent directive responses in the acute phase were directives relative to motion (52.2%), and the majority (69.0%) of those related to motion were recorded during the first half of the acute phase. Directive responses related to breathing (32.8%) were evenly distributed throughout the acute phase. Grooming and diversional activity directive responses (15%) were observed less frequently and were distributed throughout the acute phase.

An increase in directive control measures was related to an increase in powerlessness provoking events such as removal and reinsertion of a nasogastric tube, assignment of an unfamiliar nurse to her care, diarrhea, and performance of x-ray procedures.

Resistive Responses

During the acute phase, Joanne communicated a total of 57 resistive responses. The frequency of resistive responses ranged from 0 to 11 during each observation in the acute phase. The resistive responses were related to activities of daily living in the following order of frequency: motion (42), breathing (11), and grooming and diversional activites (4).

Ten of the 11 resistive responses related to breathing occurred during the first half of the acute phase. Joanne's pattern of resistive responses may indicate that her anxiety related to the vital function of breathing was at its highest level during the first portion of the acute phase. More resistive responses were noted when her powerlessness was heightened, as on days when invasive procedures (manual removal of impacted stool, replacement of the nasogastric tube) were performed.

Only four resistive responses were observed related to grooming and diversional activities during the acute phase. It is significant to note that the activities in this category involve things done with rather than to Joanne and are of a more pleasurable nature. Perhaps this accounts for her absent or minimal resistance to grooming and diversional activities.

The most frequent resistive responses in the acute phase were related to motion (73.7%), and the majority (64%) of these were recorded during the first half of the acute phase. The resistive responses related to breathing (19.3%) occurred most often (91%) during the first half of the acute phase. Resistive responses to grooming and diversional activities (7.0%) were less frequent and were evenly distributed throughout the acute phase.

Compliant Responses

During the acute phase, Joanne responded to treatments by caretakers with compliant responses a total of 35 times. Although compliant responses are perhaps less controlling responses, they are, however, chosen responses. The frequency of compliant responses ranged from 0 to 5 during individual observations. The compliant responses related to activities of daily living in the following order of frequency: motion (21), breathing (8), and grooming and diversional activities (5).

Acute Phase Summary

Controlling responses in the modalities of motion, breathing, and grooming and diversion during the acute phase are summarized in Table 4–1. Joanne manifested a high frequency of controlling responses while coping with loss of control during the acute phase. Three types of controlling responses were identified: directive, resistive, and compliant. These controlling responses varied in frequency throughout the acute phase. Directive responses were the most frequently observed during this phase, and resistive responses were the second most frequently observed. The most frequent directive and resistive responses were related to motion. The second most frequent directive and resistive responses were related to breathing. Compliance was the least frequent response observed during the acute phase. The least frequent of all the controlling responses were those related to grooming and diversional activities. Most days with a high frequency of directive responses were also days with a high frequency of resistive responses.

TABLE 4 ■ I   Summary of Controlling Responses Observed
During the Acute Phase

	Coping Responses Observed	Motion		Breathing		Grooming and Diversion	
	N	N	%	N	%	N	%
Directive	113	59	52.2	37	32.8	17	15.0
Resistive	57	42	73.7	11	19.3	4	7.0
Compliant	34	21	61.8	8	23.5	5	14.7

Phase 2: Recovery Phase

The raw data of the recovery phase consist of 16 process recordings during days 26 to 51 of the hospitalization. The recovery phases comprised events that signify the initial return of Joanne's body functions. Her tidal volume increased; weaning from the respirator began in the middle of the recovery phase and was completed within 10 days. Bladder control was regained after the removal of the urinary catheter. The nasogastric tube was removed 2 days later, and Joanne was able to eat. Near the end of the recovery phase, she could manage gross arm, hand, and finger movements.

To cope with the multiple treatments and caretakers during this gradual regain of control, Joanne continued to manifest controlling responses in her struggle for autonomy. The frequency of responses is different from that of phase 1 and is as follows: resistive (108), directive (98), and compliant (64). These controlling responses were used in relation to eating (ingestive subsystem), motion (aggressive-protective subsystem), breathing (ingestive subsystem), and grooming and diversion (restorative subsystem).

Resistive Responses

During the recovery phase, Joanne communicated 108 resistive responses. The number of resistive responses ranged from 0 to 24 during individual observations. The resistive responses related to activities of daily living in the following order of frequency: eating (37), grooming and diversional activities (26), motion (25), and breathing (20).

Eating became a function Joanne was capable of controlling, and consequently a high frequency of resistive responses was observed in relation to eating. One observation contained 11 resistive responses related to eating. This observation noted the twelfth new nurse Joanne encountered during the 41 days of hospitalization. During the first 10 minutes of observation, this staff nurse repeatedly attempted to get Joanne to eat. ("Come on, you've got to eat.") Joanne responded, "No. Why does everybody have to stuff food down my throat? I'm not hungry!" and "I wish I had some different food and a different nurse."

Within 20 minutes, and after Joanne's caretakers agreed to her request for a ride on the cart, her mood seemed to change to a more agreeable one (five compliant responses), and no further resistive responses were noted.

Joanne expressed more resistive responses related to grooming and diversional activities in the recovery phase (26) than in the acute phase (14). This seemed indicative of her concern about, and her desire to gain control over, her appearance. Her beginning of physical recovery gave her "hope," and she expressed ego strength through expressing her opinion and exerting resistance. A greater interest in diversional activities was noted in the recovery phase because of her decreased struggle over the more vital functions of breathing and so forth.

Joanne's recovery of body movement was gradual and progressed from her ability to move her head to minor motion of her shoulders and arms by the middle of the recovery phase. Toward the end of this phase, Joanne was able to perform gross arm, hand, and finger movements. She gained the ability to move her feet to a small degree. Both the gradual gains in motion and the ability to be moved in and out of her room on a cart afforded Joanne a sense of mobility by the middle of the recovery phase. It is speculated that this motion acted to decrease the frustration of her motor urge and to decrease her need to utilize responses related to motion during the last half of the recovery phase.

The same day that Joanne was completely weaned from the respirator, the decreased size of the tracheostomy tube enabled her to speak audibly. The gradual return of signficiant body function apparently facilitated Joanne's feeling of autonomy.

In the recovery phase, 20 resistive responses were related to breathing. During the weaning from the respirator, Joanne selected resistive responses to maintain some control: "No, I'm tired" and "Wait."

During the last half of the recovery phase, there were only four resistive responses related to breathing. It is speculated that the regain of respiratory functioning decreased her need to control through her resistant mode of behavior. There was no longer a struggle for physical control of this most vital bodily function and, consequently, no longer a need for manipulative control related to breathing.

In summary of resistive responses, Joanne manifested significantly more resistive responses during the recovery phase (108) than during the acute phase (57). Her most frequent resistive responses in the recovery phase were related to eating (34.3%). The resistive responses related to grooming and diversional activities (24.1%) were evenly distributed throughout this phase. Those related to motion (23.1%) occurred most often (92%) in the first half of the recovery phase. The resistive responses related to breathing (18.5%) occurred most often (80%) during the first half of the recovery phase.

Directive Responses

During the recovery phase, Joanne's directive communications totaled 98. The range of frequency for the individual observations in this phase was 0 to 28. These directives related to activities of daily living in the following order of frequency: motion (73), breathing (15), and grooming and diversional activities (10).

All 15 of Joanne's directive responses related to breathing occurred during the first half of the recovery phase. The gradual regain of respiratory function increased her feeling of autonomy which led to a decrease in her need to use directive responses.

Joanne manifested a similar number of directive responses in the recovery phase (98) as in the acute phase (113). Her most frequent directive responses were related to motion (74.5%), and the majority (78%) of these occurred in the last half of the recovery phase. All directives related to breathing (15.3%) occurred in the first half of this phase while she was still on the respirator. Directive responses to grooming and diversional activities (10.2%) were distributed evenly throughout this recovery phase.

Compliant Responses

Joanne responded to treatments and progressive rehabilitative efforts with 66 compliant responses. The frequency range for compliant responses was 1 to 13 in individual observations during the recovery phase. These compliant responses related to activities of daily living in the following order of frequency: grooming and diversional activities (28), motion (24), and breathing (12).

Participation in the weaning from the respirator was evidenced by Joanne's compliant responses. Initially, her progress was visualized with a graphic chart showing the increases in her tidal volume. Later, a chart was utilized to illustrate graphically the length of time Joanne breathed on her own power. She appeared to be proud of her achievements. Joanne's affect included smiles when progress was evident. "Yesterday I was off (the respirator) for 45 minutes," she reported one day. Joanne initially resisted being off the respirator; however, when she was given some signs of progress and when her readiness was considered, Joanne became involved with the effort to be weaned from the respirator. The graphic charts helped her increase control. These charts may have assisted her by offering a competitive and rewarding aspect to her efforts.

Joanne manifested a greater number of compliant responses during the recovery phase (64) than during the acute phase (34). Her most frequent compliant responses were related to grooming and diversional activities (43.8%). The frequency of compliant responses related to motion (37.5%) and those related to breathing (18.8%) varied throughout the recovery phase. The greatest increase of compliant responses from the acute phase (8) to the recovery phase (24) was related to motion.

Recovery Phase Summary

The controlling responses in the modalities of eating, motion, breathing, and grooming and diversion for the recovery phase are summarized in Table 4-2. Joanne manifested a high frequency of controlling responses while coping with the loss and gradual regain of control during the recovery phase. Resistive responses were the most frequently observed controlling responses during the recovery phase (108) as compared with the acute phase (57). Eating was the activity of daily living in which there were the most frequent resistive responses (34.3%). The focus of Joanne's resistive behavior changed. The frequency of resistive responses to breathing and motion decreased after she was able to breathe on her own and to experience a modified form of mobility (rides on a cart). The height of Joanne's resistive responses to all activities appeared to coincide; that is, on the day that she expressed a high resistance to eating, she also expressed a high resistance to motion, breathing, and grooming. The majority of all resistive responses occurred in the first half of the recovery phase.

Directive responses were the second most frequent controlling response observed during the recovery phase. The highest frequency (74.5%) of these directives was related to motion, and the majority (78%) of these occurred in the last half of the recovery phase after she had been given a modified form of mobility. The frequency of directive responses expressed during the recovery phase (98) was similar to the frequency expressed during the acute phase (113). The total number of compliant responses during the recovery phase (64) was almost double the total of the acute phase (34). The greatest number of compliant responses during both phases related to grooming and diversional activities.

TABLE 4 ■ 2 Summary of Controlling Responses Observed During the Recovery Phase

	Coping Responses Observed	Eating		Motion		Breathing		Grooming and Diversion	
	N	N	%	N	%	N	%	N	%
Resistive	108	37	34.3	25	23.1	20	18.5	26	24.1
Directive	98	0	0.0	73	74.5	15	15.3	10	10.2
Compliant	64	0	0.0	24	37.5	12	18.8	28	43.8

Case Study Summary

This study described the behavior of an 11-year-old girl coping with loss of control accompanying a reversible paralytic illness during the acute and recovery phases of a 3-month hospitalization. Her behaviors were analyzed and categorized for the two distinct phases. Phase 1, the acute phase, was the period of complete loss of control of body functions. Phase 2, the recovery phase, included the period of gradual regain of control of body functions.

Paralysis presented this preadolescent girl with a severe narcissistic wound involving several threats to her sense of autonomous and trusting behaviors. The child coped with threats related to loss of control of her autonomous respiratory, motor, eating and bladder functions over which she had achieved control since toddlerhood. The child's vulnerability increased since these functions became the foci of intrusions by others. Furthermore, it was necessary for the child to cope with threats due to multiple caretakers who presented a variety of approaches.

Predominant strategies that the child manifested for coping with the major threats were identified. During the acute phase, directive behavior was the predominant coping strategy. This strategy was most evident in relation to motion. The strategy of resistive behavior was demonstrated with respiratory function. Related to grooming and diversional activities (the least painful and most pleasurable activities) was the strategy of compliant behavior.

During the recovery phase, resistive behavior was the predominant coping strategy, and this was related to eating. The child's predominant coping strategy related to motor function was directive behavior. Related to grooming and diversional activities was the strategy of compliant behavior.

There were changes in the coping behaviors over a period of time. After the child gained partial control of her eating function, she was provided a new avenue for expressing resistance as a means of controlling her environment. After the child gained respiratory autonomy, partial motor function, and a modified form of mobility, she utilized directive coping strategies as a mode of control.

This child's coping strategies varied in relation to what was being done to her and by whom. There was an increased frequency of controlling behaviors when new caretakers were introduced. There was a significant increase in controlling behaviors when new or different treatments (e.g., being placed on the Circ-O-Lectric bed or being weaned from the respirator) were introduced.

Recommendations evolving from this study focus on the approaches to the nursing care of the paralyzed child and on the need for further study. It was observed that this child expressed both the need and the demand for control. Based on this observation, it is recommended that nurses who care for children suffering from paralytic illness plan for and devise approaches that allow for the child's exercise of control. These approaches include preparation for controlling events, participation, provision of emotional outlets, and development of a satisfactory mode of communication.

Each new caretaker presented a new threat to the child's sense of control. Based on this finding, it is recommended that nurses caring for children who are experiencing the threat of loss of control negotiate a plan for consistency of caretakers.

The findings also revealed that the subject had difficulty coping with the change related to weaning from the respirator. It is recommended that further study be conducted to identify clues indicating the readiness of a child for weaning from the respirator. Specific strategies to enhance control during the weaning could be tested, such as use of graphs as visual signs of improvement and reinforcement regarding ability to be off the respirator for lengthening periods.

Summary of Nursing Practice Strategies

The study and appreciation of the child's ability to cope with restricted mobility provide some understanding of the crisis of powerlessness in childhood. Both the toddler and the young adolescent suffered powerlessness, which accompanied the loss of mobility. Larry and Joanne were in critical stages of development during which mobility normally facilitates the sense of autonomy. Both patients exhibited controlling behaviors in an effort to maintain their autonomy.

The nursing approach in assisting children during the crisis of powerlessness or loss of control must be considered specifically for each child. Certain general speculative approaches are suggested in terms of preparation, participation, outlets for emotional responses, and communication.

PREPARATION

Give children time to get ready; they may feel they have some control if they have a moment to prepare and can signal the nurse when they are ready. Let them know that you are prepared and confident in treating them; telling a child that you have helped other children with certain illnesses and treatments like this may project confidence.

PARTICIPATION

Have children help choose the time of treatment and the order in which they would like it given. Providing some method of working together gives children a sense of control. Methods can be used such as counting the repetitive motions (i.e., exercises), holding onto something related to the treatment, and allowing children to cry or scream if it helps them to have a perceived sense of control.

OUTLETS FOR EMOTIONAL RESPONSES

Knowing that the restraint of mobilization causes anger and an aggressive response, the nurse should provide games and toys to act as outlets for these emotions. There may be days of withdrawal and uncooperative attitudes in children coping with the impinging force of powerlessness, and the nurse might tell the child, "It's okay to feel that way right now."

COMMUNICATION

Children communicate in a variety of ways. The toddler was not always able to verbalize what he needed, and the preadolescent could only mouth her words. Children need interpretation for understanding of their special needs.

Multiple caretakers present a threatening aspect to the child's care. Any method to provide consistency in nursing care might decrease the child's anxiety and powerlessness. The primary-nurse approach provided some consistency and some evidenced trusting behavior in both the toddler and the preadolescent after much effort was expended by the nurse to earn trust.

Johnson's model for nursing provides a framework for caring for the immobilized child. The powerlessness of immobility will cause behavioral subsystem imbalance in all subsystems: achievement, affiliation, aggression-protection, dependency, elimination, ingestion, restoration, and sexuality. Specific manifestations of subsystem imbalance are influenced by the unique situational, environmental, cultural, and family stressors impinging on the child, as well as by the child's particular stage of development.

Nursing of children coping with powerlessness related to any illness or treatment can be a challenging and rewarding experience. The coping behaviors used by both children described in this chapter were viewed as controlling behaviors and were varied. For example, although Larry was in traction, he was able to use some motion, throwing toys out of the crib and playing. Joanne was not able to use motion, but she commanded motion and used controlling behaviors of resistance, direction, and compliance. Nurses need to identify each child's needs and unique efforts to control situations. Creative methods of nursing for the sake of providing control will facilitate the child's recovery.

References

Adams, J. E., & Lindemann, E. (1974). Coping with long term disability. In G. Coelho, D. Hamburg, & J. E. Adams (Eds.), *Coping and adaptation* (pp. 127–138). New York: Basic Books.

Arnason, B. G. (1975). Inflammatory polyradiculoneuropathies. In P. J. Dyck, P. K. Thomas, & E. H. Lambert (Eds.), *Peripheral neuropathy* (pp. 110–148). Philadelphia: WB Saunders.

Auger, J. R. (1976). *Behavioral systems and nursing.* Englewood Cliffs, NJ: Prentice-Hall.

Baldwin, A. (1967). *Theories of child development.* New York: John Wiley & Sons.

Bernabeu, E. A. (1958). The effects of severe crippling on the development of a group of children. *Psychiatry, 21,* 169–194.

Blake, F. (1969). Immobilized youth. *American Journal of Nursing, 69,* 2364–2369.

Blos, P. (1979). *The adolescent passage.* New York: International University Press.

Blos, P. (1970). *The young adolescent.* New York: Free Press.

Blos, P. (1967). The second individuation process of adolescence. *Psychoanalytic Study of the Child, 22,* 162–186.

Blos, P. (1962). *On adolescence.* New York: Free Press.

Coyle, N., & Miller, B. (1966). Guillain-Barré syndrome: Nursing care. *American Journal of Nursing, 66,* 2224–2226.

Dadich, K. S. (1972). An eleven year old girl's use of control while immobilized in halo-femoral traction. *Maternal Child Nursing Journal, 1,* 67–74.

DeMello, A. R., DeFreitas, M. R., & Chimelli, L. (1989). Chronic recurrent Guillain-Barré syndrome: Report of 3 cases. *Arquivos De Neuro-Psiquiatria, 47,* 84–90.

Deutsch, H. (1944). *The psychology of women.* New York: Grune & Stratton.

Erickson, F. (1967). Helping the sick child maintain behavioral control. *Nursing Clinics of North America, 2,* 695–703.

Erikson, E. H. (1968). *Identity: Youth and crisis.* New York: WW Norton.

Erikson, E. H. (1963). *Childhood and society.* New York: WW Norton.

Erikson, E. H. (1961). *The challenge of youth.* Garden City, NY: Doubleday & Co.

Fawcett, J. (1989). *Analysis and evaluation of conceptual models of nursing* (2d ed.). Philadelphia: FA Davis.

Gallatin, J. E. (1975). *Adolescence and individuality: A conceptual approach to adolescent psychology.* New York: Harper & Row.

Greenberger, E. (1984). Defining social maturity in adolescence. In P. Karoly & J. Steffen (Eds.), *Adolescent behavior disorders: Foundations and contemporary concerns* (pp. 3–37). Lexington, MA: Lexington Books.

Langford, W. S. (1961). The child in the pediatric hospital: Adaptation to illness and hospitalization. *American Journal of Orthopsychiatry, 31,* 673–677.

Lerner, R. (1988). Early adolescent transitions: The lore and the laws of adolescence. In M. Levine & E. McAnarney (Eds.), *Early adolescent transitions* (pp. 1–21). Lexington, MA: Lexington Books.

Loveland-Cherry, C. J., & Wilkerson, S. A. (1989). Dorothy Johnson's behavioral system model. In J. Fitzpatrick & A. Whall (Eds.), *Conceptual models of nursing: Analysis and application,* (2d ed.) (pp. 147–163). Norwalk, CT: Appleton & Lange.

Low, N. L., Schneider, J., & Carter, S. (1958). Polyneuritis in children. *Pediatrics, 22,* 974–979.

Mahler, M. S. (1963). Thoughts about development and individuation. *Psychoanalytic study of the child, 12,* 307–324.

Mittleman, B. (1967). Motility in the therapy of children and adults. *Psychoanalytic Study of the Child, 12,* 284–317.

Mittleman, B. (1954). Motility in infants, children, and adults. *Psychoanalytic Study of the Child, 9,* 142–175.

Murphy, L. (1976). *Vulnerability, coping and growth from infancy through adolescence.* New Haven, CT: University Press.

Murphy, L. (1962). *The widening world of childhood.* New York: Basic Books.

Rank, B. (1949). Aggression. *Psychoanalytic Study of the Child, 3–4,* 43–48.

Riggs, J. E., Gutmann, L., & Whited, J. D. (1989). Guillain-Barré, another immune-mediated disease with a predilection for young women. *West Virginia Medical Journal, 85,* 382–383.

Robertson, J., & Robertson, J. (1971). Young children in brief separation: A fresh look. *Psychoanalytic Study of the Child, 26,* 264–270.

Seeley, E. F. (1973). Coping behavior of an immobilized eight-year-old. *Maternal-Child Nursing Journal, 2,* 15–21.

Sodaro, E., & Perlick, N. (1974). Guillain-Barré: The syndrome, patient care and some case findings. *Journal of Neurosurgical Nursing, 6,* 96–108.

Steinberg, L. (1989). Pubertal maturation and parent-adolescent distance: An evolutionary perspective. In G. Adams, R. Montemayor, & T. Gullotta (Eds.), *Biology of adolescent behavior and development* (pp. 71–97). Newbury Park, CA: Sage.

Steinberg, L. (1987). The impact of puberty on family relations: Effects of pubertal status and pubertal timing. *Developmental Psychology, 23,* 451–560.

Steinberg, L. (1981). Transformation in family relations at puberty. *Developmental Psychology, 17,* 833–840.

■

Middlescent Obese Women: Overcoming Powerlessness
■ JUDITH FITZGERALD MILLER

Middlescent individuals who have never been concerned about controlling food intake and balancing dietary discretion with adequate energy expenditure are likely to be either obese (weighing 20 percent more than their ideal body weight) or overweight (weighing more than ideal body weight but less than 20 percent more than ideal body weight). One third of middle-aged Americans are 20 percent overweight, and the majority of these are women. At least one of every five Americans is overweight. It is a discouraging fact that most obese persons will not remain in treatment. Of those who remain in treatment, most will not lose much weight, and of those who do lose weight, most will regain it (Stunkard, 1972). The efficient health professional is frustrated by not having fast, accurate answers to a problem that seems to have a simple treatment, having persons stop eating an excess amount of food. Nonetheless, this problem is complex.

Very little is known about self-control and eating behaviors. Theories by both obese subjects and scientists have been proposed, such as a carbohydrate intolerance, the belief that when some persons eat a carbohydrate, they cannot stop (Edelstein, 1977); appestat dysfunction, in which the satiety center that acts like a thermostat may be set higher than normal; underactivity (Mayer, 1968); obese eating behaviors learned as a child from obese or nonobese parents; and parents' providing food for children as a reward, a means of comfort during anxiety, or a relief from feeling blue.

This chapter will examine yet another combination of factors that influence obesity in middle-aged women: powerlessness and a developmental vulnerability to obesity. The main thrust is to present a variety of strategies that may be used to enable obese women to control food intake. Assessing obesity is the first consideration.

Obesity is determined in a number of ways. A simple measure is to look at the patient's physical appearance. A woman 5 feet 3 inches tall who weighs 180 pounds will look obese. An approximate ideal body weight can be calculated by the use of the following formula (Mahoney & Mahoney, 1976)

Approximate ideal weight for women = (height in inches $\times$ 3.5) $-$ 110

Approximate ideal weight for men = (height in inches $\times$ 4) $-$ 130

Factors not considered in this formula include whether the body frame is large, medium, or small, and the muscle content of the body. (Athletes weigh more, but this is due to increased muscle mass.) Measuring skinfold thickness is an accurate determination of body fat. The triceps skinfold is measured at a midpoint between the elbow and shoulder. A man between the ages of 35 and 50 years should have a triceps skinfold of less than 23 mm, and a woman between the ages of 35 and 40 years should have a measurement of less than 30 mm (Mayer, 1968). Any larger measurement indicates that the body mass contains more than 39 percent fat. Height and age charts according to body frame (Table 5–1) are also used as an ideal weight index.

TABLE 5 ■ I   Desirable Weights (in Pounds)*

Men of Age 25 and Over			
Height with Shoes 1-in heel	Small Frame	Medium Frame	Large Frame
5 ft 2 in	112–120	118–129	126–141
5 ft 3 in	115–123	121–133	129–144
5 ft 4 in	118–126	124–136	132–148
5 ft 5 in	121–129	127–139	135–152
5 ft 6 in	124–133	130–143	138–156
5 ft 7 in	128–137	134–147	142–161
5 ft 8 in	132–141	138–152	147–166
5 ft 9 in	136–145	142–156	151–170
5 ft 10 in	140–150	146–160	155–174
5 ft 11 in	144–154	150–165	159–179
6 ft 0 in	148–158	154–170	164–184
6 ft 1 in	152–162	158–175	168–189
6 ft 2 in	156–167	162–180	173–194
6 ft 3 in	160–171	167–185	178–199
6 ft 4 in	164–175	172–190	182–204

TABLE 5 ■ I Desirable Weights (in Pounds)* (Continued)

	Women of Age 25 and Over		
Height with Shoes 2-in heel	Small Frame	Medium Frame	Large Frame
4 ft 10 in	92–98	96–107	104–119
4 ft 11 in	94–101	98–110	106–122
5 ft 0 in	96–104	101–113	109–125
5 ft 1 in	99–107	104–116	112–128
5 ft 2 in	102–110	107–119	115–131
5 ft 3 in	105–113	110–122	118–134
5 ft 4 in	108–116	113–126	121–138
5 ft 5 in	111–119	116–130	125–142
5 ft 6 in	114–123	120–135	129–146
5 ft 7 in	118–127	124–139	133–150
5 ft 8 in	122–131	128–143	137–154
5 ft 9 in	126–135	132–147	141–158
5 ft 10 in	130–140	136–151	145–163
5 ft 11 in	134–144	140–155	149–168
6 ft 0 in	138–148	144–159	153–173

*Derived from Metropolitan Life Insurance Co. (1959) Build and Blood Pressure Study, Society of Actuaries, and from Bray, G. (1980). *Obesity: Comparative methods of weight control (p. 3). Westport, CT: Technomic Publishing.*

Developmental Vulnerability

OBESITY IN WOMEN

There are specific developmental vulnerabilities to obesity that occur during infancy, adolescence, pregnancy, the middle years, and menopause. During these phases, the individual or parent must be aware of the tendency to gain weight and must exercise restraint in overeating or overfeeding.

During infancy, the number of adipose cells increases (hyperplasia) owing to overeating. The increased number of cells stays with the individual for life, causing an extreme lifelong risk of obesity. Obesity that occurs during adolescence and adulthood results in hypertrophy of existing cells and is a less resistant form of obesity. After infancy, the developmental hazards are unique to women.

During adolescence, the growth spurt stops; however, the estrogen level in girls continues and promotes fat formation. Fat is laid down in the breasts and hips and will continue unchecked if eating is not controlled. Girls gain weight during adolescence, while boys lose weight during this time.

Pregnancy is the most vulnerable time for permanent weight gain (Edelstein, 1977). One third of obese women became obese in relation to pregnancy (Kemp, 1972). The increased appetite may remain with the woman after delivery, and breast-feeding mothers may overindulge during a time when excess calories are allowed. Once a women is 10 percent heavier than her ideal body weight, she has the lifelong potential for becoming obese and must be constantly on guard against that predicament.

During middle age (35 to 55 years old) physiologic changes occur. Muscle tone and skin tone diminish, and basal metabolic rate (BMR) decreases. Aging causes the BMR to decrease approximately 5 percent; so for every 30 years after age 25, the caloric intake should be decreased by 7.5 percent (Williams, 1970).

During the middle years, life events that were previously controlled and that provided security and comfort may now be a source of anxiety and grief, for example, role reversal (middle-aged child caring for elderly, dying parents), young adult children leaving home and entering life-styles disapproved of by parents, adolescent children experiencing developmental crises, marital strain, uncertainty of future, and feeling of unproductivity. Overeating may be the individual's means of coping with these stressors of middle years. Rosenfield and Stevenson (1988) found that both "normal" and alcoholic middle-aged women increased their food intake on stressful days.

Weight gain from overeating may be insidious. Increasing food intake by 100 calories a day without increasing exercise will result in a 10-pound weight gain in 1 year (Mahoney & Mahoney, 1976). A woman's attitude may be, "I've had three children; what do you expect my figure to look like?" This type of passive resistance blocks success in a weight-control program.

Weight gain may increase in women at menopause. At this phase of development, the obesity has been attributed to hormonal changes and decreased activity, as well as to depression (Diekelmann, 1977). In addition to developmental vulnerabilty to weight gain, powerlessness is a factor in obesity.

Powerlessness and Obesity

Powerlessness (the perception that individual behavior will not affect outcomes) is a prevalent theme in obesity in two dimensions:

1. Powerlessness results when weight loss does not occur after attempts at dieting.
2. Powerlessness is a factor that contributes to overeating.

Considering the first dimension, powerlessness is a perception that is confirmed in obese individuals after binging on "forbidden foods" or having lost no weight after a week without desserts. The lack of positive reinforcement of immediate weight loss as a result of what the obese person perceives to be a drastic change in eating behaviors contributes to

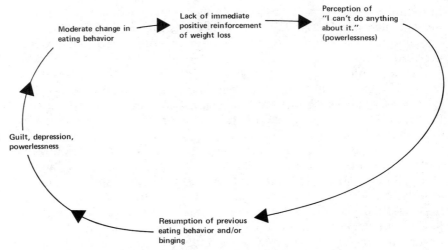

FIGURE 5 ■ I   Powerlessness obesity cycle.

powerlessness. The feeling that nothing the individual does will result in weight loss causes helplessness (powerlessness). The prevailing feeling of powerlessness causes the individual to stop trying and to return to over-eating, feeling guilt and a sense of no control. Thus the cycle (Fig. 5–1) has been completed.

The key to breaking the cycle may lie in the nurse providing reinforcement for slightly altered behavior patterns and not focusing on weight loss. The patient needs to set realistic weight loss goals—no more than an average of 2.5-pound loss per week. Helping the patient feel some sense of accomplishment in having changed the bedtime snack from an ice cream sundae to a more acceptable, lower-calorie treat is an example of positive feedback without anxiously waiting for the scale to record a 2-pound loss after 2 days of slight diet modification.

Powerlessenss may not only result from weight loss failure but may also contribute to obesity in the first place. Individuals may have a lifelong pattern of behaviors resulting from powerlessness contingencies. "Powerlessness contingencies" refer to those psychosocial states that stem from a long-term perception of being unable to influence outcomes. The psychosocial states prompt a behavior pattern that may result in overeating and little energy expenditure through exercise. These powerlessness contingencies may be categorized as self-induced and other-induced. Select contingencies of powerlessness and the resulting behavior pattern related to obesity are presented in Table 5–2. The self-induced contingencies are low tension tolerance, inability to increase activity, inability to accurately identify and express emotions, self-deprecation, unconscious positive meanings of fatness, lack of insight into eating behavior, uninvolvement in caring for self, and lack of self-confidence. Examples of

TABLE 5 ■ 2 Powerlessness Contingencies and Consequences

Powerlessness Contingencies	Behavior Pattern	Consequence
Self-induced		
Low tension tolerance	Recognizes or develops few or no alternatives for tension release	Overeating
Lacks ability to mobilize self to exercise	Moves as little as possible in daily activities. No exercise routine	Imbalance of energy intake and expenditure
Lacks ability to identify and express emotions (anger, unhappiness, frustration)	Short circuiting vague feelings without clear identification of feelings. Interprets as a need for food*	Overeating
Self-deprecation	Feelings of low self-esteem, depression	Overeating
Perceives fat as positive	Feeling comfort in being obese as a protection from sexual exploitation; keeping part of their mother; and/or protection of husband's fears and jealousy of slimmer shapely wife†	Overeating
Lacks self-insight, awareness	Unaware of eating behavior—quantity consumed, internal cues of hunger and satiation. Unaware of mood states	Overeating
Uninvolved in caring for self	Detaches own behavior from outcomes—can do nothing about it attitude. "Whatever happens is beyond my control"	Overeating
Lacks self-confidence	Unusual dependence on other persons or things for self-satisfaction	Overeating
Other-induced		
Family and society influences	Use of food as rewards, overfeeding children, clean-the-plate syndrome from childhood. Use of alcohol and food to provide an unguarded, comfortable milieu in social encounters	Overeating
Stigmatizing reaction of persons in social network	Withdrawal, reinforcement of poor self-concept	Overeating

*McCall & Siderits, 1977.
†Orbach, 1978.

other-induced powerlessness contingencies are family interactions, parents' use of food as a reward, and stigmatizing reactions of persons in the social network. Although each powerlessness contingency results in a unique behavior pattern, the consequence is the same—overeating and underexercising. Powerlessness contingencies contribute to maladaptive behavior patterns that are so ingrained that changing them may be difficult, if not impossible. The ultimate consequence is obesity.

Some research findings reinforce the fact that powerlessness is a problem in obesity. McCall (1973) noted that 169 refractorily obese women differed on the Minnesota Multiphasic Personality Inventory (MMPI) from the 181 Take Off Pounds Sensibly (TOPS) members who were successful with their weight-reduction program and who kept their weight within 5 percent of ideal body weight for 6 months. Women who were resistive to weight loss were found to have more

- Feminine dependence
- Touchiness
- Body overconcern
- Psychic hurting
- Somatization
- Rebelliousness
- Compulsive and ruminative tendencies
- Bizarre or confused thinking

Although the findings of dependence lend some support to the powerlessness theory proposed in this chapter, McCall is quick to point out that we cannot determine whether the degrees of psychologic disturbance present in refractorily obese persons are antecedent or consequent to the obesity.

Powerlessness in obese individuals is reinforced by the stigmatizing behaviors of others. Obese people are automatically categorized as sloppy, weak willed (Peternelj-Taylor, 1989), nonproductive, lazy, slow paced, easygoing, jolly, unattractive (Clayson & Klassen, 1989), and obsessed with oral gratification. Employers may view obese employees as a liability because of health risks (missed work days, insurance payments) as well as portrayal of a poor company image. In the American culture, obese persons are characterized as immature, passive, dependent, low in self-esteem, and responsible for their fatness.

"Cultural contempt" and psychosocial prejudice against obesity exist (Radvila, 1989; Wadden & Stunkard, 1987; Wright & Whitehead, 1987). Beside body image disturbances (Brodie & Slade, 1988; Gardner, Martinez, Espinoza, & Gallegos, 1988) and social discrimination, obese persons suffer no greater psychologic problems than normal-weight individuals (Radvila, 1989).

Obese persons do not appear to be assuming responsibility for adherence to prescribed weight-reduction programs. Physicians and nurses were found to have negative attitudes toward obese individuals (Maddox & Liederman, 1969; Peternelj-Taylor, 1989), which contributed to the dropout rate in weight-reduction programs. The obese subjects suffer shame and self-derogation when returning to the physician after failing to lose weight (Stunkard & Mendelson, 1967). Thin people generally do not like obese people, and obese people do not like other obese persons (Sundberg, 1978).

Reactions to condemnation by others lead the obese subject to conclude, "No one would want to be associated with me or seen in public with me." This negative self-talk reinforces individuals' perceptions that they are powerless even in maintaining close personal relationships. Stunkard and Mendelson (1967) found through interviews with 74 obese subjects that obese persons experienced two behavior disorders. First, they overate. Second, they experienced a disturbance in body image; that is, they felt their bodies were grotesque, loathsome, and viewed by others with contempt.

Eating behaviors of obese individuals may indicate no control. The fact that the obese have particular vulnerabilities and unique eating styles has been supported (Bruch, 1973; Bruno, 1972; McDonald, 1977; Stunkard & Kaplan, 1977) and refuted (Adams, et al., 1978; Mahoney, 1975). Because eating behavior may be drastically altered both in experimental conditions and when the subjects are eating in public, eating-style studies must be evaluated carefully. Obese persons overeat in privacy but seldom do so in public (Sundberg, 1978). The obese person's susceptibility to food cues includes environmental stimuli of food sights, smells, familiar binging places, and time of day without regard to internal cues of hunger and satiety as signaled by blood sugar levels, gastric motility, and gastric stretch receptors.

Binge eating is sporadic, seemingly uncontrolled eating of large quantitites of food associated with agitation and self-condemnation (Straw & Sonne, 1979). Orbach (1978) describes characteristics of obese persons who eat compulsively (binge) as eating when not physically hungry, feeling out of control around food, feeling awful about self because of being out of control, spending time thinking and worrying about food and fatness, scouting latest diets for new information, and feeling awful about their bodies. Eating is done quickly and usually furtively during binging.

Bruch (1973) describes obese individuals not only as being unable to control eating but as having the feeling that other forces are in control of their life situation. Bruch goes on to state that obese persons do not correctly identify hunger or differentiate emotional feelings from hunger. A significant relationship between control and social responsibility and weight loss was found by Hartz and coworkers (1979). Women with low control and low social responsibility scores were less successful in weight control than were women with high control and high social responsibility. Rodin (1977) found obese persons were more dependent on others and more persuadable than were persons of normal weight.

Persons who believed that they were responsible for their being overweight rather than blaming fate or others, lost weight at a significantly faster rate than those who did not hold this belief (Rodin, 1977).

Eating styles of thin persons do not have characteristics of no control. Thin persons generally do not eat very quickly, nor do they take large bites without stopping to taste the food. Life-styles and eating behaviors of thin persons need careful scrutiny so that the skills they have used to remain thin can be utilized in therapy for obese persons. Sundberg (1978) determined that thin persons' skills included ability to balance exercise with energy intake, to discriminate between adequate and excessive food intake, to adhere to regular meal patterns and control snacking (keeping frequency and type of snack food controlled), to adapt to negative emotions by means other than using food, to accurately perceive how others view them, to obtain sexual satisfaction, and to make a conscious successful effort to control weight through understanding the impact of indiscriminate eating and drinking.

SUMMARY OF POWERLESSNESS AND OBESITY

Powerlessness is a factor in causing obesity, and powerlessness is a problem that results when individuals feel they have failed in a weight-loss program. Lack of control is also evident in the obese individual's eating style (vulnerabilty to food cues and so forth). The powerlessness contingencies presented provide an analysis of the etiology of overeating (Table 5–2). The research base on powerlessness and obesity is almost nonexistent. Studies need to be done to develop the nursing diagnostic category of powerlessness and to determine the relationship between powerlessness and obesity.

The terms obese, fat, and corpulent all have negative connotations and prompt a reaction of reproach from others. Bruch (1973) describes obese persons as being under the influence of others and not in control of their bodies. Some fat people talk about their bodies as being external to themselves; some do not feel identified with the bothersome ugly physical thing. The excuses obese people use for not being able to lose weight also point to their feeling powerless, not only in having gotten fat, but also in recovering from obesity.

Middlescent Obese Women

STRESSORS CONFRONTING MIDDLE-AGED WOMEN

Most middlescent obese women became obese before reaching their middle years and the obese state is either maintained or escalated during the middle years. The stresses of middle years (ages 35 to 55 years) contribute to maladaptive behavior or successful coping. [For a thorough analysis of the middle years, see Stevenson, J. (1977). *Issues and crises during middlescence.* New York: Appleton-Century-Crofts.] Stressors are those stimuli requiring adaptation. In middle-aged women, stressors may include caring for aging parents and parents-in-law; dealing with children becoming independent; having to resolve that previous nurturing patterns are no longer needed; feeling unproductive—handling new freedom without learning new skills; experiencing role conflicts from various factors such as social pressures for liberation; dealing with changing marital intimacy; managing physical changes that result in worry and preoccupation with health; and grieving over loss of youth. Each stressor will be discussed briefly (see Figure 5–2).

The role reversal of the middle-aged daughter now having to assume responsibility for care of aging parents creates stress, affects family harmony, and may cause feelings of resentment, guilt, or despair. In some instances, an ill single parent is displaced into the daughter's home or

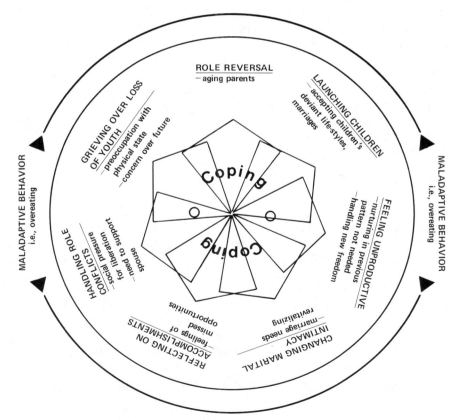

FIGURE 5 ■ 2   Stressors of middle-aged women.

into a nursing home. Disrupted family systems, conflicts, and emotional energy expenditure take place in either instance.

At the same time, young adult children may be leaving home and beginning marriages, careers, and life-styles that parents may oppose. The mother fully realizes that previous patterns of nurturing not only are no longer needed but also may be shunned by her offspring. New ways of finding satisfaction from mothering need to be learned. Obese middle-aged women who had no children may need to resolve a sense of loss over a missed opportunity to bear children.

Unless a woman has planned for and developed productive skills throughout her life, she may find herself feeling unneeded, unproductive, and unsure of her identity. Prock (1975) describes the need for women to develop multiple anchors so that when one anchor (e.g., a dependent child) is gone, other anchors still provide a sense of stability and self-worth. These anchors prevent women from feeling adrift without direction. Examples of anchors may include having a job, maintaining developed social activities, and doing volunteer work.

Marital intimacy and the source of strength that was once present in the marital bond may be waning during the middle years. As a result of schedules, communication between husband and wife may be decreasing. Husbands may have well-established patterns of confiding in business associates or fellow workers, while wives may be caught up in activities they consider of no particular interest to men—planning to advance their careers or talking about returning to school. Feelings are not shared, and sexual relationships become dull. New sources of conflict may arise, such as disagreement over each other's goals. Confirmation of affection may have disappeared from a humdrum marriage. Unless time and effort are spent to develop and share interests, few common interests will remain. The full-blown feeling of disenchantment after 20 years of marriage, although insidious in coming, has arrived. Eating may soothe the need for affection.

Coping with physical changes may precipitate a preoccupation with health. The changes may be anything from changes in the oral cavity (receding gum line), to graying of the hair, to pathologic conditions such as hypertension. These changes emphasize the realization that youth is lost.

The liberation of women in our society creates new pressures for women. Women may no longer reap self-satisfaction from supporting husbands in their successful careers. Women no longer move from school to higher education to home for child rearing, and then to low-paying jobs reserved for women when they are more stable in the work force (after childbearing years). Now women move from higher education to professions and child rearing, and remain in the productive work force. Multiple role expectations—raising children, pursuing career, taking care of spouse, and so forth—all create role strain. Women who have not been engaged in professions may feel a more intense pressure to be productive without having developed skills.

Although there may be a wide variety of responses to these stressors, one response is overeating. Obese individuals respond to stress by overeating, whereas thin people do not; on the contrary, a thin person's behavior during stress may be to eat less.

Being fat is a stressor in and of itself. Orbach (1978) recorded her observations resulting from leading a therapeutic diet group with various women participants for 5 years. Some of the connotations fat had for these obese women included

- To be fat means to compare yourself to every other woman, looking for the ones whose own fat can make you relax
- To be fat means to be excluded from contemporary mass culture, fashion, sports, and the outdoor life
- To be fat means to worry every time a camera is in view
- To be fat means having to feel ashamed for existing
- To be fat means having to wait until you are thin to live
- To be fat means to have no needs
- To be fat means to be constantly trying to lose weight
- To be fat means never saying "no"
- To be fat means to have an excuse for failure
- To be fat means to wait for the man who will love you despite the fat—the man who will fight through the layers (pp. 32–33)

Other life circumstances of middle-aged women may influence eating. There may be a change in exercise, with little physical energy expenditure taking place. The physical demands of a young family are gone. Boredom may result, with concomitant overeating. In a routinized marriage, there may be little motivation to maintain a sexually attractive appearance. There may also be misconceptions that interfere with weight loss, such as believing that losing weight may increase vulnerabilty to cancer and communicable diseases. A healthy appetite may be equated with general health, and quick complete satisfaction of appetite is needed to stay healthy. Frank rationalizations for overeating are used by some obese persons. Such rationalizations are described by Orbach (1978) and include

- Fear that food will not be available later so I must overeat now to tide me over
- Need to have something in my mouth
- Had a bad day so need to cheer up with noshing a pan of brownies
- Had a great day so I deserve one lemon pie
- Eating because it is the only way I know to give myself pleasure
- Nothing else to do in the evening

Themes of using food to alleviate bordeom and as a tranquilizer, reward, and means of oral gratification are noted in the patient comments above.

UNIQUENESS OF OBESITY IN WOMEN

Women are the fatter sex. Edelstein (1977) explains that men burn twice as many calories as women do for the same amount of exertion. A man's body contains more muscle mass than a woman's body. Muscle requires five more calories per pound to maintain itself than fat or connective tissue. However, even though the woman's body requires half as many calories as a man's, the woman's appetite is the same as a man's (Edelstein, 1977). The fat pad is necessary as a mechanism for food storage and heat protection for the fetus during pregnancy. Unfortunately, the extra fat is always with the woman, pregnant or not. Female hormones, estrogen and progesterone, are fat-producing and fat-hoarding.

Generally, women have more exposure to food stimuli than men. In most households, women are responsible for planning appealing menus and spend a good deal of their time shopping for and preparing food and cleaning up leftovers.

Obese women are more stigmatized than obese men. Fat men may be viewed as having authority and substance, whereas fat women are viewed as undisciplined (Edelstein, 1977).

In Orbach's (1978) feminist viewpoint on obesity, she proposes three explanations for overeating in women: (1) women with children are constantly giving to others, feeding the world, and feeling everyone else's needs are to be met first, the mother uses food as a means of replenishing herself; (2) becoming fat is a rebellion against pressure to look and act shapely and be sexually attractive to men, fat is a protection from sexual exploitation; (3) conflicts and ambivalences in mother-daughter relationships express themselves in fat. Eating serves as a source of love, comfort, and warmth, which may have been missing in the mother-daughter relationship. Fat may be viewed by some women as taking part of their mothers with them.

In our society, it may be more difficult for women than men to express anger in socially acceptable ways (McCall & Siderits, 1977). Women have also been socialized to be less assertive (Orbach, 1978). Women feel safer using their mouths to feed themselves rather than talking assertively and thus satisfying internal frustration.

The female giving of self is equated with food (McBride, 1988). Some women equate their role as good mother with the abilty to provide delicious baked goodies ready to satisfy an adolescent's never-ending appetite. Efforts to maintain good communication with adolescents takes place, and mother's sharing the goodies is an example of spending time trying to show interest in, understand, and communicate with the child; at the same time, this extra effort is deleterious to ideal body weight.

The yo-yo effect of losing weight, gaining it back, losing and gaining leads to giving up. The giving up phenomenon can be avoided if the refractory nature of weight loss is understood by patients and health workers. The BMR decreases by as much as 20 percent after a month of dieting (Straw & Stone, 1979). Fewer calories are used to maintain the body's metabolic function. For example, an obese woman whose daily calorie intake is 2000 calories and whose BMR is 1400 calories with 600 calories activity expenditure is maintaining her obese state. If she goes on a 1000-calorie-a-day diet, she will have lost approximately 1 kg a week. The BMR adapts to a change in calorie intake and decreases by 20 percent, so after 1 month, the BMR is not 1400 calories but 1100. If the woman's activity level decreases, despite strict adherence to the 1000-calorie-a-day diet, weight loss will not continue (Straw & Stone, 1979).

Still another reason for failure of dieting may be patients' lack of understanding that relatively unorthodox eating styles are the cause of obesity. For example, night eaters consume excessive calories from dinner time until bedtime and have morning anorexia. They take pride in not eating throughout the day but eat excessively at night. The sudden glucose load is quickly absorbed and converted to fat. Calorie intake should remain moderate and be spread throughout the day. A daily exercise routine is of paramount importance. Consuming all 1400 calories at once most likely will result in weight gain.

Whatever the underlying etiology, middle-aged obese women must struggle against weight gain and fight for control to maintain any weight loss achieved; weight control must continue for the rest of life.

Powerlessness has been described as one component contributing to obesity which results from aborted attempts at weight reduction. The first goal should be to help the obese individual feel less powerless. Empowerment strategies nurses can use to help obese women will be discussed in terms of behavior therapy, physical activity, dietary counseling, assertiveness, and rational emotive therapy to handle the stressors of middle years.

Nursing Strategies—Empowerment of the Obese Woman

BEHAVIOR THERAPY

Behavior therapy means helping the individual to change an undesirable behavior to a desirable behavior. In obese persons, the undesirable behavior is overeating. There is no emphasis on uncovering intrapsychic conflicts or changing the personality structure. The focus is on changing the maladaptive behavior. Teaching the client self-application of techniques to change behavior enables the client to be in control.

Behavior is influenced by its consequences. Brightwell, Lemon, and Sloan (1975) summarize the learning of specific behaviors through the

Stimulus ⟶	Behavior ⟶	Response
Desire to eat	Eating	Relief of hunger
Boredom, anger, anxiety	Eating	Relief of negative emotions
Depression	Eating	Alleviation of depression
Joy, elation	Eating	Continued pleasure
Food cues, sights, smells, environment	Eating	Relief of desire to eat

FIGURE 5 ■ 3   Sequence of learning eating behavior.

sequence of stimulus, behavior, event, or reward reinforcement. The sequence of eating behavior is summarized in Figure 5–3. The components of behavior therapy proposed for obesity control include obtaining an obesity profile; patient self-monitoring; environmental management; self-reinforcement; and contracts.

Obesity Profile

Obtaining a comprehensive understanding of the individual's eating behaviors, including the stimuli that prompt eating, is the first step in developing client and nurse insight into the unique patient situation. An obesity profile contains the following components: history of obesity, eating style, patient's social network, patient's knowledge, motivation, developmental stressors present, concept of self, need satisfaction and appropriate reward system, and analysis of assigned patient tasks (Fig. 5–4).

Self-Monitoring

The obese individual needs to be involved in analyzing the data gathered in the obesity profile. The goal is to begin to sensitize the client to her eating style. The client should develop an awareness of amounts and types of foods eaten, how food is eaten and in response to what stimuli, and the time of the day when the client is increasingly vulnerable to food cues and has an excessive appetite. When the appetite becomes excessive, as during the afternoon and evening, a plan for engaging in substitute activities needs to be made. For example, food preparation can take place in the early afternoon so that the woman is not exposed to food cues during the vulnerable time of day. An exercise routine can be employed during the vulnerable time. In discussing this with the woman, various

A. History
1. When did you become overweight (obese)?
2. Can you recall gaining weight associated with any particular event or period of development?
3. Family history of obesity—parents, siblings, children, spouse?
4. Health problems present (thyroid disfunction, diabetes, hypertension, coronary artery disease).

B. Eating style
1. At what time/times during the 24-hour day are you more likely to overeat?
   When is your appetite the strongest?
   When is your temptation tolerance to food cues the lowest?
2. What types of stimuli prompt eating?
3. Are you aware of your own eating behaviors:
   Amounts of food consumed, size of bites, speed of eating; automatically take seconds?
4. Do you eat until you feel full?
5. Where are you located when eating your meals?

C. Social network
1. Who prepares meals?
2. Number of family members eating meals together or separately in the same home?
3. Are your significant others a help or deterrent to weight control?
4. Relationship with spouse?

D. Knowledge
1. What are the basic food groups?
2. What are your dietary excesses and deficits?
3. Do you understand the calorie restriction according to food exchange lists?
4. Awareness of caloric value of foods routinely and occasionally consumed?
5. What are the health hazards due to obesity?

E. Motivation
1. Whose idea was it to begin a weight-control program?
2. What has been your previous involvement with weight-control programs?

3. How long did you persist in trying to be successful in previous weight-control programs?
4. OBSERVATION—Does the client present a package of excuses for not losing weight in the past as well as how any new approach will not work?
5. What do you expect to accomplish in this weight-reduction program?

F. Developmental and life stressors
1. What have been your most stressful events during the past year?
2. How do you respond, cope with stress?
3. Developmental needs—adjustment.

G. Concept of self
1. Does the client use negative self-talk?
2. How would you describe your physical appearance?
3. Do you see yourself as being fat, slightly overweight, grossly overweight, obese?
4. Do you feel you are able to influence what happens to your weight?
5. OBSERVATION—Client behavior indicate high or low self-esteem?

H. Need satisfaction and reward system
1. Do you have a need for immediate satisfaction of needs and desires in all facets of life?
2. Do you find it necessary to satisfy hunger immediately?
3. What would be a positive reward for yourself when you have done a good job? (Preferably not food.)

I. Analyses of assigned client tasks
1. Explain self-monitoring and record keeping.
2. At later sessions review diet diary (food intake, moods, times, places) for each 24-hour period. The number of days of self-recording depends upon how beneficial this direct feedback is to the client.
3. Provide appropriate feedback on analyses of client self-monitoring.

FIGURE 5 ■ 4   Obesity profile.

substitute activities that are meaningful to her can be determined, for example, practicing the piano, doing the correspondence, gardening, and doing library work. Physical activity decreases appetite, so substituting such an activity would be beneficial.

Teaching the client record keeping is a good means of self-monitoring. The record, or diet diary, helps clients become aware of their behavior; it also helps control food intake because whatever clients put into their mouths is recorded on paper for themselves and others to review. A variety of diary formats can be used. An example is given in Figure 5–5.

Date	Time	Food eaten, amounts	Calories	Place	Stimulus prompted eating	Related feelings before eating	Feelings after eating	Type and duration of exercise

FIGURE 5 ■ 5   Diet and activity diary.

Environment Management

Restricting food cues that signal eating is another aspect of behavior therapy (Stunkard & Penick, 1979). This includes avoidance of fast foods, potato chips, candy, and ice cream by not having them in the house or easily accessible. Whenever possible, places and situations contiguous with eating are to be avoided. For example, the client should be advised not to take a coffee break in the snack room where workers share home-baked treats daily.

Having the client examine what prompts eating is helpful for developing insight. This includes becoming aware of whether eating occurs in response to the time of day, seeing other people eat, smells, low blood sugar, or increased peristalsis. Clients also need to know what prompts them to stop eating, such as an extreme full feeling, having eaten all food, or seeing that eating companions have finished.

Other environmental management, or cue-suppression techniques include eating in the same room at home, using the same dishes and place mats, doing nothing else while eating, shopping from a list, setting the fork down between bites, using a smaller plate, eating with somone, and saving one item from a meal to eat later (Stuart, 1971). Eating with the nondominant hand and swallowing each bite before eating another are other techniques to help the overeater slow down. The goals of environmental management are to increase cues that support discretionary eating patterns and to decrease cues that lead to overeating.

Mahoney and Mahoney (1976) include responding to friends and family as social environment management. Significant others may be the least supportive. Mahoney and Mahoney describe four harmful patterns of reactions from loved ones:

1. Teasing about weight and size, and severely criticizing eating
2. Open sabotage by offering high-calorie foods
3. Ignoring dieter's efforts
4. Giving verbal support, yet demanding high-calorie treats to be on hand in the house

Another harmful reaction is hypervigilant scale watching by a domineering spouse.

Nurses can help family members become sensitive to their influence on obese loved ones. Because their behavior can facilitate success or failure, family members must cooperate. The assistance may include avoidance of any jokes and derogatory comments such as, "Not another diet." Family members must not offer food and eat empty calories (to be avoided by the dieter) in front of the overweight person. In some instances, open communication needs to be promoted so that food is not viewed as a display of affection. (I show my love for my husband by concocting luscious desserts.) The husband who is anxiety ridden about his wife's weight, expecting reports of foods consumed and daily weigh-in quotas while giving criticism or verbal abuse, is supporting weight gain and may be the cause of overeating in the first place. His perceptions and anxiety state need to be reviewed by the nurse.

Self-Reinforcement

To maintain accurate monitoring and changes in behavior, a method of self-rewards should be determined. Types of rewards are endless, including enjoying solitude while listening to a favorite symphony, making a phone call to a friend, spending time at a hobby, or spending extra time relaxing in a bubble bath before dinner. One client would walk to the newsstand to buy an evening paper on the days she was exceptionally good with her prescribed diet and exercise routine. Involving significant others in rewards may be very helpful. For example, a husband may participate more in unpleasant household chores, such as scrubbing floors. Another self-reinforcement technique is having clients list adverse consequences of overeating and review this list. Reviewing the adverse outcomes helps counteract the pleasure of eating.

Contracts

For some, reinforcement that is formally specified in a written contract is effective. An example of using a contract is described by Harris and Hallbauer (1973). Subjects were to decide on a reasonable amount of weight they would lose in 12 weeks and deposit a sum of money for each pound lost. Whatever amount the subject determined was acceptable. The money was refunded to the subject the week after the weight loss, providing the weight loss was maintained. The contract specified that any money remaining for failure to lose weight or dropping from the program was automatically forfeited. The forfeited money was equally divided among remaining group participants at the end of 12 weeks. Three groups with three conditions for weight control were compared after 12 weeks. Group 1 used a contract and was given information regarding diet; group 2 was given a contract and was counseled on diet and exercise; group 3 was a control group and met to discuss dieting problems. Group 2 experienced the most weight loss. The nonparticipants (dropouts) achieved significantly less weight loss than all three types of participants (Harris & Hallbauer, 1973). The contract approach weeds out obese persons who are not seriously motivated to lose weight.

TABLE 5 ■ 3 Energy Equivalents of Food Calories Expressed in Minutes of Activity*

				Minutes of Activity		
			Riding			
Food	Calories	Walking†	bicycle‡	Swimming§	Running¶	Reclining**
Apple, large	101	19	12	9	5	78
Bacon, 2 strips	96	18	12	9	5	74
Banana, small	88	17	11	8	4	68
Beans, green, 1 c	27	5	3	2	1	21
Beer, 1 glass	114	22	14	10	6	88
Bread and butter	78	15	10	7	4	60
Cake, 2-layer, ¹⁄₁₂	356	68	43	32	18	274
Carbonated beverage, 1 glass	106	20	13	9	5	82
Carrot, raw	42	8	5	4	2	32
Cereal, dry, ½ c with milk, sugar	200	38	24	18	10	154
Cheese, cottage, 1 tbsp	27	5	3	2	1	21
Cheese, cheddar, 1 oz	111	21	14	10	6	85
Chicken, fried, ½ breast	232	45	28	21	12	178
Chicken, TV dinner	542	104	66	48	28	417
Cookie, plain	15	3	2	1	1	12
Cookie, chocolate chip	51	10	6	5	3	39
Doughnut	151	29	18	13	8	116
Egg, fried	110	21	13	10	6	85
Egg, boiled	77	15	9	7	4	59
French dressing, 1 tbsp	59	11	7	5	3	45
Halibut steak, ¼ lb	205	39	25	18	11	158
Ham, 2 slices	167	32	20	15	9	128
Ice cream, ⅙ qt	193	37	24	17	10	148
Ice cream soda	255	49	31	23	13	196
Ice milk, ⅙ qt	144	28	18	13	7	111
Gelatin, with cream	117	23	14	10	6	90
Malted milk shake	502	97	61	45	26	386
Mayonnaise, 1 tbsp	92	18	11	8	5	71
Milk, 1 glass	166	32	20	15	9	128
Milk, skim, 1 glass	81	16	10	7	4	62
Milk shake	421	81	51	38	22	324
Orange, medium	68	13	8	6	4	52
Orange juice, 1 glass	120	23	15	11	6	92
Pancake with syrup	124	24	15	11	6	95
Peach, medium	46	9	6	4	2	35
Peas, green, ½ c	56	11	7	5	3	43
Pie, apple, ⅙	377	73	46	34	19	290
Pie, raisin, ⅙	437	84	53	39	23	336
Pizza, cheese, ⅛	180	35	22	16	9	138
Pork chop, loin	314	60	38	28	16	242
Potato chips, 1 serving	108	21	13	10	6	83
Sandwiches:						
Club	590	113	72	53	30	454
Hamburger	350	67	43	31	18	269
Roast beef with gravy	430	83	52	38	22	331
Tuna fish salad	278	53	34	25	14	214

TABLE 5 ■ 3   Energy Equivalents of Food Calories Expressed in Minutes of Activity* (Continued)

		Minutes of Activity				
Food	Calories	Walking†	Riding bicycle‡	Swimming§	Running¶	Reclining**
Sherbet, ⅛ qt	177	34	22	16	9	136
Shrimp, french fried	180	35	22	16	9	138
Spaghetti, 1 serving	396	76	48	35	20	305
Steak, T-bone	235	45	29	21	12	181
Strawberry shortcake	400	77	49	36	21	308

*Reprinted with permission from Konishi, F. (1965). Food energy equivalents of various activities. *Journal American Dietary Association, 46,* 186.
†Energy cost of walking for 150-pound individual = 5.2 calories per minute at 3.5 miles per hour.
‡Energy cost of riding bicycle = 8.2 calories per minute.
§Energy cost of swimming = 11.2 calories per minute.
¶Energy cost of running = 19.4 calories per minute.
**Energy cost of reclining = 1.3 calories per minute.

PHYSICAL ACTIVITY

Routine physical activities need to be reviewed by the obese woman, and a means of increasing calorie expenditure through daily exercise needs to be adopted. Obese individuals tend to expend less energy than thin persons during routine activities; that is, they move as little as possible. The mother may become aware that she is requesting the children to change the channel on the TV, bring a glass of water to her in the living room, walk to the mailbox, and so forth. The first step to increase activity is to simply move about more in daily routines. The next step is to deliberately park two blocks away from the destination, walk the stairs instead of using the elevator, and incorporate some enjoyable physical outlet into the daily routine. Unless the new exercise is viewed as pleasurable, it will not be continued. The exercise must not be contradictory to the person's health state. The routine may become more firmly established if the exercise is combined with performing other roles, such as bike riding with the children to spend time with them and get exercise at the same time. Other examples include walking, running the dog, and renewing or establishing mutual interests with a spouse by taking up tennis or some other form of exercise of common interest. This may be the beginning of a new communication pattern for the couple and may help resolve one of the stressors of middle-aged women as identified in Figure 5–2. Estimated energy expenditure for selected physical activities is presented in Table 5–3 and also in Chapter 9, Table 9–2.

DIETARY COUNSELING

Clients need a basic understanding of nutritional values of foods, for example, how fats, proteins, and carbohydrates differ in caloric values.

One gram of protein equals 4 calories, 1 gram of carbohydrates equals 4 calories, and 1 gram of fat equals 9 calories. One gram of alcohol contains 7 calories. Realizing how their own diets have deviated from required nutritional intake provides an initial insight. Edelstein suggests the following dietary changes: (1) Obese women without other pathology need to eat 1000 calories a day to lose weight. (2) Spreading calories throughout the day is important because more weight will be gained if 800 calories are consumed at dinner and 200 calories are eaten in the morning. Edelstein gives the following suggested breakdown: breakfast—250 calories, lunch—250 calories, and dinner—500 calories. (3) Approximately 40 to 50 percent of the caloric intake should be protein.

Some clients tolerate dietary change and are more adherent in the long run when changes occur gradually. One major problem may have to be eliminated each week, such as omitting the ice cream at bedtime and substituting a lower-calorie carbohydrate food such as a graham cracker.

The prescribed diet and environmental management techniques need to be given to the client in writing. The American Dietetic Association exchange list is a most effective means of teaching diet and ensuring variety in the diet. Consultation with a dietitian is needed so that an individual's calorie-restricted diet will incorporate nutritional requirements of the basic four food groups and will be individually tailored to the client's likes and dislikes.

Consuming preloads of food works for some people to decrease volume of food consumed at a subsequent meal. The preload, taken approxiamtely 30 minutes before eating, should be low in calories and high in volume, for example, two or three glasses of water or diet soda or raw vegetables (Mahoney & Mahoney, 1976).

Other strategies to control food intake may be helpful to some individuals. Have the obese client eat in front of a full-view mirror, paying attention to body size, double chin, rotund appearance, and so forth. Frustration tolerance needs to be developed so that the need for immediate satisfaction is eliminated. Teach the client that instead of gratifying a perceived need for between-meal snacks by eating, she should set a timer for 10 or 15 minutes. When the timer rings, if the snack is absolutely necessary, she can have it—ideally, a food permitted on the diet and preferably something saved from a previous meal. Creating a different response to the stimulus to eat is helpful. In response to a need to have baked goodies, bake a favorite dessert and give it away (Bruno, 1972). Leaving a bit of each type of food on the plate helps to eliminate the clean plate signal to stop eating. However, this strategy is unacceptable to individuals conscious of food costs.

ASSERTIVENESS

Assertiveness can be developed and used as a means of achieving control over life situations in general, thereby enhancing control over eating. "Assertion is any open expression in word or deed that leads others to consider seriously your desires. Assertive behavior is emotionally honest, direct, self-enhancing, and expressive" (Stuart, 1978, pp. 126–127). Assertive behavior leads to self-respect and respect from others. Open, genuine, direct means of expressing self are characteristics of assertiveness. A goal of developing assertiveness is to enhance self-worth (Gareri, 1979) to eliminate indirect, self-denying, and dishonest communication. The emotional reactions concomitant with low self-assertion are destructive to self-worth. Feelings of anxiety, anger, frustration, and guilt lead to generalized powerlessness, and the behavioral consequence may be overeating. Quereshi and Soat (1976) found that persons addicted to alcohol were low in self-assertiveness. Self-assertion needs to be studied in persons addicted to food. Obese individuals cannot affort to be passive when others are suggesting and offering forbidden foods.

The four components of teaching assertiveness as identified by Lange and Jakubowski (1976) are a useful guide in developing assertiveness in the obese individual. The components include

1. Helping individuals identify needs and their rights as well as the rights of others
2. Helping individuals differentiate among assertive, aggressive, and passive behaviors
3. Decreasing obstacles to assertive behavior—previous communication patterns learned throughout development—anxiety, guilt, low self-worth.
4. Trying out assertive behaviors in controlled-environment group practice

In order to be successful with these components, individuals need to begin to think and talk positively about themselves. "When nonassertive behavior is practiced, high anxiety and low self-esteem are the result for all participants in the interaction" (Herman, 1978, p. 129). It is hoped that obese individuals will cope with life situations by self-assertion and not by overeating.

McBride (1988) proposes that in a holistic approach to weight loss for women, multiple criteria for success be used beyond focusing on the number of pounds lost. Success may include adopting improved grooming habits, deciding not to fixate on insurance companies' weight charts, losing inches by improving muscle tone, being able to wear smaller-sized clothing, increasing energy, and eating a nutritious diet.

RATIONAL EMOTIVE THERAPY AND STRESSORS OF MIDDLE AGE

The ability to accurately recognize thoughts related to events helps one to control feelings resulting from the event. The identified stressors of middle years stimulate thoughts, feelings, and coping behaviors. Rational emotive therapy (RET) is effective in dealing with the stressors of middle years. If each stressor is rationally analyzed, the overeater's maladaptive behavior may be avoided.

The basis for RET is the assumption that control of emotions lies in the indiviudal's thoughts about the precipitating event (Ellis, 1979). A goal of RET is to help clients think rationally, developing a realistic but not self-defeating outlook regarding the event; subsequently, coping behaviors will not be self-destructive or maladaptive as in overeating. Consider a stressor of middle years as an example:

A. (Event) Chldren leaving home.
B. (Thoughts) Isn't this awful?
C. (Feelings) Anxiety, depression, guilt over missed opportunities while children were home and dependent.

The cycle continues with the symptoms being the event:

A. (Event) Anxiety, depression, guilt.
B. (Thoughts) This is awful; I can't stand these feelings. This must stop.
C. (Feelings) Deepened depression, increased anxiety, and increased guilt.

The cycle may seem to be made temporarily tolerable to the individual by overeating (or using some other maladaptive behavior). Ellis (1973) has added two more stages to RET with which the nurse can instrumentally help the client: (1) disputing the irrational thoughts and (2) analyzing effects of the disputed thoughts.

D. Disputing or challenging irrational thoughts and beliefs. Continuing with the above example: Why is this awful? Why can't I stand this change? In what way does this normal developmental progression affect my own growth?
E. Analyzing the effects of disputing the thoughts and beliefs.
   1. It is not awful for young adult children to move out on their own.
   2. This change is a mark of maturity and independence in normal young adults.
   3. Love bonds are maintained and continue to be expressed.
   4. "This developmental progression marks new opportunities for me." This is the substituted self-talk.

Each stressor of middle-aged women can be confronted using RET. The desired end is abatement of overeating, a maladaptation to the stressors of middle years.

SUMMARY

Physiologic hazards of obesity have been well documented in the literature, as have some psychosocial characteristics of obese individuals.

This chapter proposes another variable—powerlessness—to be considered in analyzing the etiology and response pattern of obese persons. It also proposes that a plan of empowerment strategies be designed and implemented as a weight-control program. The dimensions of this empowerment program for obese individuals include behavior therapy (use of obesity profile, self-monitoring, environment management, self-reinforcement, and contracts), physical activity prescriptions, dietary counseling, assertiveness training, and rational emotive therapy (RET). The goal is to have clients realize they are their own best therapists. They have the ability to control food intake and to exercise as well as to control many other aspects of their lives. Rodin and coworkers (1977) state that believing that the individual is in control has proven beneficial in achieving significant weight loss.

References

Adams, N., Ferguson, J., Stunkard, A., & Agras, S. (1978). The eating behavior of obese and nonobese women. *Behavior Research and Therapy, 16,* 225–232.

Brightwell, D., Lemon, F., & Sloan, C. (1975). *New eating behavior: Practical management of obesity.* New York: Penwalt.

Brodie, D. A., & Slade, P. D. (1988). The relationship between body-image and body-fat in adult women. *Psychological Medicine, 18,* 623–631.

Bruch, H. (1973). *Eating disorders.* New York: Basic Books.

Bruno, F. J. (1972). *Think yourself thin.* Los Angeles: Nash Publishing.

Clayson, D. E., & Klassen, M. L. (1989). Perception of attractiveness by obesity and hair color. *Perceptual and Motor Skills, 68,* 199–202.

Diekelmann, N. (1977). *Primary health care of the well adult.* New York: McGraw-Hill.

Edelstein, B. (1977). *The woman doctor's diet for women.* New York: Ballantine Books.

Ellis, A. (1979). Rational-emotive therapy, in R. Corsini (Ed.), *Current psychotherapies* (pp. 185–229). Itasca, IL: FE Peacock Publishers.

Ellis, A. (1973). *Humanistic psychotherapy: The rational emotive approach.* New York: Julian Press.

Gardner, R. M., Martinez, R., Espinoza, T., & Gallegos, V. (1988). Distortion of body image in the obese: A sensory phenomenon. *Psychological Medicine, 18,* 633–641.

Gareri, E. (1979). Assertiveness training for alcoholics. *Journal of Psychiatric Nursing and Mental Health Services, 17,* 31–36.

Harris, M., & Hallbauer, E. (1973). Self-directed weight control through eating and exercise. *Behavior Research and Therapy, 11,* 523–529.

Hartz, A., Kalkoff, R., Rimm, A., & McCall, R. (1979). A study of factors associated with the ability to maintain weight loss. *Preventive Medicine, 8,* 471–483.

Herman, S. (1978). *Becoming assertive.* New York: D Van Nostrand.

Kemp, R. (1972). The overall picture of obesity. *Practitioner, 209,* 654–660.

Konishi, F. (1965). Food energy equivalents of various activities. *Journal of the American Dietetic Association, 46,* 186.

Lange, A. J., & Jakubowski, P. (1976). *Responsible assertive behavior: Cognitive behavioral procedures for trainers.* Champaign, IL: Research Press.

Maddox, G. L., & Liederman, V. R. (1969). Overweight as a social disability with medical implications. *Journal of Medical Education, 44,* 214.

Mahan, K. (1979). Sensible approach to the obese patient. *Nursing Clinics of North America, 14,* 229–245.

Mahoney, M. J. (1975). Fat fiction. *Behavior Therapy, 6,* 416–421.

Mahoney, M., & Mahoney, K. (1976). *Permanent weight control: A total solution to the dieter's dilemma.* New York: WW Norton.

Mayer, J. (1968). *Overweight: Causes, Cost and Control.* Englewood Cliffs, NJ: Prentice-Hall.

McBride, A. B. (1988). Fat: A women's issue in search of a holistic approach to treatment. *Holistic Nursing Practice, 3,* 9–15.

McCall, R. (1973). MMPI factors that differentiate remediably from irremediably obese women. *Journal of Community Psychology, 1,* 34–36.

McCall, R., & Siderits, M. A. (1977). *Becoming a graceful loser: Psychological factors in weight control.* Milwaukee, WI: TOPS Club.

Mc Donald, M. C. (1977). Obesity: Why a losing fight? *Psychiatric News, 12,* 27.

Orbach, S. (1978). *Fat is a feminist issue.* New York: Berkley Publishing.

Peternelj-Taylor, C. A. (1989). The effects of patient weight and sex on nurses' perceptions: A proposed model of nurse withdrawal. *Journal of Advanced Nursing, 14,* 744–754.

Prock, V. (1975). The mid-stage woman. *American Journal of Nursing, 75,* 1019–1022.

Quereshi, M., & Soat, D. (1976). Perception of self and significant others by alcoholics and nonalcoholics. *Journal of Clinical Psychology, 32,* 189–194.

Radvila, A. (1989). Psychosocial aspects of obesity. *Therapeutische Umschau, 46,* 291–296.

Rodin, J. (1977). Research on eating behavior and obesity, where does it fit in personality and social psychology? *Personality and Social Psychology Bulletin, 3,* 333–335.

Rodin, J., Atkinson, R., Dahms, W., Greenway, F., Hamilton, K., & Molitch, M. (1977). Predictors of successful weight loss in an outpatient obesity clinic. *International Journal of Obesity, 1,* 1.

Rosenfield, S. N., & Stevenson, J. S. (1988). Perception of daily stress and oral coping behaviors in normal, overweight and recovering alcoholic women. *Research in Nursing and Health, 11,* 165–174.

Straw, W., & Sonne, A. (1979). The obese patient. *Journal of Family Practice, 9,* 317–323.

Stuart, R. (1978). *Act thin, stay thin.* New York: WW Norton.

Stuart, R. (1971). A three-dimensional program for the treatment of obesity. *Behavior Research and Therapy, 9,* 177–180.

Stunkard, A. (1972). Preface. In R. Stuart & B. Davis (Eds.), *Slim chance in a fat world,* Champaign, IL: Research Press.

Stunkard, A., & Kaplan, D. (1977). Eating in public places: A review of reports of direct observation of eating behavior. *International Journal of Obesity, 1,* 1.

Stunkard, A., & Mendelson, M. (1967). Obesity and the body image; Characteristics of disturbances in the body image of some obese persons. *American Journal of Psychiatry, 123,* 1296–1300.

Stunkard, A., & Penick, S. (1979). Behavior modification in the treatment of obesity. *Archives of General Psychiatry, 36,* 801–896.

Sundberg, M. (1978). Framework for nursing intervention in the treatment of obesity. *Issues in Mental Health Nursing, 1,* 25–44.

Wadden, T. A., & Stunkard, A. (1987). Psychopathology and obesity. *Annals of the New York Academy of Sciences, 499,* 55–65.

Williams, S. (1970). *Nutrition and diet therapy.* St. Louis: CV Mosby.

Wright, E. J., & Whitehead, T. L. (1987). Perceptions of body size and obesity: A selected review of the literature. *Journal of Community Health, 12,* 117–129.

▪

Powerlessness in the Elderly: Preventing Hopelessness

▪ **JUDITH FITZGERALD MILLER**
▪ **CHRISTINE BOHM OERTEL**

Aging is a process basic to the human experience. There has been a 900 percent increase in the number of Americans over age 65 (from 3 to 27 million) since 1900, with the fastest growing group being over 85 years (Russell, 1989). The losses and stresses experienced by the elderly make them vulnerable to powerlessness (Fuller, 1978; Teitelmann, 1982). The increased vulnerability of the elderly is related to their having fewer intact resources than individuals in the middle years or young adulthood. For example, the elderly may have less physical strength and reserve and diminished social support network; lower self-esteem; decreased energy; and in some instances, less motivation to improve their health or adhere to medical prescriptions. (See patient power resources model, Fig. 1–1.) Coping resources of the elderly are challenged by sociologic, physiologic, and psychologic stressors. For example, financial management is a stress because many elderly exist near poverty levels on fixed incomes through inflationary periods—approximately 18 percent of persons over age 65 are living below the poverty level (Kalish, 1975). Maintaining adequate housing may be difficult. Other sociologic stressors include maintaining social contacts, getting to and depending on public transportation, gaining access to continuous health care, maintaining nutrition, and combating stereotypes and myths imposed by a youth-oriented society (Aguilera, 1980; Lancaster, 1981).

Psychologic stressors include demands to adapt to rapid change inherent in our Western society (Eisdorfer & Wildie, 1977). In addition to the stress of living in a "fast-paced" society, the elderly have to deal with changes resulting from unexpected losses such as deaths, retirement, and relocation (a move to a different city, to retirement complexes, or to nursing homes). Decreased sensory acuity may lead to misinterpretation of stimuli, suspicion, and withdrawal (Lancaster, 1981), especially after relocation. Maintaining protection from victimization through crime (Robb, 1989) and dealing with other fears, such as personal injury from falls or accidents, are other psychologic threats.

Physiologic stressors include adapting to multiple structural and functional losses. Physiologic changes of aging will be highlighted later as a cause of perceived powerlessness in the elderly.

The purpose of this chapter is to examine powerlessness as a behavioral variable in the aging person threatened by chronic illness and hospitalization. Case studies are included to depict situational powerlessness in the elderly and to portray the devastating consequence of uncontrolled powerlessness. When powerlessness is not contained, a self-destructive cycle of powerlessness-depression-hopelessness occurs, which may hasten death (Seligman, 1975). The powerlessness-hopelessness cycle is illustrated in Figure 17–3. Identifying powerlessness in the elderly in order to intervene and prevent hopelessness is of critical importance for nurses. Being able to identify patients' perceived situational powerlessness is the first step. The initial development of a behavioral assessment tool to identify powerlessness in the hospitalized elderly is included in this chapter. It is beyond the scope of this chapter to present analyses of biologic, psychologic, and sociologic theories of aging.

Developmental Vulnerability

POWERLESSNESS IN THE ELDERLY

Various factors cause powerlessness in the elderly. Langer and Benevento (1978) classified contextual events that may render a person "helpless" including (1) being assigned a label that connotes inferiority in relation to other persons, (2) engaging in a consensually demeaning task, and (3) no longer engaging in a previously reinforcing, valued task. When applied to the elderly, examples of each contextual event easily come to mind. Elderly persons are the targets of many false labels, myths, and stereotypes (Matteson & McConnell, 1988). They are regarded as rigid, inflexible, and intolerant (Butler, 1975). Other myths that aging is a decremental process rendering the victim unteachable, asexual, less than beautiful, and unable to actively participate in their own health care (Atchley, 1981) as well as unable to grow emotionally (Lancaster, 1981), destroy self-esteem (Rodin & Langer, 1980), cause inferiority, and induce powerlessness. Many elderly persons internalize these beliefs imposed by others in their social spheres.

When assigned a consensually demeaning task, as may occur when elderly persons live with offspring or in nursing homes, the elderly individual erroneously infers self-incompetence. If a task of sealing envelopes is viewed as unimportant, elderly persons could conclude that they are incapable of doing anything more important. If elderly persons living with offspring are included in household activities only by being asked to make their own bed, when in fact, they are capable of much more, feelings of incompetence and helplessness may result.

The individual may not be able to make a transition from a work-centered role to a leisure-centered role (Robinson, 1981) and still maintain a feeling of self-worth and importance to others. No longer engaging in tasks that are reinforcing to the individual may be detrimental.

Chronic illness in the elderly is another cause of powerlessness. Kalish (1975) states that 85 percent of persons over age 65 report at least one chronic illness, and about 50 percent of these report limitation of desired activity because of chronic health problems.

Roy (1976) describes the elderly as having a constricted sphere of influence and control that increases powerlessness. "Independence, or the ability to provide for one's needs, is the most important aim of the majority of the elderly regardless of their state of health" (Culbert & Kos, 1971, p. 607). When this goal is fulfilled, a sense of control, or powerfulness, can result. Frustration of this goal leads to powerlessness. Powerlessness is frequently experienced by aging persons in our culture and is a prominent nursing diagnosis of elderly persons admitted to acute-care facilities. The aging person is vulnerable to powerlessness because of physiologic and psychosocial changes inherent in the aging process.

OVERVIEW OF PHYSIOLOGIC AND PSYCHOSOCIAL CHANGES OF AGING

Aging is a time marked by multiple losses and multiple changes. The onset of these losses varies from individual to individual and is not correlated with any specific chronologic age. There seems to be a reduction in the reserve capacity for the aged person to adapt to changes and to stress. This reduction occurs at a time when there is a corresponding increase in the number and intensity of stressors in the person's life. The changes accompanying aging demand an adaptive response and represent a potential source of powerlessness. Because the changes are multiple, only a limited overview is provided in this chapter.

As humans age, sensory changes occur. Changes in vision include decreased peripheral vision, decreased color perception, increased threshold for light stimulation, increased intraocular pressure, and presbyopia. There is a decreased pupil accommodation and diminished pupil size. Changes in hearing include lessened ability to hear high tones and to differentiate sounds. Aging also results in a marked decrease in the sense of taste. By age 75, there is a 64 percent loss of taste buds (Hayter, 1974). Taste buds that detect bitter and sour remain intact (Shore, 1976). This increased sensitivity to bitterness and decreased sensitivity to sweetness and saltiness may account for some dietary indiscretion in the elderly; however, further research is needed. Although there are reports of a marked decrease in the sense of smell, there is wide variation from person to person (Hayter, 1974; Yurick, 1989). Olfactory acuity is influenced by environmental toxins and occupational odors that have been present throughout the individual's life. The sense of touch also becomes less acute, with a steady loss of peripheral pain perception. Cataracts, glaucoma, and hearing loss increase with age (Matteson & McConnell, 1988).

The aging person must cope with an altered body image. The person in the mirror, as well as the person trying to fit into clothes, may not be the person the individual expects. It is not uncommon for older persons to remark that they still feeling like 35 until they look in the mirror or attempt to do what they were able to do at age 35. The alteration of body image results from changes such as loss of subcutaneous tissues, atrophy of muscle, skin dryness, decreased skin elasticity and thickness, decreased number of sweat glands, atrophy of hair follicles with hair loss, loss of pigment in hair and skin, increased angularity of the body, degenerative joint changes, and a shortening or stooping posture related to the narrowing of the vertebral disks. The loss of subcutaneous fat accounts for the elderly person's sensitivity to cold (Matteson & McConnell, 1988). If tooth loss occurs, it is usually due to change in supportive structures, that is, gingival recession and bone osteoporosis, not tooth decay (Rossman, 1988).

Important physiologic changes occur in the cardiovascular system. As aging occurs, there is a decrease in cardiac efficiency despite a lack of change in heart size. Heart valves become thick, rigid, and less effective. The cardiac rate at rest may be similar to that of a younger adult, but under stress it does not increase as much and takes longer to return to normal. Arterial changes include elongation, fibrosis, and calcification. There can be a decreased blood flow to organs such as the kidney, liver, heart, and brain because of arterial changes. Blood pressure may have a higher normal value resulting from increased arterial resistance.

The lung tissue of the older person becomes less elastic. This results in about a 40 percent decline in the mechanical efficiency of air exchange (Culbert & Kos, 1971). There is also a decreased capacity for oxygen uptake by the red blood cells. Respirations are further compromised by limited lung expansion related to musculoskeletal changes and resulting posture change—stooping.

The reabsorptive and excretory abilities of the kidneys decrease. The kidneys are less able to concentrate urine and thus prevent dehydration. There is a slowed compensatory response to acid-base shifts and altered chemical composition of the blood.

The individual's homeostatic mechanisms become less effective with age. Imbalances tend to develop more easily. A longer period is needed to restore equilibrium. A greater degree of deviation can result from a much lesser provocation with less tolerance. There is a diminished reserve capacity of organs and tissues.

The accumulative effect of these physiologic changes can mean decreased functional ability, diminished energy stores, and an overall lessening of speed and efficiency. Because these changes occur gradually, the individual is usually able to adapt to them, maintaining a sense of powerlessness. When these changes are complicated by the presence of one or more chronic pathologic conditions, the individual's ability to adapt successfully may be impaired.

Although statistics vary from source to source, the percentages of persons over 65 having the following chronic health problems are arthritis (65%), hypertension (42%), hearing impairment (40%), cardiac conditions (34%), cataracts (23%), and vision impairment (14%). The top three leading causes of death are heart disease, cancer, and cerebrovascular disease (Christ & Hohloch, 1988).

Loss of control or an inadequate knowledge base regarding health changes increases the aging individual's vulnerability to powerlessness. One author describes old age as "a time for savoring life, the world, and all that is in it. It is a time for making peace with oneself and the universe" (Hayter, 1974, p. 307). In reality, for many, aging may not result in such a beautiful experience.

Aging can threaten one's self-concept. The restrictions imposed by the social and cultural environment may deny the individual prestige and authority. Security may be bought at the price of loneliness and inactivity. According to Rynerson (1972), lower-level needs for food and safety may be met, while higher needs for affection, social recognition, and a role in society in which dignity, self-worth, and self-satisfaction are maintained may be neglected. Enhancing self-esteem would mean generating attitudes that lead to one's feeling of being useful and necessary in the world. Maintaining self-esteem in the elderly combats despair and promotes successful attainment of the developmental task of ego integrity versus despair (Erikson, 1975).

Psychosocial losses of aging may include loss of former roles and status, loss of family members and friends, loss of economic security, and loss of familiar surroundings. Financial strain increases with age and contributes to depression in the elderly (Krause, 1987). In addition, there may be loss of health and function. The number of significant others in the older person's life may be reduced, compromising the individual's loving support system. Death of a spouse may result in a 50 percent decrease in social contacts for the remaining partner (Rathbone-McCuen & Hashimi, 1982). Diminished physiologic reserves may force the individual into social isolation. The elderly person may be forced to face fears, dependency, chronic illness, and death alone and may respond to these overwhelming odds with perceived powerlessness and eventual despair.

As persons become more dependent on outside agencies for assistance, the individual's decision-making role and personal control are usurped (Angrosino, 1976). The stressors that alter the elderly person's perceived control are specifically pertinent for this chapter. The following discussion is limited to the perceived control in elderly subjects.

Research on Control and the Elderly

Schultz (1976) studied the effect of increased predictability and control on physical and psychologic well-being of 40 elderly subjects living in a retirement home. Subjects were randomly assigned to one of the following four conditions for visitation from college students: (1) subjects were in control of frequency and duration of visits; (2) subjects were informed when they would be visited and how long the visit would last (subjects in this group could predict this event); (3) subjects experienced a random visit schedule; and (4) subjects were not visited. Subjects in the predictable and control-visit groups had significantly higher levels of hope, less lonely time, less bored time, greater zest for life, and greater happiness, usefulness, and activity level than subjects in the no-treatment and random-visit groups. Schulz concluded that the decline in physical and psychologic status associated with aging may be inhibited or reserved by providing residents with predictable or controllable positive events. Schulz and Hanusa (1978) did a follow-up study on these same subjects. Data on physical and psychologic status were collected 24, 30, and 42 months after completion of the 1976 study. No positive long-term effects attributable to the interventions were found. Instead, those persons who initially benefited from the interventions exhibited precipitous declines after the study was terminated, and those subjects who showed no improvement in the original study remained stable in physical and psychologic functioning over time. Schulz and Hanusa (1978) warn other researchers engaged in similar field studies to provide substitute predictable and controllable events after treatment conditions of control are terminated.

The effects of enhanced personal responsibility and choice on alertness, activity participation, and overall sense of well-being were studied in 91 ambulatory nursing home residents (Langer & Rodin, 1976). Subjects were assigned to two treatment groups. The first group was given a communication by the nursing home director emphasizing self-responsibility and decision making regarding their environment and activities. Subjects in this group were given a plant they selected and were then responsible for the plant care. Subjects in the other treatment group were given a message that emphasized staff's responsibility for them. These subjects were given a plant that staff tended. Subjects in the responsibility-induced group were significantly more active, alert, happy, and generally improved. The improvement rating was determined by nurses' blind ratings. No significant difference was found on the perceived-control measure between the two treatment groups.

Rodin and Langer (1977) did an 18-month follow-up study on 26 of the subjects from Langer's 1976 study. Those subjects in the control-induced group had sustained beneficial effects. Mortality showed a striking difference in that only 7 (15 percent) of the 47 subjects in the responsibility-induced group had died during the 18 months, whereas 13 (30 percent) of the 54 subjects of the comparison (staff-controlled) group died. Significant difference was noted at the 0.01 level.

A study of 50 residents in a home for the elderly was done to determine predictors of residents' self-reported morale (Fuller, 1978). Variables considered were the resident's perceived degree of choice in moving to the home, perceived degree of choice while living in the home, and amount of time spent in social interactions weekly, as well as age, income, recent loss of a significant other, and length of time at the home. The only significant predictors of morale were perceived choice within the home and amount of time spent in social interactions each week. Those residents who perceived greater choice and who spent more time in social interactions reported higher levels of morale. Fuller emphasized that current opportunity to make choices is predictive of well-being. Opportunities for resident decision making can be provided by nurses.

Chang (1978a) found that of 30 nursing home residents studied, those who perceived themselves in control of their immediate situations as determined by the Situational Control of Daily Activities scale had higher morale scores regardless of their internal and external personality orientations. Self-determination (person's own control of daily activities) resulted in a higher morale for subjects with both internal and external locus-of-control orientations. In a similar study, Chang (1980) examined congruence of locus of control and the patient's perceived situational control with morale in 39 patients in skilled nursing facilities. All subjects completed a self-rating of their health. Internals who rated their health as "fair" and whose locus of control was congruent with their perception of having situational control had high morale compared with the incongruent group ($p = 0.04$). No significant differences were found in subjects with health ratings other than "fair." Of the externals with "fair" health ratings, incongruent subjects had low morale more frequently than did the congruent subjects ($p = 0.03$). No differences were found in terms of comparisons of race or sex. Chang also found a strong correlation between internal locus of control and high morale (0.05 level of significance).

In other studies of locus of control and the elderly, external locus of control correlated with depression (Hanes & Wild, 1977), and internal locus of control correlated with a positive self-concept (Reid, Haas, & Hawkins, 1977). Ziegler and Reid (1979) confirmed that desired control is related to psychologic adjustment. Desired control was significantly negatively correlated with depression and positively correlated with health, knowledge of services for the elderly, and use of services for the elderly in 88 elderly community residents. The researchers also studied 77 elderly men in a chronic-care hospital ward. Desired control was significantly positively correlated with life satisfaction, self-concept, tranquility, and subject senescence.

Bradley (1976) studied locus of control in 306 subjects whose ages ranged from 19 to 90 years. Locus of control in three areas of activity—intellectual, social, and physical—was studied. Bradley found that subjects over age 60 perceived themselves as having less control in the social area than did subjects in the 35- to 50-year-old age group.

POWERLESSNESS-HOPELESSNESS-DEATH

Loss of hope can have catastrophic consequences such as hastening death (Seligman, 1975). Seligman reviewed studies of death from helplessness and hopelessness in humans. Death was documented to have occurred in humans soon after the death of a spouse, parent, or other loved one; after loss of status; and during times of extreme threat. In all instances, the subjects were described as helpless. Seligman warns that loss of control that accompanies hospitalization further weakens a sick person and may cause death. "We should expect that when we remove the vestiges of control over the environment of an already weakened human being, we may well kill him" (p. 186).

Rowland (1977) completed a review of literature to determine the effect of the environmental events on death of the elderly. The three events were (1) death of significant others, (2) relocation, and (3) retirement. The research reports reviewed suggest that death of a significant other and relocation may predict death for the elderly under certain circumstances. Relocation predicted death for those elderly who were in poor physical health, which may or may not have been accompanied by poor mental health. Forced relocation may remove the last perceived control the elderly had over situations and events. Death of a significant other seems to predict death under certain conditions. The risk of death is greatest during the first year of bereavement, and Rowland's summary suggests the risk is higher for men than for women. The suggestion that those elderly who have few contacts with others may be more likely to die needs investigation. No conclusive evidence existed regarding retirement as a predictor of death in the studies reviewed by Rowland (1977).

Nursing Implications

Any action that promotes elderly persons' maximum control over their lives will maintain or improve their overall well-being (Fuller, 1978) and may have an effect on life expectancy. Simple measures to enhance perceived control in a nursing home might include providing the resident with food selection alternatives, having the resident decide on the schedule for hair appointments, or enabling the resident to request specific library books. Meaningful control measures can be assumed by residents of nursing homes according to their own desires but should not be of a temporary nature serving someone else's best interest. Meaningful activities could include

- Caring for plants
- Surveying residents for activity choices or other needs
- Providing scheduled companionship time with more disabled residents
- Delivering mail and reading it to visually impaired
- Organizing a monthly newsletter
- Recognizing residents' birthdays by planning specific events or surprises
- Sharing favorite recipes
- Conducting musical evenings (playing "old favorites" on records or piano)
- Helping others with correspondence
- Organizing discussions after and about the national news on television
- Planning field trips

The residents themselves could devise creative activity lists based on their own talents and interests. Hutchison and colleagues (1983) found that nursing home residents wanted input regarding increasing their activities and access to such activities, food selection, and resident meetings. The use of councils with residents as members enhances control for nursing home residents (Ryden, 1985).

The elderly person can be helped to realize retirement is a fulfilling, self-enriching time to "savor life." Without some specific preparation for retirement, the newly found freedom may fade into disenchantment and depression (Robinson, 1981). Nurses in all practice settings, especially community agencies, may have specific responsibilities for promoting elderly persons' health through satisfying use of leisure time, helping persons recognize leisure as a "personally significant" self-actualizing activity. Community health nurses also help the elderly take advantage of resources geared to them, for example, senior citizen centers, meal programs for the elderly, and special transporation services. The elderly are to be provided with the options for decision making for various needs, such as using resources, engaging in activities for the elderly, and relocating or modifying living environments. The emphasis is on allowing the elderly person to make the decisions.

Aging persons may need to look beyond self to find meaning and order in their lives and to resolve fears of death. To meet this need, religion may take on new importance (Brown, 1980; Moberg, 1980). The nurse can discuss spiritual well-being and ways appropriate for individuals to attain this well-being (prayer, meditation, religious rituals, reading the Bible and/or religious writings, listening to tape recordings on faith, and so forth). Despair is incongruent with spiritual well-being and having a relationship with God combats loneliness (McCreary, 1980).

Assessment of manifestations of powerlessness in the elderly is important so that early and accurate nursing diagnoses can be made and appropriate interventions can be implemented. Roy (1976) states that the indicators of powerlessness include apathy, withdrawal, resignation, fatalism, malleability, anxiety, restlessness, sleeplessness, wandering, aimlessness, and lack of decision making. Because these behaviors could be indicative of many nursing diagnoses, validation of the nurses' clinical impressions by using a valid, reliable tool is desirable.

Perceived Control Assessment Tools for the Elderly

Specific tools to measure situational control in the elderly have been developed (Chang, 1978b; Reid, Haas, & Hawkings, 1977). Chang's (1978b) tool was developed to measure elderly subjects' situational control in institutional settings. Situational control refers to the perception that either the individual or others determine the use of time, space, and resources in daily activities (Chang, 1978b). The Situational Control of Daily Activities (SCDA) scale has two factors: (1) control of socializing and privacy, and (2) control of physical care. Test-retest reliability was 0.96. Subjects respond to questions about eight activities in terms of whether they themselves or others control the activities. The activities include ambulating, dressing, eating, grooming, socializing in a group, socializing in a twosome, using the toilet, and performing solitary activities. This is a valuable tool for nurses to use in validating the elderly's perceived situational control.

A General Health Status (GHS) scale for the elderly was developed by Haney and coworkers (1981), and its validity and reliability have been established. The tool was correlated with a detailed valid Physician Assessment of Health Status scale. The GHS is a simply constructed tool in which subjects respond to 27 questions indicating whether they have trouble with the item by marking "yes," "no," or "don't know." There are 11 items related to day-to-day activities, such as "putting on or tying shoes," "going up stairs," "remembering things," "bathing," and "preparing meals." There are 16 items dealing with health problems, for example, "cannot sleep through the night," "trouble seeing," "trouble starting or stopping urine," and "swollen feet." The 11 items about daily activities are helpful in alerting the nurse to problems of control for the elderly individual.

Reid, Haas, and Hawkings (1977) developed a tool to measure locus of desire and expectancy for control in the elderly. The tool was situationally specific (instead of measuring an enduring personality trait of locus of control) and considered the immediate environment as well as desires and interests of the subjects. Subjects rated each of 14 items on a Likert-type scale. For example, "How desirable or important is it for you to be able to decide on your own daily activities?" is an item on the interest and/or desires component of the tool. Subjects rated the item as (1) not important/desirable, (2) somewhat important/desirable, (3) generally important/desirable, or (4) very important/desirable. The same question is rephrased on the expectancy component of the tool: "How often can you decide what your daily activities are going to be?" Subjects respond by answering (1) never, (2) sometimes, (3) quite often, or (4) always.

In studies of institutionalized elderly persons, internality correlated positively with nurses' ratings of subjects' happiness, and with subjects' self-ratings of contentment and happiness. Negatative correlations were found between internality and length of residency in the nursing home and age (Reid, Haas, & Hawkings, 1977).

Ziegler and Reid (1979), using the desired-locus-of-control scale, confirmed that desired expectancy for control is related to psychologic adjustment in their studies of 88 elderly community residents and 77 elderly residents in a chronic-care hospital ward.

As a result of the clinical study presented later in this chapter and a comprehensive review of the literature, a powerlessness behavioral assessment tool (Fig. 6-1) was developed. This tool is an observational guide for nurses to use in diagnosing powerlessness. The tool contains four categories of assessment data: verbal response, emotional response, participation in activities of daily living, and involvement in learning about care responsibilities. Nurses rate patient behaviors for each item on the tool using a four-point scale: (1) patient never manifests this behavior; (2) patient occasionally manifests this behavior; (3) patient frequently manifests this behavior; (4) patient always manifests this behavior.

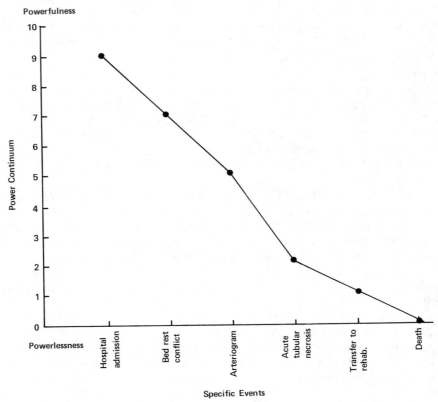

FIGURE 6 ■ 1   Powerlessness behavioral assessment tool.

Although the tool was developed as a result of field work with the elderly, its application is appropriate for adults of all ages. Nurses should validate their observations with another nurse who knows and cares for the same patient. Nurses can be alerted to potential or existing nursing diagnoses of powerlessness if patients' scores on items are three or higher. Specific nursing interventions to alleviate powerlessness are needed for a cumulative score of 57 or higher.

Many other health assessment tools can be modified for appropriate use with the elderly (Moyer, 1981). The following clinical examples further illustrate the impact of powerlessness. Patient behaviors and literature reviewed provide the base for futher development of behavioral assessment tools for powerlessness in the elderly.

Clinical Data and Nursing Strategies

The effect of powerlessness in chronically ill, hospitalized elderly persons will be depicted by two clinical examples. The first case illustrates the outcome of an ineffective intervention to counteract powerlessness in an 80-year-old woman. The second case illustrates the results of nursing interventions to counteract powerlessness in a 71-year-old woman.

■ Case I—Giving Up

Mrs. A. was an 80-year-old married woman with no children who was admitted to the hospital for arterial ulcers on both feet. Her husband was 86 years old and was unable to provide much support to Mrs. A., as he seemed to be coping with his own aging and had become accustomed to being dependent on his wife for care and household management. His normal coping behavior was to seek attention and support from his wife. Prior to admission, Mrs. A. was noted to be a warm, energetic, goal-oriented person. She expressed a perceived sense of being able to control most of the circumstances of her life in spite of her age. She boasted about being able to do all the housework, including washing, cleaning, and grocery shopping. She stated that these tasks were her responsibility and that she had no difficulty doing them.

Mrs. A.'s knowledge about her health problems was another sign of her control. She had a pacemaker and a 5-year history of non-insulin-dependent (diet controlled) diabetes. She understood the necessity for pacemaker battery replacement every 2 years, stating that it did not alter her lifestyle in any way. She was aware of longer-lasting battery cells but felt that at her age it would be "foolish" to spend the extra money.

Mrs. A. was able to define diabetes and explain its effect on the human body in simple terms. She understood the relationship between her diabetes and the lack of healing in the skin lesions of her feet. She had been doing treatments at home under her physician's orders: soaking her feet in warm water, cleansing them with pHisoHex, applying antibiotic ointment, and redressing the lesions. She had difficulty understanding the reason for activity restrictions. She had been very determined not to be hospitalized for treatment of the necrotic lesions. She stated that hospitalization meant a loss of control over her own life. She said, "In the hospital you have to do things when they tell you to do them. At home I can do things when I decide to do them."

After 3 weeks of treatment at home with little improvement of the necrotic lesions and cellulitis, Mrs. A. was admitted to the hospital. Mrs. A. had expected to remain in the hospital for about 1 week to treat the infection. Instead of 1 week, she was hospitalized for 1 month. Upon admission, Mrs. A. was placed on bedrest; oral antibiotics and chlorpropamide (Diabinese) were begun. Foot treatments were initiated; these consisted of warm-water soaks with pHisoHex and application of antibiotic ointment and dressing to the lesions three times a day.

Bedrest became an immediate source of conflict between Mrs. A and the staff. She expressed a lack of understanding of the reason for the activity restriction. She asked repeatedly to be allowed to sit up in a chair. Initially, she was given no rationale for being placed on bedrest. Mrs. A. perceived this direction as meaning that she was not allowed to move, so she moved very little in bed. When she began to express her desire to get up, the reason for the bedrest was explained more fully, and movement in bed was encouraged. The nursing staff, however, was not successful in obtaining an order for chair rest with her legs elevated during the day.

Although behavioral indicators of powerlessness were not manifested in the conflict over bedrest, Mrs. A. expressed that being in bed all the time made her feel weak and helpless. She maintained control over her environment by expressing her desire to be out of bed and by expressing her anger when that desire was thwarted. She also went to the bathroom on her own instead of using the bedpan despite the order for bedrest.

At the beginning of the conflict over bedrest, Mrs. A. remained a goal-oriented person. Her goal was to increase her activity in order to avoid becoming weak and helpless. Her appetite remained good. She took an active interest in her care. She would actively compare the treatment being done in the hospital to what she had done at home.

As the conflict over bedrest continued, subtle changes took place in Mrs. A.'s behavior. She became more quiet, making less reference to getting out of bed. Her appetite decreased; she began to pick at her food. She demonstrated less interest in the care being done for her. At the same time, she began experiencing hypoglycemic episodes that increased her feeling of weakness. The decision was made to discontinue the chlorpropamide. Mrs. A. responded by stating that she knew "those pills had been no good for me." Her hypoglycemic episodes ceased, and her blood sugar stabilized within normal limits.

The necrotic lesions on her feet were showing improvement. Necrotic tissue was debrided. Some skin granulation was apparent. There was also a decrease in the extent of edema and inflammation. At this time, the medical staff decided to do an arteriogram of her lower extremities. After the arteriogram, Mrs. A. developed acute tubular necrosis in response to the dye used. Vigorous medical treatment (peritoneal dialysis) was instituted. Mrs. A. regained normal kidney function within 3 days. Her comments included, "I don't know why they insisted on doing all those tests in the first place." Her systemic response was one of extreme weakness and fatigue.

Because of her age and lowered adaptation resources, the weakness and fatigue did not resolve quickly. Within 24 hours of her return to normal renal function, the medical staff decided to transfer Mrs. A. to the rehabilitation unit in the hospital. Mrs. A. protested that she was not ready for the transfer. The transfer was delayed another day, but the patient still felt that she was not ready for the transfer. Her protests were ignored.

More changes were noted in Mrs. A.'s behavior during the acute tubular necrosis and immediately after her return to normal renal function. She no longer took interest in her care, demonstrating apathy and resignation toward all procedures that were initiated at this time. She expressed a sense of uselessness and a fear that she was becoming a burden to everyone. Her anorexia continued. Her depression and lowered self-esteem increased. She began to verbalize her desire to die, stating that she wished the doctors would just put something into her veins that would do away with her. Her expressed desire to die was followed by the acknowledgment that she had no control over that either. She felt the assaults by the various treatments were so devastating that the staff who inflicted them could also voluntarily end her life.

After her transfer to the rehabilitation unit, Mrs. A. became more apathetic and withdrawn. She was placed on the standard rehabilitation therapeutic program. All patients were required to be out of bed by 8 a.m. and were to remain up, participating in scheduled activities until midafternoon. During the first days on the rehabilitation unit, Mrs. A. protested that she was too weak and too tired to remain up in a wheelchair for an extended period. The nursing staff was resistant to any adjustment of their routine in order to meet Mrs. A.'s request. Mrs. A. responded by withdrawing from further verbal communication. She failed to cooperate with efforts to mobilize her physically or to take an active part in her therapeutic regimen. She ceased to participate in activities of daily living, although she retained the functional capacity to perform these activities. Rapid physical deterioration began. Within 2 weeks after her transfer to the rehabilitation unit, Mrs. A. died.

The changes in behavior observed in Mrs. A. correlated with those behaviors that have been suggested as indicators of powerlessness. These behaviors include apathy, withdrawal, resignation, fatalism, malleability, anxiety, restlessness, sleeplessness, wandering, aimlessness, and lack of decision making.

Mrs. A. entered the cycle of powerlessness-hopelessness at the time of conflict over bedrest. When her attempts to control the situation failed, she felt immobilized. This sense of immobilization was reinforced by actions of the nursing and medical staffs that denied Mrs. A. control over her environment or decision-making responsibility about what was being done for her. Her perceived sense of powerlessness was exhibited by the ceasing verbal protests, decreased appetite, and apathy.

The powerlessness Mrs. A. had begun to perceive was further reinforced by the physical onslaught of acute tubular necrosis, which left her in a weakened physical condition. At this point, she began to refer to herself as "useless." Depression and hopelessness were manifested in her death wish. The perception that she would not recover was reinforced by the complications that had negated her original expectations related to her hospitalization. There was no recognition at this point by the medical or nursing staff that an elderly person needs more time to restore equilibrium within the body because of less effective homeostatic mechanisms.

Isolation developed when Mrs. A. was transferred to the rehabilitation unit. At this point, the dichotomy between her own perceived needs and the plan of care to which she was subjected was complete. Any effort on her part to achieve control over her environment had been thwarted. Figure 6–2 depicts the events with hypothetical degrees of power assigned. On the scale, 10 is maximum powerfulness, and 0 refers to complete powerlessness.

■ Case 2: Preventing Hopelessness

The second patient, Mrs. B., was a 71-year-old married woman with five children, two of whom lived in town. Her husband was an active 77-year-old man with no major health problems. The couple lived in a low-rent townhouse during the summer and spent their winters in Florida in a trailer home they owned. Before her hospitalization, Mrs. B. had managed to maintain a high level of independence, in spite of a progressive deterioration of her right hip joint.

About 3 years before this hospitalization, Mrs. B. had sustained a subcapital fracture of her right leg, which had been pinned. Within 1½ years, she began experiencing progressive pain in her right hip joint, causing an ambulatory deficit that necessitated the use of a walker. Radiologic examination revealed deterioration of the right hip joint. After more than a year and a half of continued pain and disability, Mrs. B. was admitted to the hospital for an elective total hip replacement. At the time of her admission, her health history revealed no significant findings. There was no evidence of any other chronic disease.

Upon admission Mrs. B. presented herself as an energetic person. She detailed how she and her husband were able to maintain their two homes. She did not seek outside help, expressing a perceived sense of control over most of the circumstances of her life. She demonstrated a high degree of knowledge related to the hip

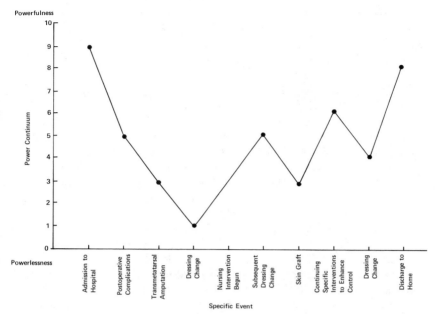

FIGURE 6 ■ 2 Degree of powerlessness and health-illness events of Mrs. A.

deterioration and the planned total hip replacement. She was able to describe the planned surgery in basic terms. Her expectation of her hospitalization was a stay of about 3 weeks.

Mrs. B. underwent surgery for the total hip replacement on May 21. For the first week, her postoperative course was uneventful. She maintained a positive, goal-oriented approach to her convalescence, participating in her care, seeking information, and complying with all that she perceived would enhance her return to health. On May 30, Mrs. B. became dyspneic and cyanotic and complained of chest pain. Diagnostic examination revealed multiple pulmonary emboli. She was transferred to the intensive-care unit and started on heparin therapy. The expected response to the heparin therapy was not achieved. Further testing revealed that Mrs. B. had a serum factor that caused platelets to aggregate in contact with heparin. On June 6, Mrs. B. developed a deep iliofemoral thrombosis of the right leg with marked edema and discoloration of the lower portion of the leg. A venous thrombectomy was performed the next day. Subsequently gangrene of the right foot developed from the impairment of circulation with ischemic changes. The right foot was treated conservatively, using pHisoHex soaks. Pulmonary status returned to normal. Mrs. B. remained hospitalized for the treatment of her right foot. Most of this time was spent on the rehabilitation unit.

During the acute crisis, Mrs. B. became withdrawn, interacting less with the persons in her environment. Her appetite decreased. She expressed a sense of being overwhelmed by her circumstances, stating, "I'm not sure what is happening to me." She also expressed a lack of previous experience to provide her with needed coping mechanisms stating, "I've never been through anything like this before." Much of the time she was quiet.

Mrs. B. returned to the surgical unit on July 18 for debridement of the lesion on her right foot and a possible transmetatarsal amputation. When she returned to the surgical unit, Mrs. B. was in a state of depression, expressing resistance to the amputation and using denial. She stated that she did not know who she was anymore and desired to go home to "find herself." In contrast to her knowledge of the original surgery, Mrs. B. had a low level of knowledge about this surgery and expressed a lack of desire to know anything about it. A transmetatarsal amputation of the right foot was performed on July 19.

Her first postoperative day was uneventful. On her second postoperative day, Mrs. B. began to exhibit acute anxiety behavior. She referred to this as her "nerves being so uptight." In her interaction with her husband, she was slightly hostile and withdrawn. The focal stimulus of her anxious behavior was the pending dressing change on her foot that had been spoken of by the surgical team during morning rounds. There was a delay of several hours before the dressing change was actually done. She stated that she wished that she "could tell them what to do and when to do it." She referred to the surgical team as "the Gestapo" and felt that no matter what she did she was "at their mercy." Her expectations of the dressing change were all negative. She perceived that it would be extremely painful, that she would not be medicated in time, and that the meperidine (Demerol) would not be effective. Mrs. B. also expressed concern that she would not be able to control her own reactions to the dressing change.

Mrs. B.'s behaviors at this point demonstrated a high degree of perceived powerlessness. The first step in intervention was to recognize the existing state of powerlessness and then to help Mrs. B. recognize her sense of powerlessness. This was done by identifying the behaviors and interpreting them to Mrs. B. An attempt was then made to reduce her global sense of helplessness to a more specific focus. This involved separating things Mrs. B. could control from things she could not control. For example, Mrs. B. could control the extent of the pain that occurred during the dressing change by requesting and receiving pain medication and by learning relaxation and refocusing techniques. She could also control the extent of the pain by using the presence of a support person in the environment. She could not control the fact that the procedure would involve pain. She also could not control the time that the surgical team would do the procedure.

As a result of these interventions, the patient became more relaxed. Her body position showed less tension. She was able to sleep for short intervals. Her verbalization was increasingly goal-directed in terms of stating that perhaps she could control the amount of pain she would experience. Although the actual dressing change was a difficult experience for Mrs. B., her sense of powerlessness was reduced. This was demonstrated in her comments the next day regarding further dressing changes: "I really screamed yesterday when they took that dressing off, but it wasn't so bad this morning when the nurses did it." Her other comments during the day revealed a much more positive, goal-oriented, hopeful approach to her circumstances. She stated that her foot was less painful, that she had decided to walk again, and that she felt like eating. She also had begun to take an active interest in herself, using part of her time in the morning to set her hair.

Because of the changes in her behavior, time was spent reinforcing her increased sense of powerfulness. Mrs. B. was helped to identify those events in her current situation that indicated improvement. These included the need for less pain medication, the discontinuation of intravenous therapy, and her increased interest in food. This nursing intervention was effective in increasing Mrs. B.'s level of hopefulness by refocusing her attention away from the series of complications that had induced the sense of powerlesness within her and toward attending to signs of improvement.

Mrs. B. continued to move from powerlessness to powerfulness. She began to exert more control over her immediate environment, although she remained on bedrest. She began deciding where things should be kept and directed her care givers accordingly. The nursing staff reinforced this behavior by allowing Mrs. B. to decide when she wanted to have her bath or have a procedure done. She began to express future-oriented thinking, planning for things she would do after her discharge. Mrs. B. also began to seek information about the effects of the amputation on her ability to walk. Her anxiety was markedly decreased, and previous signs of withdrawal and depression were absent.

Mrs. B.'s return to powerfulness was threatened when she was informed that she would need a skin graft at the amputation site. Her perception of this proposed treatment was that she was not improving. This perception reinforced her former negative expectations. She began to express uncertainty about returning home, frustration over not receiving information from her attending physicians, and reluctance to have further anesthesia. Her perceived powerlessness increased, having a more global all-encompassing effect this time. She demonstrated anxiety toward trying something new, such as using the walker. She said, "Please don't let go of me. I can't walk alone with this thing." Despair was noted in Mrs. B.'s responses, "What's the use? There have been so many setbacks."

Mrs. B.'s increased sense of powerlessness was also due to her inability to obtain answers from the surgical team to her questions about the planned skin graft ("they don't stay long enough to ask questions"). She felt a perceived loss of control in the area of decision making related to her body. She had not received sufficient information to even agree to have the skin graft. Her powerlessness resulted from a lack of knowledge about the procedure, the rationale for doing it, the time it would occur, and the expected outcome.

Again, nursing intervention began by recognizing that a state of powerlessness existed. Mrs. B. was helped to recognize her feelings of powerlessness. To increase her sense of powerfulness, the focus of her greatest concern regarding the skin graft was identified. Her identified concern was that the physicians would not give her needed information. Her right to ask questions was reinforced. A strategy was developed to obtain information from the surgical team. Mrs. B. identified specific questions she wanted answered and then set a goal to get them answered. As she focused on this task, her anxiety behaviors decreased. Her verbal comments changed from fear and depression to references to specific things she could do. Mrs. B. was able to achieve her goal, which enhanced her sense of power.

During the days before the skin graft procedure, Mrs. B. vacillated between a sense of powerfulness and powerlessness. She demonstrated a heightened anxiety level but was more realistic in approaching the problem than she had been previously. Her anxiety was not accompanied by apathy, depression, withdrawal, or pessimism. She continued to maintain control over her immediate environment and directed nursing care. She also continued her goal of walking with the walker.

Nursing interventions at this time focused on reinforcing Mrs. B.'s sense of powerfulness by supplying her with needed realistic information and encouraging her to make decisions related to her care. Anxiety was kept within limits by means Mrs. B. determined, for example, planning for physician's rounds by writing down questions and using television soap operas as a distraction from her own plight. She expressed relief to know that it was all right to feel some anxiety.

Her powerlessness increased after the skin graft at the time of the first dressing change. This was manifested by a high degree of anxiety, a lack of goal orientation, and verbalization of negative expectations. She became very angry with the surgical team during the procedure. This anger seemed to indicate her growing realization that she had a right to have control over her circumstances. She expressed her sense of the discrepancy between the words and the actions of the surgical team: "You can't trust them at all. They said that they would soak the dressing off, but instead they rush in and rip it off. They lie to you every chance they get."

During the subsequent days of hospitalization, Mrs. B.'s physical status continued to improve. Nursing interventions were directed toward helping Mrs. B. identify specific indicators of physical improvement. These included the progressive healing of the skin graft and her increased ambulation. Mrs. B. responded with increased hopefulness and futuristic, goal-oriented thinking. She became involved in activities of daily living and in her dressing changes. Her anxiety level related to the dressing changes became markedly reduced. She no longer viewed these as potential complications but as routine procedures. She retained a sense of powerlessness in response to the surgical team, commenting on their tendency to do whatever they pleased.

At the time of her discharge, Mrs. B. was ambulating well with a walker. Her foot was healed. She was doing her own dressing changes with assistance from her husband. She had begun to plan how they would manage activities of daily living at home in spite of alterations in her health. She expressed confidence in her ability to work this out. Her increased self-esteem, goal-oriented behavior, and positive responses to her situation indicated that powerlessness had been resolved and she was returning to a functional state of powerfulness.

Mrs. B. entered the powerlessness cycle at the time when multiple complications to her recovery began to occur. Within her frame of reference, these complications were seen as being outside her control. This perception led to immobilization. Her growing sense of powerlessness was reinforced by the actions of medical and nursing staffs. Their lack of perception of Mrs. B.'s need to be incorporated into decision making enhanced her perception of powerlessness. Nursing interventions that recognized Mrs. B.'s state of powerlessness and assisted her to learn new methods of control proved effective in returning Mrs. B. to a state of powerfulness. The events, with hypothetical degrees of powerlessness for Mrs. B., are depicted in Figure 6-3. No quantitative powerlessness scores were used to validate the clinical impressions depicted in Figures 6-2 and 6-3.

Nurse Rating of Behaviors

		1 Never	2 Occasionally	3 Frequently	4 Always
VERBAL RESPONSE	Verbal expressions of lack of control over what is happening.				
	Verbal expressions of doubt that self-care measures can affect outcome.				
	Verbal expressions of giving up.				
	Verbal expressions of fatalism.				
EMOTIONAL RESPONSE	Withdrawal.				
	Pessimism.				
	Undifferentiated anger.				
	Diminished patient-initiated interaction.				
	Submissiveness.				
PARTICIPATION IN ACTIVITIES OF DAILY LIVING	Nonparticipation in daily personal hygiene.				
	Noninterest in treatments.				
	Refusal to take food or fluids.				
	Inability to set goals.				
	Lack of decision making when opportunities are provided.				
	Dependency on others for activities of daily living.				
INVOLVEMENT IN LEARNING ABOUT CARE RESPONSIBILITIES	Lack of questioning concerning illness.				
	Low level of knowledge of illness after being given information.				
	Lack of knowledge related to treatment.				
	Lack of motivation to learn.				

FIGURE 6 ■ 3   Degree of powerlessness and health-illness events of Mrs. B.

DISCUSSION

As demonstrated in these two case studies, powerlessness has serious nursing implications. Powerlessness affects a person's behavioral responses. In the individual experiencing powerlessness, learning or goal achievement is not seen as helpful in affecting an outcome. "Acquisition of knowledge or goal-directive behavior is simply irrelevant or unnecessary when the individual does not perceive that future events can be controlled by his own actions," (Johnson, 1967). Knowledge or goal-directive behavior can mean the difference between successful or unsuccessful adaptation to illness. The aging patient is more vulnerable to powerlessness because of the aging process itself. In facing powerlessness, the elderly patient is less able to cope because of diminished psychosocial reserve capacity.

Powerlessness can be prevented. In the two case studies presented, there are some common factors that precipitated powerlessness. For both individuals, hospitalization meant some degree of loss of control, which they were able to limit through their expectations of a limited hospital stay. Complications in recovery precipitated a lack of fulfillment of these expectations, leading to some degree of immobilization in both patients. These complications also produced increased physical powerlessness in both patients. Both individuals viewed the complications as being outside their sphere of control.

A second factor that contributed to the development of powerlessness in both individuals was the tendency of both medical and nursing staffs to dehumanize. There was a failure to recognize the individual's right and need to be incorporated into the decision-making process, as well as failure to note special adaptive needs and limited coping capacity of the elderly. Information was not supplied fully to either individual. Decisions were made without consulting either individual. No alternatives were presented.

Because of these factors, nursing strategies for preventing powerlessness need to be aimed at preventing loss of involvement and supplying the patient with an adequate knowledge base. Preventive strategies would include involving aging individuals in planning their own care, enhancing their self-esteem by referring decisions directly to them, supplying them with cognitive control through helping them anticipate events and outcomes, and giving them time to adjust to changes. Strategies also need to be developed to help individuals understand complications that occur, bringing them into a framework that diminishes the sense of loss of control.

Summary

As demonstrated in these two case studies, powerlessness can lead to hopelessness. Hopelessness has been an accurate indicator of suicide ideation in a study of 120 depressed elderly (Hill, Gallagher, Thompson, & Ishida, 1988). Depression was more predictive of suicide ideation than hopelessness, however. Even without persistent physical decline due to illness, if hopelessness becomes a reality, suicide may result. Powerlessness affects a person's behavioral responses. When apathy and depression are pronounced, routine teaching and refocusing on goal achievement may be inadequate. Very specific concrete interventions based on individual clinical events to enable accurate and optimistic interpretations of events may be needed. Strategies to enhance elderly control have been suggested by Teitelman and Priddy (1988). These have been modified here to include

1. Promoting choice and predictability. This includes adhering to mutually determined schedules.
2. Eliminating helplessness engendering stereotypes such as "being old means being unable to participate in care." Use of negative labels needs to be avoided.
3. Avoiding severe self-blame for events. Promoting a sense of responsibility for participating in health care.
4. Promoting a feeling of success in goal accomplishment.
5. Modifying unrealistic expectations without destroying generalized hope.
6. Using control enhancing communication. The interpersonal relationship is the nurses' vehicle for care and needs to be characterized by respect, genuineness, individuation, and skill in uncovering and reviewing the elderly persons' unique assets.

For the two patients in this chapter, it was essential to foster decisional involvement since they wanted and expected it. On the other hand, nurses need to refrain from requiring decision making by persons who cannot cope with what they may interpret as added stress (Dennis, 1987). The aging patient needs more time, consistent trusting support, and repeated explanations in order to facilitate control. Alternative decisions with potential consequences need to be reviewed with patients using careful deliberation.

Reed's (1983) work prompts nurses to think about combating a mechanistic developmental view of aging as decline and substituting a view of aging as transformation to a more specialized integrated complex human being. Life span scientists pose a development theory that focuses on interaction between organismic and environmental factors. Throughout life, conflicts are encountered between the person and the environment but new energy is obtained from each successful encounter (Reed, 1983).

Russell (1989) also counters views of aging as decline. Attention must be given to the richness of being old, that is, having a wealth of life's experiences that fosters wisdom and enhances inner (not outer) direction and autonomy. Results of analysis of work by life span developmentalists disclose select themes of aging such as "self-acceptance, positive relationships with others, autonomy, environmental mastery, purpose in life and personal growth. The elderly's personality does not shift from optimism to pessimism; however, poor health does threaten the elderly's overall sense of well-being (Russell, 1989).

Powerlessness is not synonymous with aging. Membership in organizations such as the Grey Panthers and American Association for Retired Persons may provide specific enpowerment for some elderly. Age gives a person assets with which to assess life positively (Russell, 1989). The elderly have a broad range of success in changing conflicts into meaningful life experiences and thus avoiding powerlessness and hopelessness. During illness, nurses can facilitate the elderly's review of life successes.

References

Aguilera, D. (1980). Stressors in late adulthood. *Family and Community Health, 2,* 61–69.
Angrosino, M. (1976). Anthropology and the aging: A preliminary community study. *Gerontologist, 16,* 174–180.
Atchley, R. (1981). Common misconceptions about aging. *Health Values: Achieving High Level Wellness, 5,* 7–10.
Bradley, R. (1976). Age-related differences in locus of control orientation in three behavior domains. *Human Development, 19,* 49–55.
Brown, P. (1980) Religious needs of older persons. In J. Thorson & T. Cook (Eds.), *Spiritual well-being of the elderly* (pp. 76–82). Springfield, IL: Charles C Thomas.
Butler R. (1975). *Why survive?* New York: Harper & Row.
Chang, B. (1980). Black and white elderly: Morale and perception of control. *Western Journal of Nursing Research, 2,* 371–387.
Chang B. (1978a). Generalized expectancy, situational perception and morale among the institutionalized aged. *Nursing Research, 27,* 316–323.
Chang, B. (1978b). Perceived situational control of daily activities: A new tool. *Research in Nursing and Health, 1,* 181–188.
Christ, M. A., & Hohloch, F. (1988). *Gerontologic nursing.* Springhouse, PA: Springhouse Publishing.
Culbert, P., & Kos, B. (1971). Aging: Considerations for health teaching. *Nursing Clinics of North America, 6,* 605–614.
Dennis, K. (1987). Dimensions of client control. *Nursing Research, 36,* 151–156.
Eisdorfer, C., & Wildie, R. (1977). Stress, disease, aging and behavior. In J. E. Birren & J. W. Shaie (Eds.), *Handbook of the psychology of aging* (pp. 251–275. New York: Van Nostrand Reinhold.
Erikson, E. (1975). Eight ages of man. In F. Rebelsky (Ed.), *Life the continuous process, readings in human development* (pp. 23–38). New York: Alfred A Knopf.
Fuller, S. (1978). Inhibiting helplessness in elderly people. *Journal of Gerontological Nursing, 4,* 18–22.
Hanes, C., & Wild, B. (1977). Locus of control and depression among noninstitutionalized elderly persons. *Psychological Reports, 41,* 581–582.
Haney, C. A., Stephens, R. C., Cooper, H. P., Oser, G. T., & Blau, Z. S. (1981). A measure of health status in an elderly population. *Health Values: Achieving High Level Wellness, 5,* 61–66.
Hayter, J. (1974). Biologic changes of aging. *Nursing Forum, 13,* 289–308.
Hill, R., Gallagher, D., Thompson, L., & Ishida, T. (1988). Hopelessness as a measure of suicidal intent in the depressed elderly. *Psychology and Aging, 3,* 230–232.
Hutchison, W., Carstensen, L., & Silberman, D. (1983). Generalized effects of increasing personal control of residents in a nursing facility. *International Journal of Behavioral Geriatrics, 1,* 21–32.
Johnson, D. (1967). Powerlessness: A significant determinant in patient behaviors. *Journal of Nursing Education, 6,* 40.
Kalish, R. (1975). *Late adulthood: Perspectives on human development.* Monterey, CA: Brooks/Cole Publishing.
Krause, N. (1987). Chronic strain, locus of control, and distress in older adults. *Psychology and Aging, 2,* 375–382.
Lancaster, J. (1981). Maximizing psychological adaptation in an aging population. *Topics in Clinical Nursing, 3,* 31–43.
Langer, E., & Benevento, A. (1978). Self-induced dependence. *Journal of Personality and Social Psychology, 36,* 886–893.
Langer, E., & Rodin, J. (1976). The effects of choice and enhanced personal responsibility

for the aged: A field experiment in an institutionalized setting. *Journal of Personality and Social Psychology, 35,* 897–902.

Matteson, M. A., & McConnell, E. (1988). *Gerontological nursing: Concepts and practice.* Philadelphia: WB Saunders.

McCreary, W. (1980). Creative transformation and the theological resources for loneliness. In J. Thorson & T. Cook (Eds.), *Spiritual well-being of the elderly* (pp. 108–112). Springfield, IL: Charles C Thomas.

Moberg, D. (1980). Social indicators of spiritual well-being in the elderly. In J. Thorson & T. Cook (Eds.), *Spiritual well-being of the elderly* (pp. 20–37). Springfield, IL: Charles C Thomas.

Moyer, N. (1981). Health promotion and the assessment of health habits in the elderly. *Topics in Clinical Nursing, 3,* 51–58.

Rathbone-McCuen, E., & Hashimi, J. (1982). *Isolated elders.* Rockville, MD: Aspen Publications.

Reed, P. (1983). Implications of the life-span developmental framework for well-being in adulthood and aging. *Advances in Nursing Science, 6,* 18–25.

Reid, D., Haas, D., & Hawkings, D. (1977). Locus of desired control and positive self-concept of the elderly. *Journal of Gerontology, 32,* 441–450.

Robb, S. (1989). Resources in the environment of the aged. In A. Yuric, B. Spier, S. Robb, & N. Ebert (Eds.), *The aged person and the nursing process* (3d ed.). Norwalk, CT: Appleton & Lange.

Robinson, F. (1981). Leisure well-being for longer living people. *Health Values: Achieving High Level Wellness, 5,* 55–60.

Rodin, J., & Langer, E. (1980). Aging labels: The decline of control and the fall of self-esteem. *Journal of Social Issues, 36,* 12–29.

Rodin, J., & Langer, E. (1977). Long term effects of a control-relevant intervention with the institutionalized aged. *Journal of Personality and Social Psychology, 35,* 897–902.

Rossman, I. (1988). Human aging changes. In I. M. Burnside (Ed.), *Nursing and the aged* (3d ed.). New York: McGraw-Hill.

Rowland, K. (1977). Environmental events predicting death for the elderly. *Psychological Bulletin, 84,* 349–372.

Roy, C. (1976). *Introduction to nursing: An adaptation. model.* Englewood Cliffs, NJ: Prentice-Hall.

Russell, C. (1989). *Good news about aging.* New York: John Wiley & Sons.

Ryden, M. (1985). Environmental support for autonomy in the institutionalized elderly. *Research in Nursing and Health, 8,* 363–371.

Rynerson, B. (1972). Need for self-esteem in the aged: A literature review. *Journal of Psychiatric Nursing, 10,* 22–25.

Schultz, R. (1976). Effects of control and predictability on the physical and psychological well-being of the institutionalized aged. *Journal of Personality and Social Psychology, 33,* 563–573.

Schultz, R., & Hanusa, B. (1978). Long-term effects of control and predictability-enhancing interventions: Findings and ethical issues. *Journal of Personality and Social Psychology, 36,* 1194–1201.

Seligman, M. (1975). *Helplessness: On depression, development and death.* San Francisco: WH Freeman.

Shore, H. (1976). Designing a training program for understanding sensory loss in aging. *Gerontologist, 16,* 157.

Teitelman, J. (1982). Eliminating learned helplessness in older rehabilitation patients. *Physical and Occupational Therapy in Geriatrics, 1,* 3–10.

Teitelman, J., & Priddy, J. (1988). From psychological theory to practice: Improving frail elders' quality of life through control-enhancing interventions. *The Journal of Applied Gerontology, 7,* 198–315.

Yurik, A. (1989). Sensory experiences of the elderly persons. In A. Yurik, B. Spier, S. Robb, & N. Ebert (Eds.), *The aged person and the nursing process,* (3d ed., pp. 438–461). Norwalk, CT: Appleton & Lange.

Ziegler, M., & Reid, D. (1979). Correlates of locus of desired control in two samples of elderly persons: Community residents and hospitalized patients. *Journal of Consulting and Clinical Psychology, 47,* 977–979.

■ P A R T ■
III

Coping with Specific Chronic Health Problems

Stressors and coping responses of persons to specific prototypical chronic health problems are identified in this part. Particular emphases are given to etiologies of powerlessness in persons with end-stage renal disease (Chapter 7); profiles of control and coping typologies in persons with peripheral vascular disease (Chapter 8); energy deficits, a prevalent diagnosis in persons with arthritis (Chapter 9); pathophysiology, coping, and nursing care of persons with multiple sclerosis (Chapter 10); and chronic lung disease (Chapter 11). Detailed clinical examples are presented.

Hastings presents a model depicting holistic assessment, stressors, and coping resources as an overall framework for nursing care of persons with multiple sclerosis. Her research on hope, social support, and adaptation is presented in Chapter 10.

McMahon analyzes four dimensions of quality of life in persons with chronic lung disease: illness phenomena; client perceptions, functional capacity, and personal resources in Chapter 11. Detailed nursing strategies are presented.

■

Etiologies and Indicators of Powerlessness in Persons with End-Stage Renal Disease

■ SUSAN STAPLETON

Multiple stressors confront persons with end-stage renal disease (ESRD) also referred to in this chapter as chronic renal failure (CRF). Stressors can be categorized as physiologic, psychologic, role disturbance, and life change stressors. The purpose of this chapter is to present a summarized review of literature of these stressors, as well as to report observations of powerlessness in patients with CRF. Conclusions about patient responses to powerlessness will be made in order to help nurses identify behavioral indicators of the nursing diagnostic category of powerlessness in other chronically ill patients.

Stressors in ESRD

PHYSIOLOGIC STRESSORS

The toxic effects of uremia are manifested in virtually every body system. The pathophysiologic effects can be categorized as (1) disturbances in body biochemistry (altered body water homeostasis; metabolic acidosis; and elevation of serum potassium, sodium, phosphorus, calcium, magnesium, creatinine, and uric acid) and (2) organ systems disturbances (hypertension, heart failure, anemia, gastrointestinal irritation, osteodystrophy, soft-tissue calcification, clotting deficiencies, altered endocrine function, and neuropathy) (Baldree, Murphy, & Powers, 1982; Czaczkes & DeNour, 1978; Harrington & Brenner, 1973; Lancaster, 1984; Stegman, Duncan, Pohren, & Sandstrom, 1985; Ulrich, 1989). Decreased energy, impaired concentration, insomnia, weight loss, and restricted use of the extremity with the fistula contribute to stress of persons on chronic dialysis (Wright, Sand, & Goodhue, 1966). Cummings (1970) reported that the mechanisms of attention and concentration are among the first cognitive skills affected by azotemia of ESRD, impairing higher intellectual functions (e.g., abstraction, generalization). Individuals lack control over the physical changes and the course of the illness and may not be able to predict or control how they will feel and function from day to day.

PSYCHOLOGIC STRESSORS

Body Image

A psychologic stressor related to the changes in appearance and function of the body is alteration in self-concept (specifically body image). Patients on dialysis come to perceive themselves as part of the machine or endow the machine with human qualities (DeNour & Czaczkes, 1974). Abram (1969) related that patients incorporate the machines upon which they are dependent for life into their body images. Patients unconsciously think of themselves as not entirely human and therefore "freakish" (Abram, 1969). The individual may experience a temporary loss of body part at each dialysis in that blood is viewed flowing outside of the body and into the machine. This visual experience can contribute to a disturbance in body image.

Frustration in Basic Drives

A second type of psychologic stressor is the frustration of basic drives, including aggression, satisfaction of hunger and thirst, and sexual expression. Halper (1971) discussed the limitations placed on normal outlets for aggression. Persons with ESRD cannot compete as successfully at work, and their capacity to participate in physical activities and athletics is limited.

Another basic drive that is frustrated in the person with ESRD is satisfaction of hunger and thirst. Eating is a satisfying and pleasurable experience, and therefore patients have difficulty complying with dietary and fluid restrictions (Anger, 1975).

The person with ESRD frequently experiences frustration of the basic sexual drive in that there is a marked deterioration in sexual interest and/

or performance (O'Brien, 1983). Levy (1973) found that hemodialysis patients of both sexes, but particularly males as well as male transplant recipients, had substantial deterioration in sexual functioning. Levy, as well as Abram and associates (1975), found a further decrease in sexual performance in about 35 percent of the patients after the initiation of dialysis. Some degree of sexual dysfunction contributes to patient and spouse depression and marital discord in most couples (Davison, 1986; Finkelstein, Finkelstein, & Steele, 1976; Shambaugh et al., 1967). Marital discord was judged to be moderate or severe in 53 percent of the couples studied. Frustration of basic drives is beyond the individual's control and may be seen as contributing to powerlessness.

Fear of Death, Fear of Life

Beard (1969) labeled another psychologic stressor "fear of death and fear of life." It is essential to keep in mind that the prolongation of life involves not only adding to the length of life but also involves the matter of the quality and worthwhileness of the life that is prolonged. Individuals with ESRD fear that their lives will be cut short, yet at the same time they fear that their lives may not be acceptable. In a study of life satisfaction of patients on dialysis, Jackle (1974) reported that these patients rated their present lives as slightly less satisfactory than did the normative group. They rated their past lives, however, near the top of the life satisfaction scale. There is also a strong fear that something will go wrong during dialysis—events such as hypovolemic shock, ruptured dialyzer, or separation of tubing connections. Individuals frequently feel that they are at the mercy of the machine and are powerless to control it. One patient stated that the machine "maintains a powerful hold on my life—I find it impossible to make friends with the monster" (Abram, 1968). However, the contrast of dialysis or death is a powerful one (Plough, 1986).

Dependence-Independence Conflict

A dependence-independence conflict confronts the person with ESRD. The patient is expected to comply with the treatment regimen, which requires dependent behavior; however, the patient is also told to remain independent and live a "normal life," including meeting family, job, and social obligations. Reischman and Levy (1972) state that the major feeling experienced by patients is one of helplessness. They feel trapped between the wish to be passive and dependent on the one hand and the expectation of health personnel that they be active and independent on the other. The degree of the dependence-independence conflict experienced is related to the individual's predialysis personality in that subjects who were dependent before dialysis had fewer dependence-independence conflicts after beginning dialysis; those subject who were independent had greater dependence-independence conflicts after beginning dialysis (DeNour & Czaczkes, 1974; Reischman & Levy, 1972).

ROLE DISTURBANCES

Role disturbances are closely related to both physiologic and psychologic stressors. Because of the illness, the patient may be forced to eliminate social, family, and occupational roles that are important to self-concept. Loss of membership in groups and loss of job or occupation are stressors identified by persons with ESRD (Wright, Sand, & Goodhue, 1966). These losses result in feelings of isolation and disengagement. In a study of the family unit's response to dialysis, Maurin and Schenkel (1976) described a withdrawal of the entire family from social life into an existence focused on the family and, in some instances, focused only on the patient.

Role reversal within the family is common (Anger, 1975). Three types of roles may be vulnerable in the person with ESRD: breadwinner, disciplinarian, and decision maker (Cumming, 1970). The individual may experience guilt over being unable to fulfill role expectations. This inability to perform expected role behaviors is a great threat to the individual's self-esteem (O'Brien, 1983; Ulrich, 1980) and may well contribute to powerlessness.

LIFE-STYLE CHANGES

All the previously mentioned factors contribute to life-style changes in the individual with ESRD. Loss of financial security is a major stress (Anger, 1975; Cummings, 1970; Levy, 1973; Wright, Sand, & Goodhue, 1966). Although assistance with medical expenses is provided by the Social Security Act of 1972, loss of income due to loss of jobs with a decreased standard of living remains a problem.

Uncertainty regarding future plans affects life-style. Uncertainty over the future was identified as a stressor by Baldree, Murphy, and Powers (1982) in a study of 35 persons on hemodialysis. Patients plan on a day-to-day basis, with future planning being related to transplantation. Patients describe being unable to plan for vacations, a new home, or their children's education because of the uncertainty related to illness (Wright, Sand, & Goodhue, 1966). The time required for the dialysis treatment interferes with other desirable life activities and roles. Uncertainty and ambivalence were two major problems for persons awaiting renal cadaveric transplants (Weems & Patterson, 1989).

MEASUREMENT OF HEMODIALYSIS STRESSORS

The Hemodialysis Stressor Scale (Baldree, Murphy, & Powers, 1982) is a 29-item instrument to measure incidence and severity of stressors associated with hemodialysis. The paper-and-pencil test has a five-point response format, with 0 = "not at all" and 4 = "a great deal," with a possible range of scores from 0 to 116. A higher score indicates more stress. The internal consistency alpha coefficient for the total scale is 0.89 indicating good internal reliability. Factor analysis resulted in a three-factor solution with items characterized as psychobiologic, psychosocial, and dependency-restriction stressors (Murphy, Powers, & Jalowiec, 1985). The instrument has been used in subsequent studies of persons on hemodialysis by Baker (1987); Bihl, Ferrans, and Powers (1988); Eichel (1986); and Gurklis and Menke (1988). Baker (1987) found that limitation in activity, itching, fluid restriction, and muscle cramps were the most frequently identified stressors in 81 persons with ESRD. A negative relationship existed between stress and hope and between stress and self-esteem in Baker's sample. That is, the greater the patient's stress, the lower the hope and the self-esteem. Stressors reported by both hemodialysis and continuous ambulatory peritoneal dialysis (CAPD) patients included fatigue, limitation in physical activity, muscle cramps, change in body appearance, itching, and problems with work role (Eichel, 1986). The most frequent stressor reported by hemodialysis patients in decreasing order were fluid restriction, muscle cramps, fatigue, and uncertainty over the future (a stressor not identified by the CAPD subjects) (Baldree, Murphy, & Powers, 1982).

Gurklis and Menke (1988) found that physiologic stressors were more troublesome than the psychosocial stressors to the 68 hemodialysis patients studied. These patients used problem-oriented coping strategies more often than affective strategies to deal with stress. Coping methods used by the 35 persons in the Baldree et al. (1982) study included *maintaining some control,* hope, prayer, trust in God, and looking at the problem objectively. Similar coping strategies were found in the Eichel (1986) study of persons on CAPD.

SUMMARY

Table 7–1 summarizes stressors of ESRD. It is evident that illness and its management have widespread effects on the individual's life. Many of these stressors may contribute to a feeling of powerlessness. Learned helplessness and powerlessness were identified as nursing diagnoses in persons on hemodialysis (Burns, 1983; Frank, 1988; Fuchs, 1987; O'Brien, 1983). Frank (1988) reviewed the use of Roy's (1976) adaptation model for nursing care of the hemodialysis patient. Nursing diagnoses

TABLE 7 ■ I   Summary of Stressors in End-Stage Renal Disease

Physiologic	Psychologic	Role Disturbances	Life-Style Changes
Body biochemistry changes	Alterations in body image:	Loss of group membership	Loss of financial security
Effects of uremia on organ systems	Inability to control body functioning	Loss of job or occupation	Forced acceptance of government assistance
Lack of control over symptoms	Body does not function normally	Role reversal with spouse	Time required for dialysis
Progression of illness trajectory	Incorporation of dialysis machine into body image	Decreased ability to fulfill role expectations	Limitation of activity
	Loss of body part, blood, kidneys	Marital discord and family tension	Failure of future plans
	Change in body structure—shunt or fistula		Uncertainty
	Frustration of basic drives:		
	Cannot express aggression		
	Dietary and fluid restrictions		
	Decreased sexual drive and/or performance		
	Fear of death and fear of life:		
	Uncertain life expectancy		
	Fear of death due to illness		
	Fear of death due to malfunction of dialysis machine		
	Decreased life satisfaction		
	Fear that life will not be acceptable		
	Dependence-independence conflict:		
	Expected compliance with treatment regimen		
	Dependence on others and machine for satisfaction of needs		
	Subconscious desire for dependence		
	Societal expectations for independence		

generated for the interdependence adaptive mode included powerlessness.

With increasing years on dialysis, persons reported better adjustment. As the number of hours spent on dialysis increased, patient hardiness decreased (Goodwin, 1988). The feeling of diminishing control seemed to affect the state of hardiness and resilience to life's stress. In a meta analysis of 40 studies of persons with ESRD, personality factors were the strongest predictors of adjustment. Internal control was positively related to adjustment (Olsen, 1983).

Clinical Data

Six patients with ESRD on hemodialysis were studied using a participant-observer method for a period varying from 3 to 6 months. Factors causing powerlessness and the patients' responses were identified. General indicators of powerlessness manifested in the patients were lack of information seeking, failure to share relevant health information, decreased willingness to make decisions, expression of loss of hope, crying and depression, and verbal expression of loss of control.

Specific factors that contributed to the powerlessness state in these patients were the disease process, hospitalization, relationship with health-care personnel, the dialysis procedure and medical regimen, changes in family relationships, and employment and financial concerns. Each factor contributing to powerlessness and examples of patient responses are included in the following discussion.

DISEASE PROCESS OF CHRONIC RENAL FAILURE

The disease process itself is a factor over which the individual feels little control. The symptoms of CRF are quite uncomfortable and have a marked impact on the individual's life-style. Fatigue and weakness are very disturbing symptoms and curtail the individual's activities a great deal. Comments such as "I'm always so tired—I can never get anything done" and "I'll never get this house painted if I can only do this much without getting exhausted" indicate how incapacitating the fatigue can be. The unpredictability of the energy level also contributes to feelings of powerlessness. Mrs. F. describes this, "Maybe the next day you'll have a good day and be able to get something done, and maybe not. You never know." This unpredictability makes it difficult for the individual to make plans for activities and may greatly decrease social life. Mrs. M. states, "After a while you just stop associating with other people. You lose a lot of friends. You just don't have the energy." Although the individual may desire to participate in certain activities, the physiologic status prevents the patient from doing so.

Other central nervous system manifestations of CRF include decreased alertness, memory loss, and impaired thought processes. Mrs. M. described the frustration of these symptoms: "People think you're crazy or something is wrong with you mentally. You feel so dull, aren't interested in others, and can't carry on a conversation. You forget what you wanted to say."

The general downward course of the illness causes many individuals with CRF to feel powerless. Mrs. F. stated, "It's like dying slowly when you're on dialysis. Every day you know that you're going downhill, but what can you do?" Mr. O. described himself as "feeling like I'm in a car doing downhill and the brakes don't work."

The inability to control or predict the outcome of the kidney transplant is a real cause of feelings of powerlessness in the postoperative transplant patient. This is often expressed verbally with statements such as "It's really hard not knowing what's going to happen" and "I wish I could do something to be sure the kidney keeps working." The realization that the outcome of the surgery is out of one's control may cause severe depression. Mrs. B. cried, "It's not fair! I did everything just the way I was supposed to and I still rejected the kidney." Most patients finally resign themselves to this and make comments such as, "I guess you have to get used to the idea that you really don't have much control over what happens with the transplant."

Severe pain, which may occur postoperatively as a result of the surgery or complications, may cause feelings of powerlessness. Anxiety, depression, and prolonged pain often decrease the individual's ability to control the response to pain. Mr. F. experienced severe bladder spasms postoperatively and stated, "They come so suddenly that I don't have time to get ready for them. It's all I can do to keep from screaming." When the etiology of the pain is unknown, the feelings of powerlessness are even more acute. Mr. F. repeatedly asked me what might be causing his leg pain and stated, "This really has me scared. I don't know what it is, but it must be pretty serious if it hurts this bad."

HOSPITALIZATION

Hospitalization automatically results in a tremendous loss of control for an individual. Decisions such as when to eat, sleep, exercise, and bathe are made for the patient, sometimes with little consultation. As a result of patient role expectations, individuals who are hospitalized may demonstrate passive behavior, follow staff directions without comment or question, and have difficulty making small decisions when given the opportunity to do so. These behaviors are all indicative of a feeling of loss of control, or powerlessness. Even individuals who have previously managed their medical regimens alone without difficulty suddenly have them managed by others. Nurses administer medications, which the patient may take without knowing or asking what they are. The dietitian calculates the patient's diet, while other staff members weigh the patient and record intake and output.

One aspect of this management by others that contributed to feelings of powerlessness in Mrs. M. was her dependence on the nurses for pain medication. She often had to wait longer than she felt was necessary, and she expressed the feeling that the staff was "taking advantage of me because I'm so helpless." This feeling was strengthened when Mrs. M. was told by a nurse, "Your imagination can make you think that you're having pain."

Frequently, hospital routines and efficiency are given higher priority than patient needs, resulting in patient feelings of powerlessness. A nurse on the renal transplant unit told Mr. F., "You'll have to eat breakfast and wash up later. Radiation therapy is ready to do your treatment now." Mr. F. started to protest, "But I'm hungry . . .," then shrugged his shoulders, and walked over to the wheelchair. When Mrs. Z. was told that she had to move to a different room because her private room was needed for another patient, she said, "I'm low man on the totem pole, so I don't have anything to say about whether or not I move." She was told to hurry her packing so the room could be cleaned, and then she sat in the lounge for 6 hours because no one was available to clean rooms. Mrs. Z. merely accepted this passively and said, "I'm being evicted."

Because of a malfunctioning machine, Mr. F. experienced a long wait in the x-ray department while he was in severe pain. He was not told the cause for the delay, and he worried, "Waiting this long makes you worry that they've forgotten you and you'll end up sitting here all day before someone notices you." Although he made this statement to the author upon her arrival in the department, he had not attempted to ask any x-ray personnel the reason for the delay or to remind them of his presence.

Hospitalized patients, as well as those on dialysis, often exhibit behaviors indicative of powerlessness that can affect their ability to learn. Individuals who feel powerless often demonstrate a marked failure to seek information about their health states. They seem to feel that any action they might take based on such information will not influence what happens to them; therefore, the information seems useless. Although Mr. O. had kept careful records of his weight and blood pressure before starting dialysis, he never asked what they were before or after dialysis runs. The staff contributed to this by failing to volunteer this information to him. At times, hospitalized individuals do not ask questions of health-care professionals, even though they do not understand something about the management of their illness.

In addition to lack of information seeking, the individual who feels powerless often displays a lack of information sharing. When Mrs. M. was reprimanded because she had gained too much weight between dialysis runs and was told to weigh herself at home daily, she did not inform the nurse that she had no scale. Miss L. allowed the medical staff to proceed with the scheduling of pretransplant tests, without telling them that she had serious reservations about having a transplant. When the physician and social worker informed Mr. O. that he was to be transferred to another dialysis center, he was quite unhappy, but he did not discuss this with them or tell them that going to the proposed center would present difficult travel problems for him. When the author asked him why he had not discussed this with the physician, Mr. O. responded, "It wouldn't do any good. If they want me to go there, then I'll have to go."

PATIENT-STAFF RELATIONSHIPS

Interactions with the staff and routines of the hospital or dialysis unit play a large role in causing powerlessness. One patient expressed frustration and feeling of lack of control over the scheduling of appointments in the outpatient department: "They just tell me when to come in, and since the doctors are only here on certain days, it doesn't matter whether the day is convenient for me." This statement also reflects the fact that the medical-care system has control. The patient's options are limited, since survival depends on compliance with the health-care system demands.

The fact that the health-care personnel have more knowledge than the patient about CRF and its management can contribute to feelings of powerlessness in the patient. Patients feel that they must depend on the personnel to tell them what to do. A dialysis patient with diabetes stated, "I just do what they tell me. I don't even try to adjust my insulin dose the way I used to."

Just before the institution of dialysis, Mr. O. expressed anxiety about the level of competence of the dialysis staff. He stated, "But I guess I'll just have to trust them since I don't know enough to tell if they're competent or not. And I can't request only the good ones anyway."

The individual may express feelings that the staff is in control in a joking manner, such as referring to mistreatment by the staff. Mr. O. verbalized this feeling directly when he said, "I guess I'd better not give him (dialysis technician) a hard time while he has me on this thing (dialysis machine)." Although Mr. O. knew that the technician would not "retaliate," the fact remained that the technician had the power to do so.

This feeling that the staff is in control may make the individual reluctant to express anger. Mr. F. reported, "You have to be nice to them—can't get along without them." After three unsuccessful attempts to insert a needle for dialysis, Mr. O. said angrily, "This is your last chance." Then he said, "Oh, I guess I can't say that, can I? I have to have this." Even when the individual attempts to express anger, the staff may not acknowledge it, thus subtly telling the patient that this expression is not appropriate. When Mr. F., a diabetic patient who had had a transplant, said, "I'm sick and tired of getting stuck for these blood sugars," the nurse laughed and said, "Yeah, we're really mean to you, aren't we?"

Health-care personnel may increase the individual's feelings of powerlessness by comments that accentuate the control they have over the patient. A dietitian teased Mr. F. as she helped him fill out his menu, "You're lucky you have that kidney, or I'd never let you order those tomatoes."

DIALYSIS PROCEDURE

Not only does the individual feel controlled by the dialysis and hospital staff, but the individual often feels controlled by the dialysis machine, too. People on dialysis commonly refer to the machine as "the monster" or "that thing." One patient stated, "It's scary to think of being attached to that thing—to be at its mercy." He joked about needing a screwdriver "to take the machine apart if I want to, so I can stay in control." His wife gave him a tiny screwdriver, which he wore on a chain around his neck, and he often brought it out when the alarm sounded on the dialysis machine.

The immobility imposed by dialysis contributes to a loss of control by preventing individuals from meeting some of their own needs for several hours. They must ask to have their food cut up, their beds lowered, or a blanket put over them. Mr. O. expressed frustration when trying to eat or hold a book while on dialysis. "You're so doggone helpless when you're hooked up to that thing!"

Once dialysis is begun, the individual has little power to stop it. Mrs. M. cried before and during dialysis, "I don't want to do this. I want to leave." Individuals sometimes experience uncomfortable symptoms during dialysis, such as leg cramps, weakness, and nausea. But no matter how uncomfortable or inconvenient dialysis is, if an individual wants to live, the patient is dependent upon a machine. Most patients on dialysis are acutely aware of this dependency. As Mrs. A. stated, "You can't get very far from a dialysis machine or stay for very long. It's like there's a chain tying you to that machine." Mr. O. said resignedly, "I guess I'll just have to get used to this (dialysis). I really have no choice." The feeling of having no choice about the institution of dialysis is a common one, and individuals often express the feeling that "things are moving too fast." This is particularly true if the individual was too ill to participate in the decision to start dialysis.

MEDICAL REGIMEN

Other aspects of the medical regimen, besides dialysis, also may contribute to the individual's feelings of powerlessness. Although following the regimen may provide some feeling of power by helping with symptom control, there is still the knowledge that the regimen is necessary for life. Most individuals seem to feel that they have no choice as to whether or not they will follow the regimen.

Dietary management, in particular, poses many difficulties, and feelings of dissatisfaction are often expressed. Mrs. F. cried, "They say I can live a normal life, but I can't. I won't be able to eat or drink what I want and join in the fun." Mrs. Z. reported, "We've stopped eating out completely, and we really miss it. But it was just too hard to stick to my diet." The desire to eat or drink favorite foods is sometimes overwhelming. Mrs. S. repeatedly exceeded her fluid limitation, in spite of the severe discomfort from fluid overload. She expressed the feeling that she was unable to control her fluid intake. "I try not to drink too much—I swell up so bad—but it's really hard. I'm thirsty all the time."

The dependence on medications also contributes to feelings of powerlessness. Although there may be uncomfortable side effects, the individual must take the medications. Mr. O. stated, "Sometimes I think I'll just stop all of them, but I know I can't do that."

FAMILY RELATIONSHIPS

In addition to factors directly related to the illness and its treatment, the individual with CRF often experiences changes in family relationships that contribute to feelings of powerlessness. Role reversal commonly occurs, with the spouse and children taking on many of the individual's previous role tasks. At the same time, the patient takes on a more dependent role in the family.

The individual often expresses guilt at being unable to fulfill previous role obligations. As Mrs. O. reported, "I can't pull my share of the weight at home." Mrs. S. lamented, "My husband puts in a long day at work. He shouldn't have to do my work, too." Dependency on one's children seems to produce particularly strong feelings. Mrs. Z. said, "My daughter had to wash my hair when I had the shunt. Isn't that a terrible thing to put that job on a 12-year-old for a whole year? But I had no choice." Regarding her young daughters' helping with housework, Mrs. Z. said, "They're just kids. They shouldn't have to work all the time." Many of these individuals express the fear that they have become, or will become, a "burden" to their families.

In spite of the guilt, however, the individual usually recognizes the need for dependence on others. Mrs. S. said, "You can't complain. After all, you're lucky to have someone to help you." This comment was made after Mrs. S. had expressed frustration that her housework was not being done as well as she would like.

The central nervous system manifestations of CRF produce irritability and mood changes that also can influence family relationships. Mr. O.

reported, "I get so depressed and irritable. It bothers me a lot, but I can't control it."

The individual's symptoms and treatment regimen also frequently prevent participation in enjoyable family activities. Camping and hiking with his family had been an important part of Mr. O.'s life, and he became very depressed when he was unable to continue these activities. Mrs. S. cried over her inability to join in previously enjoyed physical activities with her daughters. "I used to skate and swim with my daughters, but now I'm a real dud. All I can do is sit. I told them, 'If I can't keep up, please understand.'" Mr. O. regretted having missed some of the family activities on vacation because of dialysis. "I was stuck with that machine while they were out sightseeing. Then after I'd finished, they'd already seen everything and didn't want to go back."

The incidence of impotence in men and decreased libido in both men and women with CRF interferes with sexual intimacy and provokes marital strain.

All of these examples indicate that the individual with CRF has less control over family relationships and activities than before the illness. Because of the value most individuals place on family relationships, this is an important factor contributing to an overall sense of powerlessness.

EMPLOYMENT AND FINANCIAL CONCERNS

The individual with CRF may experience changes in work role and resulting financial concerns, which contribute to feelings of powerlessness. Time is often lost from work because of physician's appointments and dialysis. Mr. O. expressed fear that his employer would eventually tire of these absences: "They're agreeable now, but I don't know how much longer they'll put up with me missing so much work." This fear, combined with a feeling that his job performance had decreased, caused much anxiety about his job security. He stated, "I'm losing my creativity. I feel thick-headed. I forget things all the time." Although he was unhappy with his job, he also feared losing it. He lamented, "I'm stuck here. I could never get another job with my kidney disease and my age. I'm lucky to have this one, but sometimes I feel like I'm trapped." One indication of Mr. O's feelings of powerlessness is his failure to make an effort to plan for the institution of dialysis with his employer, even though this scheduling was a great source of anxiety to him.

Mr. F. expressed frustration that he was no longer able to work and "support my family the way I'm supposed to." When his wife went to the welfare department to apply for assistance and was treated rudely, Mr. F. expressed extreme anger at his lack of control. "I'm stuck here (in the hospital) and can't do a damn thing about it! I'd like to go down there and just start punching." Job loss, or fear of job loss, and extraordinary expenses are significant factors contributing to feelings of powerlessness

TABLE 7 ■ 2   Factors Causing Powerlessness in End-Stage Renal Disease

Factor Category	Example of Specific Causes
Disease process	Uncertainty over relief of symptoms
	Fatigue, mental changes
	Multiple body systems involved
	Decreased sexual functioning
Hospitalization	Basic decisions are made for the patient, that is, when to perform ADLs
	Routines imposed on the patient without negotiation— timing of medications and treatments
	Loss of control over privacy
Patient-staff relationships	Patient acknowledges staff has more control than patient so fears expressing anger in order to avoid being shunned by the staff
	Staff knows more about the patient's pathology
	Patients not introduced to staff and other patients who occupy the same room
	Verbalizations by staff that they are making the decisions regarding room assignments, fluid restriction, and so forth
	Patient not informed about progress, weight, or laboratory values
Dialysis procedure	Venipunctures are painful, unavoidable
	Unpleasant side effects after dialysis may prevent functioning (headaches, dizziness)
	During procedure, patient is immobilized
	Dependent on others for all needs during dialysis
Medical regimen	Lack of patient involvement and tailoring the regimen to patient's needs beyond the pathology (scheduling dialysis procedure during work time)
Family relationships	Role reversal. Spouse assuming breadwinner and/or household-manager roles
	Increased dependence on family for needs
	Lack of full participation with family during special events
Employment and financial concerns	May miss work because of symptoms and/or treatment
	Feels loss of job security due to illness
	Job performance may be decreased or job may be lost
	Perceived inability to support family

Lack of information seeking

Failure to disclose relevant health information

Lack of willingness to make decisions

Expressions of loss of hope

Crying and other expressions of depression

Verbal expressions of loss of control

FIGURE 7 ■ I   Indicators of powerlessness in patients with chronic renal failure.

in individuals with CRF. The factors causing powerlessness in patients with CRF are summarized in Table 7–2.

SUMMARY

Some general verbal and behavioral indicators of powerlessness have been identified as a result of the author's work with individuals with CRF. Categories of these indicators of powerlessness are presented in Figure 7–1. The powerlessness seen in CRF is typical of that seen in many other chronic illnesses. An awareness of common indicators of powerlessness enables those who work with the chronically ill to recognize when individuals feel that they are not in control. These indicators also have implications for those working with individuals in acute-care settings because that environment, in and of itself, causes powerlessness.

Developing an awareness of factors that contribute to these feelings of powerlessness in patients can help health-care professionals learn to decrease this powerlessness. Many of the factors that cause powerlessness can be eliminated. Others can be offset, to some degree, by specific interventions that tend to promote a feeling of control or power. See Chapter 12 for specific nursing interventions for powerlessness in CRF.

References

Abram, H. (1969). The psychiatrist, the treatment of chronic renal failure and the prolongation of life—Part II. *American Journal of Psychiatry, 126,* 157–167.

Abram, H. (1968). The psychiatrist, the treatment of chronic renal failure and the prolongation of life. *American Journal of Psychiatry, 124,* 1351–1357.

Abram, H., Moore, G., & Westervelt, F. (1975). Suicidal behavior in chronic dialysis patients. *Journal of Nervous and Mental Diseases, 160,* 220–226.

Anger, D. (1975). The psychologic stress of chronic renal failure and long-term hemodialysis. *Nursing Clinics of North America, 10,* 449–459.

Baker, L. (1987). *Relationship among hope, self-esteem and stress of hemodialysis in persons with end stage renal disease.* Unpublished master's thesis, Marquette University, Milwaukee.

Baldree, K., Murphy, S., & Powers, M. (1982). Stress identification and coping patterns in patients on hemodialysis. *Nursing Research, 31,* 107–112.

Beard, B. (1969). Fear of death and fear of life. *Archives of General Psychiatry, 21,* 373–380.

Bihl, M. A., Ferrans, C. E., & Powers, M. J. (1988). Comparing stressors and quality of life of dialysis patients. *ANNA Journal, 15,* 33–36.

Burns, P. (1983). Learned helplessness in the renal patient. *Nephrology Nurse, 4,* 14–16.

Cummings, J. (1970). Hemodialysis: Feelings, facts and fantasies. *American Journal of Nursing, 70,* 70–73.

Czaczkes, J. W., & DeNour, A. K. (1978). *Chronic hemodialysis as a way of life.* New York: Brunner/Mazel.

Davison, N. (1986). Mourning the loss of sexuality. In M. Hardy et al. (Eds.), *Positive approaches to living with end stage renal disease: Psychosocial and thanatologic aspects* (pp. 142–151). New York: Praeger.

DeNour, A., & Czaczkes, J. W. (1974). Personality and adjustment to chronic hemodialysis. In N. B. Levy (Ed.), *Living or dying: Adaptation to hemodialysis* (pp. 102–126). Springfield, IL: Charles C Thomas.

Eichel, C. J. (1986). Stress and coping in patients on CAPD compared to hemodialysis patients. *ANNA Journal, 13,* 9–13.

Finkelstein, F., Finkelstein, S., & Steele, T. (1976). Assessment of marital relationships of hemodialysis patients. *American Journal of Medical Science, 271,* 21–27.

Frank, D. (1988). Psychosocial assessment of renal dialysis patients. *ANNA Journal, 15,* 207–210, 232.

Fuchs, J. (1987). Use of decisional control to combat powerlessness. *American Nephrology Nurses Association Journal, 14,* 11–13, 56.

Goodwin, S. (1988). Hardiness and psychosocial adjustment in hemodialysis clients. *ANNA Journal, 15,* 211–216.

Gurklis, J., & Menke, E. (1988). Identification of stressors and use of coping methods in chronic hemodialysis patients. *Nursing Research, 37,* 236–239, 248.

Halper, I. (1971). Psychiatric observations in a chronic hemodialysis program. *Medical Clinics of North America, 55,* 177–190.

Harrington, J., & Brenner, E. (1973). *Patient care in renal failure.* Philadelphia: WB Saunders.

Jackle, M. (1974). Life satisfaction and kidney dialysis. *Nursing Forum, 13,* 360–370.

Jones, K. (1987). Policy and research in end stage renal disease. *Image: Journal of Nursing Scholarship, 19,* 126–129.

Lancaster, L. (1984). *The patient with end stage renal disease.* New York: John Wiley & Sons.

Levy, N. (1973). Sexual adjustment to maintenance hemodialysis and renal transplantation. *Transactions of the American Society for Artificial Internal Organs, 18,* 138–142.

Maurin, J, & Schenkel, J. (1976). A study of the family unit's response to hemodialysis. *Journal of Psychosomatic Research, 20,* 163–168.

Murphy, S., Powers, M., & Jalowiec, A. (1985). Psychometric evaluation of the Hemodialysis Stressor Scale. *Nursing Research, 34,* 368–371.

O'Brien, M. E. (1983). *The courage to survive: The life career of the chronic dialysis patient.* New York: Grune & Stratton.

Olsen, C. A. (1983). A statistical review of variables predictive of adjustment in hemodialysis patients. *Nephrology Nurse, 6,* 16–26.

Plough, A. (1986). *Borrowed time: Artificial organs and the politics of extending lives.* Philadelphia: Temple University Press.

Reischman, F., & Levy, N. (1972). Problems in adaptation to maintenance dialysis. *Archives of Internal Medicine, 130,* 859–865.

Roy, C. (1976). *Introduction to nursing: An adaptation model.* Englewood Cliffs, NJ: Prentice-Hall.

Shambaugh, P., Hampers, C., Bailey, G., Snyder, D., & Merrill, J. (1967). Hemodialysis in the home: Emotional impact on the spouse. *Transactions of the American Society for Artificial Internal Organs, 13,* 41–45.

Steele, T., Finkelstein, S., & Finkelstein, F. (1976). Hemodialysis patients and spouses: Marital discord, sexual problems and depression. *Journal of Nervous and Mental Disease, 162,* 225–237.

Stegman, M. R., Duncan, K., Pohren, E., & Sandstrom, R. (1985). Quality of life: A patient's perspective. *American Nephrology Nurses Association Journal, 12,* 244–264.

Ulrich, B. T. (1989). *Nephrology nursing: Concepts and strategies.* Norwalk, CT: Appleton & Lange.

Ulrich, B. T. (1980). Psychological adaptation of end stage renal disease: A review and a proposed new model. *Nephrology Nurse, 2,* 48–52.

Weems, J., & Patterson, E. (1989). Coping with uncertainty and ambivalence while awaiting a cadaveric renal transplant. *ANNA Journal, 16,* 27–31.

Wright, R., Sand, P., & Goodhue, L. (1966). Psychological stress during hemodialysis for chronic renal failure. *Annals of Internal Medicine, 64,* 611–621.

Profiles of Locus of Control and Coping in Persons with Peripheral Vascular Disease

■ **PATRICIA S. SCHROEDER**
■ **JUDITH FITZGERALD MILLER**

Individuals with altered health states have been described as experiencing powerlessness. Because circumstances and events appear to be beyond the ill person's control, powerlessness is situationally determined. The chronically ill person's powerlessness may be caused by many factors—including illness-related changes, the health-care environment, and the health team's interactions with the ill individual. In addition to this situationally determined powerlessness, a personality trait (locus of control) influences the chronically ill patient's response to the health problem. Locus of control refers to the individual's perception of whether rewards are dependent on the individual's own behavior or are dependent on forces external to the individual. If outcomes (rewards) are perceived to be contingent on the individual's own behavior, the individual is said to have an internal locus of control. If events are perceived to be contingent upon external forces of fate, chance, or powerful others, the individual has an external locus of control (Rotter, 1966; 1975). (To avoid cumbersome phrases, such individuals will be referred to as "internals" and "externals" throughout this chapter.)

The purpose of this chapter is to describe behavioral indices of locus of control derived from the qualitative study of eight patients with peripheral vascular disease (PVD). Knowing the patient's locus-of-control tendency enables the nurse to anticipate:

- How independent the patient will seek to become
- How anxiety provoking the situational powerlessness will be for individuals (internals may have more anxiety in powerlessness situations than externals)
- The importance of mastering control-relevant health information for internals

It is also important for nurses to understand how coping strategies vary: internals use approach and direct confrontation strategies and externals use withdrawal, hostility, and aggression (Anderson, 1977). Understanding the patient's locus-of-control tendencies enables the nurse to have a more holistic approach to the patient.

Literature Review of Locus of Control

Locus of control has been measured by using objective tests such as Rotter's Social Attitude Survey or the I-E (Internal-External) Scale (Rotter, 1966), the Health Locus of Control (HLC) Scale (Wallston, Wallston, Kaplan, & Maides, 1976), or the Multidimensional Health Locus of Control (MHLC) (Wallston, Wallston, & DeVellis, 1978). Validation studies using cluster analysis have resulted in six clusters depicting variations in locus of control: (1) pure internals, (2) double externals, (3) pure chance, (4) yea sayers, (5) nay sayers, and (6) believers in control (Rock, Meyerowitz, Maisto, & Wallston, 1987). The advantages of using a quantitative approach to such a concept are obvious. Data are gathered by scales with established validity and reliability, and the score is a clear, definitive indication of the subject's locus-of-control tendency. However, administering written psychologic tests could be cumbersome and impractical for nurses. Traditionally, nurses have not used quantitative measures to validate clinical impressions. This type of validation will become a routine component of practice as more valid and reliable tools to measure select patient phenomena are developed.

Even though quantitative measures are not always feasible, nurses can use observational skills to note behavioral indices of locus-of-control tendencies. This chapter presents the initial progress in developing a behavioral observation index for nurses to use in assessing locus-of-control tendencies.

A participant-observer methodology was used to determine the patient's locus of control and individual coping strategies. The eight subjects studied were hospitalized for evaluation and treatment of PVD. The process of participant-observer research is well defined by Byerly (1969) as involving

> ... a sensitive awareness of the behaviors of the persons being observed, similar insight into the investigators' actions and reactions, a careful and complete recording of these events, and retrospective evaluation and analysis of data (p. 236).

Research findings on various characteristics of internals and externals provided the framework for making behavioral observations. Seeman (1963) and Seeman and Evans (1962) found that internals readily mastered control-relevant information. Lefcourt (1976) concluded from a review of literature on locus of control and cognitive activity that internals are more perceptive to, and ready to learn about, their surroundings. They are more inquisitive, curious, and efficient in processing information than are externals. Internals with high health values sought more information about a threat to health—hypertension—than did externals or the internals with low health values (Wallston, Maides, & Wallston, 1976). Fish and Karabenick (1971) studied self-esteem and locus of control in college freshmen. Their findings suggest that persons with an internal locus of control exhibit higher self-esteem.

The necessity of congruency between an individual's actual environment and locus of control was discussed by Watson and Baumal (1967). An incongruency is bound to produce anxiety. That is, a person with an external locus of control placed in a nonstructured environment and required to do a task that necessitates more self-direction will experience more anxiety than if placed in an authoritative, structured situation (Watson & Baumal, 1967). Likewise, persons with spinal cord injuries who have high preference for control have low depression when perceiving they do indeed have control in situations of importance to them (Ferrington, 1986).

Williams, Poon, and Burdette (1977) studied the effect of the cardiovascular response on 29 subjects during sensory processing, using forearm blood flow to determine response to sensory intake and sensory rejection. Forearm blood flow increased in externals but remained the same in internals during sensory intake. It was thought that the smaller forearm blood flow could be associated with active vasoconstriction during sensory intake. In accord with other research, Williams and coworkers found that the sensory intake of internals reflected a greater involvement in the task at hand than that of externals and that vascular resistance occurred in internals. The vasomotor response could be considered a means of physiologic coping. Lack of vascular resistance in externals may be significant. A number of questions can be raised, such as, Do the personality characteristics of internals serve as a prerequisite for developing vascular disease or other diseases that may have a psychosomatic component? What other psychosocial factors are involved in developing cardiovascular disease?

Lowery and DuCette (1976) found that internals with long-term diabetes were less compliant than externals with long-term diabetes. Internals were more active information seekers early in the course of their disease. Internality is also related to preventive actions such as wearing seat belts and using preventive dental care (Williams, 1972).

Health promotion and community health models emphasize personal responsibility for health (Jordan-Marsh & Neutra, 1985; Pender, 1987; Saltzer & Saltzer, 1987). Persons who used preventive health behavior had significantly lower chance locus-of-control scores than persons who did not engage in preventive health (Zindler-Wernet & Weiss, 1987). Internal health locus of control, low chance locus of control, and high self-esteem were related to a health promotion life-style in 262 women (Duffy, 1988). Although internality has been related to greater health, experience or lack of experience with the problem influences expectations about control (Saltzer & Saltzer, 1987).

Benefits of internality have been supported. Ehlke (1988) found a negative relationship between symptom distress and internal locus of control beliefs in 107 women receiving chemotherapy for breast cancer. That is, the greater the internality, the less distressing symptoms from chemotherapy were experienced (i.e., reported). Internally oriented persons were more likely to quit smoking after the release of the surgeon general's report in the 1960s than externally oriented persons (James, Woodruff, & Werner, 1965). Internals were more likely than externals to complete a weight-control program (Balch & Ross, 1975).

Arakelian (1980) proposed that exposure to planned programs can modify locus-of-control beliefs. Internal locus of control was increased by a select intervention of relaxation training in persons with hypertension (Pender, 1985).

Although the health locus-of-control research reviewed supports a health advantage for persons with an internal control tendency, caution must be used in judging this as the goal for all persons. For persons with a chronic health problem, assistance in accepting the situation without striving for absolute control over it may be necessary.

Peripheral Vascular Disease

Peripheral vascular disease includes conditions of the arteries (arterial occlusive disease due to atherosclerosis), veins (venous insufficiency or incompetency of venous valves), and lymph vessels (lymphedema due to inadequate lymph transport) (Wagner, 1986). All clinical profiles presented in this chapter are of persons having arterial occlusive disease due to atheromatous plaques on the intimal vessel surface.

CLINICAL DATA

Hospitalized patients were provided with professional nursing care by the registered nurse investigator, with careful documentation of the indicators of internal and external locus of control in a clinical journal. The following are profiles of eight subjects and their feelings of control, as well as coping behaviors observed by the investigator. Four subjects were classified as having an internal locus-of-control tendency, and four were considered to have an external locus-of-control tendency. A behavioral assessment tool of locus of control is also presented.

■ Clinical Profiles: Internals

Mr. K.

Mr. K. is a 53-year-old white man, an engineer, with an 8-year history of PVD for which he has had 10 operations, including lower-limb bypass grafts and embolectomies, before having one leg amputated above the knee. He was independent and strong-willed and had a well-developed self-care agency. His behaviors and conversations centered on how he could regain complete independence and autonomy, not just when discharged to his home but during his hospitalization. His internal locus of control was also demonstrated by statements he made during interviews:

- "I am responsible for the loss of my leg. I have continued to smoke cigarettes. If I wouldn't have gone back to work so fast after my other surgeries, maybe they could have saved it."
- "A person is only a cripple if he lets himself be one, and I won't."
- "I've been a professional person all my life, and I know that sometimes professionals can be stupid too, so I won't let my doctors railroad me. I let them know how I feel about what they're doing."
- "It's up to me to follow through on the therapy so I can get out of here (hospital)."

These statements are presented out of context, but Mr. K.'s attitudes and behaviors were compatible with the description of an internal locus of control as noted in the literature.

Mr. K. exhibited coping strategies that one would expect of a person with an internal locus of control. He read a great deal to be current and knowledgeable about his pathology, thereby enhancing his control. He actively participated in self-care and worked to be autonomous. He planned aspects of his care, such as routines to care for his remaining foot, and took special vitamins (including vitamin E) that he perceived as vital in maintaining his health. When he had nothing to do, he would daydream about inventions he could develop for amputees, "It would take someone creative and with my background to think this stuff up." Toward the end of his hospitalization, he began to act out sexually. Playful propositions to nurses and therapists, jokes about sex, and a flirtatious attitude could be interpreted as evidence of his altered body image and masculinity; by utilizing this behavior, he was able to cope with the situation and demonstrate his virility. He expressed that he was still sexually potent in spite of his impaired circulation. It seemed important to him that he reinforce the nurses' understanding of this fact.

Mrs. L.

Mrs. L. is a 50-year-old black woman, a housewife, with a 9-year history of PVD and arteriosclerotic heart disease. Like Mr. K., she has had several lower-limb bypass grafts, both aortoiliac and femoral-popliteal. Unlike him, she has not had an amputation. Mrs. L. is strong-willed and takes pride that she was able to walk unassisted in the intensive-care unit after her aortoiliac bypass surgery. Even during exacerbations of her illness, she continued to exhibit a strong self-care agency and internal locus of control. Some of the following statements show further indications:

- "I'm the strong one in my family."
- "You've got to help yourself get better around here. No one can do it but you."
- "God can give me strength and courage to do anything, even to quit smoking."
- "What I do to take care of myself will make the difference; it's not up to the nurses."

Mrs. L. coped by striving for autonomy and utilizing self-care practices. She had a daily routine of walking the halls and sitting in the lounges so that she could meet new friends, and through her encouragement to them, she herself became encouraged. She was very aware of her health regimen and felt she was more in control if she knew what was going on. Prayer and religion were very important to her and were a source of strength. In regard to her family supports, she stated that she had to support her husband and children whenever she was hospitalized because, "I am the strong one."

Mrs. B.

Mrs. B. is a 46-year-old white woman, a housewife, who has a medical history of two myocardial infarctions within the previous 2 years and began to develop intermittent claudication at the same time. She had several lower-limb bypass grafts on both legs, and because the grafts failed, she had a left above-knee amputation after a prolonged hospitalization in attempts to save the leg.

Mrs. B. speaks freely about her pathologies and hospitalizations; although she has a limited vocabulary, she uses all the appropriate medical terminology with obvious understanding. She, too, has a very strong self-care agency and works to do as much for herself as possible. She maintains control of her environment by being up in her wheelchair whenever possible. She is assertive. For example, when the medical team told her they wanted to attempt another bypass graft, she stated she would not sign the permit until her husband came. She informed them that when her husband arrived, she would page the doctors to return and have them provide her and her husband with information needed to make an informed decision.

In coping with her chronic illness, Mrs. B.'s basic strategy was to be knowledgeable about her disease and treatment. This allowed her to relate better to her caretakers and to take a more active role in decision making. She stated that when she felt "blue," she would call her husband to cry or complain, and he would be able to support her enough to allow her to regain control of herself and her surroundings. When she felt stressed, Mrs. B. would increase her smoking. Although alternate methods of tension control were encouraged, Mrs. B. stated that she has decided it was "too late" to quit smoking. She also devised ways of adapting her environment to her chronic illness, such as developing a makeshift waist restraint "in case I fall asleep in my chair." She organized her belongings within easy reach from her sitting position.

Mrs. H.

Mrs. H. is a 65-year-old white woman who has a 2-year history of PVD. She had many lower-limb bypass grafts and arteriograms, which resulted in foot-drop, acute tubular necrosis, and congestive heart failure. All these conditions have been successfully treated.

On original contact, she appeared to have an external locus of control. She had recently been transferred to a general unit from the intensive-care unit after femoral-popliteal bypass surgery that resulted in a cardiac arrest during surgery. While she was receiving intravenous medications, the intravenous infiltrated, and her left hand became ecchymotic and very edematous. This additional complication proved to be very traumatic for Mrs. H., and she became withdrawn and did not remember events or visitors from one day to the next. She was passive to treatment by the health-care team and did not participate in her own care. Although her short-term and long-term memory was accurate on various subjects, she stated, "They must have given me too much anesthetic because it takes so long after surgery for my mind to clear."

About 1 week after surgery, when it was obvious that she was improving physically, she began to exhibit indications of an internal locus of control. She asked questions about her condition and prognosis, and she became more involved in self-care. When assistance was offered in bathing, she stated, "I have to learn to do this myself. It bothers me terribly to be dependent on my husband."

She also began to take a very active role in the rehabilitation of her left hand. Before discharge, she questioned her doctor as to when she could discontinue physical therapy. When he replied "One to 2 weeks," she stated, "One will be enough; I'm doing very well."

Mrs. H. is an excellent example of the hypothesis proposed by Smith. At a time of life crisis, one is more likely to react with an external locus of control, and as it resolves, one again becomes more internally oriented. Consideration could also be given to the fact that during the acute episode, the behaviors manifested resulted from situational powerlessness. In the long run, her behaviors indicated an internal locus of control. An interesting question to consider is, Do internals display apathy and give up more readily than externals when placed in powerless positions?

When she was externally oriented, Mrs. H. coped by being passive and dependent. She also slept a great deal, perhaps indicating a lack of energy and physical debilitation, or depression. When she became more internally oriented, she took an active role in her care and stated that she received satisfaction in her ability to exercise her hand or meet her own hygienic needs. She received support from her husband but directed his actions when he offered help.

■ Clinical Profiles: Externals

Mrs. E.

Mrs. E. is a 56-year-old white woman who exhibits an external locus of control. She has diabetes and reportedly did not take her hypoglycemic medications for 4 years because of the cost. She also reports that because of poor heating in her home, she wore boots for several months without caring for her feet. On admission, she had a large necrotic area on the inner aspect of her right foot, probably caused by the boots, and subsequently had a below-knee amputation of the right leg.

Mrs. E. is hesitant to do anything for herself and feels hopeless. Although she is not "submissive" to authority, she relies on persons in authority to make all decisions. Her physical condition improved greatly since admission, and psychologically she became more pleasant and has learned a small amount about diabetes. When asked her attitude about herself, she replies

- "I know I'm helpless, and I'll always be helpless."
- "My husband won't wait on me when I get home, so I don't know what I'll do."

- "I lost my leg because my husband didn't repair the furnace."
- "Do you think my wearing boots for those months made my foot bad, or do you think it was the diabetes?"

Mrs. E. exhibits behaviors that, in general, demonstrate a very dependent role. Initially, Mrs. E. coped with noncompliance through total immobility or dependence. She was disinterested in learning self-care practices and refused to attempt them. She was withdrawn and depressed. Later she became more responsive to teaching but remained far from becoming an information seeker. She socialized minimally but did follow directions. She had no help-ing relationships with any supportive significant others in her life.

Mrs. R.

Mrs. R. is a 58-year-old white woman who reportedly had psy-chotic episodes during several hospitalizations. She has had periph-eral vascular problems for 4 years that required four femoral-popli-teal bypass procedures. She now has had a right above-knee amputation and previously had a left transmetatarsal amputation. Mrs. R. also has an external locus of control. She exhibits helpless-ness and uses religion unrealistically.

- She complained of being tired from taking Librium more often than at home. When encouraged to refuse the extra dose, she stated, "The doctor ordered it, so I have to take it."
- You have to eat everything they give you or they'll get mad."

Mrs. K.

Mrs. K. is a 48-year-old white woman who has had PVD for 2 years for which she had a femoral-popliteal bypass on the left leg. Her disease had increasingly limited her activity, and she was hos-pitalized to be evaluated for a graft on the right leg. Although she had much pain, she did not elect to have surgery at that time because of the uncertainty of its long-range success.

Mrs. K. lacked knowledge of her disease and the treatments. She was unsure why these painful tests were being performed, yet she consented to them. She stated there was nothing she could do to "alter the course of her fate" and prayed that medical science would find a cure for diabetes and her vascular problems. Her con-versations were laced with statements such as "You can't win—there's no way you can come out on top with this (disease)." She took all her medications at home but was unable to identify their names or actions. When discussing her plan of care, she stated, "You have to do what they say."

The coping behaviors Mrs. K. used appear to be based heavily on denial and expressions of guilt. She did not look to ways she could function maximally despite her disease but instead focused on praying for a cure and expressed much guilt at her inability to fulfill her roles within the home. She used religion in a basically unrealistic way. She avoided confronting the realities of her situation.

Mrs. T.

Mrs. T. is a 61-year-old white woman, a widow, who lives with her daughter and family. She has had PVD for 3 years and had a femoral-popliteal bypass graft on the left leg approximately 1 year ago. She now has been hospitalized for the same procedure on her right leg.

Mrs. T. is a very passive woman who generally agrees with anything that is said, even if it is contradictory. When asked how she felt about impending surgery, she stated, "I don't know. You've got to do what they say." Although her surgery was canceled three times because of laboratory tests not being completed or scheduling difficulties, she never became overtly angry. Postoperatively, she participated little in self-care, even to the day of discharge.

Religion was used by Mrs. T. as a coping strategy. She would pray for relief of pain and strength to handle it, which was quite realistic. When Mrs. T. was stressed, she closed her eyes and turned her head away as if to block out the undesired stimuli. Her coping reflected nonverbal avoidance. She remained dependent and tolerant of everything because "you have to go along with it."

BEHAVIORAL INDICATORS OF LOCUS OF CONTROL

In examining these data as a whole, commonalities specific for internals and externals were noted. Based on the review of research on locus of control, patient behaviors were categorized as indicating an internal or external control tendency. Two nurse educators who had knowledge of locus-of-control research and had conducted locus-of-control studies independently rated the behaviors. Only those behaviors for which there was 100 percent agreement were included on the assessment tool. Items that prompted a discrepancy between the raters were omitted. The assessment tool provides a framework for the organization of observations of behavioral indices of internal and external locus-of-control tendencies. See Table 8–1.

Patients may not exhibit behaviors related to each category noted in Table 8–1, as was true of the patient examples presented in this chapter; however, through observation of some of these behaviors, a general tendency toward internal or external control can be discovered.

Caution needs to be used to avoid rigidly categorizing patients as being at one or the other extreme of locus of control. Locus of control is

TABLE 8 ■ 1   Behavioral Indicators of Locus of Control

	Internals	*Externals*
Role definition and satisfaction	More clearly defined, more satisfying	Less clearly defined, less satisfying
Relating to authority	Peer-like interactions	Passive-like interactions
Self-esteem	Higher or more stable self-esteem	Lower or less stable self-esteem
Responsibility for self-care	Active knowledge-seeking behavior	Do not actively seek information, accept what is given
Compliance with health-care regimen	Manipulate regimen	Compliant
Confidence in abilities	Self-confident	Lack self-confidence
Problem-solving abilities	More successful	Less successful
Goal-setting behavior	Realistic in goals set	Unrealistic
Level of motivation	Motivation	Tend toward helplessness at times
Involvement in decision making	More involvement	Less involvement

to be viewed as a continuum, with most persons falling somewhere between the extremes. Although quick interpretation of Table 8–1 may lead nurses to believe that externality is negative, this may not be the case in terms of patients' experiences of anxiety, recovery rates, and select patient outcomes after illness episodes. Too little data exist to draw conclusions at this point. Strickland (1979) suggests that type A patients with cardiovascular disease may be extremely internally oriented. Increasing internality in the type A person may increase personal striving, stress, and eventually maladaptation (Wallston, Wallston, & DeVellis, 1978).

In a review of literature on locus of control and health, Wallston, Wallston, and DeVellis (1978) concluded that although internals seemed to engage in more positive health- and sick-role behaviors than externals did, findings are contradictory, and in some instances it is more functional to hold external beliefs. In general, internals were more positive in seeking health information, adhering to prescribed medications, keeping physician appointments, maintaining a diet, and giving up smoking. Lack of consistency in findings may stem from use of Rotter's I-E scale without validating findings using other locus-of-control measures as well as not using convenience samples and not controlling samples' variance in terms of severity and length of illness (Arakelian, 1980).

Careful study is needed to determine the desirability of internality training and the circumstances that warrant strategies to develop patients' internality. Arakelian (1980) reviewed literature on locus of control and suggested means of internalization. Three types of internalization strategies include (1) reconstruction of stimuli—helping patients change their perceptions of stimuli (reinterpretation of stimuli); (2) action orientation—helping patients learn problem-solving techniques and eliminate self-defeating behaviors; and (3) counseling—helping patients recognize contingencies between their own behavior and outcomes.

COPING BEHAVIORS

The case examples in this chapter suggest that the coping strategies used by internals are similar, as are those used by externals. Internals obtained strength from maintaining control over their environment, if only through their knowledge of what was occurring. This knowledge provided internals with the opportunity to make informed choices and accept, reject, or supplement their therapy. Internals also worked to develop self-care abilities. Religion or spouses were frequent sources of support that were generally aimed at returning the patient's strength to handle the situation rather than removing the situation.

Externals more frequently coped through the use of denial or expression of guilt feelings, which was not followed by actions to alter the situation. They were passively accepting and did little to increase their own self-care abilities. Religion was used by some externals but was directed at unrealistic goals such as a "cure" for their chronic disease or a return of an amputated part. In general, the externals' coping strategies did not deal directly with the situation. The use of denial did seem to decrease anxiety for the externals.

Similar findings of coping behaviors of internals and externals were found by Ewig (1979) who used two quantitative locus-of-control measures. Ewig studied coping behaviors of patients who had chronic pain to determine differences in coping between internals and externals. Subjects were classified as internal or external based on both a modified Rotter scale (Seeman & Evans, 1962) and the original Rotter scale (Rotter, 1966). Ewig's findings support the descriptive research presented in this chapter. Externals used passive coping behaviors (withdrawal, lack of goal setting, lack of self-care involvement, denial, lack of information seeking). Internals used active coping behaviors (initiation of action based on self-care knowledge and skills, goal setting, use of appropriate decision-making strategies, purposeful use of relaxation and/or distraction, pride in self-care strides, and information seeking). A comparison of the coping behaviors of internals and externals is presented in Table 8–2.

NURSING IMPLICATIONS

Because of the uncertain course of PVD, like any chronic illness, patients are placed in "uncontrollable" situations. How chronically ill patients react to their health problem is very individual. This chapter has

TABLE 8 ■ 2   Coping Behaviors of Internals and Externals

Internals	Externals
Active in self-care	Passive dependence
Helped others recognize self-care strides, boasted of ability	Sleeping
Planned for care needs, made suggestions to health worker	Lack of self-care skills
	Disinterested
Social interaction	Social isolation
Active interest in others, helped them solve problems	Withdrawn
	Focused on unrealistic cures
Set goals	
Modified environment, planned for safety needs	Refused therapies that increase mobility (physical therapy)
Used problem solving	
	Verbal expressions such as there is nothing more to be done
Information seeking	
Asked specific, relevant questions	
Read about condition	
Shared perceptions of self as being important	
Described positive role as strong person in family	
Deliberate use of prayer to provide strength	
Purposeful distraction	

reinforced the idea that knowledge about patients' locus of control is important in understanding patients' behavioral response. Knowledge of a patient's locus-of-control tendency can give direction for appropriate nursing approaches. For example, in interpersonal relationships, persons with an internal locus of control might best respond to "one-to-one" collaborative planning with the nurse in which maximum involvement of the patient is encouraged. Persons with a more external locus of control might be more responsive to an "authority-to-subordinate" approach, as this is in accord with their perceived view of success in interaction with authority figures. The nurse would need to demonstrate competence and knowledge and share experience so that the patient can surrender planning and involvement and look to the nurse as the authority.

Internals may be more capable of dealing with situations that affect their concepts of themselves. They may be able to preserve a positive self-concept in the face of chronic illness, whereas externals may be in greater need of nursing interventions to maintain a positive self-concept. Externals perceive physical disorders as more disabling than mental disorders, and internals perceive mental disorders as more disabling than physical disorders (MacDonald & Hall, 1971). Likewise, self-esteem of externals may be more vulnerable to physical health changes than is the self-esteem of internals.

Responsibility for self-care is a major area with divergent approaches based on the patient's locus of control. Internally oriented persons might be eager to receive as much information as possible about their health and plan of care. They could then approach prescribed regimens with confidence and enthusiasm and feel better able to deal with unforeseen situations. Much of the health education could be unstructured or self-directed. Externally oriented persons, however, might be best approached by a structured teaching plan including only the information that is absolutely necessary for safely implementing self-care. Externally oriented persons can be anticipated to be initially unsure of abilities, to need more direction in assuming self-care responsibilties, and to have potentially greater difficulty in problem solving regarding unplanned situations.

The amount of structure and self-direction did influence internals' and externals' success in a weight-control program (Wallston, Maides, et al., 1976). Wallston and coworkers found that externals lost more weight in a group-structured, externally controlled program, whereas internals lost more weight in a self-directed, internally oriented program.

Goal-setting behaviors of internally oriented persons are generally more realistic, requiring an honest and supportive approach by the nurse. Throughout the problem-solving process, the patient would benefit optimally from being the focal point of decision making. Because of a higher level of motivation, internals have a good chance of achieving realistic goals that tend to be self-determined. Externals can be expected to be responsive to having some decisions made for them. Because of externals' tendency to set unrealistic goals, they may need more assistance in identifying achievable outcomes and support in believing that the goals are actually attainable.

Locus of control is a fertile area for research and is relevant for nursing. Controversy exists over appropriate means of measuring locus of control and the desirability of internal versus external tendencies. Both qualitative and quantitative studies are needed on locus of control in the chronically ill. Health professionals must continue to develop locus-of-control theory through use of pooled data, validation of observations, and testing of hypotheses. Valuable studies could include how individuals' locus-of-control tendencies influence compliance, help seeking, anxiety levels, health-maintenance behaviors, perceived vulnerability to diseases, and other sick-role behavior.

Although specific care plans are not the focus of this chapter, prevalent nursing diagnoses are outlined. Herman (1986) identified nursing diagnosis for each of the following functional patterns of Gordon (1987).

1. Nutrition-metabolic pattern
   • Impaired skin integrity
2. Activity-exercise pattern
   • Activity intolerance
   • Alteration in tissue perfusion

3. Cognitive-perceptual pattern
   - Alteration in comfort
   - Pain self-management deficit
   - Knowledge deficit
4. Self-perception self-concept pattern
   - Anxiety
   - Reactive depression
   - Powerlessness
   - Body image disturbance
5. Coping-stress tolerance pattern
   - Ineffective coping
6. Health-perception health-management pattern
   - Noncompliance
   - Health-management deficit

Nursing care for patients with PVD may include interventions directed at risk modification and prevention. These include reduction of hypercholesterolemia through diet, exercise and weight control, blood pressure control, smoking cessation, and anxiety reduction. Patient teaching includes information about medication regimens (vasodilators), monitoring exercise tolerance, foot care, and control of related health problems such as diabetes (Beaver, 1986; Turner, 1986). Avoidance of trauma to legs and feet by avoiding use of warming devices (heating pads), changing elastic stocking daily, inspecting skin for breakdown, and examining calves of legs for tenderness due to thrombophlebitis all need nursing emphasis. Patient's altered comfort state needs to be managed with medications and/or adjunctive modalities (distraction, imagery, relaxation). A drug used when claudication is a problem is Trental. This is a rheologic agent which increases the red blood cells flexibility and decreases platelet aggregation and blood viscosity. Microcirculation is improved with use of Trental (pentoxifylline) (Turner, 1986). New surgical treatment modalities now include the use of laser surgery (Cox & Jacobs, 1987; Webber & Jenkins, 1988).

Summary

Emphasis in this chapter is on analysis of clinical data of eight patients with PVD on their control tendencies. For a summary of nursing assessment, diagnostic testing, and therapies, refer to Doyle (1986), Ekers (1986), Fahey (1987), Herman (1986), and Massey (1986).

Planning and providing care appropriately designed for the individual patient's unique needs and personality are dependent on understanding the patient's control tendency. By developing sensitivity to their own locus-of-control tendencies, nurses will not expect similar control behaviors in their patients. It is possible that an astute practitioner may be routinely assessing patients' locus of control and coping behavior; however, few nurses choose to organize care plans considering the locus-of-control variable. Omitting locus-of-control data in the assessment may lead to inappropriate nursing approaches that are incongruent with the patient's unique control tendency. The patient's behavior may be one of noncompliance unless effort is made to tailor nursing approaches congruent with the patient's control tendencies.

References

Anderson, C. (1977). Locus of control, coping behaviors and performance in a stress setting: A longitudinal study. *Journal of Applied Psychology, 62,* 446–451.

Arakelian, M. (1980). An assessment and nursing application of the concept of locus of control. *Advances in Nursing Science, 3,* 25–42.

Balch, P., & Ross, W. (1975). Predicting success in weight reduction as a function of locus of control. A unidimensional approach. *Journal of Consulting and Clinical Psychology, 43,* 119.

Beaver, B. M. (1986). Health education and the patient with peripheral vascular disease. *Nursing Clinics of North America, 21,* 265–272.

Byerly, E. (1969). The nurse researcher as participant-observer in a nursing setting. *Nursing Research, 18,* 230–236.

Cox, J., & Jacobs, C. P. (1987). Laser-assisted angioplasty. *AORN Journal, 46,* 835–846.

Doyle, J. (1986). Treatment modalities in peripheral vascular disease. *Nursing Clinics of North America, 21,* 241–253.

Duffy, M. (1988). Determinants of health promotion in midlife women. *Nursing Research, 37,* 358–362.

Ehlke, G. (1988). Symptom distress in breast cancer patients receiving chemotherapy in the outpatient setting. *Oncology Nursing Forum, 15,* 343–346.

Ekers, M. A. (1986). Psychosocial considerations in peripheral vascular disease. *Nursing Clinics of North America, 21,* 255–263.

Ewig, J. (1979). *The relationship between locus of control and pain coping style.* Unpublished master's thesis, Marquette University, Milwaukee.

Fahey, V. (1987). *Vascular nursing.* Philadelphia: WB Saunders.

Ferrington, F. (1986). Personal control and coping effectiveness in spinal cord injured persons. *Research in Nursing and Health, 9,* 257–265.

Fish, B., & Karabenick, S. A. (1971). Relationship between self-esteem and locus of control. *Psychological Reports, 29,* 784.

Gordon, M. (1987). *Nursing diagnoses: Process and application* (2d ed.). New York: McGraw-Hill.

Herman, J. A. (1986). Nursing assessment and nursing diagnosis in patients with peripheral vascular disease. *Nursing Clinics of North America, 21,* 219–231.

James, W., Woodruff, A. B., & Werner, W. (1965). Effect of internal and external control upon changes in smoking behavior. *Journal of Consulting Psychology, 29,* 184–186.

Jordan-Marsh, M., & Neutra, R. (1985). Relationship of health locus of control to lifestyle change programs. *Research in Nursing and Health, 8,* 3–11.

Lefcourt, H. (1976). *Locus of control: Current trends in theory and research.* Hillsdale, NJ: Lawrence Erlbaum Associates.

Lowery, B., & DuCette, J. P. (1976). Disease-related learning and disease control in diabetics as a function of locus of control. *Nursing Research, 25,* 358–362.

MacDonald, A. P., & Hall, J. (1971). Internal-external locus of control and perception of disability. *Journal of Consulting and Clinical Psychology, 36,* 338–343.

Massey, J. (1986). Diagnostic testing for peripheral vascular disease. *Nursing Clinics of North America, 21,* 207–218.

Pender, N. (1987). *Health promotion in nursing practice* (2d ed.). Norwalk, CT: Appleton-Lange.

Pender, N. (1985). Effects of progressive muscle relaxation training on anxiety and health locus of control among hypertensive adults. *Research in Nursing and Health, 8,* 67–72.

Rock, D., Meyerowitz, B., Maisto, S., & Wallston, K. (1987). The derivation and validation of six multidimensional health locus of control scale clusters. *Research in Nursing and Health, 10,* 185–195.

Rotter, J. B. (1975). Some problems and misconceptions related to the construct of internal versus external control of reinforcement. *Journal of Consulting and Clinical Psychology, 43,* 56–57.

Rotter, J. B. (1966). Generalized expectancies for internal versus external control of reinforcement. *Journal of Consulting and Clinical Psychology, 21,* 56–67.

Saltzer, E., & Saltzer, E. (1987). Internal control and health. Which comes first? *Western Journal of Nursing Research, 9,* 542–554.

Seeman, M. (1963). Alienation and social learning in a reformatory. *American Journal of Sociology, 69,* 270.

Seeman, M., & Evans, J. (1962). Alienation and learning in a hospital setting, *American Sociological Review, 27,* 772–782.

Strickland, V. R. (1979). IE and cardiovascular functioning. In L. C. Perlmuter and R. A. Monty (eds.), *Choice and Perceived Control* (pp 221–231). Hillsdale, NJ: Lawrence Erlbaum Associates.

Turner, J. A. (1986). Nursing intervention in patients with peripheral vascular disease. *Nursing Clinics of North America, 21,* 233–240.

Wagner, M. (1986). Pathophysiology related to peripheral vascular disease. *Nursing Clinics of North America, 21,* 195–206.

Wallston, K. A., Maides, S., & Wallston, B. S. (1976). Health-related information seeking as a function of health-related locus of control and health value. *Journal of Research and Personality, 10,* 215–222.

Wallston, B. S., Wallston, K. A., Kaplan, C. D., & Maides, S. A. (1976). Development and validation of the Health Locus of Control (HLC) Scale. *Journal of Consulting Clinical Psychology, 44,* 580–585.

Wallston, K. A., Wallston, B. S., & DeVellis, R. (1978). Development of the Multidimensional Health Locus of Control (MHLC) Scales. *Health Education Monographs, 6,* 160–170.

Watson, D., & Baumal, E. (1967). Effects of locus of control and expectations of future control upon present performance. *Journal of Personality and Social Psychology, 6,* 212–215.

Webber, M., & Jenkins, N. (1988). Laser treatment of peripheral vascular disease: Implications for nursing care. *Progress in Cardiovascular Nursing, 3,* 81–88.

Williams, A. F. (1972). Personality characteristics associated with preventive dental health practices. *Journal of the American College of Dentistry, 39,* 225–234.

Williams, R. B., Poon, L., & Burdette, L. (1977). Locus of control and vasomotor response to sensory processing. *Psychosomatic Medicine, 39,* 127–133.

Zindler-Wernet, P., & Weiss, S. (1987). Health locus of control and preventive health behavior. *Western Journal of Nursing Research, 9,* 160–179.

■

Energy Deficits in Chronically Ill Persons with Arthritis: Fatigue

■ JUDITH FITZGERALD MILLER

Energy is the capacity to do work. Within the complexity of the human system, work takes place on a variety of planes. In a biologic sense, energy is a requirement for cell metabolism. Energy is needed for mobilizing psychologic defense mechanisms. Cognitively, energy is needed for learning, generating ideas, solving problems, and striving for goal attainment. Social energy includes being able to interact with others as members of family and community systems. Social energy is needed for interacting with persons for whom the individual has a cathexis as well as with persons for whom there is no attachment.

Energy as a Power Resource

Energy is viewed as a power resource because of the vastly important role it plays biologically, psychologically, cognitively, and socially. Energy provides power in the following ways: It is a resource for mobility (Fagerhaugh, 1975), a factor in promoting well-being and a feeling of physical reserve, a means of providing confidence in task accomplishment, and a means of responding to unexpected stress. An energy deficit contributes to powerlessness. When the capacity to do work is lacking, powerlessness exists. The term entropy is used to describe disorganization resulting from energy loss (Putt, 1978). When a state of entropy exists, the organism is powerless. Energy deficits are a common problem in chronically ill patients.

196

In nursing care of chronically ill patients, helping the patient to become aware of energy resources and to manage energy deficits is an empowerment strategy. Specific aspects of energy as a power resource will be examined closely.

ENERGY IS A BASIC MOBILITY RESOURCE

Fagerhaugh (1975) describes energy, time, and money as basic mobility resources. Individuals draw on basic mobility resources for physical mobility and sociability. The individual's needs for physical mobility and sociability are easily met during various states of health, if adequate financial resources are present. However, basic mobility resources are decreased and continue to dwindle in persons with chronic health problems. Persons who have low energy resources but sufficient money resources can purchase the basic mobility resources of another. Mobility assistants can be hired (Fagerhaugh, 1975) to help with various living tasks—cleaning, cooking, transportation, and so forth.

Typically, the chronically ill person suffers from a deficit of energy— the basic mobility resource. Furthermore, when the ill person also lacks sufficient financial resources, the only remaining basic mobility resource is time. Having all the time available that is needed, the patient will spend it to accomplish the mobility task. For example, the patient with emphysema may require the entire morning to get dressed and perform normal morning hygiene activities. The same patient may also spend twice as much time performing routine errands such as walking to the store, since the patient may have to stop to "catch a breath" at puffing stations along the way. Figuring out which route has the least resistance (terrain not requiring walking uphill) and allowing sufficient time to avoid the routes with difficult terrain are ways of using time as a basic mobility resource (Fagerhaugh, 1975).

ENERGY PROMOTES WELL-BEING

A sense of self-satisfaction and well-being is felt when energy is present. The individual can control interactions with the environment and engage in meaningful activities, which provide positive feedback about self and a sense of joy. Exercise enhances well-being; however, lack of energy may prohibit this.

ENERGY ENABLES TASK ACCOMPLISHMENT AND ABILITY TO RESPOND TO NEEDS

Energy is a basic necessity for task accomplishment. Whether the tasks are providing self-care, learning new skills, working on the job, performing other roles, or responding to unexpected stress, energy gives the individual confidence in being able to complete the task successfully. Fatigue is the physical and psychologic manifestation of energy deficits; it is a subjective feeling of tiredness that is influenced by circadian rhythm and varies in unpleasantness, duration, and intensity (Piper, 1986). There is a progression from tiredness, to fatigue, to exhaustion, a total decompensated state (Rhoten, 1982). Fatigue interferes with coping, optimal participation in treatment programs, social activities which are important for positive feedback about self, role performance, and sexual activities.

Etiologies for fatigue are classified by Rhoten (1982) as (1) physical—posture, sedentary life; (2) mental—monotony or boredom; (3) environmental—noise, temperature; (4) emotional—anxiety, frustration, depression, conflicts; (5) physiologic—nutritional deficits, sleep-rest disturbance, select medications; and (6) pathologic—inflammation, disease processes.

Fatigue has been identified as a prevalent response to varied chronic health problems including cancer (Kaempfer & Lindsey, 1986; Kobashi-Schoot, Hanewald, Van Dam, & Bruning, 1985; Haylock & Hart, 1979; Jamar, 1989), multiple sclerosis (Hart, 1978), cardiac problems (Hertanu, Davis, & Focseneanu, 1986; Winslow, Lane, & Gaffney, 1985), end-state renal disease (Baldree, Murphy, & Powers, 1982; Eichel, 1986; Srivastava, 1989), and respiratory problems. Analysis of the energy state of the chronically ill is important.

Energy Analysis Format

ENERGY SOURCES AND TRANSFORMATION

Ryden (1977) presents a comprehensive format to examine energy. Three constructs proposed in Ryden's energy utilization model are (1) energy sources, (2) energy transformation, and (3) energy expenditure or storage. Energy sources include nutrients, oxygen, and water; other sources are rest and motivation. Motivation promotes perseverance, interest, and determination. These as well as pleasure and satisfaction derived from an activity or task serve to counteract fatigue (Hart & Freel, 1982). Energy transformation refers to the body's physiologic processing and distribution of energy sources (Ryden, 1977). In chronically ill persons, energy is affected by pathophysiologic changes that may interfere with digestion, circulation, respiration, endocrine balance, and cellular metabolism. The third construct is energy expenditure. According to Ryden, energy expenditure takes place on three levels: compensation, mobility, and growth. At the compensation level, energy is used for restoration of physical and psychosocial equilibrium. At the mobility level, energy is spent in work, hobbies, and dealing with the external environment. At the growth level, energy is spent in learning. Figure 9–1 contains Knoebel's interpretation (1978) of Ryden's model (1977).

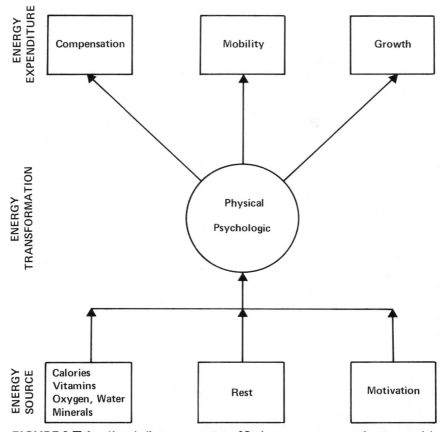

FIGURE 9 ■ 1   Knoebel's interpretation of Ryden energy source-utilization model.

ENERGY REQUIREMENTS IN CHRONICALLY ILL PERSONS

In order to understand the energy deficits in chronically ill persons, a more specific analysis of energy requirements is needed. Energy requirements will be discussed in terms of restoration of physical integrity; role expansion and coping with the effects of illness; daily activities that cannot be omitted; and activities that provide social stimulation, recreation, exercise, and learning. In this light, energy requirements include specific energy needs above and beyond that energy needed for basal metabolism. The model presented in Figure 9–2 is the basis for discussion throughout this chapter.

Restoration of physical integrity refers to wound healing (soft tissue and bones), recovering from inflammatory processes, achieving a metabolic balance (as between nutrients, insulin level, and exercise), generating new cells after cell destruction from medical therapy (chemother-

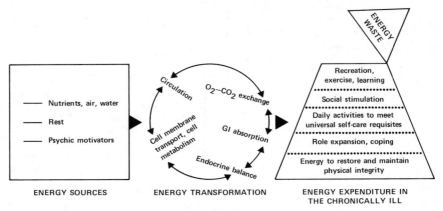

FIGURE 9 ■ 2   Energy analysis model for chronically ill persons.

apy and radiation therapy), and participating in physical therapy regimens to restore muscle strength. Pathophysiologic and therapy demands create a compromised energy state in chronically ill persons.

Role expansion and coping with the effects of illness require energy. Illness demands the individual learn new self-care practices, monitor self-response to therapy, and become sensitive to cues that need action to avert a crisis. Role expansion includes learning the goals, behaviors, and sentiments of the new role. For chronically ill patients, the new role is self-care agent. A self-care agent is the individual (or designate) who carries out self-care practices to meet requisites presented to the individual. Such requisites arise from therapies, developmental needs, and universal needs (Orem, 1985). The role of self-care agent includes varied activities, for example, administering prescribed medications or irrigating a wound.

The new role expectations of the self-care agent are beyond the continuing roles and role expectations. Those continuing roles may include mother, housewife, participant in children's school events, member of the symphony women's league, and part-time teacher of an adult art education course. The role expansion increases energy demands, adding new time pressures, problem solving, and anxieties because of role insufficiency. Role insufficiency is any difficulty in learning and/or performing new role behavior.

Coping with the tasks of a chronic illness requires energy. Coping is discussed in detail in Chapter 2 and only examples of energy depletion and coping are presented here; these examples are those that do not require extreme physical exertion such as jogging. Coping strategies such as self-disclosure, examining feelings, developing insights, and relating feelings to behaviors are challenging and energy draining. Other preferred verbal modes of expression used as coping mechanisms—such as laughing, crying, and singing—may be especially taxing to a person with a chronic condition such as severe pulmonary emphysema. The coping tasks of chronic illness identified in Chapter 2 and the psychosocial challenges of illness discussed later in this chapter all require energy.

Energy is required for daily activities that satisfy basic needs. These can be considered synonymous with the universal self-care requisites proposed by Orem (1985), including air, water, food, elimination, activity and rest, solitude and social interaction, and protection from harm. Maintaining personal hygiene and getting dressed are other examples of activities of daily living.

Activities that may not be required daily but are essential to preventing loneliness, low self-esteem, or distorted self-concept are those that provide for social interaction. The indirect result of communication is feedback about one's self. The person may feel, "I was successful in relating to another; she seemed to enjoy my company; I was able to be of assistance to another; and I received positive feedback about how I am doing." Recreation, exercise, and learning are essential for enjoying life. Adequate energy sources are needed for all three activities to take place.

ENERGY WASTERS

While energy expenditure in the above categories is required, energy is depleted or wasted in many ways in chronically ill persons.

Preventing energy depletion by eliminating energy waste is a responsibility of nursing. Energy is wasted through physical means, lack of environmental management, and unchanneled psychologic reactions and feelings (Table 9–1). Nursing interventions can be directed toward alle-

TABLE 9 ■ 1   Energy Depletion from Waste

Physical	Lack of Environmental Management	Psychologic
Pain—inadequate pain-management resources	Uncoordinated efforts directed at a variety of tasks to be accomplished	Uncontrolled anxiety
Anorexia	Lack of planning before engaging in physical activities	Unexpressed anger, hostility
Fever	No priorities identified so as to eliminate frustration when least important tasks are not accomplished	Unresolved grief
Infection		
Diarrhea		
Interrupted sleep	Procrastination; working at avoiding getting started	
Forced immobility—traction, casts, bedrest	Giving up quickly, necessitating repetitious starting over in task-accomplishment efforts	

viating physical discomforts that waste energy, including inadequate pain management, anorexia, fever, infection, diarrhea, and interrupted sleep. Forced immobility, which occurs when patients are in traction or casts or on bedrest, causes diminished muscle strength and muscle atrophy. Lack of environmental management by poor planning—for example, by making unnecessary trips up and down stairs—or by lack of priority setting in undertaking the day's activities can be alleviated by the nurse. Nurses can help patients gain insight into their behavior and recognize specific ways their environment can be managed to eliminate energy waste. Psychologic energy wasters may include uncontrolled anxiety, unexpressed anger, and unresolved grief. Identifying the patient's energy wasters is an important component of the energy-analysis format (see Fig. 9–1). It is nursing's responsibility to assess energy sources, transformation, and expenditure. Specific nursing diagnoses describing energy deficits can be identified.

NURSING DIAGNOSES AND PATIENT-IDENTIFIED DILEMMAS

Specific descriptive nursing diagnostic statements related to energy can be made as a result of the energy analysis, for example:

- Guilt due to an inability to fulfill expected roles according to personally established criteria
- Anxiety due to lack of knowledge regarding the meaning of energy depletion
- Unpredictable daily work-rest patterns due to changing energy availability
- Inability to recognize depleted energy states due to lack of internal awareness
- Helplessness due to a perceived lack of control over energy expenditure
- Frustration related to inability to complete desired tasks within a specified time

Although it is easy to empathize with patients who may have to curtail activities because of energy deficits, the real impact of energy dilemmas can be felt and expressed only by the patients themselves. Consider the following abbreviated descriptions of dilemmas that occur in patients with rheumatoid arthritis.

A 56-year-old woman described the difficulty she felt when she could not even plan ahead during a day. A friend called her at 9:00 a.m. and suggested that they meet for lunch. Because the patient was feeling stiff with increased pain and fatigue at that particular time, she refused lunch, only to be symptom-free by noon. The patient described the inability to predict how she would feel or how much energy she would have, being unable to plan ahead, feeling somewhat embarrassed over having misjudged her status, and being unable to explain the dilemma to her healthy friend. She regretted needlessly missing an opportunity to alleviate her loneliness (she lived in a rural area, her husband was at work all day, and there were no neighbors who dropped by). She was hesitant, therefore, to initiate social plans with others because of her uncertainty in being able to carry out the plans.

A middle-aged woman who had studied music enjoyed playing classical music on the piano but she was forced to give it up because of lack of strength and dexterity, and increased pain in her hands. As someone who had taught music and interpretation of musical works, this posed a difficult problem for her. She had to refrain from playing for months at a time during arthritic changes in order to protect her joints and provide them with rest. Absence of this important part of her life caused her real grief.

Another woman expressed role insufficiency because of the weakness and fatigue caused by her arthritis. She stated, "Now that I finally have grandchildren, I am unable to enjoy them. With my arthritis, I'm afraid I will drop the baby. I looked forward to running in the backyard with them; by the time they're old enough to run, I'll be lucky if I'm able to get myself to the table to eat." She expressed feeling deprived of a role that belonged to her and foresaw a future filled with disability and dependence.

John was a middle-aged factory worker with newly diagnosed rheumatoid arthritis. For a number of years, John and his fellow workers played cards during breaks and lunch hour, keeping a running tally of wins and losses. Now, instead of playing cards, John uses the time to rest and relax in a lounge chair within view of the card playing. John feels his buddies resent his behavior and view it as an abnormal withdrawal. He feels it is impossible to convince the other men of his necessity to rest so he can complete his 8-hour shift. The fellow workers have commented to him, "You're making too much of this arthritis thing. You don't look any different than you ever did." John feels socially isolated at work as a result of his careful use of time to restore energy.

A grade-school teacher in her thirties discovered that standing outside for playground duty in the morning and at noon precipitated pain and unnecessarily depleted energy. She felt guilty trying to be excused from this duty even though she could exchange this activity with lunchroom monitoring. She felt it was a reflection that she was inadequate as a teacher.

The feelings of being a burden are readily described by Mrs. T. Since her rheumatoid disease has progressively worsened, she has been unable to keep up her own apartment. "Now I have to live with my son, daughter-in-law, and their family. They don't like it any more than I do. I feel in the way, so always present—someone extra who is monitoring their fights and their times of intimacy."

The defining characteristics of energy-deficit diagnoses identified by

Pinekenstein (1979) in her study of patients with cancer have relevance for analysis of energy states in general. Two categories of defining characteristics of the nursing diagnosis "energy deficits" were patient verbalizations and nonverbal responses. Patients' verbalizations of actual or perceived changes in energy level included references to past energy, "I used to be able to work all day, make supper, and attend an evening class. Now it's difficult to set the table." Patients' references to present energy level may include, "I'm weak, just don't have any strength." Patients may verbalize hopelessness by stating, "I'm just the same, as weak as ever, despite the physical therapy. It's no use."

The nonverbal responses to energy changes include decreased social involvement (irritability, use of frequent rest periods, decreased socialization with family and friends), weight loss and muscle wasting, decreased activity tolerance, excessive use of routine patterns, and use of others' basic mobility resources.

Analysis of energy in patients with rheumatoid arthritis serves as a prototype for energy analysis in chronically ill persons. The unique problems of patients with arthritis are discussed.

NURSING DIAGNOSES AND ETIOLOGIES

The American Nurses' Association and Arthritis Health Professions Association have developed Outcome Standards for Rheumatology Nursing Practice (1983). The nursing diagnoses that provide the framework for the standards are as follows:

- Pain management deficit
- Alteration in comfort: stiffness
- Alteration in energy level: fatigue
- Self-care deficit
- Knowledge deficit regarding physical mobility (ambulation)
- Knowledge deficit regarding self-management decisions
- Ineffective individual or family coping
- Disturbance in self-concept

The rationales for each diagnosis, outcome statement, and outcome criterion have been described in detail (ANA, 1983; Pigg & Schroeder, 1984). For example, the outcome statement for the energy alteration diagnosis is "the individual incorporates as part of daily activities, those measures necessary to modify fatigue" (ANA, 1983, p. 5).

Energy Depletion in Patients with Arthritis

Arthritis afflicts more than 31 million Americans, and 6.5 million of these have rheumatoid arthritis (National Center for Health Statistics,

1989). Rheumatoid arthritis is a systemic autoimmune disease that affects joints and connective tissue. The effects of the disease can be widespread and completely debilitating. The outstanding patient challenges are to maintain comfort, preserve joint mobility and function, protect joints during exacerbations, complete prescribed exercise routines to maintain muscle strength and joint function, adhere to medicine regimens, pace activities to conserve energy, and obtain emotional and systemic rest. Because of these challenges, the patient with arthritis is described as a prototype for understanding energy deficits in chronically ill patients. Etiologies for fatigue in persons with arthritis may include

- Anemia
- Increased physical exertion
- Increased disease activity
- Muscle atrophy
- Pain
- Emotional stress
- Inadequate nighttime rest
- Lack of knowledge (about importance of rest, ways to rest, pacing, joint protection, and medication regimen) (Pigg, Driscoll, & Caniff, 1985)

Energy depletion in patients with arthritis results from physiologic and psychologic processes.

PHYSIOLOGIC ENERGY DEPLETION

Physiologically, energy depletion in arthritis is due to inflammation, metabolic changes, and pain. The connective tissue and joint become inflamed. The resultant swelling, stiffness, and muscle spasm cause pain that depletes energy. In rheumatoid arthritis, metabolic changes occur, such as synovial membrane hypertrophy, articular cartilage destruction, and invasion of pannus into the bone. Other systemic effects of the disease include muscle atrophy, myositis, fever, anorexia, and malaise. The inflammatory process can be widespread, as in arteritis, iritis, pneumonitis, and carditis (Groer & Shekleton, 1979). Anemia contributes to poor energy reserve in patients with arthritis and results from the blockage of iron release from the reticuloendothelial cells to the erythropoietic cells (Tobe, 1978).

Joint protection and work simplification directed at reducing stress and pain in affected joints result in decreased inflammation and ultimately in less energy loss. Joint protection includes resting painful swollen joints, balanced body mechanics, avoidance of excess loads, frequent change in body position, and proper use of prescribed corrective devices (Wegener & Kulp, 1988).

Although evening exercise has proved effective in decreasing the arthritis patient's morning joint stiffness and immobility (Byers, 1985), changes in fatigue states due to this or other interventions have not been systematically studied. Pain-coping studies have indicated that active pain-coping behaviors correlated with less pain whereas passive pain coping is related to greater pain (Brown & Nicassio, 1987). Again, fatigue was not a variable included in the pain studies.

Because arthritic pain is chronic, the patient cannot anticipate an end to it; relief would be a pleasant outcome, as in the healing of a surgical incision or the birth of a baby. However, as Swartz (1970) puts it, "Arthritis is so damned daily."

ENERGY IS AFFECTED BY PSYCHOLOGIC STATE

The psychologic and social processes and characteristics that accompany chronic illness deplete energy. Psychologic characteristics of individuals with chronic illness and those specifically prevalent in patients with arthritis may include anger, contained hostility, depression, hypochondriasis, hysteria, and mourning (Spergel, Ehrlich, & Glass, 1978; Zeitlin, 1977). Energy is wasted in anxiety. Patients have anxiety over uncertainty of energy availability from day to day. Anxiety is also present in pain control and sleep interference. Patients ask themselves, "Where will it hit next? How bad will it be? What residual weakness and deformity will I suffer?"

Fatigue is one manifestation of depression related to learned helplessness of chronic illness (Potempa, Lopez, Reid, & Lawson, 1986). Potempa and colleagues suggest that fatigue may be combated in part by perceived self-efficacy; that is, a conviction that one can successfully produce outcomes for oneself (Bandura, 1977). Persons with low self-efficacy have less coping ability and have exaggerated perceptions of fatigue.

Burckhardt (1985) found that positive self-esteem, internal control over health, perceived support and low negative illness attitude contribute directly to a higher quality of life in persons with arthritis. Persons with osteoarthritis had lower life satisfaction than persons on chronic hemodialysis (LaBorde & Powers, 1980). Chronic pain, being socially isolated, and a preoccupation with illness were posed as factors explaining low life satisfaction of persons with arthritis. Likewise, Bradbury and Catanzaro (1989) found that internal control over health and low negative illness attitude correlated with quality of life in men with arthritis. Loneliness was a predictor of pain in persons with arthritis (DeVellis, DeVellis, Sauter, Harring, & Cohen, 1986). Psychosocial factors in adapting to physical disability are said to include social support, positive self-concept, internal health control, and hardiness (Swanson, Cronin-Stubbs, & Sheldon, 1989). Lambert and associates (1989) confirmed that social support and hardiness were significant predictors of psychologic well-being in 122 women with arthritis.

Psychosocial tasks of persons with rheumatoid arthritis include managing role change, lack of control, poor self-esteem, hopelessness, altered body image, and challenged coping ability (Ignatavicius, 1987). Use of "wish fulfilling fantasy" was noted to be a prevalent coping strategy of 84 persons with rheumatoid arthritis (Parker et al., 1988). This strategy was associated with higher levels of depression, helplessness, and more daily stress. The tendency to use self-blame was also associated with greater psychologic distress (Parker et al., 1988).

Understandably, behaviors of anger, frustration, anxiety, and depression result from the symptoms and disability of the disease. There are some unique differences in responses between patients with arthritis and patients with other health problems. Patients with rheumatoid arthritis anticipate the course of their disease to get worse, whereas patients with peptic ulcers do not believe this is the future course for the illness (Williams & Krasnoff, 1964).

DISABLING THEMES IN ARTHRITIS

The diagnosis of rheumatoid arthritis is accompanied by disabling themes in that the patient fears becoming crippled, being perceived as being old and nonproductive, and not being understood by loved ones—being unable to obtain empathy from significant others. Mayville (1979) proposed reasons some patients with newly diagnosed rheumatoid arthritis display disabled behaviors after the diagnosis although they had not changed in gait, posture, pace of movement, and joint dexterity prior to diagnosis. She states their behaviors are due to previous knowledge of arthritis and associations with others who have the disease, patient efforts to reduce joint movement to control pain, low energy levels and joint stiffness, self-concept change of perceiving self as being old and disabled, and acting out a need for empathy as a signal to others to try to understand their plight. Some of the identified responses may be a positive means of coping and a way of decreasing joint aggravation. Other behavior reflecting a distorted self-image may need nursing intervention.

Normalizing

The patient endeavors to normalize the expending of energy (described as a coping task in Chapter 2). Wiener (1975) described the components of this behavior, which she identifed in a study of 21 subjects with rheumatoid arthritis. Normalizing refers to behaviors an individual uses to continue what the individual perceives to be a normal life. The categories of normalizing identified by Wiener were covering up, keeping up, justifying inaction, pacing, eliciting help, and balancing the options.

Covering up allows patients with arthritis to view themselves as they would prefer to be viewed by others. It includes keeping the signs and symptoms of the disease (assistive devices, slowed gait, painful expressions) out of view of others.

Keeping up refers to carrying on with the same schedule one kept before the diagnosis, resulting in exhaustion, excessive time for rest to restore energy, and, in some cases, exacerbation of symptoms and fever. Wiener (1975) identifies a paradox in patients who cover up and keep up. These patients long for understanding and sensitivity. They verbalize, "Nobody really knows how bad it is," yet state, "If I acted the way I feel, nobody would want to be around me." The patients use energy in wishing for caring and empathy while at the same time use energy to guard against turning off family and friends.

Justifying inaction includes providing rationale to others for not being able to engage in activities or meet their expectations. Justifying inaction may be necessary in cases of pain, stiffness, and uncertainty that accompanies the illness. However, justifying inaction becomes especially problematic after a history of covering up and keeping up. Imagine the dilemma of the woman who in the morning refused an afternoon bridge club engagement and then is seen shopping later in the afternoon. With the uncertainty of severity of symptoms, with increased morning stiffness on this particular day—"one of her bad days"—the patient's worry about being able to cover up and keep up during the social event caused her to refuse the social activity. Yet when symptoms subsided and she faced real demands of household management, she proceeded to do her grocery shopping.

Pacing is the balancing of activities of "keeping up" with rest. This is the desired normalizing strategy and one with which nurses can help patients. Pacing is an energy conservation behavior. Patients can be helped to analyze their daily activities, to provide for complete rest of all joints at some point during the day, and to get 8 to 10 hours of sleep at night.

Balancing the options available to the patient requires energy. Balancing the options includes deciding "whether to keep up and suffer the increased pain and fatigue; whether to cover up and risk inability to justify inaction when needed; whether to elicit help and risk loss of normalizing . . ." (Wiener, 1975, p. 102).

Clinical Data and Nursing Interventions for Energy Conservation and Restoration

The modified Ryden model provides a framework for nursing intervention for patients with energy deficits. Energy sources can be restored, problems in transformation can be referred for medical therapy, and energy expenditure can be managed. A patient example will be used to demonstrate nursing care (see Figure 9–2).

Mrs. S. is a 54-year-old Mexican-American woman with an 18-year history of rheumatoid arthritis. Her ankles, knees, hands, wrists, and shoulders are the most seriously involved joints. Ms. S. weighs 205 pounds and is 5 feet 4 inches tall. Her most recent hospitalization was for rest, weight reduction, and the fitting of hand-wrist splints for nighttime use. Currently, she is receiving health care in an ambulatory arthritis center. Mrs. S. resides with her Mexican-American husband, two or more teenage grandchildren, and nieces and nephews. The exact number of household occupants had been changing from week to week. Neither Mr. S. nor Mrs. S. was employed outside of the home, but Mrs. S. cared for three infant and toddler grandchildren (all in diapers) while their parents worked. This work was physically taxing and frustrating as Mrs. S. could not easily manipulate diaper changes and the other routine child care demands.

ANALYSIS OF ENERGY SOURCES

Nutrients

Mrs. S.'s energy sources were inadequate. Despite her obesity, she was malnourished. Her intake of milk, fruit, vegetables, and lean protein was lacking. Dietary counseling with her cultural needs in mind enhanced her understanding but did not change her pattern of overeating.

Rest

Mrs. S. was not able to obtain any rest during the day in her current home situation; at night her sleep was interrupted by what Mrs. S. describes as "the same old pains and worry." In completing a sleep history, data regarding time of retiring, bedtime rituals, sleep environment, and the patient's perception of sleep disturbance were obtained. Mrs. S. described her worries as interfering with her sleep.

Mrs. S.'s psychic state served as an energy depleter rather than an energy source. She was filled with anxiety over the care of her many grandchildren and in anticipating how to inform her children that she could no longer keep up the pace the grandchildren demanded. She resented her husband's seeming lack of understanding of her pain, fatigue, and slow mobility; his lack of productivity; and his lack of help with the children. Mrs. S. was worried about their finances. Their gas had already been turned off on one previous occasion.

Mrs. S.'s psychologic state accounts for her difficulties with energy sources in all three categories (nutrients, rest, and psychic energizers). To help with underlying anxieties about finances, Mrs. S. was referred to a social worker. The nurse acted as a liaison and accompanied Mrs. S. to the first social-work interview. Mobilizing social-services resources was an initial step in alleviating the financial worries.

Mrs. S.'s concept of self as having been a source of strength within the family (maintaining the family network) was enhanced by enabling her to discuss her perceptions of her role and receiving honest praise for a job well done.

Helping Mrs. S. give up her role of care provider for the babies (her final decision after difficult deliberation) was important for Mrs. S. to rest and alleviate her guilt over her grandchildren's care. Mrs. S. needed help with eliminating role strain by reviewing the alternatives and making a decision. She determined that giving up the role of care provider would help her obtain needed rest during the day and would alleviate her guilt over not being able to adequately manage the children. Her role transition was helped by having her rehearse how she would inform her daughters and by giving her a mental picture of what her day would be like without this responsibility (Meleis & Swendsen, 1978).

Family counseling was begun. This therapy helped increase Mr. S.'s participation in household tasks and increased his empathy for his wife. The teenaged grandchildren, who had been truant, are less of a behavior problem because their parents and grandparents became more sensitive to the teenagers' needs and demonstrated interest in them and their school activities.

Now that Mrs. S. is less anxious, data obtained in the sleep history can be used to plan strategies to promote sleep. She needed help in reestablishing a bedtime routine. Her pain management at bedtime needed improvement—to take the prescribed sulindac (Clinoril) and aspirin in the evening. Mrs. S. assumed these contributed to her wakefulness. She was taught progressive relaxation through autosuggestion (Benson, 1975), which promoted rest and well-being and conserved energy.

Since pain-control strategies conserve energy, other means of helping Mrs. S. were to identify and attempt to eliminate the pain promoters that were part of her routine. For example, she was encouraged to avoid extended exposure to cold weather, such as she experienced standing outside waiting for public transportation. She was taught principles of joint protection and to avoid joint strain during routines, that is, to avoid struggling to open screw-top jars and to seek assistance from Mr. S. The necessity of complying with wearing the night splints for joint alignment was reinforced.

As the psychosocial energy expenditure was controlled, Mrs. S. was more motivated to improve her nutritional energy source and to lose weight, thereby further alleviating joint strain that is caused by excessive weight.

ENERGY TRANSFORMATION

Although there was no real energy transformation problem with Mrs. S., the excessive intake of calories needed to be controlled. There was no other pathologic problem requiring medical intervention.

ENERGY EXPENDITURE

Energy to Restore and Maintain Physical Integrity

Although Mrs. S. was extremely anxious, she was noncompliant with the night splints, diet, and follow-up clinic visits. Now that her psychologic stresses were less, she completed her prescribed exercise routine twice daily and followed through with other therapeutic requirements. Less energy was wasted when she was compliant.

Role Expansion and Coping

Mrs. S.'s role expansion (learning self-care practices) was accompanied by role contraction—giving up the child care and related pressures. She was also receiving more attention from her husband, which was a psychic energizer for Mrs. S. Her means of coping was through prayer. Although she no longer attended Mass daily, her active prayer life contributed to her energy source. The positive effect of prayer was emphasized.

Daily Activities to Meet Universal Self-Care Requirements

Mrs. S. was taught to use her present energy efficiently by planning for what she would be doing and where she would be and collecting what she needed in one trip. For example, she was encouraged to complete her personal hygiene and loosening-up exercises in the warm shower in the morning before descending the stairs to make breakfast. (The bedrooms and bathtub are on the second floor.) She was instructed to plan ahead and take downstairs in the morning what she would need for the rest of the day. When she was working in the kitchen, she was taught ways of supporting her joints and reminded to sit down while working whenever possible. Good body mechanics for proper joint alignment were reviewed.

Social Stimulation

Many of Mrs. S.'s neighborhood friends were members of the Mexican-American culture. These women provide a support group for one another through weekly meetings at each other's houses. Mrs. S. was encouraged to tell them of her uncertainty of being with them for every get-together. The social and morale benefits of this group of friends were reviewed with Mrs. S., and it was determined that the energy expenditure was worthwhile. She received feedback from the group members about being a worthwhile person. She was also able to express her concerns to people of her own culture and felt truly understood by them. When Mrs. S. is in an energy-depleted state, expenditure in this category could be restricted or eliminated.

Recreation, Exercise, and Learning

Mrs. S. used little, if any, energy for recreation, exercise, and learning. Her sole recreation was watching television. Her exercise was necessarily confined to her prescribed routine of range-of-motion exercises to maintain joint mobility. Developing new enjoyable outlets would assist her psychologic well-being, which might include singing in the church choir, participating in the weekly Bible study class, and corresponding with residents in her native Mexican village.

Energy Waste

Mrs. S. wasted energy through anxiety and immobilized problem solving. Ways to handle anxiety (practicing relaxation exercises, verbalizing feelings to nurse, taking problems one at a time) were discussed. Mrs. S. was helped to feel self-confident and to have increased self-esteem so that she could resume family decision-making responsibilities. During periods of disease exacerbations, the increased pain and occasional fever wasted energy. Eliminating routine exercises and increasing rest and analgesics during exacerbations helped conserve energy.

Although not needed for Mrs. S., other nursing strategies can be used to conserve energy for patients with arthritis.

General Nursing Interventions for Energy Conservation and Restoration

A comprehensive nursing approach to conserving and restoring energy includes restoring energy sources, helping the patient evaluate energy expenditure, increasing energy reserve, and eliminating energy waste.

The energy sources of nutrients (food, vitamins, minerals, and water) have been discussed in relation to Mrs. S. Patients need to be advised of the necessity to make diet adjustments because of deficiencies or excesses of certain foods. Maintaining intact, healthy autoimmune systems to prevent infections and therefore prevent energy waste depends in part on adequate nutrition. The energy sources of sleep-rest have also been described in relation to Mrs. S. Using a sleep history, promoting relaxation at bedtime, and helping the patient establish a bedtime routine are helpful nursing activities.

The role of psychic energizers in restoration of energy states needs further emphasis. Energy is obtained through psychic renewal. Psychic renewal takes place through meditation (prayerful or other), routine progressive relaxation, creative imagery, and autogenic suggestion.

Physiologic changes during meditation that indicate a calming effect are decreased respiratory and heart rates, decreased oxygen consumption, lowered or stabilized blood pressure, and decreased skin conductivity (Pelletier, 1977). Autogenic training is a self-induced meditation-relaxation procedure (Luthe, 1969). Briefly, the procedure includes six stages. During the first stage, the individual focuses "passive attention" (Pelletier, 1977) on each limb, while repeating, "My right arm feels heavy," and progressing throughout the body—all limbs, torso, neck, jaw, forehead. In the next stage, the same progression of limbs is used to review warmth: "My right arm feels warm." In the third stage, the individual is to emphasize, "My hearbeat is calm and regular." Focusing on depth and ease of respiration takes place in the fourth stage, while the individual repeats the phrase, "It breathes me." During the fifth stage, the individual focuses on warmth in the upper abdomen (solar plexus), stating, "My solar plexus is warm." Instructions for the last stage are to repeat, "My forehead is cool." Pelletier states that after practice ranging from 2 months to 1 year, the entire series of six stages can be completed in 2 to 4 minutes.

Progressive relaxation in which the person is taught to focus on the extremes of muscle tenseness and complete relaxation of the same muscle group is another relaxation method.

Mental imagery is a device for promoting calmness and well-being. By creating tranquil images in the mind, mind-body pathways extend this feeling from a mental state to an actual physical state. For example, the patient with arthritis may visualize lying on a warm, sunny beach at the ocean. The patient pictures the warm sun and sand easing out the joint stiffness and imagines the ocean waves washing in and out, washing away the pain. The patient feels the body to be very light, agile, and floating. The outcome should be deep relaxation and renewed energy. The autosuggestion may have improved the comfort state as well.

Facilitating psychic energizers includes helping patients with motivation. Their eagerness to accomplish something, to establish goals, and to anticipate desired outcomes is a psychic energizer.

Any discussion on restoration of energy would be incomplete without referring to the work of Krieger (1979). Krieger's premise is that energy from one human being (healer) can be transferred through touch to another (healee). Energy from the healer helps "repattern the patient's energy level to a state that is comparable to that of the healer" (Krieger, Pepper, & Ancoli, 1979). Although countless cases of improved health after therapeutic touch have been documented, the only quantifiable variable that increases significantly at the 0.01 level of significance after treatment with therapeutic touch is hemoglobin (Kreiger, 1979). The group receiving therapeutic touch had significantly higher hemoglobin than the control no-touch group. Perhaps what was once a maneuver to comfort, share an experience, and reassure that dependence is allowed through touch can now be viewed as a powerful transfer and repatterning of energy from someone who is healthy to someone who is ill. The healing act of touch is not understood scientifically, and no attempt will be made to speculate about what actually happens. For a description of the technique, readers are referred to *The Therapeutic Touch* (Krieger, 1979).

ENABLING THE PATIENT TO EVALUATE ENERGY EXPENDITURE

Helping patients plan more precisely for energy utilization in various activities is now possible through use of METs. MET refers to metabolic equivalents, the amount of oxygen used per minute per kilogram of body weight. One MET equals 3.5 mL oxygen per kilogram of body weight per minute. Table 9–2 contains a list of activities and their approximate energy expenditure in METs.

Although MET assignment has been used as a specific energy prescription for patients with cardiac disease, specific energy expenditure analysis using METs is helpful for all patients striving to understand energy use and planning for bursts of energy expenditure. Planning includes providing for extra rest and avoiding excessive MET expenditure in a 24-hour period. The anxious patient uses more METs per activity than the individual who is not anxious.

INCREASING ENERGY RESERVE AND DECREASING ENERGY WASTE

Energy reserve is increased through physical conditioning. A regular exercise program strengthens muscles (increases muscle fiber size, endurance, and flexibility); burns calories; improves lung aerobic capacity; and affects fat metabolism by increasing high-density lipoproteins (HDL), which is helpful in ridding harmful very low density lipoprotein (VLDL) from the body. Exercise increases strength of cardiac contraction and decreases blood pressure and heart rate. In addition, exercise promotes a feeling of well-being. For some, physical exercise not only builds up energy reserve but also decreases an energy waster—anxiety.

Eliminating energy waste as summarized in Table 9–1 in the areas of physical waste, or environmental management, and psychologic waste is a nursing responsibility. For patients with arthritis, pain is a typical energy waster. Eliminating pain promoters, such as joint strain, damp environment, inadequate rest, and ineffective analgesic schedules, eliminates energy waste due to pain.

Establishing avenues for self-expression and ventilation of hostility may help alleviate psychologic energy wasters—anxiety, anger, and unresolved grief or guilt. Eliminating disabling themes (person's self-perception of being old, crippled, and dependent) will also eliminate some psychic energy waste.

Fatigue may be lessened by select energy conservation methods: rest, planning for activities and priority setting, pacing, using splints and assistive devices. Pain management, adequate nutrition, and controlling other means of energy waste are important. Anxiety may be controlled by expanding patient's coping skills. Adherence to medical regimen is necessary to control the disease process (increased disease activity is related to increased fatigue).

Furst and colleagues (1987) proposed an energy conservation program that included teaching persons about predisposing factors for energy loss; developing new skills and reinforcing these learned behaviors. Predisposing factors include developing knowledge about arthritis and the benefits of balancing rest and activity. Attitudes about possible behavior changes are reviewed with emphasis on personal ability to change behaviors. Enabling skills include developing ability to (1) analyze activities in terms of energy expenditure; (2) identify activity related to pain and fatigue; (3) understand desired good posture and body mechanics; and (4) use joint protection measures. Reinforcement includes helping family and patients recognize behavior changes as positive (Furst, Gerber, Smith, Fisher, & Shulman, 1987; Furst, Gerber, & Smith, 1985).

FATIGUE ASSESSMENT

Instruments to measure fatigue have been developed. The Piper Fatigue Self Report Scale (PFS) is a 69-item visual analog scale designed to measure patterns of fatigue including temporal, intensity-severity, affective, sensory, evaluative, associated symptom relief, and fatigue relief (Piper, Lindsey, Dodd, Ferketich, Paul, & Weller 1989). Other fatigue scales include the Fatigue Symptom Checklist (Yoshitake, 1978) and the fatigue subscale for the Profile of Mood States (McNair, Lorr, & Droppleman, 1971). The Pearson Byars Fatigue Feeling checklist consists of a list of 10 adjective phrases describing fatigue. Clinical assessment of fatigue can be completed by observing appearance, communications, activity, and attitude as well as using a 10-point response format on a single line (visual analog scale) with 0 indicating not tired, full of energy, peppy; to 10 indicating total exhaustion (Rhoten, 1982).

Other related instruments specific for the chronically ill or persons with arthritis are listed for the reader's further review and critique prior to use in research. The Arthritis Helplessness Index (AHI) is a 15-item instrument measuring perceived control (Nicassio, Wallston, Callahan, Herbert, & Pincus, 1985; Stein, Wallston, & Nicassio, 1988; Stein, Wallston, Nicassio, & Castner, 1988). The AHI has a modest internal consistency alpha of 0.69. Construct validity tests reveal negative correlations between high helplessness and self-esteem and negative correlations between helplessness and internal locus of control (Nicassio, Wallston,

TABLE 9 ■ 2 Approximate Energy Expenditure in METs (activities of 70-kg Individual)*

Category of Activity	Light (1–3 METs)		Moderate (3.5–6 METs)		Heavy (7+ METs)	
	Rest	1	Showering	3.5	Ambulation with braces or crutches	6.5
	Sitting	1	Using bedpan	4.0	Walking upstairs with 17-lb load	7.5
	Standing (relaxed)	1	Walking downstairs	4.5		
	Eating	1	Conditioning exercises	4.5		
	Conversation	1	Walking 3.5 mph	5.5		
	Dressing-undressing	2				
	Wash hands, face	2				
	Propelling wheelchair	2				
	Shaving	2.8				
	Bedside commode	3				
	Walking 2.5 mph	3				
Personal care activities	Walking level, slowly 1 mph	1.2	Walking level 3 mph	3.5	Tennis	6.0
	Painting, sitting	1.5	Bowling	3.5	Trotting horse	6.5
	Playing piano	2.0	Cycling 5.5 mph	3.5	Spading	7.0
	Driving	2.0	Badminton	3.5	Jogging level 5 mph	7.5
	Canoeing 2.5 mph	2.5	Canoeing, sailing	3.5	Skiing	8.0

Category	Activity	Value	Activity	Value	Activity	Value
Recreational activities	Horseback riding slow	2.5	Golfing	4.0	Squash	8.5
	Volleyball	2.5	Swimming	4.0	Basketball	8.5
			Dancing	4.5	Tennis	8.5
			Gardening	4.5	Cycling 13 mph	9.0
					Gymnastics	10.0
					Football competition	10.0
Housework activities	Hand sewing	1.0	Ironing, standing	3.5	Mowing lawn by hand	6.5
	Sweeping floor	1.5	Scrubbing floors	3.5	Shoveling	7.0
	Machine sewing	1.5	Hanging wash	3.5	Ascending stairs with 17-lb load	7.5
	Polishing furniture	2.0	Cleaning windows	3.5	Planting	7.5
	Peeling potatoes	2.5	Beating carpets	4.0	Construction physical worker	6.5
	Washing small clothes	2.5	Plowing with tractor	4.5	Pick and shovel work	8.0
	Kneading dough	2.5	Lifting, carrying 20–44 lb	4.5	Splitting wood by hand	10.0
	Cleaning windows	3.0	Carpentry	5.5		
	Making beds	3.0	Using pneumatic tools	6.0		
	Desk work	1.2				
	Typing (electric)	1.2				
	Radio-TV repair	1.2				
	Draftsman	1.8				

*Adapted from Clark (1978); Krusen, Kottke, and Ellwood (1971); and Karvonen and Barry (1967).

Callahan, Herbert, & Pincus, 1985). Exemplar items include, "Arthritis is controlling my life." "I can do a lot of things to cope with my arthritis" (Nicassio et al., 1985, p. 463). The AHI was modified slightly by removing the term arthritis from the items and renaming the scale to Rheumatology Attitudes Index (RAI), (Callahan, Brooks, & Pincus, 1988). Criterion validity of the RAI was established by significant correlations with ADLs, disease activity, and physical function measures. Again only a modest internal consistency of 0.68 was obtained.

Perhaps the most widely used arthritis functional assessment tool is the Arthritis Impact Measurement Scale (AIMS) (Meenan, Gertman, & Mason, 1980). The AIMS evaluates functional status in terms of physical activity, mobility, ADLs, household activity, and manual dexterity. The AIMS also measures psychologic well-being, depression, and anxiety.

Lorig and colleagues (1989) developed a scale to measure perceived self-efficacy in persons with arthritis. It is based upon Bandura's (1977) theory that persons' beliefs in their ability to perform tasks or behaviors positively influences their performance. Continued refinement and psychometric review of this scale may be of benefit for nursing research.

Summary

Energy is a power resource. A deficit in energy is often present in individuals with chronic health problems. Analysis of energy states can be guided by using the modified Ryden model (1977), in which energy sources, transformation, and expenditure are determined. Nursing diagnoses are identified, and strategies to alleviate the diagnoses are carried out. Alleviation of energy deficits results in alleviation of a degree of powerlessness. The patient with arthritis is described in this chapter as a specific prototype in applying the energy analysis model summarized in Figure 9–2.

References

American Nurses' Association and Arthritis Health Professions Association (1983). *Outcome standards for rheumatology nursing practice.* Kansas City, MI: American Nurses' Association.

Baldree, K. S., Murphy, S. P., & Powers, M. J. (1982). Stress identification and coping patterns in patients on hemodialysis. *Nursing Research, 31,* 107–113.

Bandura, A. (1977). Toward a unifying theory of behavioral change. *Psychological Review, 84,* 191–215.

Benson, H. (1975). *The relaxation response.* New York: Morrow.

Bradbury, V. L., & Catanzaro, M. L. (1989). The quality of life in a male population suffering from arthritis. *Rehabilitation Nursing, 14,* 187–190.

Brown, G., & Nicassio, P. (1987). Development of a questionnaire for the assessment of active and passive coping strategies in chronic pain patients. *Pain, 31,* 53–64.

Burckhardt, C. (1985). The impact of arthritis on quality of life. *Nursing Research, 34,* 11–16.

Byers, R. (1985). Effect of exercise on morning stiffness and mobility in patients with rheumatoid arthritis. *Research in Nursing and Health, 8,* 275–281.

Callahan, L., Brooks, R., & Pincus, T. (1988). Further analysis of learned helplessness in rheumatoid arthritis using a Rheumatology Attitudes Index. *Journal of Rheumatology, 15,* 418–426.

Clark, N. F. (1978). Disturbances in the blood pumping mechanism. In D. Jones, C. F. Dunbar, & M. M. Jirovec (Eds.), *Medical-surgical nursing: A conceptual approach* (pp. 813–839). New York: McGraw-Hill.

DeVellis, R. F., DeVellis, B. M., Sauter, S. V., Harring, K., & Cohen, J. L. (1986). Predictors of pain and functioning in arthritis. *Health Education Research, 1,* 61–67.

Eichel, C. J. (1986). Stress and coping in patients on CAPD compared to hemodialysis patients. *ANNA Journal, 13,* 9–13.

Fagerhaugh, S. (1975). Getting around with emphysema. In A. Strauss (Ed.), *Chronic illness and the quality of life* (pp. 99–107). St. Louis: CV Mosby.

Furst, G., Gerber, L., & Smith, C. (1985). *Rehabilitation through learning: Energy conservation and joint protection: A workbook for persons with rheumatoid arthritis.* Bethesda, MD: U.S. Department of Health and Human Services, National Institutes of Health Publication No. 85-2743.

Furst, G., Gerber, L., Smith, C., Fisher, S., & Shulman, B. (1987). A program for improving energy conservation behaviors in adults with rheumatoid arthritis. *American Journal of Occupational Therapy, 41,* 102–111.

Groer, M., & Shekleton, M. (1979). *Basic pathophysiology: A conceptual approach.* St. Louis: CV Mosby.

Hart, L. (1978). Fatigue in the patient with multiple sclerosis. *Research in Nursing and Health, 1,* 147–157.

Hart, L., & Freel, M. (1982). Fatigue. In C. Norris (Ed.), *Concept clarification in nursing* (pp. 251–261). Rockville, MD: Aspen Systems.

Haylock, P., & Hart, L. (1979). Fatigue in patients receiving localized radiation. *Cancer Nursing, 2,* 461–467.

Hertanu, J. S., Davis, L., & Focseneanu, M. (1986). Cardiac rehabilitation exercise programs: Outcome assessment. *Archives of Physical Medicine and Rehabilitation, 67,* 431–435.

Ignatavicius, D. (1987). Meeting the psychosocial needs of patients with rheumatoid arthritis. *Orthopaedic Nursing, 6,* 16–21.

Jamar, S. C. (1989). Fatigue in women receiving chemotherapy for ovarian cancer. In S. Funk, E. Tornquist, M. Champagne, L. A. Copp, & R. Wiese (Eds.), *Key aspects of comfort: Management of pain, fatigue and nausea* (pp. 224–233). New York: Springer.

Kaempfer, S. H., & Lindsey, A. (1986). Energy expenditure in cancer: A review. *Cancer Nursing, 9,* 194–199.

Karvonen, M., & Barry, A. (1967). *Physical activity and the heart: Proceedings of a symposium, Helsinki, Finland.* Springfield, IL: Thomas Publishers.

Kaye, R., & Pemberton, R. (1976). Treatment of rheumatoid arthritis. *Archives of Internal Medicine, 136,* 1023–1228.

Knoebel, P. (1978). An analysis of energy utilization through the implementation of the Ryden Model. Unpublished paper. Marquette University, Milwaukee, WI.

Kobashi-Schoot, J., Hanewald, G., Van Dam, F., & Bruning, P. (1985). Assessment of malaise in cancer patients treated with radiotherapy. *Cancer Nursing, 8,* 306–313.

Krieger, D. (1979). *The therapeutic touch.* Englewood Cliffs, NJ: Prentice-Hall.

Krieger, D., Pepper, E., & Ancoli, S. (1979). Therapeutic touch: Searching for evidence of physiological change. *American Journal of Nursing, 79,* 660–662.

Krusen, F., Kottke, F., & Ellwood, P. (1971). *Handbook of physical medicine and rehabilitation.* Philadelphia: WB Saunders.

LaBorde, J., & Powers, M. (1980). Satisfaction with life for patients undergoing hemodialysis and patients suffering from osteoarthritis. *Research in Nursing and Health, 3,* 19–24.

Lambert, V., Lambert, C., Klipple, G., & Mewshaw, E. (1989). Social support, hardiness and psychological well-being in women with arthritis. *Image: Journal of Nursing Scholarship, 21,* 128–131.

Lorig, K, Chastain, R., Ung, E., Shoor, S., & Holman, H. (1989). Development and evaluation of a scale to measure perceived self-efficacy in people with arthritis. *Arthritis and Rheumatism, 32,* 37–44.

Luthe, W. (1969). *Autogenic therapy.* New York: Grune & Stratton.

Mayville, K. (1979). The significance of crippling response to rheumatoid arthritis. Unpublished Master's Thesis. Marquette University, Milwaukee, WI.

McCaffery, M. (1979). *Nursing management of the patient with pain* (2d Ed.). Philadelphia: JB Lippincott.

McNair, D. M., Lorr, M., & Droppleman, L. F. (1971). *POMS: Manual for Profile of Mood States.* San Diego: Educational and Industrial Testing Service.

Meenan, R. F., Gertman, P. M., & Mason, J. H. (1980). Measuring health status in arthritis: Arthritis Impact Measurement Scales. *Arthritis and Rheumatism, 23,* 146–152.

Meleis, A.I. & Swendsen, L.A. (1978). Role supplementation: An empirical test of a nursing intervention. *Nursing Research, 27,* 11–18.

National Center for Health Statistics. (1989). *Vital and Health Statistics Series 10: Data from the National Survey.* Bethesda, MD: U.S. Public Health Service Publication No. 173.

Nicassio, P., Wallston, K., Callahan, L., Herbert, M., & Pincus, T. (1985). The measurement of helplessness in rheumatoid arthritis: The development of the Arthritis Helplessness Index. *Journal of Rheumatology, 12,* 462–467.

Orem, D. (1985). *Nursing: Concepts of practice* (3d ed.). New York: McGraw-Hill.

Parker, J., McRae, C., Smarr, K., Beck, N., Frank, R., Anderson, S., & Walker, S. (1988). Coping strategies in rheumatoid arthritis. *Journal of Rheumatology, 15,* 1376–1383.

Pelletier, K. (1977). *Mind as healer, mind as slayer.* New York: Dell Publishing.

Pigg, J. S., Driscoll, P. W., & Caniff, R. (1985). *Rheumatology Nursing: A problems oriented-approach.* New York: John Wiley & Sons.

Pigg, J. S., & Schroeder, P. S. (1984). Frequently occurring problems of patients with rheumatic diseases. *Nursing Clinics of North America, 19,* 697–708.

Pinekenstein, B. (1979). Energy alterations in: Deficiencies, identfication and comparison of defining characteristics in five hospitalized clients. Unpublished Master's Essay. Marquette University, Milwaukee, WI.

Piper, B. (1986). Fatigue. In V. Carrieri, A. Lindsey, & C. West (Eds.), *Pathophysiological phenomena in nursing: Human responses to illness* (pp. 219–234). Philadelphia: WB Saunders.

Piper, B., Lindsey, A., Dodd, M., Ferketich, S., Paul, S., & Weller, S. (1989). The development of an instrument to measure the subjective dimension of fatigue. In S. Funk, E. Tornquist, M. Champagne, L. A. Copp, & R. Wiese (Eds.), *Key aspects of comfort: Management of pain, fatigue and nausea* (pp. 199–208). New York: Springer Publishing.

Potempa, K., Lopez, M., Reid, C., & Lawson, L. (1986). Chronic fatigue. *Image: Journal of Nursing Scholarship, 18,* 165–169.

Putt, A. (1978). *General systems theory applied to nursing.* Boston: Little Brown.

Rhoten, D. (1982). Fatigue and the postsurgical patient. In C. Norris (Ed.), *Concept clarification in nursing* (pp. 277–300). Rockville, MD: Aspen Systems.

Ryden, M. (1977). Energy: A crucial consideration in the nursing process. *Nursing Forum, 16,* 71–82.

Spergel, P., Ehrlich, G., & Glass, D. (1978). The rheumatoid arthritic personality: A psychodiagnostic myth. *Psychosomatics, 19,* 79–86.

Srivastava, R. H. (1989). Fatigue in end-stage renal disease. In S. Funk, E. Tronquist, M. Champagne, L. A. Copp, & R. Wiese (Eds.), *Key aspects of comfort: Management of pain, fatigue and nausea* (pp. 217–284). New York: Springer Publishing.

Stein, M., Wallston, K., & Nicassio, P. (1988). Factor structure of the Arthritis Helplessness Index. *Journal of Rheumatology, 15,* 427–432.

Stein, M., Wallston, K., Nicassio, P., & Castner, N. (1988). Correlates of a clinical classification schema for the arthritis helplessness subscale. *Arthritis and Rheumatism, 31,* 876–881.

Swanson, B., Cronin-Stubbs, D., & Sheldon, J. (1989). The impact of psychosocial factors on adapting to physical disability: A review of the research literature. *Rehabilitation Nursing, 14,* 64–68.

Swartz, F. (1970). The rehabilitation process as viewed from the inside. *Rehabilitation Literature, 31,* 203–204.

Tobe, R. (1978). Anemia. In C. Leitch and R. Tinker (Eds.), *Primary care.* Philadelphia: FA Davis.

Wegener, S., & Kulp, C. S. (1988). Fatigue and sleep disturbance in arthritis. In J. Sands & J. Matthews (Eds.), *A guide to arthritis home health care* (pp. 185–205). New York: John Wiley & Sons.

Wiener, C. (1975). The burden of rheumatoid arthritis: Tolerating the uncertainty. *Social Science and Medicine, 9,* 97–104.

Williams, R. L., & Krasnoff, A. G. (1964). Body image and physiological patterns in patients with peptic ulcers and rheumatoid arthritis. *Psychosomatic Medicine, 26,* 708.

Winslow, E. H., Lane, L. D., & Gaffney, F. A. (1985). Oxygen uptake and cardiovascular responses in control adults and acute myocardial infarction patients during bathing. *Nursing Research, 34,* 164–169.

Yoshitake, H. (1978). Three characteristic patterns of subjective fatigue symptoms. *Ergonomics, 14,* 175–186.

Zeitlin, D. (1977). Psychological issues in the management of rheumatoid arthritis. *Psychosomatics, 18,* 7–14.

■

Adjustment, Coping Resources, and Care of the Patient with Multiple Sclerosis
■ DEBRA HASTINGS

Considered to be the number one health problem in the United States, chronic illness is actually a twentieth century phenomenon. Approximately 14 percent of the United States population are limited in activity to some degree because of chronic conditions (National Center for Health Statistics, 1985; 1986; 1987). Prior to this century, illness was generally acute in nature and limited in duration. Improved medical technology has resulted in gains over acute illnesses which were once fatal. As a result, society contains larger proportions of aging individuals, and the effects of chronic illness continue to increase (Brooks & Matson, 1982; Dimond, 1983; Forsyth, Delaney, & Gresham, 1984).

Multiple sclerosis (MS) is the most predominant of the human demyelinating diseases. It is the most common severe neurologic disease of young adults, attacking men and women in their productive years while they are planning for and participating in activities involving the major aspects of their present and future lives such as the selection of their life work and the consideration of marriage and family planning. It is a chronic degenerative demyelinating disease which is sometimes progressive and oftentimes unpredictable in its course. It attacks the central nervous system (CNS) and can have crippling effects upon such vital functions as mobility and balance, vision, speech, coordination, cognitive and emotional abilities, and bowel and bladder control. Like many other chronic diseases, it is characterized by periods of remissions and exacerbations.

Because of increased technology and better supportive care, persons with MS now live longer than before, and individuals in the community and long-term care facilities can be found coping with the effects of this chronic illness for 30 years or more (Kelly & Mahon, 1988). Therefore, nurses in a variety of clinical settings may come in contact with individuals afflicted with MS. Since MS strikes during the productive years and can be expected to continue over the course of a lifetime, a special challenge is presented to nurses in all settings. The chronic aspects of this disease stress the need for care that cuts across varied settings and includes the maintenance of physical, psychologic, social (Catanzaro, 1980), and spiritual health. Symptom evaluation and management with appropriate referrals are needs of the chronically ill. The physiologic, social, spiritual, and behavioral responses of the person to the illness are essential components of nursing care.

This chapter will be presented in three sections. An overview of MS is included in Section 1. In Section 2 adjustment to chronic illness and related research, including the results of this author's recently completed study on adjustment to MS, will be discussed. A case study along with appropriate nursing diagnoses and interventions, utilizing the Neuman Systems Model (Neuman, 1989), is described in Section 3. Neuman's model is a comprehensive systems-based conceptual framework for nursing.

Section I: An Overview of Multiple Sclerosis

PATHOLOGY

Multiple sclerosis is a disease of inflammation and degeneration of myelin with relative sparing of the axon. Myelin, which is derived from oligodendroglia that surround nerve axons in a winding process, functions to control the passage of ions on which the transmission of nerve impulses depend and also serves as insulation. Therefore, myelin is responsible for the speed of nerve impulse conduction. Demyelination is responsible for the conduction failure representative of MS. Complete conduction failure is related to severe demyelination, where slow and intermittent conduction indicates less complete destruction of myelin.

The characteristic pathologic feature of MS is the occurrence of irregularly shaped plaques of demyelination, both active and sclerotic, in the cerebellum, white matter of the brain, cranial nerves and spinal cord, the optic nerves, and around the third and fourth ventricles. Recent lesions show partial or complete degeneration of myelin and perivascular infiltration with lymphocytes and other mononuclear cells, suggestive of the inflammatory process. Areas of inflammation that interrupt the myelin occur in unpredictable patchy distributions which can be as tiny as a pin point. Brief exacerbations followed by complete remissions in 2 or 3 weeks are thought to indicate early inflammatory depression of neurotransmission without irreversible myelin destruction.

Long-standing lesions, caused by repeated and progressive attacks and the resultant inflammation, are hard, sclerotic plaques that exhibit no inflammatory reaction. Chronic lesions appear gray and shrunken, and myelin has been removed by phagocytosis, with the degree of myelin loss being dependent upon severity of the inflammation. Axis cylinders are lessened in number, and there is a lack of cellularity and a marked gliosis.

While the axons are usually preserved, especially in the early stages of the disease, there may be some axonal degeneration in severe, long-standing MS. When axons do become involved, secondary degeneration of the wallerian type takes place in the long tracts of the spinal cord (Pallett & O'Brien, 1985; Schneitzer, 1978; Slater & Yearwood, 1980; Sutherland, 1986).

PREVALENCE

It is estimated that there are about 250,000 persons with MS in this country. The prevalence of the illness in some areas of the United States is as high as one per 1000. The prevalence may be higher including incidental cases diagnosed at postmortem examination (Franklin & Burks, 1985). Multiple sclerosis occurs most frequently in people between the ages of 15 and 50, with its onset generally occurring between the ages of 20 and 40 (Holland, McDonnell, & Wiesel-Levison, 1981; Slater & Yearwood, 1980). According to Kritchevsky (1988) the mean age of onset is 33 years with the mean age of diagnosis being 37 years. The disease rarely appears before the age of 10, and approximately 10 percent of cases begin after the age of 50.

While the disease strikes both sexes, females may be affected as often as two times that of males, while whites are affected twice as often as blacks, with an insignificant distribution among other racial groups. Individuals of northern European ancestry are at greater risk of contracting MS, possibly due to immunogenetic factors (Holland, Wiesel-Levison, & Madonna, 1984; Slater & Yearwood, 1980).

One of the more puzzling aspects of MS is its uneven geographic distribution, as there is a wide prevalence of MS (30 to 80 cases per 100,000 population) in the northern, temperate zones in North America and Europe, especially above the 40th north parallel, as well as in the southern portions of New Zealand and Australia. It occurs less frequently in countries near the equator (Franklin & Burks, 1985; Whitaker, 1983). It is felt that geographic locale is significant until age 15. Movement after this age does not alter the risk factors (Holland et al., 1981).

ETIOLOGY

While the specific cause of MS is not known, there are several schools of thought as to why an individual develops the disease. One theory is that MS is caused by a slow viral infection acquired in late childhood or early adolescence, with a long interval or latency period before clinical symptoms manifest themselves. Exposure to this viral agent in early life leads to the formation of protective antibodies and immunity. The resultant reinfection or infection in adult life depends upon genetic vulnerability or the possibility of exposure to an overwhelming infection (Schneitzer, 1978; Sutherland, 1986; Whittington, 1983).

While MS is neither contagious nor hereditary, a familial tendency to develop MS has been noted, without the confirmation of any true genetic pattern. Although there is a twelve- to twentyfold increase in the frequency of MS among first-degree relatives of the MS victim, the genetic effect manifests itself as one that will increase the predisposition for acquisition rather than supporting a definite pattern of inheritance. It is felt that this predisposition may indicate exposure to shared environmental factors. In addition, recent studies of the distribution of histocompatability antigen (HLA) genetic marker in MS patients disclosed an overrepresentation of A3, B7, and Dw2 types. In Europe, North America, and Australia HLA-A3 and HLA-B7 and related antigens Dw2 and DR2 occur in a large proportion of MS patients and their relatives, while the frequency of HLA-Dw2 and DR2 individuals is much less common in a control population and in ethnic groups in whom MS is less common. However, the exact relationship of these factors to the etiology of the illness is not as yet known (Holland et al., 1981; Kritchevsky, 1988; Pallett & O'Brien, 1985; Sutherland, 1986; Whitaker, 1983).

Immune and autoimmune responses are being explored as illness etiologies. It is felt that the disease process may result from an antigen-antibody reaction, immune response to a previous illness, or an immune process (Holland et al., 1981). Sutherland (1986) notes that an abnormality of cerebrospinal fluid (CSF) immunoglobulins has been found in the majority of MS patients. Gamma globulin is increased, while the proportion of the total protein which consists of IgG is increased. Following electrophoresis, diffuse protein bands (the oligoclonal pattern) occur in the gamma globulin region. However, investigation of the general immune status of persons with MS has not shown a consistent blood abnormality, although when more sensitive tests are used, regulatory lymphocytes (cells that promote an immune response or suppress it) have been found to be abnormal (Whitaker, 1983).

According to Morgante, Madonna, and Pokoluk (1989) recent research has implicated a retrovirus in the disease process, precisely, HTLV-1. However, they state that further study is needed to substantiate this finding, which may someday facilitate an effective treatment for the illness.

DIAGNOSIS

A medical diagnosis of MS is usually based on the presenting history and physical examination as there is no specific diagnostic test for MS. The physician usually makes the diagnosis when there is evidence of multiple lesions in time and space. Table 10–1 presents formal diagnostic criteria that have been proposed to aid in establishing a diagnosis of MS. However, the vast symptomatology exhibited by those individuals who present for diagnosis make it necessary to first rule out various other neurologic disorders such as tumors and vascular and degenerative diseases.

Establishing a diagnosis can be both difficult and frustrating for the patient and clinician. In the early stages of the disease, symptoms are often transient, lasting not just hours or days, but sometimes only minutes. They may be bizarre and are often dismissed as irrelevant by both the patient and physician.

Some patients do not exhibit symptoms that meet the diagnostic criteria, and for others, symptoms may be obvious but neurologic deficits minimal. Diagnostic testing for these individuals may be helpful. According to Franklin and Burks (1985) the tests that most often serve as important diagnostic adjuncts are evoked potential testing and CSF evaluation. Patients are frequently given a lumbar puncture to obtain spinal fluid as almost all people with MS exhibit an increase in antibody (IgG). Eighty-five percent of patients with clinically definite MS have abnormal oligoclonal bands in the IgG zone on CSF electrophoresis (Davison, 1982; Kritchevsky, 1988). Other CSF abnormalities include (1) an elevated total protein, (2) increased white blood cells, (3) an abnormal colloidal gold curve, and (4) the presence of IgM (Fischbach, 1988; Holland et al., 1981; Thompson, McFarland, Hirsch, Tucker, & Bowers, 1989).

Evoked potentials are computer-averaged electrical impulses that permit measurement of the rate of nerve impulse transmission through the CNS. Slowed conduction in the visual, auditory, or somatosensory pathway is evidence for the presence of demyelination in that tract even

TABLE 10 ■ 1 Proposed Diagnostic Criteria for the Diagnosis of MS

1. Neurologic examination must reveal objective abnormalities that can be attributed to dysfunction of the CNS
2. Examination or case history must supply evidence that two or more parts of the CNS are involved
3. Evidence of CNS disease must predominantly reflect involvement of white matter
4. Involvement of the neuraxis must have followed one of two time patterns:
   (*a*) Two or more episodes of worsening, each lasting 24 hours or more, and each a month or more apart
   (*b*) Slow or stepwise progression of signs and symptoms over at least 6 months
5. At onset, the patient must be from 10 to 50 years old
6. A physician competent in clinical neurology should decide that the patient's condition could not be better explained on the basis of some other disease

Source: Adapted from Holland et al.(1981); Poser (1983); and Schneitzer (1978).

without the presence of associated symptomatology. For example, the evoked visual response tests the rate of the visual signal from eye to brain. An abnormal finding would be a delayed blink reflex. The test is most valuable in identifying clinically silent lesions. If all three tests are performed, nearly 80 to 85 percent of patients with a clinically definite diagnosis will have an abnormality on at least one of the tests (Franklin & Burks, 1985; Kritchevsky, 1988; Slater & Yearwood, 1980).

Other diagnostic tools include the use of computerized axial tomography (CAT) scan and magnetic resonance (MR) imaging. CAT scanning displays a sectional x-ray of the brain tissue, and increased concentrations of the contrast medium used for the test appear in the areas of demyelination. The test may show ventricular enlargement and cerebral atrophy with long-term disease, and areas of low attenuation around cerebral ventricles. However, this test does not provide information about the cause of the lesions, and only 20 percent of patients with clinically definite disease will have CAT scan abnormalities (Kritchevsky, 1988; Whittington, 1983; Wierenga, 1986).

Magnetic resonance imaging of the brain and spinal cord may be especially valuable as unsuspected abnormalities can be detected, especially those in the periventricular area and the brain stem, and other CNS disease disorders which may mimic MS can be excluded. The test frequently shows characteristic MS lesions within the white matter of the CNS and may demonstrate a second lesion, making MS the probable diagnosis (Davison, 1982; Kritchevsky, 1988).

SIGNS AND SYMPTOMS

The signs and symptoms of MS are related to the areas of demyelination and duration of the lesion, and since demyelination may occur anywhere in the CNS, the patient may manifest a variety of signs and symptoms. The lesions of MS may be located almost anywhere in the white matter of the CNS neuraxis, which includes the white matter of the cerebral hemispheres, optic nerves, brain stem, cerebellum, and spinal cord. The symptoms of MS can mimic those of stroke or tumors, and the sometimes bizarre and transient nature of the symptoms may be mistaken for a psychiatric disorder. While some individuals present with evidence of widespread disease from the onset, others may present with isolated focal involvement (Kritchevsky, 1988).

According to Gulick (1989), signs of the illness have been categorized into eight neurologic functional systems. Table 10–2 presents these signs and symptoms.

CLINICAL COURSE AND PROGNOSIS

Multiple sclerosis in and of itself is almost never a cause of death. On the average, those individuals with MS survive for 35 years after the onset

TABLE 10 ■ 2   Eight Categories of Neurologic Functional Systems and Their
Related Signs and Symptoms

System	Signs and Symptoms
Pyramidal	Positive Babinski, paralysis of one or more limbs, stiffness, weakness, paralysis, fatigue
Cerebellar	Intention tremor, hypotonia in any limb with truncal ataxia and broad-based gait, dizziness, clumsiness, slurred speech
Brainstem and cranial nerves III to XII	Weakness in facial structures, nystagmus, diplopia, scanning speech
Sensory	Disruptions in touch, vibratory, and position sense including numbness, tingling, pins and needles
Bowel/bladder	Hesitancy, urgency, frequency, urinary and/or bowel retention
Visual/optic	Blurred vision and visual field defects as central or paracentral scotoma (Pallett & O'Brien, 1985)
Mental/cerebral	Depression, memory loss, disorientation
Miscellaneous	Includes those not mentioned above such as seizures, aphasias, spasticity

Source: Adapted from Gulick (1989).

of illness. While the course of the disease can be unpredictable, there are certain patterns in which the course of the disease can fit. About 20 percent of the cases fall into the *benign* form which is characterized by few, mild, early attacks and complete or nearly complete clearing. Twenty-five percent of the cases are classified as *exacerbating-remitting* that exhibit more frequent early attacks with less complete clearing. Roughly 40 percent of the cases are of the *chronic-relapsing* type, characterized by fewer and less complete remissions after attacks and by disability which is cumulative and more significant than the other types mentioned above. The *chronic-progressive* form has a more insidious onset with a course that is slowly progressive without remissions and that is seen in about 15 percent of the cases. A small proportion of MS patients develop an acute form of the illness that progresses rapidly with incomplete remissions of short duration. This type of MS can be fatal within a few months or years, and it is mainly a result of severe brainstem disease, especially pertaining to the medulla (Scheinberg, 1983; Wierenga, 1986).

While 50 percent of those with MS will be employed 10 years after diagnosis, by 20 years after diagnosis, only 30 percent will remain employed (Slater & Yearwood, 1980). If the disease shortens the life span, it is usually a result of infection affecting the lungs, urinary tract, or skin due to the paralyzed state (Pallett & O'Brien, 1985; Scheinberg, 1983).

TREATMENT MODALITIES

There is no specific preventive or curative treatment for MS, so efforts must focus on supportive therapeutic measures (Slater & Yearwood,

1980). Like the disease itself, treatment efforts are very frustrating because the cause of MS is not known, and one can only guess as to the mechanism of tissue damage. There are, however, various treatment modalities that may be used to ease the symptoms or shorten an exacerbation. All the treatment approaches center around an attempt to stabilize the MS patient who is advancing through different manifestations of the ongoing disease process (Holland et al., 1981).

Scheinberg and Geisser (1983) divide treatment regimens into four categories:

1. Pharmacologic: Includes the use of steroids and corticotropin, thought to be useful in decreasing the severity and duration of exacerbations in certain cases. Used only on a short-term basis because of their potent side effects, they do not seem to have an effect on long-term outcome (Franklin & Burks, 1985). Immunosuppressive medications such as azathioprine (Imuran) and cyclophosphamide (Cytoxan) comprise another mode of treatment, but they cause side effects such as bone marrow depression, bleeding due to reduced platelet counts, and various gastrointestinal problems (Whittington, 1983). Other medications used to treat the various symptoms of MS include baclofen (Lioresal) and diazepam (Valium) for spasticity; oxybutynin (Ditropan) and propantheline (Pro-Banthine) for bladder dysfunction; and tricyclic antidepressants such as amitriptyline (Elavil) for depression.
2. Surgical treatment: May consist of cutting nerves or tendons to decrease spasticity.
3. Physical therapy: To maintain muscle tone and strength.
4. Psychologic treatment: Includes individual counseling, support group membership, and peer support.

NURSING DIAGNOSES

Using grounded theory methodology, Gould (1983) discovered that the most frequently occurring nursing diagnosis in 15 persons with MS was self-esteem disturbance related to altered body image (occurring in seven subjects in the sample). Other frequently occurring diagnoses were (1) self-care deficit level I: bathing, (2) social isolation related to impaired mobility, (3) potential ineffective family coping, and (4) sleep pattern disturbance related to anticipatory grieving.

Kelly and Mahon (1988) identified a variety of nursing diagnoses based upon the pathophysiology and psychosocial ramifications of the illness which include (1) impaired physical mobility related to muscle weakness, (2) alterations in comfort related to physical pain, (3) bowel and bladder incontinence and sexual dysfunction all related to altered nerve innervation, and (4) potential for alterations in individual coping related to multiple stressors.

In addition to a nursing diagnosis framework, two other authors offer different approaches to the care of the MS patient. Cantanzaro (1980) discussed the care of the patient with MS in terms of the American Nurses' Association (ANA) Standards of Nursing Practice as they provide criteria for evaluating the quality of care, regardless of the setting. Gulick (1984) utilized Orem's self-care model as an organizing framework for a case study of an MS patient with the progressive form of the illness which illustrated a number of self-care deficits typically experienced by MS patients and their families.

Further explication of nursing diagnoses along with appropriate interventions and outcomes specific to the MS patient, organized by a systems nursing framework, will be explored in the case study presented in Section 3 of this chapter.

The next section of this chapter will explore the concepts of psychosocial adjustment to chronic illness, and more specifically, adjustment to MS. Because of the unpredictability of MS, including (1) the potential for remissions and exacerbations, (2) variability in symptomatology, (3) the lack of a known cause, and (4) the disturbing knowledge that there is no cure, adaptation to MS can be difficult and frustrating. A working knowledge of these phenomena is important for the nursing practitioner who is responsible for providing professional care in conjunction with the planning and implementation of appropriate and strategic nursing interventions.

Section 2: Adaptation to Chronic Illness

When individuals are diagnosed as having a chronic and/or disabling illness, they go through a process of adapting to a disease that can be fraught with unpredictability, remissions, and exacerbations. Adaptation is a complex process varying from one illness to another and is influenced by both internal and external factors ranging across the biologic, psychologic, interpersonal, and sociocultural spheres of life. While life demands for the chronically ill remain the same, or are greater than before the onset of the illness, the capacity to respond in a satisfying way is often diminished (Dimond, 1979; 1983; Pollock, 1986).

Various definitions or conceptualizations of adaptation are noted in the literature (Derogatis & Lopez, 1983; Mechanic, 1977). The following conceptualization offered by Feldman (1974) (referred to as readaptation) is appropriate for nursing's holistic focus. Readaptation presupposes the ability of the individual to reach a high level of wellness through the use of positive dependency, that is, relying upon others appropriately while honestly accepting one's differences and the special needs and conditions the illness imposes:

> . . . coming to terms existentially with the reality of chronic illness as a state of being, discarding both false hope and destructive hopelessness, restructuring the environment in which one must now function. Most importantly, readaptation demands the reorganization and acceptance of the self so that there is a meaning and purpose to living that transcends the limitations imposed by the illness (p. 290).

The intrusion of a chronic and disabling illness is a significant life crisis, posing a major challenge (Feldman, 1974). The salient features of chronic illness, including its long-term nature, uncertainty, expense, and the proportionately greater efforts at palliation; the associated problem such as symptom control, preventing and/or living with social isolation, and the prevention and management of medical crises; in addition to the unpredictable dilemmas of symptom exacerbation, failure of therapy, and physical deterioration despite adherence to the prescribed regimen, result in a lack of control in all its aspects. These factors counteract successful adaptation to illness (Miller, 1983; Strauss et al., 1984).

Individuals with MS may experience feelings of powerlessness due to any of these factors in addition to (1) multiple and unpredictable symptomatology, (2) inability to perform own self-care, (3) forced dependency on others, (4) difficulty in establishing a definitive diagnosis, including anxiety related to the diagnostic process, and (5) the possibility of giving up a career.

The factors that may precipitate powerlessness among persons with MS, along with other attributes of the disease can also potentiate poor illness adjustment. Difficulty with adjustment to MS has been substantiated. Surridge (1969) found 25 percent of a sample of 108 MS patients to be depressed. In a sample of 30 MS patients Whitlock and Siskind (1980) noted that these subjects manifested more depression before and since their illness onset as compared with a group of 30 patients experiencing other neurologic afflictions with a similar degree of disability. Gould (1983) also noted the existence of emotional disturbances in 15 MS patients, while Hart (1978) found that in samples of 335 MS patients and 39 healthy subjects, a greater percentage of the MS group experienced anxiety, nervousness, and emotional stress. Harper, Harper, Chambers, Cino, and Singer (1986) noted that a sample of 301 MS patients had significantly lower states of health than comparison groups in terms of (1) physical activity, (2) social health, (3) emotional health, and (4) perceived quality of life. Tan (1986) found that 37 adult MS patients had difficulties in emotional and interpersonal adjustment and in overall psychosocial functioning as compared to 68 epileptics and 42 healthy adults.

MODELS OF ADAPTATION TO MS

It is apparent that adapting to and living with MS can be difficult. As with any of the chronic illnesses, the adjustment process itself can be lengthy, perhaps compounded by the psychologic implications of the disease. Matson and Brooks (1977) developed a model of adaptation to MS based upon their study of the social-psychologic adjustment of 174 MS patients. The stages of adaptation included (1) denial, (2) resistance, (3) affirmation, and (4) integration. In the stage of *integration,* which is lengthy and must be reestablished with each exacerbation, the patient is spending energy on matters other than health and can find certain beneficial aspects of the situation, such as a deeper sensitivity to life's experience.

LaRocca, Kalb, and Kaplan (1983) outlined four stages MS patients follow in the process of adjustment. The first stage is that of *uncertainty* which may predominate after the symptoms first appear and before a diagnosis is made. The person may feel nervous and confused, and since establishing a diagnosis may take an indefinite period of time, this stage can be lengthy. However, because of the nature of the illness, uncertainty never ends. Once the diagnosis has been made, the patient will go through the stage of *acceptance,* where feelings such as shock, disbelief, denial, and confusion may be experienced. Acceptance is difficult as it means coming to grips with forced change due to loss which is both painful and upsetting. Once acceptance has begun, and some degree of change has started to take place, *adaptation* will begin. Reactions may include shifts in self-concept and body image, anger, and depression. The task of this stage is the preservation of one's quality of life while being able to incorporate the physical, psychologic, and social changes brought about by the illness into everyday life. The patient tackles the most critical emotional task involved in adjustment: grieving, such as for lost abilities and experiences. Eventually the disease is successfully woven into the facets of everyday life. Once the necessary adjustments take place, *emergence* can begin where there is a lessening of nervousness and anger and a widening of perspective. The major task to be accomplished is to place the illness in perspective as one carries on with everyday life. The physical, emotional, and social changes that have been required have been met and integrated as much as possible into the person's life-style. Adaptation is ongoing and lifelong, requiring constant investments of energy to keep life changes and a sense of self intact.

COPING RESOURCES: FACTORS INFLUENCING ADAPTATION TO CHRONIC ILLNESS

Adaptation to MS has been shown to be influenced by such factors as duration of disease (Matson & Brooks, 1977), physical dysfunction, stressful life events, and marital status (Zeldow & Pavlou, 1984). Coping resources are important to a person's response to the diagnosis of a chronic illness and its subsequent treatment. Three coping resources that have been noted in the literature to have a significant impact on adjustment to chronic illness and are congruent with nursing's holistic framework are spirituality, hope, and social support.

Spirtuality

Colliton (1981) defines spirituality as "the life principle that pervades a person's entire being, including volitional, emotional, moral-ethical, intellectual, and physical dimensions, and generates a capacity for transcendent values" (p. 492). It can be perceived in terms of personal views and behaviors that signify a sense of relatedness to a transcendent dimension or to something greater than oneself. Spiritual transcendence emphasizes an openness to a perceived environment that goes beyond its spatial and temporal boundaries (Reed, 1987).

While spirituality can be viewed as a human need defined in terms of a search for meaning and purpose in life (Sims, 1987), it also encompasses the need for love and relatedness, and the need for forgiveness (Shelly & Fish, 1988). According to Shelly and Fish (1988):

> . . . a person who knows God's forgiveness can be at peace with God, himself and other people. He has a new awareness of God as his Father who gives life meaning and purpose. He can also experience God's love, which will in turn enable him to love God, himself and others (p. 53).

Spirituality goes beyond the boundaries of organized religion. However, according to Ruffing-Rahal (1984) religion is the principal aspect of spiritual experience and is "an institutional haven of strength, serenity, and faith against life crises" (p. 12), while O'Brien (1982b) states that most of humankind has had spiritual needs met through the functions of organized religion.

According to Soeken and Carson (1987) nursing's holistic perspective views the patient as a balance of mind, body, and spirit, with each dimension affecting or being affected by the others. The spiritual dimension can be viewed as the unifying force that integrates all the other dimensions of the human. The crises brought on by chronic illness may cause impaired functioning of mind-body-spirit systems (Miller, 1985; Soeken & Carson, 1987). The impaired functioning of these integrated systems can result in spiritual distress, a disruption of one's spiritual well-being.

As the wholeness of body or mind can be considered a state of well-being, the wholeness of one's spirit can then be considered spiritual well-being (Soeken & Carson, 1987). Spiritual well-being is a "sense of harmonious interconnectedness between self, others, nature, and Ultimate Other, which exists throughout and beyond time and space" (Hungelmann, Kenkel-Rossi, Klassen, & Stollenwerk, 1989, p. 394). Spiritual well-being has been viewed as the cornerstone of health that enables holistic integration of a person's inner resources (Stuart, Deckro, & Mandle, 1989). Persons who have spiritual health have (1) an inner state of peace and joy, (2) freedom from abnormal anxiety and guilt, and (3) a sense of security and direction in the quest for life's goals and activities (O'Brien, 1982b).

Chronic illness can have either a detrimental or a positive effect on one's spiritual well-being. Because of the uncertainty and long-term nature of a chronic illness, in addition to the potential for certain illness outcomes such as pain and alteration in body image, the disruption of a patient's once healthy spiritual state may occur. Some individuals find themselves turning away from God as they are unable to comprehend the occurence of their illness and have difficulty finding meaning and purpose in life. On the other hand, many individuals seek strength and comfort from their relationship with the Lord and may find that the illness has enhanced the quality of this relationship. Others who have never sought a relationship with God or who previously turned away from the Lord find themselves seeking a spiritual life.

While there has been little research in the area of spirituality and spiritual well-being and adjustment as it relates to chronic illness, several studies attest to the importance of this relationship. O'Brien (1982a) found religious faith to be a variable of importance to illness-related and treatment-related adjustment in a sample of 126 chronic dialysis patients, while Miller (Chapter 2) found prayer and faith to be the second most frequent coping strategy used by a sample of 56 chronically ill adults. Thirty-one women receiving their initial chemotherapy course for breast cancer were studied by Brandt (1987) who found a statistically significant negative relationship between hopelessness and religious beliefs. Those women who perceived their spiritual beliefs as helpful in coping tended to have lower levels of hopelessness. Sodestrom and Martinson (1987) interviewed 25 nurses and 25 oncology patients to ascertain their perspectives on patients' spiritual strategies and found that of 96 percent of patients who professed a religious affiliation, 88 percent found their meaning and purpose in life through their belief in and relationship with God. A significant relationship between hope and coping in 120 adult cancer patients was found by Herth (1989) who also found that strength of religious convictions was significantly related to the variables of hope and coping.

Only one MS adjustment study discussed spirituality and adjustment to MS (Matson & Brooks, 1977). Based upon a sample of 174 adults with MS, religion was found to be a highly rated coping strategy, and several subjects gave several insightful comments such as, "God will not give us a cross heavier than we can bear. Either you survive or you succumb. If you survive, you profit from the experience" (p. 248). The researchers concluded that using religion was a common and effective way of adjusting to the disease and that the illness had afforded some subjects the time to get in touch with the more essential values.

Hope

Slater and Yearwood (1980) state that because of the complex elements in the coping process of MS patients, health professionals must be able to thwart a natural tendency toward depression and negativism in patients and family. Optimizing the belief that someone cares and that there is *hope* for a return of self-esteem and self-control are fundamental to the management of MS

Hope is an essentially positive phenomenon necessary for healthy coping whose key purpose is the avoidance of despair (Korner, 1970). It can be thought of as a complex human experience; a mixture of feelings and thoughts that center on the fundamental belief that there are solutions to important human needs and problems (Lange, 1978). The opposite end of the hope continuum is hopelessness. It is a sense of the impossible; what one wants to do is beyond reach. There are feelings that life is too much to handle, and a person may feel a sense of overwhelming defeat or loss of control over oneself. There may also be feelings of intense despair and futility (Lange, 1978; Roberts, 1978; Schneider, 1980).

To inspire hope is an acknowledged part of nursing care. Stoner (1982) stated that nursing authors have written more about hope and have possibly done more to describe and define hope than have other health professionals.

Craig and Edwards (1983) note that the preservation of a sense of hope is essential for the chronically ill in the face of an uncertain future, and Miller in Chapter 2 classifies the maintenance of hope despite uncertainty or a downward illness course as a coping task or challenge. While illness can be viewed as a crisis situation leading to a state of despair, at the same time the situation can also provide conditions for hope. Hope nurtures a person's transition from being weak and vulnerable to that of functioning or living as fully as possible. Hope allows a person to utlize a crisis as an opportunity for growth (Miller, 1985).

A relationship between health and/or illness and hope has been noted in the literature. Forsyth and coworkers (1984) interviewed 50 hospitalized chronically ill adults and found that they fought to maintain hope and the feeling that they were winning over the disease by adopting specific attitudes that convinced them that they were not helpless victims of the illness. Rideout and Montemuro (1986) studied 23 patients with congestive heart failure and found that those individuals who were more hopeful maintained their involvement with life. Baldree, Murphy, and Powers (1982) and Gurklis and Menke (1988) found hope to be a highly rated coping strategy used by two samples of hemodialysis patients, while Brockopp, Hayko, Davenport, and Winscott (1989) found significant correlations between perceived level of control and eight issues related to hope and information seeking in 56 adult cancer patients. There were no studies found in the literature which examined hope and adjustment in relation to MS.

Social Support

Interest in social support has escalated since the 1970s as noted by the increased amount of research and the number of disciplines studying the concept. Several reasons for this interest are (1) its possible role in the etiology of disease and illness, (2) the role it may play in the rehabilitation and treatment of illness, and (3) the function it may have in helping with the conceptual integration of the literature regarding psychosocial factors and illness (Cohen & Syme, 1985).

Social support is actually a set of concepts or a multidimensional construct. It can be viewed as "resources provided by others" (Cohen & Syme, 1985, p. 4) or individuals as interpersonal resources who provide gratification of basic human needs in relationships (Hubbard, Muhlenkamp, & Brown, 1984). Weiss (1974) conceptualized social support as six categories of relational provisions: (1) attachment, (2) social integration, (3) opportunity for nurturance, (4) reassurance of worth, (5) a sense of reliable alliance, and (6) obtaining guidance.

Sources of support can be formal or informal. Formal sources include professional helpers, and informal sources consist of those such as spouses, friends, and relatives (Tilden, 1986).

Social networks can be defined as the number and types of ties one maintains with others (Gottlieb & Green, 1984), or a subset of persons upon whom one relies for socioemotional, instrumental, or informational aid (Hibbard, 1985). Social networks are viewed from two perspectives: structural, which refers to network links, and functional, which refers to the quality and nature of the links. The structural properties of social networks most appropriate to social support are (1) size, (2) strength of ties, (3) density, (4) homogeneity of membership, (5) dispersion of membership, (6) frequency of contact, (7) multiplexity, (8) ratio of kin to nonkin, and (9) reciprocity of links (Dimond & Jones, 1983).

According to Cohen and Syme (1985) there are two main hypotheses of interest regarding social support and its relationship to health. The buffering hypothesis states that social support protects individuals from the harmful effects of stress. It is felt that increases in the amount of stress places people at risk for illness but that the presence of adequate levels of support should buffer this stress.

The second hypothesis states that support enhances health regardless of the level of stress (Cohen & Syme, 1985). According to Hibbard (1985) social support may actually lessen the likelihood of exposure to stressful events, for example, through group norms and feedback. Individuals with adequate support are more apt to practice positive health behaviors as they receive encouragement or pressure to do so from within their network (Tilden, 1986).

While previous research has shown an association between social support and adjustment to chronic illness (Corbin & Strauss, 1988; Northouse, 1988), several studies have also indicated that a significant relationship exists between social support and adjustment to MS. Crawford and McIvor (1985) studied the benefits of group psychotherapy for MS patients in terms of illness adjustment. Based upon a battery of test results examining depression, anxiety, locus of control, and self-esteem, 41 patients were placed in one of the three following groups: (1) insight-oriented, (2) current events, or (3) control. After 50 sessions, the results indicated that those individuals in the insight-oriented group demonstrated significantly less depression than the others, and both the current events and insight-oriented groups were significantly more internally oriented than the control group. The authors feel this may be due in part to the buffering effects provided by the social support system that may be developed within the group setting.

Fifty adults with MS were studied by Braham, Houser, Cline, and Posner (1975) to assess their social needs (nonmedical support or action). Findings of the study indicated that the greatest number of needs were found in (1) subjects' and spouses' reactions to the illness, (2) the marital relationship, and (3) children's adjustment. Eighteen subjects said they adjusted without any outside help, or with the help of their families, while 34 spouses had needs that were met through their own adjustments or from within or outside the family.

McIvor, Riklan, and Reznikoff (1984) studied depression in a sample of 120 MS patients and noted that the most significant correlation was between severity of depression and perceived social support from family and friends. The more depressed a subject was, the more likely he or she was to perceive little or no social support.

HOPE, SOCIAL SUPPORT, AND ADAPTATION TO MS

Since there were no studies noted in the literature that examined hope and adjustment to MS, and since there is a paucity of research related to social support and MS, a descriptive correlational study was done to determine if there was a relationship between hope and adaptation to MS and between social support and adaptation to MS in a convenience sample of 30 adults (Hastings, 1989). Secondary purposes of the study were to ascertain if the select demographic variables of severity of disability, support group membership, and length of time since diagnosis were related to adaptation, hope, and social support. Pearson product moment correlation coefficients were calculated to see if relationships existed among the variables. An exploratory qualitative component was also utilized to determine patterns or themes that were descriptive of the process of adjustment to MS and to define the factors important to personal adjustment from the patients' own perspectives. Data were collected by tape-recorded interviews that were transcribed verbatim. The data were analyzed using a content analysis, data-reduction approach.

Analysis of the data demonstrated significant negative relationships between adaptation and hope ($r = -.5151$; $p = .002$), and adaptation and social support ($r = -.4186$; $p = .011$). *Lower scores on the adaptation measure indicate more successful adaptation.* Those who have better adaptation have higher levels of hope and perceived social support. In addition, a significant positive relationship was found between hope and social support ($r = .6413$; $p = .000$). A significant negative relationship also existed between adjustment and support group membership ($r = -.4541$; $p = .006$). The more adaptation increased, the more likely it was that subjects would belong to a support group. Other correlations between adaptation, hope, and social support and the demographic variables were not significant.

Analysis of the qualitative data revealed that reactions to the diagnosis of MS ranged from relief to denial, and subjects felt such emotions as fear and sorrow. The work of adaptation was found to be difficult; however, most subjects came to either accept or adapt to the process. Adaptation was described as a continual, daily process which for some had beneficial outcomes but also involved having to pace oneself and make life-style modifications.

Four categories of coping resources emerged from the data: (1) social support resources, (2) religion or faith, (3) inner strengths such as self-determination and a positive attitude, and (4) knowledge about the disease. Support from family and friends was the most important means of assisting with the adaptation process for the sample (Hastings, 1989).

Implications for nursing practice emerged from the study findings. In light of the correlations between hope and adjustment, and social support and adjustment, it is felt that patients could benefit from a more thorough investigation of their hope states and social support resources as part of a routine nursing assessment. Findings from a hope assessment could be used as a basis from which hope-inspiring strategies could be generated. The social support assessment could pinpoint inadequacies or problems in the patient's social support system for which appropriate nursing interventions could be instituted. Understanding the factors that are significant to an individual's illness adaptation will help nurses focus on personal strengths that will facilitate the adjustment process.

The last section of this chapter will present an in-depth case study that deals with adaptation to MS. Nursing assessment and interventions are based upon use of the Neuman Systems Model (Neuman, 1989).

Section 3: Case Study Utilizing the Neuman Systems Model

Ann is a 40-year-old caucasian female, married with two children, ages 10 and 14, who was diagnosed with MS 8 years ago. She was referred to a nurse-managed MS clinic at a large teaching hospital by her physician for evaluation of her inability to adapt to the illness-related disabilities which include progressive upper and lower extremity weakness, intention tremor, and bladder dysfunction. She has also admitted to having difficulty in maintaining a supportive marital relationship.

The clinic utilizes an interdisciplinary holistic framework, with a nurse practitioner as primary care giver and manager as described by Winters, Jackson, Sims, and Magilvy (1989). They state that the uniqueness of this multidisciplinary approach is that a patient has one evaluation conducted concurrently by several professionals who are then able to coordinate their efforts to construct a thorough plan of care. Other health-care professionals include a neurologist, physiatrist, physical therapist, psychologist, and occupational therapist.

Nursing care in the clinic is based upon the Neuman Systems Model, a comprehensive systems-based conceptual framework which, according to the author, "fits well with the wholistic concept of optimizing a dynamic yet stable interrelationship of mind, body, and spirit of the client in a constantly changing environment and society" (Neuman, 1989, p. 10). Based upon the concepts of stress and the reactions to it, the model views the client as a composite of five interacting and interrelated variables: (1) physiologic, (2) psychologic, (3) sociocultural, (4) developmental, and (5) spiritual, ideally existing in harmony with internal and external environmental forces to which the system is subjected to at any given point in time (Neuman, 1989). Environment, both internal and external, therefore, is a critical element of the model. Stressors, which comprise the environment, are either intrapersonal, interpersonal, or extrapersonal (Harris, Hermiz, Meininger, & Steinkeler, 1989). Health is viewed as optimal system stability or the best possible wellness state at a given time, while nursing's major concern is stability of the client system through accurate assessment of actual and potential effects of environmental stressors as well as assisting clients to achieve optimal levels of wellness. Nursing intervention is based upon the point in time at which the stressor is suspected or identified. Intervention typology includes primary, secondary, or tertiary prevention (Neuman, 1989).

NURSING HISTORY

Ann came to the MS clinic for her first appointment with her husband, but he did not participate in the intake interview and waited in another room. The initial interview was done by the nurse practitioner who used Neuman's (1989) assessment and invervention tool to ascertain the perceived patient stressors. The nurse practitioner noted that Ann, a heavy, very well dressed woman, whose hair and makeup were poorly done, entered the room in a motorized wheelchair, and as they began to speak, she noted that the patient had difficulty keeping eye contact with her. The patient stated that her husband was a successful attorney and that she had never had to work, although she held a degree in elementary education. She described her two children as "what I live for. They give me a reason for waking up in the morning."

Stressors as Perceived by the Client

The patient stated that her health status was the major stressor in her life as it has only been within the last year that the disease has had such an impact on her life. Her life-style had completely changed. Until then she was able to ambulate independently, with occasional wheelchair use if she was to walk for long distances. Because of progressive weakness in her legs, she has had to use a motorized wheelchair for the last year while progressive upper extremity weakness and intention tremor have made performance of activities of daily living (ADLs) difficult. She stated, however, that she refuses to have anyone come in to help her with grooming, although she admits to the difficulties her attitude is causing. She must make frequent trips to the bathroom, and transferring has become difficult. Ann admitted to having frequent "accidents" due to her difficulty getting to the toilet.

She stated that her greatest joy in life was caring for her husband and children. Now she is forced to have domestic help for meal preparation and cleaning except for weekends when the family is home. "I've always prided myself on how well I cared for my family and how tidy my house was. Now I can hardly use a feather duster. My daughters are a tremendous help on the weekends. They clean and cook for the family. They've given up many activities to help me out. They want to help me bathe and wash my hair for me, but I can't let them see that their mother can't do this for herself, and I just can't give up everything. They would also see how fat their mother has gotten. I'm so ashamed of myself. I just look terrible." She stated that she was 5 feet 2 inches and weighed 165 pounds. She has had a significant weight gain within the last year since using the wheelchair. "I smell terrible, too, no matter how much I clean myself; the odor from the urine is overwhelming."

The nurse practitioner asked her if she had ever experienced any other significant life events and how she had handled them in the past. Ann stated that her diagnosis of MS was certainly significant but that previously since she did not have the deficits she was now experiencing, she had been able to push problems out of her mind. "If there was nothing tangible, then it did not exist." She did, however, compare this time in her life to the lingering death of her mother of cancer when Ann was 25 years old. While she stated that it was very difficult for her, her main coping strategy was her faith in the Lord and her daily readings from the Bible. When asked if she still had strong religious beliefs, Ann stated that she felt the Lord had deserted her. "While I'm still a Christian, I do not want to go to church. He must be terribly angry with me to have let this happen." When asked what else she does to relieve stress, Ann stated that she'll watch television and eat candy. "I used to go out and work in the garden or call a good friend if something was bothering me. But, what else is there to do when you're in a wheelchair? I have no friends anymore. It's not that they don't want to be friends with me, I just can't do the things that they want to do. Besides, why should they be burdened with a cripple. As least when I eat, I can have something that I choose. Of course, it isn't doing much for my waistline, and watching TV is certainly not productive, but when you're sitting in a wheelchair, what does it matter?"

When asked what she anticipates for the future, Ann laughed. "You're seeing the future sitting before you. This is the future, only it will probably be worse. This situation is hopeless. When you have MS, there is no future."

The nurse practitioner then asked Ann what she was doing to help herself at this time. Ann stated, as she did previously, that caring for her own needs, as difficult as it may be, was the only thing she could do to help herself at this time. "I am not capable of doing anything else." When asked to state what else she felt she could be doing for herself, she said, "As I just told you, I am not capable of doing anything else."

When Ann was asked what she felt others could be doing for her, she replied, "As I said, my children do a lot for me and would do more if I let them. My husband, on the other hand, well, I'm surprised he even came here with me. He's too busy with his clients to do a thing for me. It's the children that help me get into bed and make sure I'm comfortable, not him. He hasn't touched me in a year, not that I can blame him. There's not much I can do in that realm anymore, and, besides, I look so awful now. I think he stays with me out of obligation and for the children's sake. Not that he does much with them, either. Before the MS got so bad, we did everything together as a family. He may be at home with us, but he's really not. Do you know what I mean?"

When the interview was over, the nurse practitioner made a second appointment with Ann so that they could discuss the interview and her other evaluations which would be done this same day and devise a plan of care. The nurse practitioner also asked that Ann's husband be present at the next session. Ann, however, felt that at this time, it would not be a good idea to involve him.

Stressors as Perceived by the Care Giver

After Ann left, the nurse practitioner reviewed the interview data to evaluate her own perception of the client stressors. The nurse agreed with Ann's perception of her declining health status being the major stressor. Several other significant stressors flowed from the pivotal stressor. The client's deteriorating relationship with her husband was seen as significant. It appears that he is unable to adjust to the change in his wife's health status and avoids interactions with her as a way of coping with the situation. His avoidance sets up tensions within the household, and Ann must turn to her children for the support she wants and needs from her husband. His attitude in turn affects her adjustment to the illness.

While Ann's continued pursuit of accomplishing her own self-care needs could be viewed as a strength, the nurse also viewed this as a source of stress since the energy used to complete her ADLs will lead to increased fatigue. The nurse noted a study by Hart (1978) which found that MS patients when fatigued had an accentuation of disease symptoms and greater indications of emotional stress.

Self-esteem and body image were noted to be stressors. The nurse saw that Ann derived the majority of her self-esteem needs from caring for her family and home, and this was no longer possible. Ann mentioned no outside interests during the interview. While the nurse felt Ann saw her altered body image as due to her weight gain, the nurse also saw Ann's body image alteration in terms of her perception of being wheelchair bound and, perhaps, only seeing herself as an extension of the wheelchair. Her decreasing bladder function was also felt to have an effect on her body image perception. All the data pointed to very significant lifestyle changes for both Ann and her family.

According to the client, she was able to cope successfully with her mother's illness and eventual death because of her belief in God. However, she is now experiencing spiritual distress and is unable to utilize this once effective coping mechanism. She apparently has no other means of effective coping, an area which, if Ann is willing, will need improvement.

The nurse felt that Ann was experiencing feelings of hopelessness and powerlessness due to her present situation. Ann's perception of the future is one that someone experiencing feelings of hopelessness would describe; that is, she does not have a future orientation, and what she does see is related to a worsening of the situation. Feelings of powerlessness were apparent in the client's statements regarding her inability to do anything but care for her own needs. She felt inadequate since she was unable to care for her home and family and did not give any suggestion of what else she could do. The nurse thought that the feelings of powerlessness and hopelessness were tied to Ann's level of self-esteem.

Finally, it was evident that Ann expected much more from her husband than he was either willing or capable of giving. In addition, their sexual relationship had completely deteriorated, although it was hard to determine from the client's comments how this situation had evolved. She intimated that she was unable to satisfy his needs in this area but also spoke of his lack of affection toward her.

While Ann only spoke of care givers in terms of family, the nurse felt her perception of outside care givers was important. Since Ann was not willing to accept outside help for her personal needs, the nurse felt that her refusal might be an issue of control. By allowing someone to help with her care, she would be giving up the only control she feels she has over the situation. This would increase her feelings of powerlessness.

Summary of Impressions

After completing her evaluation of client stressors, the nurse wrote her summary of impressions.

Intrapersonal Factors

Physical factors influencing the client situation that were noted by both the nurse and the patient were the progressive MS symptomatology that included progressive lower extremity weakness impeding mobility, progressive upper extremity weakness, intention tremor, and bladder dysfunction impacting achievement of ADLs. The nurse also saw the bladder dysfunction affecting body image and both the lower extremity weakness and bladder dysfunction potentially affecting skin integrity.

Psychosocial evaluation included the nurse's perception of the client's spiritual distress as evidenced by her feelings that God was angry with her. The nurse also felt that the patient utilized ineffective coping mechanisms to deal with stress. The client was in partial agreement when she stated that her eating was affecting her weight.

Developmentally, tasks of this client's age group include (1) acceptance of self and a stabilizing self-concept and body image; (2) establishment of an intimate bond with another; (3) establishment of and management of a home; (4) finding a congenial social group; (5) deciding whether or not to have a family; (6) formulating a meaningful philosophy of life; and (7) becoming established in a vocation or profession that makes one feel that he or she is making a contribution to society (Murray & Zentner, 1979). It was evident to the nurse that the patient was having difficulty achieving some of these developmental tasks.

1. Self-concept and body image were significant problems.
2. Maintaining an intimate spousal relationship was difficult.
3. Ability to maintain the family home was unachievable because of the patient's physical and emotional condition.

4. A supportive social network was not maintained.
5. No vocation has been pursued posteducation, and the client has disclosed that at this point in time, she does not see herself as a productive member of society.
6. Client's philosophy of life is difficult to ascertain since everything seems rooted in the here and now; she sees no future.

As noted earlier, the client is suffering from spiritual distress, which according to Burnard (1987) is the "result of total inability to invest life with meaning" (p. 377) and can be demotivating, painful, and the cause of anguish. The client's feelings of hopelessness and powerlessness may be related to her spiritual distress, as hope is predicated on a belief in God's control over a situation and His ability to support an individual through the crisis. Meaning and purpose in life and in suffering can be found in one's relationship with God and having knowledge of His control. However, this relationship and knowledge cannot provide hope forever without the possibility of a meaningful and purposeful future as hope ultimately depends on the promise of eternal fellowship with the Lord (Shelly & Fish, 1988).

Interpersonal Factors

Interpersonal factors related to the situation include the relationships the client has with both her spouse and daughters. Spousal support has been shown to be a significant factor in adjustment to chronic illness. Strauss and coworkers (1984) note that the most important work that a caring spouse does for the mate who is ill is "psychological" work, that is, those tasks which are basically uncomplicated, such as bolstering spirits to those that involve complex maneuvering (p. 103). Corbin and Strauss (1984; 1988) studied 63 couples managing chronic illness at home and found that those who collaborated in managing the illness felt that they had the internal and external resources to continue the work, no matter what may happen in the course of the illness, and that their relationships had grown even closer from having to work together. Klinger (1984) found that social support was the single most helpful factor in complying with the medical regimen, for 60 postmyocardial infarction patients, with spousal support being cited most often. Dimond (1979) found a positive relationship between spousal support and morale in a study of 36 patients undergoing hemodialysis, and Northouse (1988) found that adjustment to breast cancer was facilitated by higher levels of spousal support in a sample of 50 mastectomy patients.

The difficulty of spousal adjustment as noted in the intake interview correlates with the findings of Braham and coworkers (1975) who found that of 47 MS patients and their families both the subject and the spouse had the most difficulty accepting the disease, and 32 couples had need for help with their marital relationships. Because of the specifics of the disease, perhaps the adjustment needs of MS patients and their spouses are different than those of other chronic illnesses.

The nurse noted as did the client that her children were her main source of support. In the study by Hastings (1989) children were found to be sources of help and encouragement for the MS patient. However, in a qualitative study of three mothers with MS and their daughters, Friedmann and Tubergen (1987) found that while parenting patterns were distinct in each family, all mothers had high expectations of the daughter who was described as the "good" child (p. 47). All three daughters experienced either physical or emotional symptomatology, which suggests the presence of stress within the family. All three daughters were excellent students, which may be a reflection of the children's efforts to live up to their mothers' expectations. This study led the nurse to question further the dynamics of Ann's family.

Extrapersonal Factors

The extrapersonal factors related to Ann's situation and that influence both the intrapersonal and extrapersonal variables were the use of outside agencies and Ann's inability to sustain social relationships. It is evident that by having a home health aide assist Ann with her personal care, less energy would be expended by the patient, leaving her with more time and less fatigue so that perhaps outside interests might be more enticing. The family should also feel a sense of relief knowing that someone would be of assistance, and the daughters may not feel as obligated to help with personal needs. However, the nurse questioned if Ann was ready to give up this source of independence.

Friends have been shown to be significant sources of support. Hastings (1989) found that several persons with MS stated that friends, both those with MS and others, have helped in the adjustment process. McIvor and coworkers (1984) found that a significant correlation existed between severity of depression and perceived social support from family and friends in a sample of 120 MS patients. According to these authors the loss of emotionally significant persons, be it family or friends, apparently adds a further threat to the severe burden of loss of functional ability and knowledge of the presence of MS. This apparently is one more loss Ann is sustaining in addition to the independence she seems to crave.

Nursing Diagnoses

Based upon this assessment, the nurse practitioner decided that since symptomatology was already present, secondary prevention was the appropriate level of intervention. Secondary prevention is aimed at providing treatment of symptoms so that optimal client stability or wellness

TABLE 10 ■ 3   Nursing Diagnoses Appropriate for MS Patient, Ann

Nursing Diagnosis	Etiologies
1. Potential for total self-care deficit	Increased tremor of the upper extremities and weakness of the lower extremities
2. Alteration in urinary elimination	Altered nerve innervation (Kelly & Mahon, 1988)
3. Potential for alteration in skin integrity	Increased immobility and incontinence
4. Potential for injury	Increased lower extremity weakness and upper extremity tremor
5. Self-esteem, low: situational	Inability to accomplish usual homemaking and family tasks
6. Body image disturbance	(*a*) Substantial weight gain, (*b*) difficulty accepting wheelchair confinement, (*c*) bladder dysfunction
7. Spiritual distress	Perception of the Lord's desertion and anger
8. Ineffective individual coping	Inability to utilize past successful coping mechanisms
9. Diversional activity deficit and social isolation	Altered self-concept (seeing self as a cripple and burden)
10. Hopelessness	Inability to perceive any positive outcomes for the future
11. Sexual dysfunction	Altered nerve innervation (Kelly & Mahon, 1988) and dissatisfaction with the marital relationship
12. Powerlessness	Declining physical capabilities leading to the perception of the inability to have control over own life
13. Impaired adjustment	Increasing disability and perceived lack of spousal support
14. Possible ineffective family coping	Spouse's perceived inability to accept wife's declining health (The nurse was not able to speak with the husband who would have been able to assist in validating the diagnosis.)

and energy conservation are attained (Neuman, 1989). Table 10–3 lists the nursing diagnoses which were felt to be appropriate for Ann's situation.

Multidisciplinary Evaluation

When Ann returned for her second visit, she and the members of the interdisciplinary team discussed the results of their respective assessments. It was decided that Ann would come to the clinic two times weekly for physical therapy for upper and lower extremity strengthening exercises to facilitate ADL completion and transferring and to prevent lower extremity contractures, and to see the occupational therapist for help with the fitting and use of adaptive devices and techniques necessary for use because of the intention tremor. The neurologist felt that Ann should see a urologist for urodynamic studies and measurement of postvoiding residual urine to define the type of bladder dysfunction and determine the appropriate therapy (Kritchevsky, 1988). The psychologist suggested that

Ann and her husband begin counseling sessions as a means of helping to strengthen their marital and sexual relationships. At a later date, the children would be included in therapy sessions.

It was felt that it would be more appropriate to have physical and occupational therapy treat the self-care deficit and injury potential while ineffective family coping would be best left to the psychologist. Physical and occupational therapy would also facilitate the avoidance of a disruption in skin integrity. Alteration in urinary elimination would be explored after Ann saw the urologist. Sexual dysfunction would be dealt with after the urology consult and after the psychologist was able to make an evaluation of the couple's progress in counseling. The nurse practitioner would coordinate all efforts by the team.

Nursing Care Plan

The nurse and Ann reviewed the nursing diagnoses and prioritized them in terms of immediate and long-term importance. While all the diagnoses were believed to be significant, it was felt that by resolving hopelessness, spiritual distress, and powerlessness, work on the other diagnoses would be facilitated. The three nursing diagnoses are intricately intertwined with one another as spiritual distress can promote both feelings of hopelessness and powerlessness. Figure 10–1 represents a diagrammed version of holistic nursing assessment and intervention for the MS patient. As noted in Neuman's model (Neuman, 1989) the MS patient is viewed from a systems perspective as an integrated whole being composed of interactive and interrelated components. One can appreciate the reciprocal nature of the assessment and intervention phases as both the client and nurse are integral and active participants in the entire process. In the assessment phase, both the client and nurse identify perceived stressors. After the stressors are identified, both parties collaborate on the actual plan of care.

The following nursing care plan was devised by the nurse, with full acceptance by the client.

Hopelessness

Short-term Goals

The client will be able to list factors promoting feelings of hopelessness.

The client will be able to name personal resources necessary to help inspire hope.

Long-term Goal

The client will successfully integrate and utilize hope-inspiring strategies.

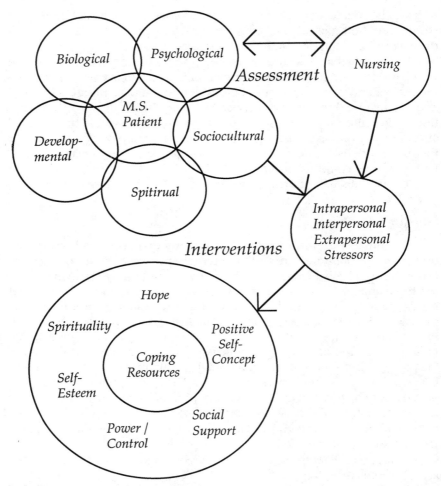

FIGURE 10 ■ 1   A framework for holistic nursing assessment and intervention for care of the MS patient.

Interventions

1. Utilize a life-promoting framework so that the client is viewed as a potentially powerful and productive person with illness being only one facet of personality (Miller, 1985).
2. Help the client to explore those factors that contribute to feelings of hopelessness (Lederer, Marculescu, Mocnik, & Seaby, 1990).
3. Explore in depth the reasons why the above factors are felt to promote hopelessness, and determine those factors that have given the client hope in the past.

4. Facilitate client's use of past successful hope-inspiring mechanisms.
5. Teach reality surveillance, the reconstructing of past events and assigning logic and reasoning to them, so that the client is able to avoid thinking about negative outcomes while looking for clues that affirm the maintenance of hope is possible (Miller, 1985).
6. Assess client for potential success of utilizing relaxation techniques as a means of stress reduction and to facilitate coping so that other hope-inspiring strategies are reinforced.
7. Suggest the use of MS support group membership. Spiegelberg (1980) noted that MS support groups play an important role in allaying fears, helping members to utilize their strengths, and in helping to reach other patients.
8. Based upon the results of the psychologic counseling sessions, potentially include the family relationships as a way of further inspiring hope. According to Miller (1985) one way to inspire hope is through emphasizing to the patient that the presence and hopefulness of his or her sustaining relationships is important, since patient's loved ones have the strongest influence on helping a patient sustain hope.
9. Assist the client to set small, measurable goals so that a future orientation may be established.
10. Integrate interventions from both the spiritual distress and powerlessness nursing diagnoses.

Spiritual Distress

Short-term Goal

The client will verbalize the reasons why chronic illness may precipitate distress of the human spirit.

Long-term Goal

A renewed and more meaningful relationship with the Lord will emerge.

Interventions

1. Perform a thorough spiritual assessment to determine past religious and spiritual practices.
2. Assist the client to examine the consequences of MS, which may arouse feelings of anger and of being abandoned by God.
3. Allow the client to express feelings of anger and abandonment.

4. Facilitate exploration of the client's past relationship with the Lord and how it was successful in helping to manage stress-inducing situations.
5. Explain how a meaningful and purposeful relationship with God can help to maintain feelings of hope and control.
6. Establish the therapeutic use of self by employing listening, empathy, vulnerability, humility, and commitment (Shelly & Fish, 1988).
7. Facilitate the use of prayer and scripture as a means of comfort and support.
8. Integrate appropriate interventions from the hopelessness and powerlessness diagnoses.

Powerlessness

Short-term Goals

The client will identify those factors and situations which precipitate feelings of powerlessness.

The client will actively participate in decision making related to her plan of care.

Long-term Goal

The client will begin to express feelings of control over her present situation and will identify actions that she feels are within her control.

Interventions

1. Collaborate with the other members of the multidisciplinary team to help encourage the client's participation in decision making regarding her plan of care and her own self-care needs, in addition to keeping her informed of her ongoing progress.
2. Encourage the client to express her feelings about her current illness situation facilitating the view of illness as an experience, thereby promoting feelings of personal significance (Roberts, 1978).
3. Once the client is comfortable participating in decision making regarding her care, encourage her to participate in family-related decision making (also considering her progress in counseling).
4. As maintenance of positive self-esteem has been determined to be an area of difficulty, and since positive self-esteem has been noted to be a power resource, utilize strategies to enhance self-esteem such as the promotion of positive self-statements and encouraging positive social experiences

(tying into the problem of social isolation and diversional activity deficit) (Chapter 1).

5. As powerlessness is a factor contributing to overeating, an identified patient problem related to body image, help the client to further explore the reasons for overeating and begin to assist her to establish healthy eating habits.

6. Integrate the appropriate interventions related to the diagnoses of hopelessness and spiritual distress. The maintenance of hope and spiritual well-being both facilitate an empowered state.

Summary

MS and its potential for a downhill trajectory can promote a situation in which a person can feel vulnerable and experience a loss of control. Adjustment to a chronic illness such as MS is a dynamic, complex process influenced by a diverse number of variables, all needing further research. Despite the course that the illness may take, nurses can facilitate adjustment to chronic illness, and specifically MS, through the use of a holistic systems framework and assist the patient toward developing effective coping resources such as hope, spiritual well-being, and social support.

References

Baldree, K. S., Murphy, S. P., & Powers, M. J. (1982). Stress identification and coping patterns in patients on hemodialysis. *Nursing Research, 31,* 107–112.

Braham, S., Houser, H. B., Cline, A., & Posner, M. (1975). Evaluation of the social needs of nonhospitalized chronically ill persons. *Journal of Chronic Diseases, 28,* 401–419.

Brandt, B. T. (1987). The relationship between hopelessness and selected variables in women receiving chemotherapy for breast cancer. *Oncology Nurses Forum, 14,* 35–39.

Brockopp, D. Y., Hayko, D., Davenport, W., & Winscott, C. (1989). Personal control and the needs for hope and information among adults diagnosed with cancer. *Cancer Nursing, 12,* 112–116.

Brooks, N. A., & Matson, R. R. (1982). Social-psychological adjustment to multiple sclerosis. *Social Science and Medicine, 16,* 2129–2135.

Burnard, P. (1987). Spiritual distress and the nursing response: Theoretical considerations and counselling skills. *Journal of Advanced Nursing, 12,* 377–382.

Cantanzaro, M. (1980). Nursing care of the person with MS. *American Journal of Nursing, 80,* 286–291.

Cohen, S., & Syme, S. L. (1985). Issues in the study and application of social support. In S. Cohen & S. L. Syme (Eds.), *Social support and health* (pp. 3–21). Orlando, FL: Academic Press.

Colliton, M. A. (1981). The spiritual dimension of nursing. In I. L. Beland, & J. Y. Passos, *Clinical nursing. Pathophysiological and psychosocial approaches* (4th ed.) (pp. 492–501). New York: Macmillan.

Corbin, J. M., & Strauss, A. L. (1988). *Unending work and care: Managing chronic illness at home.* San Francisco: Josey-Bass.

Corbin, J. M., & Strauss, A. L. (1984). Collaboration: Couples working together to manage chronic illness. *Image: Journal of Nursing Scholarship, 16,* 109–115.

Craig, H. M., & Edwards, J. E. (1983). Adaptation in chronic illness: An eclectic model for nurses. *Journal of Advanced Nursing, 8,* 397–404.

Crawford, J. D., & McIvor, G. P. (1985). Group psychotherapy: Benefits in multiple sclerosis. *Archives of Physical Medicine and Rehabilitation, 66,* 810–813.

Davison, A. N. (1982). Multiple sclerosis—recent advances in research. *Physiotherapy, 68,* 151–153.

Derogatis, L. R., & Lopez, M. C. (1983). *The psychosocial adjustment to illness scale. Administration, scoring, & procedures manual-I.* Baltimore: Clinical Psychometric Research.

Dimond, M. (1983). Social adaptation of the chronically ill. In D. Mechanic (Ed.), *Handbook of health care and the health professional* (pp. 636–654). New York: Free Press.

Dimond, M. (1979). Social support and adaptation to chronic illness. The case of maintenance hemodialysis. *Research in Nursing and Health, 2,* 101–108.

Dimond, M., & Jones, S. L. (1983). *Chronic illness across the life span.* Norwalk, CT: Appleton-Century-Crofts.

Feldman, D. J. (1974). Chronic disabling illness: A holistic view. *Journal of Chronic Diseases, 27,* 287–291.

Fischbach, F. (1988). *A manual of laboratory diagnostic tests* (3d ed.). Philadelphia: JB Lippincott.

Forsyth, G. L., Delaney, K. D., & Gresham, M. L. (1984). Vying for a winning position: Management style of the chronically ill. *Research in Nursing and Health, 7,* 181–188.

Franklin, G. M., & Burks, J. S. (1985). Diagnosis and medical management of multiple sclerosis. In F. P. Maloney, J. S. Burks, & S. P. Ringel (Eds.), *Interdisciplinary rehabilitation of multiple sclerosis and neuromuscular disorders* (pp. 32–47). Philadelphia: JB Lippincott.

Friedmann, M. L., & Tubergen, P. (1987). Multiple sclerosis and the family. *Archives of Psychiatric Nursing, 1,* 47–54.

Gottlieb, N. H., & Green, L. W. (1984). Life events, social network, life-style, and health: An analysis of the 1979 National Survey on Personal Health Practices. *Health Education Quarterly, 11,* 91–105.

Gould, M. T. (1983). Nursing diagnoses concurrent with multiple sclerosis. *Journal of Neurosurgical Nursing, 15,* 339–345.

Gulick, E. E. (1989). Model confirmation of the MS-related symptom checklist. *Nursing Research, 38,* 147–153.

Gulick, E. E. (1984). Multiple sclerosis: The nurses' role using a self-care framework. *Journal of Community Health Nursing, 1,* 247–255.

Gurklis, J. A., & Menke, E. M. (1988). Identification of stressors and use of coping methods in chronic hemodialysis patients. *Nursing Research, 37,* 236–239, 248.

Harper, A. C., Harper, D. A., Chambers, L. W., Cino, P. M., & Singer, J. (1986). An epidemiological description of physical, social and psychological problems in multiple sclerosis. *Journal of Chronic Diseases, 39,* 305–310.

Harris, S. M., Hermiz, M. E., Meininger, M., & Steinkeler, S. E. (1989). Betty Neuman systems model. In A. Marriner-Tomey, *Nursing theorists and their work* (2d ed.) (pp. 361–388). St. Louis: CV Mosby.

Hart, L. K. (1978). Fatigue in the patient with multiple sclerosis. *Research in Nursing and Health, 1,* 147–157.

Hastings, D. (1989). *Hope, social support, and adaptation to multiple sclerosis.* Unpublished master's thesis, Marquette University, Milwaukee.

Herth, K. A. (1989). The relationship between level of hope and level of coping response and other variables in patients with cancer. *Oncology Nurses Forum, 16,* 67–72.

Hibbard, J. H. (1985). Social ties and health status: An examination of moderating factors. *Health Education Quarterly, 12,* 23–34.

Holland, N. J., McDonnell, M., & Wiesel-Levison, P. (1981). Overview of multiple sclerosis and nursing care of the MS patient. *Journal of Neurosurgical Nursing, 13,* 28–33.

Holland, N. J., Wiesel-Levison, P., & Madonna, M. G. (1984). Community care of the patient with multiple sclerosis. *Rehabilitation Nursing, 9,* 18–20.

Hubbard, P., Muhlenkamp, A. F., & Brown, N. (1984). The relationship between social support and self-care practices. *Nursing Research, 33,* 266–270.

Hungelmann, J., Kenkel-Rossi, E., Klassen, L., & Stollenwerk, R. (1989). Development of the JAREL spiritual well-being scale. In R. M. Carroll-Johnson (Ed.), *Classification of nurs-*

ing diagnoses. Proceedings of the eighth conference (pp. 393–398). Philadelphia: JB Lippincott.

Kelly, B., & Mahon, S. M. (1988). Nursing care of the patient with multiple sclerosis. *Rehabilitation Nursing, 13,* 238–243.

Klinger, M. (1984). Compliance and the post-MI patient. *The Canadian Nurse, 80,* 32–36.

Korner, I. N. (1970). Hope as a method of coping. *Journal of Consulting and Clinical Psychology, 34,* 134–139.

Kritchevsky, M. (1988). Multiple sclerosis. In W. C. Wiederholt (Ed.), *Neurology for nonneurologists* (2d ed.) (pp. 177–186). Philadelphia: Grune & Stratton.

Lange, S. P. (1978). Hope. In C. E. Carlson & B. Blackwell (Eds.), *Behavioral concepts & nursing interventions* (2d ed.) (pp. 171–190). Philadelphia: JB Lippincott.

LaRocca, N., Kalb, R., & Kaplan, S. R. (1983). Psychological changes. In L. C. Scheinberg (Ed.), *Multiple sclerosis. A guide for patients and their families* (pp. 175–194). New York: Raven Press.

Lederer, J. R., Marculescu, G. L., Mocnik, B., & Seaby, N. (1990). *Care planning pocket guide. A nursing diagnosis approach* (3d ed.). Redwood City, CA: Addison-Wesley Nursing.

Matson, R. R., & Brooks, N. A. (1977). Adjusting to multiple sclerosis: An exploratory study. *Social Science and Medicine, 11,* 245–250.

McIvor, G. P., Riklan, M., & Reznikoff, M. (1984). Depression in multiple sclerosis as a function of length and severity of illness, age, remissions, and perceived social support. *Journal of Clinical Psychology, 40,* 1028–1033.

Mechanic, D. (1977). Illness behavior, social adaptation, and the management of illness. A comparison of educational and medical models. *The Journal of Nervous and Mental Disease, 165,* 79–87.

Miller, J. F. (1985). Inspiring hope. *American Journal of Nursing, 85,* 22–25.

Miller, J. F. (1983) *Coping with chronic illness. Overcoming powerlessness.* Philadelphia: FA Davis.

Morgante, L. A., Madonna, M. G., & Pokoluk, R. (1989). Research and treatment in multiple sclerosis: Implications for nursing practice. *Journal of Neuroscience Nursing, 21,* 285–289.

Murray, R. B., & Zentner, J. P. (1979). *Nursing assessment & health promotion through the life span* (2d ed.). Englewood Cliffs, NJ: Prentice-Hall.

National Center for Health Statistics (1987). *Current estimates from the National Health Interview Survey, United States 1986.* (Series 10, No. 164. DHHS Publication No. 87–1592). Hyattsville, MD: Department of Health and Human Services.

National Center for Health Statistics (1986). *Current estimates from the National Health Interview Survey, United States 1984.* (Series 10, No. 156. DHHS publication No. 86–1584). Hyattsville, MD: Department of Health and Human Services.

National Center for Health Statistics (1985). *Current estimates from the National Health Interview Survey, United States 1982.* (Series 10, No. 156. DHHS Publication No. 85–1578). Hyattsville, MD: Department of Health and Human Services.

Neuman, B. (1989). *The Neuman systems model* (2d ed.). East Norwalk, CT: Appleton & Lange.

Northouse, L. L. (1988). Social support in patients' and husbands' adjustment to breast cancer. *Nursing Research, 37,* 91–95.

O'Brien, M. E. (1982*a*). Religious faith and adjustment to long-term hemodialysis. *Journal of Religion and Health, 21,* 68–79.

O'Brien, M. E. (1982*b*). The need for spiritual integrity. In H. Yura, & M. B. Walsh (Eds.), *Human needs 2 and the nursing process* (pp. 85–113). Norwalk, CT: Appleton-Century-Crofts.

Pallett, P. J., & O'Brien, M. T. (1985). *Textbook of neurological nursing.* Boston: Little Brown.

Pollock, S. E. (1986). Human responses to chronic illness: Physiologic and psychosocial adaptation. *Nursing Research, 35,* 90–95.

Poser, C. M. (1983). The diagnosis. In L. C. Scheinberg (Ed.), *Multiple sclerosis. A guide for patients and their families* (pp. 17–33). New York: Raven Press.

Reed, P. G. (1987). Spirituality and well-being in terminally ill hospitalized adults. *Research in Nursing and Health, 10,* 335–344.

Rideout, E., & Montemuro, M. (1986). Hope, morale, and adaptation in patients with chronic heart failure. *Journal of Advanced Nursing, 6*, 157–169.

Roberts, S. (1978). *Behavioral concepts and nursing throughout the life span.* Englewood Cliffs, NJ: Prentice-Hall.

Ruffing-Rahal, M. A. (1984). The spiritual dimension of well-being. Implications for the elderly. *Home Healthcare Nurse, 2*, 12–16.

Scheinberg, L. (1983). Introduction. L. C. Scheinberg (Ed.), *Multiple sclerosis. A guide for patients and their families* (pp. 3–6). New York: Raven Press.

Scheinberg, L., & Geisser, B. S. (1983). Drug therapy. In L. C. Scheinberg (Ed.), *Multiple sclerosis. A guide for patients and their families* (pp. 45–55). New York: Raven Press.

Schneider, J. S. (1980). Hopelessness and helplessness. *Journal of Psychiatric Nursing and Mental Health Services, 18*, 12–20.

Schneitzer, L. (1978). Rehabilitation of patients with multiple sclerosis. *Archives of Physical Medicine and Rehabilitation, 59*, 430–436.

Shelly, J. A., & Fish, S. (1988). *Spiritual care. The nurse's role* (3d ed.). Downers Grove, IL: InterVarsity Press.

Sims, C. (1987). Spiritual care as a part of holistic nursing. *Imprint, 34*, 63–65.

Slater, R. J., & Yearwood, A. (1980). MS. Facts, faith, and hope. *American Journal of Nursing, 80*, 276–281.

Sodestrom, K. E., & Martinson, I. M. (1987). Patients' spiritual coping strategies: A study of nurse and patient perspectives. *Oncology Nurses Forum, 14*, 41–46.

Soeken, K. L., & Carson, V. J. (1987). Responding to the spiritual needs of the chronically ill. *Nursing Clinics of North America, 22*, 603–611.

Spiegelberg, N. (1980). Support group improves quality of life. *Association of Rehabilitation Nurses, 5*, 9–11.

Stoner, M. J. H. (1982). Hope and cancer patients. (Doctoral dissertation, University of Colorado, 1983). *Dissertation Abstracts International, 44*, 115B.

Strauss, A. L., Corbin, J., Fagerhaugh, S., Glaser, B. G., Maines, D., Suczek, B., & Wiener, C. L. (1984). *Chronic illness and the quality of life* (2d ed.). St. Louis: CV Mosby.

Stuart, E. M., Deckro, J. P., & Mandle, C. L. (1989). Spirituality in heath and healing: A clinical program. *Holistic Nursing Practice, 3*, 35–46.

Surridge, D. (1969). An investigation into some psychiatric aspects of multiple sclerosis. *British Journal of Psychiatry, 115*, 749–764.

Sutherland, J. M. (1986). Multiple sclerosis—clinical. In Downie, P. A. (Ed.), *Cash's textbook of neurology for physiotherapists* (4th ed.) (pp. 383–397). Philadelphia: JB Lippincott.

Tan, S. Y. (1986). Psychosocial functioning of adult epileptic and MS patients and adult normal controls on the WPSI. *Journal of Clinical Psychology, 43*, 528–534.

Thompson, J. M., McFarland, G. K., Hirsch, J. E., Tucker, S. M., & Bowers, A. C. (1989). *Mosby's manual of clinical nursing* (2d ed.). St. Louis: CV Mosby.

Tilden, V. P. (1986). New perspectives on social support. *Nurse Practitioner, 11*, 61–62.

Weiss, R. S. (1974). The provisions of social relationships. In Z. Rubin (Ed.), *Doing unto others* (pp. 17–26). Englewood Cliffs, NJ: Prentice-Hall.

Whitaker, J. N. (1983). What causes the disease? In L. C. Scheinberg (Ed.), *Multiple sclerosis. A guide for patients and their families* (pp. 7–16). New York: Raven Press.

Whitlock, F. A., & Siskind, M. M. (1980). Depression as a major symptom of multiple sclerosis. *Journal of Neurology, Neurosurgery, and Psychiatry, 43*, 861–865.

Whittington, L. (1983). Multiple sclerosis. Dealing with reality. *The Candian Nurse, 79*, 34–38.

Wierenga, M. (1986). Alterations in motor function. In C. M. Porth (Ed.), *Pathophysiology. Concepts of altered health states* (2d ed.) (pp. 847–867). Philadelphia: JB Lippincott.

Winters, S., Jackson, P., Sims, K., & Magilvy, J. (1989). A nurse-managed multiple sclerosis clinic: Improved quality of life for persons with MS. *Rehabilitiation Nursing, 14*, 13–16.

Zeldow, P. B., & Pavlou, M. (1984). Physical disability, life stress, and psychosocial adjustment to multiple sclerosis. *Journal of Nervous and Mental Disease, 172*, 80–84.

■

Coping with Chronic Lung Disease: Maintaining Quality of Life
■ **ANNE McMAHON**

Adults with chronic lung disease experience a succession of distressing physical, psychologic, and spiritual responses that challenge personal resources for coping. Progressive dyspnea and fatigue impair functioning in physical, emotional, and social dimensions of daily living. Human responses commonly experienced by adults with emphysema and chronic bronchitis and interventions designed to promote optimal coping are described in this chapter. Pathophysiologic changes, challenges to quality of life, and a case study are reviewed. A model of quality of life for persons with chronic obstructive pulmonary disease (COPD) described in this chapter provides a framework for organizing research and nursing interventions.

Patients have identified the sense of mastery, or feeling of control, over the disease as an important aspect of quality of life in coping with impaired breathing (Guyatt, Townsend, Berman, & Pugsley, 1987). Nursing interventions during all phases of disease progression are directed at enhancing this sense of mastery.

Pathophysiologic Changes

Human responses to chronic lung disease are related to alterations in the structure and function of the airways and lungs (Carrieri & Janson-Bjerklie, 1986*a*; Porth, 1986; West, 1987). Chronic bronchitis and emphysema cause irreversible changes that result in obstruction to the normal

255

flow of air, hence the term *chronic obstructive pulmonary disease*. Persons who have one of these conditions often have both, in part because the causative factors of cigarette smoking and air pollution are common to both. Persons with these conditions often also have some degree of asthma, which causes episodes of airflow obstruction in response to irritating stimuli.

The pathophysiologic changes that accompany chronic bronchitis cause three main effects: hypertrophy of mucous glands in the large bronchi, hypertrophy of the bronchial smooth muscle surrounding the airways, and chronic inflammation and edema of the small airways. These changes obstruct airflow by narrowing the airways and by impairing the mucociliary system that normally clears foreign bodies from the airways. Persons with chronic bronchitis experience a chronic cough, productive of sputum that is purulent during acute exacerbations. In the later stages, ankle edema and fluid retention characteristic of right ventricular failure commonly appear.

The obstruction to airflow that accompanies emphysema has a different etiology. Pathophysiologic changes cause the eventual destruction of alveolar walls, a process that destroys the capillary bed in which diffusion of respiratory gases occurs. This process weakens the supporting structure of the lungs and reduces the radial traction that maintains the patency of airways. Persons with this condition have "air-trapping," a condition in which there is overinflation of the lungs and obstruction to airflow during expiration. Loss of the lung's normal elastic recoil causes bronchioles to collapse during exhalation, trapping air in the distal bronchioles and alveoli. Eventually the shape of the thorax becomes distorted and movement of the diaphragm during breathing is impaired.

Persons whose lung disease has an asthmatic component experience acute episodic obstructions to airflow, caused by spasms of the bronchial smooth muscle. Bronchospasm may be precipitated by irritating stimuli such as dusts, aerosols, or other allergens; exercise; exposure to cold air; or stressful psychologic stimuli. Bronchoconstriction, which is responsive to treatment by bronchodilators, is labeled *reversible* airflow limitation. The airflow obstruction in asthma is compounded by edema of the bronchial walls and by thick, tenacious mucus produced by hypertrophied mucuous glands.

Pulmonary function tests (PFTs) provide clinical measures of the airflow impairments caused by COPD. Patients achieve low values for measures of expiratory airflow such as forced expiratory volume in 1 second (FEV_1), the forceful, timed exhalation of vital capacity. High values for residual volume (RV) provide evidence of air-trapping.

Arterial blood gases (ABGs) provide data on impaired diffusion of respiratory gases across the alveolar-capillary membrane and on the mismatching of ventilation and perfusion in the lung. Hypoxemia, hypercarbia, and respiratory acidosis are common patterns. Hypoxemia, with arte-

TABLE 11 ■ 1   Nursing Assessment for Patients with Pulmonary Disorders

---

Activity-exercise pattern
 Dyspnea
  Self-report of experience
  Rating on visual analog scale (Gift, 1989)
  Frequency
  Precipitating factors
  Patterns from dyspnea log (Carrieri, 1989)
  Improvement or worsening (Mahler et al., 1984)
 Cough
  Frequency
  Sputum: appearance, amount
  Precipitating factors
  Relieving factors
 Daily activities
  Functional independence in self-care activities
  Driving or alternative transportation
  Has handicapped parking permit
  Exercise patterns
  Access to fitness equipment
  Work: current, past
  Hobbies and recreation
  Other health problems that limit activity and mobility
  Former activities given up because of lung disease
 Chest
  Inspection
   Anterior-posterior diameter
   Breathing pattern
    Rate
    Depth
    Inspiration:expiration ratio
    Coordination of abdomen and chest muscles
    Use of intercostal, neck, and shoulder muscles
  Percussion
   Hyperresonance
  Auscultation
   Breath sounds: diminished, bronchial
   Adventitious sounds: crackles, rhonchi, wheezes
 Pulse: rate, rhythm
 Neck vein distention
 Color
  Skin
  Mucous membranes
  Nailbeds
 Skin turgor
 Edema
 Posture and positioning
  Sitting
  Standing
 Exercise tolerance
  Six-minute walk test (Guyatt et al., 1985; McGavin et al., 1976)
  Rating of dyspnea: Borg Scale (Borg, 1982)
  Pulse oximetry: resting, walking
 Data from medical assessment
  Pulmonary function testing
   Tidal volume
   Vital capacity
   Residual capacity

TABLE 11 ■ 1   Nursing Assessment for Patients with Pulmonary Disorders
(Continued)

Total lung capacity
Forced expiratory volume in 1 second (FEV_1)
Diffusing capacity for carbon monoxide (D_LCO)
Arterial blood gases
  Oxygenation
  Acid-base balance
Chest x-ray
Diagnosis
Medical management
Other health problems
Nutritional-metabolic pattern
  Appetite
  Diet
    Normal day's or week's intake: types and amounts
    Recent changes
    Diet log, if indicated
  Usual fluid intake
  Weight gains or losses within past year
  Dyspnea with meals
  Abdominal discomfort
  Drug and alcohol consumption
  Weight, height, ideal weight
  Appearance: Body build
  Oxygen saturation while eating, if indicated
Elimination pattern
  Bowel elimination patterns
  Bladder elimination patterns
    Stress incontinence
Sleep-rest pattern
  Usual sleep and rest patterns, including naps
  Number of pillows used
  Paroxysmal nocturnal dyspnea
  Feel adequately rested
  Factors that prevent rest
  Factors that promote rest
  Sleep study data, if available
Cognitive-perceptual pattern
  Sensory deficits
  Memory: short-term, long-term
  Ability to concentrate
  Decision-making ability
  Education
  Self-care knowledge
Self-perception–self-concept pattern
  Feelings of anxiety, restlessness, being down or blue, powerlessness
  Sense of mastery in managing disease
  Activities that provide a sense of accomplishment, satisfaction, of "being me"
  Body image concerns:
    Sputum
    Shortness of breath
    Noisy respirations
    Presence of oxygen
    Appearance
  Motivation for rehabilitation
  Goals
Coping-stress tolerance pattern
  Current sources of stress
  Factors that relieve stress

TABLE 11 ■ 1   Nursing Assessment for Patients with Pulmonary Disorders
(*Continued*)

Family support available
Other resources for coping with stressors
Communication
    Verbal
    Nonverbal
Role-relationship pattern
  Significant other(s)
  Positive aspects of relationship(s)
  Changes related to lung disease
  Other roles and relationships:
    Family
    Work
    If retired, past work history
    Clubs, hobbies
  Concerns about roles and relationships
Sexuality-reproductive pattern
  Changes related to impaired breathing
  Satisfaction with present patterns
Health perception–health management pattern
  Past medical history, hospitalizations
  Current treatments
    Medications
    Oxygen
    Nebulizer
    Chest physiotherapy
    Respiratory muscle training (Kim, 1984)
  Adherence to prescribed treatments
  Risk factors
    Respiratory irritants: smoke, aerosols, sprays, dusts, allergens
      At home
      Away from home
    Response to environmental conditions
    Smoking history, if applicable
      Currently smoking?
      Attempts to quit
        Methods used
        Successes
  Prevention practices
    Immunizations for influenza, pneumococcus
    Use of air conditioner, humidifier, air cleaners
Value-belief pattern
  Spiritual resources
  Feelings of hope or hopelessness
  Religious affiliation and practices
  Sources of strength to transcend suffering

rial Po$_2$ below 55 mm Hg, predisposes to the development of right-sided heart failure (Porth, 1986; West, 1987).

COMPREHENSIVE ASSESSMENT

A guide for nursing assessment of the person with a pulmonary disorder is summarized in Table 11–1. The assessment format is based on Gordon's (1987) eleven functional patterns.

The nursing diagnoses Ineffective Airway Clearance, Ineffective Breathing Patterns, and Impaired Gas Exchange summarize the principal alterations in pulmonary function that accompany COPD. Each diagnosis may have one or more causes for a given individual.

Ineffective airway clearance is defined as a state in which an individual is unable to clear secretions or obstructions from the respiratory tract to maintain airway patency. Causes may include airflow limitation, airway infection, the presence of an artificial airway, or other conditions that disturb the production or clearance of mucus. An effective cough requires the ability to collect a large volume of air in the chest and to exhale forcefully and rapidly. Persons with COPD have difficulty coughing to clear the airways effectively because of weakness of the respiratory muscles and the production of excessive, abnormally viscous mucus (DeVito, 1985; Kim & Larson, 1987).

Ineffective breathing patterns are defined as states in which the individual's inspiratory and/or expiratory pattern does not provide adequate ventilation. Causes may include airflow limitation, respiratory muscle fatigue, or decreased lung expansion. Aspects of normal breathing patterns which are altered may include respiratory rate, tidal volume, ratio of inspiratory time to expiratory time, and the coordinated motion of respiratory muscles. For COPD patients, the altered breathing pattern usually produces rapid shallow breathing, a pattern which increases the work of breathing by increasing ventilation of physiologic dead space. This pattern is inefficient and eventually ineffective in meeting ventilatory needs (Kim & Larson, 1987).

The diffusion of oxygen and carbon dioxide in the pulmonary capillaries is impaired by the loss of surface area in the lungs and by uneven distribution of air in the lungs. Hypoxemia results when blood flows past poorly aerated areas of lung tissue. Hypercarbia and acidosis result from impaired excretion of carbon dioxide. Patients with impaired gas exchange may have tachycardia, weakness, fatigue, restlessness, and confusion (DeVito, 1985).

Quality of Life and COPD

For persons with a chronic illness, quality of life is dependent upon changes related to illness phenomena, perceptions, functional capacity, and personal resources. *Illness phenomena* refers to individuals' subjective responses to the changes induced by disease. Disease comprises the structural and pathophysiologic changes that can be evaluated using objective clinical measures, such as pulmonary function testing and ABGs. Illness phenomena encompass individuals' subjective experiences, such as dyspnea and fatigue, related to these changes. *Perceptions* refers to individuals' unique interpretations of their health status, functioning, well-being, and life quality. *Functional capacity* refers to the ability to perform activities in the physical, emotional, and social aspects of daily living. *Personal resources* refers to physical, cognitive, emotional, social, and economic assets available to the individual (Dracup & Raffin, 1989; Gilson et al., 1975; Padilla et al., 1983; Wenger, Mattson, Furberg, & Elinson, 1984).

As a progressive disease affecting the vital supply of oxygen to muscle, brain, and other body cells, COPD affects all four aspects of life quality discussed. The broad range of responses experienced by patients is indicated by the nursing diagnoses associated with each of the four aspects (see Table 11–2). Nursing interventions are directed at modifying patients' responses in each of the four areas.

ILLNESS PHENOMENA IN COPD

Dyspnea

Dyspnea is a prevalent response reported by persons with chronic lung disease. Sometimes used interchangeably with the term "breathlessness," dyspnea is the sensation of difficult or uncomfortable breathing, as perceived and interpreted by the individual. It occurs when the demand for ventilation, as perceived by the individual, is out of proportion to the ability to respond to that demand. For persons with COPD, the increased demand for ventilation is related to inefficient pulmonary gas exchange. The reduced ability to respond to ventilatory needs is caused by abnormal mechanics of the lung, diaphragm, and other respiratory muscles and by respiratory muscle fatigue (Carrieri, Janson-Bjerklie, & Jacobs, 1984; West, 1987).

Persons with emphysema typically describe their dyspnea as a constant, unrelenting pervasive body sensation of difficulty breathing or "difficulty getting the air out" (Carrieri & Janson-Bjerklie, 1986). Persons with asthma more commonly refer to sensations of constriction and chest tightness in describing their experience of dyspnea (Janson-Bjerklie, Carrieri, & Hudes, 1986). In recalling episodes of acute dyspnea, COPD patients have reported concomitant feelings of fear, helplessness, loss of vitality, preoccupation, and concern about having difficulty convincing others of the seriousness of their distress (DeVito, 1990).

In the early stages of COPD, patients experience dyspnea as a response to strenuous activity or intense emotions. As the disease progresses, dyspnea occurs with minimal activity in the absence of emotional arousal, and eventually dyspnea is present during rest. Changes in dyspnea over time can be assessed using tools such as the Baseline Dyspnea Index and the Transition Dyspnea Index, which quantify dyspnea in relation to the activities which provoke it and the effort expended (Mahler, Weinberg, Wells, & Feinstein, 1984).

The severity of dyspnea reported by patients does not correlate directly with physiologic measures, such as PFT results and ABG values.

TABLE 11 ■ 2   Dimensions of Life
Quality and Associated Nursing
Diagnoses* for Persons with COPD

Illness phenomena
   Decreased cardiac output
   Constipation
   Fatigue
   Fluid volume deficit
   Fluid volume excess
   Potential for infection
   Potential for aspiration
   Ineffective airway clearance
   Ineffective breathing patterns
   Impaired gas exchange
   Alteration in oral mucous membrane
Perceptions
   Anxiety
   Altered comfort
   Ineffective denial
   Fear
   Grieving, actual and anticipatory
   Dysfunctional grieving
   Hopelessness
   Powerlessness
   Self-concept disturbance
   Body-image disturbance
   Self-esteem disturbance
Functional capacity
   Activity intolerance
   Impaired verbal communication
   Diversional activity deficit
   Potential for disuse syndrome (end-stage)
   Altered health maintenance
   Impaired home maintenance management
   Potential for injury
   Impaired physical mobility
   Altered role performance
   Self-care deficit
   Altered sexuality patterns
   Impaired social interactions
   Social isolation
Personal resources
   Ineffective individual coping
   Ineffective family coping
   Compromised family coping
   Defensive coping
   Altered family processes
   Knowledge deficit
   Noncompliance
   Altered nutrition: less than body
     requirements
   Sleep pattern disturbance
   Spiritual distress
   Impaired swallowing
   Altered thought processes

*Nursing diagnosis labels based on Carpenito
(1989).

This observation supports the notion that dyspnea is a multidimensional phenomenon rather than a purely physiologic one (Gift, Plaut, & Jacox, 1986; Hudson & Pierson, 1981).

Episodes of acute dyspnea are often accompanied by an intensely distressing sensation of panic (Janson-Bjerklie et al., 1986). Patients learn to prevent such dyspnea-panic episodes by avoiding the physical exertion and emotional experiences which precipitate them. This pattern of behavior leads to a progressively restricted life-style, in which the individual may eventually be unable to perform basic ADLs, such as bathing, dressing, preparing meals, or even eating. Deconditioning of the cardio-respiratory system and the skeletal muscles then limits activity beyond the restrictions imposed by the pathophysiologic changes (Glass, 1981).

Persons experiencing chronic dyspnea report using a variety of coping strategies. Problem-focused strategies include modifying grooming, eating, and other ADLs; modifying activities by planning ahead or using breathing stations; self-selected treatments, such as adjusting medications; and protective behaviors. Emotion-focused strategies include emotional distancing, adopting a positive attitude, social isolation, and tension-reduction strategies. Seeking social support is a mixed problem-emotion–focused strategy (Carrieri & Janson-Bjerklie, 1986*b*).

Fatigue

Another response frequently experienced by persons with chronic lung disease is fatigue, a pervasive sense of energy depletion that affects many aspects of functioning and well-being. It is related to hypoxemia, dyspnea, altered sleep and rest patterns, and altered mood states. It is aggravated by the process of cardiovascular and skeletal muscle deconditioning that often accompanies the experience of chronic dyspnea. Patients report feeling low in energy, worn out, and sluggish. Fatigue is associated with reports of psychologic distress (Guyatt et al., 1987; Janson-Bjerklie et al., 1986; Kinsman et al., 1983).

Fatigue and the accompanying management tasks present a challenge to patients' resources of time, energy, and money. For persons fortunate enough to have a dependable support system, the problem of energy depletion strains the resources of the members and necessitates ongoing trade-offs of one resource for another. It becomes increasingly necessary to utilize the energy of family members, other care givers, and community agenices for household maintenance and for meeting basic needs (Fagerhaugh, 1973).

PERCEPTION: SENSE OF MASTERY

Patients' perceptions of their illness and its impacts are important aspects of life quality. This emphasis on patients' subjective interpretations is consistent with the phenomenologic view that individuals' perceptions of reality are more important than the reality itself (Dracup & Raffin, 1989).

A perception rated as important by persons with COPD is the sense of mastery over symptoms and functioning (Guyatt et al., 1987). The sense of mastery is threatened by dyspnea, fatigue, and altered mood states that accompany disease progression. Diminution of the sense of mastery can precipitate feelings of powerlessness and depression. There is evidence that persons who have a diminished sense of mastery use emergency services more than other COPD patients (Traver, 1988).

Empirical observations indicate that the sense of mastery is bolstered by effective medical management and by developing competence with skills, such as controlled breathing patterns and energy-conservation techniques, which help to avert or attenuate the experience of dyspnea. A primary goal of nursing care is to assist patients in maintaining or enhancing the sense of mastery by mobilizing their resources for coping. The sense of mastery is influenced by perceived changes in one's physical self (body image) and self-worth (self-esteem).

Altered Body Image

Physical changes that accompany disease progression may require coping with alterations in body image. As the anterior-posterior diameter of the chest increases and accessory muscles of breathing in the neck hypertrophy, patients note that shirts and blouses no longer fit properly and can no longer be buttoned at the neck.

Embarrassment related to symptoms and treatments can be problematic. Patients report feeling embarrassed by coughing and noisy breathing and by using medications or breathing treatments in public places (Guyatt et al., 1987). For patients receiving continuous oxygen by cannula, the presence of nasal prongs and tubing gives unspoken evidence of disability.

Diminished Self-esteem

A number of threats to self-esteem accompany the progression of COPD. Patients may experience guilt about having smoked or being unable to quit smoking. The need to accept assistance with transportation, household chores, and, eventually, self-care activities threatens autonomy and may induce feelings of diminished self-worth. Inability to fulfill role expectations on the job, at home, and in social settings presents the need for the patient to redefine his or her sense of identity and to find alternative sources of self-affirmation.

FUNCTIONAL CAPACITY

The progression of COPD is characterized by a steady deterioration in function, with episodic acute exacerbations which may require hospitalization. Because effective breathing is essential to physical, cognitive, psychologic, and social functioning, persons with impaired breathing experience difficulties with functioning in many aspects of daily living. Typically in the fifth and sixth decades of life, persons with COPD may have coexisting health problems, such as arthritis, heart disease, or sensory deficits, which compound functional limitations. Psychologic responses such as depression or ineffective coping may further limit energy levels and vigor.

Human responses to chronic lung disease are a unique product of the pathophysiologic changes caused by the disease and the personal resources of the individual. Pathophysiologic processes produce typical patterns in clinical testing, as previously discussed. But these data alone are not predictive of the physical, emotional, cognitive, social, or occupational functioning of a given individual. Persons with identical abnormal pulmonary function and ABG results may differ greatly in their level of functioning and quality of life (Foxall, Ekberg, & Griffith, 1987; McSweeney, Grant, Heaton, Adams, & Timms, 1982; Prigatano, Wright, & Levin, 1984).

Functional capacity can be viewed as a quotient of the opposing effects of disease progression on one hand and individuals' personal resources for coping on the other. The relationship of these factors is illustrated by the model in Figure 11-1, which is based on the concept of trajectory formulated by Strauss and coworkers (1984). Pathophysiologic changes are associated with a trajectory or course of progressively declining functional capacity. This decline in functioning is characterized by fluctuations, which are related to acute exacerbations, to the effects of atmospheric conditions on breathing, and to physical and psychologic factors. Individuals may have a level of actual functioning that is considerably below their potential functional capacity. Actual functioning is enhanced by personal resources for coping, including physical, cognitive, social, economic, and spiritual resources. Persons with optimal resources, including knowledge and motivation, are able to achieve a level of actual functioning that approaches or matches their potential functional capacity. According to this model, deficits in resources are correlated with impaired functioning, an observation supported by clinical studies (McDonald, Borson, Gayle, Deffebach, & Lakshminarayan, 1989; Moser, Bokinsky, Savage, Archibald, & Hansen, 1980). A goal of nursing care and of pulmonary rehabilitation is to assist patients in mobilizing their resources to maintain functioning at the maximal level allowed by disease progression. Assessment modalities and research findings related to each component of functioning will be reviewed.

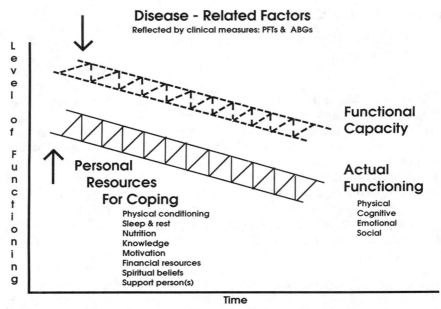

FIGURE 11 ■ 1 Proposed model of factors affecting functioning for persons with COPD.

Assessment of Functional Capacity

Because of the pervasive effects of dyspnea and fatigue on functioning in all aspects of daily living, a comprehensive assessment of patients' functioning is essential. Standardized questionnaires such as the Sickness Impact Profile (SIP) (Bergner, Bobbitt, Carter, & Gilson, 1981), the Pulmonary Impact Profile Scale (PIPS) (Weaver & Narsavage, 1989), and the Chronic Respiratory Disease Questionnaire (CRQ) (Guyatt, Berman, Townsend, Pugsley, & Chambers, 1987) are useful adjuncts to the comprehensive initial nursing assessment in Table 11–1. These tools provide comprehensive data on patients' functioning in ADLs, including physical, emotional, and cognitive aspects. They can be readministered for subsequent evaluation of patients' responses to intervention programs or to disease progression. The PIPS and CRQ were designed specifically for the assessment of adults with chronic lung disease.

Several studies of large groups of patients have documented the broad range of functional impairment accompanying COPD. A study of quality of life for 985 COPD patients with mild hypoxemia revealed moderate to severe impairment of function in most dimensions of daily living measured by the SIP, including ambulation, mobility, social interaction, communication, alertness behavior, emotional behavior, sleep and rest, home management, recreation and pastimes, and employment. Patients with COPD differed significantly from control subjects on all measures except the two dimensions of body care and movement, and eating (Prigatano et al., 1984). Also responding to the SIP, 203 patients with advanced COPD reported impaired life quality on all parameters assessed. Areas severely affected included home management, ambulation, mobility, sleep and rest, and recreation and pastimes. Eating and communication were moderately affected (McSweeney, Grant, Heaton, Adams, & Timms, 1982).

Noting the increasing incidence of COPD among women, Sexton and Munro (1988) investigated the life quality of 72 women with COPD. One third of COPD subjects reported shortness of breath and fatigue as their biggest problems. The ADLs most affected were physical activity and sleep. Fear of having a dyspnea attack while away from home restricted activity for many of the women. Because energy fluctuated widely from day to day, many reported difficulty in planning household and social activities.

EMOTIONAL DYSFUNCTION

Patients with COPD have indicated that changes in emotional functioning are an important factor affecting their quality of life (Guyatt et al., 1987). In coping with COPD, they encounter a succession of stressful experiences. Those mentioned in a support group discussion included being unable to do previously enjoyable activities, aging-related changes, family stresses, the effects of weather on breathing and energy levels, unrealistic family expectations, the distress of symptoms, financial concerns, and dietary changes. The anxious thoughts that accompany stressful experiences can precipitate rapid, shallow breathing. The result may be an escalating episode of anxiety, dyspnea, and panic, which is typically very difficult to interrupt. Episodes of acute anxiety are accompanied by other stress responses, such as poor appetite. Patients also report a more chronic state of anxiety, which is characterized by feeling worried, tense, restless, and fidgety (Gift et al., 1986; Janson-Bjerklie et al., 1986; Sexton & Munro, 1988).

Episodes of acute dyspnea are accompanied by both anxiety and depression (Gift & Cahill, 1989). Clinical observations and research data indicate high incidences of anxiety and depression among persons experiencing chronic dyspnea. Other responses reported by patients include episodes of anger, hostility, frustration, and responses indicating repression of feelings and cognitive impairments. Emotional dysfunction is attributed in part to an inadequate supply of oxygen to the limbic system and other areas of the brain that mediate emotional behavior (McSweeney et al., 1982).

Empirical observations support the theory that COPD patients live in an "emotional straitjacket" (Dudley, Wermuth, & Hague, 1973). According to this theory, emotional states are directly related to breathing. Active emotional states, such as anger and anxiety, increase metabolic demands for oxygen to levels that eventually exceed the limited oxygen supply available to persons with chronically impaired breathing. Conversely, inactive emotional states, such as depression, diminish breathing to the point that ventilation is inadequate. In both cases, the subsequent distress causes patients to limit their expression of, and eventually even their experience of, these emotions. The result is learned patterns of emotional repression and social isolation.

Feelings of helplessness, hopelessness, and depression are commonly reported by persons with unremitting dyspnea. Reactive depression may occur in response to physical dysfunction, job loss, disruptions in family life, or thoughts about impending death. Depression has been attributed in part to fatigue, which depletes physical and psychic energy, and to a pattern of social isolation commonly adopted by persons experiencing chronic dyspnea. Indications that might signal depression in persons with COPD include insomnia, decreased appetite, social withdrawal, indecisiveness, a sense of failure or disappointment in oneself, sadness, difficulty in concentrating, dyspnea, suicidal ideation, lethargy, and feelings of helplessness or hopelessness (Janson-Bjerklie et al., 1986; Kinsman et al., 1983; McSweeney et al., 1982; Prigatano et al., 1984; Light, Merrill, Despars, Gordon, & Mutalipassi, 1985; Sandhu, 1986; Sexton & Munro, 1988).

IMPAIRED COGNITION

Problem solving, abstract thinking, and judgment are important resources for successful coping with life events. These intellectual skills can be impaired by the hypoxemia and respiratory acidosis that accompany advanced COPD. A study of 121 patients with advanced COPD revealed cognitive impairments in three fourths of the subjects. The skills most frequently affected were abstracting ability, perceptual-motor integration (problem solving and other complex skills), simple motor skills, and attention. Skills involving language and memory remained generally intact (Grant, Heaton, McSweeney, Adams, & Timms, 1980). Long-term oxygen therapy for these patients resulted in small but definite improvements in cognitive function (Heaton, Grant, McSweeney, Adams, & Petty, 1983). Patients in another study reported forgetfulness, confusion, and difficulty with concentrating, focusing attention, reasoning, and solving problems (Guyatt et al., 1987).

ALTERED ROLE FUNCTIONING: IMPACTS ON PATIENT AND FAMILY

Spouse, employee, parent, club member, friend, neighbor, grandparent, community member—these roles and others change for individuals with COPD. Successful coping entails grieving the losses that accompany changes and establishing new balances of personal and family resources (McSweeney et al., 1982; Sexton & Munro, 1985; 1988).

Patients and their support networks face the tasks of adapting to diminished energy reserves, mobilizing the resources of family members and community services, and finding a new equilibrium in response to the progressive nature of the disease. Optimal coping necessitates setting priorities, making decisions, and trading off one resource for another. For the patient, this may mean allocating time for rest in order to maintain roles central to one's self-concept, coping with feelings of loss and social isolation, and learning energy-conserving techniques to use in maintaining selected roles and responsibilities. For the family it may mean reallocating roles and responsibilities, spending money to pay for help with household chores, giving up some social and recreational activities, and finding new diversional activities.

As the roles of the ill member contract, the role of family members and others must correspondingly expand or help must be obtained from outside sources. The wives of 46 men with COPD reported taking on the roles of caretaker, decision maker, financial manager, and errand runner, while maintaining previous roles in the household (Sexton & Munro, 1985). Role synchrony is facilitated when the patient, family, and others are realistic about the extent of disability (Barstow, 1974).

For care-giving spouses, COPD presents a number of challenges. The disease occurs at a time in life when the care-giving spouse may also be experiencing acute or chronic health problems. Wives of men with COPD reported personal health problems that included arthritis, hypertension, cataracts, and heart disease (Sexton & Munro, 1985). The tasks of care giving can aggravate health problems or limit time and financial resources for managing health problems. During even a short-term illness or hospitalization, care givers may find it difficult to find reliable assistance with household maintenance and care-giving roles.

Social isolation can become a problem for both patient and spouse. Spouses must deal with the losses of social and recreational activities, especially when shared activities such as dancing, traveling, or bridge-playing are affected. Successful coping involves exploring new pastimes that match the affected partner's energy and tolerance.

Driving is a role that can provide not only mobility, but self-esteem. When the patient is the only driver in the household, mobility and social interaction for both patient and spouse may be restricted. Transportation problems can restrict access of both persons to needed supplies and services, including groceries, medications, banking, and health-care appointments. Limited access to social contacts can affect the well-being of both partners.

Some couples have reported positive responses to some of the effects of COPD. The changes that accompany the disease bring a slower pace of life and a sense of the tenuous nature of life, factors which have increased the closeness and interdependence in some marriages (Hanson, 1982). Of the married women studied by Sexton and Munro (1988), over half indicated that their illness had increased their closeness with their husbands. Only one tenth indicated that their disease had caused distance from spouses.

OCCUPATIONAL ROLE

The stresses associated with a planned and timely retirement are well known. As a progressive disease occurring during the productive decades of middle adulthood, COPD often necessitates premature retirement due to disability. The individual may experience isolation from a network of significant social contacts and the loss of a role central to identity. These losses may be compounded by the econmic impact of the job loss (Stollenwerk, 1985).

A positive correlation has been found between IQ and successful coping with the occupational changes consequent to COPD. This has been attributed to the fact that persons with higher IQ scores are more likely to have less physically strenuous jobs, which can be maintained further into the disease process (Daughton, Fix, Kass, Patil, & Bell, 1979). Persons with a higher IQ may have greater resources of time and money to facilitate their coping.

Women carrying out traditional roles in the household may have special problems in adapting to the limitations imposed by COPD. Because of the constant nature of household responsibilities, retirement is usually more difficult for these individuals. Women studied by Barstow (1974) continued to perform household chores despite functional impairments. They reported incorporating pauses for rest and seeking help with heavy chores.

RECREATIONAL ACTIVITIES

While experiencing the progression of COPD, patients and families may note several changes in the time available for recreational activities. Early in the disease process, while maintaining occupational roles, patients may conserve energy by reducing recreational activities and hobbies. As function is further impaired, some persons who are required to retire early report having increased time for recreational activities, a change seen as a short-term positive side-effect of the disease (Foxall et al., 1987).

As fatigue and dyspnea advance, minimally strenous activities such as sewing or card-playing can become luxuries for the person with COPD. The loss of hobbies and pastimes curtails sources of recreation, identity, and socialization that make life pleasurable.

Social and recreational activities often involve exposure to second-hand smoke, which can precipitate dyspnea and coughing. Even in restaurants, public transportation, and public areas where smoking is restricted, small amounts of smoke can impair breathing in persons who are sensitive to inhaled irritants. For many COPD patients and families, this factor restricts social and recreational activities.

SEXUAL DYSFUNCTION

Because of its physical and psychologic effects, chronic lung disease may impair sexual and affectional expressions. A group of 128 patients studied by Hanson (1982) rated this impact of the disease a highly important one. Correlational data indicate that worsening of lung disease is accompanied by worsening of sexual dysfunction (Fletcher & Martin, 1982). Both male and female patients have reported fear of becoming too tired or dyspneic during intercourse to continue (Dudley, Glaser, Jorgenson, & Logan, 1980). Other physical causes of sexual dysfunction include hypoxemia, inadequate cardiopulmonary reserve, coughing, wheezing, and effects of medications. Psychologic responses including anxiety, depression, repression of emotions, social isolation, and diminished self-esteem also have detrimental effects on sexual function (Campbell, 1987; Timms, 1982).

Sexual dysfunction in one partner integrally affects affection, identity, and self-esteem for both. Of 46 wives of COPD patients, more than half reported that they no longer engaged in sexual intercourse. Some women identified this as a problematic change and others did not (Sexton & Munro, 1985).

EFFORTS TO ADAPT TO ALTERED FUNCTIONAL CAPACITY

Individuals adapt to changing energy levels in ways that may or may not promote optimal functioning. Both denial of the disability and exaggeration of it can result in behaviors that compound the physiologic deficits and restrict functioning unnecessarily. Denial is a common early response, in part because dyspnea is by nature a subjective experience that may not be accompanied by overt signs. Affected persons may engage in activities that tax their energy reserves beyond capacity and subject them to episodes of extreme fatigue, frustration, and feelings of anger or depression (Dudley et al., 1980). Early in the disease process, family members may also deny the illness and place undue expectations on the ill member (Sexton & Munro, 1988).

Exaggeration of activity intolerance can cause patients to restrict their functioning prematurely in the disease process. Family dynamics may be a contributing factor. A spouse experiencing guilt may be overly protective and solicitous and may unconsciously foster dependence. Such patterns can compound the loss of function associated with physical deconditioning. These patterns may contribute to emotional dysfunction and diminished self-esteem.

Patients interviewed in depth by Barstow (1974) reported a number of alterations used in managing ADLs. Most entailed "planning ahead to maximize economy of effort." Patients employed the concept of simplification of activities, for example, eating only easily prepared foods, wearing slip-on shoes to avoid stooping and bending, and bathing less frequently. They applied the concept of pacing, for example, by bathing and dressing in stages with rest pauses.

In interviews using a grounded theory approach, Fagerhaugh (1973) found that patients used similar adaptations in coping with breathlessness. They used the process of "routing" to set priorities and efficiently expend limited reserves of energy. They described complex systems of planning ahead for shopping and household chores, using "puffing stations" to unobtrusively recover from breathlessness in public places, and carefully monitoring energy expenditure. Their lives were characterized by careful balancing of the resources of time, energy, and money to maintain equilibrium. One resource essential in this dynamic process was the use of "mobility assistants," family members and others who provided energy-conserving transportation and assistance.

For persons requiring continuous oxygen, portable oxygen systems bring mixed blessings for physical mobility and daily functioning. For some individuals the oxygen systems are portable reservoirs of energy. Carts, shoulder straps, and backpacks enhance the systems' portability, allowing such activities as golfing, shopping, travel, and even swimming. Other persons paradoxically limit their activity after receiving oxygen systems. Some perceive the systems as cumbersome. Others see them as a symbolic burden and a sign of disability. Uninformed and insensitive comments by others who identify oxygen as a risk for explosion or fire can aggravate the social isolation.

PERSONAL RESOURCES

The physical, psychologic, social, and spiritual resources of patients and families determine the responses and options available as pathophysiologic changes progress. Functioning and quality of life are integrally related to these resources.

Nutrition

Optimal nutritional status is essential for effective breathing and for functioning of the immune system. Malnourishment puts individuals at risk for respiratory muscle fatigue and for infections affecting the lungs and other body systems. These problems can necessitate hospitalization and mechanical ventilation and may be life-threatening (Openbrier & Covey, 1987).

Weight loss and malnutrition are commonly seen with advancing COPD. These responses are attributed to increasing metabolic demands and to decreasing ingestion of needed calories and nutrients. Metabolic requirements are elevated by the increased work of breathing associated with chronic airflow limitation. Smoking further increases metabolic rates (Braun et al., 1984).

Appetite and eating can be adversely affected by a number of factors including fatigue, dyspnea, expectoration of sputum, and dry mouth. Taste and smell are blunted by malnutrition and by smoking. Gastric irritation is a common side effect of bronchodilating agents and steroids. Ineffective breathing patterns cause difficulty with simultaneously breathing and eating, resulting in meal-related dyspnea. Some patients experience oxygen desaturation during meals, attributed to ineffective diaphragmatic function associated with gastric fullness (Openbrier & Covey, 1987).

Sleep and Rest

Sleep and rest promote coping by restoring physical and psychic energy. The physical and psychologic responses which accompany COPD interrupt normal sleep and rest patterns.

Sleep disturbances and daytime somnolence compound the problem of fatigue for many persons with COPD. Problems reported by patients include difficulty with initiating and maintaining sleep, nightmares, and excessive daytime sleepiness (Kinsman et al, 1983; Klink & Quan, 1987; Sexton & Munro, 1988). Oxygen desaturation due to disordered breathing during sleep is one probable cause for sleep disturbances (Douglas & Flenley, 1990; Fulmer & Snyder, 1984). Sleep is also disrupted by orthopnea, coughing, and shortness of breath.

For couples, the sleep disturbances of one partner can have adverse effects for both. The patient's nocturnal restlessness, coughing, and orthopnea make it necessary for the patient and spouse to sleep in separate beds or even separate rooms (Sexton & Munro, 1985). A related challenge for couples is finding alternative expressions of closeness and affection.

Support Person

A vital resource in successful coping with chronic lung disease is the assistance of a competent and dependable person, usually a spouse or other family member. In the stages before the patient requires direct assistance and care, the support person becomes a valuable source of energy for meeting daily needs for food, clothing, household maintenance, and illness management. This person often helps to attenuate fluctuations in mood, give encouragement, foster motivation, and provide surveillance in observing daily changes in appearance, energy, and response to treatment. Specific functions performed by this person include helping with household chores, assisting with treatments, and discussing feelings and choices (Barstow, 1974; Fagerhaugh, 1973; Hanson, 1982; Sexton & Munro, 1988).

Deficits in or absence of a dependable support system will have a dramatic impact on quality of life as the disease progresses. Persons without reliable help in the home require earlier referral for home care and other resources, whose availability often depends upon ability to pay. Nursing home placement, with the attendant changes and losses, becomes necessary earlier in the disease process for individuals lacking assistance from family and other care givers.

Financial Resources

Energy is a valuable commodity for persons with COPD. As personal reserves of energy are depleted, financial resources can be used to purchase needed assistance with home maintenance, transportation, household chores, and care of personal needs.

The financial impact of COPD is an important concern for many patients and families. For those who must reduce work hours or retire prematurely, income may be unexpectedly diminished. Discretionary expenditures may be greatly altered as money is needed for medications, oxygen, modifications of the home environment, help with home maintenance chores, and home care. Medications alone can become a major monthly expense. Patients often express frustration at the expense accompanying frequent changes in prescriptions.

Health insurance that covers home care services can lengthen the time patients are able to remain at home. Persons lacking this resource need to seek care in a long-term care facility earlier in the disease process.

Values and Belief System

Persons with advancing COPD may find it difficult to sustain inner resources at the very time when they are experiencing threats to hope and spiritual well-being. Fatigue and episodes of coughing or labored breathing may preclude attendance at church services. Awareness of personal vulnerability and mortaility may cause doubts about beliefs previously unquestioned, precipitating hopelessness, powerlessness, or spiritual distress. Awareness of the importance of breathing as a powerful symbol of life and health can intensify this distress.

Nursing Interventions

A case study at the end of this chapter discusses the application of specific interventions in the care of a patient coping with the progression of COPD. Interventions related to each of the four components of life quality are presented here.

A goal of nursing care is to identify, mobilize, and augment patients' and families' resources for coping with the changes related to illness phenomena, perceptions, and diminished functional capacity. Nursing care is often provided in the context of a pulmonary rehabilitation program, a holistic multidisciplinary program that might include a pulmonary nurse specialist, physician, respiratory therapist, physical therapist, occupational therapist, dietician, social worker, vocational counselor, psychiatrist or psychologist, the individual with COPD, and a family member or care giver. Other disciplines may be available for referral. In most such programs, roles are not mutually exclusive and team members work cooperatively to meet patient needs. Members of each discipline reinforce patient compliance with the interventions provided by other members of the rehabilitation team. A nurse often serves as coordinator for the pulmonary rehabilitation program (Borkgren, 1989; Hahn, 1988; Kirilloff, Carpenter, Kerby, Kigin, & Weimer, 1986).

Participation in a pulmonary rehabilitation program is associated with a number of beneficial effects. These positive outcomes include improved functioning in ADLs, enhancement of self-concept, and decreased depression and anxiety (Emery, Leatherman, & MacIntyre, 1989; Kersten, 1989a; Moser et al., 1980; Shenkman, 1985).

Whenever possible, interventions should include both patient and family. Even patient-centered interventions, such as breathing exercises, are enhanced by the understanding and reinforcement of family members. Other interventions, such as postural drainage and chest percussion, may require assistance from a care giver in the household.

INTERVENTIONS RELATED TO ILLNESS PHENOMENA

Breathing Retraining

Breathing retraining interventions can help patients to modify dyspnea and to increase functional capacity. Pursed-lip breathing—exhaling slowly through pursed lips—increases tidal volume, slows respiratory rate, and decreases the collapse of small airways by increasing intra-airway pressure. Diaphragmatic or abdominal breathing involves relaxing the abdominal muscles during inspiration and mildly tightening them during expiration to augment the diaphragm's upward movement. The result is to increase the use of the diaphragm during inspiration (Lareau

& Larson, 1987). After patients master these breathing patterns, they can be taught to integrate them into exercises and ADLs. Such coordinated breathing involves inhaling during the resting phase of activities and exhaling during the exertion phase, for example, while placing groceries on shelves, dressing, cleaning, or getting into a car. Mastery of this skill can remarkably improve quality of life by increasing activity tolerance and daily functioning. Although these breathing patterns are widely used, their long-term efficacy has not been systematically studied (Carrieri et al., 1984).

Bronchial Hygiene

To enhance airway clearance, patients can be taught about exercise and adequate fluid intake. Supervised practice with coughing maneuvers can assist patients in clearing airways effectively without breathlessness and fatigue. Controlled coughing involves inhaling by sniffing, followed by pursed-lip exhalations to move secretions into large airways. The final exhalation is a staggered huffing effort, which keeps intrathoracic pressure low, preventing premature airway closure. Bronchial hygiene measures such as chest percussion and postural drainage may be necessary for persons unable to cough effectively (DeVito, 1985).

Inspiratory Muscle Training

Inspiratory muscle training involves a program of exercise for the diaphragm and other respiratory muscles, similar to training for skeletal muscles. Patients on such a program breathe for 15 to 30 minutes daily through a small hand-held device that increases inspiratory pressure loads (Larson, Kim, Sharp, & Larson, 1988). There is evidence that such a program may be useful in preventing respiratory fatigue and improving exercise tolerance, effects thought to be mediated by increased strength and endurance of the respiratory muscles (Kim, 1984).

Oxygen Therapy

For patients with impaired gas exchange, therapeutic use of low-flow supplemental oxygen may be necessary to maintain arterial Po_2 at about 60 mm Hg (Porth, 1986). The Nocturnal Oxygen Therapy Trials (NOTT) demonstrated the efficacy of continuous low-flow oxygen in prolonging life for persons with hypoxemia (Nocturnal Oxygen Therapy Group, 1980). The goal of oxygen therapy is to maintain arterial oxygen levels without supressing the patient's hypoxic drive to breathe. This requires careful monitoring of ABG measurements.

Oxygen sources for home use include cylinders, liquid oxygen systems, and oxygen concentrators. Selection of the optimal system requires careful assessment of the patient's mobility and the flow rates needed (O'Ryan & Burns, 1984).

Patients receiving oxygen who are concerned about the appearance of conventional nasal cannulas may be candidates for trans-tracheal oxygen systems. These systems deliver oxygen directly into the trachea through a small flexible tube implanted surgically under local anesthesia. The tube provides an efficient method of supplying oxygen that can be hidden under clothing. Advantages include the cosmetic effects, cost savings due to reduced oxygen consumption, and improved mobility resulting from use of smaller portable reservoirs. Patients must be well informed about self-care of the catheter and must be carefully assessed for motivation to comply (Christopher et al., 1987; Lucas, Golish, Sleeper, & O'Ryan, 1988).

Care During Acute Episodes

In a qualitative study of hospitalized patients' experiences during episodes of acute dyspnea, 96 patients recalled nurse behaviors they perceived as helpful. These included directly communicating acknowledgment of patients' fear, demonstration of simple breathing techniques for patients to imitate, assisting with self-care activities, validation of the severity of the dyspneic episode, and facilitating patients' concentrating on breathing (DeVito, 1990).

INTERVENTIONS RELATED TO PERCEPTIONS

Self-monitoring

Self-monitoring is an essential skill for successful coping with chronic lung disease. Self-monitoring interventions often precipitate spontaneous changes in individuals' behavior patterns (Ryan, 1989). By recognizing triggering events and early signals of dyspnea and anxiety, patients can learn to avert acute episodes. Recognition of the slight changes in sputum and breathing that herald a respiratory infection is a requisite skill in securing prompt treatment and avoiding hospitalization.

Even slight variations in air quality, temperature, and humidity can affect breathing for persons with COPD (Fagerhaugh, 1973). Becoming attuned to the sensations of breathing, breathing patterns, and the effects of changing weather conditions is a first step in learning to plan activities to maximize breathing and functioning.

A useful initial intervention in promoting a sense of mastery over symptoms is having the patient keep a detailed log of daily activities and the accompanying sensations, symptoms, and weather conditions. This tool can help to identify patterns and precipitating factors that might otherwise go undetected. An adaptation of this idea is a dyspnea log, in which

Mark the line at the point that best describes your breathing.

_____

No difficulty   *Extreme difficulty*
breathing   *breathing*

FIGURE 11 ■ 2   Dyspnea visual analog scale.

patients record the time, severity, and factors related to all episodes of dyspnea (Carrieri, 1989; Kersten, 1989*b*). In using such a log one patient discovered that she often experienced dyspnea episodes in the early afternoon, on days when she prepared and ate a large midday meal. By getting accustomed to smaller meals that are more easily prepared and digested, she was able to alter this pattern of dyspnea and achieve a sense of mastery.

Patients' experiences of dyspnea, fatigue, exertion, and anorexia can be rated on a visual analog scale. A common format is a vertical or horizontal line, usually 100 millimeters in length, with verbal descriptors such as "extreme difficulty breathing" and "no difficulty breathing" at either end (see Fig. 11–2). The patient is directed to make a mark indicating present, usual, or worst dyspnea. Measuring the interval marked on the scale provides an objective measure of this subjective experience; it can be used to compare episodes of dyspnea and to evaluate the effects of interventions. Because of their simplicity, such scales can be used by

Circle the number that best matches your shortness of breath.

0	*None at all*
0.5	*Very, very slight (just noticeable)*
1	*Very slight*
2	*Slight*
3	*Moderate*
4	*Somewhat Severe*
5	*Severe*
6	
7	*Very Severe*
8	
9	*Very, very severe (almost maximal)*
10	*Maximal*

FIGURE 11 ■ 3   Modified Borg Scale. (SOURCE: *Borg, 1982.*)

acutely dyspneic patients, including those in emergency rooms or on ventilators (Brown, 1988; Gift, 1987, 1989; Lush, Janson-Bjerklie, Carrieri, & Lovejoy, 1988; Openbrier & Rogers, 1989).

In using the Modified Borg Scale patients indicate their experience of dyspnea or other symptoms by using numbers from 0 to 10 to correspond to verbal descriptions (see Fig. 11–3). This scale is useful for rating changes in dyspnea, exertion, or fatigue during exercise (Borg, 1982).

Biofeedback tools can be used to demonstrate the efficacy of interventions. Pulse-oximetry monitors give immediate feeback on the effects of diaphragmatic breathing patterns on oxygen saturation (Tiep, Burns, Kao, Madison, & Herrera, 1986). Patients are often surprised to learn that they can significantly increase saturation levels during an initial effort at controlled breathing. Pulse monitoring can be useful in observing the effects of relaxation techniques and exercise.

Teaching

Patients can benefit from information about comfort measures. Temperature extremes affect oxygen demand and consumption. Maintaining humidity at about 40 percent, using an air conditioner or humidifer if necessary, and keeping room temperature at 68 to 72°F is optimal (Curigan & Gronkiewicz, 1988). Patients who experience a sense of suffocation with impaired breathing often find some relief with an electric fan blowing on the face.

Living with lung disease involves adapting to and using the tools of its medical treatment. Patients need to adjust treatment modalities to their life-styles and to make decisions about using these treatments in response to self-assessments. Knowledge can promote a sense of mastery in using these resources. A teaching program for COPD patients utilizing principles of adult education has demonstrated short-term increases in knowledge and skills for coping (Perry, 1981). Areas in which patients may need information include medications and use of metered dose inhalers, nebulizer devices, oxygen delivery systems, bronchial hygiene techniques, and use of inspiratory muscle training (IMT) devices (Davido, 1981; Kersten, 1989*b*; Larson et al., 1988; Lindell & Mazzocco, 1990; Lucas et al., 1988; Openbrier, Fuoss, & Mall, 1988; Openbrier, Hoffman, & Wesmiller, 1988; Sexton, 1990). Patients who are candidates for trans-tracheal oxygen require carefully tailored assessment and teaching (Christopher et al., 1987; Heimlich & Carr, 1989).

Patients on continuous oxygen who are interested in traveling need specialized teaching and referral to medical equipment vendors (Sleeper, 1988; Traver, 1985). Information about cruises for persons with pulmonary disease may be appropriate for many patients, including those receiving continuous oxygen (Burns, 1987).

INTERVENTIONS RELATED TO PHYSICAL AND EMOTIONAL FUNCTIONING

Exercise Program

A program of progressive exercise is a key component of pulmonary rehabilitation. Many patients with mild to moderate disease have restricted their activity in response to fear of dyspnea and are surprised to learn that they can comfortably exercise at more intense levels than prior to rehabilitation. Therapeutic exercise should be designed to promote the functional activities needed by the individual. Arm exercises, such as using an arm ergometer or arm lifts using dowels or weights, promote the upper body strength needed for self-care, household, and recreational activities. Walking and exercising on a stationary bicycle promote cardio-pulmonary conditioning and are exercises suited to the life-styles of most individuals. Using a treadmill and water exercises are other options (Hughes & Davison, 1983; O'Hara et al., 1987; Ries, Ellis, & Hawkins, 1988).

Regular exercise is correlated with significant improvements in function in daily activities, self-care, sense of well-being and mastery, and control over the fear of dyspnea. Although exercise conditioning is not associated with improvement in pulmonary function parameters or ABGs, its positive effects on exercise tolerance and daily functioning are associated with improved quality of life (Braun, Fregosi, & Reddan, 1982; Holden, Stelmach, Curtis, Beck, & Stoller, 1990; Stratton, 1989). Progressive exercise supervised directly by a health-care professional may have the effect of deconditioning patients to the fear of dyspnea, resulting in increasing tolerance of activity (Glass, 1981).

Energy-Conservation Techniques

Persons who live with chronic lung disease devise ways of conserving vital energy by, for example, using carts for carrying groceries and laundry, planning rest stops during strenuous activities, wearing clothing that is easy to put on, and using energy-saving devices such as microwave ovens and remote-controlled television. Even very resourceful individuals can benefit from discussing principles of energy conservation and planning ways to apply them in meeting present and future needs. Calling ahead to stores, shopping centers, and office buildings can yield important information about accesses with few stairs, merchandise available, and locations of offices or items. Obtaining and using a handicapped parking permit decreases the amount of walking needed for completing errands. Getting into and out of cars can be eased by placing a large plastic bag on the seat to reduce the adherence of clothing and upholstery. Combing hair and applying makeup consume less energy and tax breathing less when elbows are supported on a table. Group discussion of energy conservation techniques can provide a lively exchange of energy-saving ideas.

PROMOTING EMOTIONAL FUNCTIONING

Relaxation Techniques

Anxiety can trigger dyspnea and tax cardiopulmonary function. To gain mastery over these distressing responses, many patients benefit from reflecting on their responses to stress and applying principles of behavior modification to respond in ways that place fewer demands on cardiopulmonary reserves. Relaxation training and meditation techniques can be effective tools in the relief of anxiety. Progressive muscle relaxation has been shown to be effective in helping patients to slow breathing rates. This technique can be taught in one session and reinforced with a tape recording, before following up with two or three weekly outpatient sessions (Renfroe, 1988). Such techniques can be supplemented by the use of biofeedback to control tension in respiratory and peripheral muscles (Sandhu, 1986).

Patient and Family Counseling

Resources are best utilized when the patient, family, and others are realistic about the disease and its impacts. Counseling skills can be used to assist both patient and family to acknowledge the thoughts and feelings accompanying limitations and losses. For patients overwhelmed by losses, summarizing the coping resources they and their support network possess can provide needed affirmation.

Sudden, unexplained changes in behavior may be related to physical or psychologic factors. Nurses can apply advanced skills in assessment and counseling to assist families to understand and cope with this source of frustration (McDonald, 1981). To interrupt patterns of blame and anger, patients and families can be taught to attribute the emotional effects of COPD to the disease process and not to one another (McSweeney et al., 1982). They can be guided to increase their exposure to experiences that are psychologically rewarding.

A multidisciplinary approach can be used for patients with impaired emotional functioning. Pulmonary patients with depression have shown positive responses to antidepressant medications, including improvements in functional ability and quality of life (McDonald et al., 1989). Nurses can play a key role in recognizing signs of depression, making referrals for medical treatment, and evaluating patient responses. Patients with severe depression or potential for suicide should be referred to a mental health professional.

Assertiveness Training

Patients who learn and apply principles and techniques of assertive communication exhibit enhanced physical and emotional functioning. Such skills can help patients take effective action to communicate their needs, conserve energy, avoid exposure to respiratory infections, and control episodes of dyspnea. Success with assertive communication can bolster self-esteem.

One patient coined the phrase "I need to 'take ten,'" to briefly communicate to family and friends her needs for rest or relaxation. She used this technique, along with self-monitoring, to arrest episodes of dyspnea and anxiety before her symptoms become severe. Another patient, pleased with new-found skills in assertive communication, commented, "Sometimes the best medicine is saying 'No!'"

Sexual Counseling

For persons with COPD, planning ahead is an essential coping skill applicable to most activities, including sexual expression. A program of exercise conditioning can result in improved breathing and energy levels during sexual activity. Like other exercises requiring energy expenditure, sexual activity is optimized at times of day when breathing is best, often in late morning or early afternoon. In the early morning, coughing may be a problem because respiratory secretions accumulate during the night. Sexual activity can be planned to coincide with the peak action of medications. Breathing is enhanced when patients avoid a large meal or physical exertion before sexual activity. Shared pleasure is heightened when both partners are relaxed and approach encounters by pacing, going slowly, and adopting an attitude of playfulness (Hahn, 1989).

Inhaled bronchodilators can be taken before or during sexual activity. Patients receiving oxygen should maintain usual flow rates or increase flow by 1 liter (Cooper, 1986). Pursed-lip breathing and diaphragmatic breathing should be used to improve breathing. Positions that will minimize pressure on the chest, such as side-lying or sitting, may be necessary (Katzin, 1990).

INTERVENTIONS RELATED TO PERSONAL RESOURCES

Promoting Optimal Nutrition

Because malnourishment predisposes patients to impaired breathing and infections, dietary intake and nutritional status should be carefully assessed. Assessment should include factors in the social history which predispose to malnutrition: inadequate income, absence of a person with whom to eat, inadequate facilities, smoking, and impaired mobility and dexterity (Openbrier & Covey, 1987).

Measures to maximize oral intake include snacks and meals high in calories and nutrients, using hard candy or gum to stimulate salivation before meals, planning the largest meal when hunger is greatest, and cooking aromatic foods to stimulate appetite. Meal-related oxygen desaturation can be assessed with oximetry and treated with increased liter flows. Stabilizing the chest by resting elbows on the table can facilitate breathing. Relaxation techniques and a general exercise program can relieve anxiety and promote appetite. Medication and treatment schedules can be revised to minimize gastric irritation, dry mouth, or expectoration of sputum. Gas-forming foods that impair function of the diaphragm should be identified and avoided.

Diet supplements can be used to provide calories and nutrients. There is an abundance of products available tailored to meet individual needs. One product, formulated in response to concerns about carbon dioxide production after ingestion of carbohydrates, contains 28 percent carbohydrate and 55 percent fat (Openbrier & Covey, 1987).

Enhancing Sleep

Measures that provide some relief from sleep-disturbing orthopnea include elevating the head of the bed on blocks, procuring a hospital bed, or sleeping or napping in a reclining chair. Patients with severe orthopnea may sleep best at a table, with the arms and upper body supported on pillows. Patients often report that a fan blowing on the face minimizes the sense of suffocation that accompanies dyspnea. Keeping the temperature comfortably warm and controlling humidity minimize oxygen demands and promote comfort and rest. Previously used habits and bedtime rituals should be identified and encouraged. Nocturnal oxygen administration is indicated for persons with sleep-related hypoxemia (Douglas & Flenley, 1990).

Social Support

Because an effective support system is essential for optimal coping, nursing care encompasses assessment of the support system, mobilization of their resources, and interventions directed at maintaining the well-being of the entire network. The nurse can help patients identify what type of support would be most helpful during a given phase of illness and which expressions of support are not perceived as helpful (Woods, Yates, & Primomo, 1989).

Support groups for both patients and those affected by their disease can be a source of affirmation, sharing, and problem-solving ideas. Groups

TABLE 11 ■ 3   Topics for Educational Programming for Pulmonary Support Groups

Topic	Resource
Using humor in coping Expressing love and sexuality Expressing anger constructively Decisions about life-support Coping with change and loss Coping with stress	Nurse

Energy conservation
  At home
  Away from home
	Occupational therapist

Medications, effects, and side effects	Pharmacist, physician, nurse
Air quality	Meteorologist
Options for exercise	Physical therapist
Optimal nutrition	Dietician
Nebulizers for aerosol therapy Home oxygen systems Traveling with oxygen	Respiratory therapist
Trans-tracheal oxygen	Nurse and respiratory therapist
Financial aspects Community resources Home-care options Long-term care options Family relationships	Social worker and nurse
Personal safety at home and away from home	Hospital security officer

Source: Adapted from White, 1989.

may employ a variety of formats. Members of the rehabilitation team and other community experts can present educational programs on topics of interest. Examples are summarized in Table 11–3. With a competent group leader, discussions of experiences, resources, and problem-solving methods can be helpful. Structured group exercises can be used to point out the psychosocial aspects of COPD and suggestions for coping with them. Both patients and family members can benefit from informal communication with persons sharing similar experiences, in a group setting or during a refreshment break.

Financial Resources

Lost earnings combined with illness-related expenditures can be a source of distress. A social worker can provide invaluable assistance in evaluating financial assets and providing information about programs of assistance for which patients qualify. To control the costs associated with frequent changes in prescriptions, patients may ask the pharmacist to fill only part of a prescription at a time. The resultant savings must be weighed against the need for more frequent trips to the pharmacy. Individualized assessment of costs should be a part of the selection of oxygen systems and other treatment modalities (Openbrier et al., 1988).

Spiritual Resources

Spiritual beliefs and practices can provide meaning and sustenance for patients confronting the changes and losses accompanying COPD. Nurturing this resource can avert or lessen the distress experienced by COPD patients and families.

Life review, with emphasis on achievements and accomplishments, can be a useful tool in providing a sense of purpose and order to patients' experiences (Stollenwerk, 1985). For persons experiencing spiritual distress, interventions include prayer and discussion of concerns. A referral for pastoral care may be indicated. Patients unable to attend church services may benefit from home visits by a pastor and church members.

Care Giver Support

Because the long-term assistance of one or more support persons is critical to successful coping, planning may be necessary to maintain the resources of these individuals. Age and the stresses of care giving put the care giver, usually a spouse, at risk for health problems. The nurse should plan with the spouse for personal health management. Interventions may include stress management and relaxation techniques, referral to a support group, or attention to personal health needs. Volunteers may be available for weekly visits or for assistance with shopping and home maintenance. For patients with advanced disease, respite care in the home or an inpatient facility can assist the care giver during times of stress or illness (Sexton & Munro, 1985).

PLANNING FOR LONG-TERM CARE

As the progression of illness impairs function, patient and family may need assistance in making arrangements for long-term care. Coping tasks include acquiring information, setting priorities, allocating financial resources, and confronting the feelings accompanying multiple changes. In making decisions about home care or admission to a long-term care facility, patients and family members can benefit from the expertise of a social worker in evaluating financial assets and insurance coverage. Care in the home, even with ample assistance from other professional care givers, requires a competent and dependable primary care giver (Heslop & Bagnall, 1988; White & Briggs, 1980).

PREPARING FOR DEATH

Preparing for the eventuality of death involves other coping tasks for the patient and family. These include dealing with feelings and the accompanying behaviors, such as repression of fears and withdrawal from spouse and family members. Patients may need help in anticipating possible episodes of acute respiratory insufficiency and discussing with the physican how aggressively these will be treated. The implications of intubation and mechanical ventilation can be discussed before an acute problem occurs. Hospice care, at home or in an inpatient facility, is a resource that can be suggested and explored before the disease is at end-stage. Living Will and power-of-attorney documents can be used by patients to communicate their wishes to family members and care givers. After death, bereavement visits can assist family members in accepting changes and the associated feelings and integrating these into their life experience.

■ Case Study

Ruth P.

The experiences of Ruth P., summarized below, illustrate some of the changes in quality of life experienced by an individual coping with COPD and some of the interventions which can be used to enhance quality of life at successive stages of the disease.

Ruth P., age 72, reminisces during a home visit. Her narrative is cut short by dyspnea, but her story unfolds in subsequent visits. In her early sixties, after over 40 years of smoking twenty to thirty cigarettes per day, Ruth became increasingly aware of her "smoker's cough" and occasional shortness of breath. Her doctor told her she had emphysema. For several years, the diagnosis had little impact on her life. Widowed with three adult children, she maintained her large first-floor flat, made and sold quilts, entertained and went out with friends.

The changes began insidiously. In her late sixties, Ruth noticed increasing shortness of breath while walking to the grocery store. She became so fatigued while shopping that upon arriving home she collapsed exhausted into a chair. After resting, she was able to put the groceries on cupboard shelves. She experienced increasing dyspnea while climbing the stairs to her daughter's second-floor apartment. Eventually this became so uncomfortable that she went up only with great effort and felt fatigued for the rest of the day. She now required help with heavier household chores, such as washing floors and carrying baskets of laundry up and down the basement stairs.

"By this time," Ruth said, "the term 'emphysema' had personal meaning for me." She took an oral theophylline preparation and digitalis as prescribed and saw the physician when her sputum increased or became yellow-tinged, signs she knew indicated a respiratory infection.

She had repeated visits to the emergency room for episodes of acute dyspnea and the panic which invariably accompanied them. She was hospitalized with increasing frequency for treatment with intravenous and aerosol bronchodilators and oxygen and medical management of heart failure.

At the urging of her physician, Ruth reluctantly accepted a referral to an outpatient pulmonary rehabilitation program. At her first appointment, she received an overview of the 12-week program. At this visit the nurse did an assessment and interview, focusing on Ruth's experience of her lung disease and its impact on her life. Ruth manifested compromised quality of life in all areas: illness phenomena, perceptions, functional capacity, and personal resources. Team members collaborated in identifying Ruth's current problems and her resources for coping with her lung disease (see Tables 11–4 and 11–5). Based on her personal goals, needs, and resources, they identified objectives and developed a plan of care (see Table 11–6). Over the next 3 months, Ruth had individualized weekly appointments with members of the rehabilitation team, for monitored walking, breathing exercises, and teaching and counseling.

When asked to identify her greatest problem in living with lung disease, Ruth immediately mentioned episodes of acute breathing difficulty, which she experienced with increasing frequency and acuity. While eating in a restaurant, a pleasure she savored, she would suddenly experience dyspnea and panic so acute that she would rush outside panting and pale, leaving her meal untouched, her companion deserted, and Ruth exhausted for the rest of the day. The sense of powerlessness evoked by these episodes was a distressing aspect of the illness. She admitted taking extra puffs of her metered-dose inhaler at these times but found that this offered limited relief. When told that pulmonary rehabilitation might provide help in gaining control over these episodes, Ruth was skeptical but willing to participate.

Ruth was taught controlled breathing patterns, designed to make more effective use of her diaphragm and other respiratory muscles. First she learned diaphragmatic breathing, relaxing her abdomen while inhal-

TABLE 11 ■ 4   Nursing Diagnoses of Ruth P.

Ineffective breathing patterns related to airflow limitation
Anxiety related to episodes of dyspnea
Impaired mobility related to dyspnea, fatigue, and deconditioned state
Altered self-esteem related to reliance on family members
Altered health maintenance: neglect of other health needs (dental, podiatry) related to dyspnea and fatigue
Potential for noncompliance related to cost of medications and difficulty getting to pharmacy
Self-care deficit: bathing, cooking, laundry, related to dyspnea and deconditioned state
Knowledge deficit about self-assessment, medications, energy conservation, breathing exercises
Impaired health maintenance related to smoking

TABLE 11 ■ 5   Assessment of Resources for Coping with Lung Disease for Ruth P.

Assets	*Deficits*
PERSONAL	
Sense of humor	Limited skills in assertive communications
Personal and family experience with illness	Little knowledge of lung disease and
Cognitive skills	coping strategies
Trust in physician, medications	
Age and life-experience: effects on expectations	
Low-energy hobbies	
SOCIAL	
Significant person: daughter	Concern about other daughter's impending
Son, daughter-in-law	divorce and finances
Sister in Arizona	
Other family members	
Network of friends	
Pet dog	
SPIRITUAL	
Faith	Difficulty attending church
Good relationship with pastor	
PHYSICAL	
Good appetite	Cardiorespiratory pathology
Prepares well-balanced meals	Deconditioned state
	Arthritis
	Obesity
	Smoking
	Hearing deficit
FINANCIAL	
Income supplemented by hobby (selling her quilts)	Gaps in insurance coverage
	Cost of medications
Financial resources for energy-saving devices	Expenses of maintaining large home
ENVIRONMENTAL	
No other smokers in home	Maintenance of large home
	Use of sprays and aerosols

ing and moderately tightening abdominal muscles while exhaling. In later visits she learned and practiced pursed-lip breathing, exhaling slowly through lips tightened almost into a whistling position. The pulse oximeter was used as a biofeedback tool, to give Ruth immediate visual evidence of the efficacy of her new breathing pattern. She was able to increase her oxygen saturation from 86 to 94 percent with a few minutes of pursed-lip breathing.

TABLE 11 ■ 6   Plan of Care for Ruth P.

Personal goals identified by Ruth
1. To receive a medication or treatment to control panic attacks
2. To depend less on family members for household chores
3. To visit sister in Arizona, if possible
4. To remain in home for as long as possible

Objectives developed by Ruth and rehabilitation team. Ruth will:
1. Verbalize awareness of her resources for coping with effects of her lung disease
2. Demonstrate knowledge and skill in maintaining an effective equilibrium of physical and psychologic resources including:
    Knowledge for coping with lung disease
    Management of dyspnea-panic episodes
    Health maintenance: optimal nutrition, rest, and exercise
    Self-care of personal needs
    Home management skills
    Effective self-administration of prescribed medications, including oxygen if needed
    Stress management
    Satisfying relationships
    Financial resources
3. Use resources for smoking cessation
4. Demonstrate improved exercise tolerance
5. Exhibit increased function in ADLs
6. Lose 20 pounds
7. Consider plans and options for making a trip to Arizona to visit her sister
8. Report increased satisfaction with her quality of life

Interventions. Teaching and counseling related to:
1. Living with lung disease
    Awareness of energy, fatigue, and early sensations of dyspnea
    Recognizing and promptly reporting signs of infection
    Avoiding respiratory irritants
        In the home environment
        In public places
        Seasonal conditions
            Ozone, humidity in summer
            Cold weather in winter
2. Breathing retraining exercises
    Diaphragmatic breathing
    Pursed-lip breathing
    Coordinated breathing
    Inspiratory muscle training (IMT) as prescribed
3. Stress management
    Identification of stressors
    New responses to stress
    Assertive communication principles and skills
    Relaxation techniques
4. Smoking cessation:
    Quit-smoking message
    Exploring personal motives to quit
    Referral
    Individualized program
5. Energy-conservation techniques
    Planning ahead
    Rest periods
    Work simplification
    Organizing supplies
    Positioning for efficiency
    Saying "no"

TABLE 11 ■ 6   Plan of Care for Ruth P. (*Continued*)

6. Nutritional assessment and counseling
       Control of obesity
             Behavior modification
             Cognitive restructuring
       Prevention of muscle atrophy
       Control of CO_2 production
             Decreasing carbohydrates
             Increasing polyunsaturated fats
7. Exercise program
       Progressive exericse
             Walking
             Stationary cycling
             Arm exercises
       Application of coordinated breathing
       Self-monitoring, safety precautions

Next she learned coordinated breathing, integrating the controlled breathing patterns into movements and ADLs. The effort-expending portion of activities, she learned, should be done while exhaling slowly. She demonstrated her skill in applying this pattern while placing groceries on shelves, inhaling while resting and exhaling while lifting items to shelves. At the nurse's suggestion, she placed smiling-faced stickers as visual cues in her home environment to remind her to use controlled breathing patterns while bathing and dressing, preparing meals, changing bed linens, and performing other ADLs.

With some reluctance, Ruth participated in learning relaxation techniques, using tape-recorded exercises twice a day to progressively relax muscle groups and induce a state of mental quietude. Focusing attention on herself was a new experience for her, and she needed regular encouragement to continue with this. As she became attuned to the feeling of tension in her neck and shoulder muscles, she could see how this affected her breathing and how she could prevent episodes of dyspnea by arresting the developing tension. She continued to experience episodes of dyspnea, but the frequency and acuity were notably lessened through the practice of relaxation.

Ruth's variable level of energy was a daily problem, which she felt powerless to control. She could not anticipate what her energy level would be on any given day or time of day. Her fluctuating energy level seemed to be affected by how well she had slept, the air quality, humidity, and her psychologic state. When she pushed herself too hard, the ensuing exhaustion reinforced the need to take control of this aspect of her disease. A goal for this problem was for Ruth to balance rest and activity to prevent episodes of extreme fatigue and dyspnea. Interventions involved helping Ruth to learn new skills: sensitivity to her body's sense of energy or fatigue and the ability to identify factors which affected her energy level. She was helped to adopt new attitudes: accepting her fluctuations in energy and learning to consider all plans tentative. She was taught to apply skills in assertive communication in making her needs known to family and friends. Like her, they needed to learn that coping with lung disease may require last-minute changes in plans. Ruth learned to be flexible, changing plans when her energy level was unexpectedly low and, when necessary, canceling appointments or plans with friends.

During summer, when air quality in the city could deteriorate, Ruth learned to monitor meteorologists' reports of ozone levels, air quality, and humidity, available on radio and television news and on telephone recordings by the local weather service and the Department of Natural Resources. When ozone levels were high or the air-quality index was low, she avoided going out if possible. She learned to schedule appointments and do shopping early in the morning, to avoid peak ozone levels which usually occur in the afternoon. She found humidity oppressive and on particularly bad days sought refuge in her air-conditioned bedroom.

SMOKING CESSATION

During the first 6 years after diagnosis of her emphysema, Ruth had made five aborted attempts to quit smoking. She attended a group program with a friend, but her hearing deficit made it difficult to participate. On her own, she cut back to about fifteen cigarettes a day but was unable to quit. "I truly enjoy those cigarettes!" she said with conviction. While attending the pulmonary rehabilitation program, she half-heartedly agreed to participate in individualized counseling by a graduate nursing student. Through this program, supplemented by exercises from the American Lung Association's (1986) booklet "Freedom from Smoking in 20 Days," she was eventually successful in total smoking cessation. Especially helpful to her was her list of smoking substitutes: activities she enjoyed that did not involve smoking (Table 11–7). During this time she

TABLE 11 ■ 7 Ruth's List of Things I Enjoy That Do Not Involve Smoking

Sewing a square for quilt-making
Caring for my plants
Eating a gooey dessert
Working a jigsaw puzzle
Combing the dog's coat
Taking a warm bath
Drinking a cup of tea
Playing solitaire
Crocheting a section of an afghan
Typing a letter
Making popcorn
Playing cards with a friend
Making holiday decorations

TABLE I I ■ 8   Ruth's List of Things I
Enjoy That Cost Less Than 5 Dollars

Watching the "Today" show
Reading a biography from the library
Buying flowers
Calling my sister in Arizona
Staying in my robe and slippers all morning
Going out to lunch with my daughter
Doing light gardening
Reading "People" magazine
Sitting out in the yard
Watching the late movie
Listening to music
Having a neighbor over for coffee

became a connoisseur of teas and sugar-free candies; she immersed herself in her hobbies, making piles of quilts and afghans. She commented, "Sometimes I get so absorbed in my sewing that I don't think of smoking for several hours."

Ruth discussed her ambivalence about quitting smoking. "I surprised myself. I never believed I'd quit." She also saw this as a loss of one of her greatest pleasures, at a time when her life was becoming constricted by her disease. One of the nursing goals at this time was for Ruth to view her smoking cessation more as a successful achievement and less as a loss. Principles of patient contracting (Steckel, 1982) were used to help her to reinforce nonsmoking. Weekly goals were set, with the main criterion that they be easily achievable. The first goal was for Ruth to make a list of ten things she enjoyed that cost no more than 5 dollars. She readily agreed to this and returned the next week with her list (see Table 11–8).

She learned to use these rewards to reinforce her nonsmoking behavior and to build her sense of self-esteem as a nonsmoker. She continued to find it especially difficult to avoid smoking during the first hour of the morning. She was instructed to build into her environment cues which stimulated behaviors other than smoking. For example, she set the table for breakfast before going to bed. Upon arising she brushed her teeth and proceeded immediately to prepare breakfast, avoiding cues to her former habit of reading the newspaper in the living room with a cup of coffee and a cigarette. After getting through that first hour smoke-free, she was instructed to reinforce her behavior with a reward from her list. She grew to relish using these rewards to reinforce her nonsmoking behavior and reported satisfaction at her hard-won victory over smoking.

EXERCISE PROGRAM

Ruth attempted to participate in the physical-conditioning aspect of the rehabilitation program. In favorable weather she would begin a walking program but had difficulty sustaining the effort. Inclement weather limited her walking, and she had no interest in the stationary bicycle which was recommended. "I've never been one to exercise much," she said, "and, to be honest, I have trouble believing it can help me now." Interventions were designed: a discussion and demonstration by a client who experienced markedly increased exercise tolerance after beginning a walking program, and a demonstration of the effects of exercise on Ruth's pulse rate.

Ruth agreed to participate in a program of arm exercises, designed to help her to prevent the limitation of arm function which often accompanies chronic lung disease. During clinic visits, she used the arm ergometer in supervised exercise sessions with the physical therapist. At home, she did exercises taught by the therapist, lifting a 36-inch wooden dowel overhead repetitively while using coordinated breathing. Ruth was motivated to comply with the arm exercise program because "My arms are stronger and that makes a difference in my life. I can see that it's easier to lift big pieces of fabric, bathe myself, comb my hair, and cook."

ENERGY CONSERVATION

The aspect of the program which Ruth enjoyed most was learning about energy-conservation techniques, taught by the occupational therapist. She learned ways to simplify daily activities, which soon became habits, such as rolling laundry in a sheet and pushing it down the basement stairs, and placing clean laundry on hangers in the basement to be carried up later by visiting family members.

She completed the 12-week rehabilitation program, participating in the components with varying degrees of enthusiasm. The most salutary outcome for her was a marked increase in her daily activities. "The coordinated breathing has made all the difference for me," she reported in a postprogram evaluation. "I've learned to pace myself. Now I can do things that I hadn't done for the past year—vacuum my own carpet, put my groceries away without getting exhausted, enjoy time with my grandchildren again." She was exhilarated at the liberation of again being able to climb stairs, exhaling through pursed lips while climbing and pausing to inhale and rest on every third stair.

GROUP SUPPORT

Ruth began attending the monthly meetings of a support group for patients with chronic lung disease and their families and friends, coordinated by the nurse manager of the pulmonary rehabilitation program. The format of meetings consisted of a brief practice of breathing exercises, an educational program on an aspect of living with lung disease, group discussion, and informal conversation and refreshments. Ruth and her daughter attended meetings when possible. It was a new experience for Ruth to see other people coping successfully with lung disease more advanced than hers. She was heartened to hear a man with portable oxygen discussing his golf score. She empathized with group members who discussed the hazards of using Handicapped Parking permits when one has an "invisible handicap." She cheered their stories of using assertive communication in responding to unfeeling comments by strangers in restaurants and shopping centers. She incorporated information from the educational sessions into her own self-care practices.

RELOCATION

Over the next 2 to 3 years, her lung disease became the central fact of Ruth's life. She experienced a series of changes and losses and came to rely heavily on her daugher's daily assistance.

As Ruth became unable to maintain her home, her daughter searched for a satisfactory elderly housing unit, completed the extensive application forms, sold much of her furniture, packed, moved, and set up the new household in a way that would conserve Ruth's now limited energy. The pulmonary rehabilitation nurse assisted with planning for energy conservation. She recommended investing in several new appliances—a microwave oven, a remote-control television, and an apartment-sized air conditioner. A reclining chair was also suggested, to provide for rest periods with feet elevated. Ruth and her daughter were advised to set up "living stations," that is, chairs in two or three areas of the home where needed supplies would be within easy reach. Ruth's daughter set up a chair by the bathroom sink and placed all toiletry supplies within arm's reach. In the kitchen, she placed frequently used articles on countertops or in waist-level drawers, to minimize bending and reaching which impair ventilation and consume energy. In the living room, the reclining chair was placed within easy reach of a floor lamp, magazine rack, and a table which held commonly used items: telephone, television remote control, writing supplies, crocheting and sewing supplies, nail file, and tissues. In the bedroom, the sewing machine was similarly equipped with all needed items within easy reach.

Ruth experienced fatigue and difficulty sleeping, which were attributed to nocturnal oxygen desaturation. This was documented using oximetry, and nocturnal oxygen was prescribed. The oxygen proved to be a mixed blessing, increasing Ruth's energy while presenting several new challenges.

When Ruth's associates in the building saw the "Oxygen in Use" sign on her apartment door, some of them expressed anxiety and began avoiding her. The nurse suggested having a question-and-answer session on oxygen presented for her friends, the building manager, and other interested tenants. Ruth sent invitations and was happily surprised when twelve people appeared at the appointed time. They listened attentively to the nurse's explanation of the system and raised questions about the combustibility of oxygen, the possibility of a cylinder exploding, and the belief that only terminally ill people are treated with oxygen. Several expressed relief in learning that oxygen is a safe treatment which poses no threat to people nearby. Their altered beliefs enabled Ruth to demonstrate that nothing essential had changed despite the oxygen cylinder and nasal cannula.

As Ruth's hypoxemia progressed, her pulmonologist prescribed continuous oxygen therapy. It now became necessary for Ruth to let the delivery person from the durable medical equipment (DME) company into her apartment every 3 to 4 days to replace empty cylinders. Ruth experienced this as an intrusion into her privacy and schedule. On delivery days, Ruth would be certain to be dressed by mid-morning. Because of her hearing deficit, she worried that she would fail to hear the doorbell, especially when she was resting. She curtailed rest periods until the oxygen had been delivered. Walking to the door and carrying on a short conversation consumed precious energy. In discussing principles of energy conservation, Ruth admitted, "This is all too fatiguing." With her approval, the nurse arranged for Ruth's friend across the hall to have a key to her apartment and to let the delivery person in.

With Ruth now receiving continuous oxygen, the DME supplier suggested an oxygen concentrator as an option. At the nurse's next visit, Ruth raised questions about concentrators and expressed reluctance to make a change. The nurse explained the function of the concentrator, removing nitrogen and other gases from the air to provide a concentrated supply of oxygen. She pointed out the advantages for someone on continuous, low-flow oxygen: it would be less costly and require less frequent service, helping Ruth to conserve energy. About the size of an end table, with a wood grain finish, the concentrator would be more pleasant to look at. She also made Ruth aware of the differences from her present system. Because concentrators are powered by electricity, Ruth would still require an oxygen cylinder as a backup system in case of power failure. She could expect to become accustomed to the low-pitched mechanical humming sound of the concentrator after the first few days.

Upon trying the concentrator, Ruth realized its smooth functoning allowed her to plan her daily rest periods without the previously bothersome interruptions. She expressed anxiety about the possibility of a power failure. "I'll just have to call the paramedics," she said, revealing anger at her sense of powerlessness. The nurse used demonstrations, with return demonstrations by Ruth, to teach her to disconnect her tubing from the concentrator and connect it to the cylinder in the closet, after turning the flow meter to 2 liters. Reliance on the oxygen delivery system induced in Ruth feelings of vulnerability, dependency, anger, and depression. During home visits, Ruth was encouraged to express these feelings. An effective strategy was providing Ruth with feedback and summaries of her successful coping behaviors, aimed at helping her to maintain her self-esteem and sense of autonomy despite increasing limitations. She learned to accept the oxygen and to successfully make the life-style adjustments associated with it.

At first, the oxygen therapy caused Ruth to restrict her mobility outside of her apartment building. The nurse taught Ruth's daughter to manage the portable cylinder and procured a wheelchair. Ruth enjoyed the freedom of short outings, for a meal at a restaurant and for appointments.

At the outset of her pulmonary rehabilitation program, Ruth had expressed a tentative wish to travel to Arizona to visit her sister. "I know it's probably too late," she had said, "but some days I think I could do it." With considerable support and coordination by the rehabilitation team, this dream became a reality for Ruth. She traveled by train, accompanied by her daughter. Liquid oxygen was supplied along the route and in Phoenix by vendors carefully orchestrated by the respiratory therapist. Upon her return, Ruth expressed gratitude for this opportunity. "The things I learned in the rehab program gave me the energy and confidence to make the trip," she said. Her sense of personal accomplishment was evident.

DECLINING TRAJECTORY

For the next 10 months, Ruth enjoyed a high level of function in her daily activities. She then developed a fever and acute dyspnea, diagnosed as pneumonia. Hospitalized in the intensive-care unit, she received intravenous and aerosol bronchodialators and intravenous antibiotics. Blood gases were monitored frequently and a ventilator was on standby. When asked if she had fears, Ruth said to her nurse, "This is the closest I've ever come to dying. I'm afraid I'll suffocate. But I don't want to be put on any machines. And I don't want a tube in my throat." Aware of the physician's plans for intubation if necessary, the nurse consulted the clinical nurse specialist (CNS). The CNS asked Ruth about her impressions of intubation and mechanical ventilation, pointed out the need to support respiratory muscles during episodes of fatigue, and clarified Ruth's misconceptions. Ruth held firmly to her insistence on "no tubes or machines for breathing." The CNS communicated Ruth's wishes to the physician, who met with Ruth and her family and reluctantly agreed to comply with her wishes for no intubation. Ruth recovered from this episode and returned home.

Over the coming months, the quality of her life declined precipitously as Ruth experienced greater energy deficits and constant dyspnea. She required the help of a home health aide for laundry, housecleaning, meal preparation, and bathing. In the shower she experienced acute feelings of suffocation, so a hand-held shower and shower chair were supplied. Most of her limited energy was now directed at easing her breathing. As dressing became exhausting, she wore only a nightgown and slippers. She spent much of her time sitting with her elbows propped on the kitchen table, a position that best eased her dyspnea. A fan blowing on her face provided some relief from the constant feeling of suffocation. As Ruth experienced impairment of her attention span and short-term memory, her reading was limited to short magazine articles. Television provided some diversion, but eating aggravated her shortness of breath. Because the effort of chewing impaired her breathing, she ate mainly soft foods, augmented with diet supplements. Within a 10-week period she lost 25 pounds, despite meal assistance. To ease orthopnea, the head of her bed was elevated on blocks and she used several pillows. Her sleep was fitful and she napped intermittently, night and day, in the reclining chair. Digitalis and diuretics had little effect on her pitting edema. Eventually a commode became necessary, as walking to the bathroom became too great an effort.

Nursing care during this time was directed at meeting Ruth's basic needs, supporting her and her family in adapting to the changes imposed by her disease, and planning for her future needs. At times Ruth and her family coped ineffectively with the losses, stresses, and demands of illness. Some family members began avoiding Ruth. The nurse interpreted their behaviors, reminding Ruth that they loved her, felt powerless to make her comfortable, and feared losing her. She encouraged Ruth to discuss her feelings with them. Ruth's family sometimes expressed frustration at her irritability and forgetfulness. When they recognized these as signs of hypoxia, they were better able to accept her without blaming and to help in planning for her safety. When Ruth recognized her powerlessness to control her body and the changes brought by her now end-stage disease, she attempted to control family members through demanding and manipulative behaviors. The nurse supported family members in setting realistic limits. She helped Ruth and her family to express their feelings about loss and death. Ruth's daughter later said, "The turning point for me was when the nurse said our job is to care for Mom, not to get a cure for her. After that I could put my energy into trying to make her comfortable."

During this time Ruth experienced times of spiritual distress, questioning the need for her suffering and expressing hopelessness about the prayers which had previously sustained her. The nurse contacted a nearby parish, and Ruth began receiving weekly visits from the priest. She appreciated the opportunity to receive Communion, to pray with the priest, and to discuss concerns.

It became evident to Ruth and her family that her needs would soon exceed the resources available at home. Ruth feared being left alone, even for short periods. Her daughter was becoming exhausted from spending nights with her mother, working full-time, and maintaining her own family and household. They acknowledged that a nursing home would be needed. After weighing the assets of available homes and prioritizing Ruth's needs—proximity to family and space for a small table where Ruth could sit with her arms supported and feet elevated with a fan blowing on her face—a home with these requisites was found.

Ruth's cardiopulmonary function continued to decline. Her breathing became increasingly labored, her skin became taut with edema fluid, urine output lessened, and her awareness became obtunded. During her third night in the nursing home, Ruth died of acute heart failure caused by her lung disease.

Her daughter later reflected, "One difficult part of having a chronic illness is not knowing what is ahead, when an acute episode may occur in the middle of the night, when the end is coming. We thought Mom probably had weeks or months to live. If we had known her death was so near, we would have stayed with her for those 3 days at home. There was no way of knowing. Having a chronic disease gives you a chance to prepare and to lose a loved one in pieces, instead of all at once. At each stage, the nurses helped us to anticipate and plan for the problems of the next stage."

Summary

Quality of life for persons with COPD is affected by illness phenomena, perceptions, functional capacity, and personal resources. Changes experienced by patients and families can be ameliorated by nursing strategies, provided within the framework of a rehabilitation team approach. Such strategies are associated with significant improvements in the four aspects of quality of life. Continued research is needed to evaluate the efficacy of specific interventions and to refine the selection of interventions for groups of patients having common characteristics.

References

American Lung Association. (1986). *Freedom from smoking in twenty days.* New York: American Lung Association.

Barstow, R. E. (1974). Coping with emphysema. *Nursing Clinics of North America, 9,* 137–145.

Bergner, M., Bobbitt, R. A., Carter, W. B., & Gilson, B. S. (1981). The Sickness Impact Profile: Development and final revision of a health status measure. *Medical Care, 19,* 787–805.

Borg, G. A. V. (1982). Psychophysical bases of perceived exertion. *Medicine and Science in Sports and Exercise, 14,* 377–381.

Borkgren, M. W. (1989). Diversity in pulmonary rehabilitation: A geographic survey study. *Journal of Cardiopulmonary Rehabilitation, 9,* 63–71.

Braun, S. R., Fregosi, R., & Reddan, W. G. (1982). Exercise training in patients with COPD. *Postgraduate Medicine, 71,* 163–173.

Braun, S. R., Keim, N. L., Dixon, R. M., Clagnaz, P., Anderegg, A., & Shrago, E. S. (1984). The prevalence and determinants of nutritional changes in chronic obstructive pulmonary disease. *Chest, 86,* 558–563.

Brown, M. L. (1988). Measuring dyspnea. In M. Frank-Stromberg (Ed.), *Instruments for clinical nursing research* (pp. 369–378). Norwalk, CT: Appleton & Lange.

Burns, M. R. (1987). Cruising with COPD. *American Journal of Nursing, 87,* 479–482.

Campbell, M. L. (1987). Sexual dysfunction in the COPD patient. *Dimensions of Critical Care Nursing, 6,* 70–74.

Carpenito, L. J. (1989). *Nursing diagnosis: Application to clinical practice.* Philadelphia: JB Lippincott.

Carrieri, V. K. (1989). *Will the self-management/cognitive behavioral strategies used in the pain model decrease dyspnea?* Paper presented at the meeting of the American Thoracic Society, Cincinnati, OH.

Carrieri, V. K., & Janson-Bjerklie, S. (1986a). Dyspnea. In V. K. Carrieri, A. M. Lindsey, & C. M. West, *Pathophysiological phenomena in nursing: Human responses to illness* (pp. 191–218). Philadelphia: WB Saunders.

Carrieri, V. K., & Janson-Bjerklie, S. (1986b). Strategies patients use to manage the sensation of dyspnea. *Western Journal of Nursing Research, 8,* 284–301.

Carrieri, V. K., Janson-Bjerklie, S., & Jacobs, S. (1984). The sensation of dyspnea: A review. *Heart and Lung, 13,* 436–447.

Christopher, K. L., Spofford, B. T., Petrun M. D., McCarty, D. C., Goodman, J. R., & Petty, T. L. (1987). A program for transtracheal oxygen delivery: Assessment of safety and efficacy. *Annals of Internal Medicine, 107,* 802–808.

Cooper, K. (1986). Sexual counseling of the patient with chronic lung disease. *Focus on Critical Care, 13,* 18–20.

Curgian, L. M., & Gronkiewicz, C. A. (1988). Enhancing sexual performance in COPD. *Nurse Practitioner, 13,* 34–35.

Daughton, D. M., Fix, A. J., Kass, I., Patil, K. D., & Bell, C. W. (1979). Physiological-intellectual components of rehabilitation success in patients with chronic obstructive pulmonary disease (COPD). *Journal of Chronic Diseases, 32,* 405–409.

Davido, J. (1981). Pulmonary rehabilitation. *Nursing Clinics of North America, 16,* 275–283.

DeVito, A. J. (1990). Dyspnea during hospitalizations for acute phase of illness as recalled by patients with chronic obstructive pulmonary disease. *Heart and Lung, 19,* 186–191.

DeVito, A. J. (1985). Rehabilitation of patients with chronic obstructive pulmonary disease. *Rehabilitation Nursing, 10,*12–15.

Douglas, N. J., & Flenley, D. C. (1990). Breathing during sleep in patients with obstructive lung disease. *American Review of Respiratory Disease, 141,* 1055–1070.

Dracup, K., & Raffin, T. (1989). Withholding and withdrawing mechanical ventilation: Assessing quality of life. *American Review of Respiratory Disease, 140,* S44–S46.

Dudley, D. L., Glaser, E. M., Jorgenson, B. N., & Logan, D. L. (1980). Psychosocial concomitants to rehabilitation in chronic obstructive pulmonary disease. *Chest, 77,* 413–420, 544–551, 677–684.

Dudley, D. L., Wermuth, C., & Hague, W. (1973). Psychosocial aspects of care in the chronic obstructive pulmonary disease patient. *Heart and Lung, 2,* 389–393.

Emery, C. F., Leatherman, N. E., & MacIntyre, N. R. (1989, November). *Psychological effects of a pulmonary rehabilitation program.* Paper presented at the meeting of the Gerontological Society of America, Minneapolis, MN.

Fagerhaugh, S. Y. (1973). Getting around with emphysema. *American Journal of Nursing, 73,* 94–99.

Fletcher, E. C., & Martin, R. J. (1982). Sexual dysfunction and erectile impotence in chronic obstructive pulmonary disease. *Chest, 81,* 413–421.

Foxall, M. J., Ekberg, J. Y., & Griffith, N. (1987). Comparative study of adjustment patterns of chronic obstructive pulmonary disease patients and peripheral vascular disease patients. *Heart and Lung, 16,* 354–363.

Fulmer, J. D., & Snyder, G. L. (1984). American College of Chest Physicians/National Heart, Lung, and Blood Institute national conference on oxygen therapy. *Heart and Lung, 13,* 550–562.

Gift, A. G. (1989). Visual analogue scales: Measurement of subjective phenomena. *Nursing Research, 38,* 286–288.

Gift, A. G. (1987). Dyspnea: A clinical perspective. *Scholarly Inquiry for Nursing Practice, 1,* 73–85.

Gift, A. G., & Cahill, C. A. (1989). Psychophysiological aspects of dyspnea in COPD. *American Review of Respiratory Disease, 139,* A245.

Gift, A. G., Plaut, S. M., & Jacox, A. (1986). Psychologic and physiologic factors related to dyspnea in subjects with chronic obstructive pulmonary disease. *Heart and Lung, 15,* 595–601.

Gilson, B. S., Gilson, J. S., Bergner, M., Bobbitt, R. A., Kressel, S., Pollard, W. E., & Vesselago, M. (1975). The Sickness Impact Profile: Development of an outcome measure of health care. *American Journal of Public Health, 65,* 1304–1310.

Glass, L. B. (1981). Exercise therapy for the patient with pulmonary dysfunction. *Topics in Clinical Nursing, 3,* 87–93.

Gordon, M. (1987). *Nursing diagnosis: Process and application* (2d ed.). New York: McGraw-Hill.

Grant, I., Heaton, R. K., McSweeney, A. J., Adams, K. M., & Timms, R. M. (1980). Brain dysfunction in COPD. *Chest, 77S,* 308–309.

Guyatt, G. H., Berman, L. B., Townsend, M., Pugsley, S. O., & Chambers, L. W. (1987). A measure of quality of life for clinical trials in chronic lung disease. *Thorax, 42,* 773–778.

Guyatt, G. H., Thompson, P. J., Berman, L. B., Sullivan, M. J., Townsend, M., Jones, N. L., & Pugsley, S. O. (1985). How should we measure function in patients with chronic heart and lung disease? *Journal of Chronic Diseases, 38,* 517–524.

Guyatt, G. H., Townsend, M., Berman, L. B., & Pugsley, S. O. (1987). Quality of life in patients with chronic airflow limitation. *British Journal of Diseases of the Chest, 81,* 45–54.

Hahn, K. (1989). Sexuality and COPD. *Rehabilitation Nursing, 14,* 191–195.

Hahn, K. (1988). A nursing framework for multidisciplinary rehabilitation. *Rehabilitation Nursing, 11,* 6–10.

Hanson, E. I. (1982). Effects of chronic lung disease on life in general and on sexuality: Perceptions of adult patients. *Heart and Lung, 11,* 435–441.

Heaton, R. K., Grant, I., McSweeney, A. J., Adams, K. M., & Petty, T. L. (1983). Psychologic effects of continuous and nocturnal oxygen therapy in hypoxemic chronic obstructive pulmonary disease. *Archives of Internal Medicine, 143,* 1941–1947.

Heimlich, H., & Carr, G. (1989). The Micro-Trach: A seven-year experience with transtracheal oxygen therapy. *Chest, 95,* 1008–1012.

Heslop, A. P., & Bagnall, P. (1988). A study to evaluate the intervention of a nurse visiting patients with disabling chest disease in the community. *Journal of Advanced Nursing, 13,* 71–77.

Holden, D. A., Stelmach, K. D., Curtis, P. S., Beck, G. J., & Stoller, J. K. (1990). The impact of a rehabilitation program on functional status of patients with chronic lung disease. *Respiratory Care, 35,* 332–341.

Hudson, L. D., & Pierson, D. J. (1981). Comprehensive respiratory care for patients with chronic obstructive pulmonary disease. *Medical Clinics of North America, 65,* 629–645.

Hughes, R. L., & Davison, R. (1983). Limitations of exercise reconditioning in COLD. *Chest, 83,* 241–249.

Janson-Bjerklie, S., Carrieri, V. K., & Hudes, M. (1986). The sensations of pulmonary dyspnea. *Nursing Research, 35,* 154–159.

Katzin, L. (1990). Chronic illness and sexuality. *American Journal of Nursing, 90,* 55–59.

Kersten, L. (1989a). Changes in self concept during a pulmonary rehabilitation program. *American Review of Respiratory Disease, 139,* A194.

Kersten, L. (1989b). *Comprehensive respiratory nursing: A decision making approach.* Philadelphia: WB Saunders.

Kim, M. (1984). Respiratory muscle training: Implications for patient care. *Heart and Lung, 13,* 333–339.

Kim, M., & Larson, J. L. (1987). Ineffective airway clearance and ineffective breathing patterns: Theoretical and research base for nursing diagnosis. *Nursing Clinics of North America, 22,* 125–134.

Kinsman, R. A., Yaroush, R. A., Fernandez, E., Dirks, J. F., Schocket, M., & Fukuhara, J. (1983). Symptoms and experiences in chronic bronchitis and emphysema. *Chest, 83,* 755–761.

Kirilloff, L. H., Carpenter, V., Kerby, G. R., Kigin, C., & Weimer, M. P. (1986). Skills of the health team involved in out-of-hospital care for patients with COPD. *American Review of Respiratory Disease, 133,* 948–949.

Klink, M., & Quan, S. E. (1987). Prevalence of reported sleep disturbances in a general adult population and their relationship to obstructive airways diseases. *Chest, 91,* 540–546.

Lareau, S., & Larson, J. L. (1987). Ineffective breathing pattern related to airflow limitation. *Nursing Clinics of North America, 22,* 179–191.

Larson, J. L., Kim, M. J., Sharp, J. T., & Larson, D. A. (1988). Inspiratory muscle training with a pressure threshold breathing device in patients with chronic obstructive pulmonary disease. *American Review of Respiratory Disease, 138,* 689–696.

Light, R. W., Merrill, E. J., Despars, J. A., Gordon, G. H., & Mutalipassi, L. R. (1985). Prevalence of depression and anxiety in patients with COPD: Relationship to functional capacity. *Chest, 87,* 35–38.

Lindell, K. O., & Mazzocco, M. C. (1990). Breaking bronchospasm's grip with MDIs. *American Journal of Nursing, 90,* 34–39.

Lucas, J., Golish, J. A., Sleeper, G., & O'Ryan, J. A. (1988). *Home respiratory care.* Norwalk, CT: Appleton & Lange.

Lush, M. T., Janson-Bjerklie, S., Carrieri, V. K., & Lovejoy, N. (1988). Dyspnea in the ventilator-assisted patient. *Heart and Lung, 17,* 528–535.

Mahler, D. A., Weinberg, D. H., Wells, C. K., & Feinstein, A. R. (1984). *Chest, 85,* 751–758.

McDonald, G. (1981). A home care program for patients with chronic lung disease. *Nursing Clinics of North America, 16,* 259–273.

McDonald, G., Borson, S., Gayle, T., Deffebach, M., & Lakshminarayan, S. (1989). Nortriptyline effectively treats depression in COPD. *American Review of Respiratory Disease, 139,* A11.

McGavin, C. R., Gupta, S. P., & McHardy, G. J. R. (1976). Twelve-minute walking test for assessing disability in chronic bronchitis. *British Medical Journal, 1,* 822–823.

McSweeney, A. J., Grant, I., Heaton, R.K., Adams, K. M., & Timms, R. M. (1982). Life quality of patients with chronic obstructive pulmonary disease. *Archives of Internal Medicine, 142,* 473–478.

Moser, K. M., Bokinsky, G. E., Savage, R. T., Archibald, C. J., & Hansen, P. R. (1980). Results of a comprehensive rehabilitation program. *Archives of Internal Medicine, 140,* 1596–1601.

Nocturnal Oxygen Therapy Group. (1980). Continuous or nocturnal oxygen therapy in hypoxemic chronic obstructive lung disease. *Annals of Internal Medicine, 93,* 391–398.

O'Hara, W. J., Lasachuk, K. E., Matheson, P. C., Renahan, M. C., Schlotter, D. G., & Lilker, E. S. (1987). Weight training benefits in chronic obstructive pulmonary disease: A controlled crossover study. *Respiratory Care, 32,* 660–667.

Openbrier, D. R., & Covey, M. (1987). Ineffective breathing pattern related to malnutrition. *Nursing Clinics of North America, 22,* 225–247.

Openbrier, D. R., Fuoss, C., & Mall, C. C. (1988). What patients on home oxygen therapy want to know. *American Journal of Nursing, 88,* 198–201.

Openbrier, D. R., Hoffman, L. A., & Wesmiller, S. W. (1988). Home oxygen therapy: Evaluation and prescription. *American Journal of Nursing, 88,* 192–197.

Openbrier, D. R., & Rogers, R. M. (1989). Validity and reliability of visual analog scales (VAS) used to measure symptoms in patients with COPD. *American Review of Respiratory Disease, 139,* A244.

O'Ryan, J. A., & Burns, D. G. (1984). *Pulmonary rehabilitation: From hospital to home.* Chicago: Year Book Medical Publishers.

Padilla, G. V., Presant, C., Grant, M. M., Metter, G., Lipsett, J., & Heide, F. (1983). Quality of life index for patients with cancer. *Research in Nursing and Health, 6,* 117–126.

Perry, J. A. (1981). Effectiveness of teaching in the rehabilitation of patients with chronic bronchitis and emphysema. *Nursing Research, 30,* 219–222.

Porth, C. M. (1986). *Pathophysiology: Concepts of altered health states* (2d ed.). Philadelphia: JB Lippincott.

Prigatano, G. P., Wright, E. C., & Levin, D. (1984). Quality of life and its predictors in patients with mild hypoxemia and chronic obstructive pulmonary disease. *Archives of Internal Medicine, 144,* 1613–1619.

Renfroe, K. (1988). Effect of progressive relaxation on dyspnea and state anxiety in patients with chronic obstructive pulmonary disease. *Heart and Lung, 17,* 408–413.

Ries, A. L., Ellis, B., & Hawkins, R. W. (1988). Upper extremity exercise training in chronic obstructive pulmonary disease. *Chest, 93,* 688–692.

Ryan, P. (1989). Noncompliance. In J. M. Thompson, G. K. McFarland, J. E. Hirsch, S. M. Tucker, & A. C. Bowers, *Clinical Nursing* (pp. 1612–1615). St. Louis: CV Mosby.

Sandhu, H. S. (1986). Psychosocial issues in chronic obstructive pulmonary disease. *Clinics in Chest Medicine, 7,* 629–642.

Sexton, D. L. (1990). *Nursing care of the respiratory patient.* Norwalk, CT: Appleton & Lange.

Sexton, D. L., & Munro, B. H. (1988). Living with a chronic illness: The experience of women with chronic obstructive pulmonary disease (COPD). *Western Journal of Nursing Research, 10,* 26–44.

Sexton, D. L., & Munro, B. H. (1985). Impact of a husband's chronic illness (COPD) on the spouse's life. *Research in Nursing and Health, 8,* 83–90.

Shenkman, B. (1985). Factors contributing to attrition rates in a pulmonary rehabilitation program. *Heart and Lung, 14,* 53–58.

Sleeper, G. (1988). Traveling with oxygen. In J. Lucas, J. A. Golish, G. Sleeper, & J. A. O'Ryan (Eds.), *Home respiratory care* (pp. 95–108). Norwalk, CT: Appleton & Lange.

Steckel, S. (1982). *Patient contracting.* New York: Appleton-Century-Crofts.

Stollenwerk, R. (1985). An emphysema client: Self care. *Home Healthcare Nurse, 3,* 36–40.

Stratton, B. F. (1989). Pulmonary rehabilitation: For the breath of your life. *Journal of Cardiopulmonary Rehabilitation, 9,* 80–86.

Strauss, A., Corbin, J., Fagerhaugh, S., Glaser, B., Maines, D., Suczek, B., & Weiner, C. (1984). *Chronic illness and the quality of life.* St. Louis: CV Mosby.

Tiep, B. L., Burns, M., Kao, D., Madison, R., & Herrera, J. (1986). Pursed lips breathing training using ear oximetry. *Chest, 90,* 218–221.

Timms, R. M. (1982). Sexual dysfunction and chronic obstructive pulmonary disease. *Chest, 81,* 398–399.

Traver, G. A. (1988). Measures of symptoms and life quality to predict emergent use of institutional health care resources in chronic obstructive airways disease. *Heart and Lung, 17,* 689–697.

Traver, G. A. (1985). *Information for home respiratory therapy patients: Traveling with oxygen.* Deerfield, IL: Travenol Laboratories.

Weaver, T., & Narsavage, G. (1989). Reliability and validity of the Pulmonary Impact Profile Scale. *American Review of Respiratory Disease, 139,* A244.

Wenger, N. K., Mattson, M. E., Furberg, C. D., & Elinson, J. (1984). Assessment of quality of life in clinical trials of cardiovascular therapies. *American Journal of Cardiology, 54,* 908–913.

West, J. B. (1987). *Pulmonary pathosphysiology: The essentials* (3d ed.). Baltimore: Williams & Wilkins.

White, H. A., & Briggs, A. M. (1980). Home care of persons with respiratory problems: Optimazation of breathing and life potential. *Topics in Clinical Nursing, 2,* 69–77.

White, P. (1989, October). *Pulmonary support groups.* Paper presented at the meeting of the Nursing Assembly of the American Lung Association/Wisconsin, Milwaukee.

Woods, N. F., Yates, B. C., & Primomo, J. (1989). Supporting families during chronic illness. *Image, 21,* 46–50.

■ P A R T ■
IV

Select Nursing Strategies

Select categories of nursing strategies are developed in this section. Generalized nursing strategies and an exemplar plan for decreasing powerlessness are presented by Stapleton in Chapter 12. Innovative strategies to enhance quality of life of the chronically ill are presented by prescribing the use of literature (Chapter 13) and imagery (Chapter 14). Hobus presents selected literature passages and poems to be used as therapy. Storytelling, use of metaphors, and journal writing are included in Chapter 13. The theoretical bases and psychotherapeutic effects of imagery are described by Stephens in Chapter 14. A case study including a script for guided imagery is also included.

Ryan presents a framework for selecting strategies to facilitate behavior change in the chronically ill in Chapter 15. Theories that have been proposed to explain behavior change are reviewed, including self-efficacy, social support, social-cognitive theory, and macrosocial theory. Types of changes needed to improve and maintain health are described. Knowledge is the power resource that is developed in this chapter.

Detailed analyses of self-esteem and hope (two power resources) are included in Chapters 16 and 17. Newly developed models of nursing strategies to enhance self-esteem and inspire hope are presented. Clinical assessment and research instruments to measure these phenomena are reviewed.

■

Decreasing Powerlessness in the Chronically Ill: A Prototypical Plan

■ SUSAN STAPLETON

Powerlessness is a prevalent nursing diagnosis in chronically ill patients; it can have physically and mentally detrimental effects on the individual. As has been noted in previous chapters, prolonged powerlessness leads to anxiety, depression, and hopelessness, and eventually, may hasten physiologic deterioration and death. The alleviation of powerlessness is, therefore, an important nursing goal. General categories of nursing strategies to decrease powerlessness are discussed in this chapter, as are specific nursing measures based on the unique characteristics inherent in patients with end-stage renal disease (ESRD). Although the strategies are related to specific factors causing powerlessness in patients with ESRD, the strategy categories are general and can be used for any chronically ill patients experiencing powerlessness.

The categories of nursing strategies aimed at decreasing powerlessness include (1) modifying the environment, (2) helping the patient set realistic goals and expectations, (3) increasing the patient's knowledge, (4) increasing the sensitivity of health-team members and significant others to the imposed powerlessness, and (5) encouraging verbalization of feelings. These five general strategies provide guidance in developing specific measures to decrease powerlessness in the chronically ill individual.

Nursing Strategies

MODIFYING THE ENVIRONMENT

As a means of increasing control, chronically ill individuals can modify the environment. These measures may include simple routines taken for granted, such as having the call bell and telephone within reach and arranging the environment of the hospital room for the patient's convenience. At home, persons can control visitors during rest or times of dialysis treatments by informing others of their routines and schedules and requesting that there be no visits or other interruptions during these times. A note pad to receive messages can even be attached outside the door at home.

Other control measures relate to patients' feelings of deference and inferiority in communicating with physicians and other health-care workers. Specific measures to increase patients' security and comfort when relating to physicians decrease powerlessness. The nurse may emphasize to patients that their needs are the first priority of the health team. Reviewing with patients their medical concerns before the physician visit is helpful in assisting patients to prioritize and formulate their questions and receive needed reassurance. Nurses can interpret esoteric language for patients. Although partnership in medical-care decisions may not be accomplished, patients should not feel inferior, or be unable to verbalize concerns, or be uninvolved in decisions made about their health.

In implementing specific measures to enhance patient control, the nurse may need to reiterate, "You do have control," and to review specific examples of that control.

Identifying situations that cause feelings of powerlessness and recognizing these feelings in oneself are examples of other control measures. If the patient realizes that long waits in an impersonal outpatient department precipitate feelings of powerlessness, substitute activities can take place during this waiting time. The patient can become resigned to the fact that the visit will take no less than 2½ hours and so during that time can accomplish other goals, for example, balancing the checkbook, reading a book or newspaper, writing letters, or organizing the meal plan for the week. Being sensitive to the factors causing powerlessness enables the patient to prepare for the situation. The nurse should keep the waiting patient informed as to the approximate waiting time remaining and reasons for the delay. These courtesies are easily overlooked in institutional settings.

Mr. C. identified two aspects of his visit to the outpatient department that caused him to feel powerless. They were (1) the long wait before seeing the physician and (2) the physician's failure to supply him with all the information he wanted about his health and treatment plan. The author suggested meeting Mr. C. in the clinic waiting room before each appointment and using the time to help him write down a list of specific questions for the physician. Mr. C. was told to take the list from his pocket while talking with the physician and check off each question after it had been answered to his satisfaction. The effectiveness of this strategy in decreasing Mr. C.'s powerlessness was seen in several ways. He exhibited less anxiety during his clinic visits, as evidenced by a decrease in such motor activity as pacing, drumming his fingers, and looking at his watch. He also began to speak more positively of upcoming clinic visits, instead of dreading them. He expressed a sense of satisfaction that he had exercised some control during the visits and obtained the information he wanted. Mr. C. stated, "Now I feel more like I have something to say about what happens to me, instead of just waiting for them to do something to me."

SETTING REALISTIC GOALS

Individuals who can set realistic goals feel less powerless as the goals are achieved. Chronically ill individuals often need assistance in setting realistic goals and in rehearsing possible outcomes. Depression and feelings of hopelessness may inhibit patients from setting goals at all. Lack of information about illness or use of denial as a coping mechanism may lead patients to set goals they are unable to achieve. Never achieving the goals reinforces powerlessness.

Patients should be given the opportunity to participate in their total plan of care by mutually identifying goals with the nurse, validating assessment of self-care skills, and confirming with the nurse that they do have unique strengths that empower them to assume responsibility to achieve desired outcomes. Nurse-patient collaborative decisions increase perceived control (Fuchs, 1987).

Laborde and Powers (1980) compared 20 patients with osteoarthritis and 20 patients undergoing hemodialysis on their ratings of past, present, and future life satisfaction using the Cantril Self-Anchoring Life Satisfaction Scale. No differences were found on past and future ratings; however, the patients on dialysis had significantly higher present life satisfaction scores (at the 0.05 level). Considering the extensive body-system involvement with multiple symptoms in chronic renal failure (CRF), this finding is surprising. The dialysis procedure provides a predictable outcome of temporary alleviation of symptoms. Patients on dialysis may have been helped to set realistic expectations of dialysis as an extension of life and a provider of temporary relief of symptoms. For some patients on dialysis, the relief of symptoms gave them a "new lease on life" compared with predialysis states. The pain experienced by patients with arthritis so interfered with present quality of life that their scores were significantly lower than those of the patients on dialysis. Nurses can use specific verbal reinforcers with the patient on dialysis to decrease powerlessness, such as "the dialysis will control symptoms by restoring fluid and electrolyte balance, eliminate wastes, and so forth." Careful explanation of the desired therapeutic effects of the medical regimen, which helps the patient have realistic expectations from the treatment, will enhance control.

The following is an example of helping the individual develop pacing behaviors to cope with the fatigue of CRF. Mrs. A. expressed feelings of powerlessness from fatigue that interfered with her ability to do her housework. She was asked to keep a list of her activities and her required rest periods for one week. At the same time, Mrs. A. made a list of the things she wanted to do in order of their importance to her. Using these lists, Mrs. A. was assisted in evaluating her tolerance of specific activities and planning her activities according to her energy level. For example, she discovered that she could perform only one major task each day, such as grocery shopping or vacuuming. She planned her weekly schedule so that these especially tiring tasks were done, one each day, on the days after dialysis, when her energy level was highest. This was a more realistic goal than trying to do several major tasks in one day, and Mrs. A.'s feeling of powerlessness decreased when she was able to reach this goal. At the same time, Mr. A. suggested that his wife plan her arrival from the grocery store to coincide with his arrival home from work so that he could carry the bags of groceries into the house. This decreased her energy expenditure so that she was still able to participate in family activities that evening. The list of activities according to priority also enabled her to determine which activities she could delegate to other family members, or eliminate completely, without damaging her self-esteem. A goal for increasing physical activity may be appropriate. Improving physical fitness through regular exercise programs has helped increase energy levels and self-satisfaction in persons with ESRD (Jagusch & Butchart, 1989; Snyder, 1989).

INCREASING KNOWLEDGE

Knowledge is a power resource. Control in a given situation increases with increasing knowledge about the situation. When individuals experience powerlessness, they may subsequently fail to seek information about their situations, further increasing feelings of powerlessness. Chronically ill individuals need knowledge about their illness and its management so that they can make decisions and take actions relative to the illness. This ability to make decisions and act on them gives individuals some control over what happens to them, thereby decreasing powerlessness. Being informed of physiologic changes, positive responses to therapy, and expected results from therapy increases the perception of control. Nurses need to assume major responsibility for increasing patients' knowledge.

Devins' (1989) study confirmed that higher levels of ESRD-relevant information are significantly associated with increased levels of perceived control over nonillness aspects of life. He also recommends forewarning patients about impending changes in treatment to control powerlessness and decrease uncertainty.

The value of knowledge in the reduction of powerlessness can be noted in Mr. C. When Mr. C.'s renal function deteriorated to the extent that the institution of dialysis was imminent, he began to express feelings of powerlessness about the arrangements for dialysis. He had expressed an interest in home dialysis, but the social worker, after discussing it with Mrs. C., told him, "That's not for you." Mr. C. felt that choices were being made without consulting him. A strategy for reducing this feeling of powerlessness involved providing him with information about the various dialysis alternatives: in-center, home, and in-center self-care dialysis. Mr. C. was given specific information about each type, with the advantages and disadvantages of each. Mrs. C. was also involved in these discussions, as she would play an active role in the latter two types of dialysis. Mr. and Mrs. C. were helped to examine what each of the choices would mean to their lives and to discuss their individual feelings about each choice. Mr. C. came to the same decision reached by the social worker, that in-center dialysis was the best choice for him. An important distinction, however, was that now he felt the decision was his own and not one made for him. His feelings of powerlessness were decreased by having information needed to make a decision about what would happen to him. Knowledge about select coping strategies such as relaxation and guided imagery is another type of information to be given (Horsburgh & Robinson, 1989).

INCREASING THE SENSITIVITY OF HEALTH TEAMS AND SIGNIFICANT OTHERS TO IMPOSED POWERLESSNESS

Factors within the health-care system itself are often the most significant causes of powerlessness in the chronically ill. These include unexplained delays and waiting in various hospital departments (x-ray) and brisk, insensitive verbal interaction by admitting clerks, outpatient receptionists, or home health aides. The sterile environment of a hospital with clearly identified boundaries promotes powerlessness (e.g., the nurses' station is off limits for patients; patients cannot review their records without obtaining special permissions as established by hospital policy). Health-care professionals need to develop sensitivity to these and other causes of powerlessness. Efforts need to be made to be humanistic and to avoid depersonalizing patients.

Role playing is a valuable strategy for sensitizing health-care workers to factors in the environment that contribute to the patient's powerlessness. The more realistic the role playing the better. Placing health-care workers in a situation in which they experience an actual loss of control, and then providing the opportunity for them to share their feelings, can provide excellent insights into the concept of powerlessness. Role playing can be a part of planned staff conferences. A focus of the conference could be a discussion of the factors causing powerlessness (Chapter 7) and specifically how personnel can cause powerlessness. Strategies to alleviate powerlessness for specific patients could be devised in this group setting.

Health-care workers may need to review principles of therapeutic communication in addition to simply remembering to introduce themselves to the patient. Personnel need to wear name tags on which their titles are clearly indicated. Acute-care nurses describe persons with ESRD as presenting difficult care challenges, creating a tendency in some nurses to avoid these patients (Wolfsen, 1989).

In order for patients to monitor physiologic progress, having access to the dialysis record on which weight, vital signs, and laboratory values are recorded is important. Some patients achieve control by keeping detailed records and graphs of blood chemistry values. By noting a controlled creatinine level and having a visual representation of the creatinine level over time on a graph, the patient realizes that no physiologic deterioration is occurring. This is a positive-feedback mechanism for the patient to continue to engage in the present therapeutic plan as well as a sign of physiologic control. Teaching the patient the significance of the laboratory values must be included in this control strategy.

Increasing the sensitivity of persons at home, at work, and in social settings is important to decreasing powerlessness in the patient. Dimond (1979) found a positive correlation between the hemodialysis patient's morale and the presence of social support (family environment, spouse support, and the presence of a confidant). A negative correlation was found between the family cohesion (one aspect of family environment), presence of a confidant, and the amount of change in social functioning in adjusting to the chronic illness. Social changes since beginning dialysis were less if the patient had family cohesiveness and a confidant available. The nurse can work with families to help them realize how significantly they can influence adaptation and control in their ill family member. The greater the family cohesiveness and open expression, the higher the patient's morale and the fewer medical problems occurred. Nurses can help families improve communication, increase expressions and types of support, and demonstrate caring and affection. Nurses can also devise specific mechanisms the family can use to increase the patient's perceived and/or actual control. Decisions can be referred to the patient; the family can encourage the patient's resumption of family maintenance tasks, such as paying the bills. The task of planning for maximal use of leisure time and family togetherness activities can be assumed by the ill family member (in this case the patient on dialysis).

Social support has been identified as a resource for chronically ill patients and contributes to psychologic well-being in persons with ESRD (Christensen, Turner, Slaughter, & Holman, 1989; Dimond, 1979; Muthny, 1984; Siegal, Calsyn, & Cuddihee, 1987). Reviewing with family members the important sustaining role they play may help them enhance patient well-being and control.

VERBALIZATION OF FEELINGS

When the chronically ill individual is able to verbalize feelings of powerlessness, a basis for beginning problem solving to increase feelings of control is established. The patient may be able to identify factors contributing to the present state and pose alternate solutions. Through discussion, feedback is solicited from the nurse. The verbalization is a sharing of feelings and provides the nurse with an opportunity to demonstrate understanding.

Open admission of feeling powerless may be too threatening to some individuals for whom control is extremely important. These patients frequently deny any feelings of powerlessness and report that they feel very much in control. Direct confrontation regarding powerlessness can increase anxiety in these patients. On the other hand, when powerlessness is due to deteriorating health that cannot be controlled, discussion of these feelings enables the nurse to share them, lessening the patient's burden. When patients hear their feelings verbalized, the distortion that occurs through mental rumination about the situation is controlled—feelings and concerns are brought into perspective. Reactions from others and empathy are solicited and alternate solutions to problems are generated as a result of verbalization.

An example of a situation in which verbalizing feelings of powerlessness seemed to help decrease these feelings is that of Mr. F. His illness and the resulting financial problems forced Mrs. F. to apply for public assistance while Mr. F. was still hospitalized. She was treated rudely at the welfare office and was quite upset by her experience there. Mr. F. was extremely angry and expressed frustration regarding his powerlessness: "I'm stuck here and can't even help her! I feel like going down there and punching someone!" The strategy of encouraging him to express his feelings, not responding negatively to or denying his anger, was very effective in decreasing his feelings of powerlessness. He was visibly less agitated and stated, "It's good to get it all out." He also indicated that he felt less helpless, although the actual situation had not changed.

Developing a Plan to Decrease Powerlessness

In using these strategies to decrease powerlessness in the chronically ill individual, the nurse must carefully develop strategies specific for each

TABLE 12 ■ 1 Plan of Care to Alleviate Powerlessness in Patients with Chronic Renal Failure

Situation or Factor Causing Powerlessness	Patient Indicators of Powerlessness	Strategies to Decrease Powerlessness	Criteria for Evaluation
		PATIENT-STAFF RELATIONSHIPS	
Appointments in outpatient department: a. Long waits before seeing physician b. Difficulty in obtaining desired information from physician	1. Verbalizing the feeling that cannot control when patient sees physician and that patient's time is not seen as important 2. States, "The doctor never tells me anything. I can't get him to answer my questions"	1. Meet patient in clinic waiting room before each appointment 2. Help patient to formulate a list of specific questions for the physician for that visit 3. If necessary, see physician with the patient to assist patient in asking questions 4. Suggest that patient take the list of questions out of pocket and refer to it while talking with the physician	1. States that the time in waiting room is spent productively 2. Appears calm while waiting: no pacing, tapping fingers, picking at nails 3. Makes list of questions and uses list while talking with physician 4. Verbalizes satisfaction with the amount of information received from the physician about illness and treatment
Enforced dependence during dialysis and dependence on dialysis staff and machine for life Health-care personnel have a much greater knowledge about CRF and its management than patient Staff expression of anger toward the patient; patient unable to show anger in return	1. Expresses fear that some dialysis staff members are less competent than others and that patient cannot judge them 2. Jokes that patient wants a screwdriver "so I can take the machine apart if I want to and stay in control" 3. Expresses the feeling that patient is at the "mercy" of the dialysis machine and staff 4. Refers to dialysis machine as "the monster" 5. States that patient can't get angry at the staff because "I can't get along without them"	1. Provide organized, individualized teaching program that includes the following content: normal kidney function, basic CRF pathophysiology, laboratory values and their significance, purpose of dialysis, dialysis procedure, diet, medications 2. Explain and demonstrate alarm system on machines 3. Arrange for patient to meet some of the other patients to discuss dialysis from patients' point of view 4. Arrange for patient to observe the start and ending of dialysis on another patient (movie or in person) before beginning dialysis	1. Correctly explain dialysis to someone else in simple terms 2. Remains calm when alarm on machine goes off 3. Demonstrates confidence in dialysis staff 4. Asks questions when patient does not know something about CRF and its management 5. States present weight and range of blood pressure 6. Asks for weight, blood pressure, and lab values

if this information is not volunteered by staff

7. Assists with some aspects of dialysis
8. Freely expresses anger toward staff when appropriate and in an appropriate way

5. As dialysis is started, explain each step and reinforce prior teaching. Continue to provide opportunities for questions as they occur to patient and family
6. Utilize primary nursing or assign patient to the same one or two people for the first few weeks
7. Give patient a screwdriver on the day dialysis starts
8. Keep patient informed of progress during dialysis—weight, lab values, blood pressure—and explain their significance
9. Encourage patient participation in dialysis as patient is ready—holding tubings, applying pressure to puncture sites, taking pulse
10. Give patient as much responsibility as patient is ready for—bringing any medications to be taken while on dialysis, arranging own transportation (including driving self), explaining dialysis to own family or new patients
11. Encourage patient to keep own record of blood pressure and pre- and postdialysis weight
12. Encourage verbalization of feelings about dialysis machine and staff and patient's dependence on them
13. Allow for joking or expression of anger during dialysis as a means of maintaining some control
14. Avoid ignoring patient's expressions of anger or responding with anger in return. Use accepting manner

TABLE 12 ■ 1 Plan of Care to Alleviate Powerlessness in Patients with Chronic Renal Failure (*Continued*)

Situation or Factor Causing Powerlessness	Patient Indicators of Powerlessness	Strategies to Decrease Powerlessness	Criteria for Evaluation
		PATIENT-STAFF RELATIONSHIPS	
		15. Avoid comments by staff, even joking ones, that emphasize the control staff has over patient during dialysis	
Physician tells patient that patient will be transferred to a different dialysis center without asking patient's approval	1. Verbalizes feelings of not having control over where patient will go for dialysis 2. Does not tell physician that the planned dialysis center is very inconvenient for patient	1. Assist patient in weighing the pros and cons of each center 2. Serve as a liaison in planning a visit to the other center to meet the staff and discuss routines 3. Support the patient in decision to agree or disagree with the physician's decision 4. Serve as patient advocate, if needed, in explaining patient's decision to physician	1. States the advantages and disadvantages of each center for patient 2. Visits the other dialysis center and asks questions there to obtain the information needed to make a decision about the two centers 3. Questions the physician as to the rationale for switching to the other center 4. Determines, on the basis of all the above information, which dialysis center is best for patient 5. Discusses the decision with the physician, explaining the reasons for choice
Patient severely reprimanded because	1. Accepts reprimand and anger from staff without comment—	1. State amount of weight gain in a matter-of-fact, nonscolding manner	1. Explains, in simple terms, basic CRF

patient gained too much weight between dialysis runs

1. hangs head and looks at floor
2. Later remarks that "they're always yelling at me, but I can't afford to yell back"
3. When told to weigh self daily at home, did not inform staff that patient has no scale
4. States, "I try to follow my diet and not drink too much, but I'm always so thirsty. I just can't help myself"

2. Explore with patient possible reasons for excess weight gain
3. Ask patient to keep a list of everything eaten and drunk for 1 week—including time of day, amounts, what patient was doing at the time and how patient felt at the time
4. Explore with patient the meaning of food and drink to patient
5. Assist patient to identify own eating and drinking patterns
6. Teach basic pathophysiology of CRF and the physiologic effects of excess fluid retention if patient does not already know this
7. Suggest that patient weigh self daily at home, keep record of weights and bring this to dialysis. Help patient get scale
8. Assist patient to correlate weight changes with food and fluid intake
9. Assist patient to identify how patient feels when patient has excess fluid retention
10. Work with patient, dietitian, and physician to develop diet pattern that is most acceptable to patient, considering previous patterns, and meets the criteria of the medical treatment plan
11. If patient eats or drinks in response to stimuli other than hunger or thirst (e.g., tension or boredom), teach other methods of coping with these feelings (e.g., relaxation techniques, self-hypnosis, physical activities)

pathophysiology and the effects of fluid retention on the body
2. Identifies various reasons for eating and drinking patterns: hunger, thirst, tension, boredom
3. Verbalizes what food and drink mean to self and own feelings about food and fluid restrictions
4. Keeps record of daily weights and brings to dialysis
5. Correlates changes in weight with food and fluid intake
6. Identifies how it feels to have excess fluid retention
7. Actively participates in development of a diet pattern
8. Reports that new diet pattern is more acceptable and there is more success in complying with it
9. Practices, on a regular basis, some type of relaxation technique

TABLE 12 ■ 1 Plan of Care to Alleviate Powerlessness in Patients with Chronic Renal Failure *(Continued)*

Situation or Factor Causing Powerlessness	Patient Indicators of Powerlessness	Strategies to Decrease Powerlessness	Criteria for Evaluation
		DISEASE PROCESS	
Patient expected to take care of her A-V shunt before feeling ready	1. Cries and states, ''I don't want to do this,'' while shunt care is done, but does not refuse to do it if staff insists 2. Asks no questions about shunt	1. Assess patient's stage in the grieving process and in adaptation to an altered body image 2. Explore with patient the meaning of the shunt to self 3. Observe for verbal and behavioral clues that patient is ready to learn shunt care—looking at shunt, asking questions, watching while care is done 4. Follow this sequence to develop self-care: Explain care as done, patient assists with care, patient describes procedure verbally, patient performs care with help, patient performs care with observation by nurse, patient takes full responsibility for care 5. Assist patient in explaining procedure to significant other—especially what to do if shunt comes apart 6. Encourage patient to verbalize feelings and fears regarding shunt and its care 7. Discuss ways of covering the shunt 8. Role play with patient the explanation of the shunt to a friend 9. Role play dealing with questions from a curious stranger	1. Looks at shunt 2. Asks questions when some aspect of the care of the shunt is unknown 3. Correctly teaches shunt care to significant other 4. Correctly describes actions to be taken if shunt comes apart and teaches this to significant other 5. Reports ability to cope with stares and questions of others about the shunt

Irritability from the central nervous system manifestations of azotemia Feels weak and tired constantly; must take frequent naps Cannot plan activities because of uncertainty of symptoms Cannot see printed instructions on diet, kidney disease, dialysis	1. States an inability to control moods as easily as before illness 2. Expresses guilt about irritability with family 3. Says, "I'm always tired, I can't get anything done" 4. Reports decrease in social activities, never being able to plan ahead 5. States, "How can I help myself, I cannot even see the instructions?"	1. Discuss the etiology of the irritability with patient and significant others 2. Explore with patient effective ways of dealing with anger and depression without damaging relationships with family members 3. Allow for verbalization of feelings of guilt about irritability 4. Teach specific activities to relieve tension and help deal with stress 5. Support family members in understanding and dealing with patient's mood changes 6. Assist family members in identifying sources and effects of stress on each of them, and explore ways of meeting the needs of each family member 7. Plan for balancing energy expenditure with energy conservation 8. Set priorities; engage in activities that confirm self-worth, and have the highest value for the patient 9. Provide with large print, magnifying glass, and verbal reinforcement of instructions	1. Correctly explains, in simple terms, the physiologic basis for the irritability 2. Practices some form of relaxation technique on a regular basis 3. Significant others explain physiologic basis for patient's irritability 4. Significant others describe ways in which they provide for meeting their own needs 5. Adheres to specific sleep-rest pattern throughout the day 6. Verbalizes understanding; asks appropriate questions
Inability to predict or control the outcome of renal transplantation	1. States, "I guess you just have to get used to the idea that you really don't have much control over how the surgery turns out" 2. Does not ask questions about present health state 3. States, "It's not fair—I did everything I was told and I still rejected the kidney"	1. Provide patient with as much data as possible about patient's level of physiologic control (lab values, weight, vital signs, results of diagnostic tests) 2. Allow patient to verbalize feelings about lack of control of the outcome of the surgery 3. Explore with patient the meaning of the kidney transplant to self 4. Assist patient in recognizing and	1. Demonstrates an interest in present health state by asking for information such as test results, urine output, vital signs, weight 2. Verbalizes realistic expectations about how the transplant will affect own life 3. Indicates an ability to

TABLE 12 ■ 1 Plan of Care to Alleviate Powerlessness in Patients with Chronic Renal Failure *(Continued)*

Situation or Factor Causing Powerlessness	Patient Indicators of Powerlessness	Strategies to Decrease Powerlessness	Criteria for Evaluation
		DISEASE PROCESS	
		dealing with any incongruences between expectations and the actual results of surgery	cope satisfactorily with the possibility of rejection and the uncertainty of prognosis 4. Expresses a sense of hope in relation to the prognosis
		FAMILY RELATIONSHIPS	
Decreased ability to participate in social activities with family and friends Missed part of family activities while on vacation because of dialysis Spouse repeatedly reminds patient to rest and not to do any strenuous activities Role reversal—spouse takes over many of the patient's roles: paying bills, shopping, yard work	1. Expresses guilt and regret over inability to participate in activities with family: "I used to skate with my daughters, but now I'm a read dud—all I can do it sit" 2. "I was stuck with that machine while they were out sightseeing. Then after I'd finished, they'd already seen everything and didn't want to go back" 3. States, "Sometimes I feel like doing something, but she gets upset, so it's easier just to do nothing"	1. Ask patient to make a list of previous activities and their importance to patient 2. Assist patient in setting priorities regarding those activities that patient would most like to continue 3. Explore with patient the meaning to self of participation in family activities 4. Assist patient and family in realistically evaluating the patient's abilities and limitations 5. Encourage spouse to avoid unnecessarily restricting patient's activities 6. Explore with spouse feelings and fear that cause spouse to "shelter" the patient 7. Assist patient in developing new interests and/or modifying previous	1. Lists activities in which participation is desired according to priority 2. Identifies which activities are most important and why they are important 3. Realistically identifies own abilities and limitations 4. Uses the above information to decide which activities will be continued 5. Significant others realistically identify patient's abilities and limitations and encourage patient to continue activities

activities according to present
abilities and limitations
8. Assist patient and family in
developing new ways of interacting
that are compatible with the patient's
limitations
9. Encourage family members to
continue their own activities and
interests as much as possible, and
allow for the expression of any guilt
that may be associated with these
activities
10. Provide family members with a safe
outlet for the expression of any anger
which might be felt toward the
patient
11. Allow for the expression of any
feelings of anger or resentment the
patient may have toward family
members as they continue with
activities in which patient cannot
participate
12. Encourage verbalization about
feelings related to role reversal;
determine significance of previous
role expectations

patient can tolerate
6. Modifies activities as
necessary to
accommodate any
changes in health
7. Significant others
continue with some
activities that meet their
own needs, even if
patient is unable to
participate
8. Expresses the feeling that
patient is coping
satisfactorily with any
changes in activities and
roles required by illness

EMPLOYMENT

Effect of dialysis on ability
to retain job
Effect of CRF symptoms on
job performance
Inability to work requires
family to apply for public
assistance

1. Verbalizes fear of inability to
continue working after starting
dialysis
2. Doesn't like job, but also fears
loss of job; states, "I'm stuck
here. I can never get another job
with my age and kidney disease.
I'm lucky to even have this one,

1. Provide patient with specific
information about dialysis: number of
times a week, number of hours for
each dialysis run, tentative day and
time
2. Assist patient in making plans with
employer for when dialysis starts
3. Explore meaning of job with patient

1. Makes specific plans with
employer about fitting
dialysis into work
schedule
2. Indicates a decrease in
anxiety level about
continuing to work after
starting dialysis

TABLE 12 ■ 1 Plan of Care to Alleviate Powerlessness in Patients with Chronic Renal Failure (Continued)

Situation or Factor Causing Powerlessness	Patient Indicators of Powerlessness	Strategies to Decrease Powerlessness	Criteria for Evaluation
		EMPLOYMENT	
	but sometimes I feel like I'm trapped" 3. Feels that job performance has decreased. States, "I'm losing my creativity. I feel thick-headed. I forget things all the time" 4. Has made no effort to plan for dialysis with employer, even though this is a source of great anxiety for patient	and encourage verbalization of fears about being unable to continue working 4. Ask if patient would like nurse to talk with personnel at company (supervisor or company nurse) to communicate information about dialysis schedule, symptoms of CRF, patient's health-care needs, patient's concern about retaining job 5. Support the patient in obtaining feedback from employer about his job performance, e.g., role play how patient will approach supervisor, suggest that patient do own evaluation first 6. Explore with patient the effects of being unemployed on self-esteem 7. Allow patient to verbalize feelings regarding inability to support family 8. Allow patient and family to verbalize feelings about receiving public assistance 9. Explore with patient and significant others alternate ways of enhancing patient's self-esteem (other than functioning as breadwinner in the family) 10. Assist patient in identifying own strengths and provide positive reinforcement to enhance self-esteem	3. Identifies why job is important to self 4. Discusses job performance wtih supervisor and obtains feedback as to own performance 5. Begins to consider alternative ways of meeting needs now met by job in the event that it will be difficult to continue working 6. Identifies the effects that being unemployed have had on self-esteem 7. Explores alternative ways of enhancing self-esteem—what patient can do to feel better about self

individual. The first steps are to recognize patient indicators of powerlessness and identify the factor(s) causing powerlessness (see Chapter 7), specific strategies can then be developed to decrease powerlessness. These strategies must fall within one or more of the five categories already discussed but must be very specific if they are to provide adequate guidance for those working with the patient. Finally, criteria for evaluation of the strategies must be identified. The criteria are specific patient behaviors that can be expected to occur if the strategies are to be effective.

The care plan in Table 12–1 contains examples of strategies used in working with individuals with CRF who were experiencing powerlessness. Some dealt with situations that occurred once, others dealt with broader, recurring factors that caused powerlessness. The stressors or factors causing powerlessness in CRF patients discussed in Chapter 7 provide the basis for the plan. The types of factors promoting powerlessness included in the care plan are patient-staff relationships, disease process, family relationships, and employment. Although the strategies on the care plan are specific to the patient's situation or specific precipitant of powerlessness, the types of strategies used can be classified as (1) modifying the environment, (2) helping the patient set realistic goals, (3) increasing the patient's knowledge, (4) increasing the sensitivity of health-team members and significant others to the imposed powerlessness, and (5) encouraging verbalization of feelings. Lack of personal control over health and nonillness aspects of life has a negative impact on psychosocial well-being (Devins, 1989). A negative relationship was noted between hope and stress of 81 persons with ESRD (Baker, 1987), adding yet another challenge for nurses to inspire hope and control stress.

Although the strategies discussed in this chapter were developed specifically for individuals with CRF, they provide a prototype for health professionals and significant others working with individuals with any chronic illness. The strategies to decrease powerlessness in patients with

TABLE 12 ■ 2 Empowerment Strategies

Patient education
Individual approach to the patient and patient teaching
    Assessment of and emphasis on each person's uniqueness
    Emphasis on self-care assets and personal strengths
    Setting realistic goals
Behavior modification
Environment modification
    Removal of barriers to patient control
Involvement of significant others
    Sensitizing them to importance of their reactions
    Helping them devise means of permitting patient control
Facilitate verbalization of feelings
Eliminate misperceptions
Develop coping skills

CRF described in this chapter are collectively labeled *empowerment strategies* and are sumarized in Table 12–2. These strategies are specific for strengthening the power resources of psychologic stamina and social support network, motivation, and knowledge. (Refer to the power resource model, Chap. 1.)

References

Baker, L. (1987). *Relationship among hope, self-esteem and stress of hemodialysis in persons with end stage renal disease.* Unpublished master's thesis. Marquette University, Milwaukee.

Christensen, A., Turner, C. Slaughter, J., & Holman, J. (1989). Perceived family support as a moderator of psychological well-being in end-stage renal disease. *Journal of Behavioral Medicine, 12,* 249–265.

Devins, G. (1989). Enhancing personal control and minimizing illness intrusiveness. In N. Kutner, D. Gardenas, & J. Bower (Eds.), *Maximizing rehabilitation in chronic renal disease* (pp. 109–136). New York: PMA Publishing.

Dimond, M. (1979). Social support and adaptation to chronic illness: The case of maintenance hemodialysis. *Research in Nursing and Health, 2,* 101–108.

Fuchs, J. (1987). Use of decisional control to combat powerlessness. *ANNA Journal, 14,* 11–13, 56.

Horsburgh, M., & Robinson, J. (1989). Relaxation therapy and guided imagery in ESRD. *ANNA Journal, 16,* 11–14, 19.

Jagusch, W., & Butchart, B. (1989). A conducted exercise program for the ESRD patient at an outpatient dialysis center. In N. Kutner, D. Gardenas, & J. Bower (Eds.), *Maximizing rehabilitation in chronic renal disease* (pp. 79–86). New York: PMA Publishing.

Laborde, J., & Powers, M. (1980). Satisfaction with life for patients undergoing hemodialysis and patients suffering from osteoarthritis, *Research in Nursing and Health, 3,* 19–24.

Muthny, F. A. (1984). Postoperative course of patients during hospitalization following renal transplantation. *Psychotherapy and Psychosomatics, 42,* 133–142.

Siegal, B. R., Calsyn, R. J., & Cuddihee, R. M. (1987). The relationship of social support to psychological adjustment in end stage renal disease patients. *Journal of Chronic Disease, 40,* 337–344.

Snyder, B. (1989). An exercise program. *American Journal of Nursing, 89,* 362–364.

Wolfsen, C. (1989). Acute care nurses' perceptions of hemodialysis patients. *ANNA Journal, 16,* 329–336.

■

Literature

A Dimension of Nursing Therapeutics*

■ RUTH HOBUS

The use of literature is one of many innovative nursing interventions. Creative and selective use of readings, written journals, and storytelling is therapeutic in terms of enabling persons to cope with health alterations, to have hope and feel comforted, and to manage their health-related or life demands.

Literature, as a treatment modality, may empower the spirit, enable problem solving, provide fresh understanding of an event, or simply reassure (Gorelick, 1987; Mazza, 1988; Hobus, Hansen, Evans, & Woodard, 1987). Literature that focuses on the meaning of existence, transitions in health (Travelbee, 1971), or passages of time can "mirror well the life situation of clients" (Chavis, 1988, p. 232).

Varied terms referring to therapeutic use of literature include the following:

1. *Bibliotherapy* (from the Greek words for book and healing). A bibliography that may be used, sometimes in a prescriptive fashion, to bring new thoughts to an individual or to determine the content of existing thought.
2. *Transitional reading*. Readings especially suited to those experiencing a change in their life cycle, such as the birth of a child, sudden incapacitation, illness, or injury, or a loss by death (Hobus, 1987).

*Special recognition and thanks to A. Thomas Hansen, Humanist and Associate Professor of English, Northern State University, South Dakota, for his contributions, manuscript review, and support in development of this chapter. The author also thanks D. Evans, T. Hansen, L. Hasselstrom, and K. Norris for making their manuscripts from the Humanities in the Healing Arts Dialogue Series available.

3. *Interactive bibliotherapy.* A dialogue between a therapist and a client relative to the literary work to bring about a therapeutic interaction.
4. *Reading bibliotherapy.* A newer concept consisting of assignment of self-help guided reading without discussion groups or a bibliotherapist (Cohen, 1989).

Bibliotherapy may restore the mind and spirit just as medical and other nursing interventions restore the body. Poetry therapy, journal writing, oral stories, teaching tales, and use of metaphors are some of the strategies used in bibliotherapy that will be discussed.

Body-Mind-Spirit Unity

The unity of body, mind, and spirit is a fundamental principle for nursing. A body-mind-spirit model can be conceptualized as an equilateral triangle. The base of the triangle is the physical body; the two sides of the triangle, representing mind and spirit, are equal in value to the base. At the apex, the values of mind and spirit represent a person's highest aspirations—the quest for self-actualization. A keen mind and strong spirit are enhanced by the empowerment of a strong physical base, but the unity remains, even in illness. Nursing accountability increasingly demands care of the whole person, a being who is more than the sum of these parts.

All human interactions encompass a spiritual component (Tournier, 1965). The life a person lives in the body is evidenced in the mind and the spirit and reflects the client's belief systems (Nagai-Jacobsen & Burkhardt, 1989). It is not possible to be in a position of therapeutic helpfulness if one disregards the reality of the spirit (Nagai-Jacobsen & Burkhardt, 1989; Travelbee, 1967).

Literature and Health through the Ages

Ancient medical practice in the time of Socrates and Asclepius included drama in the form of tragic plays (Cohen, 1988; Gorelick, 1987). Elaborate temples had chambers in which "healing dreams" were induced. Hippocrates, the father of modern medicine, learned the Asclepian traditions and linked them with careful observation of signs and symptoms and patient temperament and environment. The myths of Hygeia and Asclepius, the comic and the tragic masks, symbolize opposing points of view in medicine (Schunior, 1989). Hygeia sought natural law which would ensure a healthy mind in a healthy body. The more skeptical followers of Asclepius believed that the chief role of medical practice was to treat disease and the imperfections caused by accidents of birth and life-style (Schunior, 1989).

During the last two centuries social forces have tended to undermine inquiry into spirituality as a domain of nursing care and nurturance. Stuart and coworkers (1989) state that Cartesian dualism (mind-body separatism) and the task-oriented nursing of an industrial society were at least partly to blame.

In addition, nurses in American society have been grounded in separation of church and state to such an extent that, for a number of years, patient spirituality was confused with "religion" (Newman, 1989). As such, the spiritual well-being of the patient was not considered a valid focus of the nursing process. Belief systems were thought to be the exclusive property of the patient, and it was feared that any inquiry might invade religious privacy. The patient's belief system, spirit, and spirituality have been ignored for decades because of this confusion.

Proliferation of modern medical technology during the twentieth century, the discovery of miracle drugs, and the perfecting of ever more daring and innovative surgeries caused great optimism for scientific medical cures. The advent of health insurance made health care available to more people. Although the medical model flourished, the spiritual dimension of patients received little attention.

As medical costs began to soar in the late 1970s and through the 1980s, the quality of life and the costs of care for the chronically ill whose lives had been extended by modern medicine became the source of a national debate. It was found that the cure had often been an optimistic and "loveless misuse of language" (Lange, 1990). There often were no cures for chronic illness.

Encouraging the humanistic aspect of medicine became a focus of inquiry during the 1970s. Fox (1979) wrote that there is a spirituality in compassion—meaning to suffer with, or to undergo and to share with; however, Rogers and Barnard (1979) stated that patient care had often been characterized by "dehumanization, denial and distancing" (p. 5). Lifton (1979) named this phenomenon "technicism," and the distancing "psychic numbing," not unlike the guilt of survivorship (Lifton, 1979). Rogers (1979) suggested that overattention to health-monitoring and life-support systems implies psychologic denial of the importance of human engagement in the healing process, while Rogers and Barnard (1979) concluded that the balance between compassion and technologic expertise was never more seriously skewed than in health care in the 1970s and 1980s.

Spirituality in Literature

"Spirituality is the unifying force, or vital principle . . . that integrates all manifestations of the human being" (Burkhardt, 1989, p. 69). Carpenito (1989) and the North American Nursing Diagnosis Association (NANDA) include spiritual distress (distress of the human spirit) in their taxonomies of nursing diagnoses. Current research-based literature describes the influences of mind and spirit on human responses to illness.

For the purpose of this chapter the following definitions apply: The *spirit* is "the essential quality" of a person, or the "animating principle" (Burkhardt, 1989). *Spirituality* is described as a process and a sacred journey (Mische, 1982), a sense of connectedness with a higher power, God, or ultimate other (Burkhardt, 1989; Fox, 1983). *Spiritual distress* is a state in which "an individual experiences, or is at risk of experiencing disturbance in belief systems or value systems that ordinarily would provide strength, hope, or meaning to one's life" (Carpenito, 1989, p. 155). Chronic illness may provoke challenges to beliefs and values and create uncertainty regarding the meaning of life. Use of literature can bring hope, encouragement, instruction, or a model for persons to follow.

Coping with Chronic Illness

Coping with powerlessness is a major demand of chronic illness (Chap. 2). The changes are far-reaching and are psychologic and spiritual, as well as physical, in nature. The patient's adaptive capabilities are considerably strained if matters of control, understanding of treatment, and decision making are kept from them and are solely the agency of the health-care providers (Rogers, 1979). Loss of control may lead to hopelessness, depression, and immobilization, as seen in Miller's model (Chap. 17). With no remaining hope, the most valuable power resource is lost.

The chronically ill person requires psychologic and spiritual interventions, often before other empowering strategies can be attempted. The client with a chronic illness or disability must be encouraged to discard both false hope and destructive hopelessness (Feldman, 1974). Restructuring the environment in which the patient must now function will require courage and continual reframing of the situation by the client and the nurse. Literature which parallels the patient's needs or condition, addressing spiritual needs or encouraging a quest for the meaning in the illness, is often one of the first and most available interventions. Modeling behavior displayed in the reactions of characters in a story may suggest new ways of responding to the patient.

Choice of Therapeutic Literature

Literature, in the context of therapy, may include anything that will be of probable value in helping the client and the care giver to understand, to come to terms with, or to therapeutically redirect (reshape) a situation. Literary contributions can also bring humor to the situation (Shunior, 1989).

A common misconception is that nurses are not equipped to use literature as therapy because of inadequate knowledge of "good" or classical literature. Nurses in fact have a rich repertoire of personal interactions and previous experiences from which to draw either comforting, amusing, or teaching anecdotes. A point may be illustrated with a newspaper or magazine clipping or something from a journal. Literature used as therapy may include classics such as Tolstoy's *Ivan Ilych* or Robert Frost's *The Road Not Taken*, depending on the client's needs, interests, and reading ability.

What is important in the selection of literature for a specific patient is that it reflect his or her environment and understanding. Regional writers are especially useful in this realm (Hasselstrom, 1990). Regional writers discuss areas, topics, and values that are familiar and may be comforting or instructive. Poems, articles, and stories about the feelings of war veterans or the topics of growing old, abuse, women's issues, or the disabled are useful. Many anthologies are available by topic. *Despite This Flesh: The Disabled in Stories and Poems* is an example (Miller, 1985). Prescriptive readings by developmental life stages (Gold, 1988) can be found in Table 13–1.

"What you will look for in a poem," or writing of any type for therapy purposes, "is a statement of concentrated and psychic power, an inward-looking vision which expresses the dynamic conflicts and tensions of the inner life and one which will appear to fit many particular situations" (Jaskoski, 1987, p. 9). Such writing expresses universal truths: truths which endure and are valid for people of all ages. Literature which provokes reminiscences is generally a good choice, even if the memories are painful. Literature can assist recall and catharsis through the reminiscing process (Clements, 1986). Clements recommends this as an aid to families in distress, whose children are hospitalized because of a serious illness or accident.

Short stories and short prose poems have the advantage of being compressed and getting a thought across in a few lines (Gorelick, 1987). Brevity can be an important factor for persons who are doing their own reading and may have a short attention span because of pain or medication. Others, with long hours to spend, such as in rehabilitation settings, may enjoy more lengthy writings.

Gorelick (1987) described how literature can be of help with family crises. The family tragedy may be abuse, addiction, chronic disease, or prolonged aftermath of an accident. The family at such an impasse "must discover a way to move their situation or they will ultimately succumb to defeat, despair or whatever else is fated by genes or the environment" (p. 42). A poem or good short piece may tell the story with sufficient power to give the reader a shock of recognition and offer new solutions to the patient as reshaping takes place in the reader's mind (Gorelick, 1987).

Hasselstrom (1990) detailed this use of literature from a personal experience. A friend called one day with the intention of saying one last farewell, after having taken a large overdose of tranquilizers. The friend lived hundreds of miles from Hasselstrom, who was not sure that she could get help to the friend in time. However, the friend was rescued and taken to a hospital. As soon as Hasselstrom determined that her friend was out of danger, she sent the woman a copy of Victoria Tokareva's *Centre of Gravity.* This is a warm-hearted story of a Russian woman who tried several ways to commit suicide, unsuccessfully, since she always got sidetracked doing a good deed for someone. In the end she was offered a helping hand, from a stranger, to get back to the safety of her apartment. This helping hand reminded her of the times she had stretched out her hands to others. In a few days Hasselstrom called her friend, who was then able to talk about her feelings and reevaluate her life. The story had intervened in a nonthreatening way.

Sometimes a poem may be written as part of a group therapy activity where each person furnishes input into the poem's construction. The result may not be a good poem from a literary viewpoint, but it often exquisitely meets the needs of the group (Hasselstrom, 1990).

Poems and short stories written by nurses, aides, and victims of abuses and chronic illness may often say very well what the client has not been able to articulate. This author has participated in workshops in which the participants have said, "How can I describe how I feel? I have no words for it." Literature of various kinds can help clients to focus and give voice to their innermost thoughts by furnishing the words.

Literature is a form of empowerment. By giving a voice and words to the client so that the experience, frustrations, and emotions can be shared, one enables the person to name the distress. "Naming" is an important aspect of psychologic and spiritual care. Once clients can recognize and deal with their principal spiritual distress, other areas of care often fall into line. A clinical synopsis at the end of this chapter will illustrate this point.

Stories from literature often contain guidance as well as being a form of diversion and entertainment. Judeo-Christian stories, Christian and Zen parables, and the stories of Hans Christian Anderson and Walt Disney are all examples of guidance embedded in stories. These forms are an indirect and nonthreatening means of instruction. "Direct teaching of behavioral laws and principles is often met with resistance" on the part of those being taught "because the message is too direct, too personal, too shocking . . . or too hard to understand" (Barker, 1985, p. vii).

Basis for Use of Literature as Nursing Therapeutics

There are rich indicators for the use of literature therapy within the traditions of nursing. Travelbee (1971) advised nurses to use parables, metaphors, and personal experiences in a therapeutic use of self. The goal was to assist patients to cope with the illness and to accept their own humanness. Travelbee's basic assumption is that illness is a part of life, and finding meaning in illness or suffering can be a growth experience for both the client and the nurse (Travelbee, 1971). Meleis (1985) summarized two other noteworthy assumptions of Travelbee's theory:

1. Human beings are motivated to search for meaning and understanding in life's experiences.
2. Illness and suffering are not only physical encounters but are emotional and spiritual as well.

Paterson and Zederad's (1988) humanistic nursing model recognized the need for patients to know how other persons experience their own existence. They recognized literature as a realistic source of this information, stating that the commonalities of suffering and other dilemmas of the human condition described in poetry, drama, and fiction surpass textbooks in being concrete and realistic. Younger (1990) thought of literature as a way for nurses to learn compassion.

Recent studies in the survival value of hope have documented that the lack of hope can correlate with an early demise (McGee, 1984). Miller (Chap. 17) spoke of prompt nursing intervention to fortify hope as a priority in overcoming powerlessness and preventing early death.

Moch (1989) expressed the need for the patient to "get in touch with the message within illness" (p. 23) in an effort to find what remains of health within the illness. In Moch's plan treatment would be decided by the client and would include bibliotherapy, journal keeping, meditation, and aesthetic art experiences.

Literature Use with the Chronically Ill

There are at least two ways in which one can contemplate why literature, metaphor, and story forms are of help to the chronically ill. First, they empower. Stapleton (Chap. 12) named five categories of nursing strategies aimed at empowering the client. The use of literature and journal writing can fit into each of the strategies, depending on choice of materials. Stapleton's five categories include (1) modifying the environment, (2) helping the patient set realistic goals and expectations, (3) increasing the patient's knowledge base, (4) increasing the sensitivity of health-team members and significant others, and (5) encouraging the verbalization of feelings.

The second way to consider the enabling power of literature is to understand how it is taken in and processed by the brain. Reports on the functions of the right brain and left brain have provided some important links between metaphor, patient's symptoms, and therapeutic interventions; the left brain is associated with analytic, orderly, and cognitive processing of information (Mills & Crowley, 1986). Barker (1985) states, "the left brain processes literal, sequential, and logical aspects of language" while "metaphor is the language of the *right* cerebral hemisphere. . . . Therapy methods that address the right brain directly—such as the use of stories, . . . metaphor," and "embedded statements . . . seem to produce results more quickly" (p. 21). The right brain is also active in processing emotional information and physical symptomatology (Mills & Crowley, 1986). Right-hemispheric mediation of both client symptomatology and embedded suggestion through metaphors, or stories, allows this type of information to go "straight to the target area, the right-brain processes" (pp. 17–18). Flowers (1988) states this concept aptly: "We could say that poetry calls the brain cells together, making the image-processing of the right brain collaborate with the word-processing of the left brain, and enticing the mind to dance with the heart and the body" (p. 27).

Metaphor has been variously defined as "a figure of speech that makes an implicit comparison between two unlike entities" (Lankton & Lankton, 1983, p. 78); "a story which means more than it appears to say, and says more than it appears to mean" (McAbee, 1987, p. 2); and "personal experiences or make-believe tales told to illustrate a particular viewpoint, make some concept clear by comparison, or lead someone's thinking toward a particular conclusion" (Laborde, 1984, p. 173).

The therapeutic benefits of storytelling and metaphor have been acknowledged because of the work of psychotherapist Milton Erickson, whose teaching tales and use of metaphors are now well known (Mills & Crowley, 1986; Rosen, 1982; Barker, 1985; Wallas, 1985). The uses of metaphors, imagery, and literature are also found in the family therapy of Minuchin, Satir, and Andolfi (Mazza, 1987).

Schrodes (1949) developed an early model for bibliotherapy as an interaction between the reader and literature in which the "readers see similarities between their own problems and those of characters in literary works" (Cohen, 1989, p. 79). "Schrodes listed the curative elements of bibliotherapy as identification, catharsis and insight" (p. 79). (See Fig. 13–1.) Yalom (1985) identified therapeutic factors found in group therapy. Cohen recognized a relationship between Schrodes's curative elements of bibliotherapy and Yalom's therapeutic components of group therapy and merged the two models, as seen in Figure 13–1. Yalom's elements of cure, altruism, universality, cohesiveness, and transference can take place in Schrodes's category called identification. Yalom's group tasks of socialization, instillation of hope, imparting of information, and so forth, fit in with Schrodes's view of the insight one gathers from reading (Cohen, 1989).

Exemplars: Literature in Clinical Use

The author began to use literature as therapy in a variety of areas in 1985. The following poems and incidents will illustrate some of the ways

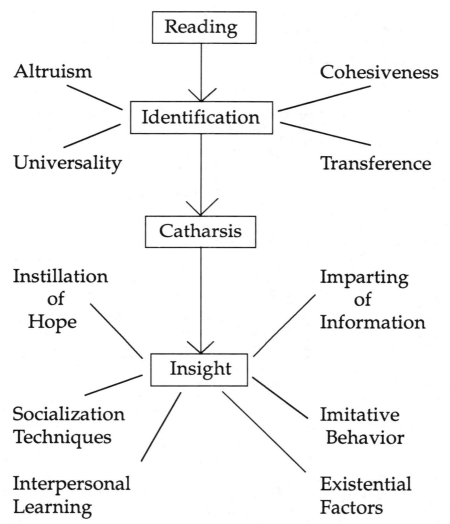

FIGURE 13 ■ 1 Proposed model for healthy pathway of bibliotherapy. [From Cohen (1989), with permission.]

in which bibliotherapy can be used for clients and for health-team members.

A small, close-knit community that had never experienced any losses of small children to accident or violent death, suddenly experienced the death of two children and a traumatic leg amputation of a third child. These accidents occurred over 3 months in a summer. Staff members and the physician all grieved. Many of the health-team members were parents of children the same ages as those who died, some of whom had been friends. Throughout the summer, many emergency-room nurses voiced anxiety and verbalized feelings of not wanting to come to work. In nursing reports and in individual sessions the following poem helped several members of the health team.

Sad Summer*

We must have been eight or nine then,
because Jess was twelve, neighbor kid,
an authority on marbles, and other things.
We last saw him in the crowd on the 4th of July
at Bohson Park; he was laughing and excited,
and there was money in his pocket,
because he bought a boat ride and we only watched.

Remember when Dad came home and said
that Jess was dead!
We listened through the screen-door
while he talked to Mom.
Jess had gotten a rifle for his birthday,
climbed the hayloft in the barn to shoot pigeons. . . .
We had to guess the rest.

That night we got into the Model A
and drove over to their farm.
Mom went in and Dad went to the barn. . . .
In a sandy spot by the house, we could tell the place
where Jess always drew the circle,
set his marbles, and aimed his shooter.
Real slow and low you said, "Jess shoulda
stayed with marbles."

Our family sat in the second row,
Too close to the whiteness of the flowers,
and the cold coffin and the dreary sermon.

That night we pooled our marbles in a shoe-box
and pushed it far back in the dark upstairs closet.
But all the rest of that summer
we saw the pigeons
that had always flown back and forth
from our barn to his.

The universality of experience found in this poem provided comfort to the health team. They were helped to see that they were not isolated. Members of the staff who had lost their enjoyment in coming to work could empathize with the children in the poem who put their marbles away. It was seen as a form of distancing. Health-care workers decided that, metaphorically, they "had been putting their marbles away." Once

---

*Carlee Swann, 1977, with permission.

this was named, it afforded considerable relief. A final metaphor was found in the pigeons, likened to memories, which would continue to fly back and forth all summer between the farms (Hobus, 1987).

This poem changed the internal environment for the health-care workers as their understanding increased; it sensitized the health-team members to each other's anguish, and it encouraged verbalization of feelings.

The following poem exemplifies what an elderly or chronically ill client may be feeling. This is a desirable type of distancing (Lazarus, 1979) in which the client was able to help herself escape when the realities of critical care overpowered her.

Through the Window*

A colorless canopy
Covers the town tonight,
The arms of the elm
are lost in the lingering fog;
The bell in the clock tower
measures its might
By the answering bark
of the dog. . . .

I have passed my limit of
three-score years and ten,
And I hear the nurse as she walks
the sterile hall;
But she doesn't know that I'm sitting
across the street
Swinging my feet against
A wet brick wall.

"Through the Window" was written after Swann had been discharged from a regional medical center. In addition to being a form of therapy for the client, it instructs and sensitizes the health-care team about the feelings of that client. It is universal.

The next poem, "Darkness," is useful in instructing one about the feelings of an elderly client, awake in the nursing home at night. All that is being asked is relief from loneliness. Imposed powerlessness is implicit. The author has used this poem in a number of workshops to sensitize family and health care providers to needs of the elderly.

Darkness*

I lay securely positioned
curled up in an unfamiliar bed
in a dark unfamiliar room.

---

*Carlee Swann, 1978, with permission.
*L. S. Pike, 1979, with permission.

I feel empty, weak, old and alone.
I cannot sleep.
I see the call bell dangling on
the rails that surround my bed.
I push the bell and wait.
And wait.
The light goes on and a white figure
scolds, "What do you want?"
I want to be in my own home again,
surrounded by my own things
and the people I love.

I want to be young and alive again,
to feel and touch and move and create.
I want another day laughing with my friends
or scolding my children, or a walk in the wood,
or an evening by a bright fire.
What do I say?
Touch me. Hold me.
Reach out and reassure me that I am still alive.
Please, just a smile to warm me
so I don't feel so alone.
What do I say?—I say
"I feel cold."
I am covered. The room darkens.
Again I lay alone, imprisoned.

Barker (1985) reviews clinical uses of anecdotes and stories. They can make or illustrate a point, suggest solutions to problems, help people recognize themselves, seed ideas, reframe or redefine a problem, model a way of communicating, embed directions in a pleasant manner, help to build egos, decrease resistance, allay fear, or remind people of their own resources. The following poem does several of these, depending on whose point of view is taken when reading it.

What Have You Done to My Mother?*

How often these words are directed to me.
As they search for the "Mother" that used to be.
"Have you given her drugs or spoken unkindly?"
"I brought her some cookies, she stared at me. Blindly—"
"Not seeing the daughter who loves her dearly."
"She seems not to care that I've come all this way."
"What's wrong with this place, anyway?" . . .
"She strikes out in anger and curses my name."
"I know she can't mean it—it hurts just the same!" . . .
"But, if I leave now, will she be here tomorrow?"
Call it pain or grief—call it guilt or fear.
It sounds the same when it reaches my ear.
It's love, pure and simple, needs no explanation—
Will it be the same in the next generation?

---

*L. G. Davey, 1983, with permission.

> "What have you done to my mother," they say.
> "She's not the same person I left yesterday!"

The author, a nurse at the time this was written, gives voice to the universal phenomenon of parental decline and the pain that it brings to adult children. Many adult children have seen themselves in this poem.

Literature can help to name an experience so that one can consciously think about it and discuss it (Kissman, 1989). Naming the experience also implies the universality of the experience so that one no longer feels alone against overwhelming loss. Literature can be a way of knowing, informing, and finding oneself (Pies, 1988), as associations are made with the central story characters or with the voice of the poet.

"In time of loss, it is important to see what remains in our lives" (Woodard, 1987). Woodard (1990) illustrates the efficacy of literature in understanding overwhelming loss with a personal experience. A very close friend of his died suddenly without warning, leaving a wife and small child. Woodard was asked to go to his friend's city and arrange for the memorial service.

In the days that followed, alone with his deep grief, Woodard found that he was angry at people around him for no apparent reason. This vague, unsettling anger followed him everywhere he went. He was perplexed and unhappy with himself for feeling this way. Surely he had expected grief, but why this vague anger, always ready to surface?

Then, out of his literary background came the scene from *King Lear,* in which the old king held his beautiful, dead, youngest daughter in his arms. Woodard recalled these words from the king at that terrible moment: "Why should a dog, a horse, a rat, have life, and thou no breath at all? Thou'lt come no more, Never, never, never, never, never!" (Shakespeare, *King Lear*).

Anger and frustration are often seen in the face of untimely death. When he remembered the scene from *King Lear,* Woodard stated that it comforted him. He realized that his grief reaction was universal. Remembering this scene from the play empowered him by giving permission for and understanding of the anger; it clarified his problem; it provided a rationale for understanding the anger; it gave him words with which to verbalize the pain.

A second example of the rage which one feels in the loss of a loved one is eloquently expressed in the words of Dylan Thomas (1957) at the death of his father:

> Do not go gentle into that good night,
> Old age should burn and rave at close of day;
> Rage, rage against the dying of the light.
>
> Though wise men at their end know dark is right. . . .
>
> And you, my father, there on the sad height,
> Curse, bless me now with your fierce tears, I pray.

> Do not go gentle into that good night.
> Rage, rage against the dying of the light.

Death is the prototype of all injustices (May, 1975). Many clients and their families need permission or the words to voice rage, even if the death was of a parent whose timely end was to be expected. There is also rage in the permanent loss of abilities, as in chronic illness. To the extent that there is sufficient rapport between the client, or family, and the nurse, the poem may be comforting.

For those who enjoy classic literature, *King Lear* has other applicable themes for therapy. Some of them include pessimism, evil, failure as a king, feelings of failure as a father, and the "incompatibility between rational man and an absurd universe" (Trilling, 1967, p. 129). These qualities continue to make it a favorite.

Adolescents often face losses that forever change their world. Poetry therapy and interactive bibliotherapy for adolescents is reported by Morris-Vann (1983), Mazza (1981), and Cohen-Morales (1989). This therapy covers a wide range of conditions. Chronic disability, spinal cord injury, incest, and deaths of loved ones are several of the topics which have been discussed in the literature.

A therapeutic result of poetry writing is naming the pain when the client is ready, thus setting the stage for discovering meaning out of the experience (Bardarah-McCandless, 1989). Control is in the hands of the writer. "Poetic imagery may perform a distancing function without denying the existence of the problem" (p. 148). The story of the giraffe with purple spots, discussed later in this chapter, will illustrate this helpful distancing.

Finally, as the patient moves into integration of the experience there is an accepting of "previously forbidden feelings . . . such as rage, loneliness . . . fear" and a reinterpretation of the earlier situation in the light of new understanding (Bardarah-McCandless, p. 149). The following poem expresses some of the rage and pain felt by a young man who lost his father to cancer.

A Farmer Dying*

> What is there of justice, Father,
> in the 57 years of droughts and blizzards
> you have coughed up onto my bedroom floor?
> What is left for me at 16
> when you have told me
> there is no room for God
> in malignant tumors,
> that a heart attack
> would have been prettier
> and much more quiet?

---

*Kevin Woster, 1978, with permission.

Can you see better than I
In this candle-lit darkness?
I ask you this, Father,
before I go
to my Hail Marys.

Norris (1987) writes that younger children will reveal the truth through their poetry and that you can discover events that are taking place in the children's lives, some of their longings and their fears. Norris described working as a poet-in-residence in a classroom. A poem, "My Very First Dad," by one of the young students described the father in glowing terms, "like God in my heart." In fact, the father had abandoned the child and the mother on the day the child was born. "The poem revealed, as perhaps nothing else could, that the child was carrying a load of pain" (Norris, 1990, p. 2). Norris states that this is typical of the "self-healing children engage in. It told the truth about the burden the child was carrying within and confronted the adults with a cry for help" (Norris, 1990, p. 2). Through poetry therapy the child was able to name a pain which no one had suspected. Leedy (1973), Kramer (1987), and Gorelick and Monser (1988) are among those in support of poetry therapy as a therapeutic intervention for children.

Norris speaks of listening attentively to children and suggests that "listening sometimes requires a leap of the imagination. Sometimes the truth of what a child is saying is so unpleasant that our instinct is to deny it" (Norris, 1990, p. 3). The following prose poem illustrates Norris's own catharsis of a troubling event concerning a child.

Saturday Afternoon at the Library*

I let him climb on my lap
Because he wanted to be held
by a woman;
he'd lost three already
by the age of five.
His mother in a wreck
when he was a baby
then his grandmother
who'd taken care of him;
and then
just last week
the stepmother, young,
with a baby of her own.
She was a sweet thing
who read self-help books;
Norman Vincent Peale,
How To Be Your Own Best Friend.
His dad beat her

---

*Kathleen Norris, 1988, with permission of the author.

and was drinking up
most of their money. . . .

What does the boy understand
of this? He knows
that she and the baby were gone
one day, when he and his dad came back from town.

He holds me tightly and says:
"I'm going to kill you.
"I'll shoot you
and cut you up in little pieces
and keep you in my refrigerator."
I look at him and say
"Don't put me there,
I'll be too cold."
He says: "I'll keep you
in my closet then."
I say: "Closets are too dark."
He giggles, slides down and away,
out the door.

And the boy just wanted
to be held close
to soft woman flesh
and loved. That was all he wanted.

Norris (1990) says of this incident, ". . . they were words he needed to say and someone needed to hear them" (p. 4). Norris speaks of sharing anecdotes and personal stories, as suggested by Travelbee. A child who grieved over being abandoned by the father was helped with an account of poet Diane Wakoski's similar experience and her subsequent choice of George Washington as her symbolic father. A child who grieved over a family suicide gained solace from hearing Norris share a similar family experience (Norris, 1990).

Smith (1989) has compiled an excellent annotated bibliography of reading resources for children regarding death and grieving. Gold (1988) reported on the value of fiction as a mediator of the developmental life stages. The prescriptive reading suggestions for the various developmental states may be found in Table 13–1 (Gold, 1988).

Successful use of stories, anecdotes, and metaphors in clinical practice have been documented by Barker (1985), Rosen (1982), Mills and Crowley (1986), and Larkin and Zahourek (1988). Rosen (1982) identified advantages for using anecdotes and stories in patient communication:

1. Anecdotes are interesting, hold attention, and "tag memory."
2. Anecdotes are nonthreatening and are told in the third person.
3. Stories and anecdotes bypass natural resistance to change because they are only a story.

4. Control over what is heard is in the ear of the client. One will hear only what the psyche will allow it to pick up.

Metaphors and Storytelling

Larkin and Zahourek (1988) point out that metaphors and stories are easily incorporated into many areas of nursing practice. The authors give a negative example of this in the horror stories patients hear from friends and relatives, including stories pregnant women hear. Positive stories, of course, are more therapeutic and can help to instill positive expectations of the treatment outcome (Larkin & Zahourek). The authors point out that the phrase "I had a patient once . . ." is similar to "Once upon a time . . ." and sets the stage to illustrate how the healing process occurs or how someone will be encouraged.

Larkin and Zahourek (1988) also report that indirect healing suggestions may be used in a number of acute care settings. "Waking suggestibility," according to the authors, is a time when the patient is comfortable following medication for pain relief and is a prime time for the introduction of indirect metaphoric suggestion. Morgan (1988) suggests doing this in a very offhand way, almost as an afterthought. One lead-in is "I remember a patient who . . ." This is also the ideal time to intersperse needed information and embedded suggestions with the story.

Larkin and Zahourek (1988) related their use of therapeutic storytelling and of metaphors in pediatric clinical practice. A case study is presented of a 9-year-old leukemic boy who was dying in a pediatric intensive-care unit. He was in much pain and afraid of approaching death. Larkin told him the story of "another boy who learned to go inside his mind and find a special big tree with a hidden opening. . . . So he went into the opening and found the warm, comforting home of a friendly chipmunk. It felt really peaceful there" (p. 50). Messages of "feeling comfort, feeling better and sitting by the fireside, talking to your friend" (p. 50) were interspersed throughout the story as embedded suggestion. The boy was encouraged to go within this sanctuary whenever the pain was too intense or he needed comfort. The child was able to die with little apparent distress (Larkin & Zahourek, 1988).

Mutual storytelling is also a strategy to keep the mind occupied when painful debridement and change of burn dressings must be done (Larkin & Zahourek, 1988). A story of a giraffe with purple spots was used to help a child explore the idea that her scars would make her somewhat different from other children when she was discharged from the hospital (Larkin & Zahourek, 1988).

"The most important requirement for an effective metaphor is that it meet the client at his model of the world. . . . The metaphor preserves the structure of the client's problematic situation" (Gordon, 1978, p. 171).

TABLE 13 ▪ I   A Tentative Formulation of Developmental Tasks—General Development Tables

Life Stage	General Tasks and Skill Growth	Goals, Needs, and Activities	A Sample of Reading Prescriptions
Infancy	Learning a sense of trust; object differentiation, phonic and visual coordination, etc.	Holding on/letting go, mother tongue, physical senses, and identity.	Finger games, rhythm and rhyme, peek-a-boo-repetition, "this little pig," "ride a cock-horse," "rock-a-bye baby"
Early and middle childhood	A sense of initiative; family relations and roles; I/thou reality and rules, power, etc.; fears of desertion	The simplest adventure stories—projected danger and exploring—testing—feeling small stories. Identity	Enid Blyton, Beatrix Potter, Babar, fairy tales, folk tales, animal sameness and differentiation, Disney, Just So Stories, Aesop's Fables, Toad and Ratty, Sendak
Preadolescence	Achieving a sense of industry, responsibility, social skills, body acceptance, competition	Living concepts, political and moral awareness, socialization, sexual awareness preparation, concepts of group structure and institutions; achieving personal independence, tastes and personal goal awareness, values adoption	Judy Blume, Nancy Drew, Hardy Boys, C. S. Lewis, L. M. Alcott, L. M. Montgomery, V. and B. Cleaver, Robert N. Peck, Farley Mowat
Adolescence	Sexual roles, economic independence, negotiation skills, achieving emotional stability, body awareness, clothing styles, skills and talents discoveries, deepening friendships, religious questioning	Acquiring information, developing power, sexual adjustment, modeling on chosen figures, developing language power, leaving home, career planning, future fantasies	S. E. Hinton, Betsy Byars, Mark Twain, Stephen King, Jane Austen, Charles Dickens, Lewis Wyndham

Early adulthood	Achieving intimacy, sharing, self-knowledge, mate selection, starting a family, education and training	Learning parenting and planning, investment, recreational skills and selection, social volunteer role selection, self-acceptance, and understanding	John Steinbeck, Philip Roth, Alice Munro, the Brontes, D. H. Lawrence, Margaret Atwood, Ernest Hemingway, Helen Keller
Middle adulthood	Rearing children, vocation and family planning, estate management, vocation stabilization, civic responsibility, social group formation, mediating, grandparenting, and family obligation	Coping with family stress, possible group work, values transmission, job anxiety, marriage enrichment or divorce, life review, physiological adjustment, reality acceptance	F. Scott Fitzgerald, Mordecai Richler, Nancy Thayer, Iris Murdoch, Mavis Gallant, George Eliot, Thomas Hardy, Erica Jong, James Carrol, Judith Guest, Virginia Woolf
Late adulthood	Grief for loss of friends, etc., retirement, reduced income, grandparenting, diminishing strength or health, loss of power, social or civil service interests, death planning	Normalizing loss and loneliness, aging and frustration; keeping mentally alert and interested, networking with peers, accepting failed plans and disappointments; coping with death, doubts, and fears; appropriate recreation	Margaret Laurence, Mavis Gallant, Charles Dickens, biographies of famous people, Bernard Malamud, Doris Lessing, Morley Torgov, May Sarton

Source: Gold (1988), with permission.

Metaphors can be derived from any acceptable source including folklore, Biblical tales, mythology, Mother Goose, or one's own personal experiences.

Journal Writing

Writing in a journal is another means of validating self, testing ideas, ventilating feelings, or expressing pain in privacy. "The journal becomes a therapy tool where a person's own emotions can be voiced without fear" (Hasselstrom, 1987).

Advantages in journal writing as a therapy form are

1. A journal is liberating.
2. A journal can be a best friend and confidante.
3. A journal builds esteem as one later looks back and identifies solutions and power to cope with past problems (Hasselstrom, 1990).

There are people who have great difficulty expressing their deepest and most troublesome or even therapeutic thoughts in a group. If these clients have any interest in writing, prescriptive bibliography may include journal writing, which they may or may not discuss with a therapist. The client may never read it. The point of the therapy is to gather thoughts and clarify and dispose of the painful emotions. Occasionally a prescriptive therapy may include assigning the client to read literature and to record his or her reactions in a journal (Aleksychik, 1989).

A clinical application of journal writing from the author's practice concerns a young male client who had just graduated from high school and was in a tragic motorcycle accident with a truck. He remembered nothing of the first weeks after the accident, but the young man's mother started a journal recounting his struggle to survive. After he was able to return to his home, with surgeries and rehabilitation still ahead of him, he began to keep the journal for himself.

Several years have passed, and the young man has enrolled in college, with some residual injuries. "When I have a bad week, I read the journal. The issues then were would I ever be continent? Would I walk? Reading the journal shows me how far I have come. It becomes a good attitude adjustment" (personal communication to the author, 1990).

The young man had been a football player in high school and also had a close relationship with his family, especially the father. During the 2 years of convalescence and rehabilitation the following poem by David Allan Evans helped to sustain him.

The Touchdown in Slow Motion*

. . . Here I go
in the shape

---

*David Allan Evans, 1974, with permission.

> of my father's hope
> on a 30 sweep right
> ranging out cutting
> now turning it on
> turning the corner
> to give up turf and
> snatch what I need to be nifty
> with a last fake
> in a farewell wave of my hand
>
> Stretching out
> I find my light
> and a way to move
> in the green world.

There was sustaining power in thinking about issues of rehabilitation as a different kind of football game. It implied to the client the need to give the strenuous rehabilitation routine as much dedication as had gone into football. This game was even more important. A final empowering image was the idea that he would walk again, "in the shape of his father's hope," a love that was there to sustain him just as it had been in his football victories.

This anecdote illustrates that, as an outcome, the young man has grown spiritually and found meaning in his illness as Travelbee suggests. It also supports Hasselstrom's observation (1990) that confidence and empowerment are gained as the client looks back into the journal and can finally see the almost imperceptible gains.

The lines, "Here I go/in the shape/of my father's hope" are an applicable introduction of hope for victims of any number of conditions. Many patients who suffer chronic illness persevere in treatment largely because of their loved ones' enabling hope.

Healing of War Veterans

Veterans often have special needs in therapeutic literature. In addition to the chronic illness or injury which is the focus of their medical treatment, the spiritual component may include a load of guilt and pain from service-related incidents, unresolved conflicts, and survivor guilt.

Most veterans no longer talk about their experiences since the general perception is that no one is interested. Nurses are poorly prepared to discuss these issues with clients who are veterans. A good strategy is to enroll in a course in war literature within a college humanities department. This will allow the care giver to discover some of the issues in a relatively pain-free environment as Younger (1990) previously suggested.

In choosing literature for the veteran who is still dealing with service-connected spiritual and emotional conflicts, poems of Wilfred Owen and carefully chosen poems of Walt Whitman, such as *The Wound-Dresser*, may be useful. Anthologies of war literature and poetry are available.

The veterans of the Vietnam era have special problems that have been addressed under post-traumatic stress syndrome in *Military Medicine* and the nursing journals. Significant works of prose about the Vietnam experience include: *Going After Cacciato* (O'Brien), *In Country* (Mason), *Dispatches* (Herr), *Meditations in Green* (Wright), and *Short Timers (Full Metal Jacket)* (Hasford). "Each truthfully reveals important aspects of the Vietnam experience while maintaining its integrity as an achieved work of art" (Stewart, 1988, p. 123). Others of interest are: *American Experiences in Viet Nam: A Reader* (Sevy, 1989) and *Carrying the Darkness: American Indochina Poetry of the Vietnam War* (Erhardt, 1985).

Stewart (1989) suggests the potential of story making as a means of coming to terms with Vietnam war experiences. The obvious therapeutic nursing intervention is to encourage the veteran to write his own story, even if it is never shared with others. Others who are willing to preserve their story for family and friends might find it a source of empowerment. Reminiscences may be recorded as an oral history.

Enhancing Self-Esteem and Enabling Hope

Literature can aid survival by creating good feelings and enhancing self-esteem (Evans, 1990). Self-esteem is necessary for hopefulness and for empowerment. Evans believes that there is an example of enhancement of self-esteem in this poem by Emily Dickinson.

It Dropped So Low in My Regard*

It dropped so low-in my Regard—
I heard it hit the Ground—
And go to pieces on the Stones
At the bottom of my Mind—

Yet blamed the Fate that fractured—less
Than I reviled Myself
For entertaining Plated Wares
Upon my Silver Shelf—

There is a convincing imagery, a metaphoric example of someone else's values or opinions which are "silver-plated wares" compared to the "silver shelf" of the author's own insight and understanding (Evans, 1990). "The poem says, give yourself credit; trust yourself; what else can you do but trust yourself?" (p. 2).

This poem can also serve as a warning to nurses who might think of this poem as paralleling the readiness of a client to adopt a new health

---

* Emily Dickinson, 1960, with permission .

style. To the extent that the client may not be convinced of the value of the new information, the health teaching may drop so low in the client's judgment that it does "go to pieces . . . at the bottom" of the hearer's mind.

Sometimes it is comforting to "know the problems can't be completely solved, you just have to do the best that you can" (Evans, 1987). There is a Zen parable about a man who drops over a cliff while trying to escape a tiger and clings tightly to a vine. But there is another tiger below him, snapping and snarling. "All he can do, then, is with his free hand pluck a strawberry on that same vine and eat it, and enjoy its sweetness! To be an adult is to realize that some problems and dilemmas simply cannot be 'worked out.' You might as well make the most of what you have left in life" (Evans, 1990, p. 3). This metaphorically restates Moch's concept; find any elements of health left within the illness.

Connectedness is important in establishing hope. Poetry and literature deal with connectedness of family and friends. "Bess," by William Stafford, may bring courage to family members grieving over the loss of a mother. "Bess would have no meaning without her relationships with others. She is defined by those relationships" (Evans, 1990, p. 2).

Bess*

Ours are the streets where Bess first met her
cancer. She went to work every day past the
secure houses. At her job in the library,
she arranged better and better flowers, and when
students asked for books her hand went out for help.
In the last year of her life
she had to keep her friends from knowing
how happy they were. She listened while they
complained about food or work or the weather. . . .

Pain moved where she moved. She walked
ahead; it came. She hid; it found her. . . .
It was almost as if there was no room
left for her on earth. But she remembered
where joy used to live. She straightened its flowers;
she did not weep when she passed its houses. . . .

Another poem about connections is "A Flat One," by W. D. Snodgrass (1968) about an old man in a veterans' hospital who wasted away to nothing and then died. The voice is that of the male aide who attended the veteran. He "felt the old man's energy, learns from him, responds to him, even if he thinks there is no hope for his surviving" (Evans, 1990, p. 4).

A final and important source of empowerment and hope for many people is found in the words and music of hymns or readings from the

---

*William Stafford, 1977, with permission.

Bible; many reassuring portions can be read to satisfy varied needs such as love, hope, and self-worth.

Hansen (1990) states, "Those who have suffered utterly devastating losses might find themselves tempted (or encouraged by others) to read the story of Job, whose life seems to be a case study in unrelenting disaster" (p. 1). Far from providing easy answers, the story of Job shows us how false and how "wrong" easy answers can be (Hansen, 1990). "Job lost his wealth, his life's work and his children. His wife told him to curse God and die. His friends suggested to him that he was being punished for his sins. He rejected that notion, but finally demanded an explanation from God" (Hansen, 1987, p. 2).

The story can teach compassion. Job suffered through no fault of his own as many patients in today's world suffer. Job did eventually have his fortune and children restored to him—a happy ending which can be misleading. "This is the popular view of the story of Job—that it is inspiring because it gives hope to the hopeless. But we all know that goodness is rarely rewarded in the here and now. People suffer and don't know why, and unlike Job they are unlikely to get the kind of clear and unequivocal answer God gave to Job" (Hansen, 1990, p. 4).

The role of literature in the healing arts, as stated by Hansen (1990), is not to give comfort by falsifying, even if there is much to be said for positive thinking. "The role of literature in healing is to get the feelings out in the open, to articulate painful emotions we too often can't put into words. It admits that our sorrow is sometimes inconsolable, that our problems are sometimes unsolvable. . . . Even when it does this, it shows us that we are not alone—that others have been there before us and have found ways of living with what they could not change" (p. 4).

Clinical Synopsis

Mr. B. was admitted to acute care after a 2-year battle with leukemia. He had been under the care of an oncologist and a surgeon. A splenectomy had been done 1 year previously, after which he had gone back to managing his business. He had several admissions to the hospital for complications of immunosuppression, pneumonia that would not clear, weakness, and fatigue. His white count was extremely low. With this admission he was placed in protective isolation.

For some time his primary physician had wanted him to transfer to a large university medical center for consultation and advanced care. Medical team members were convinced that he needed technologies available in a designated cancer treatment center. Mr. B. refused to go, telling the physician that he had unlimited faith in him. Mr. B. had not drawn up a will in the 2 years of illness and was currently talking of expanding his business. The team helplessly watched Mr. B.'s symptoms of lung involvement heighten and his blood studies deteriorate.

The author started a program of bibliotherapy and guided reading to suggest to Mr. B. that he really needed to set his affairs in order. Mr. B. was bored with the protective isolation and could not find enough to read or do. The author's first step, as primary nurse, was to spend as much time with him as possible, to build rapport with the client, who could receive few visitors in isolation. Mr. B.'s interests were assessed. He liked a certain cowboy humorist of national renown.

The author brought Mr. B. cassette tapes of those books. The next step was to bring humorous poems by the same author and regional poetry about the Midwest. The visits were continued whenever possible, allowing the client to vent his frustrations concerning his continued and worsening symptoms of pneumonia. He was not emotionally ready to hear the interspersed suggestions that we wished for him to go out for highly advanced care. He could not "hear" us. Over the next few days his reading was guided from purely recreational to regional literature, then to occasional stories or poems about men who had retired or had left their land, all from regional authors. On the fifth day, as the author stopped for the daily visit, the client looked up and said, "These stories are taking a strange twist. Are you trying to tell me something?" He had understood the stories intuitively, and with his psychologic and spiritual battle behind him, that of denial, he was now ready to make arrangements for his physical care. He put his affairs in order that afternoon and sought care the next day.

Conclusion

As with any nursing intervention, the first step in using bibliotherapy or transitional reading is to establish rapport with the client and the family. Determine the reading interests and the reading skills of the client through a progression of short stories or poems. How receptive is the patient to guided reading? A comment like, "I just happen to have a story about . . . at home," will give you valuable clues to this receptivity. Think of your own bookshelves as storerooms of untapped creative energy for your patient (Cohen, 1988). Save, clip, and collect for future use. Some general guidelines about literature include (Cohen, 1988):

1. The readings should be enjoyable.
2. Short excerpts are effective. The whole book is not necessary.
3. Never force a book on a client.
4. Select literature that reflects as closely as possible the situa-

tion the client is facing. First-person accounts of similar experiences are helpful to some clients.

5. Know the literature you recommend. The client could be offended by alternative values.

6. Make friends with a research librarian and ask about book lists by topic, such as aging, life transitions, or loss.

7. Consult therapy resource lists such as "Poetic Resources" found in the *Journal of Poetry Therapy.*

A list of prescriptive readings is included at the end of this chapter for use with clients at varied ages and stages of health and illness.

References

Aleksychik, A. (1989). Bibliotherapy: An effective principal and supplementary method of healing, correcting and administering relief. *Journal of Poetry Therapy, 3*(1), 19–21.

Bardarah-McCandless, J. (1989). Agony, a womb of poetry. *Journal of Poetry Therapy, 2*(3), 145–154.

Barker, P. (1985). *Using metaphors in psychotherapy.* New York: Brunner/Mazel.

Berger, A. (1988). Working through grief by poetry writing. *Journal of Poetry Therapy, 2*(1), 11–19.

Burkhardt, M. A. (1989). Spirituality: An analysis of the concept. *Holistic Nursing Practice, 3*(3), 69–77.

Carpenito, L. J. (1989). *Handbook of nursing diagnosis* (p. 155). Philadelphia: JB Lippincott.

Chavis, G. G. (1988). Poetic resources. *Journal of Poetry Therapy, 1*(4), 232.

Clements, D. B. (1986). Reminiscence: A tool for aiding families under stress. *Maternal Child Nursing, 11,* 114–117.

Cohen, L. J. (1989). Reading as a group process phenomenon: A theoretical framework for bibliotherapy. *Journal of Poetry Therapy, 3*(2), 73–83.

Cohen, L. J. (1988). Bibliotherapy: The right book at the right time. *Journal of Psychosocial Nursing and Mental Health, 26*(8), 7–12.

Cohen-Morales, P. J. (1989). Poetry as a therapeutic tool within a group adolescent setting. *Journal of Poetry Therapy, 2*(3), 155–160.

Davey, L. G. (1983). What have you done to my mother? *Journal of Gerontological Nursing, 9*(2), 133.

Dickinson, E. (1960). It dropped so low in my regard. In T. H. Johnson (Ed.): *Complete Poems of Emily Dickinson.* Boston: Little, Brown.

Erhardt, W. D. (1985). *Carrying the Darkness: American Indochina Poetry of the Vietnam War.* New York: Avon.

Evans, D. A. (1990). *Notes on nursing and literature.* Unpublished manuscript. Brookings: South Dakota State University.

Evans, D. A. (1987, November). *The use of literature in healing.* Address presented at Humanities in the Healing Arts Dialogue #2, Sioux Falls, SD.

Evans, D. A. (1974). The touchdown in slow motion. *Train windows* (p. 35). Athens: Ohio University Press.

Feldman, D. (1974). Chronic disabling illness: A holistic view. *Journal of Chronic Disability, 27,* 287.

Flowers, B. S. (1988). Poetry, healing and making whole. *Journal of Poetry Therapy, 2*(1), 25–31.

Fox, M. (1983). *Original blessing* (p. 85). Santa Fe, NM: Bear.

Fox, M. (1979). *A spirituality named compassion and the healing of the global village, Humpty Dumpty and us* (pp. 1–35). San Francisco: Harper & Row.

Gold, J. (1988). The value of fiction as a therapeutic recreation and developmental mediator: A theoretical framework. *Journal of Poetry Therapy, 1*(3), 135–147.

Gordon, D. (1978). *Therapeutic metaphors* (p. 19). Cupertino, CA: Meta Publications.

Gorelick, K. (1987). Greek tragedy and ancient healing: Poems as theater and Asclepian temple in miniature. *Journal of Poetry Therapy, 2*(1), 41–45.

Gorelick, K, & Monser, R. (1988). Consultation corner. *Journal of Poetry Therapy, 2*(1), 41–45.

Hansen, A. T. (1990). *The story of Job and the use of literature in the healing arts.* Unpublished manuscript, Aberdeen, SD: Northern State University.

Hansen, A. T. (1987, September). *Literature pertaining to parenting, home and family, and the story of Job.* Address presented at Humanities in the Healing Arts, Dialogue #1, Aberdeen, SD.

Hasselstrom, L. (1990). *Using journals as therapy.* Unpublished manuscript.

Hasselstrom, L. (1987, November). *Writing in a journal: How to turn blank pages into your private physician, personal psychiatrist and best friend.* Address presented at Humanities in the Healing Arts, Dialogue #3, Pierre, SD.

Hobus, R. M. (1987). *A professional framework for the application of literature in nursing.* Address presented at Humanities in the Healing Arts, Dialogue #1, Aberdeen, SD, and Dialogue #2, Sioux Falls, SD.

Hobus, R. M., Hansen, A. T., Evans, D. A., & Woodard, C. L. (1987). *Humanities in the healing arts.* A dialogue series. South Dakota Committee on the Humanities. Box 7050, University Station, Brookings, SD, 57007.

Jaskoski, H. (1987). Artesan or genius: Two views of poetic process. *Journal of Poetry Therapy, 1*(1), 5–13.

Kissman, K. (1989). Poetry and feminist social work. *Journal of Poetry Therapy, 2*(4), 221–230.

Kramer, A. (1987). Poetry as a key to unlocking self. *Journal of Poetry Therapy, 1*(2), 77–87.

Laborde, G. L. (1984). *Influencing with integrity.* Palo Alto, CA: Science and Behavior Books.

Lange, J. P. (1990). *Closer walk.* Wheaton, IL: Chapel of the Air Press.

Lankton, S. R., & Lankton, C. H. (1983). *The answer within.* New York: Brunner/Mazel.

Larkin, D. M., & Zahourek, R. P. (1988). Therapeutic storytelling and metaphors. *Holistic Nursing Practice, 2,* 45–53.

Lazarus, R. S. (1979). Positive denial: The case for not facing reality. *Psychology Today, 13*(4), 44–45, 47–48, 51–52, 57, 60.

Leedy, J. J. (1973). *Poetry as healer.* Philadelphia: JB Lippincott.

Lifton, R. (1979). Advocacy and corruption in the healing professions. In W. R. Rogers & D. Barnard (Eds.), *Nourishing the humanistic in medicine* (pp. 53–72). Pittsburgh: University of Pittsburgh Press.

May, R. (1975). *The courage to create* (p. 29). New York: Bantam.

Mazza, N. (1988). Poetry and technical proficiency in brief therapy: Bridging arts and science. *Journal of Poetry Therapy, 2*(1), 3–10.

Mazza, N. (1987). Editor's note. *Journal of Poetry Therapy, 1*(2), 65.

Mazza, N. (1981). The use of poetry in treating the troubled adolescent. *Adolescence, 62*(3), 403–407.

McAbee, P. (Ed.). (1987, Fall). *Brochure on the magic of metaphor.* (Available from the Philadelphia Training Institute for Neuro-Linguistic Programming, 569 North Main St., Doylestown, PA, 18901.)

McGee, R. F. (1984). Hope: A factor influencing crisis resolution. *Advances in Nursing Science, 6*(4), 34–43.

Meleis, A. I. (1985). *Theoretical nursing: Development and progress* (pp. 254–263). Philadelphia: JB Lippincott.

Miller, V. (1985). *Despite this flesh: The disabled in stories and poems.* Austin: University of Texas Press.

Mills, J., & Crowley, R. (1986). *Therapeutic metaphors for children and the child within.* New York: Brunner/Mazel.

Mische, P. (1982). Toward a global spirituality. In *The whole earth papers,* No. 16, East Orange, NJ: Global Education Associates.

Moch, S. D. (1989). Health within illness: Conceptual evolution and practice possibilities. *Advances in Nursing Science, 11*(4), 23–31.

Morgan, L. B. (1988). Metaphoric communication and psychotherapeutic process. *Journal of Poetry Therapy, 1*(3), 169–181.

Morris-Vann, A. M. (1983). The efficacy of bibliotherapy on the mental health of elementary students who have experienced loss. *Dissertation Abstracts International, 44* 676A (University Microfilms No 83-15616).

Nagai-Jacobsen, M. G., & Burkhardt, M. A. (1989). Spirituality: Cornerstone of nursing practice. *Holistic Nursing Practice, 3*(3), 18–26.

Newman, M. A. (1989). The spirit of nursing. *Holistic Nursing Practice, 3*(3), 1–6.

Norris, K. (1990). Healing in the classroom: A memoir. Unpublished manuscript.

Norris, K. (1988). Saturday afternoon at the library. *The Year of Common Things* (pp. 2–3). Denver: Wayland Press.

Norris, K. (1987, September). Poetry therapy in classroom and acute care settings. Address to Humanities in the Healing Arts, Dialogue #1, Aberdeen, SD.

Paterson, J., & Zederad, I. (1988). *Humanistic Nursing.* New York: John Wiley & Sons.

Pies, L. S. (1988). The poet and the therapist. *Journal of Poetry Therapy, 2(2), 84–88.*

Pike, L. S. (1979). Darkness. *Journal of Gerontological Nursing, 5*(2), 46.

Rogers, W. R. (1979). Helplessness and agency in the healing process. In W. R. Rogers & D. Barnard, (Eds.), *Nourishing the humanities in medicine: Interactions with social sciences* (pp. 25–52). Pittsburgh: University of Pittsburgh Press.

Rogers, W. R., & Barnard, D. (1979). The interaction between humanistic social sciences and medical education. In W. R. Rogers & D. Barnard (Eds.), *Nourishing the humanities in medicine: Interactions with social sciences* (pp. 3–24). Pittsburgh: University of Pittsburgh Press.

Rosen, S. (1982). *My voice will go with you: The teaching tales of Milton H. Erickson.* New York: WW Norton.

Schrodes, C. (1949). Bibliotherapy: A theoretical and clinical experimental study. Unpublished doctoral dissertation. University of California, Berkeley.

Schunior, C. (1989). Nursing and the comic mask. *Holistic Nursing Practice, 3*(3), 7–17.

Sevy, G. (1989). *American experiences in Vietnam: A reader.* Norman: University of Oklahoma Press.

Shakespeare, W. (1605). *King Lear,* Act V, Scene 3, Lines 307–309.

Smith, A. C. (1989). Reading guidance: Death and grief. *Journal of Poetry Therapy, 3*(1), 23–28.

Snodgrass, W. D.(1968). The flat one. *After experience.* New York: Harper & Row.

Stafford, W. (1977). Bess. *Stories that might be true.* New York: Harper & Row.

Stapleton, S. R. (1983). Decreasing powerlessness in the chronically ill: A prototype. In J. F. Miller (Ed.), *Coping with chronic illness: Overcoming powerlessness* (pp. 257–274). Philadelphia: FA Davis.

Stewart, M. D.(1989). Making sense out of chaos: Prose writing, fictional kind and the reality of Vietnam. *Dissertation Abstracts International* (University Microfilms No. DA 8908032).

Stuart, E. M., Deckro, J. P., & Mandle, C. L. (1989). Spirituality in health and healing: A clinical program. *Holistic Nursing Practice 3*(3), 35–46.

Swann, C. (1978). Through the window. *Pasque Petals, 52.* Sioux Falls: South Dakota State Poetry Society.

Swann, C. (1977). Sad Summer. *Wanna go to Sally's?,* Aberdeen, SD: North Plains Press.

Thomas D. (1957). Do not go gentle into that good night. *The collected poems of Dylan Thomas* (p. 128). New York: New Directions.

Tournier, P. (1965). *The healing of persons* (pp. 6–61). San Francisco, Harper & Row.

Travelbee, J. (1971). *Interpersonal aspects of nursing* (2d ed.) Philadelphia: F. A. Davis.

Trilling, P. (1967). *The experience of literature* (pp. 124–132). New York: Holt, Rinehart, & Winston.

Yalom, E. D. (1985). *The theory and practice of group therapy* (3d ed.). New York: Basic Books.

Younger, J. B.(1990). Literary works as a mode of knowing. *IMAGE: Journal of Nursing Scholarship, 22*(1), 39–42.

Wallas, L. (1985). *Stories for the third ear.* New York: WW Norton.

Woodard, C. L. (1990, March). *Spirituality in literature.* Address to the United Campus Ministries, Brookings, SD.

Woodard, C. L. (1987). *The power of literature in healing.* Address presented at Humanities in the Healing Arts, Dialogue #1, Aberdeen, SD.

Woster, K. (1978). A farmer dying. *Oakwood, 4,* 17. Brookings: South Dakota State University.

Prescriptive Reading Suggestions
Edited by Ruth Hobus

I. Death of a Loved One, Incapacitation, and Aging

Chekov, Anton — "A Lament" (story on the loss of a son)

Dickinson, Emily — "Apparently, with No Suprise"

Dickey, James — "The Hospital Window" (about dying father)

Hughes, Langston — "Dreams" (Hold fast to dreams)

Ignatow, David — "Sunday at the State Hospital"

Masters, Edgar Lee — "Fiddler Jones"
"The Hill"

Stafford, William — "Bess"
"At the Grave of My Brother"

Swann, Carlee — "A Sad Summer"

Thomas, Dylan — "Do Not Go Gentle into That Good Night"

Williams, William Carlos — "The Last Words of My English Grandmother"

Woster, Kevin — "A Farmer Dying"

II. The Need for Peace, Self-Contentment

Berry, Wendell — "The Peace of Wild Things"

Frost, Robert — "The Pasture"
"The Road Not Taken"

Jeffers, Robinson — "To the Stone Cutters"

Masters, Edgar Lee — "Albert Schirding" (go for the simple things)
"Paul McNeeley" (about a nurse who gave peace to a dying man)

King James Bible — 23 Psalm

III. Birth of A Handicapped Child

Miller, Vassar (Ed.) — *Despite This Flesh* (an anthology of the handicapped) Some of the selections include:

Williams, Miller — "The Ones That Are Thrown Out"

Tyler, Anne — "Average Waves in Unprotected Waters"

Jacobsen, Josephine — "The Glen"

IV. Child's Awareness of Death

Conrad, Pam — *My Daniel* (a book about death of a brother)

Donnelly, Elfie — *So Long Grandpa* (death of a grandparent)

Woolverton, Linda · *Running before the Wind* (death of an abusive father)

Zindel, Bonnie · *A Star for the Latecomer* (mother died of cancer)

V. Death of A Child

Aiken, Conrad · "All Lovely Things"
Dickey, James · "The Lifeguard"
Field, Eugene · "Little Boy Blue" (widely anthologized)

Frost, Robert · "Home Burial" (widely anthologized)

VI. Midlife and Marital Discord

Justice, Donald · "Men at Forty"
Ciardi, John · "Suburban Homecoming"
Lyell, Ruth · *Middle Age, Old Age* (short stories, poems, and plays on aging)

Mueller, Lisel · "A Voice in the Dark"
Plath, Sylvia · "Mirror" (aging)
Snodgrass, W. D. · "Heart's Needle" (divorce)

VII. Journals

Thoreau, Henry David · *Journal*
Sarton, May · *Journal of a Solitude*
Simons, G. F. · *Keeping Your Personal Journal*

West, Celeste · *Words in Our Pockets*

VIII. Selected Books

Bly, Carol (1985). *Backbone*. Minneapolis: Milkweed Editions. (Short stories, one about a woman who ran away from a nursing home.)

Daniels, Kate (1984). *The White Wave*. Pittsburgh: University of Pittsburgh Press. (Poems about a children's ward and other family relationships.)

Dwyer, David (1976). *Ariana Olisvos: Her Last Works and Days*. Amherst: University of Massachussetts Press. (Many poems are about cancer.)

Gold, Joseph (1990). *Read for Your Life*. Ontario, Canada: Fitzhenry & Whiteside. (Sometimes humorous poems and readings through the developmental cycle.)

Hasselstrom, Linda (1987). *Roadkill*. Spoon River Poetry Press: Peoria, IL. (Poems about life. Concludes with "Hannah: Dying In a Hospital.")

Lloyd, Roseanne (1985). *Tapdancing for Big Mom*. Minneapolis: New Rivers Press. (Many poems about incest and how it haunts survivors.)

Norris, Kathleen (1988). *The Year of Common Things*. Wayland Press: Denver. (Memorable poems about family, love, abuse and answered prayers.)

Norris, Kathleen (1981). *The Middle of the World*. Pittsburgh: University of Pittsburgh Press. (Miscellany of poems; includes "At Killian's Grave" about the death of a child.)

Olds, Sharon (1983). *The Dead and the Living*. New York: Knopf. (Honest poems about child abuse and how it affects a family.)

Woodard, Charles (1989). *As Far As I Can See*. Windflower Press, Lincoln, NE. (Inspiring anthology of memories, home, legacy, and loss.)

Zweig, Paul (1985). *Eternity's Woods*. Middletown, CT: Wesleyan University Press. (Thoughtful volume; last poems of a poet with cancer.)

■

Imagery as a Means of Coping

■ REBECCA STEPHENS

New knowledge about cognitive processes is expanding nursing's repertoire of interventions. This chapter contains a review of imagery as a nursing strategy to facilitate client coping and positive responses to altered health states. The review of imagery contained in this chapter is relevant for the practitioner who believes that attitudes, beliefs, and reactions to life experiences influence whether persons get sick and how quickly they recover.

Clients look to nurses to help them face the challenge of long-term health problems. Initially, the nurse manages the demands generated by the altered health state; ultimately, successful management of the health regimen falls on the client. In order to take charge of their own health care, clients must have the feeling that their own actions will significantly affect what happens to them. Repeated studies have shown that helping clients gain control or a perceived sense of control over their lives is essential for successful adjustment to chronic illness (Christman, McConnell, Pfeiffer, Webster, Schmitt, & Reis, 1988; Mishel, 1984; Frank, 1985; Smith, Wallston, Wallston, Forsberg, & King, 1984).

Averill (1973) outlined three categories of control:

1. *Behavioral control.* Client takes actions to change his or her environment.
2. *Cognitive control.* Client interprets or appraises the event.
3. *Decisional control.* Client makes choices about the plan of care.

Imagery is a strategy that can enhance all three types of control. Different types of imagery can be used for different needs. *Guided imagery* helps

353

the client appraise his or her situation. *End-result imagery* and *process imagery* help redefine the client's situation, allowing rehearsal of new behaviors and changing the perceived powerlessness caused by the threatening diagnosis.

This chapter explores the use of imagery as a cognitive tool to reduce pain and stress, alter the course of disease, and/or improve health-seeking behaviors. Imagery techniques are doubly effective because they can be taught while the client is under the care of the nurse and can later help the client maintain control, reduce stress, and alleviate pain with minimal assistance at home.

Imagery techniques involve the use of images or of fantasy to achieve health-related goals. Imagery can be used to achieve altered states of awareness, change the client's perception of the situation, and facilitate control of the autonomic nervous system and other physiologic mechanisms. In addition, it can be used for bypassing neurologic mechanisms in order to give generalized instructions to the body.

Furthermore, imagery can be used to enhance other medical and nursing therapies. For example, in patients with cancer, imagery can be combined with chemotherapy and radiation to improve the client's prognosis. It is effective in helping to control the debilitating symptoms of nausea and vomiting that accompany these treatments (Frank, 1985). Imagery is predominantly an adjunctive therapy, rather than a primary therapy.

Imagery helps in the control of pain, both acute and chronic, by augmenting relaxation, providing distractions, and inducing a state of auto-hypnosis. Stressors associated with illness include inability to tolerate ambiguity, delayed gratification, fatalistic ideation, feeling out of control, and viewing oneself as inadequate to fight the illness. Imagery effectively reduces these stressors.

While imagery has its roots deep in cultural and religious beliefs as an ancient healing technique (Samuels & Samuels, 1975), recently the anecdotal evidence in academic literature strongly supports the use of imagery in modern-day medicine and suggests that it has great potential as a therapeutic intervention in nursing. Formal nursing research studies on imagery are beginning to appear in the literature as well.

Definition of Imagery

Imagery is only one of several mental processes that can be used to develop cognitive control and promote stress reduction. Other processes include biofeedback, meditation, and relaxation. While biofeedback has also proven effective in stress reduction (Brown, 1984) and continues to be used today, meditation was primarily used in the 1960s. Benson and Klipper's (1975) work documented the physiologic changes produced by relaxation. This paper will discuss the use of imagery and the use of relaxation to augment that imagery.

Achterberg (1985) defines imagery as an ancient healing technique whereby purposeful or therapeutic use of mental images are used to achieve a specific, desired goal. These thought processes invoke and use the senses: vision, audition, smell, taste, and the senses of movement, position, and touch. They are a communication mechanism between perception, emotion, and bodily change and act as a bridge between body and mind. Sometimes the subject is alert, concentrating intensely, participating with his or her whole being and visualizing the scene as if it is real. At other times imagery is done in a relaxed state.

Although frequently used together, imagery and relaxation are different. Brown (1974) states, "the release of the body's tension during relaxation stimulates a dream-like trance in which many mental images are released" (p. 143). In relaxation, the thoughts are free flowing and intentionally undirected. This state of relaxation calms the body, promotes rest, and provides an escape from daily pressures.

On the other hand, with imagery the individual channels the energy generated by the images by performing a goal-directed activity. In this instance, the initial part of the guided imagery uses a relaxation exercise followed by a combination of process imagery and/or end-result imagery. Process images are images of the actual or fantasized mechanism by which a desired effect can be achieved. End-result imagery has a concrete image of the desired result as having already taken place (Dossey, 1988).

Process imagery is more complex and very difficult to study. Holden-Lund (1988) used process imagery with 24 cholecystectomy patients. She found significantly lower state anxiety, lower cortisol levels 1 day post-surgery, and less surgical wound erythema in the treatment group than in the control group.

An example of how imagery could be operationalized in this situation follows. Place the client in a relaxed state using progressive relaxation as described by Snyder (1984). With the nurse as the guide, have the client with a recent skin graft visualize this image. The new skin and the graft site have hands reaching out to each other. Each day the hands move closer together until they can grasp each other in a firm handshake with complete closure at the suture line.

Many practitioners believe that this kind of physiologic change is possible with mental imagery (Simonton, Matthews-Simonton, & Sparks, 1980; Holden-Lund, 1988; Blandhard, McCoy, Wittrock, Musso, Gerardi, & Pangburn, 1988). To individualize process imagery, the nurse must (1) have a fundamental knowledge of the physiology involved in disease, (2) know the interaction of all treatments, such as medications and surgery, (3) understand the client's belief systems, and (4) have a complete assessment of the client's psychophysiologic condition (Achterberg & Lawlis, 1980).

End-result imagery can be illustrated by the following example. Clients who are severely overweight might visualize themselves at their ideal weight, listen to family and friends rave over their new figure, and experience how it feels to be slim. Clients can picture with clarity trying on a new bathing suit and looking really great. This process can be used by clients who suffer from only minor complaints as well. Whatever the symptomatology, clients imagine their bodies healing (process imagery) and/or cured of the disease and healthy again (end-result imagery).

Imagery serves as a powerful tool for altering one's physiologic processes, mental state, self-image, performance, or behavior. Achterberg (1985), a foremost researcher of imagery, contends, "Imagine the type of person you wish to become . . . and you will most likely reach your goals" (p. 7).

Although imagery as a therapeutic technique in nursing is new, all clients use various forms of imagery in their lives. Memory, daydreams, dreams, and hallucinations are all forms of imagery. Some of these states are voluntary, like memory and daydreams. Others, including the alpha periods that occur just before sleep or upon awaking, are only partially under voluntary control. Alpha periods also occur naturally after intense periods of concentration (Samuels & Samuels, 1975). When persons are staring out of a window, they are probably in an alpha period. Other types of imagery such as dreams and hallucinations are totally beyond voluntary control.

Carl Jung (1963) was one of the first psychologists to address the idea of imagery as a form of therapy. Jung believed that new insights could be gained by actively using alpha times to bypass the censorship of the ego. Imagery directly connects the mind to bodily processes, thus making physiologic change possible. Clients can be taught to organize and use alpha periods to enhance the image they are working on such as weight loss.

Thus imagery, with or without relaxation, can help clients regain a sense of control over their lives, a renewed sense of purpose to face the limitations of their illness, and the strength to make the necessary lifestyle changes. Imagery can be used in a generalized form with no reference to the client's presenting symptoms, or it may be tailored to address specific problems. This technique is helpful to clients with a chronic illness as a means of maintaining or regaining psychologic stamina.

THEORETICAL RATIONALE

Theoretical speculation about how imagery works has evolved in the fields of medicine and psychology. While an exhaustive review is not feasible here, one early model that has been useful will be shared. While this framework may not be consistent for all the different views of imagery, it is useful for explaining how different people have varying success with imagery.

Horowitz's (1978) conceptual framework examines the three modalities in which thought represents meaning: the enactive, lexical, and imagic modes. *Enactive thought* represents motor response memories. Thinking about lifting a heavy book lying on the table stimulates enactive thought, and a mild tensing of the muscle groups in the shoulders and arms occurs. Control of an enactive mode of thought lies in the limbic system. The limbic system controls emotions that manifest themselves through the tensing of facial muscles. The enactive mode can be accessed by way of the imagic mode. Images may be connected with emotions, which trigger enactive thought followed by observable behavior.

The *lexical mode* uses words and grammar to think about objects. Lexical thought makes it possible to communicate clearly. The left hemisphere of the brain controls this mode. Studies of right- and left-hemispheric function indicate that the right and left hemispheres of the brain process information differently. The left hemisphere analyzes, abstracts ideas, counts, marks time, and plans logically, thereby forming lexical thought.

In the *imagic mode,* persons perceive and process perceptual information in the form of dreams, fantasies, and images. Primarily, right-hemisphere activity controls imagic thought. The right hemisphere of the brain shows us how things exist in space and how pieces fit together (Whitrock, 1977). This mode creates ideas and draws new conclusions. Paradigm shifts and leaps of understanding—an "Ah! Huh! Now I understand" type of learning—characterizes right-brain functioning.

Imagic mode of thought develops greatly before the child learns to speak (Singer, 1974). After the child learns to express him- or herself, language takes on greater importance and the imagic mode of thought decreases. Our school systems develop the functions of the left hemisphere, logic and reasoning, while ignoring the function of the right-hemisphere. In most individuals, the lexical mode of thought is dominant, while the imagic mode of thought is underdeveloped from lack of use.

Researchers believe that images held by the brain may be lost when we try to translate them into language (Samuels & Samuels, 1975). For example, when one awakens from a dream, the meaning and image of that dream is clear. However, the meaning becomes confused and lost when the individual tries to share the dream in words to another person. The translation of an image into lexical thought can distort or change the image. That does not indicate that the person did not have a clear understanding of the dream, but simply that putting it into words obscured the meaning. Western culture often disregards or belittles ideas that cannot be articulated well in words. Eastern culture values this form of thinking, believing it demonstrates great wisdom.

The mind, by way of the senses in the form of images, transforms all stimuli into the enactive, lexical, or imagic modes of thought. All are equally important to cognitive functioning. Persons call upon the various modes of thought for different purposes, but each individual has a pre-dominant mode of thought. For example, an athlete may use enactive thought more frequently and an artist may have a higher refined ability to use imagic mode of thought. Accountants and lawyers use predominantly lexical thought.

Consequently, individuals differ in their ability to elicit visual or auditory images. Some persons report they are unable to experience visual or auditory images, even with detailed descriptions. Kunzendorf (1981) studied individual differences in imagery abilities and control of skin temperatures. Kunzendorf suggests that those who frequently use visual, auditory, and tactile-proprioceptive images facilitate imagery and may have more control over their autonomic nervous systems.

Finally, reframing is a theoretic framework which is helpful in explaining imagery. Reframing is a technique to help persons contact parts of their minds that are keeping them stuck. Reframing suspends a person's old belief system; allowing reorganization of a problem or experience. In this manner, the person can move toward a healthier state (Stanton, 1989).

Dossey (1988) describes this process in the following way:

> The dramatic psychophysiologic changes that occur in hypnosis and imagery result from gaining access to state-dependent memory, learning, and behavior systems and making their encoded information available for problem solving. Every access of information can be seen as a reframe. When one gains access to state-dependent memory, it then can be re-associated, reorganized, or reframed in a manner that resolves the negative memory (pp. 226–227).

While theories of how imagery functions appear in the literature, little agreement exists at this time among researchers. Nevertheless, practitioners continue to find imagery effective, despite this academic dilemma, and use it in their practice.

Literature Review

Imagery appears in the literature in four areas, psychotherapy, cognitive behaviorist studies, sports literature, and medical literature, especially immunology and nursing. Articles unique to nursing appear less frequently.

IMAGERY AND PSYCHOLOGY

Many studies in the psychotherapy literature are in anecdotal form, unique to a specific client situation. Most of these studies look at imagery as a therapy for pathologic conditions (Singer, 1974; Ashen, 1983) and to improve the client's health (Sheikh, 1984). Meichenbaum (1983) attempts to provide order from psychotherapy studies by identifying commonalities among therapies. The underlying mechanisms contained in these therapies are (1) a feeling of control gained from image rehearsal, (2) a change in the internal dialogue associated with maladaptive behavior, (3) mental rehearsal of adaptive responses, and (4) the consequent decrease of fear.

The educational literature revealed three behavioristic studies of imagery as a treatment for anxiety. Weissberg (1977) found that "coping imagery" increased the effectiveness of desensitization therapy. Hymen and Warren (1978) combining imagery with rational emotive therapy found test anxiety lowered in the experimental imagery group. Ayres and Hopf (1985), while studying speech anxiety, found imagery more effective when persons visualize themselves having a problem and working through it to a successful completion (process imagery) than when they pictured the task accomplished (end-result imagery). No studies were found that used imagery as a primary intervention in the treatment of anxiety.

IMAGERY AND HEALING

The connection between imagery and the immune system has been studied with increasing frequency. Simonton and coworkers (1980) first used imagery as a psychologic intervention in the treatment of clients with advanced cancer. Comparing the survival rates of their study population to nationally established survival times for breast, bowel, and lung cancer, they found that clients using imagery combined with traditional medical treatment had a prolonged life expectancy. The study followed 159 patients diagnosed with incurable cancer and a 1-year life expectancy. Sixty-three subjects remained alive after 2 years. In addition, 22.2 percent showed no evidence of cancer and 19.1 percent demonstrated tumor regression. The median survival for these clients was 8 to 19 months longer than the national average (Simonton et al., 1980).

Interest in imagery for treating patients with terminal cancer grew. Studies found great discrepancies in the effectiveness of similar traditional cancer treatments. Yet, these differences did not seem connected to the location or the type of cancer under treatment. Life span also varied drastically (Simonton et al., 1980).

The client's hardiness and desire to live seemed to play a major role in the client's recovery or, at the very least, an increase in life span (Justice, 1987). Imagery therapy was designed by the institute (Simonton et al., 1980) to foster the client's sense of control over life and ability to enact change in this frightening situation. This program to foster wellbeing and teach imagery strategies has gained worldwide recognition.

In no way did Simonton and coworkers (1980) claim that imagery explained all the differences found in this study. However, they did feel that the program increased motivation, mobilized internal resources, and increased the expectation that the treatment results would be positive.

Studies by Greer and Morris (1978), Maguire (1981), and Frank (1985) found that personal coping strategies significantly influenced patient outcomes in breast cancer treatment. Frank (1985) and Bridge, Benson, Pietroni, and Priest (1988) reported that patients practicing "guided imagery/relaxation" felt less emotional distress and nausea or vomiting following chemotherapy infusion. Both studies used control groups.

Researchers are now beginning to study the effects of imagery on physiologic changes in the immune system. Halliburton (1986) studied changes in the T-cell activity of cancer patients who practiced relaxation with guided imagery. The role of the B and T cell is to recognize the presence of an antigen and to initiate specific mechanisms of disposal, a process vital to fighting of cancer cells. After 1 year, the subjects' blood samples showed improved T-cell activity, increased killer cell activity, and changes in some B-cell measures. Similarly, Kiecolt-Glaser (1987) studied the impact of imagery on killer cells in a healthy elderly population and found improved T-cell function. In addition, the subjects had lower resting heart rates, slower respirations, and diminished perspiration. They reported feeling more in control of their lives.

IMAGERY AND DISCOMFORT

Anxiety

Stephens (manuscript submitted for publication) studied the effectiveness of imagery on moderate levels of nonpathologic anxiety. Using a quasiexperimental pretest/posttest design, Stephens randomly assigned 159 undergraduate nursing students to two treatment groups and a control group. One treatment group listened to an audiotape containing guided end-result imagery. The second group used an audiotape with the same imagery combined with relaxation. The third group was a control group. Findings showed both treatment groups had significantly lower levels of anxiety than the control group, using Speilberger and coworkers' (1983) State-Trait Anxiety Inventory.

Surprisingly, imagery alone was as effective as the imagery combined with relaxation. This contradicts most of the findings in the literature which indicate that imagery combined with relaxation is more effective than imagery alone. In practice, if imagery could be used effectively without having to put the client into a relaxed state, imagery could be used in many more settings. Further study is needed. Relaxation requires sitting alone in a quiet place and entering a trancelike state. In some situations audiotapes with relaxation would be highly dangerous, such as when driving a car. People would practice an imagery technique more frequently if they could combine it with a routine mundane task.

King (1988) tested Donovan's Relaxation with Guided Imagery Tool with 33 graduate nursing students and also found imagery to be effective in lowering anxiety. The effect was short-lived in that subjects had returned to preimaging levels within a 2-week interval.

Pain

Imagery has been used in acute clinical pain experiences such as childbirth, abortion, and minor surgery. Anecdotal reports indicate that imagery is very effective in reducing pain, but surprisingly few formal studies have been done. Donovan (1980) used imagery to decrease anxiety and pain in cancer patients. Weinstein (1976) found imagery effective in lowering anticipatory pain in burn patients.

Most strategies employed pleasant imagery as a distraction. Maltzman (1988), however, found that viewing unpleasant slides increased pain tolerance more than viewing pleasant slides of landscapes. Perhaps, the unpleasant slides were more distracting and mentally absorbing, therefore holding the subjects' attention for longer periods of time.

QUALITATIVE STUDIES OF IMAGERY

Qualitative studies in this area enhance understanding of the nature of imagery and its therapeutic value. Achterberg and Lawlis (1980) outlined the beginning steps on the use of art to clarify images. They have found that when the client pictures the white blood cells as stronger than the cancer cells, there is a high predictor of success in persons with cancer and other forms of chronic illness.

Using drawings is an effective way to evaluate clients' reactions to imagery. Following instructions to imagine their cancer cells, immune system, and medical intervention, the subject is asked to draw his or her thoughts. Central themes emerging from this qualitative data include vividness, activity, strength, concreteness versus symbolism, and effectiveness. The researchers believe that persons' experiences as seen through their drawings have major implications for treatment. A prognostic tool is under development.

CONTROVERSIES

While guided imagery holds promise as a therapeutic tool, researchers are critical of imagery studies because of inconsistent methodologic protocols. Studies define imagery differently, combining imagery with other treatment modalities, such as rational emotive therapy, and vary the length of relaxation training and the number of imagery sessions. Nonprobability sampling techniques and control groups were not used in early studies. These factors make interpretation of the data difficult and cloud the question, Is imagery a legitimate intervention strategy?

Differences in conceptual labels such as guided imagery, relaxation with guided imagery, hypnosis, and pleasant imagery also lead to wide variations in the way guided imagery can be operationalized in a study. These factors make it difficult to compare treatment effects from one study to another.

Implications for Nursing Practice

Despite the methodologic issues, data continue to accumulate to support the therapeutic effectiveness of guided imagery. Nurses will continue to study the potential of guided imagery as a therapeutic modality and will find imagery useful in varied situations. The outcome desired helps the nurse and client determine the imagery technique that is appropriate.

When nurses wish to aid the client to modify physiologic function, they use techniques involving deep relaxation and the symbolic representation of physiologic control mechanisms. Such techniques expound on the placebo effect enhancing the healing process. Rossman (1988) points out ". . . placebo does not mean the response isn't real. It simply means the results stem from the belief of the patient in therapy, rather than from the therapy itself. The important thing about the placebo response is that it demonstrates beyond doubt that thoughts can trigger the body's own healing abilities" (p. 48).

The previous example of the skin graft shows how imagery uses symbolism. The placebo effect of the imagery enhances healing. However, imagery in this situation is only an adjunctive therapy combined with more traditional medical therapy such as sterile dressing changes, good nutrition, and antibiotic therapy.

If the goal of the imagery is to develop insight or increase personal resources to combat stress, symbolic representation of conflict and its resolution is used. End-result imagery can be used for conditions such as weight loss or smoking cessation.

The ability of the client to use imagery will vary, and the client will need assistance in development of the technique. Still, clients of all ages find imagery effective. Anyone who can think can imagine. Success will be determined by the willingness of the client to learn and practice the process. Nurses need to remember that imagery needs energy, and, therefore, a well-rested client increases the chance of success.

Uses and Techniques

CHRONIC PAIN

Imagery helps clarify the client's perception of the pain experienced. Pain can be labeled and described more vividly with the use of imagery.

Clients become aware of how the pain can be manipulated and changed. Then the practitioner can use imagery to relieve discouragement and increase hopefulness, changing the expectation that the pain will continue forever, shifting the focus of the client's life away from the pain, and helping increase the client's energy level needed to deal with the pain.

Guided imagery can be used to create a place of safety from the pain. Visual and auditory images seem more effective than kinesthetic images (Sodergren, 1985). For example, find the sights and sounds that are pleasing to the client. Imagining a wave hitting the beach, the wind moving through the trees, or lying on a soft cloud under a clear blue sky may relax a client and provide a retreat from continual pain. McCaffery (1989) calls this "taking a vacation from the pain."

Do not talk to the client during the guided imagery process unless the client has a question that must be answered immediately. The client is guided to release feelings and images during this time. Talking as a logical process will interfere with the flow of the images.

Precede the script with a general relaxation script. An example is given at the end of the chapter. Pick up cues, such as restlessness, from the client's behavior and add words like "pleasant," "warm," or "comfortable" to help promote relaxation. Tell the client that imagery is a fast way to connect the body, mind, and spirit by quieting the body and focusing on a particular event.

The following script illustrates a way to promote pain reduction:

> Let your imagination choose a place that is safe and comfortable . . . retreat to this place of comfort . . . experience the warmth of the sun as you float on your own special cloud under a splendid blue sky . . . this is a healthy technique that you can use at any time to escape from the pressures of daily life which cause or increase pain . . . allow yourself the privilege of coming to your special place frequently . . . at the beginning it may take you longer to create a state of pain-free enjoyment, but with practice you will reach this state with increased ease.

REHABILITATION

Korn's (1983) work with neurologic patients demonstrated that after a cerebrovascular accident clients can use imagery to relearn how to swallow or regain sitting balance, speech, and memory. Korn suggests that helping the client reexperience the psychomotor task activates sensory and neuromuscular mechanisms. This simulates the original task. Experiments with athletes produced the same results.

RELAXATION

Effective relaxation improves with guided imagery. Subjects can reach a relaxed state faster, achieve deeper relaxation, and remain for longer periods. Imagery augments outcome behaviors such as a decrease in blood pressure, anxiety, and muscle tension. Participants exposed to pleasant guided imagery experience a sense of timelessness and transcending boundaries. Butcher and Parker (1988) believed timelessness is an expansion and increased motion in the human energy field, thus enhancing patterning and harmony with the environment. They used Roger's Theory of Unitary Human Beings as a framework for their study.

Meichenbaum (1983) found combining relaxation and imagery more effective as a treatment for phobias. Through imagery techniques, the meaning of the phobic object is changed and the client can rehearse confrontation with the phobia.

PROBLEM SOLVING

Imagery is helpful when adjusting to drastic bodily change. A client with a new amputation can be asked to visualize himself or herself going home for the first time. With the use of imagery the client confronts previously ignored realities. A client with an amputation can resolve the problem of getting from the car to the house. While identified new problems are difficult, the result is to help the client successfully prepare for discharge.

Similarly, rehearsal of a stressful conversation allows the client to act out various scenarios and try out new behaviors. The client and the nurse explore the situation, identify what is causing the anxiety, and modify the client's response to the situation or the meaning of the situation to the client. This allows the client to gain a feeling of control in a situation that has been frightening in the past.

STRESS MANAGEMENT

Using imagery to identify areas of conflict or concern and to gain insight into common thinking patterns is within the nurse's domain, provided the clients are mentally healthy. Imagery which employs free-flowing and unstructured techniques should be used with caution. Clients must be told at the outset of each session that they can come out of the exploration at any time. The practitioner should have qualifications in the advanced mental health field to do psychotherapy with imagery. It is not clear if utilizing imagery with psychotic clients is harmful, but most practitioners warn against its use (McCaffery, 1989).

Summary

Imagery as a field of study is in its infancy. This combined with the lack of replicated studies with control groups limits the information available to the practitioner about expected client outcomes. Frequently, practitioners use information from case studies and consult with one another. Most importantly, imagery must produce no harmful physical and psychologic effects for the client.

While using guided imagery, nurses are to pay close attention for any signs of client's distress, such as agitation. If the client is hesitant about beginning, explore what the experience might be like first. Some casual suggestions about how to proceed may help the client to continue. Relaxation will make the imagery more effective. Clients should be told that they are in complete control of the imagery and can change it at any time or discontinue the treatment by opening their eyes.

Imagery techniques to improve the body's ability to fight off disease appear frequently in the literature. Clients who feel they are at the mercy of a medication, the physician, or the agency can use imagery to bring back a much needed sense of control. It is important to allow the client to create and individualize the images.

A word of caution: Imagery, as an adjunct to chemotherapy, can occasionally cause problems. Some clients may feel guilty if the imagery is not effective in attenuating tumor growth. Nurses must be alert for this reaction. A client with a poor prognosis is vulnerable to magical thinking. Severe side effects from the chemotherapy may tempt a client to end conventional treatment. Clients should understand that the use of imagery alone is inadvisable. Imagery should give the client a sense of power, not provide an additional stressor. Stop the imagery therapy if distress occurs.

Case Study

Imagery can be effective in reducing pain and stress, altering the course of disease, and/or helping clients develop healthy behavior patterns. At the same time, a secondary theme emerges, empowerment of the client. Individuals experience renewed self-confidence, increased feelings of control, and a healthier outlook on their lives.

Individuals who need to lose large amounts of weight frequently experience difficulty making this life-style change. Weight loss may be necessary to help control some disease conditions and because weight may escalate when exercise is restricted by illness. Overeating is frequently used as a source of comfort, leaving even healthy clients with a weight problem. All these situations can lower the client's self-esteem and cause depression. This case study explores the needs of an obese client and her struggle to gain control over her weight.

The nurse uses imagery throughout to help clarify the client's perceptions. The assessment data contain quotes from the client to allow for analysis of the data in relationship to the concept of powerlessness.

Guided imagery used to gather assessment data, process imagery used to stimulate the client's metabolism, and end-result imagery used to picture a new slim self all demonstrate ways imagery enhances nursing practice. The author combines imagery with more traditional nursing interventions.

BACKGROUND DATA

Mrs. Holland, a 46-year-old white female executive in public relations, complained of persistent inability to lose weight. She was 5 feet 5 inches tall and, when first seen, weighed 254 pounds. Her usual adult weight of 125 pounds had increased following the development of arteritis. Her hospitalization in intensive care included high doses of steroids, and convalescence resulted in prolonged periods of total bedrest.

One year after diagnosis, she weighed 192 pounds and decided, with her physician's consent, to try one of the physician-administered weight-loss programs. The diet consisted of liquid drinks containing protein and other essential supplements. She successfully lost 47 pounds during this time but failed to use the maintenance plan because of the overwhelming expense of the program. Relating her feelings at the time, she said,

> I desperately wanted to lose the weight gained during my illness. Finally, I decided to use starvation. (laughs.) That's what a protein liquid diet is you know. A very expensive way to starve.
> The diet program cost my family more than $50 a week, can you believe it? Boy! What a waste. I felt so guilty, I decided to forego the maintenance plan. I was confident that I could maintain my weight myself. Eight months later and 25 pounds heavier, I felt like a total failure. I couldn't even control what I put in my mouth.
> It brought back all of the feelings of being sick and scared to death in the intensive care unit with all those machines. I became so depressed, I could hardly get out of bed. . . . I even considered liposuction. Pretty drastic, huh? The surgery frightened me and besides, why should my family spend more money on me?

During the next 2 years, Mrs. H. suffered from yo-yo dieting. She alternated long periods of starvation with binging, resulting in a weight of 254 pounds and a very low self-esteem. Recently, an endocrinologist determined she had hypothyroidism. Being diagnosed with a thyroid problem gave Mrs. H. new hope and prompted a visit to the nurse using imagery therapy.

> Maybe I'm not just lazy with no will power. It's nice to know that there was a reason why I had such a hard time losing the weight. But, I need to lose 110 pounds. (laughs.) Well, at least 100.
> I've heard you work with imagery and I could certainly use a change of image. (laughs.) No quick fixes this time.

A general health assessment was completed by the nurse, using the Gordon's format (Gordon, 1987). The physical exam included blood

TABLE 14 ■ 1   Guided Imagery Technique*

---

1. Ask the client to sit or lie down with eyes closed
2. Induce relaxation
3. Reinforce relaxation by suggesting peaceful images
4. Suggest deeper relaxation
5. Describe the motif
6. Have the client elaborate on the setting
7. Have the client describe the situation experienced using symbolic images
8. Help the client resolve any conflicts
9. Bring the client out of the fantasy situation
10. Discuss the client's interpretation of the fantasy excursion
11. Ask the client to comment on insights gained during the session

---

*If the client becomes agitated during the imagery session, suggest thinking about visualization.
   For a brief period after any guided imagery exercise using deep relaxation, the client should sit quietly and stretch and move both arms and legs before arising. Most clients express a feeling of well-being and release after the session.

chemistry, serum thyroid hormone levels, and urine analysis. The lab work was normal, including thyroid function. A treadmill test revealed no cardiac abnormalities but revealed a very low exercise tolerance.

During assessment, guided imagery helped clarify the client's self-image, determine her level of self-esteem, and explore her feelings about her illness and past health-care experience. Guided imagery helped her express painful feelings and experiences. Steps used in the guided imagery technique are summarized in Table 14–1.

EVALUATION OF THE CASE STUDY

Accurate records describing the interventions help the practitioner determine the effectiveness of the imagery. The short-term and long-term goals, used as outcome criteria, determine the client's progress. Modifications in the interventions are made as problems arise and the nurse knows the client's individual needs better. Decisions about the treatment plan are made in collaboration with the client. Helping the client to control her health-care plan starts with the first visit. From the beginning the goal is client independence.

Imagery is a flexible, creative means of diagnosing and intervening in health-care situations. In a subtle approach, the nurse interweaves imagery questions and concepts into routine conversation, educational discussions, and discharge planning sessions. Imagery serves to heighten the nurse's awareness during assessment and paints mental pictures to clarify new ideas for the client.

In the more systematic approach, the nurse uses process and end-result imagery as a potential healing tool. In both cases, imagery gains power from the physiologic actions it has on the body as a natural healing mechanism. It is in effect a self-healing technique, and the nurse serves as the guide for this impressive pathway.

SUMMARY OF ASSESSMENT DATA

Biologic Responses	Psychosocial Responses
* 110-pound weight gain * Sleep disturbance * Limited physical ability (difficulty tying shoes, inability to garden) * Does not feel rested upon awakening * Is unable to work as desired * Low energy levels	* Reluctant to speak in front of a group * Decreased sexual contact with husband * Plays less with children * Low self-esteem * Blames self for weight gain * Difficulty expressing feelings * Has distanced self from friends * Under prolonged stress * Exhibits isolation behaviors

Cognitive Responses	Spiritual Responses
* Has difficulty concentrating * Exhibits anxiety * External locus of control * Lack of confidence in ability to problem solve	* Lack of belief in care givers * Feels helpless * Feels hopeless

Nursing Diagnoses

* Activity Intolerance related to obesity
Ineffective Individualized Coping related to low self-esteem
* Alteration in Role Performance related to low energy levels
* Altered Health Maintenance related to increased food consumption in response to stress and insufficient energy expenditure
Potential for Injury related to decreased ability to maintain balance
* Powerlessness related to yo-yo dieting and persistent weight gain
Body Image Disturbance related to excessive weight gain
Sleep Pattern Disturbance related to depression
Social Isolation related to being self-conscious about appearance
Hopelessness related to prolonged inability to lose weight

*A treatment plan follows for these nursing diagnoses.

NURSING DIAGNOSIS   Activity Intolerance Related to Obesity

Goals	Nursing Interventions
Short-Term The client will 1. Walk for 20 minutes 6 days per week 2. Use taped music while walking one time in the evening **Long-Term** The client will 1. Increase walks to 4 miles six times per week	1. Start walking for 20 minutes three times a week. 2. Increase walking to six times per week. 3. Gradually lengthen the walk 5 minutes at a time as tolerated. 4. Make a tape for the client using up-beat music of client's choice 5. Have the client listen to the tape while she walks

NURSING DIAGNOSIS   Activity Intolerance Related to Obesity (*Continued*)

Goals	Nursing Interventions
Rationale: The tape is developed to set up a rhythm that will stimulate metabolism and help lower the client's set point Exercise helps the client to gain immediate control over one aspect of her treatment. It also stimulates the body to burn fats and helps alleviate depression If the client will follow the exercise program, she will have a strong sense of accomplishment	6. Also have client listen one other time during the day to increase metabolism and help lower the client's set point 7. Make frequent phone contacts to provide encouragement. 8. Provide safety tips, suggest that good walking shoes be worn

NURSING DIAGNOSIS   Alteration in Role Performance Related to Low Energy Levels

Goals	Nursing Interventions
Short-Term The client will 1. Spend 30 minutes of quality time with her children each day 2. Plan a date with her husband once a week *Long-Term* The client will 1. Return to speaking in front of an audience in her work setting 2. Work with her family on an outdoor project 3. Return to church and take an active role in her Sunday school class *Rationale:* End-result imagery can be used to help the client prepare for speaking in her work situation or rehearsal of play or sexual activities.	1. Discuss the roles in her life and their importance 2. Determine which role she wishes to work with first 3. Plan activities that she would like to do with her children 4. Rehearse approaching her husband for a date 5. Discuss fears about public speaking 6. Using end-result imagery, have the client picture herself giving a speech to a group of coworkers 7. Explore with the client what she is feeling while she gives her speech. Problem-solve any difficulties with her 8. Practice building a positive image by using process imagery daily to work toward her goals

NURSING DIAGNOSIS Altered Health Maintenance Related to Increased Food Consumption

Goals	Nursing Interventions
Short-Term The client will: 1. Eat three meals a day and snacks when hungry 2. Eat mostly complex carbohydrates, small amounts of protein, limit fats 3. Drink six glasses of water a day *Long-Term* The client will 1. Maintain a weight loss of 1 to 2 pounds per week 3. Differentiate between hunger and desire to eat 4. Eat only when truly hungry	1. Keep a food log to determine eating patterns. The client should not eat differently. First the present eating pattern must be discovered. Record level of hunger on a scale of 1 to 4 before eating anything 2. Teach the importance of protein, the role of fat in weight gain, what foods are high in fat, the role of complex carbohydrates, and importance of drinking water for waste removal 3. Tell client to weigh herself only once a week 4. Teach exercise role in metabolism of food 5. Use an imagery tape daily describing how the client will look after weight loss, activities that can be done when slim, attention of others to her new self, feelings of self-confidence and self-approval

NURSING DIAGNOSIS Powerlessness Related to Yo-Yo Dieting with Persistent and Excessive Weight Gain

Goals	Nursing Interventions
Short-Term The client will: 1. Express a willingness to follow the exercise plan, believe that walking will help her lose weight 2. Identify times when she eats and is not hungry 3. Express feelings of anger and frustration without using food 4. Give herself a non-food-related reward for each week that she meets her exercise goal *Long-Term* The client will 1. Express a feeling of control over the amount of food she eats 2. Look forward to increasing her exercise program and adding her own modifications 3. Plan a reward for every 10 pounds lost 4. Make new friends and plan activities with them biweekly 5. Look daily at pictures of herself when she was at her goal weight 6. Carry herself with pride and renewed confidence	Teach or encourage client to: 1. Express feelings about past weight loss attempts 2. Read about the role of exercise and food in weight loss. Learn about rebound weight gain 3. Make decisions about how to change her exercise program and the amount and types of foods to eat 4. Discuss frustrations and setbacks with the nurse and client's family openly and identify support systems to help handle disappointments 5. Emphasize how much progress she has made (how far she can walk) instead of how much weight she has left to lose 6. Express confidence in reaching her goal weight and set a target date that is realistic 7. Plan small vacations to anticipate and buy new clothes to improve self-image 8. Seek out a new business challenge

Script for Relaxation and End-Result Imagery

SESSION 1

Your goal today is to master abdominal breathing. Sit upright or lie with your spine straight. Relax a moment. Place your hands an inch or two above your waist, your fingers extending across your rib cage. Inhale and exhale several times, feeling the abdominal muscles tense and release around your navel.

Now close your eyes and feel your abdomen with your hands. Breathe in deeply, feeling your abdomen expand. Then breathe out, feeling it fall and relax. Inhalation and exhalation should be connected in a smooth circular pattern. Keep breathing in and out slowly and deeply for several minutes, feeling the rise and fall of your abdomen with your hands. Continue for 3 to 5 minutes . . . (observe the client for signs of restlessness and encourage him or her to continue breathing slowly and effortlessly if necessary)* . . . Feel the tension draining from your neck and shoulders as you breathe . . . experience the warmth that spreads throughout your body as you relax and enjoy this experience.

When you have had enough, rest quietly for a few minutes. Open your eyes. Breathe normally and stretch your arms and legs. Tell me how you feel . . . Practice this several times before the next session.

SESSION 2

Your goal for today is to learn the process of *emptying* in which you clear your mind of distracting thoughts and emotions. Repeat the abdominal breathing you learned last time. Place your hands lightly on your rib cage. Begin to breathe slowly and rhythmically. When you feel completely relaxed, nod your head so that I will know you are ready to continue . . . (allow the client to set the pace, but if he or she is too impatient, encourage him or her to continue to breathe in the same manner for a longer period of time).

Continue to focus on your breathing. Breathe in as quietly and slowly as possible so that if I held a thread in front of your nose, it would not move . . . (allow time to pass) . . . Exhale even more slowly. Leave a tiny pause or even hold your breath a moment between exhalation and inhalation. This fixation on your breathing helps stop intrusive thoughts. Inevitably, some feelings and impressions or physical sensations will invade. Let them float away in the movement and rhythm of your breathing. Gradually your thoughts will slow to only several per minute.

Now picture a clear pool of water. A pool so clear that you can see way down into the bottom, far, far away. Gradually take your worries and

---

*Instructions for the imagery guide are contained in parentheses.

concerns and release them into this pool. Watch them disappear from sight. Warmth and peace invade your body as you give up your worries and concerns. Let this emptiness and calm wash above you. Experience the energy that is released when your burdens are given up to the cool blue pool of water, washing you clean and ready for a new experience. Relax and enjoy this sensation.

Gradually as I count to three you will awake and feel refreshed and ready to continue your day. Open your eyes. Stretch your arms and legs. Describe to me how it felt to give up your worries and concerns . . . Practice your breathing and this new technique of emptying during this week. Each time you practice this technique you will learn to reach your place of peace and calm more quietly and will experience a greater feeling of relaxation.

SESSION 3

Our goal for today is to introduce a new mental picture of yourself. The following vision is what motivates you to accomplish your goals. Vision is what gives you the drive and ambition to get started. This session will help you see and feel the new you in each detail. This crystal-clear vision will instill in you the drive to carry out your exercise and weight-loss program . . . (In order for the imagery to paint a vivid mental picture for the client, the imagery must stimulate all the senses: sight, sound, touch, smell, and sense of position.)

Begin your abdominal breathing with your hands resting lightly on your rib cage . . . Begin emptying your mind of worries and concerns . . . (Move at the client's pace.) When you feel completely relaxed and at peace, nod your head so that we can begin the imagery . . . (If the client has not practiced the first two techniques enough and does not seem to be relaxed, you may need to repeat session 2 and postpone the imagery for a week.)

Imagine that you have already reached your goal weight. You feel lean and energetic and have for some time. See your lean, supple body. See how slim your legs and thighs are, how small your hips, how flat your stomach, slim arms, a graceful neck, a radiant healthy face with clear eyes and well-defined features.

Now imagine you are standing on a scale. Your feet are bare and the plastic feels cold below them. You are looking down at the numbers on the scale. The needle lands solidly on your ideal weight. You move from side to side, but the needle doesn't budge.

You move to your closet and look at an old pair of jeans. You are now so slim that it is hard to imagine that you could ever wear those pants. You say to yourself, "I can hardly believe that I was ever that fat. These clothes could never have belonged to me."

Imagine yourself trying on a new bathing suit in a small size. You examine yourself in a full-length mirror. Your lean, trim body looks great in your new one-piece swimsuit. You allow your hands to move down your firm, flat stomach. You try to grab on to some fat at the side of your waist, but there is no fat there, not even a little bit. The air conditioning feels cool against your bare back.

Imagine yourself striding confidently down the beach with your friends. People turn and look at you as you walk across the warm sand to the water's edge. You swim for 20 minutes and come out of the water refreshed and full of energy. Exercise is now a wonderful part of your daily life.

You take a drink of water from your thermos. It tastes cold and refreshing. You are amazed that you no longer crave sweet soda or candy and junk food. Now you look forward to salads and fruit, eating only when you feel hungry.

Now walk briskly into the large conference room at work. Twenty of your coworkers look up expectantly. You smell the rich aroma of coffee as you enter. You feel confident in your new, silk suit. You begin your presentation. You have all the facts you need and your presentation is applauded by your colleagues when you finish. You are smiling and everyone is smiling with you.

Your husband is waiting in your office when you finish to take you to lunch. As you walk hand in hand with your husband to the elevator, you think, "My presentation really went well. I never thought I would be able to do that again. I am proud of my work and the weight I have lost. Things are really looking up."

References

Achterberg, J. (1985). *Imagery in healing: Shamanism and modern science.* Boston: New Science Library.

Achterberg, J., & Lawlis, F. (1982). Imagery and health interventions. *Topics of Clinical Nursing, 3*(4), 55–60.

Achterberg, J., & Lawlis, G. F. (1980). *Bridges of the body-mind: Behavioral approaches to health care.* Champaign, IL: Institute for Personality & Ability Testing.

Ashen, A. (1983). Eidetic imagery. In A. A. Sheikh (Ed.), *Imagery: Current theory, research and application.* New York: John Wiley & Sons.

Averill, J. (1973). Personal control over aversion stimuli and its relationship to stress. *Psychological Bulletin, 88,* 286–303.

Ayres, J., & Hopf, T. S. (1985). Visualization: A means of reducing speech anxiety. *Communication Education, 34*(4), 318–323.

Blandhard, E., McCoy, G., Wittrock, D., Musso, A., Gerardi, R., & Pangburn, L. (1988). A controlled comparison of thermal biofeedback and relaxation training in the treatment of essential hypertension. II. Effects on cardiovascular reactivity. *Health Psychology, 7*(1), 19–33.

Benson, H., & Klipper, M. X. (1975). *The relaxation response.* New York: William Morrow.

Brown, B. B. (1974). *New mind, new body.* New York: Harper & Row.

Brown, J. M. (1984). Imagery coping strategies in the treatment of migraine. *Pain, 18,* 157–167.

Bridge, L. R., Benson, P., Pietroni O. C., & Priest, R. G. (1988). Relaxation and imagery in the treatment of breast cancer. *British Medical Journal, 297*(5), 1169–1172.

Butcher, H. K., & Parker, N. I. (1988). Guided imagery within Rogers' science of unitary human beings: An experimental study. *Nursing Science Quarterly, 1*(3), 103–110.

Christman, N. J., McConnell, E. A., Pfeiffer, C., Webster, K. K., Schmitt, M., & Reis, J. (1988). Uncertainty, coping, and distress following myocardial infarction: Transition from hospital to home. *Research in Nursing and Health, 11*(2), 71–82.

Donovan, M. I. (1980). Relaxation with guided imagery: A useful technique. *Cancer Nursing, 3*(1), 27–32.

Dossey, B. M. (1988). Awaking the inner healer. In B. M. Dossey (Ed.). *Holistic nursing* (pp. 223–261). Denver: Aspen Publishing.

Frank, J. M. (1985). The effects of music therapy and guided visual imagery on chemotherapy induced nausea and vomiting. *Oncology Nursing Forum, 12*(5), 47–52.

Gordon, M. (1987). *Nursing diagnosis: Process and application.* New York: McGraw-Hill.

Greer, S., & Morris, T. (1978). The study of psychological factors in breast cancer: Problems of method. *Social Science Medicine, 12,* 129–134.

Halliburton, P. (1986). Impaired immunocompetence. In V. Carrieri, A. M. Lindsey, & C. W. West (Eds.), *Pathophysiological phenomena in nursing: Human responses to illness* (pp. 319–342). Philadelphia: WB Saunders.

Holden-Lund, C. (1988). Effects of relaxation with guided imagery on surgical stress and wound healing. *Research in Nursing and Health, 11,* 235–244.

Horowitz, M. J. (1978). *Image formation and cognition.* (2d ed.). New York: Appleton-Century-Crofts.

Hymen, S. P., & Warren, R. (1978). Evaluation of rational-emotive imagery as a component of rational-emotive therapy in treatment of test anxiety. *Perceptual and Motor Skills, 46*(3), 847–853.

Jung, C. G. (1963). *Memories, dreams, reflections.* New York: Pantheon Books.

Justice, B. (1987). *Who gets sick: Thinking and health.* Houston: Peak Press.

Kiecolt-Glaser, R. (1987). Cited in Squires, A. Visions to boost immunity. *American Health, 6*(6), 54–61.

King, J. V. (1988). A holistic technique to lower anxiety: Relaxation with guided imagery. *Journal of Holistic Nursing, 6*(1), 16–20.

Korn, E. R. (1983). The use of altered states of consciousness and imagery in physical and pain rehabilitation. *Journal of Mental Imagery, 7,* 25–34.

Kunzendorf, R. G. (1981). Individual differences in imagery and autonomic control. *Journal of Mental Imagery, 5,* 47–60.

Maguire, P. (1981). Psychological and social consequences of cancer. In C. J. Williams & J. W. Whitehouse (Eds.), *Recent advances in clinical oncology* (pp. 236–254). London: Churchill Livingston Press.

Maltzman, S. (1988). Visual stimuli in distraction strategies for increasing pain tolerance: The confounding of affect with other stimulus characteristics. *Pavlovian Journal of Biological Science. 23*(2), 67–74.

McCaffery, M. (1989). *Nursing management of the patient in pain* (3d ed.). Philadelphia: JB Lippincott.

Meichenbaum, D. (1983). Why does using imagery in psychotherapy lead to changes? In J. Singer and K. S. Pope (Eds.), *The power of the human imagination.* New York: Plenum Press.

Mishel, M. H. (1984). Perceived uncertainty and stress in illness. *Research in Nursing and Health. 7,* 163–171.

Rossman, M. L. (1988). The healing power of imagery. *New Age Journal, 5*(2), 47–54.

Samuels, M., & Samuels, N. (1975). *Seeing with the mind's eye: The history, techniques and uses of visualization.* New York: Random House.

Shiekh, A. (1984). *Imagery and human development series: Imagination and healing.* Farmingdale, NY: Baywood Publishing.

Simonton, O. C., Matthews-Simonton, S., & Sparks, T. F. (1980). Psychological intervention in the treatment of cancer. *Psychosomatics, 21,* 226–235.

Singer, J. L. (1974). *Imagery and daydream methods in psychotherapy and behavior modification.* New York: Academic Press.

Smith, R. A., Wallston, B. S., Wallston, K. A., Forsberg, P. R., & King, J. E. (1984). Measuring desire for control of health care processes. *Journal of Personality and Social Psychology, 17*(2), 415–426.

Snyder, M. (1984). Progressive relaxation as a nursing intervention: An analysis. *Advances in Nursing Science, 14,* 47–58.

Sodergren, K. M. (1985). Guided imagery. In M. Snyder (Ed.), *Independent nursing interventions* (pp. 103–124). New York: John Wiley & Sons.

Speilberger, C. D., Gorsuch, R. E., & Lushene, R. W. (1983). *STAI Manual.* Palo Alto, CA: Consulting Psychologists Press.

Stanton, H. (1989). Ego-enhancement: A five-step approach. *American Journal of Clinical Hypnosis, 31*(3), 192–198.

Stephens, R. L. (1990). *Imagery: A treatment for adult student anxiety.* Manuscript submitted for publication.

Weinstein, D. J. (1976). Imagery and relaxation with a burn patient. *Behavior Research and Therapy, 14,* 481.

■

Facilitating Behavior Change in the Chronically Ill
■ POLLY RYAN

Whether it begins dramatically with a myocardial infarction, or insidiously with osteoarthritis, living with a chronic illness changes one's life. The individual, with assistance from significant others and health professionals, must deal with the symptoms, monitor the illness trajectory, and implement treatment. Additionally, he or she is advised to change behaviors which directly contribute to the illness or place one at increased risk for developing other illnesses. Therefore, in addition to living with chronic illness, redefining personal and social self-concepts, managing symptoms, carrying out treatments, and compensating for taxed resources, persons with chronic illness benefit from making a number of long-term behavior changes.

At the time when persons with chronic illness are most vulnerable, they are also most challenged to change life-long behavior patterns. Failure to change behavior not only risks physiologic consequences but may affect one's self-concept and social functioning. Repeated failure to lose weight, quit smoking, take medication, and/or exercise can erode the individual's self-concept and self-respect resulting in social withdrawal. Repeated failures at maintaining behavior change can be degrading and threaten access to continuing care. The managing health professional might conclude, "There is really nothing more I can do for you until you are able to make these changes." Repeated failure and a seeming rejection by health professionals further erodes one's self-confidence.

376

Therefore, inability to change behavior can decrease one's sense of power. Feelings of powerlessness contribute to failed attempts at behavior change, and the problem becomes cyclical: Powerlessness leads to failure and failure leads to an increased sense of powerlessness. Successfully changing behavior can break the cyclical nature of failure and despair.

Individuals can learn to change their behavior. Behavior change does not happen because of need or desire: rather behavior change results from special skills and adequate support. Persons with chronic illnesses must learn the skills which facilitate behavior change, and they need professional and social support during the process.

The purpose of this chapter is to identify how persons with chronic illness can be assisted in changing behavior. The following areas will be discussed: (1) definition and types of change, (2) select theories, (3) chronic illness and behavior change, and (4) a framework for selecting strategies which facilitate change. All strategies presented have been tested; however, the framework for organizing the strategies is still being studied.

Definition

Although behavior change can occur spontaneously and unconsciously, the type of behavior change discussed in this chapter occurs when a habitual pattern of behavior is deliberately altered. The behavior pattern is changed because it represents a risk to the individual's health. The ultimate responsibility for change lies with the individual; however, the health-care professional must identify a need for the change, identify desired outcomes, suggest strategies which facilitate change, and provide continued care during the change process. Depending on the setting and outcome, behavior change has been termed compliance, alliance, adherence; prevention or life-style modification; or recovery and/or cure (Ryan, 1990).

At the turn of the century little was known about behavior change. The major health problems were infectious diseases and injuries. Diagnostic tests, medications, and treatments were limited; as a result people died from acute illness or injury. As antibiotics were discovered and technology advanced, many acute illnesses were curable and life expectancy increased. Currently, persons live longer, but they may accrue multiple chronic illnesses. Patient management of these illnesses requires behavior change. Additionally, epidemiologists have targeted behaviors which place persons at risk for development of disease. Consequently, behavior change is an integral component of the treatment and prevention of chronic health problems.

Types of Behavior Change

There are three types of behavior change: removal, replacement, and addition. *Removal* refers to behaviors which must be completely eliminated; for example, the use of any form of tobacco or street drugs or uncontrolled use of alcohol. *Replacement* refers to behaviors for which a substitute behavior is needed; for example, dietary habits, whether for caloric or nutrient substitutes. *Addition* refers to behaviors which supplement or expand usual behavior pattern and includes taking medications, scheduling and keeping appointments, and exercising. Selecting strategies which effect behavior change partly depends upon the type of behavior being modified. While there is overlap, some strategies are specifically appropriate for removing behavior, replacing behavior, or adding behavior. These strategies will be discussed in more detail in the intervention section of this chapter.

Theories of Behavior Change

Within the past 2 decades numerous theories of change have been proposed. Extensive research has tested the ability of these theories to both explain and predict change. The theories of behavior change describe change from multiple perspectives, including causation and the process of change. An overview of select theories from these two perspectives will be discussed. Theories effecting behavior change include (1) Sociodemographic Model, (2) Medical Model, (3) Health Belief Model, (4) Social Support, (5) Social Cognitive Theory, (6) Self-efficacy, and (7) Macrosocial forces. The process of behavior change discussed includes work by Prochaska and DiClemente (1983) and Marlatt and Gordan (1985).

Factors Influencing Behavior Change

SOCIODEMOGRAPHIC CHARACTERISTICS

One of the earliest explanations for compliance (adherence to recommended change) was based on sociodemograhic characteristics (Haynes, Taylor, & Sackett, 1979; Marston, 1970). The relationship of age, gender, education, race, income, social status, psychologic status, and religion to compliance was studied. These studies demonstrated that extremes of age and a diagnosis of paranoid schizophrenia correlated positively with noncompliance. Gender, education, race, ethnicity, income, social status, or religious affiliation did not correlate with behavior change.

THE MEDICAL MODEL

The Medical Model (DiMatteo & DiNicola, 1982; Haynes, 1979; Koltun & Stone, 1986) assumes that an individual would comply with medical prescription if the disease was serious. To study this assumption, physicians ranked characteristics of the disease (i.e., type of illness, complexity of regimen, discomfort associated with the illness, the duration of therapy) and the gravity of illness (i.e., seriousness, duration, associated disability). Actual compliance was then compared with these rankings. The results demonstrated no significant correlation between the physician's assessment of the characteristics or gravity of an illness and compliance.

THE HEALTH BELIEF MODEL

The Health Belief Model (HBM) (Becker, 1974; Becker et al., 1979; Janz & Becker, 1984) was developed to determine what factors influenced preventive health behaviors. It was later used to study illness and compliance. The HBM states that motivation to change behavior equals perception of the reward minus the perceived cost and the perceived barrier.

$$\text{Motivation} = \text{reward} - (\text{cost} + \text{barriers})$$

Essentially, behavior change depends on the attractiveness of the goal, the estimation of one's likelihood of success, and occurrence of a cue to change behavior. The HBM uniquely focuses on the patient's perceptions rather than on the professional's. The major components of the HBM are health and willingness to accept medical direction; subjective estimates of susceptibility, vulnerability, and extent of bodily harm; interference with social roles; and perception of the efficacy and safety of the proposed regimen. (Multiple studies document a significant positive correlation between the HBM and compliance. However, the HBM does not *predict* compliance with health-care recommendations.)

SOCIAL SUPPORT

Social networks and support are positively or negatively related to behavior change (Berkman, 1984; Bruhn & Phillips, 1984; Cohen & Syme, 1985; Cwikel, Dielman, Kirscht, & Israel, 1988; DiMatteo & DiNicola, 1982; Gottlieb & Green, 1984; Jacobson, 1986). Specifically social support relates positively to behaviors that lead to a healthy life-style (Aaronson, 1989; Boyd-Franklin, 1987; Coppotelli & Orleans, 1985; Hansen et al., 1987; Hubbard, Muhlenkamp, & Brown, 1986; Mermelstein, Cohen, Lichtenstein, Baer, & Kamarck, 1986; Muhlenkamp & Sayles, 1986) and sometimes to behavioral change associated with illness (Glasglow & Toobert, 1988; Morisky, DeMuth, & Field-Fass, 1985; Somer & Tucker, 1988; Stanton, 1987). The relationship between health beliefs and social influence is reported by the Ajzen and Fishbein Theory of Reasoned Action which states that an individual's intention to act is a function of the person's beliefs and attitudes toward that behavior and his or her beliefs about others' expectations. Although this theory has had limited testing compared to the HBM, a number of studies have demonstrated a positive association between attitudes and subjective norms (Ajzen & Fishbein, 1972; Ajzen & Fishbein, 1980; Ajzen & Madden, 1986; Pender & Pender, 1986; Saltzer, 1980).

SOCIAL COGNITIVE THEORY

The Social Cognitive Theory (Bandura, 1986), based on the Social Learning Theory (Bandura, 1977a), proposes a reciprocal relationship between cognition and other personal factors, environment, and behavior. Each factor is interdependent. Essential to this theory are the beliefs that people can use symbols, think about things before they happen, learn from personal and communal experiences, make decisions based on personal and communal standards, and reflect on their own past. To facilitate change, the professional influences cognition, environment, behavior, or all three. A component of this theory currently being tested widely is self-efficacy.

SELF-EFFICACY

In order to change behavior the individual must know what to do, believe it is beneficial, and believe it is attainable. Self-efficacy is defined as belief in one's ability to perform a task. Bandura (1977b) defined self-efficacy as "the conviction that one can successfully execute the behavior required to produce the outcomes" (p. 193). A number of studies have tested self-efficacy and found that persons with high self-efficacy are likely to initiate and maintain a specific behavior change (Baer, Holt, & Lichtenstein, 1987; Bandura, 1982; Barrios & Niehaus, 1985; Coelho, 1984; Colletti, Supnick, & Payne, 1985; DiClemente, Prochaska, & Gibertini, 1985; Godding & Glasgow, 1985; Yates & Thain, 1985).

MACROSOCIAL FACTORS

In addition to personal relationships, macrosocial forces affect behavior change (Lefebvre & Flora, 1988; Hymowitz, 1987; Killen et al., 1989; McLeroy, Bibeau, Steckler, & Glanz, 1988; Minkler, 1989; Syme & Alcalay, 1982). Several macrosocial forces which affect behavior are workplace (Hallett, 1986; Peterson et al., 1988), laws (such as the Clean Indoor Air Act), public policy (Breslow, 1982), warnings from authorities (e.g., Surgeon General), and mass communication such as television, radio, and newspaper (Best, 1980; Cummings, Sciandra, & Markello, 1987).

Process of Behavior Change

PROCHASKA AND DiCLEMENTE

Prochaska and DiClemente (1983) have proposed five stages of behavior change: precontemplation, contemplation, action, mainte- nance, and relapse. Persons in a precontemplation stage avoid thoughts or actions related to behavior change. They are defensive and hold firm to old beliefs and behaviors. Persons contemplating behavior change are interested in changing behavior and actively gather opinions by talking, listening, and reading. Persons in the action stage are actively engaged in changing behavior. Once the change has occurred, it is either maintained or relapse occurs; if relapse occurs, the individual returns to precontem- plation or contemplation.

During each stage individuals engage in behaviors consistently. Pro- chaska and DiClemente have concluded that particular strategies are most effective during particular stages of behavior change. Education and feed- back are most effective during contemplation. As individuals are in tran- sition from contemplation to change, self-reflection is effective. During the stage of action, persons change their environment, rely on social sup- port, and use reinforcements for their behaviors. During maintenance persons decrease their use of reinforcements but continue to use envi- ronmental control.

MARLATT AND GORDON

Rather than five stages of behavior change, Marlatt and Gordon (1985) proposed three stages of change: commitment and motivation (preparation for the change), implementation, and long-term mainte- nance of the behavior change. Their unique and significant contribution has been the reframing of relapse as an opportunity to learn rather than a failure. They also suggest specific strategies during specific stages includ- ing the relapse stage.

SUMMARY OF THEORIES

There is no singular theory that consistently predicts behavior change. Many new and revised theories of behavior change combine con- cepts from multiple theories. While there is no singular theory explaining and predicting behavior change, there are select dimensions which pre- dictably influence behavior change. The two major factors influencing behavior change are personal characteristics and social characteristics.

Personal characteristics include such factors as knowledge, beliefs, attitudes, meaning and purpose, motivation, and past experiences. Social factors influencing behavior change include environment; interpersonal social relationships such as social networks, social support, social influences; and macrosocial factors, such as work site, community, and communication media.

Behavior change is a process with identifiable stages. Although individual theorists differ in the actual name and number of stages, they generally agree that preparatory activity precedes change. Once change occurs it must be maintained. Relapse frequently follows behavior change. Relapse can be viewed as failure, or it can be an invaluable learning opportunity when the individual can identify those aspects of change which they were not prepared to manage.

Behavior change may be viewed as a multidimensional, dynamic process. Personal and social characteristics influence initiation and maintenance of behavior but differ during various stages of change. The initiation and maintenance are associated with altered personal and social characteristics. Normally, the individual deliberately and consciously alters personal and social characteristics in order to change behavior. However, behavior change for persons with a chronic illness can differ.

Chronic Illness and the Change Process

Behavior change is recommended or prescribed by a health-care professional as a component of treatment for the chronic illness. Failure of the patient to change erodes the efficacy of the treatment plan and can cause a downward trajectory of the chronic illness. Frequently individuals are advised to make several changes simultaneously and to actively change their behavior soon after the diagnosis is made. The change is monitored by the health-care professional. Behavior change in chronic illness is characterized by external recommendation for change, health risk of unmodified behavior, continued external monitoring, multiple simultaneous changes, and lack of preparatory phase.

Framework for Selecting Interventions

The framework to determine which strategies will most likely effect behavior change is based on the stage of behavior change, personal characteristics, and social characteristics. Once these factors have been identified, specific strategies can be chosen (Bandura, 1986; Barofsky; 1977; Comoss, 1988; DiMatteo & DiNicola, 1982; Dishman, 1988; Falvo, 1985; Frenn, Borgeson, Lee, & Simandl, 1989; Green, Kreuter, Deeds, & Partridge, 1980; Haynes, Taylor, & Sackett, 1979; Health and Public Policy Committee, American College of Physicians, 1986; Leventhal & Cleary, 1980; Pender, 1987; Ryan, 1987; Trower, Casey, & Dryden, 1988).

Strategies need to match the stage of change, the personal characteristics, and social characteristics. If the personal characteristics are inadequate to initiate or maintain the desired change, individuals can be provided with strategies which strengthen or alter personal characteristics during that stage of change. If social characteristics are inadequate, strategies which strengthen or alter social characteristics are desirable. If both the personal and social characteristics are inadequate to initiate or maintain the desired change, the individual can be provided with strategies which strengthen or alter both.

The categories of strategies include universal strategies, strategies specific to stages of change, and strategies for persons choosing not to engage in the change process. The strategies specific to the stages of change are subdivided into those strategies specific to personal and social characteristics.

UNIVERSAL STRATEGIES

Some strategies are universal. The goals of the universal strategies include: to provide persons with the knowledge of what, why, and how changes should be made; to assure the individual's familiarity with available resources; and to provide continued care. The respective strategies are teaching, identification of resources, and continued supervision.

All persons whose treatment for chronic illness requires behavior change(s) should be taught the rationale for change, consequences of not making the change, specific behaviors involved in the change, and intended outcomes (Bartlett, 1982; Devine & Cook, 1983; Lorig & Lourin, 1985; Marshall, Penckofer, & Llewellyn, 1986; Mazzuca, 1982; Powers & Wooldridge, 1982; Ruzicki, 1989). Information should be presented in a manner consistent with the individual's coping style and locus of control. Structured educational programs are more effective than unstructured programs, but individual and group learning are equally effective. When possible, information should be prepared in at least two methods (e.g., written and small group) as the combined methods facilitate cognitive, affective, and psychomotor learning (Cohen, 1981; Falvo, 1985; Redman, 1984; Simonds, 1983; Wilson-Barnett & Osborne, 1983). According to Ley (1976) information is most effective if it has six characteristics:

1. *Primacy.* The most important facts should be presented first.
2. *Brevity.* Information should be presented succinctly.
3. *Organization.* Material should be organized in topics or categories; as like information which is clustered will be remembered longer than information presented randomly.
4. *Specificity.* Directions should be clear.
5. *Repetition.* Important information should be repeated frequently and presented in a variety of ways.

6. *Level.* Information should be presented at the individual's level of comprehension.

Written material prepared for use by the general public should have a reading level between third and sixth grade (Doak, Doak, & Root, 1985; Redman, 1984). The reading level can be determined by sentence length and number of polysyllable words. Therefore, in order to prepare written material for a lower reading level, one should shorten the sentence and word length and use simple pictures and diagrams.

It is equally important to consider the comprehension level of groups and audiences. Again it is helpful to keep sentences short and words simple. Pictures and diagrams can be used as an aid to concept explanation.

Teaching can also be done in a manner which takes into account the individual's coping style (Thornburg, 1982) and locus of control. For example, persons who cope with an illness by using minimization should be given only essential information. Extensive explanations and detailed descriptions are generally counterproductive. On the other hand, those individuals who cope through vigilant focusing benefit from explanations and detailed descriptions.

All persons changing behavior should be encouraged to know, find, and use the available resources. Lists of compiled resources are most helpful; for example, a listing of all local smoking cessation programs or listings of alternate modes of transportation to clinics. People need to be informed of services available through various associations (e.g., The American Heart Association, The American Lung Association, and American Cancer Society). They should be apprised of published information dealing with the management of chronic illness and related behavior changes.

And, finally, all persons should be seen regularly during the phase of active change, and periodically during maintenance. Everyone should have accurate information regarding follow-up care and access to a contact person for questions and emergencies.

CHANGE STRATEGIES DEPENDENT ON STAGE AND PERSONAL AND SOCIAL CHARACTERISTICS

Some individuals successfully initiate and maintain change by knowing what to do and receiving regular care. However, most people require additional help and support. The following framework has been proposed as one method of selecting strategies which best match the individual's stage in the change process with their personal and social characteristics (see Table 15–1).

The goal of strategies is to facilitate the change process by altering personal beliefs and social characteristics influencing behavior change during a specific stage. For the purposes of this discussion, four stages of

TABLE 15 ■ 1   Strategies to Facilitate Change

Stage	Personal	Social
Preparation	Consciousness raising Discussion Value clarification Self-monitoring Problem solving Reframing	Reference Groups Assertiveness
Actual change	Goal setting Tailoring regimens Self-monitoring Cognitive restructuring Time management Management of withdrawal Thought stopping	Planned social and environmental change
Maintenance	Relaxation Exercise Self-monitoring	Involvement with formal programs
Relapse	Reframing Relapse preparation	Increased support

change will be used: preparation, actual change, maintenance, and relapse. Although this is an implied order of occurrence, it has not been tested. It is likely that change is fluid and dynamic, rather than a linear process, and that several stages occur simultaneously or in different sequences, depending on the behavior being changed and the individual.

Preparation

The common sequence in chronic illness is diagnosis followed by recommendation or prescription to change several behaviors. Ideally these changes should occur immediately following diagnosis. When the sequencing of diagnosis and prescribed changes are immediate, individuals are expected to skip preparation. Possible consequences of skipping preparation are a higher rate of relapse, increased difficulty of change, increased distress in making change, increased use of resources to change, and higher rates of refusal to change.

However, for some, the physiologic need for change outweighs the need for gradual preparation (e.g., the need for insulin, anti-arrhythmic medication, or dialysis). Therefore, in order to facilitate behavior change in persons with a chronic illness, both the normal change process and therapeutic requirements of the illness need to be blended in a manner consistent with the physical and psychosocial needs and desires of the individual. Professional judgment is required when selecting behavioral change strategies.

Persons in the preparatory phase are contemplating behavior change. At this time they are most receptive to specific information about behavior. Personal characteristics needed to effect a change include a desire for more information, belief in the value of changing behavior, belief in ability to change behavior, belief that the behavior change will result in the desired outcomes, and willingness to bring habitual behaviors to a conscious level. Social characteristics needed to change include the involvement with social networks which will allow and support behavior change. Therefore, strategies are directed toward the achievement of these characteristics.

Examples of strategies which affect personal characteristics during preparation include consciousness raising (value clarification, discussion, self-monitoring), problem solving (identification of intended and unintended consequences), and reframing. Strategies that affect social characteristics and are effective during this stage include assertiveness skills and involvement in reference groups.

Consciousness-raising strategies bring aspects of behavior to awareness. Included among the techniques are discussions, value clarification techniques, and self-monitoring. In discussion, the principles of guidance and counseling are used to enable the individual to explore feelings and beliefs about the desired behavior change.

With value clarification, the individual is assisted to identify multiple alternative behaviors and to explore their values related to specific alternatives (Berger, Hopp, & Raettig, 1975; Steele & Harmon, 1979; Uustal, 1977). One value clarification technique is the Pie of Life. Two circles or pies are drawn. The individual is instructed to cut the first pie into slices that represent those behaviors they believe are associated with their health. The individual is then instructed to cut the second pie into slices that represent those behaviors that they regularly perform. Once this is done, the individual can visualize the discrepancy between what they believe they should do and what they do. This enables the person to make a conscious choice to perform behaviors that are more consistent with values and beliefs. It also provides them with an opportunity to identify why they have engaged in behaviors which are inconsistent with their values and beliefs.

Self-monitoring (Carnahan & Nugent, 1975; Mahoney, 1974; Oldridge & Jones, 1983), when used in the preparation phase of behavior, enables the person to identify the patterns of a behavior. Self-monitoring employs a written record which enables the individual to identify cues and consequences of a particular behavior. Although behavior patterns can generally be identified in 3 to 5 days, it will be the individual's tolerance for self-monitoring which determines the extent of information logged. A self-monitoring log can be as limited as identification of the frequency and time of a behavior or it can be as detailed as the place, persons, feelings, and activities associated with the behavior. These records are reviewed and patterns of behavior emerge, enabling the individual to become aware of the habitual, frequently unrecognized, aspects of their behaviors. This insight prepares them for making specific plans for change.

Reframing is a technique in which one sees alternative perspectives of a behavior change. For example, instead of viewing smoking cessation or dieting as a loss, one can see them as a gift to oneself. When individuals reframe their thinking, they are freed to act differently.

If persons are surrounded with social influences which oppose or fail to support a behavior change, the individual will benefit by enlarging social support to include persons who foster the desired change. Reference groups, or persons with shared concerns, can provide essential support. Examples of reference groups include Weight Watchers, Alcoholics Anonymous, or Mended Hearts Club. Additionally, people will benefit from using assertiveness skills to manage the negative messages and pressures from their support systems. People need to identify the inconsistent messages given by social groups. For example, their significant other may express a desire for them to lose weight, yet be displeased with the individual when he or she chooses not to share the dessert. Assertiveness skills enables one to manage the conflict without alienating the significant other.

Macrosocial messages, especially if consistent, can be very influential in preparing persons to change. For example, during the spring of 1990 there was a major television, radio, and written media campaign on saving the earth. Local governments provided people with specific information on how and what to recycle. The amount of material recycled increased significantly.

Actual Change

Habits, such as smoking, drinking, and overeating, occur automatically. These behaviors are so ingrained that they occur without thought. That is, people generally do not consciously decide to smoke every cigarette or eat every cookie. In order to change a behavior, individuals must become consciously aware of the behavior and make a deliberate choice to change the behavior. This process requires time, energy, and focus. Failure to remain focused places the individual at risk for returning to habitual behaviors. Likewise, new behaviors are added by the individual consciously electing to perform the behavior.

Active change occurs by consciously attending to actions. The stage of active change can last from weeks to months. During this period, time and energy remain focused on behavior. In addition to being very preoccupied with behavior, the person must deal with side effects of changing behaviors. The withdrawal symptoms of some behaviors, like smoking and drinking, are clearly recognized. But all behavior change has associated effects. Dietary changes are associated with food cravings, hunger, and gastrointestinal symptoms. There are intended and unintended effects of the medication. Exercise programs are associated with various levels of fatigue and muscle soreness or injury. Constantly focusing on one's behavior, is in itself, tiring and disorganizing.

Examples of strategies affecting personal characteristics that are appropriate during the stage of active change include goal setting (Czar, 1987; Eiser & Gentle, 1988; Haller & Reynolds, 1982), tailoring, self-monitoring, cognitive restructuring, time management, preparation for and management of withdrawal, reminders, relaxation (Donovan, 1980; Scandrett & Uecker, 1985), and thought stopping. Examples of strategies that affect social characteristics and are effective during active change include planned social and environmental changes.

Behavior change must be tailored to the individual's life-style. That is, new behaviors should fit with routines and preferences. Self-monitoring was discussed under the preparatory phase of behavior change. During active change, self-monitoring is done in the same way, but its purpose changes. Rather than for identification of the cues and rewards for behavior, self-monitoring is now done to assist the individual to be aware of his or her behavior. If a written food diary is kept daily, the individual will remain aware of everything eaten. When a behavior is monitored, the individual is aware of actions, and the performance of the behavior becomes increasingly consistent with the desire to change the behavior.

Individuals should prepare for and manage withdrawal symptoms. The effect of sensory preparation on withdrawal symptoms is currently being tested. Sensory preparation is an intervention which apprises persons of potential noxious symptoms by informing them prior to the experience about the anticipated sensations. Additionally, people need suggestions on coping with specific withdrawal symptoms. For example, taking a long, slow, deep breath is very helpful to persons experiencing an urge for a cigarette.

Behavior patterns can be changed by actually altering the behaviors associated with the pattern (as discussed in altering cues and using alternative rewards), or they can be changed by altering one's perspective of the behavior, its causes, the perceived loss and distress, and the perceived consequences. A number of cognitive coping skills (e.g., cognitive restructuring, framing, thought stopping) effectively alter one's perspective (Bandura, 1986; Davis, Eshelman, & McKay, 1980; Ellis, 1988).

Reminders are stimuli that cue a desired behavior (Gabriel, Gagnon, & Bryan, 1977). Reminders are effective for problems associated with forgetting. They are effective only for a few days; when used consistently and as reminders become routine, they lose their effectiveness. Postcards or telephone calls have been an effective method to decrease the number of missed appointments or increase the number of rescheduled follow-up visits. Self-sticking labels can also be affixed to grocery lists to remind persons of ingredients to be avoided.

Any individual planning to change behavior should also be assisted to develop realistic plans during the period of active change. Any new behavior takes time. A new diet requires additional time to plan menus, shop, substitute foods, and prepare meals. Additionally, the occasional fast food solution to a busy day needs to be reworked. Increased attention by health-care professionals is an effective strategy for facilitating behavior change.

During active change it is essential to alter environmental and social factors. Deciding what to alter is based on understanding the behavior pattern. Social and environmental cues are associated with behavior. Additionally every behavior has consequences which both reward and reinforce the behavior. Therefore, once the cues are identified they can be altered in a fashion more consistent with the desired change. For example, a woman has been advised to quit smoking because she has chronic obstructive pulmonary disease. She agreed to try and monitored her smoking behavior for a week. Based on the results of monitoring, it became apparent that she only smoked in the kitchen or outside, always smoked on the telephone, always smoked after meals and with coffee, and considered the cigarette a reason to take a break from her work. She worked with the nurse to identify specific environmental factors which could be changed to make cessation easier. These changes consisted of limiting time in the kitchen by using television and telephone in the living room, brushing her teeth immediately after eating, temporarily substituting tea for coffee, and using preplanned breaks in her daily schedule.

The social factors associated with maintenance of the smoking habit also need to be identified and changed. For example, if one always smokes while bowling, perhaps one could request to play with a team of nonsmokers or enlist the support of a team member who has successfully quit smoking.

Smoking cigarettes and eating are self-reinforcing behaviors. Once these behaviors are changed, one may experience a loss due to absence of the reinforcement. Frequently the rewards of a new behavior are not evident. It can take months to feel good from exercise. Therefore, it can be helpful during the stage of active change to teach the individual to use artificial rewards (i.e., use rewards that are not normally associated with the behavior). Persons can identify a list of rewards prior to initiating change. Initially persons should use these rewards every time they perform the new behavior; later the rewards should be used intermittently. Intermittent rewards seem to be more effective in locking the behavior. The reward should be as small as possible, yet still be seen as rewarding. The reward should be immediate; that is, it should be paired with the behavior. Remote rewards are not effective for reinforcing new behaviors.

Examples of rewards include calling a friend, trip to the hardware store, extra minutes in the bath or shower, or setting aside time to read.

Maintenance

During maintenance, behaviors which have been consciously changed must become habituated, or done automatically (Swan & Denk, 1987). The long-term goal of maintenance is to perform the desired behavior without always making a conscious choice. Maintenance is the stage of behavior change which has been studied least. Clinically it is the stage of change which has the fewest number of programs, resources, or information. Most third-party payers do not financially support continued supervision of the maintenance phase. However, relapse remains the most frequent outcome of behavior change. Therefore, it is an area in which extensive work needs to be done.

It has been suggested that there is a positive association between persons successfully maintaining the removal of a behavior (smoking, alcohol) and the use of relaxation and exercise. Self-monitoring is an effective means of maintaining weight loss. Persons who maintain connections with formal programs, such as volunteering, experience greater success with maintenance. Successful maintenance is facilitated by environments and social systems which support the change.

Relapse

Relapse is a stage of behavior change which occurs when the individual returns to the prechange patterns of behavior (Saunders & Allsop, 1987; Wewers & Lenz, 1987). Relapse can be a slip or total reversal. For many specific behavior changes, the consequences of a slip are undetermined. However, Marlatt and Gordon (1985) have postulated that if a slip is perceived as a failure and attributed to the individual's inability to change, it is highly probable that the slip will result in total relapse.

Examples of strategies which affect personal characteristics and are appropriate to the stage of relapse include prevention and reframing (Baer, Kamarck, Lichtenstein, & Ransom, 1989; Cummings, Jaen, & Giovino, 1985; Eiser, van der Pligt, Raw, & Sutton, 1985; Harackiewicz, Sansone, Blair, Epstein, & Manderlink, 1987; Supnick & Colletti, 1984; O'Connell & Martin, 1987; Shiffman, 1984). Increasing support is a strategy which affects the social characteristics and is effective during relapse (Mermelstein, Lichtenstein, & McIntyre, 1983). Preventing relapse is facilitated by self-monitoring. Persons need to be aware of risky persons and situations. It is most helpful to know this before attempting the change, but actual experience is frequently the most effective method of identifying persons and situations which need to be altered or avoided. Rather than viewing relapse as another failure, the individual can view the relapse as an invaluable learning opportunity. Persons can prepare for relapse by preplanning alternative ways of managing the lapse (Supnick & Colletti, 1934). If a lapse is stopped and personal and social characteristics altered, a total relapse can be prevented.

Continued support from significant others and health-care professionals is essential for persons who have relapsed. The availability of a person during highly tempting situations can prevent relapse. A therapeutic person can assist the individual to reframe the lapse, provide reinforcement for positive actions and outcomes, and generate alternative ways of continuing to manage situations. Continued supervision conveys the belief that change is important and the individual, with appropriate help, can make the desired change.

MANAGEMENT OF TREATMENT FOR NONCHANGERS

For any number of reasons there will be individuals who choose not to make a change, not to change at this time, not to change in this professional relationship, or not to change in the manner recommended. Individuals have the right to choose not to change, particularly if their behavior does not directly harm others. Health-care professionals have the right to choose not to care for a person who chooses not to change, as long as other sources of care are available and the behavior is not life-threatening. However, if the individual continues to request care and if the health-care professional is willing to care for a person who chooses not to make the recommended changes, a number of strategies can be effective. If the individual fails to participate in the change process, care is directed toward achievement of these goals: (1) the establishment and maintenance of a relationship, (2) simplification and prioritizing care, and (3) identification of alternative resources.

Continued relationships enable the professional to have a foot in the door. The foot-in-the-door strategy was originally developed for marketing and sales. The individual is requested to have minimal involvement with some aspect of change, such as agreeing to take printed information. Once the individual has agreed to this minimal participation they will be more likely to continue with increasing involvement. Gradually, positive outcomes will be attained and it becomes increasingly possible to change behavior. Maintaining an open door (continued access to care), repetitive and consistent messages, and a supportive relationship set the stage for future behavior change.

For those individuals who would experience significant physiologic consequences, strategies such as negation, graduated regimen implementation, and contracting can be effective.

Graduated regimen is a strategy in which complex behavior patterns are gradually changed by successfully changing small sequential behaviors. Individuals successfully master one step at a time, mastery being required for progression to the next step. The American Heart Association Cookbook outlines step-by-step details of restricting cholesterol and saturated fats by using a graduated regimen.

Contracts have been demonstrated to be very effective in changing behavior (Herje, 1980; Lewis and Michnich, 1977; Mahoney and Thoresen, 1974; Steckel, 1980; Steckel, 1982). A contract is a process in which the practitioner and the patient select a behavior which is to be changed, specify the conditions of change, and identify a reward for successfully completing the contract. Contracts involve a negotiation process, as both the practitioner and the patient agree on the goals and specific behaviors. Contracts are most effective when written and positively stated. The target behavior needs to be measurable (i.e., counted, recorded, graphed, or observable to both parties).

Again, continued care is necessary, as the strategies effectively change behavior when used, but when stopped, the behavior reverts back to prechange patterns.

Conclusion

Behavior change is an active, powerful way of dealing with and managing a chronic illness. Successful change creates feelings of control and power, feelings which enable even greater success. Change produces hope. When someone is able to change, there is a realistic hope that the consequences of the illness can be minimized or at least contained.

Behavior change is a multidimensional process. Although there are common factors which influence behavior change, and common stages in the process of change, it is always unique for the individual, different at every moment and with every experience. Many strategies which facilitate change have been identified, yet what we know is limited by our world view, contained by our morality and ethics, and restricted by our science. With such limitations it is imperative that we proceed with caution, judge with great reluctance, and always look first to ourselves and our systems as we prescribe change.

References

Aaronson, L. (1989). Perceived and received support: Effects on health behavior during pregnancy. *Nursing Research, 38,* 4–9.

Ajzen, I., & Fishbein, M. (1980). *Understanding attitudes and predicting social behavior.* Englewood Cliffs, NJ: Prentice-Hall.

Ajzen, I., & Fishbein, M. (1972). Attitudes and normative beliefs as factors influencing behavioral intentions. *Journal of Personality and Social Psychology, 21,* 1–9.

Ajzen, I., & Madden, T. (1986). Prediction of goal-directed behavior: Attitudes, intentions, and perceived behavioral control. *Journal of Experimental and Social Psychology, 22,* 453–474.

Baer, J. S., Holt, C. S., & Lichtenstein, E. (1986). Self-efficacy and smoking reexamined: Construct validity and clinical utility. *Journal of Consulting and Clinical Psychology, 54,* 846–852.

Baer, J. S., Kamarck, T., Lichtenstein, E., & Ransom, C. C. (1989). Prediction of smoking relapse: Analyses of temptations and transgressions after initial cessation. *Journal of Consulting and Clinical Psychology, 57,* 623–627.

Bandura, A. (1986). *Social foundations of thought and action: A social cognitive theory.* Englewood Cliffs, NJ: Prentice-Hall.

Bandura, A. (1982). Self-efficacy mechanism in human agency. *American Psychologist, 37,* 122–147.

Bandura, A. (1977a). *Social learning theory.* Englewood Cliffs, NJ: Prentice-Hall.

Bandura, A. (1977b). Self-efficacy: Toward a unifying theory of behavioral change. *Psychological Review, 84,* 191–215.

Barofsky, I. (Ed.). (1977). *Medication compliance: A behavioral management approach.* Thorofare, NJ: Slack.

Barrios, F. X., & Niehaus, J. C. (1985). The influence of smoker status, smoking history, sex, and situational variables on smokers' self-efficacy. *Addictive Behaviors, 10,* 425–429.

Bartlett, E. (1982). Behavioral diagnosis: A practical approach to patient education. *Patient Counseling and Health Education, 4,* 29–35.

Becker, M. H. (Ed.). (1974). *The Health Belief Model and personal health behavior.* Thorofare, NJ: Slack.

Becker, M. H., Maiman, L. A., Kirsch, J. P., Haefner, D. P., Drachman, R. H., & Taylor, D. W. (1979). Patient perceptions and compliance: Recent studies of the Health Belief Model. In R. B. Haynes, D. W. Taylor, & H. D. Sacket, (Eds.), *Compliance in health care* (pp. 78–109). Baltimore: Johns Hopkins University Press.

Berger, B., Hopp, J., & Raettig, V. (1975). Values clarification and the cardiac patient. *Health Education Monograph, 3,* 191–199.

Berkman, L. F. (1984). Assessing the physical health effects of social networks and social support. *American Review of Public Health, 5,* 413–432.

Best, J. A. (1980). Mass media, self-management, and smoking modification. In P. O. Davidson & S. M. Davidson (Eds.), *Behavioral medicine: Changing health lifestyles* (pp. 371–390). New York: Brunner/Mazel.

Boyd-Franklin, N. (1987). Group therapy for black women: A therapeutic support model. *American Orthopsychiatric Association, 57,* 397–401.

Breslow, L. (1982). Control of cigarette smoking from a public policy perspective. *Annual Review of Public Health, 3,* 129–151.

Bruhn, J., & Phillips, B. (1984). Measuring social support: A synthesis of current approaches. *Journal of Behavioral Medicine, 7,* 151–169.

Carnahan, J., & Nugent, C. (1975). The effects of self-monitoring by patients for the control of hypertension. *American Journal of Medical Science, 269,* 69–73.

Coelho, R. J. (1984). Self-efficacy and cessation of smoking. *Psychological Reports, 54,* 309–310.

Cohen, S. A. (1981). Patient education: A review of the literature. *Journal of Advanced Nursing, 6,* 11–18.

Cohen, S. A., & Syme, S. (Eds.). (1985). *Social support and health.* New York: Academic Press.

Colletti, G., Supnick, J. A., & Payne, T. J. (1985). The smoking self-efficacy questionnaire: Preliminary scale development and validation. *Behavioral Assessment, 7,* 249–260.

Comoss, P. M. (1988). Nursing strategies to improve compliance with life-style changes in a cardiac rehabilitation population. *Journal of Cardiovasular Nursing, 2,* 23–26.

Coppotelli, H. C., & Orleans, C. T. (1985). Partner support and other determinants of smoking cessation and maintenance among women. *Journal of Consulting and Clinical Psychology, 53,* 455–460.

Cummings, K. M., Jaen, C., & Giovino, G. (1985). Circumstances surrounding relapse in a group of recent exsmokers. *Preventive Medicine, 14,* 195–202.

Cummings, K. M., Sciandra, R., & Markello, S. (1987). Impact of a newspaper mediated quit smoking program. *American Journal of Public Health, 77,* 1452–1453.

Cwikel, J. M. G., Dielman, T. E., Kirscht, J. P., & Israel, B. A. (1988). Mechanisms of psychosocial effects on health: The role of social integration, coping style and health behavior. *Health Education Quarterly, 15,* 151–173.

Czar, M. (1987). Two methods of goal setting in middle-aged adults facing critical life changes. *Clinical Nurse Specialist, 1,* 171–177.

Davis, M., Eshelman, E., & McKay, M. (1980). *The relaxation and stress reduction workbook.* Richmond, CA: Harbinger.

Devine, E. C., & Cook, T. D. (1983). A meta-analytic analysis of effects of psychoeducational interventions on length of postsurgical hospital stay. *Nursing Research, 32,* 267–274.

DiClemente, C. C., Prochaska, J.O., & Gibertini, M. (1985). Self-efficacy and the stages of self-change of smoking. *Cognitive Therapy and Research, 9,* 181–200.

DiMatteo, M. R., & DiNicola, D. D. (1982). *Achieving patient compliance: The psychology of the medical practitioner's role.* New York: Pergamon Press.

Dishman, R. K. (1988). *Exercise adherence: Its impact on public health.* Champaign, IL: Human Kinetics Books.

Doak, C., Doak, L., & Root, J. (1985). *Teaching patients with low literacy skills.* Philadelphia: JB Lippincott.

Donovan, M. (1980). Relaxation with guided imagery: A useful technique. *Cancer Nursing, 3,* 27–32.

Eiser, J. R., & Gentle, P. (1988). Health behavior as goal-directed action. *Journal of Behavioral Medicine, 11,* 523–535.

Eiser, J. R., van der Pligt, J., Raw, M., & Sutton, S. R. (1983). Trying to stop smoking: Effects of perceived addiction, attributions for failure, and expectancy of success. *Journal of Behavioral Medicine, 8,* 321–341.

Ellis, A. (1988). Psychotherapies that promote profound philosophical change foster behavioral change. *Journal of Integrative and Eclectic Psychotherapy, 7,* 397–402.

Falvo, D R. (1985). *Effective patient education: A guide to increased compliance.* Rockville, MD: Aspen.

Frenn, M. D., Borgeson, D. S., Lee, H. A., & Simandl, G. (1989). Life-style changes in a cardiac rehabilitation program: The client perspective. *Journal of Cardiovascular Nursing, 3,* 43–55.

Gabriel, M., Gagnon, J. P., & Bryan, C. (1977). Improved patient compliance through use of daily drug reminder chart. *American Journal of Public Health, 67,* 968–969.

Glasgow, R. E., & Toobert, D. J. (1988). Social environment and regimen adherence among Type II diabetic patients. *Diabetes Care, 11,* 377–386.

Godding, P. R., & Glasgow, R. E. (1985). Self-efficacy and outcome expectations as predictors of controlled smoking status. *Cognitive Therapy and Research, 9,* 583–590.

Gottlieb, N., & Green, L. (1984). Life events, social network, life-style, and health: An analysis of the 1979 national survey of personal health practices and consequences. *Health Education Quarterly, 11,* 91–105.

Green L. W., Kreuter, M. W., Deeds, S. G., & Partridge, K. B. (1980). *Health education planning: A diagnostic approach.* Palo Alto, CA: Mayfield.

Haller, K. B., & Reynolds, M. A. (1982). *Mutual goal setting in patient care; CURN Project.* New York: Grune & Stratton.

Hallett, R. (1986). Smoking intervention in the workplace: Review and recommendations. *Preventive Medicine. 15,* 213–231.

Hansen, W. B., Graham, J. W., Sobel, J. L., Shelton, D. R., Flay, B. R., & Johnson, C. A. (1987). The consistency of peer and parent influences on tobacco and alcohol use among young adolescents. *Journal of Behavioral Medicine, 10,* 559–561.

Harackiewicz, J. M., Sansone, C., Blair, L. W., Epstein, J. A., & Manderlink, G. (1987). Attributional processes in behavior change and maintenance: Smoking cessation and continued abstinence. *Journal of Consulting and Clinical Psychology, 55,* 372–378.

Haynes, R. B., Taylor, D. W., & Sackett, D. L. (Eds.) (1979). *Compliance in Health Care.* Baltimore: Johns Hopkins University Press.

Haynes, R. B. (1979b). Determinants of compliance: The disease and the mechanics of treatment. In R. B. Haynes, D. W. Taylor, & H. D. Sacket (Eds.). *Compliance in health care* (pp. 49–62). Baltimore: Johns Hopkins University Press.

Health and Public Policy Committee, American College of Physicians. (1986). Methods for stopping cigarette smoking. *Annals of Internal Medicine, 105,* 281–291.

Herje, P. (1980). Hows and whys of patient contracting. *Nurse Educator, 5,* 30–35.

Hubbard, P., Muhlenkamp, A. F., & Brown, N. (1984). The relationship between social support and self-care practices. *Nursing Research, 33,* 266–270.

Hymowitz, N. (1987). Community and clinical trials of disease prevention: Effects on cigarette smoking. *Public Health Review, 15,* 45–81.

Jacobson, D. (1986). Types and timing of social support. *Journal of Health and Social Behavior, 27,* 250–264.

Janz, N. K., & Becker, M. H. (1984). The Health Belief Model: A decade later. *Health Education Quarterly, 11,* 1–47.

Killen, J. D., Robinson, T. N., Telch, M. J., Saylor, K. E., Maron, D. J., Rich, T., & Bryson, S. (1989). The Stanford adolescent heart health program. *Health Education Quarterly, 16,* 263–283.

Koltun, A., & Stone, G. C. (1986). Past and current trends in patient noncompliance research: Focus on diseases, regimens-programs, and provider-disciplines. *Journal of Compliance in Health Care, 1,* 21–32.

Lefebvre, R. C., & Flora, J. A. (1988). Social marketing and public health intervention. *Health Education Quarterly, 15,* 299–315.

Leventhal, H., & Cleary, P. D., (1980). The smoking problem: A review of the research and theory in behavioral risk modification. *Psychological Bulletin, 88,* 370–405.

Lewis, C., & Michnich, M. (1977). Contract as a means of improving patient compliance. In I. Barofsky (Ed.), *Medication compliance: A behavioral management approach.* Thorofare, NJ: Slack.

Ley, P. (1976). Towards better doctor-patient communication. In A. E. Bennett (Ed.), *Communication between doctors and patients.* London: Oxford University Press.

Lorig, K., & Lourin, J. (1986). Some notions about assumptions underlying health education. *Health Education Quarterly, 12,* 31–38.

Mahoney, M. (1974). Self-reward and self-monitoring techniques for weight control. *Behavioral Therapy, 5,* 48–57.

Mahoney, M. J., & Thoresen, C. E. (1974). *Self-control: Power to the person.* Monterey, CA: Brooks-Cole.

Marlatt, G. A., & Gordon, J. R. (1985). *Relapse prevention.* New York: Guilford Press.

Marshall, J., Penckofer, S., & Llewellyn, J. (1986) Structured postoperative teaching and knowledge and compliance of patients who had coronary artery bypass surgery. *Heart & Lung, 15,* 82–86.

Marston, M. V. (1970). Compliance with medical regimens: A review of the literature. *Nursing Research, 19,* 312–323.

Mazzuca, S. A. (1982). Does patient education in chronic disease have therapeutic value? *Journal of Chronic Disease, 35,* 521–529.

McLeroy, K. R., Bibeau, D., Steckler, A., & Glanz, K. (1988). An ecological perspective on health promotion programs. *Health Education Quarterly, 15,* 351–377.

Mermelstein, R., Cohen, S., Lichtenstein, E., Baer, J. S., & Kamarck, T. (1986). Social support and smoking cessation and maintenance. *Journal of Consulting and Clinical Psychology, 54,* 447–453.

Mermelstein, R., Lichtenstein, E., & McIntyre, K. (1983). Partner support and relapse in smoking-cessation programs. *Journal of Consulting and Clinical Psychology, 51,* 465–466.

Minkler, M. (1989). Health education, health promotion and the open society: An historical perspective. *Health Education Quarterly, 16,* 17–30.

Morisky, D., DeMuth, N., & Field-Fass, M. (1985). Evaluation of family health education to build social support for long-term control of high blood pressure. *Health Education Quarterly, 12,* 35–50.

Muhlenkamp, A., & Sayles, J. (1986). Self-esteem, social support, and positive health practices. *Nursing Research, 35,* 334–338.

O'Connell, K. A., & Martin, E. (1987). Highly tempting situations associated with abstinence, temporary lapse, and relapse among participants in smoking cessation programs. *Journal of Consulting and Clinical Psychology, 55,* 367–371.

Oldridge, N., & Jones, N. L. (1983). Improving patient compliance in cardiac exercise rehabilitation: Effects of written agreement and self-monitoring. *Journal of Cardiac Rehabilitation, 3,* 257–262.

Pender, N. (1987). *Health promotion in nursing practice* (2d ed.). Norwalk, CT: Appleton & Lange.

Pender, N., & Pender, A. (1986). Attitudes, subjective norms, and intentions to engage in health behaviors. *Nursing Research, 35,* 15–18.

Petersen, L., Helgerson, S. D., Gibbons, C. M., Calhoun, C., Ciacco, K. H., & Pitchford, K. C. (1988). Employee smoking behavior changes and attitudes following a restrictive policy on worksite smoking in a large company. *Public Health Reports, 103,* 115–120.

Prochaska, J. O., & DiClemente, C. C. (1983). Stages and processes of self-change of smoking: Toward an integrative model of change. *Journal of Consulting and Clinical Psychology, 51,* 390–395.

Powers, M., & Wooldridge, P. (1982). Factors influencing knowledge, attitudes, and compliance of hypertensive patients. *Research in Nursing and Health, 85,* 171–182.

Redman, B. (1984). *The Process of Patient Teaching in Nursing* (5th ed.). St. Louis, MO: CV Mosby.

Ruzicki, D. A. (1989). Realistically meeting the educational needs of hospitalized acute and short-stay patients. *Nursing Clinics of North America, 24,* 629–637.

Ryan, P. (1990). *Behavior change: A concept analysis.* Unpublished manuscript. Milwaukee: University of Wisconsin–Milwaukee.

Ryan, P. (1987). Strategies for motivating life-style. *Journal of Cardiovascular Nursing, 1,* 54–66.

Saltzer, E., (1980). Social determinants of successful weight loss: An analysis of behavioral intentions and actual behavior. *Basic and Applied Social Psychology, 1,* 329–341.

Saunders, B., & Allsop, S. (1987). Relapse: a psychological perspective. *British Journal of Addiction, 82,* 417–429.

Scandrett, S., & Uecker, S. (1985). Relaxation training. In G. Bulechek & J. McCloskey (Eds.), *Nursing interventions: Treatments for nursing diagnoses.* Philadelphia: WB Saunders.

Shiffman, S. (1984). Cognitive antecedents and sequelae of smoking relapse crisis. *Journal of Applied Social Psychology, 14,* 296–309.

Shiffman, S. (1982). Relapse following smoking cessation: A situational analysis. *Journal of Consulting and Clinical Psychology, 50,* 71–86.

Simonds, S. K. (1983). Individual health counselling and education: Emerging directions from current theory, research, and practice. *Patient Counseling and Health Education, 4,* 175–181.

Stanton, A. L. (1987). Determinants of adherence to medical regimens by hypertensive patients. *Journal of Behavioral Medicine. 10,* 377–394.

Steckel, S. (1982). *Patient contracting.* New York: Appleton-Century-Crofts.

Steckel, S. (1980). Contracting with patient selected reinforcers. *American Journal of Nursing, 80,* 1596–1599.

Steele, S. M., & Harmon, V. M. (1979). *Values clarification in nursing.* New York: Appleton-Century-Crofts.

Somer, E., & Tucker, C. M. (1988). Patient life engagement, spouse marital adjustment, and dietary compliance of hemodialysis patients. *Journal of Compliance in Health Care, 3,* 57–65.

Supnick, J. A., & Colletti, G. (1984). Relapse coping and problem solving training following treatment for smoking. *Addictive Behaviors, 9,* 401–404.

Swan, G. E., & Denk, C. E. (1987). Dynamic models for the maintenance of smoking cessation: Event history analysis of late relapse. *Journal of Behavioral Medicine, 10,* 527–554.

Syme, S. L., & Alcalay, R. (1982). Control of cigarette smoking from a social perspective. *Annual Review of Public Health, 3,* 179–199.

Thornburg, K. (1982). Coping: Implications for health practitioners. *Patient Counseling and Health Education, 4,* 3–9.

Trower, P., Casey, A., & Dryden, W. (1988). *Cognitive-behavioural counselling in action.* Beverly Hills: Sage.

Uustal, D. (1977). Searching for values. *Image, 9,* 15–17.

Wewers, M. E., & Lenz, E. R. (1987). Relapse among ex-smokers: An example of theory derivation. *Advances in Nursing Science, 9,* 44–53.

Wilson-Barnett, J., & Osborne, J. (1983). Studies evaluating patient teaching: Implications for practice. *International Journal of Nursing Studies, 20,* 33–44.

Yates, A. J., & Thain, J. (1985). Self-efficacy as a predictor of relapse following voluntary cessation of smoking. *Addictive Behaviors, 10,* 291–298.

■
Enhancing Self-Esteem
■ JUDITH FITZGERALD MILLER

Self-esteem is the evaluative component of self-concept. It is a judgment about one's worth. Rosenberg (1965) states that self-esteem is an attitude of approval or disapproval of self. Self-esteem involves three principal senses of self-regard: Self-love, self-acceptance, and a sense of competence (Wells & Marwell, 1976). Self-esteem combines evaluative and affective components. Discrepancies between self-ideal (cognitions and expectations for self) and the actual attainment or fulfillment of the expectations affect self-esteem. Individuals with high self-esteem perceive themselves as worthwhile and significant; they feel confident in influencing desired outcomes. However, persons with low self-esteem feel worthless, of little importance, and unable to affect outcomes. Wells and Marwell (1976) reviewed other labels for self-esteem such as self-love, self-confidence, self-respect, self-acceptance, self-satisfaction, self-regard, self-evaluation, self-appraisal, self-worth, sense of adequacy of personal efficacy, sense of competence, self-ideal congruence, and ego or ego strength. Self-shame would be an opposing label. (Morrison, 1989).

Coopersmith (1967) specified the theoretic bases for self-esteem to include

1. *Significance.* Results from acceptance, attention, and affection from others with a sense of being valued and cared about as a worthwhile person
2. *Competence.* Perception of successful performance of important tasks
3. *Virtue.* Adherence to moral and ethical standards
4. *Power.* Ability to influence and control events, to control one's own life, and to influence others.

397

The developmental influences of self-esteem in children are acceptance of children by their parents, enforcement of clearly defined limits, and respect for children's latitude within set limits (Coopersmith, 1967).

Persons who have high self-esteem appear to be adjusted, happy, competent, and free from undo anxiety (Gilberts, 1983); take risks; interact with others with confidence (Hirst & Metcalf, 1984); and report less pain in pain-induced studies (Feldman, 1986). Persons with low self-esteem use negative self-statements (Crouch & Straub, 1983), expect rejection and failure, and project past failure into the future (Wells & Marwell, 1976). They are also dependent upon others, shy, nonexplorative, and guarded (Rosenberg, 1965). Cohen (1959) noted that persons with low self-esteem incorporate negative information into their concepts of self; they are more sensitive to negative feedback.

While self-acceptance is fundamental to high self-esteem, illness challenges self-acceptance. Chronic illness presents lifelong demands for coping with a health alteration and imposed health regimen. The diagnosis of a chronic illness may be accompanied by a change in the individual's view of self (self-perception). If the individual's view of self is one of physical strength, endurance, and wholeness, there is a greater likelihood for the individual to have a higher self-esteem than if the self-perception is one of physical weakness, lack of energy, and altered body function. A change in self-perception occurs in chronically ill persons when previous aspirations need to be modified, roles changed, and other adjustments made because of altered physical reserve. When physical ability deteriorates, individuals may conclude they are worthless, undeserving of self-respect, and generally inadequate. This lowered self-esteem is present in all patients during some phase of the health problem.

Norris and Kunes-Connell (1988, 1985) conceptualize three types of self-esteem. *Basic self-esteem* is the stable core sense of self-worth. *Functional* or *situational self-esteem* is that self-worth that varies with situations, rewards, and failures. *Defensive self-esteem* protects individuals from situational threats. It is also referred to as *pseudo self-esteem.* Although their work has focused on validating three distinct types of self-esteem as nursing diagnoses (Norris & Kunes-Connell, 1988, 1985), no attempt will be made throughout this chapter to distinguish among these three types of self-esteem. A review of self-esteem as a power resource, assessment of self-esteem, and nursing strategies to enhance self-esteem will be included in this chapter.

Power Resource

High self-esteem empowers the chronically ill individual in the following ways:

- It enables the person to be an active participant in care.
- It helps the person develop confidence in interpersonal communication.
- It provides the person with accurate internal feedback as opposed to the inaccurate, derogatory feedback that occurs in persons with low self-esteem.
- It enhances the potential for successful role performance.
- It is a resource for coping (Walsh & Walsh, 1989).

The level of self-esteem is significant in motivating patients to work on life-style modification or to follow through with rehabilitation programs (McGlashan, 1988).

Being an active participant in care decisions and assuming responsibility for care to hasten independence in self-management depend on many factors, one of which is self-esteem. Self-esteem enables the patient to assume an active role in controlling care. Being a self-care agent requires the patient to have motivation, knowledge, and self-worth (Kearney & Fleisher, 1979). Patients with high self-esteem feel that they are worth the time and effort needed to maintain and improve health and eagerly take responsibility to meet self-care needs. Conversely, individuals with low self-esteem may be unable to make self-care decisions and assume responsibility for care outcomes. For example, an obese individual with low self-esteem may feel undeserving of better health and unworthy of close dietary monitoring, health-care personnel's time, and his or her own effort.

The confidence and competence individuals have in their interpersonal relationships are positively influenced by high self-esteem. Interactions with significant others (those from whom acceptance is sought) and with strangers provide feedback about self. If the individual feels worthwhile and demonstrates self-approval during interactions, others will respond with similar feelings of respect and approval. These patients feel confident that their own concerns are not petty or foolish and are deserving of professional consultation.

High self-esteem enables individuals to more accurately interpret feedback about self, whereas low self-esteem causes individuals to distort feedback. Persons with low self-esteem may consistently engage in an internal dialogue that results in a negative interpretation about self. Guilt and self-pity may be induced. For example, consider Mr. C., who has a colostomy. When his dressing is changed on a particular day, his nurse is less talkative than usual. Mr. C. interprets this as being due to her repugnance of him. The patient may carry on a silent dialogue to reaffirm his false interpretation. It seems as though the patient seeks reinforcement for his own negative feeling of low self-worth. Instead of being open in interactions and validating the meaning of the feedback, the patient may interpret the message in a way that is destructive to self.

High self-esteem breeds success in performing life roles. Self-esteem provides confidence in undertaking new roles (such as assuming the role of self-care agent) and a recognition of personal potential for accomplishing goals associated with familiar roles. The belief in one's own ability to be successful operates as a self-fulfilling prophecy. The patient with high self-esteem confidently anticipates success, which in fact does materialize.

Coping mechanisms of persons with high and low self-esteem may be distinctily different. Cohen (1959) stated that preferred defenses (mental coping mechanisms) of persons with high self-esteem include denial and repression or ignoring conflicting impulses. Persons with low self-esteem used projective and expressive defenses. Therefore, persons who had low self-esteem before the onset of chronic illness may experience greater threats to self-esteem as a result of the illness than do persons with high premorbid self-esteem. This may be especially true if development of the illness is viewed as a personal shortcoming or a negative component of self.

Since self-esteem is a power resource, nursing efforts to enhance self-esteem help to increase the patient's perceived power (alleviating powerlessness). Ascertaining the patient's level of self-esteem is an important first step.

Assessment of Self-Esteem

To determine the nature of the patient's self-esteem, information is gathered through observation, an interview, analysis of the patient's role performance, and identification of changes in social interaction.

OBSERVATION OF SELF-DEROGATORY COMMENTS

Nursing observations of patient behavior include noting the pattern of verbal comments by the patient over time. Self-derogatory verbal comments indicate low self-esteem. Examples are the following statements:

I feel I am no longer a good person.
I can't do anything anymore. Now I am good for nothing, useless.
I feel guilt and embarrassment when I have to ask for help.
I've lost my independence; that is mighty rough.
I've lost faith in myself.
Sometimes I feel my body has turned against me.
I don't like myself this way.

These comments indicate feelings of insignificance, uselessness, and worthlessness.

Other observations of patient interaction may indicate low self-esteem. The patient may be hesitant to bother the nurse or ask for help. The person with low self-esteem may avoid direct eye contact when communicating with others, especially when interacting with authority figures. The patient's reluctance to participate in the medical plan may also indicate low self-esteem.

INTERVIEW

After a trusting nurse-patient relationship has been established, specific questions can be raised to gather information about the patient's self-esteem. Besides gathering data for self-esteem assessment, interview questions enable the patient to review existing abilities and develop self-insight, thereby providing an opportunity to enhance self-esteem. The following questions are helpful in gathering self-esteem information:

> How has having arthritis (or whatever the health problem is) changed the way you feel about yourself?
> In evaluating your abilities, how would you describe yourself?
> Would you say you had a positive or negative attitude toward yourself?
> What do you like best about yourself?
> What are your weak points?
> What do you do to feel good about yourself?
> Are you able to complete the care needed as a result of the illness?
> What changes in your life will occur as a result of the illness? Are important losses involved?
> Do you anticipate any differences in the way your family and friends will respond to you?
> Tell me about your accomplishments and disappointments in life.

Information gathered by using patient self-report (responses to the above or similar questions) can be validated with the patient by asking the questions again or by confirming responses later. The self-report is compared with observations, social interaction, and role performance.

ROLE PERFORMANCE

Role changes may be imposed by illness. Sometimes, previous work roles are no longer possible. The more important the role is in determining the person's self-concept, the more devastating the role loss is to the person's self-esteem. For example, if a symphony pianist suffered a traumatic amputation of three fingers, the concept of self as a pianist is threatened. The patient's breadwinning capacity may be threatened temporarily until the patient can accept a substitute role, for example, teaching piano or developing a related talent such as vocal music performance. Questions to be considered in assessing role performance include the following:

How threatening is the health problem to the individual's definition of self or self-concept?

Will the health problem interfere with established career goals or the present employment role?

Does the health problem cause the patient to feel less sexually attractive? (Joint deformities and decreased mobility of arthritis may limit activities the individual views as important for developing and maintaining sexual relationships.)

Does the patient perceive self to be less adequate in social relationships because of the health problem? (Patients with chronic diarrhea from Crohn's disease may hesitate to become involved in group activities to avoid the embarrassment of having to take frequent trips to the rest room.)

CHANGES IN SOCIAL INTERACTION

Although information about self-esteem and social interaction relates closely to role performance, specific changes in social interaction can be noted. Have social activities been eliminated, leisure activities changed, or relationships with family and significant others altered? Patient's family and friends may relate that the patient's interaction themes focus on negative self-talk. Self-derogatory comments may dominate conversation. Friends may eventually withdraw. The resulting social isolation may contribute to further lowering of self-esteem.

Valued social activities may be eliminated. For example, the patient with severe emphysema may avoid the weekly card party at the senior citizens' center to avoid exposure to crowds and respiratory infections. Although the decision may be a good one in terms of health maintenance, unless acceptable substitutes are found, positive feelings about self may diminish. The nurse can help the patient find an alternative activity; for example, the patient could select three friends to meet weekly at the patient's home to play cards.

Low self-esteem indicators (verbalizations and behaviors) can be summarized in three categories: changes in role performance, changes in interpersonal relationships, and presence of negative self-talk. See Table 16–1.

Assessment of self-esteem is important for designing appropriate individual strategies to enhance self-esteem. Individuals evaluate themselves highly in situations in which they achieve a sense of mastery. A sense of mastery is based on the person's behavior.

TABLE 16 ■ 1   Indicators of Low Self-esteem

Interpersonal Relationships	Negative Self-talk	Role Performance
Feels unworthy of nurses' time, care, attention	Verbalizations convey: Self-blame	Expresses having few accomplishments
Hesitant to ask for help	Guilt over disease	Expresses doubts about
Pessimistic	Self-derogatory	ability to fulfill roles
Feels undeserving of praise	comments	Feels inferior; compares self
Resentful of others who are well	Negative attitude toward self	to others
Lacks assertiveness	(physical self,	Feels own actions will have little effect on an
Lacks self-confidence in one-to-one and/or group interactions	personal self, and spiritual self)	outcome (feels ineffective)
Self-conscious	Feeling of	Feels insignificant
Expresses a sense of worthlessness	uselessness	Unable to take pride in accomplishing goals
	Lack of self-respect	Unable to set goals
		Feels has failed in life's mission
		Lacks a sense of competence

SPECIFIC TOOLS FOR SELF-ESTEEM ASSESSMENT

Paper-and-pencil tests to measure self-esteem include Rosenberg's Self-esteem Scale (1965), Coopersmith's Self-esteem Scale (1967, 1982) which has both a child and an adult version, and the Children's Self-esteem Questionnaire by Busse, Mansfield, and Messinger (1974).

Taylor (1982) developed another self-esteem assessment guide based on the four theoretic bases of self-esteem (significance, competence, virtue, and power). Questions are posed to patients about the importance of each of the four theoretic bases and the extent to which they are present in their lives.

Self-Esteem and Chronic Illness

Although the research findings about whether or not persons with chronic illness have lower self-esteem than healthy persons have been inconclusive (Wright, 1983; Weinberg-Asher, 1976), high self-esteem has been correlated with adjustment to disability and chronic illness (Burckhardt, 1985; Linkowski & Dunn, 1974). Self-esteem, low negative attitude, internal control over health, and perceived social support all contributed significantly to quality of life in 94 adults with arthritis (Burckhardt, 1985). A significant relationship between self-esteem and acceptance of disability in 55 disabled college students was reported by Linkowski and Dunn (1974). Self-esteem was also identified as a positive factor influencing medication compliance in adolescents with rheumatoid arthritis (Litt,

Cuskey, & Rosenberg, 1982). Antonucci and Jackson (1983) found in their national survey of 2264 adults that not only was self-esteem lower in those persons with a health problem, but there was also a linear relationship between severity of illness and low self-esteem. The linear relationship was stronger for men than women. Similar findings are reported for the elderly in that those with poorer health, more daily pain, and greater disability had lower self-esteem (Hunter, Linn, & Harris, 1981–1982). Persons in their sample with low self-esteem had more anxiety, greater external control, and greater depression. Lisanti (1989) found that persons with continuous chronic back pain had lower self-esteem scores than those with intermittent chronic pain. On the other hand, although subjects reported significant differences in health status, self-esteem was not significantly different among groups of women with rheumatoid arthritis, systemic lupus, and those who were healthy (Cornwell & Schmitt, 1990). Body image was significantly lower in women with lupus. Hastings (Chap. 10) found significant relationships between hope and social support, and between hope and adaptation in 30 persons with multiple sclerosis (MS). These findings were supported by Foote and associates (1990) who also found significant positive relationships between self-esteem and hope and self-esteem and social support in 40 persons with MS (Foote, Piazza, Holcombe, Paul, & Daffin, 1990). Persons with MS with severe limits in mobility (no walking) had significantly lower self-esteem than those depending upon assistive devices or a wheelchair (Walsh & Walsh, 1989). Walsh and Walsh also reported that a positive affect was predictive of high self-esteem.

CHRONIC ILLNESS AS LOSS OF SELF

Charmaz (1983) studied the nature of suffering of 57 adults with various chronic health problems. Her work illustrates the impact of chronic illness as a threat to self-perception and provides a framework for nursing care directed at preserving self-esteem in chronically ill persons. Through in-depth interviews Charmaz identified that chronic illness meant suffering a loss of self because of

1. Living a restricted life-style
2. Existing in social isolation
3. Experiencing discredited definitions of self
4. Becoming a burden

Living a restricted life-style means the individual is unable to do the things once valued and enjoyed. In the most severe stage of illness progression, it may resemble an all-consuming retreat into illness. Recall the stages of illness progression from an earlier chapter: interrupted time, time intrusion, and encapsulation.

Social isolation occurs because of a restricted social network, little ability or energy to share leisure activities, and increasing amounts of time spent on illness management. Positive feedback about self is dependent in part upon social interaction. Persons with MS who belonged to a support group had higher self-esteem than those who did not (Walsh & Walsh, 1989). Orr and associates (1989) found that of the 121 adolescents and young adults suffering burns, those who had more social support had higher self-esteem, more positive body image, and less depression.

Discrediting definitions of self occur because of feedback from others as well as from unmet expectations of the ill person. Ill persons may scrutinize encounters with others finding hints of negative self-reflections, or in some instances the negative feedback may be blatant. Charmaz (1983) found that discrediting is more likely to occur when the ill person feels vulnerable or identifies with the individual providing the discrediting message.

Becoming a burden occurs when the individual becomes more dependent and immobilized. When perceiving self as a burden, self-worth is lowered. Physical, enonomic, and psychologic dependency all play a role in perceiving self as a burden to others.

CONSTRUCTING POSITIVE VIEWS OF SELF

Wright (1983) provides a framework for disabled persons to view themselves positively and avoid the devaluation which results from losses due to illness by focusing on (1) enlarging their scope of values, (2) subordinating physique, (3) containing disability effects, and (4) avoiding emphasis on comparative asset values.

Enlarging the scope of values refers to persons recognizing their own assets or abilities and that they can participate in desired activities in their own way despite limitations. It is a moving beyond grieving over the losses due to illness. It may require accepting a new way of walking or receiving sexual gratification.

Subordinating physique means there is less psychic energy spent on worrying about the physical component of self in terms of appearance and physical prowess, and more energy is spent recognizing that an individual's definition of self extends beyond the physical self.

Containing disability means preventing the disability from consuming the entire identity of the person.

Avoiding comparative status values means spending less time ruminating and comparing self to past abilities or to others' abilities and more time on valuing and accepting self and others.

Other works are helpful in designing a model of strategies to enhance self-esteem. Turk (1979) proposed the following to be essential components for adaptation to chronic illness: (1) knowledge about the nature of the illness (including therapy), (2) ability to use coping strategies, (3) presence of a social support system, (4) problem-solving attitude in facing the challenges of illness management, (5) sense of personal control, and (6) motivation to implement the required behaviors for illness management. Development of these personal resources contributes to self-worth.

Miller (1987) recommends the following categories of strategies to enhance self-esteem of adolescents: (1) establishing a trusting relationship, (2) promoting social interaction and involvement in groups, and (3) helping the adolescent discover his or her own assets. Although few studies on strategies to enhance self-esteem have been conducted, Thomas (1988) tested the effect of a meditation-relaxation training program on 11 black women and found that it had a significant impact on self-esteem and life satisfaction. A comparison didactic stress management information group ($N = 10$) had lower scores (Thomas, 1988). Goldberg and Fitzpatrick (1980) found that the 15 elderly who participated in movement therapy had higher self-esteem and morale than the 15 persons in the control group.

Nursing Strategies to Enhance Self-esteem

Another model for enhancing self-esteem based on literature and research findings as well as on study of the chronically ill is presented here. Specific areas for enhancing self-esteem may include developing the following: cognitive control, self-affirmation, positive perception of role performance competence, interpersonal relationships, social activities, and self-care competence. It should be noted that the proposed strategies have not been systematically studied to verify the outcomes suggested.

COGNITIVE CONTROL

Helping persons become sensitized to thoughts and self-talk which are self-derogatory will reduce this self-initiated reinforcement of low self-worth. A direct reflective communication technique can be used to help the patient become aware of negative self-talk, to reappraise the statements and consequent feelings, and to find substitute positive statements. The goal is to change the person's internal dialogue as well as to change the negative thoughts and perceptions (McKay & Fanning, 1987; Meichenbaum, 1976). Examples of positive statements may have to be suggested to the person such as, "Today I'm the best me possible. Because I am human, I am worthwhile. I am special. There is no one like me in the entire world." Helping the person become aware of distorted thinking such as catastrophizing, filtering out all positive details, and maximizing negative possibilities is helpful (McKay, Davis, & Fanning, 1981). The person is to be helped to have accurate perceptions of the situation and to avoid a totally devastating, demoralizing view.

The intended *outcome* of this strategy is positive self-talk and an accurate, not a distorted perception of the situation.

SELF-AFFIRMATION

Self-rejecting behaviors as indicated above, as well as berating self, feeling embarrassed about disabilities, believing self to be unattractive, and giving credit deserved for self to others, all need to be eliminated before self-affirmation can occur. Self-affirmation includes giving self approval, talking gently to self, forgiving self, having fun without feeling guilty, rewarding self with a special treat (quiet time alone, listening to a favorite piece of music, or any appropriate reward), liking self and accepting affection from others (Bloomfield & Kory, 1980).

The *outcome* of self-affirmation is greater self-regard.

ROLE PERFORMANCE REVIEW AND ROLE MODIFICATION

Despite disability, not all roles are abolished. Preventing the negative spread of the view that the entire body is dysfunctional can be expanded beyond body image to social aspects of the individual as well. Roles which remain intact should be reviewed and role supplementation strategies should be made for roles which must be modified. Together the nurse and client review intact roles making a verbal listing. Helping the patient redefine roles may also be needed. Just because the patient is no longer able to perform the physical task according to previous criteria does not mean that he or she no longer has the role. On the other hand some roles will have to be surrendered, but this giving up of roles is necessary as well for healthy individuals at various times in their lives. An example of role modification may be the father of a 12-year-old whose fathering role was defined, in part, by his active participation in his son's soccer plays. Because of an illness progression such as arthritis, the physical participation may become more limited; however, the nurse can review how the father can fulfill this role in other ways: watching the games, taking notes regarding specific plays, reviewing game strategies, critiquing drills, and so forth.

Role performance review is akin to reminiscing used with the elderly, which has had positive results in terms of life satisfaction, adjustment, and ego integrity.

The *outcome* of role performance review is perceived self-competence.

SELF-CARE COMPETENCE

Achieving mastery in managing the health problem will enhance the patient's perception of control. Perceived control has been correlated with high self-esteem in persons with cancer for example (Lewis, 1982). Mastery includes the patient's having knowledge about the specific prescribed health regimen and desired outcomes as well as having the skill to carry out the regimen. It also includes helping the patient develop internal awareness to physiologic and psychologic cues which demand attention and at times medical intervention. Training in new skill development may need to begin with activities of daily living. Reinforcing independence with activities such as dressing and performing hygiene highlight progress and enhance self-esteem as the person becomes aware of new accomplishments.

The *outcome* of developing self-care competence is perceived control.

INTERPERSONAL RELATIONSHIPS

The nature of the relationship between the nurse and patient should be characterized by unconditional acceptance, positive regard, mutual respect, and an expectation for mutual growth because of the relationship. Eventually the nurse can share with the patient how he or she benefited from knowing the patient. Recognition of the patient's knowledge or unique abilities and expressions of appreciation for insights gained from knowing the patient enhance self-esteem. The nurse is to communicate sincere interest in the patient as a whole person and not just an interest in the health problem.

Families need to be helped to understand the powerful role they play in the self-esteem of the patient. They may need counseling to help them grieve over the losses experienced by their loved one as well as to help them see the richness of the personality of their loved one. They need to know that persons who are questioning their self-worth readily interpret messages from others as negative (Shrauger & Rosenberg, 1970), so any cues conveying a pseudo-repugnance should be avoided.

It is through relationships with others that individuals receive affirmation of their worth. Preventing alienation and isolation from previously enjoyed activities is necessary. Helping the patient conserve energy and make plans to continue whatever social activities previously contributed to positive self-esteem is worthwhile in preserving self-acceptance.

It should be noted that self-help groups do not have positive effects for all persons with disabilities. Dixon's (1981) study of 142 disabled persons revealed that group identification was strong among the visibly handicapped (persons with amputations, spinal cord injuries, and strokes), whereas persons with arthritis and emotional disorders preferred dissociation with others having the same diagnosis. Little research has been done on the specific effects of support groups for physically handicapped persons. The results of one study of 34 women with rheumatoid arthritis concluded that group counseling had a significant effect on improving the self-concept and knowledge of the women (Kaplan & Kozin, 1981).

The *outcome* of experiencing healthy interpersonal relationships is positive feedback about self. Patients may realize that others accept and enjoy them despite the illness. Self-acceptance is the desired end result.

The model in Figure 16–1 summarizes the strategies to enhance self-esteem. Outcomes for each strategy are suggested. Although not discussed in this text, the impact of each opposing strategy and specified outcome are presented in the model. For example the strategies and outcomes leading to decreased self-esteem include

- Cognitive distortion resulting in negative self-talk
- Self-denial and self-doubt resulting in self-rejection
- Fixation on role incompetence resulting in reinforced self-incompetence
- Self-care incompetence resulting in powerlessness
- Social isolation resulting in lack of affirmation of worth

(See Fig. 16–2.)

Self-esteem has been studied as it relates to other aspects of life. Barron (1987) discovered a relationship between learned helplessness and low self-esteem in 36 women who were divorced after their first marriage. When causal explanations for the divorce were found to be internal, sta-

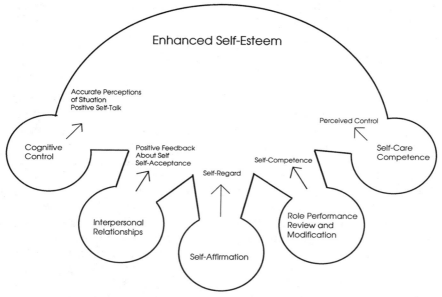

FIGURE 16 ■ 1   Strategies to enhance self-esteem.

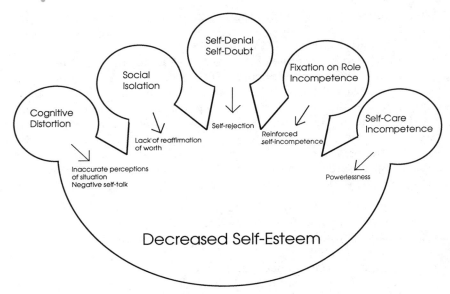

FIGURE 16 ■ 2   Mechanisms that decrease self-esteem.

ble, and global (dimensions of learned helplessness), then more emotional distress and lower self-esteem were present. Spouses have an impact on each other's self-esteem. The more positive a husband's appraisal of his wife, the higher the woman's self-esteem (Meisenhelder, 1986). Self-esteem has also been associated with positive health behaviors (Muhlenkamp & Sayles, 1986).

Summary

A basic human need is to feel worthwhile to self and others. Personal worth is needed for all individuals, sick or well. Self-esteem has been identified as a central concern influencing the behavior of all persons. Helping persons find intrinsic worth; that is, not meeting some other-stipulated criteria for what is worthwhile, is the goal. In our Protestant work ethic ideology, we may be challenged to help persons be more satisfied over being less concerned about doing. Quality of life is not possible for persons with low self-esteem. High self-esteem could insulate individuals with a disability against the debilitating psychologic problems of hopelessness and depression. Acceptance means viewing the loss due to chronic illness as nondevaluing (Dembo, Leviton, & Wright, 1975). Self-esteem levels in turn may reflect the levels of acceptance by the individual of the illness. The need for more research on self-esteem in the chronically ill is evident.

References

Antonucci, T., & Jackson, J. (1983). Physical health and self-esteem. *Family and Community Health, 6,* 1–9.

Barron, C. (1987). Women's causal explanations of divorce: Relationships to self-esteem and emotional distress. *Research in Nursing and Health, 10,* 345–353.

Bloomfield, H., & Kory, R. (1980). *Inner joy: New strategies for adding more pleasure to your life.* New York: Wyden Books.

Burckhardt, C. (1985). The impact of arthritis on quality of life. *Nursing Research, 34,* 11–16.

Busse, T. V., Mansfield, R. S. & Messinger, L. J. (1974). *Activities in child and adolescent development.* New York: Harper & Row.

Charmaz, K. (1983). Loss of self: A fundamental for suffering in the chronically ill. *Sociology of Health and Illness, 5,* 168–195.

Cohen, A. (1959). Some implications of self-esteem for social influence. In C. Hovland & I. Janis (Eds.), *Personality and persuasibility.* New Haven, CT: Yale University Press.

Coopersmith, S. (1982). *Self-esteem inventories.* Palo Alto, CA: Consulting Psychologist Press.

Coopersmith, S. (1967). *Antecedents of self-esteem.* San Francisco: Freeman.

Cornwell, C., & Schmitt, M. (1990). Perceived health status, self-esteem, and body image in women with rheumatoid arthritis or systemic lupus erythematosus. *Research in Nursing and Health, 13,* 99–107.

Crouch, M. A., & Straub, V. (1983). Enhancement of self-esteem in adults. *Family and Community Health, 6,* 65–78.

Dembo, T., Leviton, G. L., & Wright, B. A. (1975). Adjustment to misfortune: A problem of social-psychological rehabilitation. *Rehabilitation Psychology, 22,* 1–100.

Dixon, J. K. (1981). Group-self identification and physical handicap: Implications for patient support groups. *Research in Nursing and Health, 4,* 299–308.

Feldman, H. R. (1986). Self-esteem, types of attributional style and sensation and distress pain ratings in males. *Journal of Advanced Nursing, 11,* 75–86.

Foote, A., Piazza, D., Holcombe, J., Paul, P., & Daffin, P. (1990). Hope, self-esteem and social support in persons with multiple sclerosis. *Journal of Neuroscience Nursing, 22,* 155–159.

Gilberts, R. (1983). The evaluation of self-esteem. *Family and Community Health, 6,* 29–49.

Goldberg, W., & Fitzpatrick, J. (1980). Movement therapy with the aged. *Nursing Research, 29,* 339–346.

Hirst, S., & Metcalf, B. (1984). Promoting self-esteem. *Journal of Gerontological Nursing, 10,* 72–77.

Hunter, K. I., Linn, M. W., & Harris, R. (1981–1982). Characteristics of high and low self-esteem in the elderly. *International Journal of Aging and Human Development, 14,* 117–126.

Kaplan, S., & Kozin, F. (1981). A controlled study of group counseling in rheumatoid arthritis. *Journal of Rheumatology, 8,* 91–99.

Kearney, B., & Fleisher, B. (1979). Development of an instrument to measure exercise of self-care agency. *Research in Nursing and Health, 2,* 25–34.

Lewis, F. A. (1982). Experienced personal control and quality of life in late-stage cancer patients. *Nursing Research, 31,* 113–119.

Linkowski, D. C., & Dunn, M. (1974). Self-concept and acceptance of disability. *Rehabilitation Counseling Bulletin, 14,* 236–244.

Lisanti, P. (1989). Perceived body space and self-esteem in adult males with and without chronic low back pain. *Orthopaedic Nursing, 8,* 49–56.

Litt, T. F., Cuskey, W. R., & Rosenberg, A. (1982). Role of self-esteem and autonomy in determining medication compliance among adolescents with juvenile rheumatoid arthritis. *Pediatrics, 69,* 15–17.

McGlashan, R. (1988). Strategies for rebuilding self-esteem for the cardiac patient. *Dimensions of Critical Care, 7,* 28–38.

McKay, M., Davis, M., & Fanning, P. (1981). *Thoughts and feelings: The art of cognitive stress intervention.* Richmond, CA: New Harbinger Publications.

McKay, M., & Fanning, P. (1987). *Self-esteem*. Oakland, CA: New Harbinger Publications.

Meichenbaum, D. (1976). Toward a cognitive theory of self-control. In G. Schwartz & D. Shapiro (Eds.), *Consciousness and self-regulation: Advances in research* (Vol. 1.). New York: Plenum Press.

Meisenhelder, J. B. (1986). Self-esteem in women: The influence of employment and perception of husband's appraisals. *Image: Journal of Nursing Scholarship, 18*, 8–13.

Miller, S. (1987). Promoting self-esteem in the hospitalized adolescent: Clinical interventions. *Issues in Comprehensive Pediatric Nursing, 10*, 187–194.

Morrison, A. (1989). *Shame: The underside of narcissism*. Hillsdale, NJ: Analytic Press.

Muhlenkamp, A., & Sayles, J. (1986). Self-esteem, social support, and positive health practices. *Nursing Research, 35*, 334–338.

Norris, J., & Kunes-Connell, M. (1988). A multimodal approach to validation and refinement of an existing nursing diagnosis. *Archives of Psychiatric Nursing, 2*, 103–109.

Norris, J., & Kunes-Connell, M. (1985). Self-esteem disturbance. *Nursing Clinics of North America, 20*, 745–761.

Orr, D., Reznikoff, M., & Smith, G. (1989). Body image, self-esteem and depression in burn-injured adolescents and young adults. *Journal of Burn Care and Rehabilitation, 10*, 454–461.

Rosenberg, M. (1965). *Society and the adolescent self-image*. Princeton, NJ: Princeton University Press.

Shrauger, J., & Rosenberg, M. (1970). Self-esteem and the effects of success and failure feedback on performance. *Journal of Personality, 33*, 404–406.

Taylor, M. (1982). The needs for self-esteem. In H. Yura & M. Walsh (Eds.), *Human Needs 2 and the Nursing Process* (pp. 117–153). Norwalk, CT: Appleton-Century-Crofts.

Thomas, B. (1988). Self-esteem and life satisfaction. *Journal of Gerontological Nursing, 14*, 25–30.

Turk, D. (1979). Factors influencing the adaptive process with chronic illness. In E. G. Sarason & C. D. Spielberger (Eds.), *Stress and anxiety* (Vol 6.). Washington, DC: Hemisphere Publishing.

Walsh, A., & Walsh, P. A. (1989). Love, self-esteem and multiple sclerosis. *Social Science and Medicine, 29*, 793–798.

Weinberg-Asher, N. (1976). The effects of physical disability on self-perception. *Rehabilitation Counseling Bulletin, 20*, 18–20.

Wells, L. E., & Marwell, G. (1976). *Self-esteem: Its conceptualization and measurement*. Beverly Hills, CA: Sage.

Wright, B. (1983). *Physical disability: A psychosocial approach* (2d ed.). New York: Harper & Row.

■

Inspiring Hope
■ JUDITH FITZGERALD MILLER

One of a person's most valued, private, and powerful resources is hope. Hope is an intrinsic component of life, which provides dynamism for the spirit (Adams & Proulx, 1975), saving individuals from apathetic inaction. It is the affect that accompanies faith (belief system). Although faith could not be sustained without hope, the basis of hope is faith. Hope means anticipating success yet having some uncertainty. It is the negation of the worst possible outcome (Beck, Kovacs, & Weissman, 1975).

Hope as a Power Resource

Hope is a power resource in that it (1) enables transcendence (Bloch, 1970), as from earthly suffering; (2) is a buffer for stress (Korner, 1970); (3) creates a sense of well-being, combating a futile painful state of despair (Fromm, 1968); (4) enables healthy ego functioning (Heagle, 1975); (5) provides a sense of freedom during times of suffering (Lynch, 1974; Marcel, 1962); and (6) plays a role in psychotherapeutic and physical healing (Aardema, 1984; Diez-Manrique, 1984; Frank, 1968, 1975; Menninger, 1959; Pruyser, 1963).

Hope Defined

Although Stotland (1969) defines hope as an expectation greater than zero of achieving a goal, hope is more than anticipating goal accomplishment.

Hope is a state of being, characterized by an anticipation of a continued good state, an improved state or a release from a perceived entrapment. The

413

anticipation may or may not be founded on concrete, real world evidence. Hope is an anticipation of a future that is good and is based upon: mutuality (relationships with others), a sense of personal competence, coping ability, psychological well-being, purpose and meaning in life, as well as a sense of "the possible" (Miller, 1986, p. 52).

Dufault (1989) described two spheres of hope: particularized and generalized. Particularized hope refers to the anticipation of achieving a specific desired goal. Generalized hope contributes to a feeling of well-being and provides a sense that life is worthwhile. It is an impetus to carry on with life's responsibilities and to transcend any dependence on particular objects of hope (Dufault & Martocchio, 1985). There are varied characteristics and dimensions of hope including affective (sensations and emotions), cognitive (thoughts, insights, and imagination), affiliative (connectedness with others), temporal (time sense), and contextual (life circumstance) (Dufault & Martocchio, 1985). Hope cannot exist alone, but is dependent upon communion with another (Marcel, 1962). When significant others believe in the possibility of a positive outcome and convey a willingness to share the crisis, hope is enlivened. "Hope is an inner readiness, that of an intense but not yet spent activeness" (Fromm, 1968, pp. 11–12). Everything human beings do in life is based upon some level of hope.

Owen (1989) proposed six hope attributes: goal setting, positive personal attributes (courage, optimism, positive attitude), future redefinition, meaning of life, peace, and energy. Stanley's (1978) definition of hope resulted from a qualitative study of 100 college students and concluded hope to be "a confident expectation that a future good, although accompanied by doubt and fear, is realistically possible through active endeavor, supportive interpersonal relationships and a religious faith" (p. 50). Stanley proposed seven common elements of hope: (1) expectation of a significant future outcome, (2) feeling of confidence in the outcome, (3) transcendence, (4) interpersonal relatedness, (5) a comfortable feeling, (6) an uncomfortable feeling, and (7) action to affect outcomes. For additional definitions, see the matrix of 16 hope definitions derived from research, clinical practice, conceptual, and conjectural orientations in Miller (1986, appendix A). Although there are varied definitions of hope, there is consensus that hope is a multidimensional, complex construct.

LEVELS OF HOPE

Three levels of hope can be described, as shown in Figure 17–1. The first level is the most elementary, in which superficial wishes—as for basic material goods or a nice day—are included. Shallow optimism characterizes this level. When this level of hope is not actualized, little despair occurs and little psychic energy is expended.

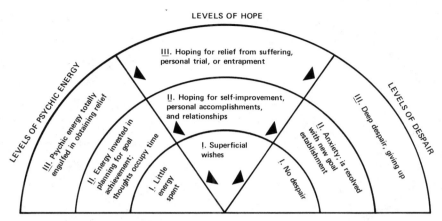

LEVELS OF HOPE

III. Hoping for relief from suffering, personal trial, or entrapment

II. Hoping for self-improvement, personal accomplishments, and relationships

I. Superficial wishes

LEVELS OF PSYCHIC ENERGY

III. Psychic energy totally engulfed in obtaining relief

II. Energy invested in planning for goal achievement; thoughts occupy time

I. Little energy spent

LEVELS OF DESPAIR

III. Deep despair, giving up

II. Anxiety; is resolved with new goal establishment

I. No despair

FIGURE 17 ■ 1   Levels of hope, despair, and psychic energy.

The second level of hope includes hoping for relationships, self-improvement, and self-accomplishments. When hope at this level is thwarted, the resultant level of despair is characterized by anxiety. The anxiety is relieved with new goal establishment. Psychic energy investment is greater than at the first level but less than at the next stage. Thoughts about goal achievement occupy considerable time and energy.

The third level of hope arises out of suffering, personal trial, or state of captivity. Marcel (1962) states that it is in a situation tempted by despair that hope has its true meaning. Deep despair or giving up occurs when relief is not imminent by the evaluation of the individual. Total engulfment of psychic energy occurs at this point.

This chapter deals with the third level of hope—hope at its most intense and powerful level. Maintaining hope despite a downward physical course is a challenge (coping task) of the chronically ill. Included in this chapter is a discussion of the assessment of hope–hopelessness and nursing strategies to inspire hope.

Chronic illness, by virtue of its unpredictable nature and concomitant losses, precipitates powerlessness. When powerlessness is not contained, hopelessness can result. As shown in Figure 17–2, the cycle of powerlessness leads to depression and low self-esteem, causing hopelessness that in turn immobilizes the individual. The cycle continues until the giving up associated with prolonged hopelessness with no relief in sight leads to total despair and thought of self-harm may occur. The hastening of death may appear desirable. See Chapter 6 for a clinical description of hopelessness leading to death.

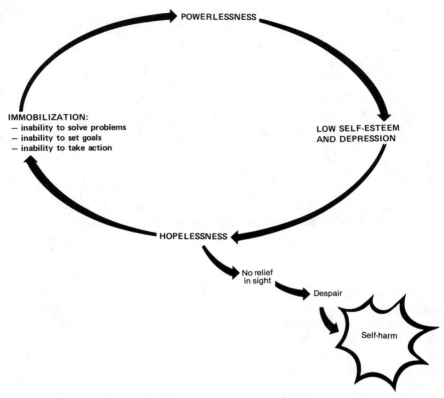

FIGURE 17 ■ 2   Powerlessness-hopelessness cycle.

LOSSES OF THE CHRONICALLY ILL

Cumulative losses suffered by chronically ill patients can lead to hopelessness. Not only does the chronically ill individual suffer from loss of health status and body-function control—for example, coordination—but also the person may suffer loss of body parts, loss of roles, loss of self-esteem, loss of certainty, loss of sexual attractiveness, loss of social relationships, loss of independence, and loss of finances. Categories of losses recorded in 81 chronically ill adults are included in Table 17–1. Grieving over these losses is a crucial process for the chronically ill person. Grief resolution may be needed to prevent the accumulated losses from becoming overwhelming, thereby causing hopelessness. The patient's degree of hopelessness can be understood by determining the patient's perceived sense of powerlessness, duration of powerlessness, and severity of losses suffered.

TABLE 17 ■ 1   Losses of Chronic Illness

Categories of Losses of the Chronically Ill
Health status losses—functions
Energy
Strength-vitality
Ability to communicate verbally
Muscle coordination
Bowel and bladder control
Loss of body parts
Organs
Hair
Weight
Loss of roles
Loss of breadwinner role
Loss of secure future
Loss of self-esteem, dignity
Loss of certainty, predictability from day to day
Loss of sexual performance abilities
Loss of intimacy
Loss of relationships with others
Loss of independence—ability to care for self
Loss of finances

CRITICAL ELEMENTS OF HOPE

Based upon an exploratory research study of hope in persons who are critically ill (Miller, 1989) and a comprehensive review of literature including the etymology of hope, theology, philosophy, sociology and anthropology, psychology, biology, nursing, and health perspectives, the following critical elements of hope were identified (Miller, 1986; Miller & Powers, 1988).

- *Mutuality and affiliation.* Interpersonal relationships which are characterized by caring, sharing, and a feeling of belonging, being needed (Lynch, 1974). Trust in another, having someone who shares the period of trial, and experiencing unconditional love are all descriptive of mutuality as an element of hope.
- *Sense of the possible.* Despairing effects of a futile attitude and a global impression that all of life is hopeless are avoided.
- *Avoidance of absolutizing.* Not imposing rigid all-or-nothing criteria on an aspect of life or hoped-for situation (Lynch, 1974).
- *Anticipation.* Looking forward to a future that is good, an expectation of a positive outcome coupled with acceptance of the necessity of patient waiting and trusting.

- *Establishing and achieving goals.* Objects of one dimension of hope.
- *Psychologic well-being and coping.* Elements that enable individuals to have psychic energy needed to sustain hope. Hope has been described as an elementary strength of the human ego (Meissner, 1973).
- *Purpose and meaning in life.* Enables individuals to have something to live for, to devote energy to, and to feel a sense of life satisfaction.
- *Freedom.* Opposite of the sense of entrapment which accompanies hopelessness (Lynch, 1974; Marcel, 1962). With hope there is a way out of difficulty and a recognition that one's own freedom may be used to influence an outcome or create a positive attitude.
- *Reality surveillance.* Cognitive task in which individuals search for clues which confirm that maintaining hope is feasible. Activities may include comparing self to others, holding out for new therapeutic discoveries, reviewing strengths, and affirming self-competence (Wright & Shontz, 1968).
- *Optimism.* Prerequisite for hope (Gottschalk, 1974; Raleigh, 1980).
- *Mental and physical activation.* Energy that combats the apathy of despair.

HOPE ANTECEDENTS, CONCOMITANTS, SOURCES, AND THREATS

Dufault (1981) studied 35 elderly persons with cancer over a 2-year period using a participant observation method to determine the critical indicators of hope: antecedents, concomitants, and sources of and threats to hope. Antecedents are those experiences and emotions present when hope arises and include the experience of captivity, loss, stress, major decision making, hardship, suffering, and challenges with uncertainty. Concomitants are those emotions and cognitions present when hope is alive and include faith, trust, love, courage, patience, uncertainty, peace, joy, humor, involvement, and well-being.

Dufault (1981) found that sources of hope were supportive behavior of significant others, spiritual factors, relief of symptoms, receiving a sense of personal worth, past positive life experiences, and having overcome adversity. Other sources of hope may include having faith in care givers and in therapy; relying on an existential philosophy—viewing human beings as having limitless potential for growth; using select mental mechanisms such as a rationalizing chain or reality surveillance; and finding meaning in suffering.

Threats to hope in persons with cancer (Dufault, 1981) in order of decreasing prevalence included evidence of deteriorating health; behavior of the physician, nurses, and family (such as despairing behaviors and abruptness); negative aspects of therapies, diagnostic tests, and hospital environment; lack of information; ambiguity; a sense of being a burden and imposing on others; spiritual distress; and past negative life experiences.

HOPE METAPHORS

Metaphoric expressions of hope were collected from books such as thesauri, dictionaries, novels, folk writings, and political speeches to provide another perspective in understanding hope (Averill, Catlin, & Chon, 1990). A total of 108 basic metaphors were categorized into eight groups depicting hope as (1) a vital principle, (2) a source of light and warmth, (3) an elevated space, (4) a form of support, (5) a physical object or thing, (6) a deception, (7) a pressure, and (8) miscellaneous metaphors. Each category has themes and subthemes. For example,

1. Hope as a vital principle has several themes, such as:
    a. Hope is the basis of life.
        (1) Where there's life there's hope.
        (2) Without hope the heart would break.
    b. Hope is a remedy for what ails a person.
        (1) Hope gives you strength.
        (2) The miserable have no other medicine but hope.
    c. Hope is itself a form of life.
        (1) Nourish hope.
        (2) Foster hope.
        (3) Keep hope alive (Averill, Catlin, & Chon, 1990, pp. 54–65).

These examples of the dynamics of hope provide increased understanding of hope and its complexities.

CAN HOPELESSNESS BE INDUCED BY OTHERS?

Jourard (1970) proposed that persons can be inspired to live or dispirited to give up and die. A person dies in response to an invitation from others to stop living such as when he or she is devalued, when his or her aims and purposes in life are diminished, and when the worth of another's existence is questioned. To dispirit another is to accerlerate his or her rate of dying. To inspirit another is to augment another's worth and meaningful life. Jourard (1970) contends that by inspiriting another we can render the person more resistant to physical and mental problems, raising the spirit titer so to speak.

Assessment of Hope and Hopelessness

Hope assessment modalities include observation of behaviors, being attentive to patient verbalizations or conversation themes, and use of paper-and-pencil tests. Lange (1978) categorized behaviors as hopeful or despairing. For example, hopeful behaviors labeled *activation* included feeling energetic, alert, interested in accomplishing goals. The opposite of activation is *hypoactivation* with example behaviors of feeling empty, drained, without energy, and being unable to take action because of feelings of heaviness. *Psychologic comfort* is present with hope and includes a sense of well-being, feeling at peace, being free from conflict, able to release tension, and able to relax and be optimistic about the future. *Psychologic discomfort* indicative of despair may include feelings of loss, deprivation, tension, and bearing a heavy burden. *Social engagement* is indicative of hope as noted by having a sense of being needed, benefiting from relationships with others, expressing interest in others. *Social distancing* (withdrawing, keeping an emotional distance from others) is indicative of despair. *Sense of competence* is having self-assuredness, positive body image, and self-confidence. The opposite, *sense of incompetence,* is indicative of despair (Lange, 1978).

Behavioral indicators of hopelessness may include lack of participation in care activities when the patient has the ability, withdrawal, despondency, lack of or change in interaction, less willingness to engage in conversation, expressions about wanting to be relieved of any more suffering, and requesting to have death hastened.

Engel (1968) has labeled the failure of coping mechanisms as the "giving-up–given-up complex." This complex includes (1) feelings of being at the end of one's rope, at an impasse, helpless and hopeless; (2) having a poor self-image and feeling incompetent and out of control; (3) having a loss of gratification from roles and relationships; (4) feeling a sense of disrupted continuity among past, present, and future; and (5) recalling memories of previous helpless states. Engel proposes that this psychologic state creates a psychobiologic condition that contributes to the emergence of disease. Engle (1971) also attributes deaths of subjects after experiencing sudden losses (e.g., death of a spouse) to the giving-up–given-up complex.

Isani (1963) described a nine-stage behavioral definition of progressive hopelessness (Table 17–2). Patient behaviors indicative of moving toward hope or moving toward despair are identified in Table 17–2.

Conversation themes indicative of hope include references about optimism over the future; receiving help, support, and sustenance from others or from self; being the recipient of good fortune, luck, or favor; achieving constructive outcomes; longevity; smooth interpersonal relationships (Gottschalk & Glesser, 1969). Conversation themes indicative of hopelessness include references about not being or wanting to be the

TABLE 17 ■ 2 Analysis of Patient Behavior According to Nine-Stage Progression of Hopelessness

Patient Behavior Indicates Moving Toward Hope	Definition of Hopelessness	Patient Behavior Indicates Moving Toward Despair
Readily establishes personal goals and anticipated positive outcomes	1. The person has anticipations of an improved state of affairs relating to achievement of goals	Unable to set goals
Continually modifies goals to allow perceived success	2. Repeatedly fails to achieve goals	Perceives unachieved outcomes as personal failure
Focuses on past successes as a sustaining force	3. Makes unfavorable comparisons of present situation of failure with past anticipations of success	Emphasizes failure in light of accomplishments while well
Modifies goals without self-punishment	4. Fails to modify goals or selected routes to goal achievement	Rigidly adheres to achieving goals possible only during healthy state
Plans for alternative action if one plan does not produce expected results	5. Reduces anticipations of finding clear-cut solutions	No effort is made to consider alternatives
Promotes peace of mind through activity and motivation toward goal	6. Increasingly limits efforts to achieve goals	Becomes increasingly agitated over accomplishing nothing
Rationalizes why solution not found	7. Despairs of finding solutions	Verbalizes doubts in self, therapy, and life
Consensually validates with friends their belief in patient	8. Loses faith in self and others	Verbalizes giving up as the only solution
Persists in motivating self, clings to positive signs and encouragement from respected others	9. Gives up trying, becomes hopeless	Gives up

Source: Adapted from Isani (1963).

recipient of God's favor or blessing; not getting help, support, sustenance; feeling hopeless, despairing; lacking ambition and interest; feeling pessimistic or discouraged (Gottschalk & Glesser, 1969).

Paper-and-pencil tests to measure hope do exist, some of which are appropriate for nursing research and/or validation of a nursing diagnosis of decreased hope or hopelessness. These instruments include The Miller Hope Scale (Miller, 1986; Miller & Powers, 1988), The Hope Scale (Erickson, Post, & Paige, 1975), the Stoner Hope Scale (Stoner, 1982), the

Hope Index Scale (Obayuwana & Carter, 1981), the Herth Hope Scale (Herth, 1989), and the Nowotny Hope Scale (Nowotny, 1989). The Miller Hope Scale does not limit the measure and definition of hope to an expectation for goal attainment as do those instruments based on Stotland's definition of hope (an anticipation of goal attainment). The intangible dimensions of generalized hope as described by Dufault (1981) are to be included in a comprehensive conceptualization of hope. The hope scales listed above have had varying degrees of psychometric evaluation and so would need careful scrutiny before their use in clinical decision making.

Research Synopses—Select Hope Studies

Hope has been credited with influencing survival against all odds, and when it is absent, recovery may be adversely affected and death may be hastened (Engle, 1968, 1971; Gottschalk, 1985; Jourard, 1970; Menninger, 1959; Richter, 1957; Seligman, 1975). The importance of hope to sustain persons through natural disasters (Henderson & Bostock, 1975; 1977), concentration camp experiences (Bettelheim, 1960; Frankl, 1962), and prisoner of war experiences (Nardini, 1952) has been well documented. Early studies noted that hope influences long-term survival in women with breast cancer (Greer, Morris, & Pettingale, 1979; Pettingale, 1984) as well as long-term survival on hemodialysis (Ziarnik, Freeman, Sherrard, & Calsyn, 1977). More recent qualitative and quantitative research has been completed.

Hope-inspiring strategies of 60 critically ill adults (ages 38 to 83) were discovered by use of a grounded theory method (Miller, 1989). A 20-item open-ended interview guide was used to solicit information about what sustained persons during a critical illness, a time when giving up was a possibility. Findings of this study provide ideas for nursing strategies to inspire hope. Transcriptions of verbatim interviews were analyzed and the following were found to maintain hope (Miller, 1989).

- *Cognitive strategies.* Thought processes individuals consciously used to change unfavorable perceptions to less threatening perceptions. These mental coping strategies included internal dialogues such as "I'd better get with it and get out of here." "I know I have to get through the tests, I am strong, I can do it."
- *Determinism.* Mental attitude reflecting a conviction that a positive outcome is possible. "There was no way I was going to give up." "You gotta aim high cause you might fall a little short and end up just where you belong." "The faintest glimmer of hope regarding recovery, even if it's recovery in a limited way, is worth going after."

- *Philosophy of life and world view.* View of life as having meaning and that growth takes place as a result of struggle and difficulty. Some patients had a deliberate day-to-day way of approaching recovery.
- *Spiritual strategies.* Those beliefs and practices that enabled individuals to transcend suffering based on a relationship with God. "It's something you feel but difficult to express. You know you're getting help from the Lord."
- *Relationship with care givers.* Care givers had a constructive view of the patient and conveyed positive expectations for competent handling of stress. "They made you feel they wanted you to win." The relationships were described as having warmth and sincerity and being filled with strong encouragement.
- *Family bonds.* Sustaining relationships with loved ones who convey a sharing of the difficulty and provide reasons for living, goals to be accomplished, and directions for living. "My children are small, they need me."
- *Sense of being in control.* Perception that one's own knowledge and actions can affect an outcome. Being informed about progress and schedules and involved in care decisions enhanced control.
- *Goal accomplishment.* Desired activities to accomplish and valued outcomes to attain. Examples ranged from being able to perform a simple physical task ("go to the bathroom by myself") to being able to enjoy retirement (see pp. 25–26).

Other miscellaneous means of maintaining hope included use of humor, relaxation to improve a sense of well-being, and use of distraction to avoid thoughts of negative consequences.

The following threats to hope were identified by these critically ill patients: physical cues interpreted as setbacks, a feeling that no one cares (family does not visit or demonstrate support, family has fatalistic attitude), and negative hospital experiences such as receiving dehumanizing messages. A patient described the experience ". . . like being put through one large-sized factory" (Miller, 1989, p. 27). Nurses can intervene in preventing these threats to hope.

Herth (1989) found a significant positive relationship between hope and level of coping in 120 persons with cancer receiving chemotherapy. Those persons categorized as having strong religious faith had significantly higher hope and coping than persons with weak, unsure, or lost faith. Persons whose disease did not interfere with performance of family role responsibilities had higher hope (Herth, 1989). Brandt's (1987) sample of 37 women on chemotherapy for breast cancer revealed that they had high levels of hope, received social support, and valued religious beliefs as helpful in coping with illness.

A significant positive relationship between hope and grief resolution was noted in 75 persons who had been widowed between 12 to 18 months (Herth, 1990). Spouses of persons who died in hospice settings had significantly higher hope than those who died in hospitals or nursing homes. Significant negative correlations were found between hope and evasive, fatalistic, and emotive coping styles (Herth, 1990).

Hope has been studied in adolescents. Hinds and Martin (1988) found that 59 adolescents with cancer relied on achieving a hopeful state as a process of comforting themselves. For these youths, hope was a component of a self-sustaining process leading to a sense of personal competence in resolving health threats. For adolescents, hope meant the degree to which the adolescent possessed a comforting, life-sustaining belief that a personal and positive future exists (Hinds, 1984; 1988).

A single core variable identified by 58 adolescents with cancer as directly promoting hopefulness was the nurses' use of humor (Hinds, Martin, & Vogel, 1987). Humor included being lighthearted, initiating or responding to teasing, and engaging in playful interactions. Using a grounded theory method, other nursing strategies identified as promoting hopefulness included the nurses' use of (1) truthful explanations, (2) participation in activities with the adolescent (cards, computer games, piano), (3) caring behaviors (hugging, demonstrating interest), (4) purposeful conversations diverted to neutral topics, (5) care competence, (6) sharing knowledge of survivors with a similar disease, (7) maintaining a future focus (Hinds, Martin, & Vogel, 1987).

Hope has been noted to be a prerequisite for effective coping and is considered by some to be a coping mechanism (Jalowiec & Powers, 1981; Korner, 1970; Stoner & Keampfer, 1985; Weisman, 1979). Maintaining hope is a coping task of the chronically ill (Greene, O'Mahony, & Rungasamy, 1982). Also refer to Chapter 2 of this text. Persons with a chronic illness perceived themselves in a "winning position" over their illness if they maintained hope (Forsyth, Delaney, & Gresham, 1984). Hope was noted to be a frequently used coping strategy by emergency-room patients (Jalowiec & Powers, 1981) and by hemodialysis patients (Baldree, Murphy, & Powers, 1982).

Hope has been identified as a primary need of family members of persons with cancer (Lewandowski & Jones, 1988; Weisman, 1979; Brockopp, Hayko, Davenport, & Winscott, 1989), of the critically ill (Coutu-Wakulczyk & Chartier, 1990; Leske, 1986; Norheim, 1989; Norris & Grove, 1986), and of brain-injured patients (Campbell, 1988). In 30 persons with multiple sclerosis and their 30 family member "carers," hope and psychologic well-being were predictive of patient adaptation (Miller & Hastings, submitted for publication.) Similar findings were noted by Christman (1990) in 55 men receiving radiotherapy for cancer, in that lower hope and more uncertainty were associated with more adjustment problems.

Nursing Strategies

Nursing strategies to inspire hope are countless in number and nature, limited only by lack of sensitivity to the uniqueness of each patient and family response as well as lack of creativity. Figure 17–3 summarizes the categories of nursing strategies described in this chapter. These strategies have been gleaned from the literature, particularly from Miller (1985; 1991). The strategies are based upon an existential frame of reference in which human beings are viewed as having a never-ending possibility of improving their own being (Marcel, 1962). Nurses can inspire hope, focusing on living the moment as fully as possible. There may not be hope of returning to previous functioning or of being cured, but hope in maximizing the moment; benefiting optimally from relationships or aesthetic surroundings. Examples of maximizing experiences include

- Savor the richness of black coffee at breakfast.
- Feel the tartness of grapefruit wake up the taste buds.
- Note the crystal-clear blue of the sky.
- Feel the warmth of a sunbeam.
- Watch activities of animals in a tree outside the window.
- Benefit from each encounter with another human being.
- Share experiences children are having.

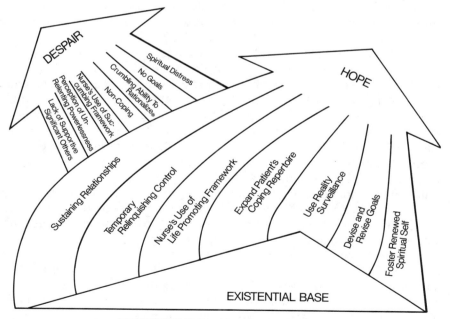

FIGURE 17 ■ 3   Hope–despair model.

- Note loving characteristics of spouse.
- Appreciate expressions of caring concern.
- Work out intricate plans, such as for rebuilding the summer cottage.
- Plan to rearrange the living room furniture.
- Build highlights into each day, such as meals, visits, Bible reading.
- Write messages to grandchildren, nieces, or nephews.
- Plan for volunteer work to help others.
- Study a favorite painting.
- Listen to a symphony as a means of escape.

It is recognized that not all patients will benefit from isolated reconstructed experiences such as the melting of snowflakes on their cheeks. However, all patients will benefit from renewed appreciation of making the most of the moment, not letting the moment pass by without appreciating its beauty. Using these experiences helps to achieve a sense of personal fulfillment.

Following are categories of strategies to inspire hope.

AFFILIATIVE DIMENSION—USE OF SUSTAINING RELATIONSHIPS

The affiliative dimension of hope means hope depends upon a sense of connectedness with others and involvement beyond self, including intimacy and attachment, mutuality and sharing, and other-directed social interaction and relationships (Dufault, 1981). Specific strategies are (1) to use attachment ideation and (2) to develop significant others' awareness of their powerful role in influencing hope states of their ill loved ones. Attachment ideation is a preoccupation with a principal attachment figure, that is with loved ones and significant others such as spouse, child, and girl friend. With attachment ideation, the nurse helps the client review attributes, that is, unique, important, and loving characteristics of the attachment figure. Reviewing patients' peak life experiences and how their relationships are caring may be helpful. Even if patients are unconscious, attachment ideation may be used by repeating the loved one's name to the patient, reviewing their special devotion and concern, relating experiences shared by the loved one as reminders of joy, and being needed throughout life as well as now. The nurse helps re-create mental images of the attached figure, enabling the patient to fixate on someone for whom to live and maintain hope.

Significant others need to realize how powerful they are in sustaining the patient. They may benefit from reviewing their role in maintaining hope which will have a reciprocal benefit for their loved one (patient). Those persons who are the closest are the most meaningful in the patient's life and have the most contagious influence in terms of hope and other mental states. Nurses may need to help family focus on goal-directed interactions that emphasize unfinished work waiting for the patient, life goals to be accomplished, and how they are vitally needed in the lives of their family. The nurse may model this type of communication and also model use of touch and closeness so that the family member is not hesitant to use these modalities. Lack of supportive significant others leads to despair.

ENHANCE CONTROL AND SUPPORT THE TEMPORARY RELINQUISHING OF CONTROL

Enhancing control by providing clients with the skills to manage self-care and monitor self, or in times of acute need assuring them that relinquishing control is temporary, may affect hope states. The perception of unrelenting powerlessness leads to hopelessness.

USE OF A LIFE-PROMOTING INTERPERSONAL FRAMEWORK

A deliberate interactional style that focuses on surviving adversity and growing as a result is a constructive life-promoting framework (Wright, 1980). Patients are regarded as potentially powerful, unique persons having coping resources that can be uncovered. Patient resources can be reviewed and their use reinforced. Confrontation with problems is interpreted as being part of life, and the patient's ability to resolve and/or adapt is emphasized. Getting on with living without undue dwelling solely on problems is the goal. The interaction that focuses on survival with discovery of new meaning in life will have an impact on hope.

The opposite approach is a succumbing framework in which the nurse concentrates on the devastation of the crisis; what the patient can no longer do, spreading a theme of disability throughout all aspects of the person's life (negative spread). A disabling theme is evident in the interaction. The problem is not that the disability is recognized but that constructive forces in the person's life are neglected (Wright, 1980).

EXPAND PATIENT AND FAMILY COPING REPERTOIRE

Persons receive a sense of strength knowing there are ways to respond (cope) in order to control negative affects and anxiety. Weisman (1979) defines coping as what one does about a problem in order to bring about relief, quiescence, and equilibrium. Noncoping leads to power-lessness, depression, and eventually despair. Coping mechanisms as described in Chapter 2 can be taught such as use of self-instructional internal language, imagery, stress innoculation, rational inquiry, and mutuality. All these mechanisms support the belief that there is a way out of difficulty and may enable anticipation of a future. Noncoping leads to despair.

REALITY SURVEILLANCE

Reality surveillance is a cognitive task in which the individual searches for clues which confirm that maintaining hope is feasible (Wright & Shontz, 1968). Also called reality or phenomenal grounding, this mental mechanism provides some tangible evidence from the real world as a basis for hope. Korner (1970) refers to constructing hope from examining bits of reality held together by logic and reasoning, using a rationalizing chain. Table 17–3 contains select categories of reality surveillance with exemplar patient behavior and the related nursing role. The opposite phenomenon is a crumbling ability to rationalize leading to despair.

DEVISE AND REVISE GOALS

Hope is energized by the belief in the ability to accomplish something (Lynch, 1974; Stotland, 1969). Patients may need help in devising goals and recognizing their accomplishments. These goals may include (1) physical strides, (2) work to be accomplished, (3) responsibility to discharge, and (4) love relationships to renew and/or sustain. Specific feedback about progress in healing, returning to previous or new levels of functioning, and so forth, needs to be consistently provided. Setting physical goals that are realistic needs to be considered, for example, walking distance and other amounts of exercise to be tolerated. Work can be accomplished through others. Patients may be helped to see that providing guidance without needing to personally carry out all work plans provides a sense of accomplishment. Having someone and something to live for inspires hope. Renewing and being able to sustain love relationships maintains hope. In hopelessness, the future is tolerable if the patient feels there is unconditional love from someone and that there is someone with whom to share the future.

FOSTER RENEWED SPIRITUAL SELF

Spiritual life is a major source of hope for some persons. This includes maintaining a relationship with God or deity and having a sense of purpose and meaning in life. Providing opportunity for prayer, reading hope-filled scripture, and creating an environment in which the patient feels comfortable expressing hope in God are examples of nursing strat-

TABLE 17 ■ 3 Analysis of Reality Surveillance

Select Categories of Reality Surveillance*	Examples of Patient Behavior Indicative of the Category	Nursing Role
Reviewing changing environmental conditions	"I must be improving; the nurses are not monitoring me as closely; they come less often"	If patient's interpretations are accurate, confirm them; that is, the V.N.A. will visit less frequently because of these signs of improvement. Review indicators of improvement
Reviewing assets	"I have a good health history; I have never been hospitalized before" "I still have one good leg" "I have always exercised to keep physically fit" "Now that I have an ileostomy, at least I won't get cancer of the bowel"	Help patient review assets, which include physical, interpersonal, and role-function abilities
Comparing self with other individuals or groups	"It took my neighbor longer to recover from his heart attack" "I didn't realize I would be able to wear my same clothes after my colostomy surgery" "The patient representative from the ostomy association was so helpful"	Information on self-help groups can be provided. Listen to patient's need to compare own better progress to other patients with slower progress
Planning for assuming self-care responsibilities	"I realize now, the diabetes will not be going away. I'd better start learning to take care of myself"	Provide assistance through teaching and support so patient gradually assumes responsibility for care and realizes that self-care is not an impossible overwhelming task
Avoiding confrontation with negative outcomes	"The chemotherapy has got to be effective after all this suffering with side effects. It's got to be killing something"	Listen with empathy; help patient with internal dialogue to increase patient's insight
Plans are contingent upon if-then events	"If I remain in remission until Christmas, I will plan the trip"	Foster positive expectations for remaining physically stable. Teach importance of optimistic mind set, influencing body response. Inform patient of mind-body pathways and holistic response to health
Holding out for future discoveries	"Who knows, maybe they will find a cure for multiple sclerosis"	Share knowledge of advances in caring for patients with debilitating diseases. Acknowledge discoveries in medicine that were unheard of years ago
Using statements of uncontestable truisms	"God will help me through this" "All that is needed is for me to do my best and to follow the medical orders"	Recognize that this verbalization is comforting to the patient and the patient is watching the nurse's response
Making testimonials	"I've read of miraculous cures of arthritis"	Demonstrate interest without scientific interrogation or "putting the patient down," repudiating the patient for the claims

*Source: Adapted from Wright and Shontz (1968).

429

egies. If appropriate, nurses can remind clients of the boundless, infinite love God has for each person. Marcel (1962) states, "Hope is the radical refusal to set limits." When all in life looks grim, that is, when what is happening is beyond the individual's influence, hopelessness is prevented by turning to God. Spiritual distress is the opposite phenomenon which contributes to despair.

Hope may also be inspired by use of humanities resources such as literature, poetry, art, and music. See Chapter 13 for poignant poems and suggested literature sources for use in comforting clients. Careful use of humor is another strategy to help put stress in perspective, alleviate excess tensions, and maintain some sense of life as having moments of lightheartedness. Helping clients find meaning in suffering, in their existence in life, in their current challenges may also be an effective strategy to mobilize hope.

Summary

"To hope" is different from "to hope that." To hope is an existential orientation to achieve a generalized state of being. "To hope that" means there is a specific object of hope, and the individual is subjected to the vulnerable insecurity of not having his or her particular object of hope realized. A focus of nursing strategies to inspire hope needs to include generalized hope and not be exclusively devoted to hope for goal accomplishment. In general, by increasing clients' levels of hope, we are empowering them to be in control of their lives, to anticipate a future that is good, and to have a restored sense of well-being.

References

Aardema, B. (1984). *The therapeutic use of hope.* Unpublished doctoral dissertation. Western Michigan University, Kalamazoo, MI.

Adams, C., & Proulx, J. (1975). The role of the nurse in the maintenance and restoration of hope. In B. Scheonberg et al. (Eds.), *Bereavement: Its psychosocial aspects* (pp. 256–263). New York: Columbia University Press.

Averill, J. R., Catlin, G., & Chon, K. K. (1990). *Rules of hope.* New York: Springer-Verlag.

Baldree, K. S., Murphy, S., & Powers, M. J. (1982). Stress identification and coping patterns in patients on hemodialysis. *Nursing Research, 31,* 107–112.

Beck, A., Kovacs, M., & Weissman, A. (1975). Hopelessness and suicidal behavior: An overview. *Journal of the American Medical Association, 234,* 1146–1149.

Bettelheim, B. (1960). *The informed heart: Autonomy in a mass age.* Glencoe, IL: Free Press.

Bloch, E. (1970). *Man on his own.* New York: Herder & Herder.

Brandt, B. (1987). The relationship between hopelessness and select variables in women receiving chemotherapy for breast cancer. *Oncology Nursing Forum, 14,* 35–39.

Brockopp, D. Y., Hayko, D., Davenport, W., & Winscott, C. (1989). Personal control and the needs for hope and information among adults diagnosed with cancer. *Cancer Nursing, 12,* 112–116.

Campbell, C. H. (1988). Needs of relatives and helpfulness of support groups in severe head injury. *Rehabilitation Nursing, 13,* 320–325.

Christman, N. (1990). Uncertainty and adjustment during radiotherapy. *Nursing Research, 39,* 17–20.

Coutu-Wakulczyk, G., & Chartier, L. (1990). French validation of the Critical Care Family Needs Inventory. *Heart and Lung, 19,* 192–196.

Diez-Manrique, J. F. (1984). Hope as a means of therapy in the work of Karen Horney. *American Journal of Psychoanalysis, 44,* 301–310.

Dufault, K. (1981). *Hope of elderly persons with cancer.* Unpublished doctoral dissertation. Case Western Reserve University, Cleveland, OH.

Dufault, K., & Martocchio, B. (1985). Hope: Its spheres and dimensions. *Nursing Clinics of North America, 20,* 370–391.

Engle, G. (1971). Sudden and rapid death during psychological stress: Folklore or folk wisdom? *Annals of Internal Medicine, 74,* 771–782.

Engel, G. (1968). A life setting conducive to illness: The giving-up–given-up complex. *Annals of Internal Medicine, 69,* 293–300.

Erickson, R., Post, R., & Paige, A. (1975). Hope as a psychiatric variable. *Journal of Clinical Psychology, 31,* 324–330.

Forsyth, G., Delaney, K., & Gresham, M. (1984). Vying for a winning position: Management style of the chronically ill. *Research in Nursing and Health, 7,* 181–188.

Frank, J. (1975). Mind-body relationships in illness and healing. *International Academy of Preventive Medicine, 2,* 46–59.

Frank, J. (1968). The role of hope in psychotherapy. *International Journal of Psychiatry, 5,* 383–385.

Frankl, V. (1962). *Man's search for meaning.* New York: Simon Delta.

Fromm, E. (1968). *The revolution of hope.* New York: Harper & Row.

Gottschalk, L. (1985). Hope and other deterrents to illness. *American Journal of Psychotherapy, 39,* 515–524.

Gottschalk, L. (1974). A hope scale applicable to verbal samples. *Archives of General Psychiatry, 30,* 770–785.

Gottschalk, L., & Glesser, G. (1969). *The measurement of psychological states through the content analysis of verbal behavior.* Berkeley: University of California Press.

Greene, S., O'Mahony, P., & Rungasamy, P. (1982). Levels of measured hopelessness in physically ill patients. *Journal of Psychosomatic Research, 26,* 591–593.

Greer, S., Morris, T., & Pettingale, K. (1979). Psychological responses to breast cancer: Effect on outcome. *Lancet, 2,* 768–787.

Heagle, J. (1975). *Contemporary meditation on hope.* Chicago: Thomas More Press.

Henderson, S., & Bostock, R. (1977). Coping behavior after shipwreck. *British Journal of Psychiatry, 131,* 15–20.

Henderson, S., & Bostock, R. (1975). Coping behaviour: Correlates of survival on a raft. *Australian and New Zealand Journal of Psychiatry, 9,* 221–223.

Herth, K. (1990). Relationship of hope, coping style, concurrent losses and setting to grief resolution in the elderly widow(er). *Research in Nursing and Health, 13,* 109–117.

Herth, K. (1989). The relationship between level of hope and level of coping response and other variables in patients with cancer. *Oncology Nursing Forum, 16,* 67–72.

Hinds, P. (1988). Adolescent hopefulness in illness and health. *Advances in Nursing Science, 10,* 79–88.

Hinds, P. (1984). Inducing a definition of hope through the use of grounded theory methodology. *Journal of Advanced Nursing, 9,* 357–362.

Hinds, P., & Martin, J. (1988). Hopefulness and the self-sustaining process in adolescents with cancer. *Nursing Research, 37,* 336–340.

Hinds, P., Martin, J., & Vogel, R. (1987). Nursing strategies to influence adolescent hopefulness during oncologic illness. *Journal of the Association of Pediatric Oncology Nurses, 5,* 14–22.

Isani, R. (1963). From hopelessness to hope. *Perspectives in Psychiatric Care, 1,* 15–20.

Jalowiec, A., & Powers, M. (1981). Stress and coping in hypertensive and emergency room patients. *Nursing Research, 30,* 10–15.

Jourard, S. (1970). Living and dying: Suicide an invitation to die. *American Journal of Nursing, 70,* 269–275.

Korner, I. (1970). Hope as a method of coping. *Journal of Consulting and Clinical Psychology, 34,* 134–139.

Lange, S. P. (1978). Hope. In C. E. Carlson & B. Blackwell (Eds.), *Behavioral concepts and nursing intervention* (pp. 171–190). Philadelphia: JB Lippincott.

Leske, J. (1986). Needs of relatives of critically ill patients: A follow-up. *Heart and Lung, 15,* 189–193.

Lewandowski, W., & Jones, S. L. (1988). The family with cancer: Nursing interventions throughout the course of living with cancer. *Cancer Nursing, 11,* 313–321.

Lynch, W. F. (1974). *Images of hope: Imagination as the healer of the hopeless.* Notre Dame, IN: University of Notre Dame Press.

Marcel, G. (1962). *Homo viator: Introduction to a metaphysic of hope.* Translated by E. Craufurd. New York: Harper & Row.

Meissner, W. W. (1973). Notes on the psychology of hope. Part I. *Journal of Religion and Health, 12,* 7–29.

Menninger, C. (1959). Hope. *American Journal of Psychiatry, 146,* 481–491.

Miller, J. F. (1991). Developing and maintaining hope in families of the critically ill. *Clinical Issues in Critical Care Nursing.*

Miller, J. F. (1989). Hope inspiring strategies of the critically ill. *Applied Nursing Research, 2,* 23–29.

Miller, J. F. (1986). *Development of an instrument to measure hope.* Unpublished doctoral dissertation. University of Illinois, Chicago.

Miller, J. F. (1985). Nursing strategies to inspire hope. *American Journal of Nursing, 85,* 22–25.

Miller, J. F., & Hastings, D. (Submitted for publication.) Family member response and patient adaptation to multiple sclerosis: The influence of hope.

Miller, J. F., & Powers, M. J. (1988). Development of an instrument to measure hope. *Nursing Research, 37,* 6–10.

Nardini, J. E. (1952). Survival factors in American prisoners of war of the Japanese. *American Journal of Psychiatry, 109,* 241–248.

Norheim, C. (1989). Family needs of patients having coronary artery bypass graft surgery during the intraoperative period. *Heart and Lung, 18,* 622–626.

Norris, L., & Grove, S. (1986). Investigation of selected psychosocial needs of family members of critically ill adult patients. *Heart and Lung, 15,* 194–199.

Nowotny, M. (1989). Assessment of hope in patients with cancer: Development of an instrument. *Oncology Nursing Forum, 16,* 57–61.

Obayuwana, A., & Carter, A. (1981). *Hope Index Scale.* Silver Spring, MD: Institute of Hope.

Owen, D. (1989). Nurses' perspectives on the meaning of hope in patients with cancer: A qualitative study. *Oncology Nursing Forum, 16,* 75–79.

Pettingale, K. W. (1984). Coping and cancer prognosis. *Journal of Psychosomatic Research, 28,* 363–364.

Pruyser, P. (1963). Phenomenology and dynamics of hoping. *Journal of Science and the Study of Religion, 3,* 86–96.

Raleigh, E. (1980). *An investigation of hope as manifested in the physically ill adult.* Unpublished doctoral dissertation. Wayne State University, Detroit, MI.

Richter, C. P. (1957). On the phenomenon of sudden death in animals and man. *Psychosomatic Medicine, 19,* 190–198.

Seligman, M. (1975). *Helplessness: On depression, development and death.* San Francisco: WH Freeman.

Stanley, A. T. (1978). *The lived experience of hope: The isolation of discrete descriptive elements common to the experience of hope in healthy young adults.* Unpublished doctoral dissertation. Catholic University, Washington, DC.

Stoner, J. (1982). *Hope and cancer patients.* Unpublished doctoral dissertation. University of Colorado, Denver.

Stoner, J., & Keampfer, S. (1985). Recalled life expectancy information, phase of illness and hope in cancer patients. *Research in Nursing and Health, 8,* 269–274.

Stotland, E. (1969). *The psychology of hope.* San Francisco: Jossey-Bass.

Weisman, A. (1979). *Coping with cancer.* New York: McGraw-Hill.

Wright, B. (1980). Person and situation: Adjusting the rehabilitation focus. *Archives of Physical Medicine and Rehabilitation, 61,* 59–64.

Wright, B., & Shontz, F. (1968). Process and tasks in hoping. *Rehabilitation Literature, 29,* 322–331.

Ziarnik, J. P., Freeman, C. W., Sherrard, D. T., & Calsyn, D. A. (1977). Psychological correlates of survival on renal dialysis. *Journal of Nervous and Mental Disease, 164,* 210–213.

■ *I N D E X* ■

An "f" indicates a figure; a "t" indicates a table.